For Marina

Rome under the surface

Maximilian Just

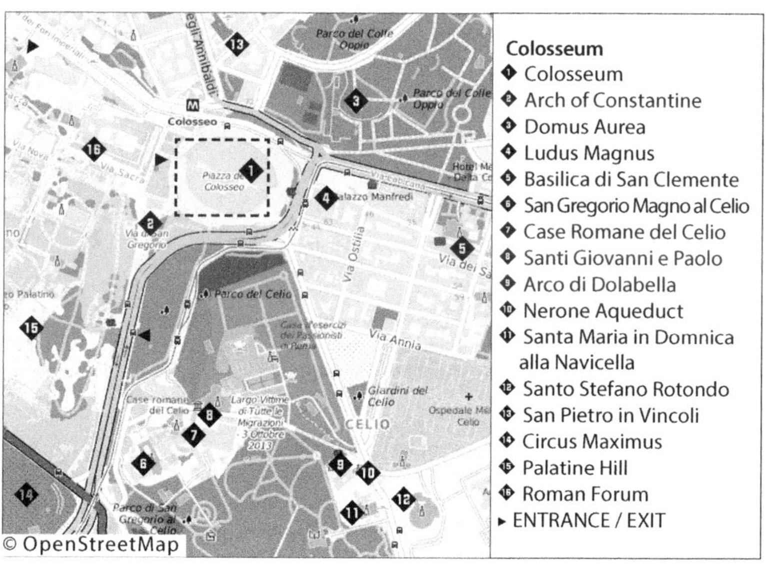

Photography © Maximilian Just
Cover and design by JUSTePublishing

Maps by OpenStreetMaps Foundation. Maps extracted from OpenStreetMap are licensed on terms of the Open Database License, „ODbL" 1.0.
www.openstreetmap.org/copyright

Translations by Una Krizmanić Ožegović

Published by JUSTePublishing
www.justepub.com

Printed in the United States of America
First paperback edition, 2022

ISBN: 978-3-9503520-0-9 (paperback)

Contents

INTRODUCTION

When in Rome, Do as the Romans Do

IMPERIAL ROME

A journey through time

In the epicenter of power

Hub of the Roman Empire

Monumental public projects of Roman rulers

A story of shifting the center of the world

HEART OF ROME

The perfect building in the heart of Rome

The most pleasant place to walk around

Breakfast area away from the traffic noise

Art of miracles and miracle of arts

Contents

List of Did you knows

Improve your knowledge about Rome, Vatican and famous artists with fascinating stories and facts about people, places and history that make you think.

Rome

Ancient Rome

Vatican City State

Famous Artists and their Artworks

List of Incredible facts about

List of Museum and Church Guides

List of Maps

La Dolce Vita

Gelateria del Teatro – Via dei Coronari 65

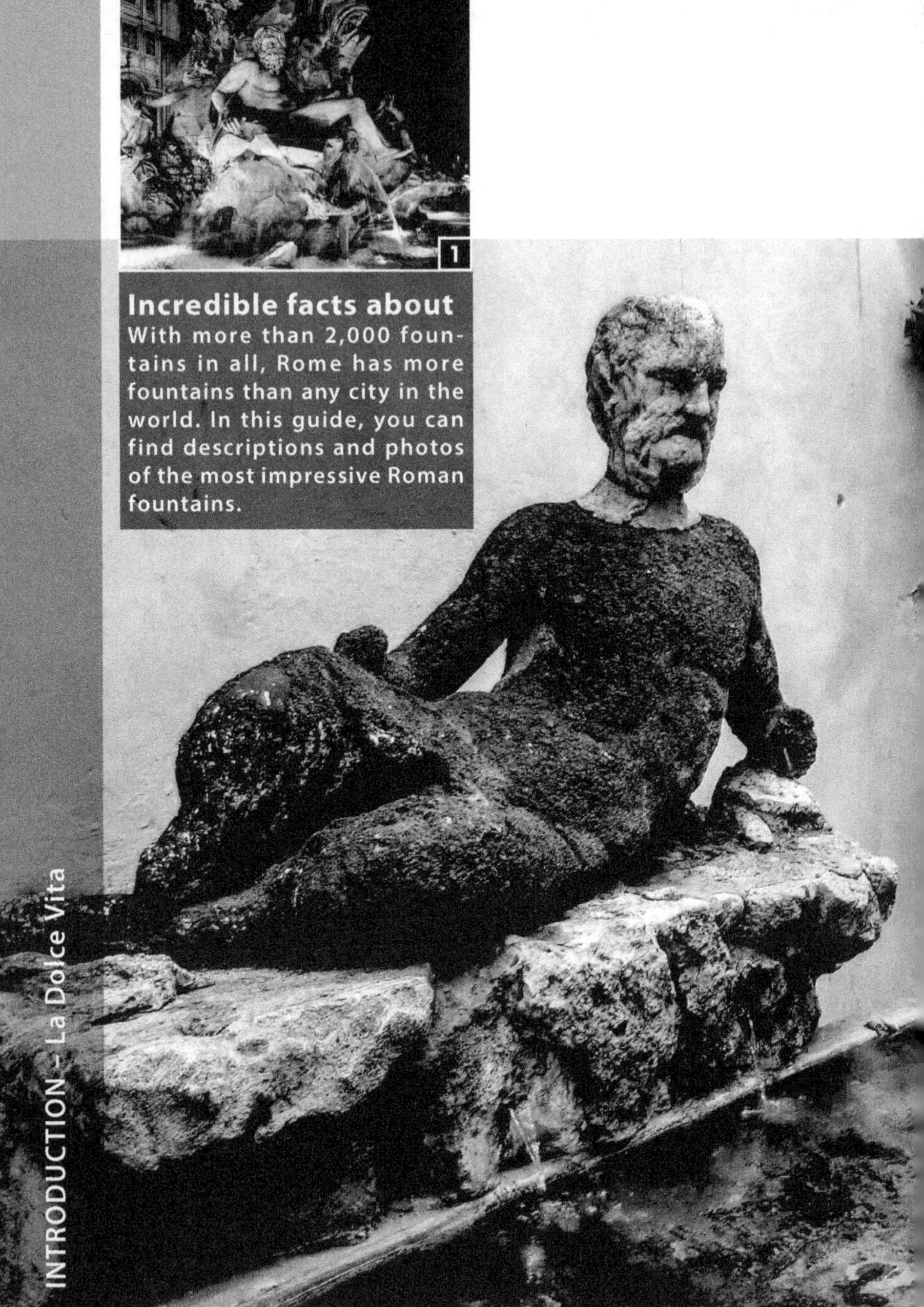

Incredible facts about

With more than 2,000 fountains in all, Rome has more fountains than any city in the world. In this guide, you can find descriptions and photos of the most impressive Roman fountains.

Fontana del Babuino – Via del Babuino

Extra Tip : : :

Entire streets of Rome are dedicated to fashion, just as others are all about antiques and food. However, it is more common to find a mix of fashion, art, antiques, churches and restaurants which add up to a unique Roman mosaic, street after street.

When in Rome, do as the Romans do

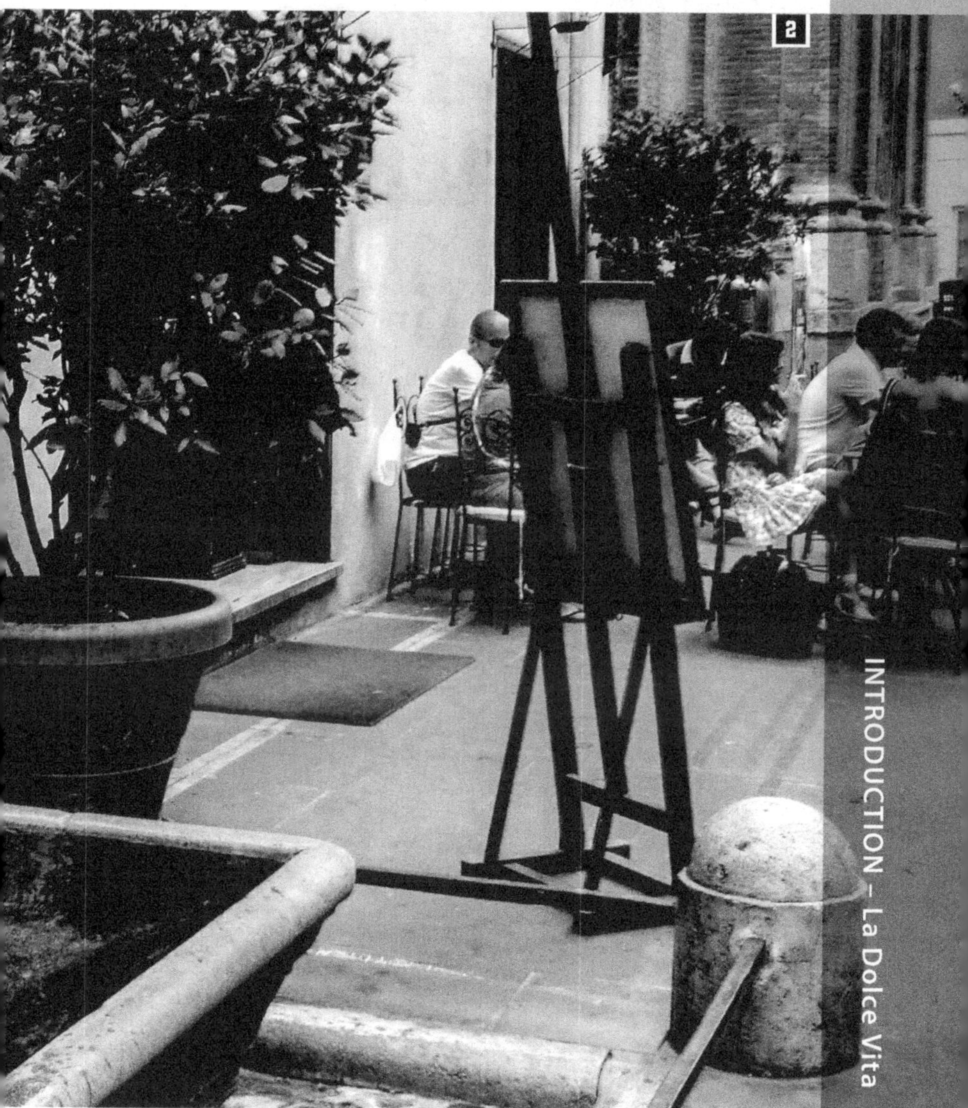

Via del Babuino
Address: Via del Babuino, Roma
Public transportation: Metro A stop Spagna or Flaminio | Bus stop Babuino: 119 | Tram stop Flaminio: 2

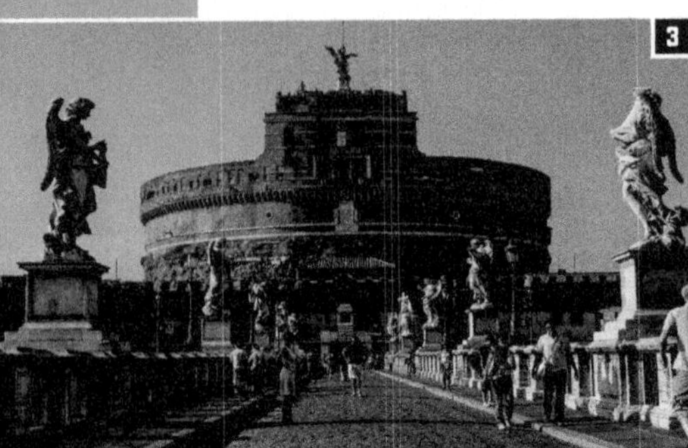

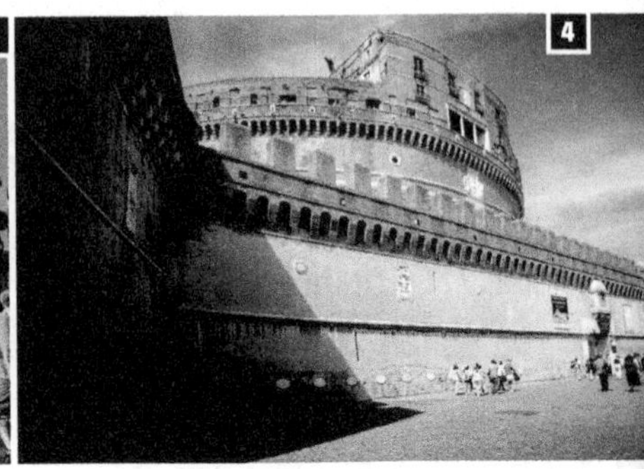

❶ Why visit Rome?

There are many reasons to visit Rome. Whether you are into art, history, archaeology, religion or simply love to travel, Rome is where you will always find more than you expected. **2**

This is why it is best to take as much as you can into account and get ready for all kinds of surprises. Rome was and remains a chaos that leaves everyone breathless. **1**

❷ Rome is a work in progress

It is impossible to find just one landmark that belongs to a single period in history. For example, when you decide to go to the Castel Sant'Angelo on the banks of the Tiber River, you are actually visiting a papal fort with luxurious suites, and a home of renaissance popes.

The quarters are connected to the Vatican Palace via a secret tunnel. At the same time, you are in the Emperor Hadrian's mausoleum, where several Roman emperors found their final resting place. **4**

Apart from being a papal residence, this imperial mausoleum also served as a prison during the inquisition.

Castel Sant'Angelo is where the philosopher and astronomer Giordano Bruno was held captive for six years. This is also where Galileo Galilei awaited sentencing and Benvenuto Cellini, a renaissance artist, practiced the art of escape. There is a small courtyard where executions took place. In order to even get to the Castel Sant'Angelo, you have to cross the Tiber over the eponymous bridge. **3**

On this old Roman bridge you will be greeted by a colonnade of oversized angels. **5**

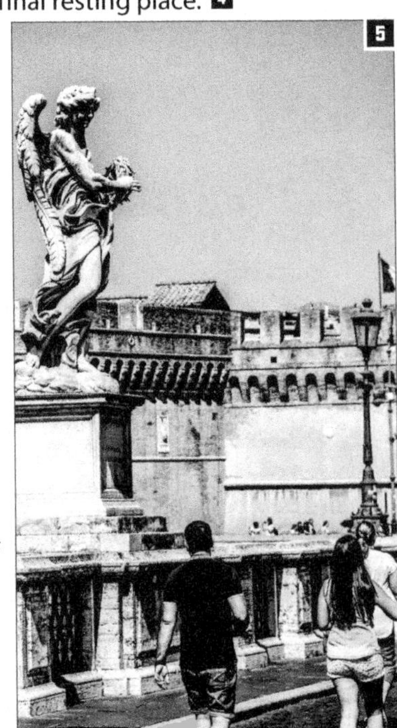

INTRODUCTION – La Dolce Vita

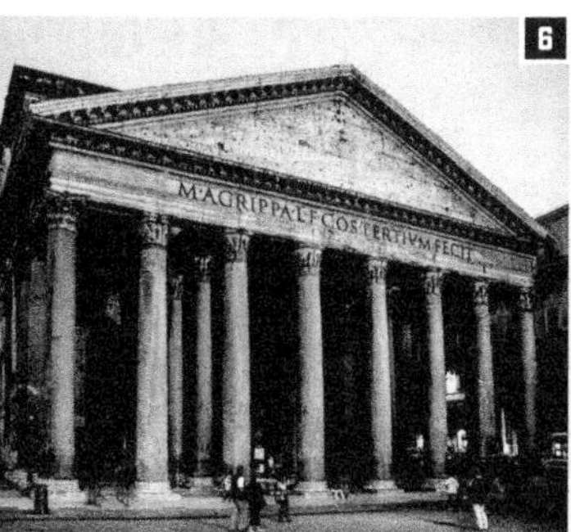

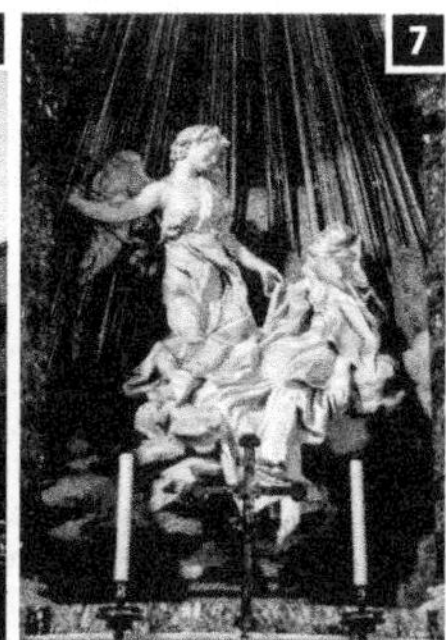

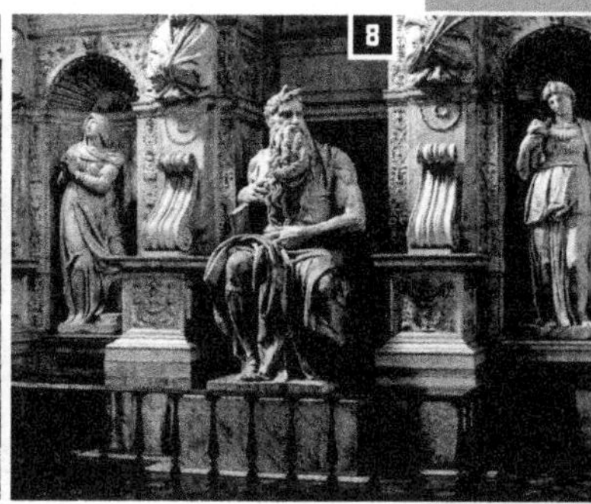

These sculptures were made by the baroque master Gian Lorenzo Bernini and his pupils.

In Rome, layers of history and art overlap wherever you go — ancient Roman temples turned into Catholic churches by papal decrees **6**, statues of female saints receive divine messages in shockingly sensual ecstasy **7**, Madonnas who are younger than their sons, linguistic errors set in stone on heads of prophets **8**, just to name a few.

Don't be shocked to see ancient city walls running straight through a fast food restaurant under the Termini train station.

❸ The trinity of everyday life

Everything in Rome revolves around three things – food, antiquities and fashion. The trinity of everyday life is the topic of every verbal and nonverbal conversation, either on the street or in the news. **9**

❹ First things first

Italian cuisine is only a name for an endless number of dishes and drinks, but also variations specific to each region.

For instance, pizza is a well-known Italian specialty. But *Pizza Romana* is something entirely different from *Pizza Napolitana*. Not to mention *Pizza Bianca*, typically found in the region of Lazio, whose capital is Rome.

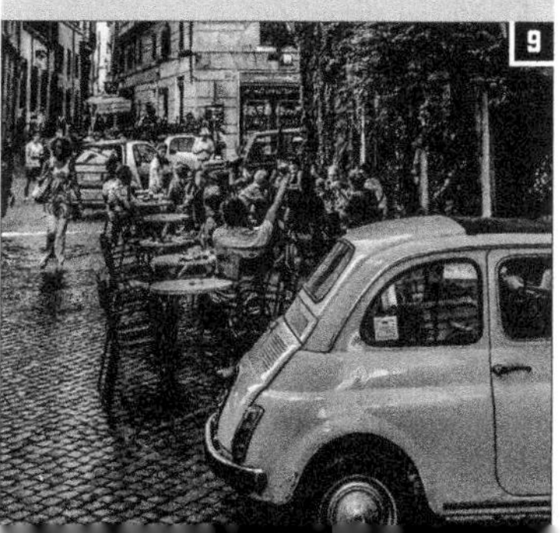

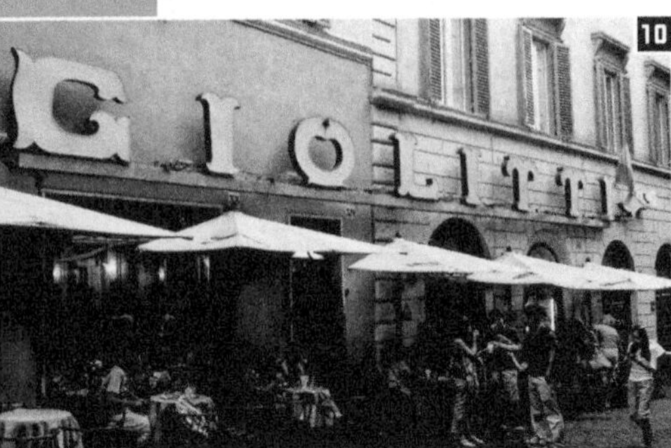

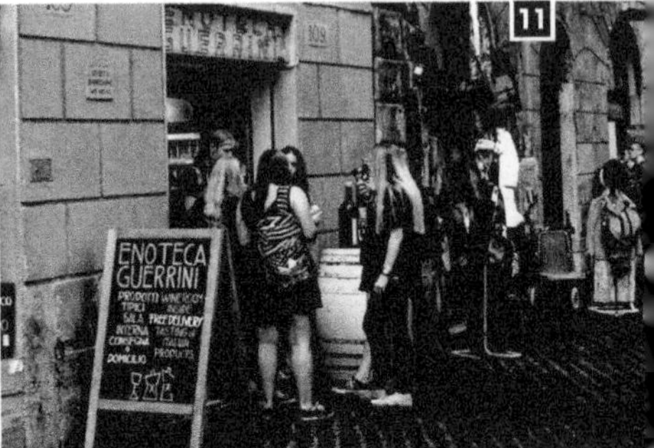

You can eat spaghetti anywhere in Italy, but only the Romans can claim *Spaghetti alla Carbonara* as their own, with *Pecorino Romano*, the local cheese — the cheese used to be the main meal of the Roman legionnaires and now it is one of the most important ingredients of Spaghetti alla Carbonara.

Another side of Roman cuisine can be found in meals made by Romans of Jewish descent. If you haven't tried *Carciofi alla Giudia* (Jewish style artichokes) or *Fiori di Zucca* (zucchini flowers), you can't really say you know Roman cuisine that well.

You may find yourself in a state of panic while trying to visit every sight on your itinerary, so you will opt to eat something on the fly. Do as the Romans do, look for a nice slice of vegetarian pizza or *porchetta* sandwich and you will not regret it.

There are many places in Rome where you can eat a good gelato. For the Romans, Audrey Hepburn in "Roman Holiday", Pope John Paul II and not just them, only one ice cream parlor in Rome is really unique. ☐

Roman wines have been popular for centuries, especially white wines. Wines such as *Frascati* and *Castelli Romani* are protected with the DOC label (Controlled designation of origin) and perfectly suited to go with Roman dishes. ☐

As far as coffee goes, the holy grail of all Roman beverages, there are three places that are said to have the best espresso or cappuccino in the world.

◆ Time after Time

In a city where façades get more beautiful the less they are restored and where there are more clocks per meter of street than anywhere in the world, the past is certainly cherished.

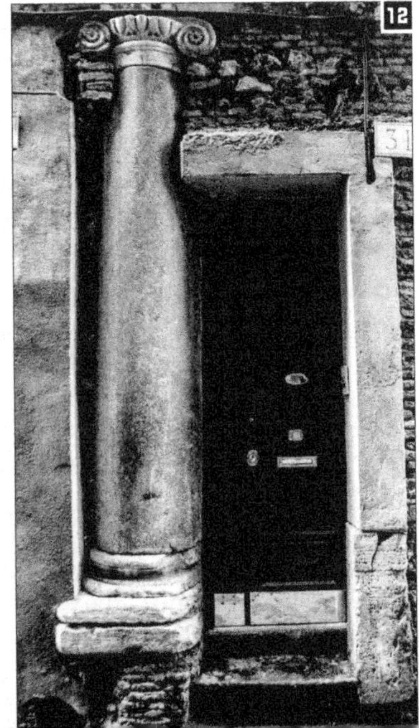

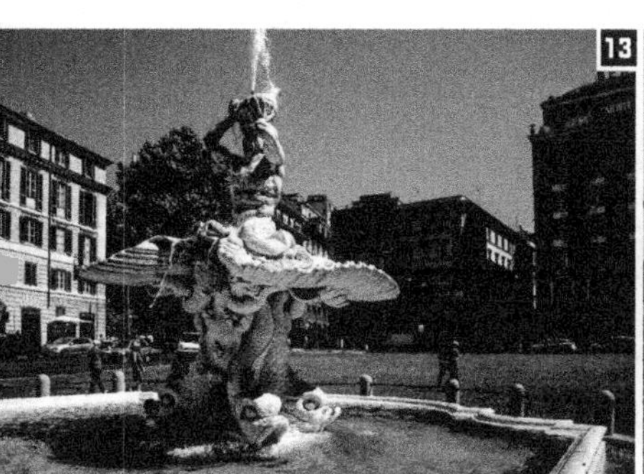

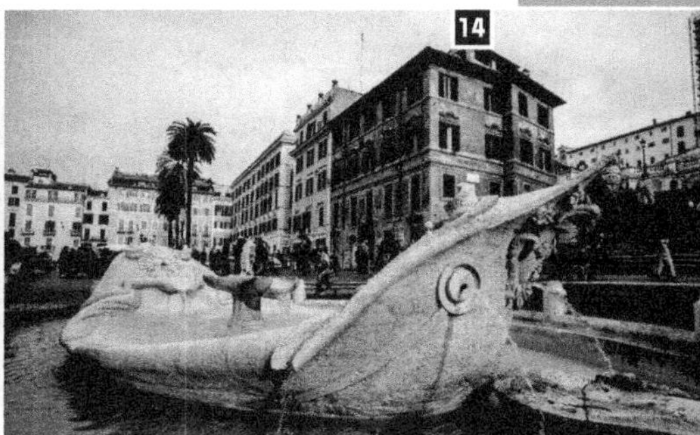

In every church, façade or courtyard, there is a piece of sculpture, column, capital, or brick from a time long gone. **13**

Each ancient remnant somehow turns into a piece of a puzzle or even a prominent part of a new building, and that has been the case since ancient times. **32**

These are called *spolia* and they are found not only as additional decoration, but also as essential parts of new buildings without which the new structure could not even exist. **12**

From the Arch of Constantine, numerous Roman churches, all the way to St. Peter's Basilica at the Vatican, each generation used the old stones to make new buildings, as if Rome had always been a giant self-service antique store.

It is no wonder that entire streets and parts of Rome are filled with antique shops, with countless objects stacked on top of each other during the last 2,700 years. **14**

And no matter how much history there is at every turn, there is also a mirror of the present moment. It is hard to find anything more up-to-date than fashion.

◆ *La Bella Figura* or Good Impression

Rome is one of four major fashion capitals, along with Milan, New York and Paris.

Did you know?

Where to find the most famous artists and their works?

► Where to see Michelangelo's architecture in Rome and Vatican? [p.78]

► Where to see Michelangelo's sculptures and frescoes in Rome and Vatican? [p.138]

► Where to see Raphael's paintings and frescoes in Rome and Vatican? [p.163]

► Where to see Bernini's architecture and fountains in Rome and Vatican? [p.110]

► Where to see Bernini's paintings and sculptures in Rome and Vatican? [p.197]

► Where to see Caravaggio's paintings in Rome and Vatican? [p.118]

► Where to see Borromini's works in Rome? [p.231]

► Where to see Domenico Fontana's architecture and fountains in Rome? [p.285]

► Where to see Cosmati mosaics in churches of Rome? [p.176]

► Where to see fountains designed by Giacomo della Porta? [p.117]

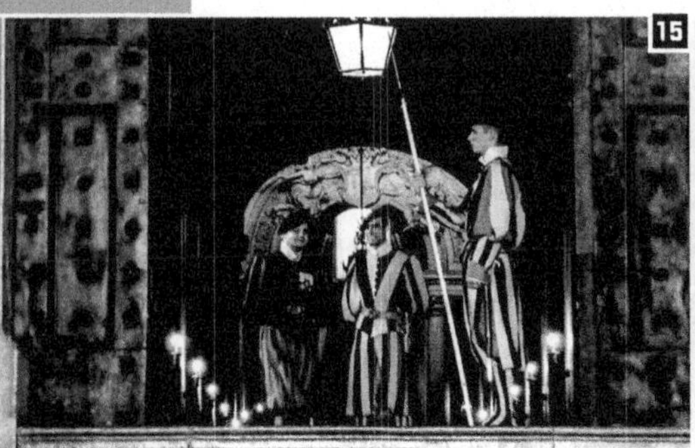

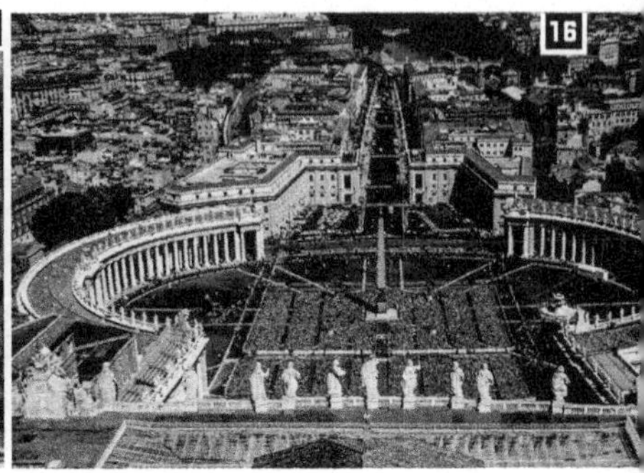

The headquarters of almost every Italian luxury brand is located in Rome and all the other famous designer brands have their stores here.

High fashion shops and perfume stores are on every corner in downtown Rome.

There is much on offer — from global fashion brands around Piazza di Spagna, which are already show their fall/winter collections in early summer, to tailors who will make you an elegant shirt in a day after they take your measurements, e.g., around the Roman Senate, between the Pantheon and Piazza Navona. **17** Whatever you take home with you, it will be something special.

❼ Fountains & Squares

Unlike other European capitals, where life courses behind the walls, life is at its most intense on the streets of Rome. Streets and squares are open air theaters and you shouldn't overlook them for the sake of indoor spaces. **18** But among streets, fountains and squares, there are those which are more interesting, gorgeous and fascinating than others.

You can explore the city by bicycle, bus or on foot, the latter still being the most attractive option, because the most interesting streets are cobbled, narrow, crowded, full of antique shops, coffee shops and restaurants with outdoor seating. **19 26**

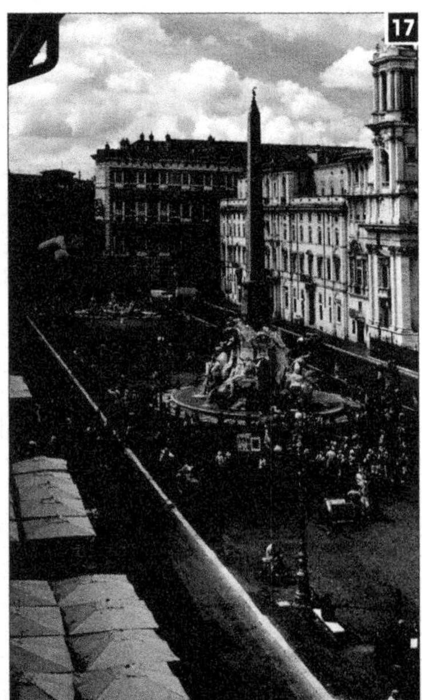

Rome is a city of fountains. In Rome, you will find some of the most famous, spectacular and artistic fountains. Not every fountain in Rome is on a square, but there is not a square without a fountain. **27 30 31**

❽ Rome for first-time Visitors

Ideally, your first trip to Rome should be four to five days long. A week in Rome would be beyond ideal. But do not fool yourself in thinking that will be enough to see everything worth seeing. **21**

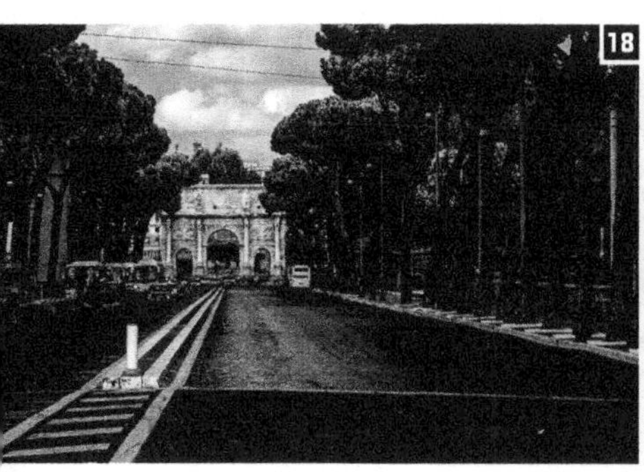

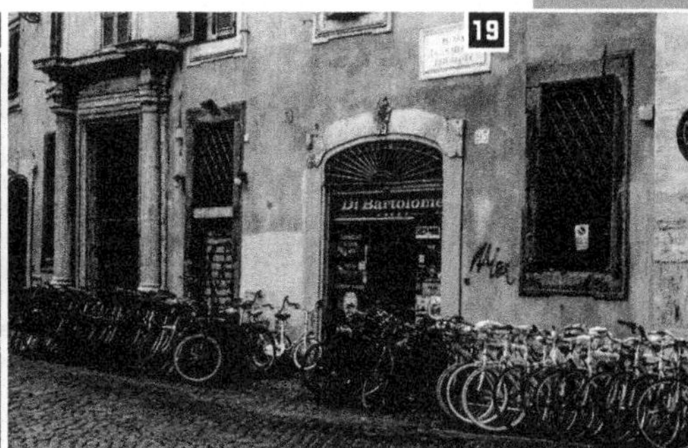

Even after two weeks in Rome, you will still not be able to say you have seen most of its sites. **20**

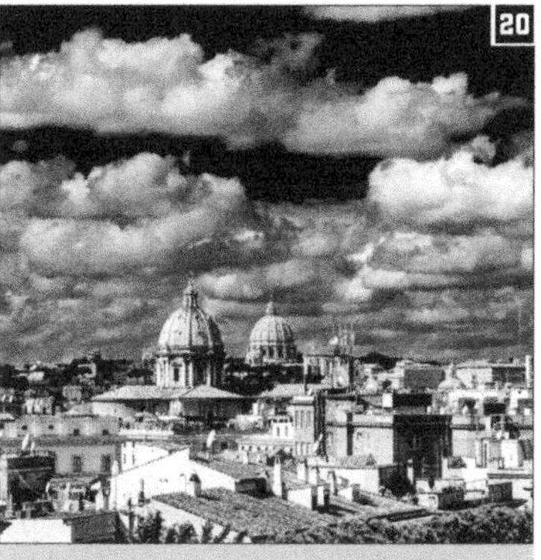

This is why you should throw a coin over your shoulder in the Trevi Fountain and make a wish to come back to Rome as soon as possible. **28**

❾ Self guided walking tours

To see as much of Rome as possible, we have compiled a seven-day list with major landmarks that should not be missed.

Each day is planned as a walk-through Rome that begins and ends at the nearest metro station. No need to grab a taxi, tram, bus or the metro between sites.

You can simply enjoy walking through the city center that has much more to offer than unique museums and churches, palaces and parks, all of them filled with works by so many famous artists, whose number is unmatched anywhere else in the world.

If you're staying only for a day, take the first walk on our list and it will be more than enough. If you're in Rome for two days, our first and second day offer an ideal selection of Roman sites, just like the rest of our walks.

You can also swap walks according to your interests and how many times you have already visited Rome.

Did you know?

Self guided walking tours [p.328]

▸ **1st day** — Imperial Rome

▸ **2nd day** — Vatican and Heart of Rome

▸ **3rd day** — Walk around – Art

▸ **4th day** — Walk around – Architecture

▸ **5th day** — Walk around – Archaeology

▸ **6th day** — Catacombs and ancient sights on the Appian Way

▸ **7th day** — On the way to the Sea

Extra Walks

▸ Along the Tiber **[p.174]**

▸ From Galleria Borghese to Trevi Fountain **[p.188]**

▸ From Baths of Diocletian to the Piazza del Quirinale **[p.208]**

▸ Trastevere and Gianicolo **[p.236]**

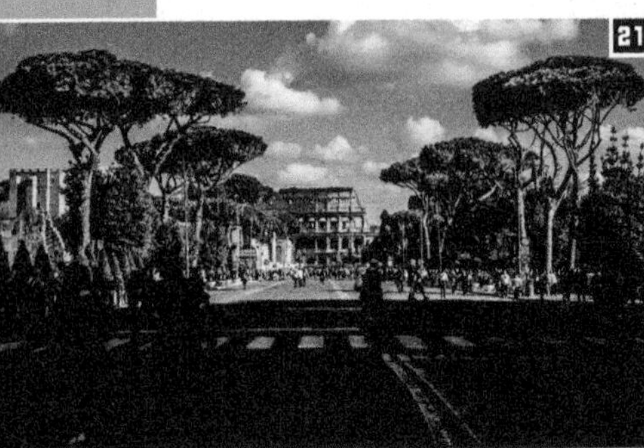

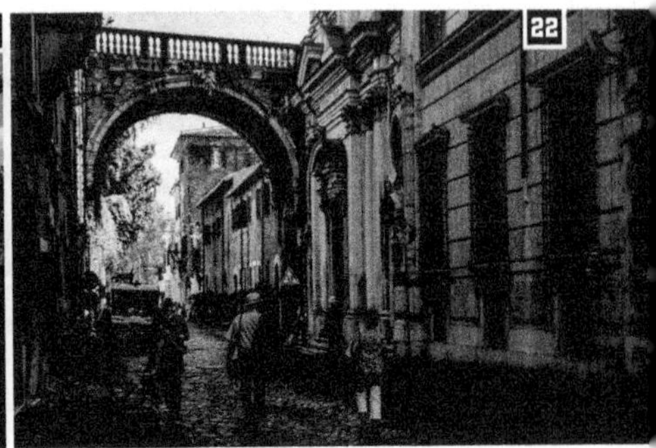

Time-saving tips

It would be great if you did a few things before your trip.

First, buy a guide that will offer you more landmarks than you plan to visit. Here's why this is crucial.

We are certain that you will change your plans several times, depending on what you will like on the spot and where you will spend more time than planned. It is important that you can change your priorities on the go.

There is no way to anticipate which landmarks you might come across by chance, which ones you will like based on what you had read about them or heard from friends. Besides, a lot depends on changes in the working hours or the weather, which is also out of your hands.

It certain sites could get closed for visitors without prior notice exactly when you plan to visit them and that's something you have to count on happening in Italy at any time.

There are also places that you will discover by accident and where you will want to stay for so long that you will end up missing out on visiting what you had already planned.

If you want an example, the Basilica of San Clemente al Laterano is only a 5 minute walk away from the Colosseum. When you walk into the church at street level, you will find yourself in the Basilica of San Clemente al Laterano, built around 1100. This church was not built on the foundations of the previous church, but literally on top of a 4th-century church which has been completely preserved right underneath the basilica, so you can go down and look around that church as well.

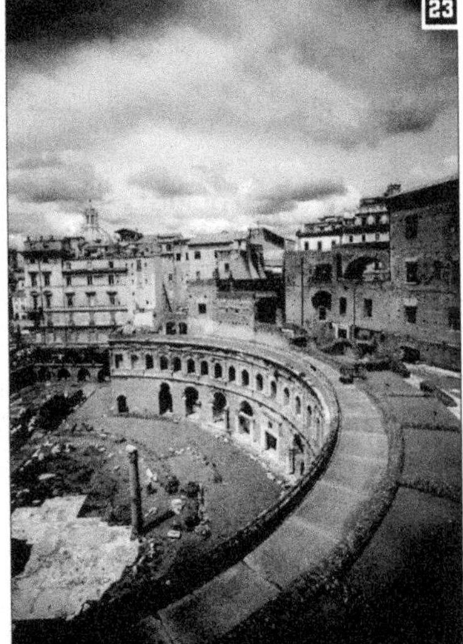

But that's not all. There is another level under with a *Mithraeum* from the 3rd century, Temple of Mithras, an especially popular god among Roman soldiers. You have to walk down an old Roman alley, which is, just like the temple, some 65 ft or 20 m under

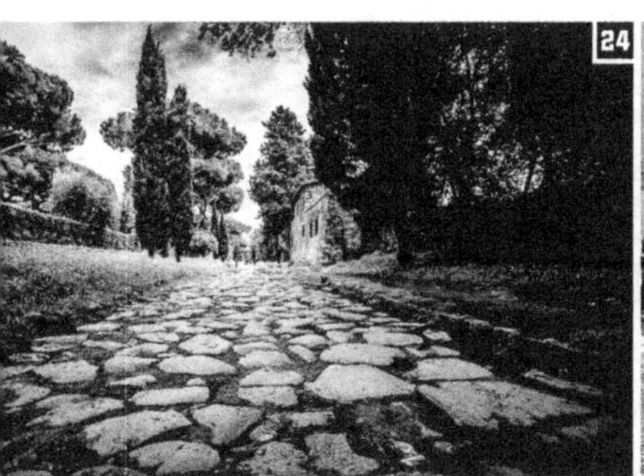

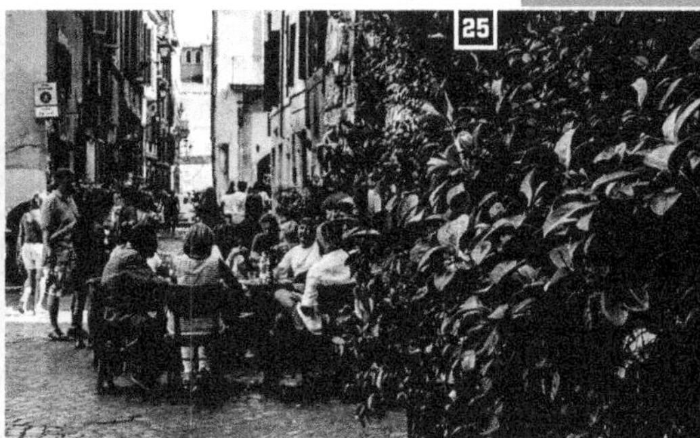

the present-day Roman streets, to get to the partially preserved Roman mint called *Moneta*, build in the 1st century AD.

Our guide provides more than a month's worth of information and landmarks according to your interests. It would be wise to buy tickets online before your trip for some of the most relevant and visited sites. This will save you a lot of time because you won't have to wait in line. All these sites are highlighted in our guide, with links to online museum ticket shops free of additional charges, ways to avoid crowds and long waiting.

Moreover, there are several extremely important sites that are impossible to visit without buying a ticket in advance. This means you will not be able to buy a ticket once you get there, even if there are not that many visitors that day.

Another thing to pay attention to is that on Mondays, much like in the rest of Europe, a lot of Roman museums are closed for visitors.

Certain sites, for example, the catacombs, have coordinated their working hours, so they are open when all the other ones around them are closed.

You can also buy combined tickets for multiple sites and save a lot of money and time.

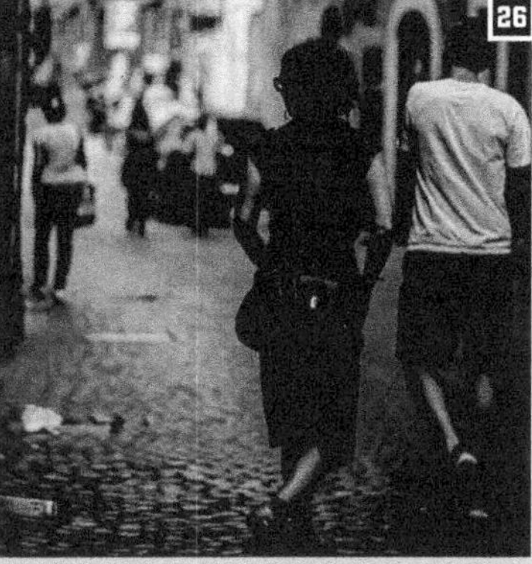

Did you know?

Getting Around

▶ On Foot

This is the most practical and the most beautiful way of getting around Rome.

▶ Metro

The subway is the fastest way to visit the most attractions and museums in the least amount of time.

▶ Bus

The bus lines are impossible to number. The timetable is rarely respected.

▶ Tram

There are only a few tram lines and they usually operate outside the city center.

▶ Taxi

Taxi is the most expensive way to get around Rome and certainly not the fastest.

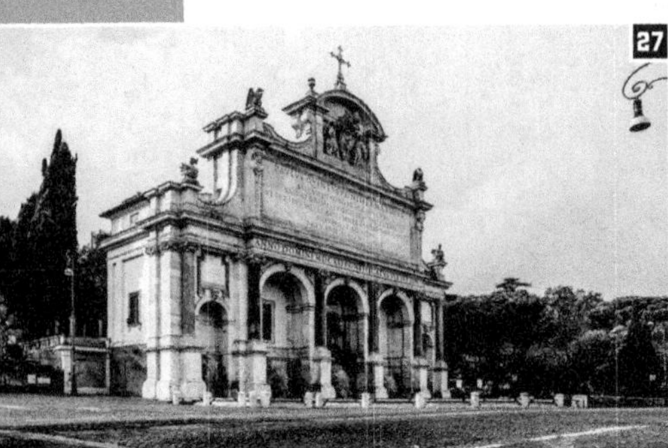

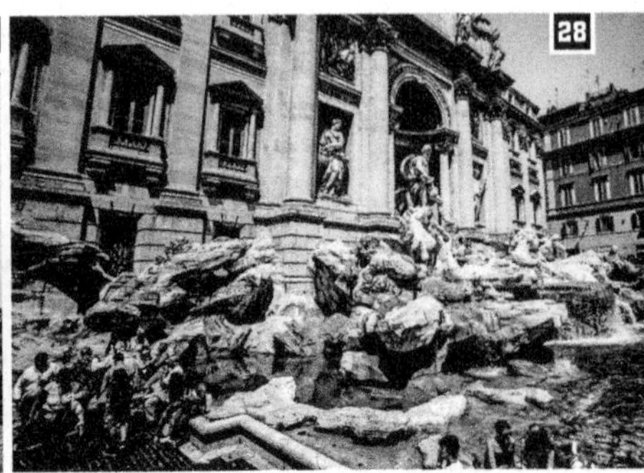

This has nothing to do with "Roma Pass" and similar discounts for public transport, museums, and shopping.

⓫ How to dress and behave

Comfortable clothes and footwear are recommended, but be careful not to use transparent clothes. This is because you will visit many churches and other religious buildings, whether you are religious or not.

Roman churches are museums you can visit for free, and it would be a shame to miss out on paintings and sculptures by Michelangelo, Raphael, Bernini, Bramante or Caravaggio just because you didn't cover your shoulders or you wore tight-fitting clothes, shorts or a revealing dress, flip-flops and so on.

What's more, unlike in most other cities, popes have declared so many ancient monuments as churches or especially important to the history of the Catholic Church, which saved them from destruction to this day.

For example, the Pantheon is also the Basilica di Santa Maria ad Martyres or Basilica of St. Mary and the Martyrs. **6**

It would be best to wear airy clothes that cover your shoulders and knees and closed shoes.

Furthermore, you will have to leave your backpack and umbrella in the museum cloakroom, and there are almost no closed spaces where you can take a photo using a tripod.

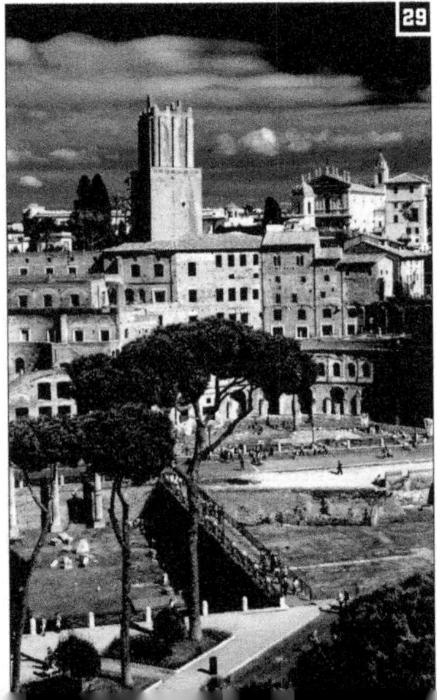

⓬ Safety measures

You will inevitably spend a lot of time in crowded Roman public places.

As far as pickpocketing goes, Rome is no exception to other large cities, so use common sense and be careful with your money and documents the same way you would in other cities.

We would recommend using money belts and travel wallets for daily cash and personal documents.

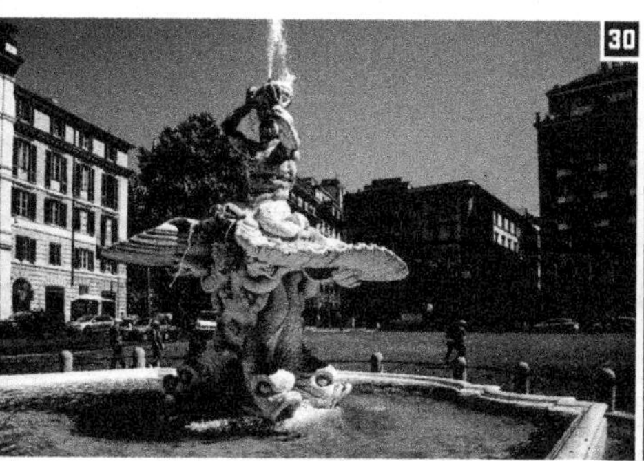

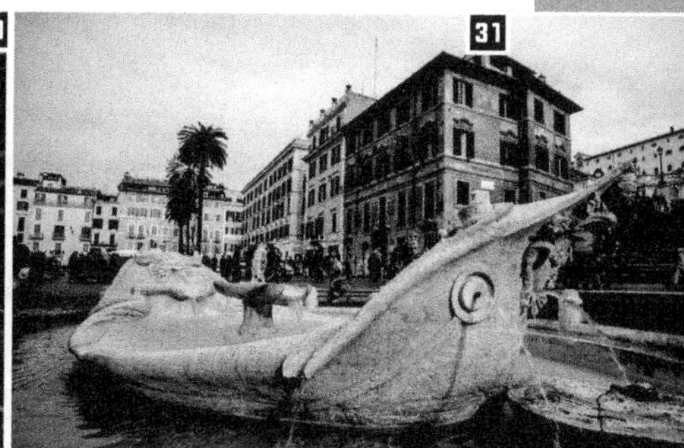

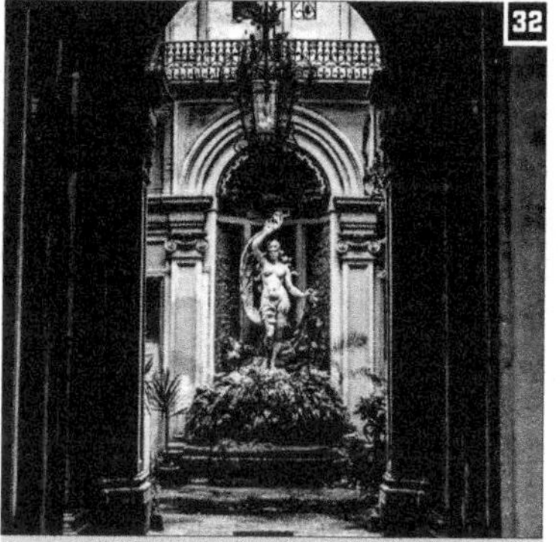

Also, do not wear anything across your shoulder that you cannot secure with your hand. The same thing goes for valuable watches and necklaces. It would be best to leave them at the hotel safe.

Since you will spend a lot of time walking in the heat, you will need a water bottle, so you should consider getting a backpack that keeps both of your hands free. Use padlocks on your zippers for extra security. When you are using public transport, make sure to take off your backpack and hold it next to your leg, no matter how many passengers there are in the vehicle.

When to visit Rome?

It would be best to avoid peak season in the summer because the heat and humidity in July and August are unbearable, so you won't be able to walk from site to site all day long.

Therefore, Rome is the most pleasant in the spring, April and May are ideal, as well as in the fall, that is, September or October.

To be precise, you should visit Rome in late April and early May, or late September and early October.

This is also when the vegetation is the most lavish — it is less crowded than in the summer, the weather is agreeable with optimal temperatures.

Did you know?

Museum and Church Guides in this Book

▸ Galleria Borghese e Museo Borghese | Borghese Gallery and Museum [p.188]

▸ Musei Vaticani | Vatican Museums [p.143]

▸ Palazzo Massimo alle Terme – The National Roman Museum [p.26]

▸ Musei Capitolini | The Capitoline Museums [p.81]

▸ Palazzo Altemps – The National Roman Museum [p.114]

▸ Via Appia Antica | The Appian Way (open air museum) [p.290]

▸ Foro Romano | The Roman Forum (open air museum) [p.50]

▸ Basilica Parrocchiale Santa Maria del Popolo | Basilica of Santa Maria del Popolo [p.195]

▸ Basilica di San Pietro | St. Peter's Basilica [p.136]

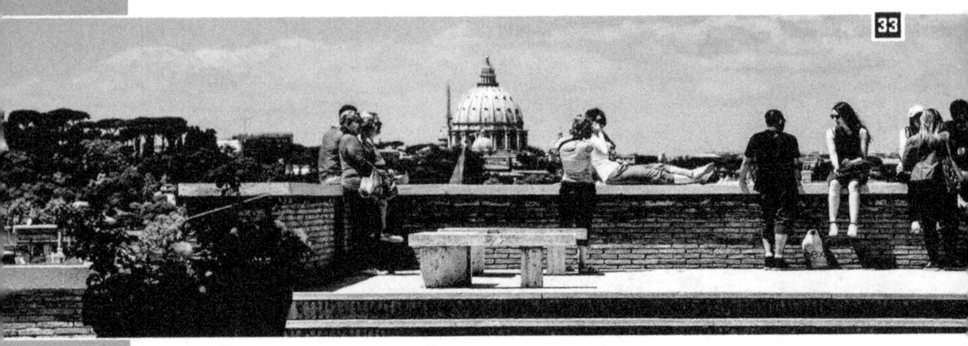

However, if you are extremely fond of museums and churches and you would like to visit them when they are the least crowded, and you would also like to book a table at a restaurant without any problems or even try your luck finding a table without a reservation, it is best to come to Rome in late November.

This is also when sightseeing is the least stressful. Here's an example of why you should consider this option. From spring to fall, at the end of the tour of the Vatican Museums, you will get a chance to go through the Sistine Chapel.

We say 'go through' because you will be told to leave after 15 minutes. Not only is this too short a time to gaze at Michelangelo's creations in a chapel which hosts, to this day, papal conclaves, but you will also be squeezed among other visitors like a canned sardine and out in 15 minutes.

On the other hand, if you visit the Vatican Museums in late November, do not leave the last 15 minutes for the Sistine Chapel. You can literally stay there for as long as you want.

Feel free to sit on the stone bench along the chapel wall for hours and watch the walls and ceiling painted by Michelangelo until your neck hurts, without any fear someone might tell you to leave. Same goes for a lot of other museums.

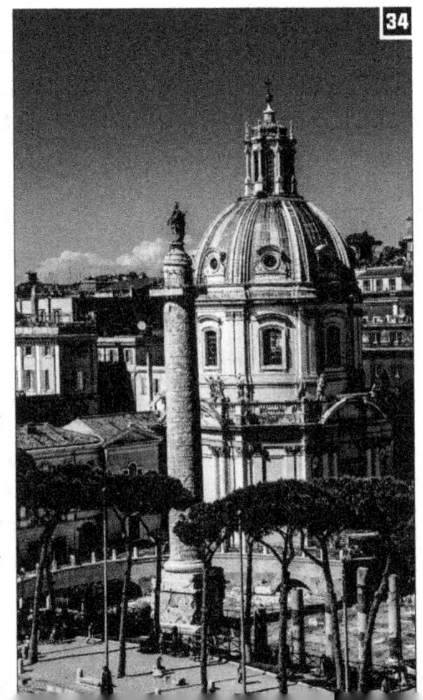

⑭ The Eternal City

Fascination with Rome is three thousand years old. Who hasn't heard that "All roads lead to Rome" or even that "Rome is the center of the world"? 🎧

Greek philosopher Aelius Aristides shared in AD 156 his excitement of Rome:

> *... everywhere fountains, marble halls, temples, workshops, schools ... bold spectacles of every kind and so many competitions.*

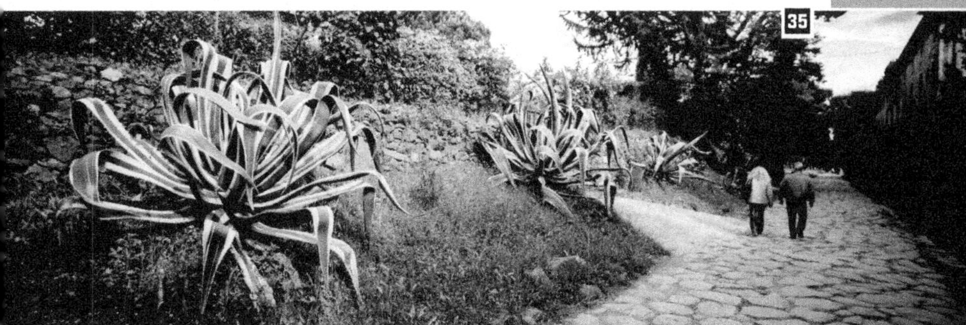

After his visit to Rome, the eighteenth-century German art historian Johann Joachim Winckelmann said:

Apart from Rome, there is virtually nothing beautiful left in the world.

Perhaps one of the best quotes on the effect Rome has on its modern visitors comes from American actor Robert De Niro:

Italy has changed. But Rome is Rome.

⑮ Why is Rome so special?

Roman churches are exceptional not only because of the artists who built them, but also because of the artists who painted them. 🄴

For example, at the church of San Luigi dei Francesi you can see three large paintings by Caravaggio, while paintings by Raphael, Caravaggio and an altar by Bernini wait only a hundred steps away at the Basilica di Sant'Agostino, along with the tomb of St. Augustine's mother, St. Monica, whose remains were transferred from Ostia.

If you walk another hundred steps, you will reach Piazza Navona, former stadium of Roman Emperor Domitian, with beautiful fountains sculpted by Bernini.

Museum buildings in Rome are pieces of art in themselves sometimes.

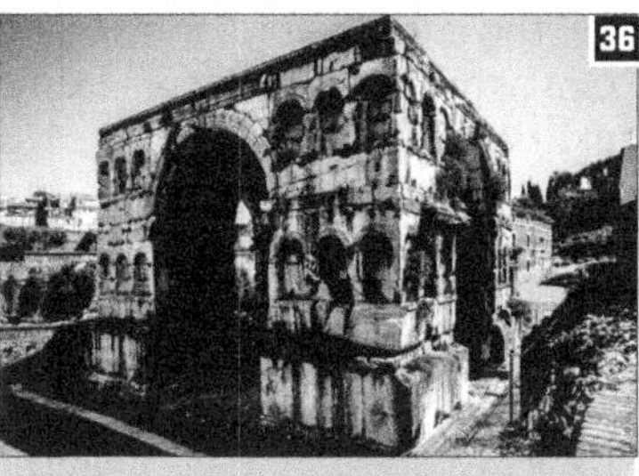

How to use this guide

★ ★ ★ ★ – Key site in the chapter

★ ★ ★ – Not to be missed

★ ★ – Worth seeing

★ – For those with specific interests

Tip ::: – Information you should pay attention to when you plan a visit to the sites described in the chapter.

► Where and what to eat in Rome?

The Food & Drink chapter introduces you to Roman cuisine and its most important dishes and drinks, as well as restaurants, trattorias and osterias where you can enjoy authentic Roman cuisine.

► Where to shop in Rome?

The Shopping chapter offers you the most important streets and neighborhoods where you can window shop, buy shoes, clothes, antiques, or food and drinks to take home as souvenirs.

► Index of People and Places

For quick reference, there is an index of people and places at the end of the guide.

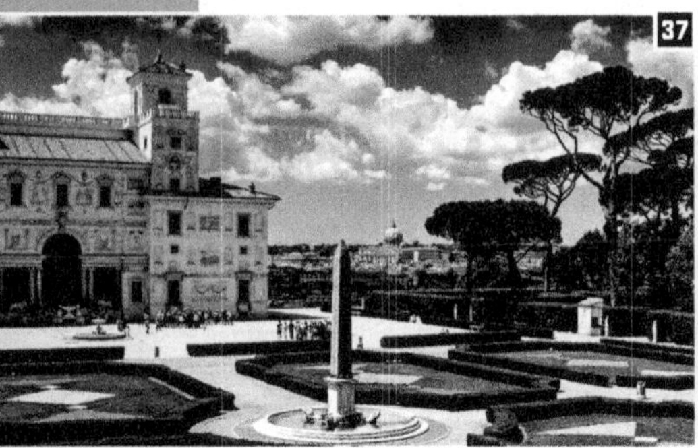

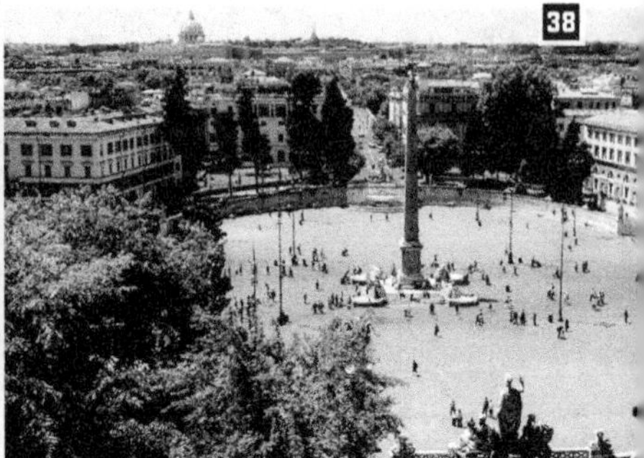

This is true of the Capitoline Museums as much as the National Museum of 21st Century Art (MAXXI).

The Barberini Palace, for example, was built by Maffeo Barberini (Pope Urban VIII) for his family.

He ordered the architect Carlo Maderno to build a representative palace for the Barberini family on the foundations of the Sforza family's palace.

Soon after the construction of the palace began, Gian Lorenzo Bernini became the head architect and builder.

Bernini's biggest rival at the time, Francesco Borromini, also participated in the construction of the palace, and created the masterpiece spiral staircase in the south wing of the Barberini Palace.

Nowadays, the Palace houses the collection of the National Gallery of Ancient Art.

If you are overwhelmed and pressed for time, not knowing whether to visit another famous museum or walk through yet another of Rome's neighborhoods, you should bear in mind that Rome in itself is the biggest and most beautiful of all Roman museums. 37 38

Did you know?

Vatican City — City of the Pope

As far as the pope is concerned, he lives in his theological state, Vatican City, surrounded by the city of Rome on all sides. 15

Every Wednesday at 10:30 a.m. you can see him at St. Peter's Square while he is greeting people and giving blessings to curious tourists, devout Christians and pilgrims. 16

You will need to book the Papal Audience in advance. 39
The tickets are free of charge: www.papalaudience.org

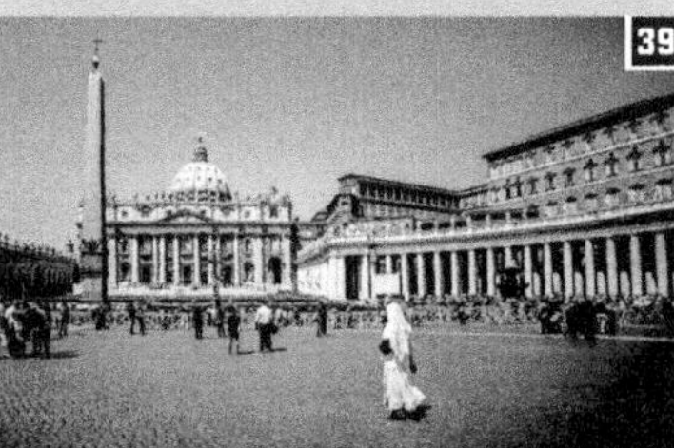

Did you know?

In the smallest state in the world

▸ The courtyard of the Vatican was the first archaeological park in the world. [p.167]

▸ The largest church in the world is in Vatican City. [p.136]

▸ Inside the walls of Vatican City you will find some of the best collections of art. [p.143]

Colosseum

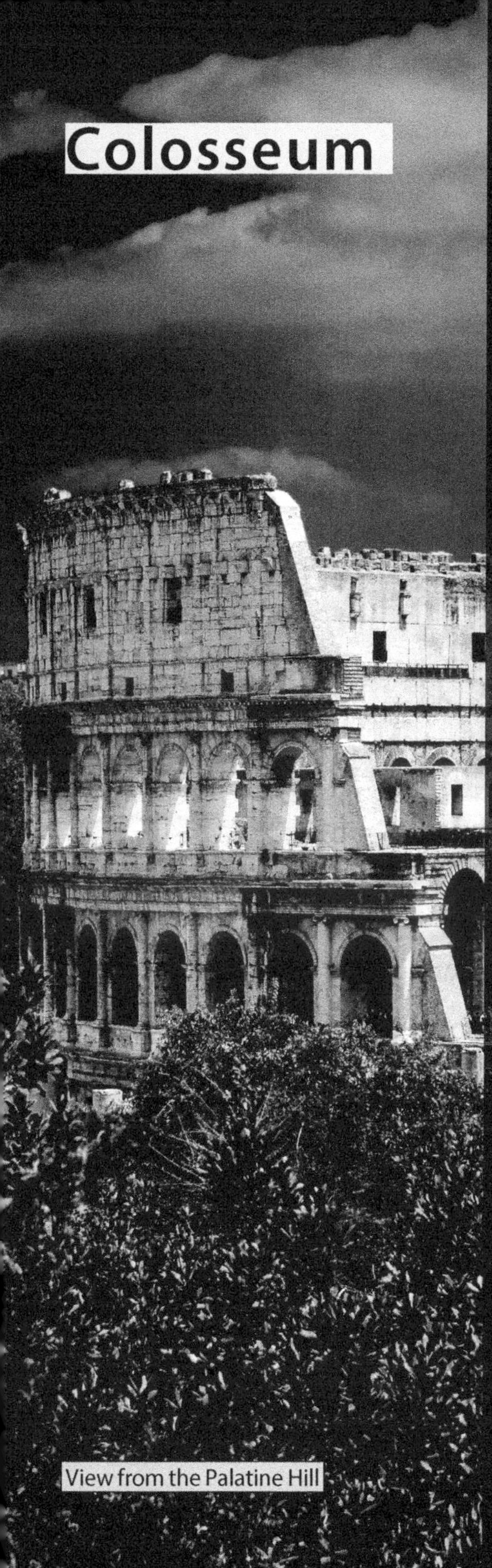

View from the Palatine Hill

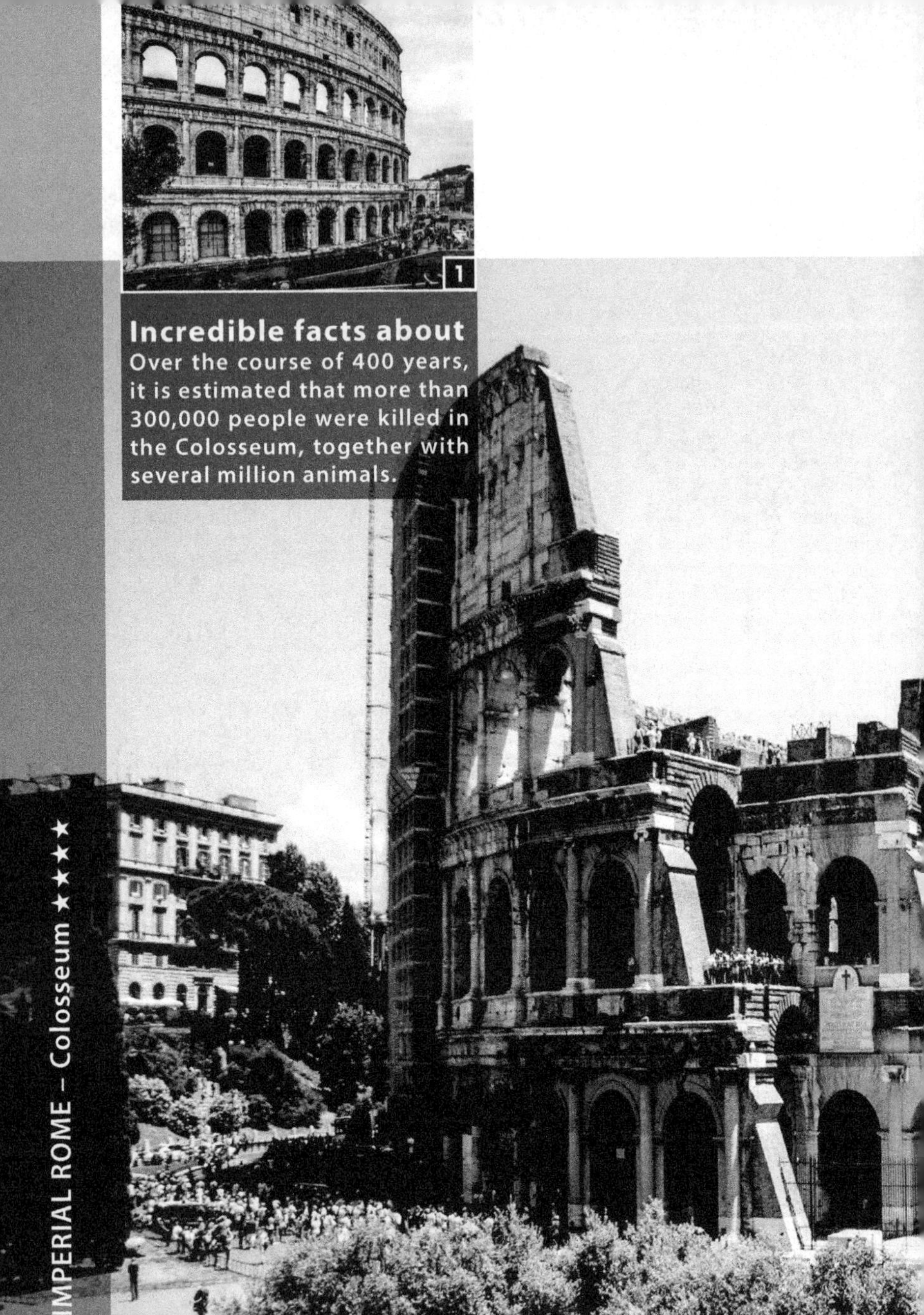

Incredible facts about

Over the course of 400 years, it is estimated that more than 300,000 people were killed in the Colosseum, together with several million animals.

View of the Colosseum from the Temple of Venus

Extra Tip : : :
The standard entrance ticket includes entrance to the Colosseum, Roman Forum and Palatine Hill. Your ticket is valid for two days but you can visit each attraction only once.

A journey through time

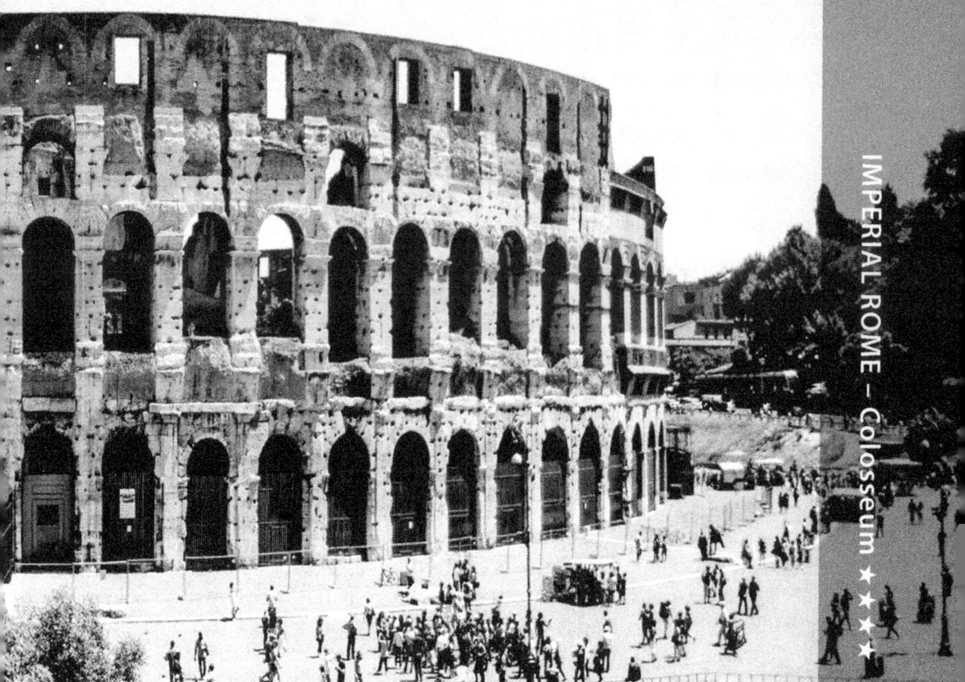

Colosseo | Colosseum
Address: Piazza del Colosseo, Roma
Public transportation: Metro B stop Colosseo | Bus stop Colosseo: 51, 85, 87, 117 |
Tram stop Piazza del Colosseo: 8
Hours and tickets: www.parcocolosseo.it/en

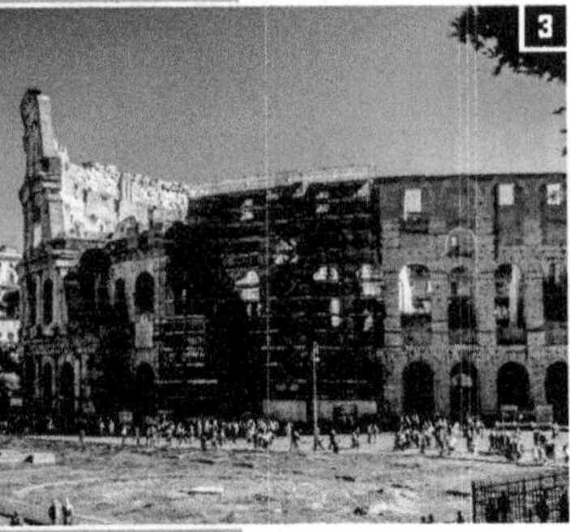
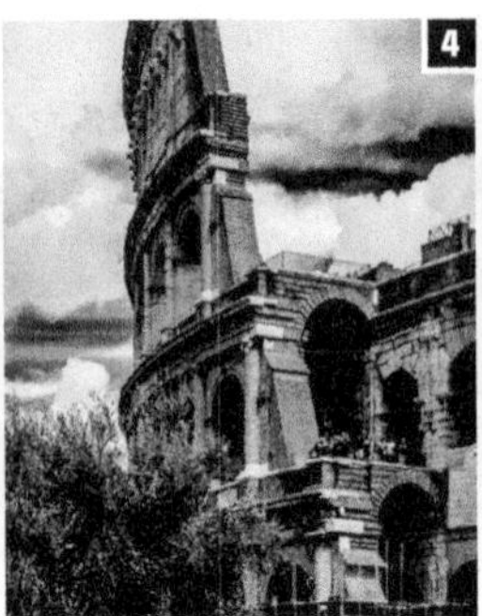
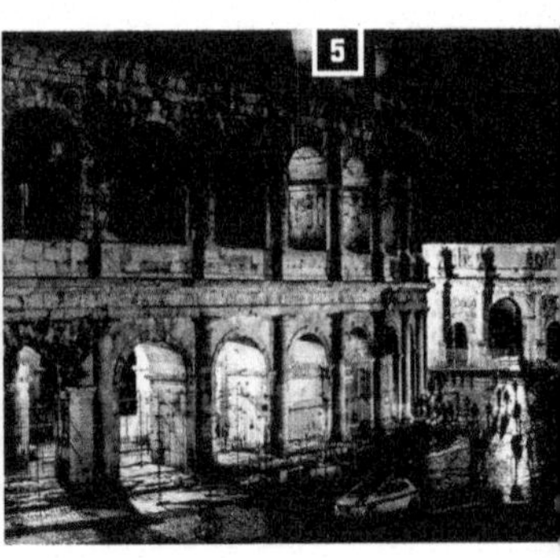

❶ Colosseum ★ ★ ★ ★

The Colosseum is the largest amphitheater in the world and the biggest closed structure Romans ever built. **1**

The construction began during Emperor Vespasian (69–79) in AD 72, followed by Titus (79–81), who finished it eight years later. Further modifications took place while another member of the Flavian family was in charge, Emperor Domitian (81– 96). This is why Romans referred to the Colosseum as *Amphitheatrum Flavium*. It is estimated that the Colosseum could hold 50,000 to 87,000 people. **2**

During Vespasian's reign, it had three tiers: the first one was Doric, second one Ionic, and the third Corinthian. Titus added another tier with rectangular windows. Outer walls were limestone and Roman travertine, while the inner walls were made of brick and tuff, i.e., solidified volcanic ash. **3**

For the grand opening ceremony, games with gladiator fights, naval battles and animal fights were scheduled for a period of a hundred days. When Emperor Trajan celebrated his victory in Dacia in AD 107 (present-day Romania), the games went on for four whole months, with more than 10,000 gladiators and 11,000 wild animals. Colosseum is another testament to incredible Roman engineering. **4**

Did you know?

The amphitheater as the most famous Roman building

The oldest Roman amphitheaters were built in the Late Republican Period (509 BC–27 BC). During the Imperial Era (27 BC–AD 476), the amphitheater became the most dominant building in a Roman city, the same way churches would dominate the cityscape in the Middle Ages or skyscrapers in the 20th century. The Colosseum is 187 ft (50 m) high, which is almost as high as a twelve-story building.

Public spectacles held at amphitheaters, circuses and theaters started to lose their appeal with the spread of Christianity. Roman Christians did not place such a high value on games and fun and the wealthy members of society stopped investing in construction of public venues, which used to help them attain higher status and receive honors. The Roman Christians wanted to be rewarded by God in Paradise, so they started giving to charity rather than public venues and games. This is how gladiator fights started disappearing in the third century, while animal fights and horse racing finally disappeared in the sixth century.

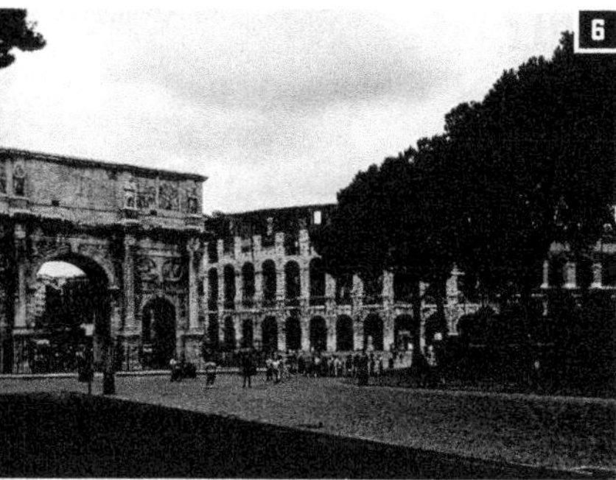

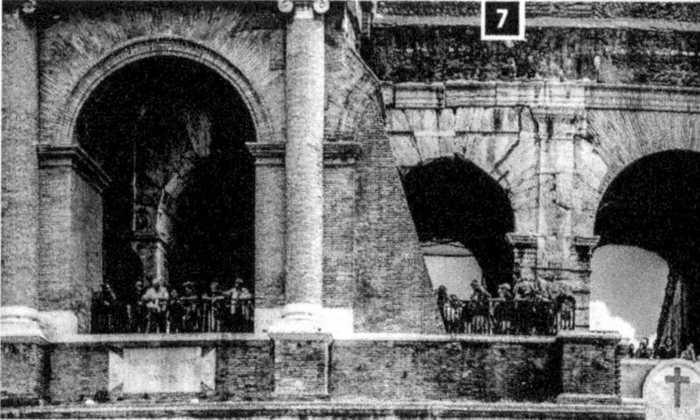

Anyone entering the arena can find a seat within ten minutes thanks to 80 gates. **7**

There were four VIP entrances, for the emperor, senators, priests and Vestal priestesses. A special lodge was erected for the emperor, called the *pulvinar*.

Distinguished Roman citizens sat behind the senators according to rank and wealth. The poorest men and women of Rome had to stand on the very top of the arena.

Two-story basements are located below the arena where gladiators and animals waited before the show. A spectacular entrance for the animals was secured by eight shafts. **5**

Underground halls led all the way to the stables outside the arena and to the gladiator training school, the Ludus Magnus.

Colosseo | Colosseum
Address: Piazza del Colosseo, Roma
Online: www.coopculture.it/en

Public transportation: Metro B stop Colosseo | Bus stop Colosseo: 51, 85, 87, 117 | Tram stop Piazza del Colosseo: 8

Opening hours and tickets: www.parcocolosseo.it/en

Colosseum
1. Colosseum
2. Arch of Constantine
3. Domus Aurea
4. Ludus Magnus
5. Basilica di San Clemente
6. San Gregorio Magno al Celio
7. Case Romane del Celio
8. Santi Giovanni e Paolo
9. Arco di Dolabella
10. Nerone Aqueduct
11. Santa Maria in Domnica alla Navicella
12. Santo Stefano Rotondo
13. San Pietro in Vincoli
14. Circus Maximus [p.45]
15. Palatine Hill [p.40]
16. Roman Forum [p.50]
► ENTRANCE / EXIT

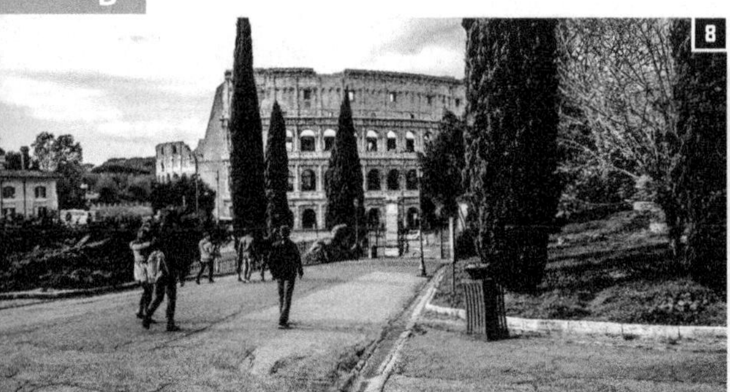
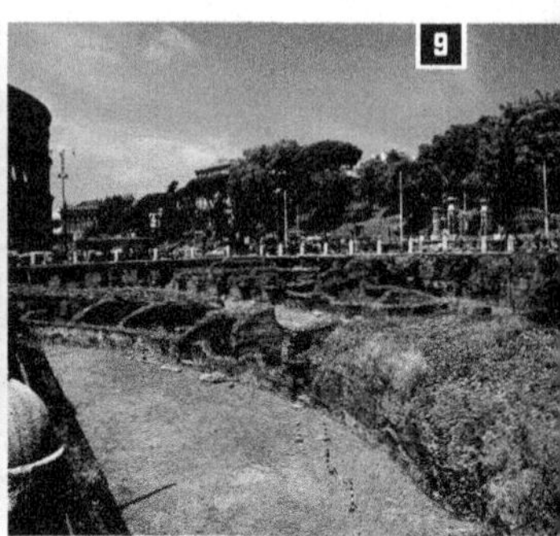

Walk around Colosseum

❷ Arch of Constantine ★★

This is the biggest triumphal arch in Rome. ❻

It was erected on the exact spot where Via Triumphalis joins Via Sacra. This was the path of triumph for centuries.

The procession would start at the Circus Maximus, headed by the emperor, pass the Palatine all the way to Via Sacra and continued across the Roman Forum to the Capitoline Hill.

The Arch of Constantine was erected to celebrate the ten years of Emperor Constantine the Great's rule, as well as his victory in the Battle of Milvian Bridge in AD 312 when he defeated Emperor Maxentius.

The Roman Senate is signed as the commissioner of the arch, in the name of all Roman citizens.

There was not a lot of time for thoughtful decoration of the arch, because this message had to circulate immediately.

Reliefs were taken off the surrounding buildings, dedicated to the "good emperors" Trajan, Hadrian and Marcus Aurelius. Unlike the "good emperors", appreciated for their wisdom and good government, Constantine the Great built the arch to commemorate the triumphal victory over the people of Rome, which had been a taboo for the entirety of Roman history up to that point.

The part that was made especially for this arch is a relief below Hardian's medallions, which greatly differs in style from the rest of the arch. Here, we have Constantine the Great sitting high on his throne among the Romans. Everyone is turned to him and he is giving them money.

Only Constantine the Great is facing the viewer. Lack of perspective is obvious and typical of early Christian art, marking the beginning of the Middle Ages. However, reliefs still belong to the classical style, hands are in perspective, so it is safe to say this is also the Late Classical period.

❸ Domus Aurea ★★

Domus Aurea (Lat. Golden House) was a grandiose complex of palaces, envisioned by the Emperor Nero. It burned down in AD 64.

The Baths of Trajan were built on some of its ruins. As far as the ruins of Nero's Domus Aurea are concerned, the remains consist of the basement, large dining rooms, an octagonal courtyard and mosaics which inspired Raphael when painting the Vatican Stanzas. ❽

Domus Aurea
Address: Via della Domus Aurea 1, Roma
Online: www.coopculture.it/en

Public transportation: Metro B stop Colosseo | Bus stop Colosseo: 51, 85, 87, 117 | Tram stop Piazza del Colosseo: 8

Opening hours and tickets:
www.parcocolosseo.it/en

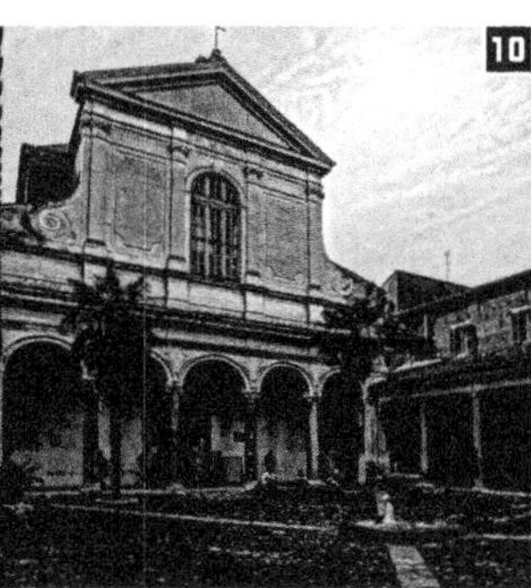

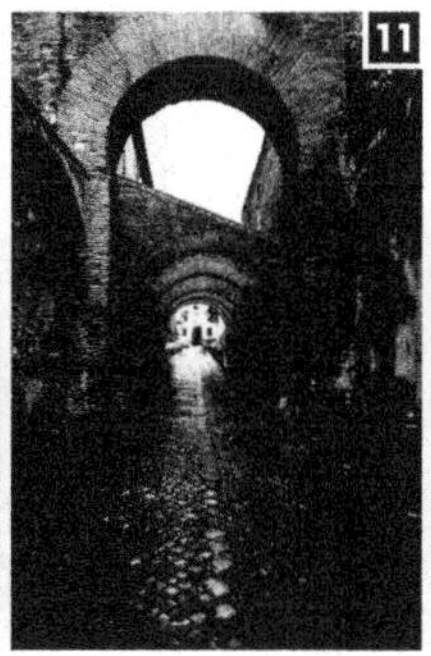

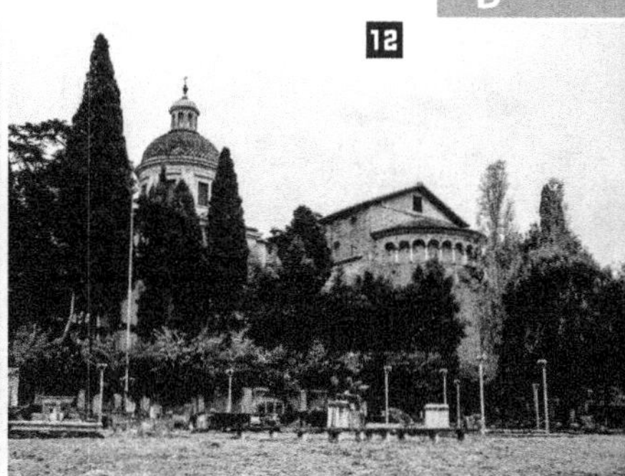

◆ Ludus Magnus ★

Underground halls of the Colosseum lead all the way to the great gladiator training school called Ludus Magnus. The Ludus Magnus was built by the emperor Domitian (81–96) for the performances to be held at the Colosseum.

At the center of the Ludus Magnus was an ellipsoidal arena in which the gladiators practiced. It was circumscribed by the steps reserved for a limited number of spectators. **9**

◆ Basilica di San Clemente ★ ★ ★

This is the first church you should visit in Rome. By going through the layers of this place, you can see millennia of history. [p.20] Basilica of San Clemente was built on a two-story Roman palace which is located below the church. **10**

The ancient palace is still there! It used to be a *Moneta*, or an ancient mint. In turn, the palace was built on an old house from the Republican era that burnt to the ground in the Great Fire of AD 64. On the ground floor of the Roman palace, that is, two levels below the present-day church, there is a Temple of Mithras from the second century.

Between the Temple of Mithras and the Basilica of San Clemente, there is a church from the fourth century. Let's build our way up through all this.

◆ San Gregorio Magno al Celio ★

Pope Gregory I (590–604) ordered the construction of a Benedictine monastery on his father's land. This is where the original church was raised around 1000. The church and the monastery are on the Celio, one of seven legendary Roman hills. St. Augustine of Canterbury went on his Christian campaign to England in 597 with the Benedictines from this place. The interior features a *Cosmatesque floor*, and the church owes its appearance today to construction work in 1725. The church has three oratories, among which the Oratorio di Sant'Andrea and the Oratorio di Santa Barbara date back to Pope Gregory I. Oratorio di Santa Silvia was only added circa 1600.

The Oratory of Saint Andrew is the central oratory with the following frescoes:

► Flagellation of Saint Andrew by Domenichino,

Basilica di San Clemente al Laterano
Address: Via Labicana 95, Roma
Online:
www.basilicasanclemente.com

Public transportation: Metro B stop Colosseo or Metro A stop Manzoni | Bus stop Labicana: 51, 75, 85, 87, C3 | Tram stop Labicana: 8

Opening hours: *see online*

San Gregorio Magno al Celio
Address: Piazza di San Gregorio al Celio 1, Roma
Online:
www.monasterosangregorio.it/en

Public transportation: Metro B stop Circo Massimo | Bus stop S. Gregorio: 51, 81, 85, 87, C3 | Tram stop Parco Celio: 8

Opening hours: *see online*

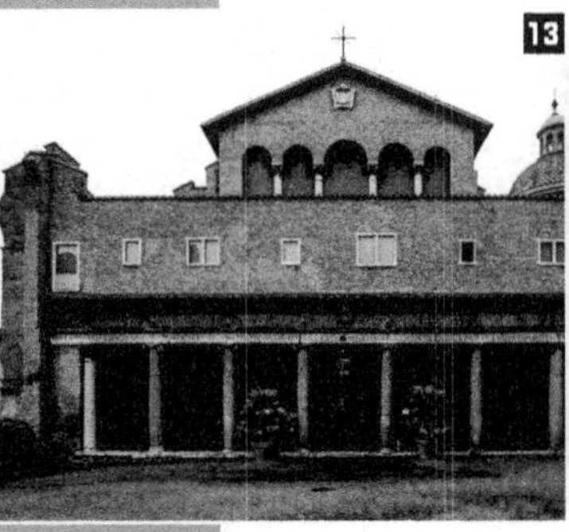

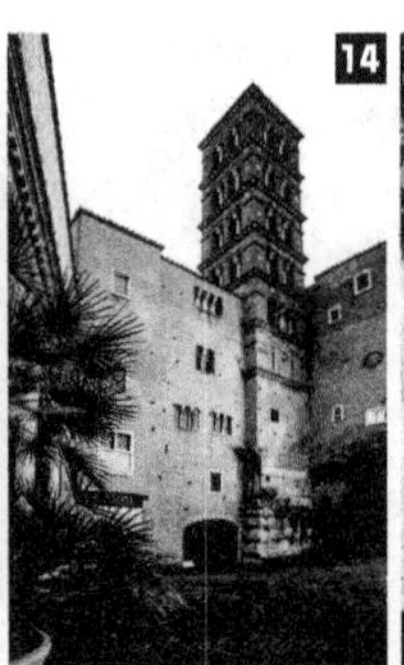

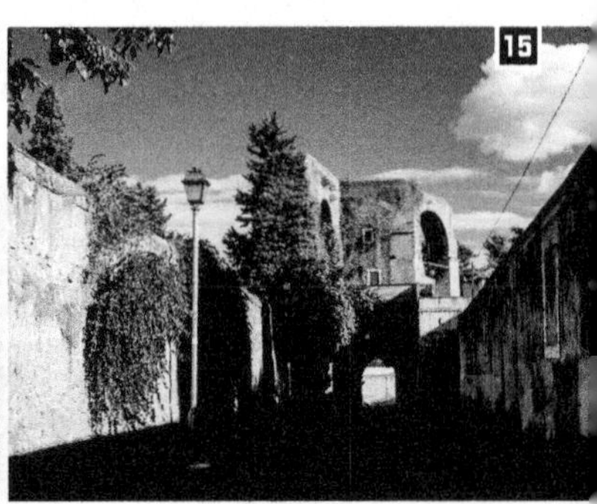

▸ Saint Andrew brought to the temple and Saints Peter and Paul by Reni,

▸ Virgin with Saints Andrew and Gregory by Il Pomarancio,

▸ Saint Silvia and Saint Gregory by Giovanni Lanfranco,

▸ The Oratorio di Santa Barbara features frescoes by Antonio Viviani,

Frescoes in the Santa Silvia oratory are:

▸ Concert of Angels by Guido Reni,

▸ Isaiah by Sisto Badalocchio.

The statue of Aphrodite of Menophantos was discovered underneath the monastery. It is kept at the National Roman Museum or Museo Nazionale Romano. Right next to the basilica and the monastery there is a homeless shelter run by the Order of the Blessed Mother Teresa of Calcutta.

❼ Case Romane del Celio or the Roman Complex Houses at the SS. Giovanni e Paolo ★★★

At the underground sites of the fifth-century Basilica Santi Giovanni e Paolo, Father Germano di San Stanislao discovered in 1887 twenty decorated rooms belonging to at least five different buildings dated between the first and the fourth century. These five buildings comprise one of the best conserved Roman era residential building complexes still standing today.

❽ Santi Giovanni e Paolo ★

The church was not named after the apostles, it owes its name to the patron saints of Rome. The first Christian building here was an oratory built in the third century. The church that we see today dates back more or less to the mid-twelfth century. 🔟 The street leading up to the church, Via di San Giovanni e Paolo, is still paved with the original ancient stones. 🔟

The Romanesque tower was built on the foundations of an ancient Roman temple dedicated to Claudius the Divine (AD 54). 🔟 The anteroom is supported by eight ancient columns, six of which have Ionic capitals, and two have Corinthian capitals. 🔟 The interior of the church is shaped like a basilica, with three naves and no dome. The most interesting thing about this building is its underground from the days of ancient Rome.

Case Romane del Celio | The Roman Complex Houses at the Basilica Santi Giovanni e Paolo
Address: Clivo di Scauro, Roma

Public transportation: Metro B stop Circo Massimo | Bus stop S. Gregorio: 51, 81, 85, 87, C3 | Tram stop Parco Celio: 8

Opening hours: www.coopculture.it/en/poi/roman-houses-of-the-celio-hill

---

Basilica Santi Giovanni e Paolo
Address: Piazza Santi Giovanni e Paolo 13, Roma
Online:
www.santigiovanniepaolo.it/en

Public transportation: Metro B stop Circo Massimo | Bus stop S. Gregorio: 51, 81, 85, 87, C3 | Tram stop Parco Celio: 8

Opening hours: *see online*

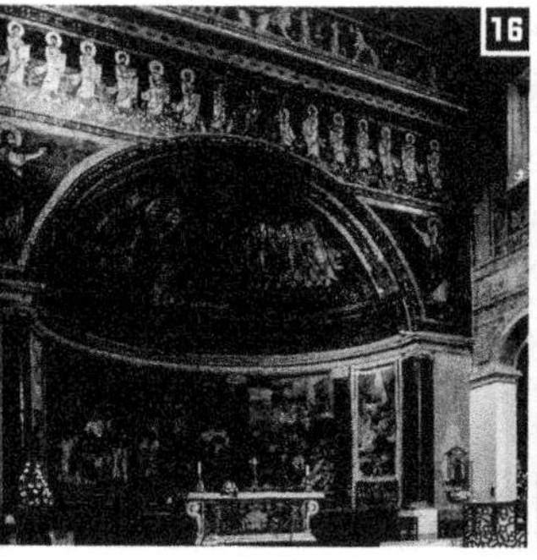

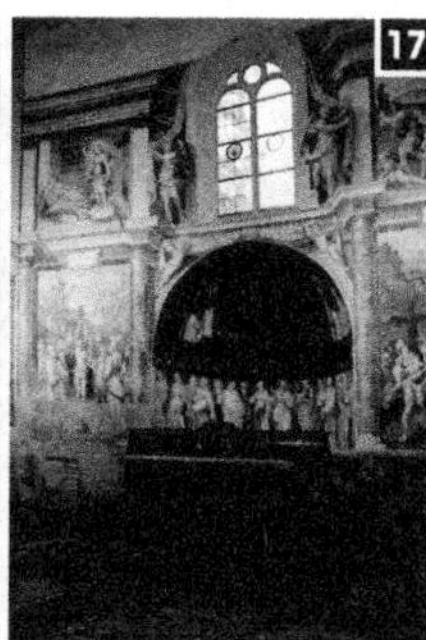

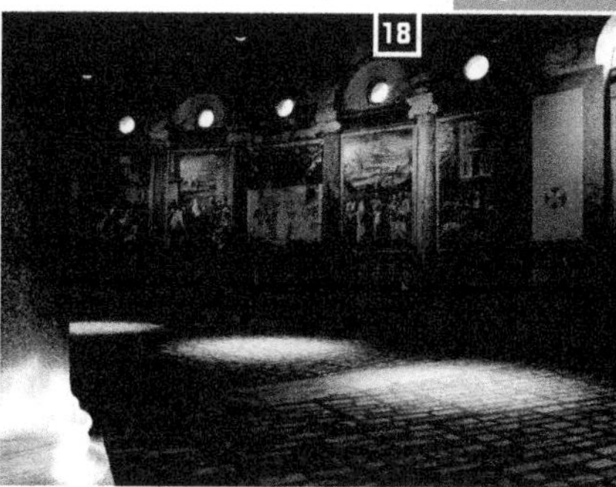

❾ Arco di Dolabella at Silani ★

These ancient city gates go back to the time of the Roman Republic as part of the Servian Wall (4th century BC). 🅖 Originally, they were called Porta Caelimontana. They were restored during the period of Augustus, visible from the inscription on top of the gates (AD 10) with the names of consuls Publius Cornelius Dolabella and Gaius Iunius Silanus.

❿ Nerone Aqueduct ★

During Emperor Nero the extension of the Aqua Claudia aqueduct was built over the arch of the gates. When you go from Arco di Dolabella towards Santa Maria in Domnica, you will come across the remains of an aqueduct from Nero's era, known today as Nerone Aqueduct.

⓫ Santa Maria in Domnica alla Navicella ★★

The name *in Domnica* comes from an ancient marking Dominicum, which was used to label the places of Christian worship. *Navicella*, which means "little boat" in Italian, refers to the votive offering of sailors in the Temple of Isis, which used to be here. The little boat is still in front of the church. Pope Paschal ordered a new, three-nave basilica to be built in 820, decorated with spolia and Ionic and Corinthian capitals. The mosaic in the apse dates back to Cardinal Giovanni de' Medici, who later became Pope Leo X and renovated the church in 1513 in the Renaissance style. 🅖 The cassette ceiling is from that period. The same pope hired the architect Andrea Sansovino to make the façade and the fountain.

⓬ Santo Stefano Rotondo ★★★

This church was consecrated during Pope Simplicius (468–483) and dedicated to the first Christian martyr Saint Stephen. Pope Gregory I built a monastery next to the church and Pope Theodore I (642–649) ordered the transfer of Felician's and Primus' relics from the catacombs to the church of Santo Stefano. This was also the first transfer of martyrs' relics to a church in the history of Christianity. 🅗 For that purpose, an apse was built, the only thing that has been preserved from that period. A dramatic representation of their torture

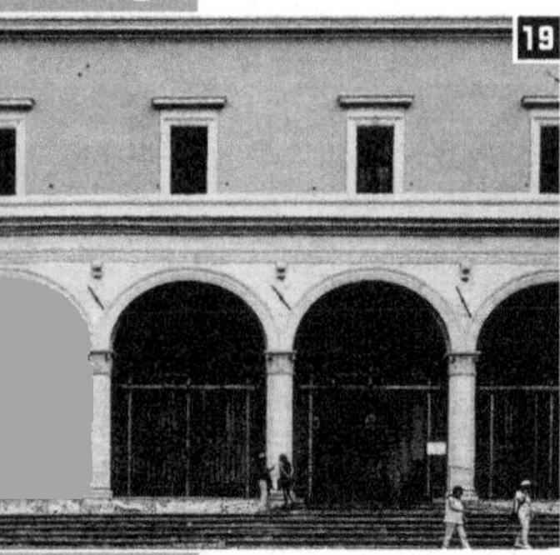

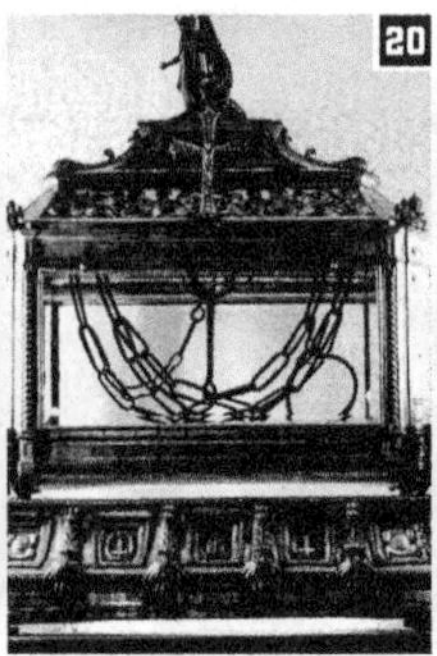

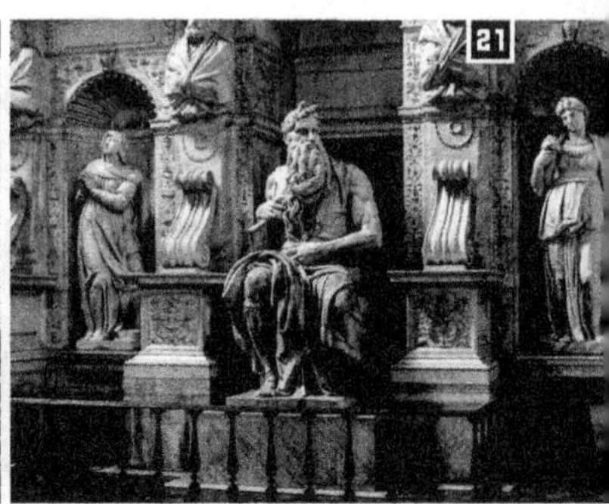

in 32 scenes was rendered by Niccolò Circignani detto il Pomarancio and Matteo da Siena (1582–1583).

Matteo da Siena also painted the landscapes in the background. The Chapel of St. Felician and Primus was painted by Antonio Tempesta in 1580. **18**

⑬ San Pietro in Vincoli ★★★

This church was built in the 5th century on the remains of a 2nd century church. It went through extensive change in the following centuries. It was remodeled by Francesco Fontana, under the orders of Cardinal Giuliano della Rovere. **19** The cardinal became Pope Julius II in 1503 and he then decided to build his tomb here as well. For this purpose, he hired Michelangelo.

① St. Peter's Chains ★

The relic of this church is already present in its name — in Vincoli means "in chains," traditionally belonging to St. Peter. The chains are kept in a glass niche below the main altar. **20**

② Moses by Michelangelo ★★★

Michelangelo represented Moses fresh back from Mount Sinai when he saw the Israeli dancing around the Golden Calf. At first, the sculpture of Moses was supposed to be on the left and this is why Moses is facing in the opposite direction, towards the sarcophagus. The most confusing are his horns. These are the result of a translation error of the Old Testament from Hebrew. Hebrew writing omits vowels, so the word in question was spelled *krn*.

The translator added two E's between the consonants. Krn turned into *keren*, which means "with horns." **21**

The translation was still in use while Michelangelo was working on Moses. It took centuries for the E's to be replaced by A's to make the word *karan*, which means "brilliant." Moses' horns are a linguistic error set in stone. The same "linguistic" horns can be seen on the statue of Moses at the Fontana dell'Acqua Felice (1588), next to the Church of Santa Maria della Vittoria. **[p.225]** Michelangelo also made the figures in the niches. They are Leah, personification of love, and Rachel, personification of faith.

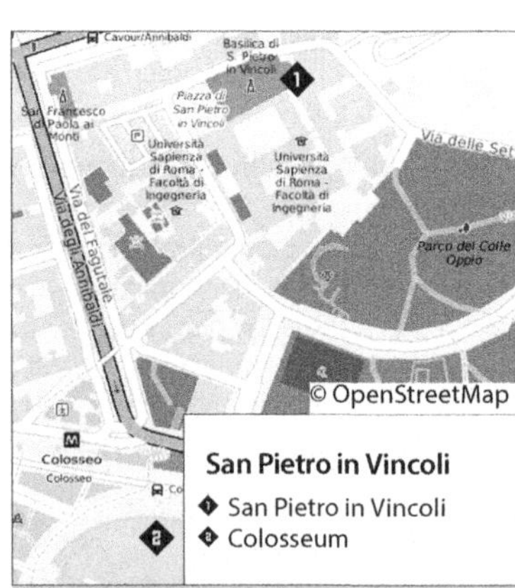

San Pietro in Vincoli
❶ San Pietro in Vincoli
❷ Colosseum

San Pietro in Vincoli
Address: Piazza San Pietro in Vincoli 4a, Roma

Public transportation: Metro B stop Cavour | Bus stop Cavour 75

Opening hours: www.rome.net/san-pietro-in-vincoli

Palatine Hill

In the Flavian Palace on the Palatine Hill

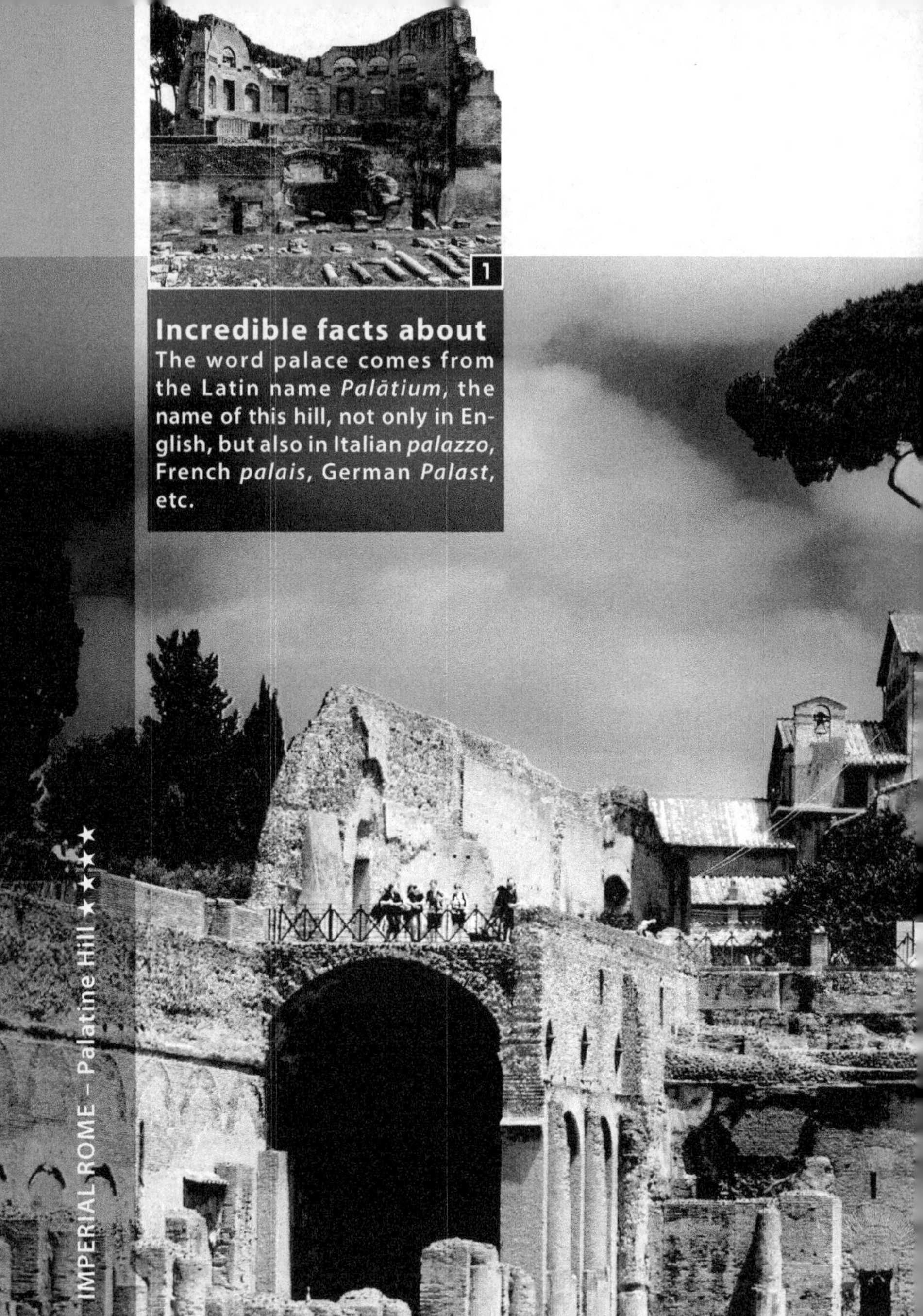

Incredible facts about
The word palace comes from the Latin name *Palātium*, the name of this hill, not only in English, but also in Italian *palazzo*, French *palais*, German *Palast*, etc.

Hippodrome of Domitian – Palatine Hill

Extra Tip : : :
Palatine is a steep hill rising 130 ft or 40 m above Circus Maximus on one side and the Roman Forum on the other. If you are coming to Circus Maximus, go to the Arch of Constantine that you can see at the end of Via di San Gregorio.

In the epicenter of power

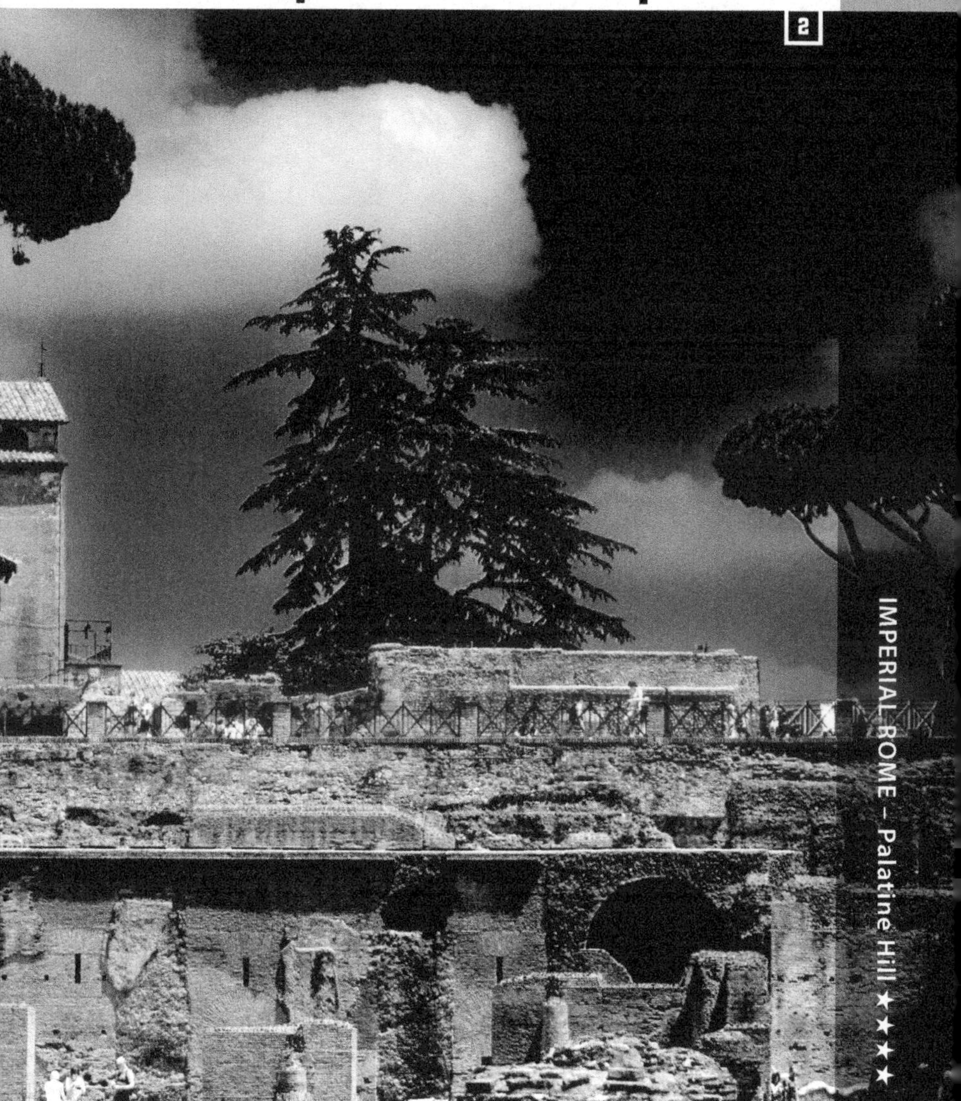

Palatino | Palatine Hill
Address: Via di San Gregorio 30, Roma
Public transportation: Metro B stop Circo Massimo | Bus stop S. Gregorio: 51, 81, 85, 87, C3 | Tram stop Parco Celio: 8
Opening hours and tickets: www.parcocolosseo.it/en

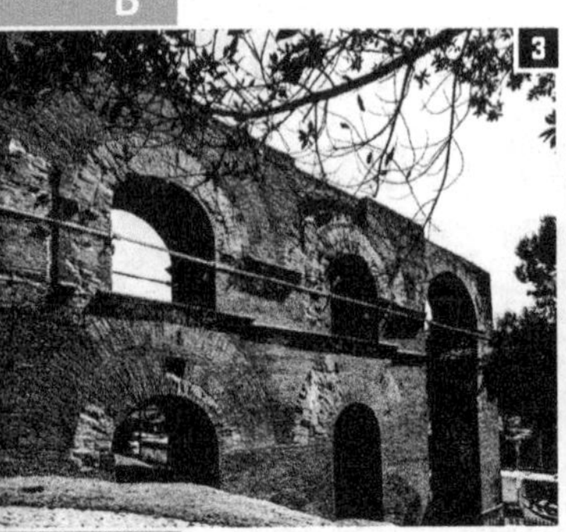

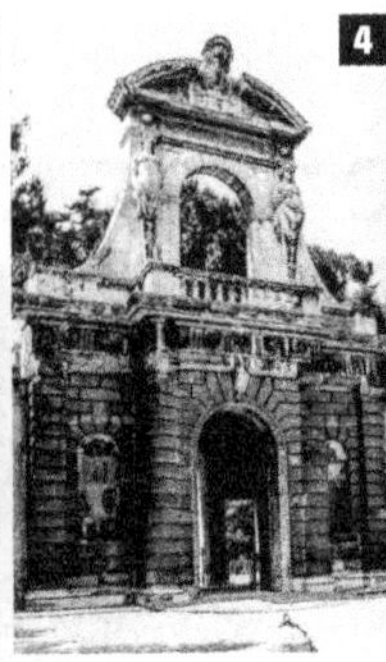

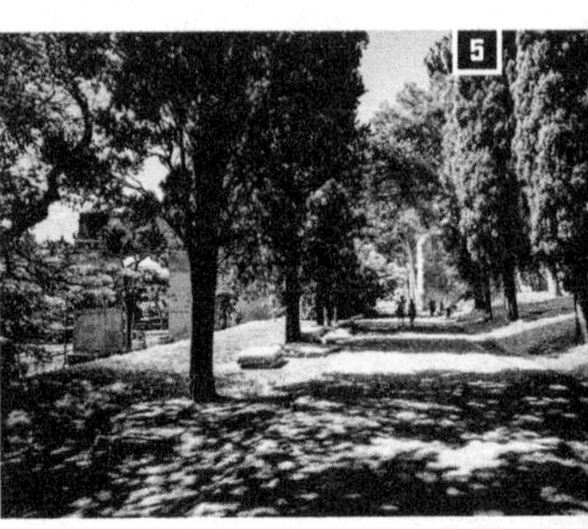

❶ Palatine Hill ★ ★ ★ ★

The Palatino was the center of Roman power. According to the legend Romulus and Remus, twins raised by a she-wolf, founded Rome on this very hill. This is where the first royal hut of Romulus was built. The legendary date is April 21, 753 BC. Archaeological excavations concluded that there was a settlement on the Palatine Hill going back to the tenth century BC. Every emperor built his own residence on the Palatine Hill without tearing down the old ones. So, with time, the whole of Palatine turned into a monolithic complex of palaces with open courtyards, hippodrome, numerous shrines and fenced terraces.

① Aqua Claudia ★

The Arch that you are walking towards and that you will pass on your way to the Palatine, was once part of an aqueduct called Aqua Claudia. **3** It was built by the Emperor Caligula in AD 38. Water was drained from the mountains called Monti Simbruini, 45 miles (69 kilometers) east of Rome in the so-called "Rome's Alps". Ancient Romans referred to that area as *Sub imbribus*: i.e., "under the rain." Emperor Domitian (51–96) ordered the construction of the part that you are passing under right now. **6** This branch supplied the Palatine with water.

② Domus & Baths of Septimius Severus ★ ★

The first ruins you will come across are on your right. They belong to a building complex constructed by Emperor Septimius Severus (145–211). **8**

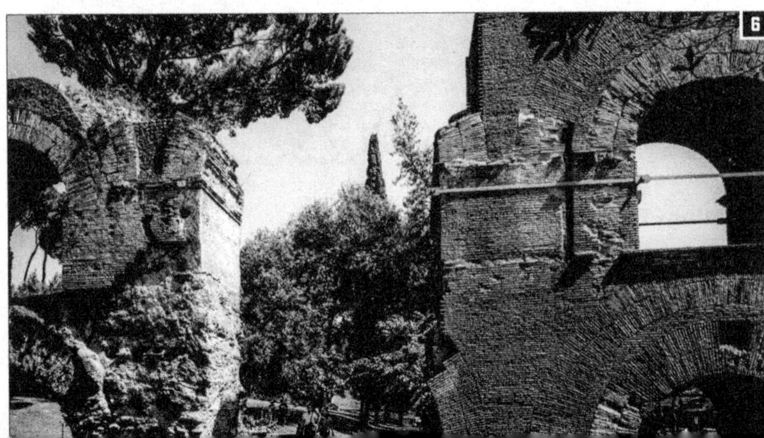

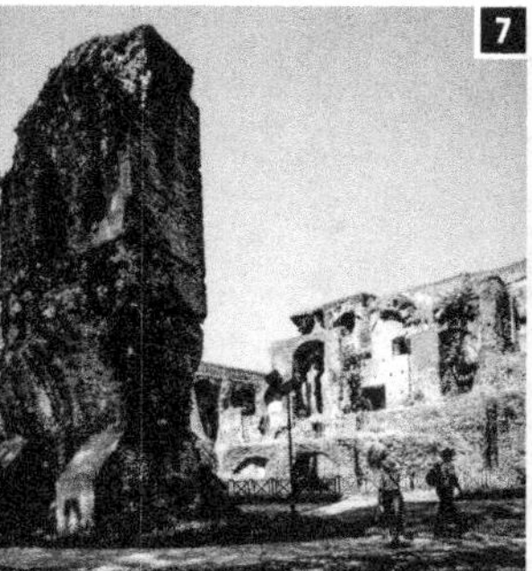
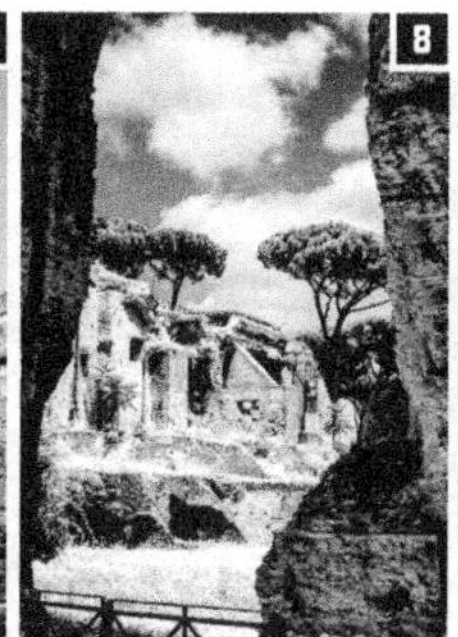
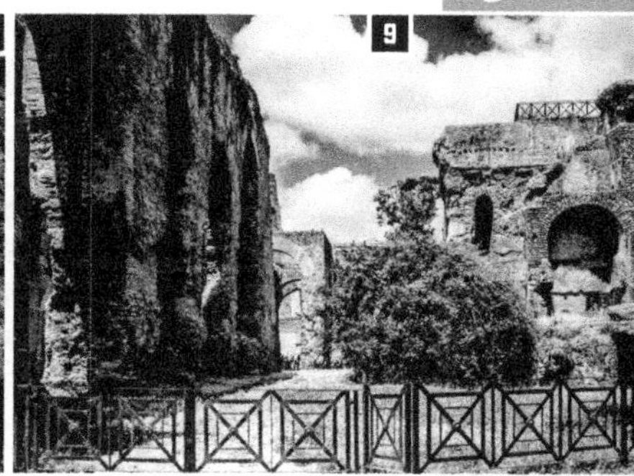

His palace, Domus Severina, is next to the ruins of the Severus Baths. Arches of the Severus Palace are preserved and typical of the architecture of Roman baths. **9**

Since the whole Palatine had been covered in palaces by the time Severus arrived, there was nothing left for him to do but build terraces to expand the Palatine. This is how he got more room for his own palace.

Did you know?

The Roman Aqueduct

The aqueduct was another wonder of Roman engineering.

They used gravity to build pipes with a gradual one-foot drop (30 cm) every 300 ft (91 m).

③ Stadium of the Emperor Domitian ★★★

After you walk under the arches of the Severus Palace, you will find yourself on a long, rectangular clearing. This is the so-called "Domitian's stadium" or hippodrome. It stands between Domus Augustana or the Emperor's Palace and Severus Baths. It is shaped like a Roman circus, but it is more similar to a Greek stadium because it is a lot smaller, 160 by 48 ft or 49 m by 14.5 m. It could not hold horse races with chariots, that's for sure. It is more likely that this was an athletic venue. **2**

Did you know?

How to Get to the Palatine Hill

Palatine is a steep hill rising 130s ft or 40 m above Circus Maximus on one side, and the Roman Forum on the other.

If you take the subway Line B to the Circus Massimo Station, go to the Arch of Constantine that you can see at the end of Via di San Gregorio.

The Colosseum is right behind the Arch.

After you pass Circus Maximus, cross Via dei Cerchi and continue on the Via di San Gregorio. Stick to the fence of the Palatine Hill area with antique ruins and enjoy your walk underneath the signature pines. **5**

After you buy the ticket, turn left and take the path parallel to the street that you had just walked on. **4**

The same ticket is valid for visiting the Palatine Hill, Roman Forum, and the Colosseum.

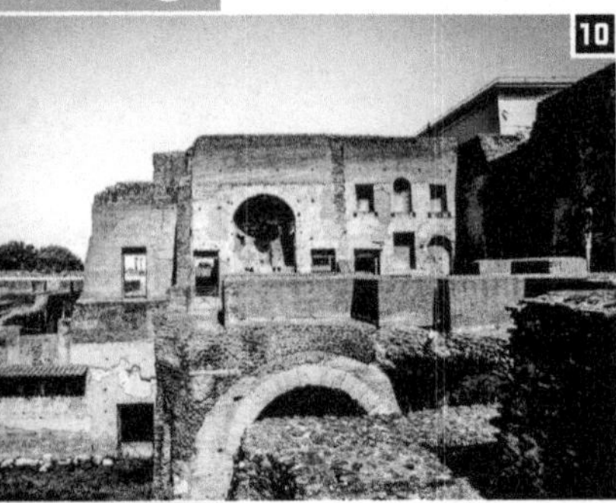

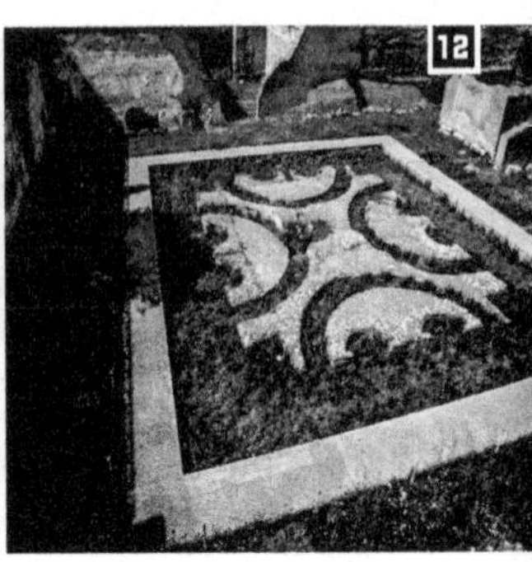

According to others, it may have been a large park for religious and profane shows that the emperor watched from his lodge. There was a *portico* — a colonnade with a roof structure around the stadium. Only the bases of the columns have been preserved.

Walk on the portico until you find a semicircular protrusion. That is the *pulvinar* or the emperor's lodge. On the other side of the hippodrome, climb the plateau where you have an amazing vista of the hippodrome. On the right, there is Domus Augustana.

Behind, you can see the Colosseum between the pines. Let's turn right towards Domus Augustana.

Domus Augustana of the Emperor Domitian ★★

It was built by Domitian in AD 92, alongside Domus Flavia. Unlike Domus Flavia, which was built purely for representative purposes, Domus Augustana was designed as emperor's private residence.

Domus Flavia of the Emperor Domitian ★★

Domus Flavia is a palace arching towards Circus Maximus. Basilica and Aula Regia have been preserved.

Basilica consisted of three chambers. Aula Regia was the largest room in the palace.

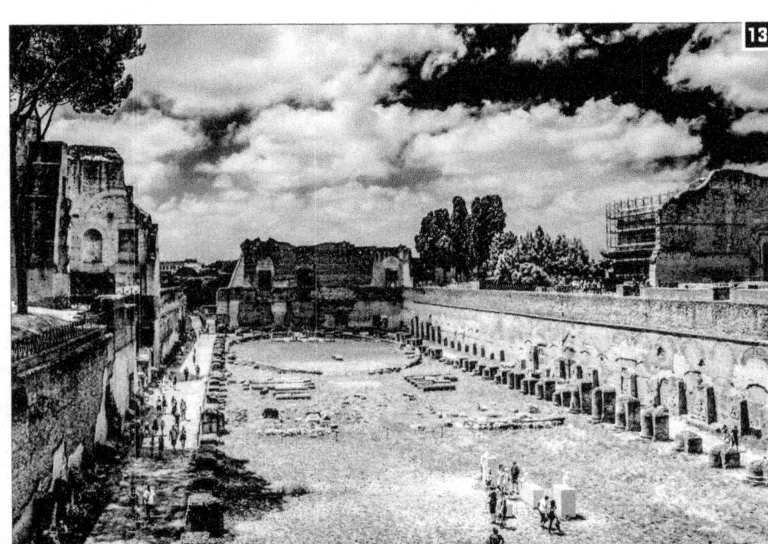

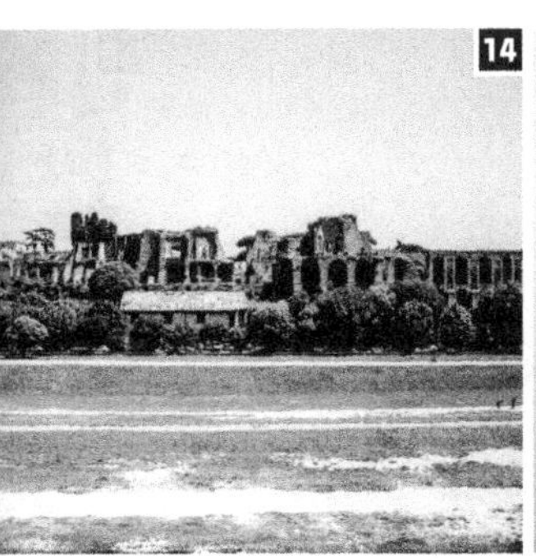
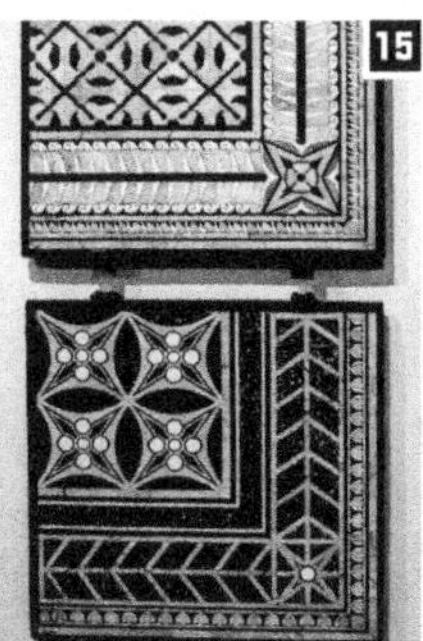
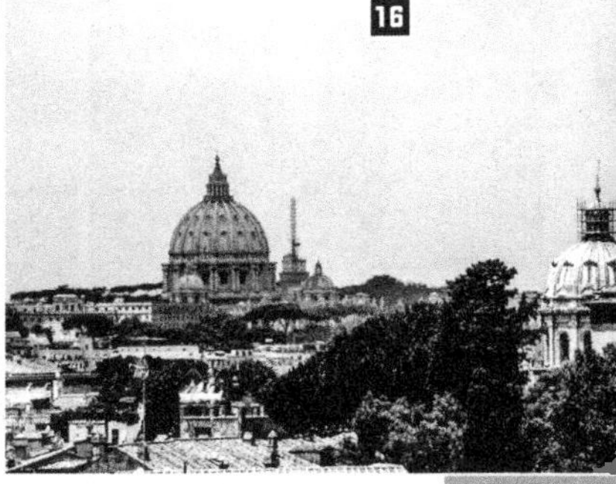

◇ Museo Palatino | Palatine Museum ★★

In the Suore della Visitazione monastery from the nineteenth century, which was built on the foundations of Domus Flavia, there is the Palatine Museum or Museo Palatino. Most of the statues in the museum were found on Domitian's hippodrome. Additionally, this small museum holds the frescoes from the Palatine, as well a reconstructed archaic hut and terracotta reliefs.

Apollo is holding a chitara

There is a particularly interesting fresco fragment from the Augustan period (27 BC – AD 14). Apollo is holding a *chitara*, a string instrument from Greece of the lyre variety. This is typical of the Classicist style — the imitation of artistic expression from the classical period in Greek art. Apollo was the personal protector of Emperor Augustus. The emperor was grateful to Apollo for the victory over Mark Antony in the Battle of Actium in 31 BC. Right next to the imperial residence, the first Roman emperor built a monumental temple in honor of Apollo with this fresco.

Mosaics from Domus Transitoria

The museum also holds colorful mosaics from Domus Transitoria, which was Emperor Nero's palace (37–68), destroyed in the great fire in AD 64. **15**

◇ Domus Augusti of the Emperor Augustus ★★★

When you exit the museum, go towards Domus Augusti, Emperor Augustus's palace. Beautiful frescoes were found inside, especially in the so-called "Room of Masks", or *ambiente delle maschere*. These frescoes are kept in the Palazzo Massimo alle Terme. [p.208]

This museum also holds frescoes from the house of Livia, Augustus's wife. Domus Livia is in close proximity to Domus Augusti.

In the days of ancient Rome, the hut of Romulus, the founder of Rome, was also located in this part of the Palatine Hill.

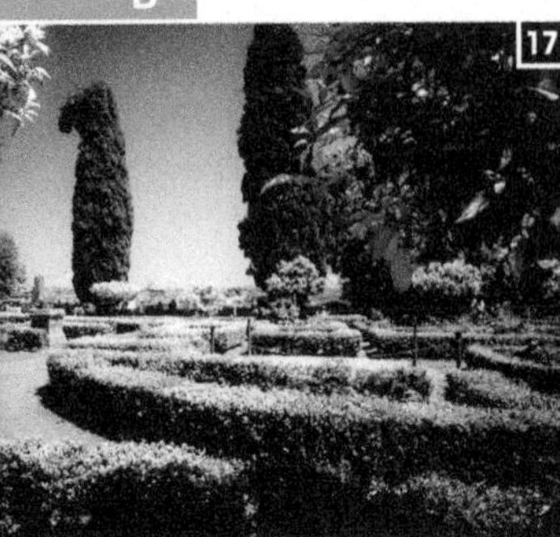

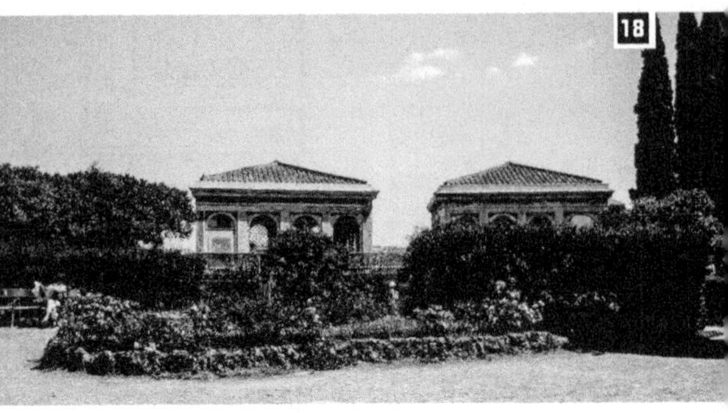

◈ Farnese Gardens ★★

After feasting your eyes over the rooftops of Rome, go towards the Roman Forum through the Farnese Gardens. These gardens were designed by cardinal Alessandro Farnese around 1550. Farnese Gardens are considered one of the first private botanical gardens in Europe. **17** Today, only a small portion remains. **18** Cardinal Farnese employed Giacomo Barozzi da Vignola, a famous architect, to build the gardens. Don't forget to step on the edge of the Farnese Gardens where you will find a unique view of the Roman Forum. It's best to make this a starting point for your tour of the Roman Forum. **19**

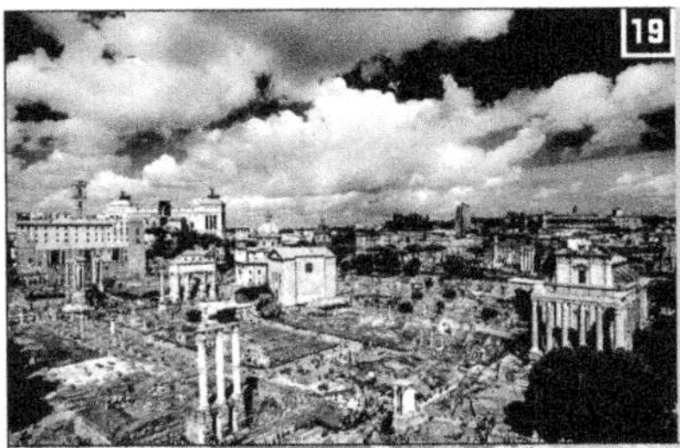

Palatino | Palatine Hill
Address: Via di San Gregorio 30, Roma
Online: www.coopculture.it/en

Public transportation: Metro B stop Circo Massimo | Bus stop S. Gregorio: 51, 81, 85, 87, C3 | Tram stop Parco Celio: 8

Opening hours and tickets:
www.parcocolosseo.it/en

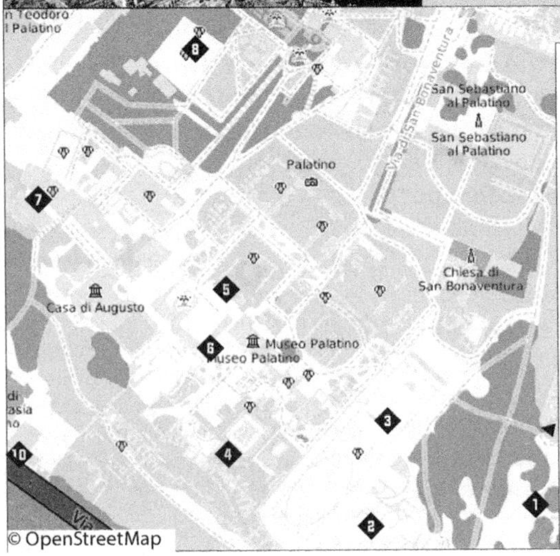

Palatine Hill
❶ Aqua Claudia
❷ Domus & Baths of Septimius Severus
❸ Stadium of the Emperor Domitian
❹ Domus Augustana of the Emperor Domitian
❺ Domus Flavia of the Emperor Domitian
❻ Museo Palatino | Palatine Museum
❼ Domus Augustana of the Emperor Augustus
❾ Colosseum
❿ Circus Maximus
▶ ENTRANCE / EXIT

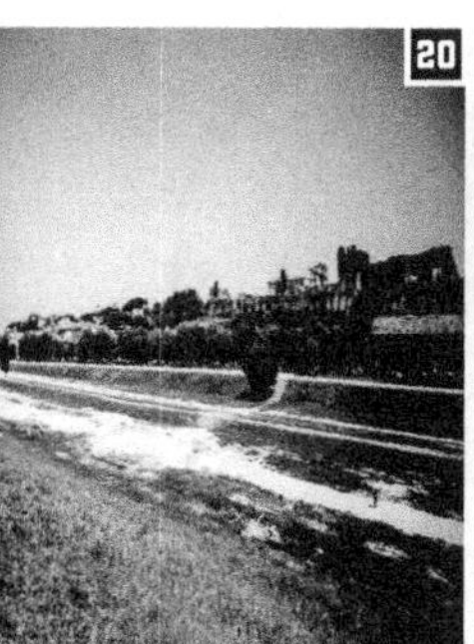
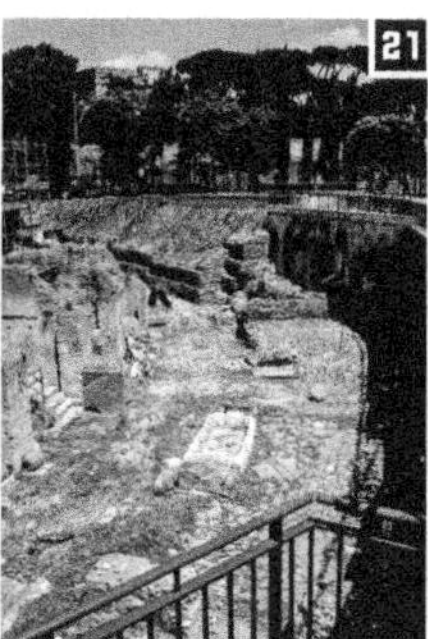
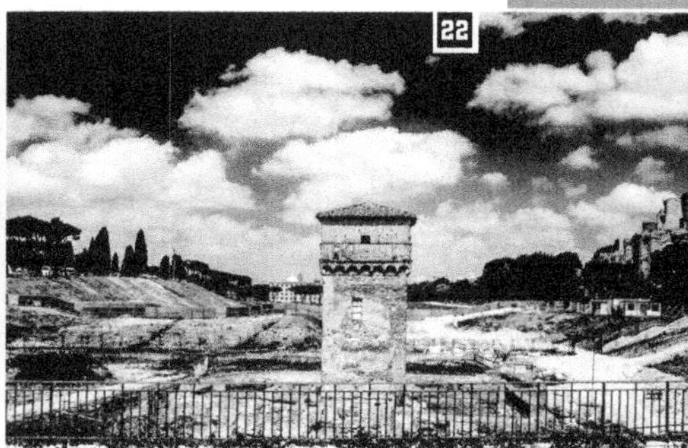

Walk around Palatine Hill

❖ Circus Maximus ★★

The scale of the Circo Massimo alone speaks volumes about the extreme popularity of chariot racing. Circus Maximus is still the largest man-made stadium. **20** Including the arena and the stairs, Circus Maximus is 2,037 ft long and 387 ft wide (621×118 m). Today, due to floods, the original track is 20 ft or 6 m below ground. During the reign of Gaius Julius Caesar (100–44 BC), it could receive around 150,000 spectators. The auditorium was constantly expanding. **21** During the Late Classical period (4th–7th century) there were roughly 385,000 seats.

In Caesar's days, the city had one million dwellers and two hundred years later the number rose to 1.5 million people. According to a legend, King Lucius Tarquinius Priscus started building it in early sixth century BC when the first wooden stands were put in place. Since these stands would regularly cave in under the weight of so many eager spectators, Caesar was the first ruler who started replacing wooden stands with marble ones. His stepson, Emperor Augustus (27 BC – AD 14) decided to build a marble city. He expanded Circus Maximus and replaced wood with marble. But it was only during Emperor Trajan's reign until AD 103 that the last timbering in the Circus was replaced with stone, concrete and brick. Trajan was the first one to place an obelisk in the center of the race track.

Today, this obelisk is located at the Piazza del Popolo. [p.194]

On the same *spina*, another obelisk was set by Constantius II (317–361). That one can be seen in front of the Lateran Palace. [p.270]

In the Roman Empire, the frequency rose to 24 races per day. Each race consisted of seven laps around the spina, a longitudinal barrier in the center that allowed the chariots and the horses to move in circles. **22** The spina had two obelisks, as mentioned, and a stop light. The stop light was made of seven bronze dolphins. One by one, the dolphins would dive, indicating the remaining number of laps to the audience. Roman emperors had a special lodge under the Palatine Hill.

However, the emperor could watch the races directly from his palace on the Palatine, from a terrace overlooking the stadium.

Races at Circus Maximus took place from mid-fifth century BC all the way to AD 449, when the Ostrogoth king Totila conquered Rome and the final races took place.

Circo Massimo | Circus Maximus
Address: Via del Circo Massimo, Roma

Public transportation: Metro B Circo stop Massimo | Bus stop Circo Massimo: 51, 81, 85, 87, 118, 160, 628, C3 | Tram stop Aventino – Circo Massimo: 8

Opening hours:
Public place – always open

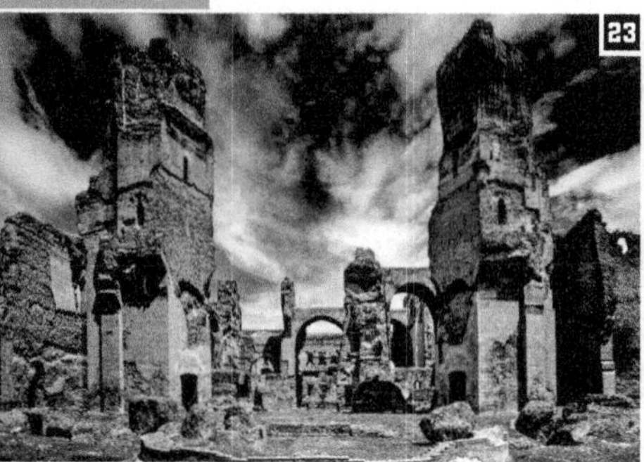

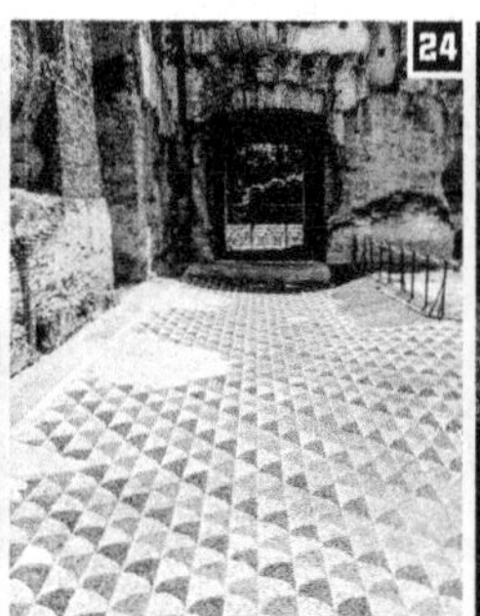

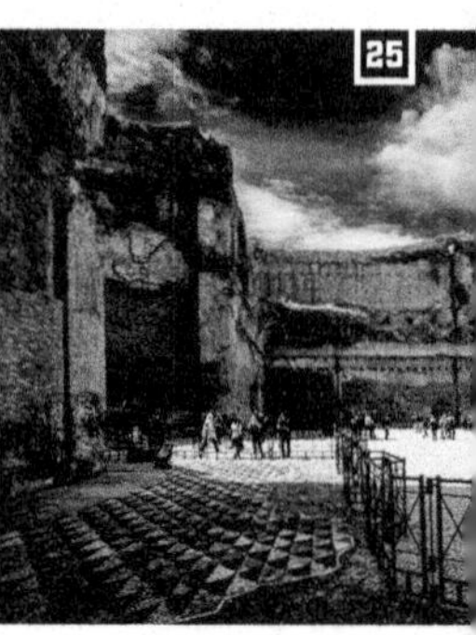

Apart from the grassy track, there is very little left of what was once the largest construction of the Roman Empire. Marble seats were used to build St. Peter's Basilica, and obelisks were removed by Pope Sixtus V in 1587.

❸ Baths of Caracalla ★★★ 23

The Terme di Caracalla were built between 212 and 216 during emperors Septimius Severus and Caracalla. The facilities occupied 25 acres and the building was 748 ft (228 m) long, 381 ft (116 m) wide and 125 ft (38 m) high. The baths could fit 1,600 bathers. Apart from bathing, visitors had two public libraries at their disposal: one with Latin and the other one with Greek texts. The whole structure was raised 20 ft or 6 m above ground to fit the furnaces for heating water and pipes for floor heating. 24 The baths were used until 537, when Aqua Marcia as well as all other aqueducts were destroyed by the Ostrogoths. Today, we only have monumental remains, with floor mosaics and partial sculptures. *Farnese Hercules* and *Farnese Bull* were found here, now on display at the National Archaeological Museum in Naples.

If you decide to go further towards Via Appia Antica, make sure to walk the ruins of these baths. 25

Terme di Caracalla | Baths of Caracalla
Address: Viale delle Terme di Caracalla 52, Roma
Online: www.coopculture.it/en

Public transportation: Metro B stop Circo Massimo | Bus stop Terme Caracalla – Porta Capena: 118, 628 | Tram stop Aventino – Circo Massimo: 8

Opening hours and tickets: *see online*

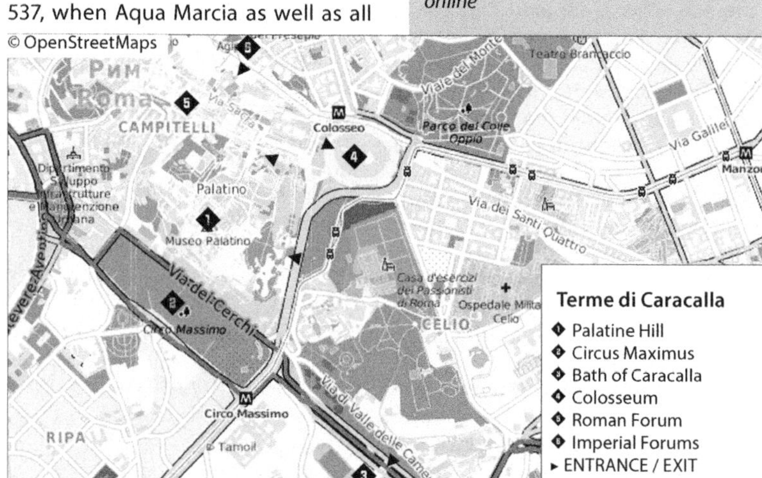

Terme di Caracalla
- ❶ Palatine Hill
- ❷ Circus Maximus
- ❸ Bath of Caracalla
- ❹ Colosseum
- ❺ Roman Forum
- ❻ Imperial Forums
- ► ENTRANCE / EXIT

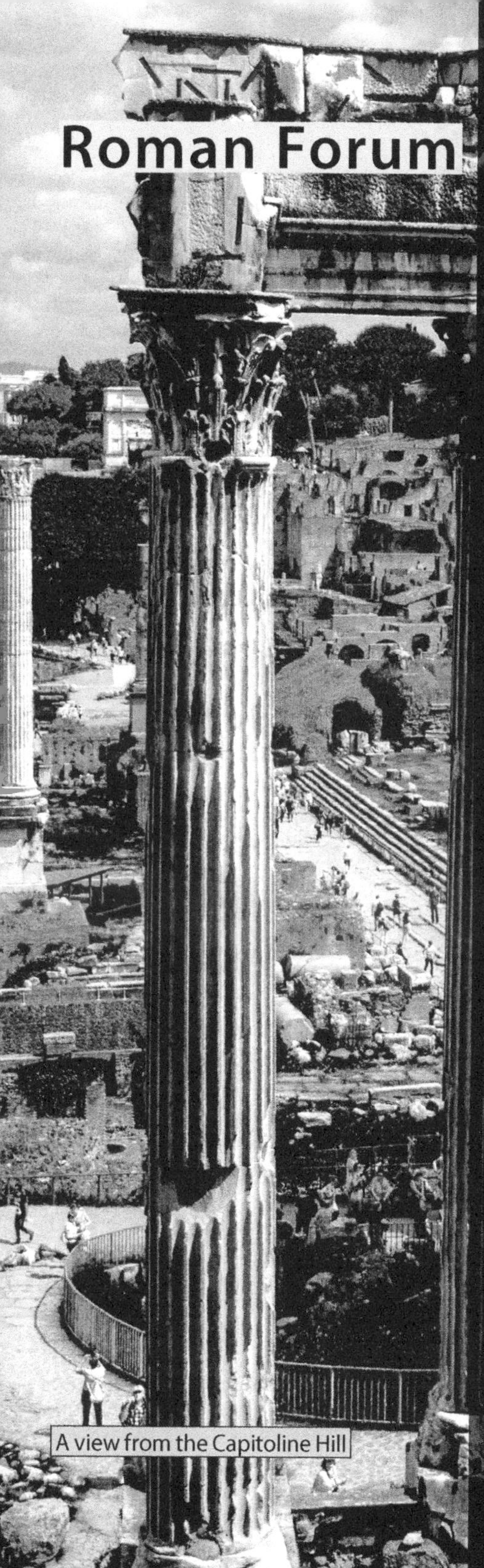

Roman Forum

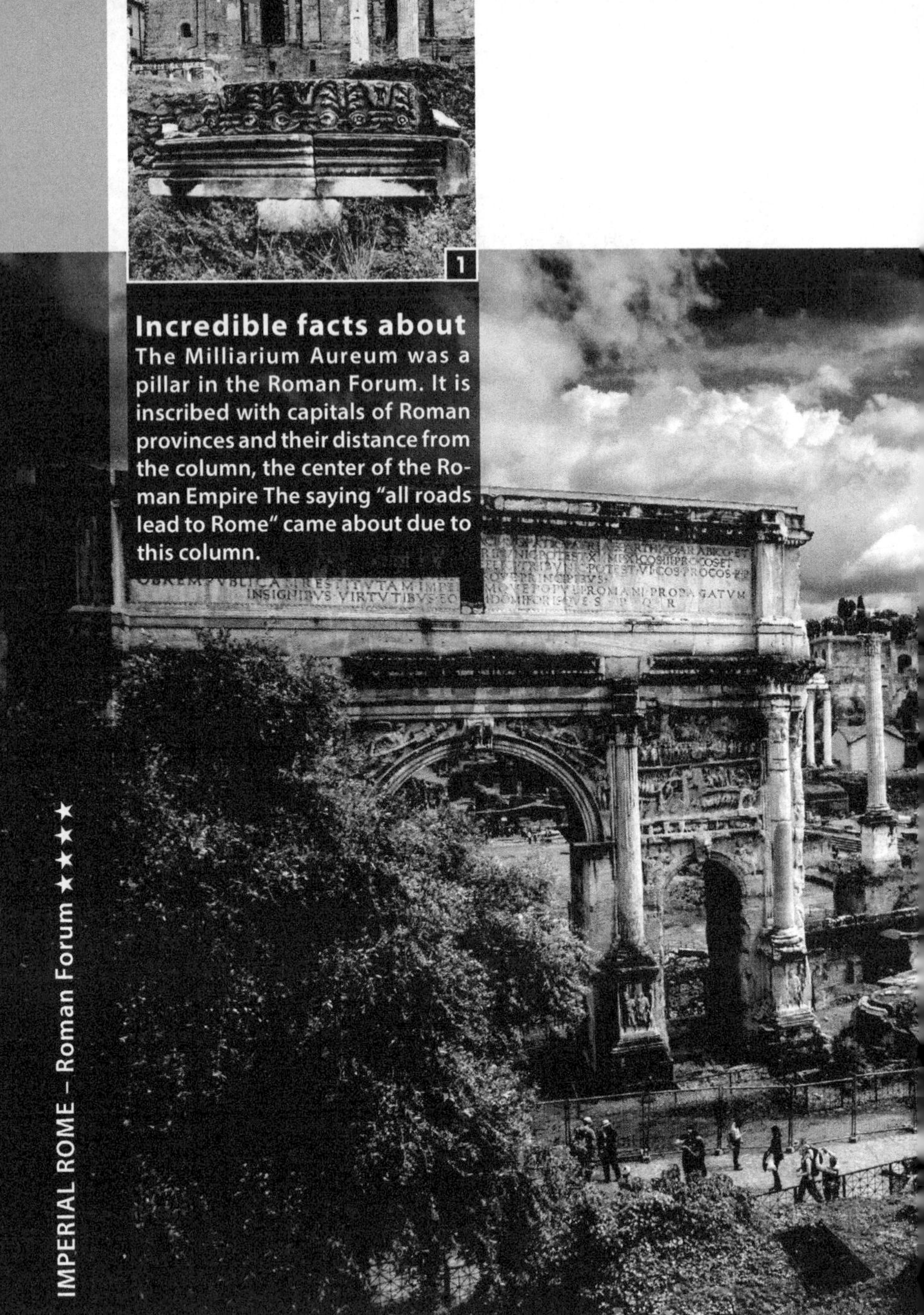

Incredible facts about
The Milliarium Aureum was a pillar in the Roman Forum. It is inscribed with capitals of Roman provinces and their distance from the column, the center of the Roman Empire The saying "all roads lead to Rome" came about due to this column.

The Arch of Septimius Severus on the Roman Forum

Extra Tip : : :
You can see the Roman coins that melted in the fire glued to the floor of Basilica Aemilia. The coins had imperial figures on them, so it was easy to reconstruct the time and circumstances of Basilica Aemilia's final destruction.

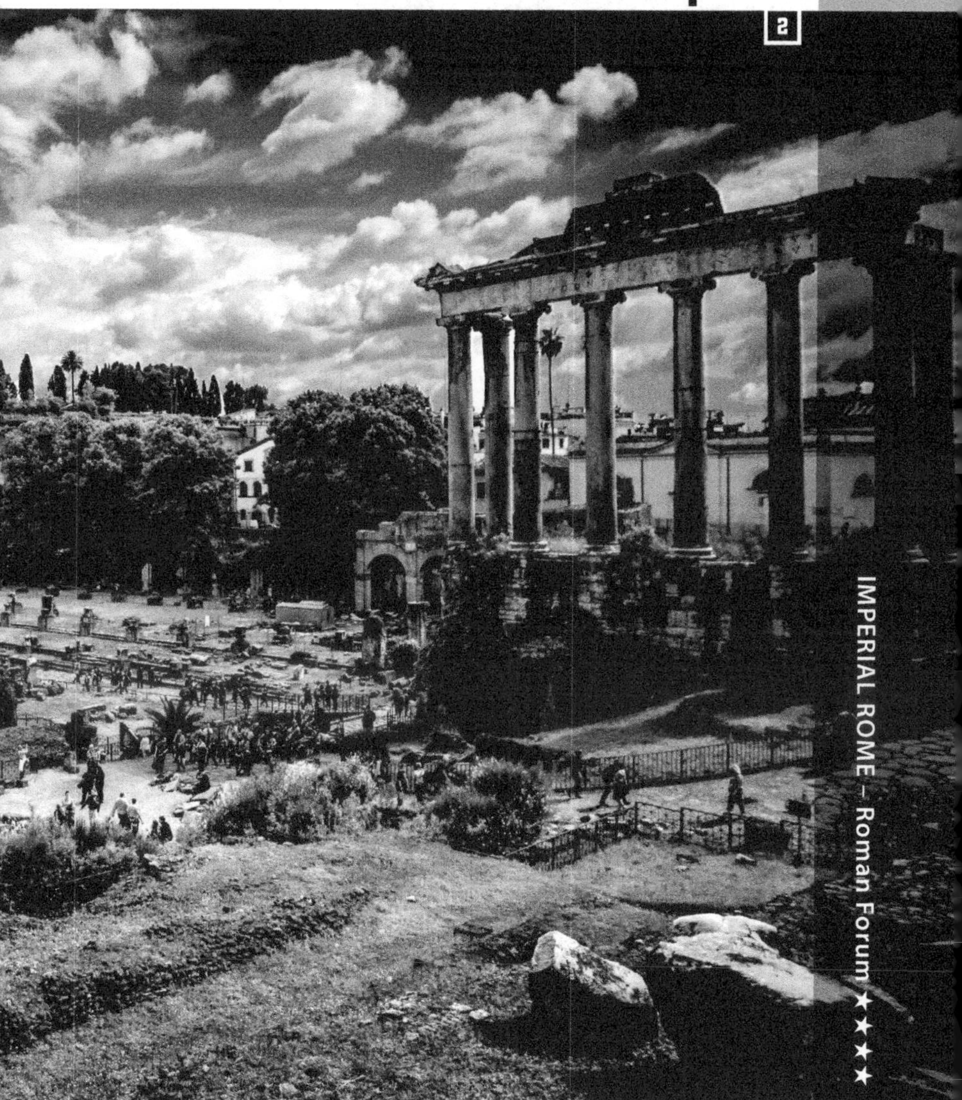

Hub of the Roman Empire

Foro Romano | Roman Forum
Address: Via della Salara Vecchia, Rome
Public transportation: Metro B stop Colosseo | Bus stop Fori Imperiali or Colosseo:
51, 85, 87, 118
Opening hours: www.parcocolosseo.it/en

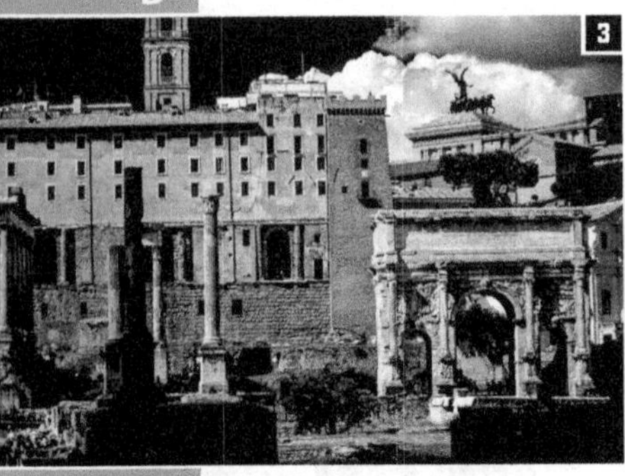

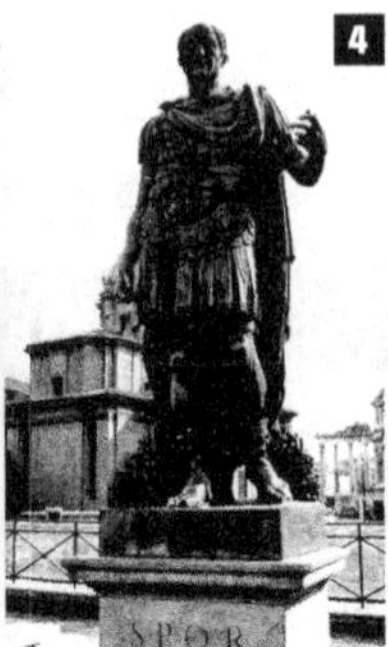

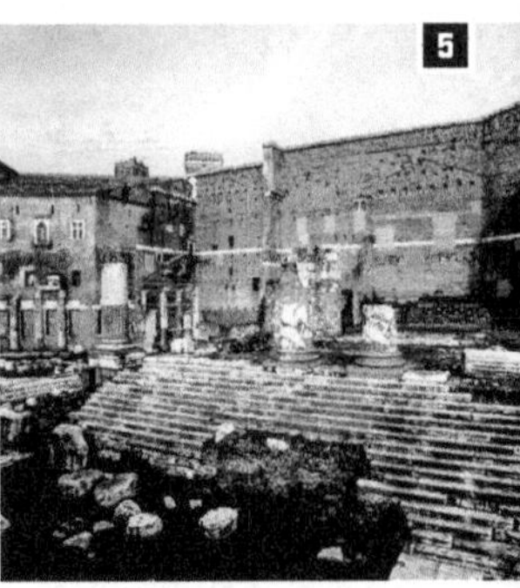

❶ The Roman Forum ★★★★

Roman Forum was the center of social, economic, political, judiciary and spiritual life of Rome, which means of the entire Roman Empire. **2**

Some of the most important and largest temples were located here. Consuls of the Roman Republic and Roman emperors stepped behind a podium on the Forum to declare vital decisions to the Senate and the people. **3** An eternal fire burned for more than a thousand years as the religious symbol of everlasting Rome. As the city was experiencing an unstoppable growth spur, the Forum needed to be expanded. Therefore, Caesar (100–44 BC) decided to build an entirely new forum right next to the old one. **4**

His example was followed by emperors Augustus **5**, Nerva and Trajan, adding different complexes, from basilicas, to shopping districts, squares and temples. The forums built by Roman emperors are called Imperial Forums.

◇ The Arch of Titus ★★★

The Arch of Titus is the oldest preserved arch in Rome. It was erected in AD 82 by Emperor Domitian, following the death of Titus, his older brother, to celebrate Titus's victories, including the Siege of Jerusalem in AD 70. **6**

This arch also became a model for many modern arches, such as the *Arc de Triomphe de l'Étoile* in Paris, built in 1836. Although the Arch of Titus is not mentioned in classical literature, the inscription on its east side, the one facing the Colosseum, provides the relevant time and context:

SENATUS

POPULUSQUE ROMANUS

DIVO TITO DIVI VESPASIANI F(ILIO)

VESPASIANO AUGUSTO

Senate
And the people of Rome (built this arch)
To the divine Titus, the son of the divine Vespasian Augustus

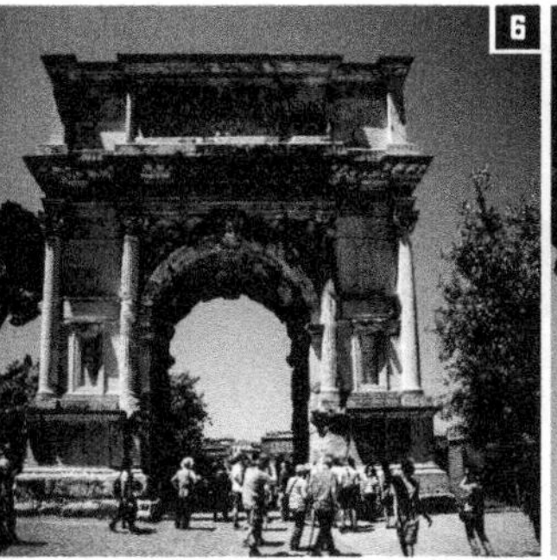

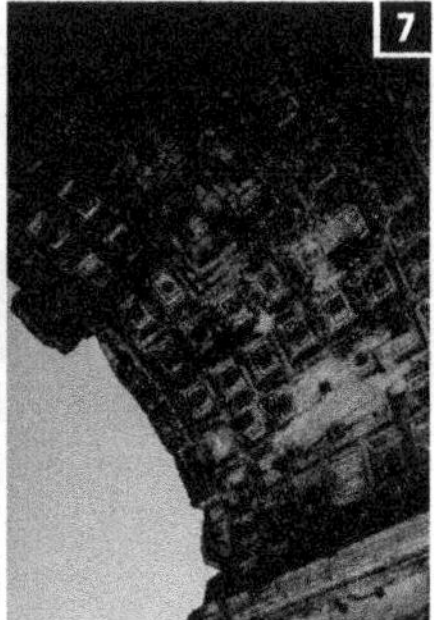

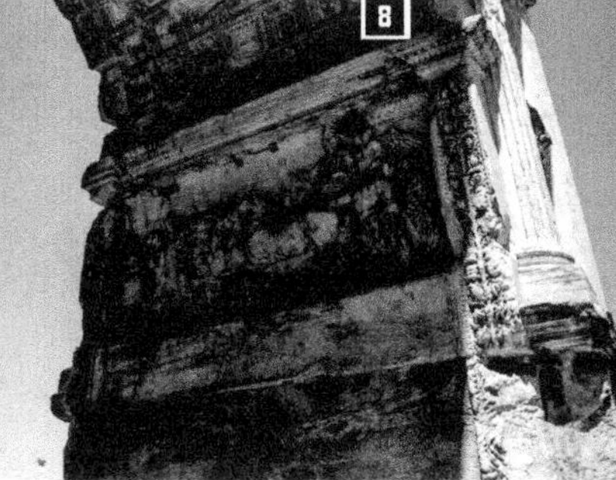

The arch is historically relevant because it contains a depiction of victory over the Jews by Vespasian and Titus in AD 70. **7**

The victory is commemorated by two reliefs in the upper parts of the arch.

▸ On the north side, the lateral side of the arch closer to Via dei Fori Imperiali, there is Titus on a *quadriga*, a chariot drawn by four horses, crowned with a laurel wreath by goddess Victory. Virtus, divine personification of military courage, is leading the horses. **8**

Honos, the embodiment of a noble citizen, together with twelve *lictors*, Titus's personal guards, are following the victor.

Formally speaking, however, these reliefs do not belong to the time of construction, they were added in approximately AD 190.

▸ On the south side of the Arch, closer to the Palatine Hill, there is a scene of victors carrying their plunder from the Jerusalem Temple.

Did you know?

The Arch of Titus and Jewish history

In the twentieth century, the Arch turned into a symbol of the Jewish diaspora.

When the Israeli state was founded (1948), the Jewish community gathered around the Arch of Titus.

That was the first time that Jews walked under the arch of their own accord, but they walked backwards. Symbolically, they wanted to demonstrate that 2,000 years of slavery and Roman exile were finally over.

IMPERIAL ROME – Roman Forum ★★★★

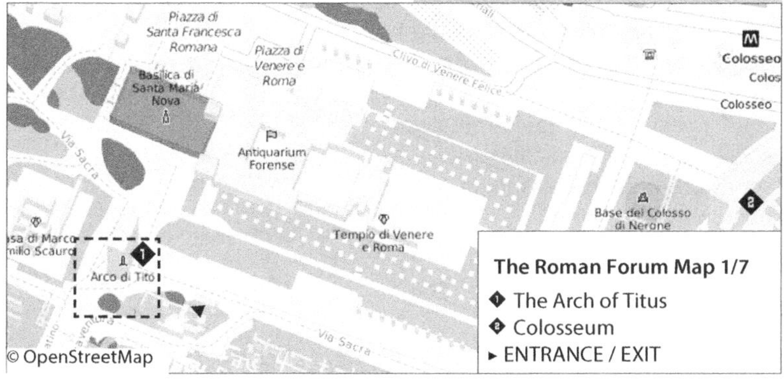

The Roman Forum Map 1/7

❶ The Arch of Titus
❷ Colosseum
▸ ENTRANCE / EXIT

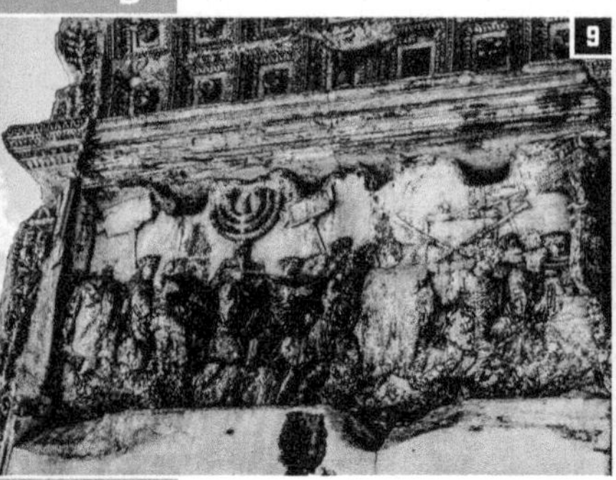

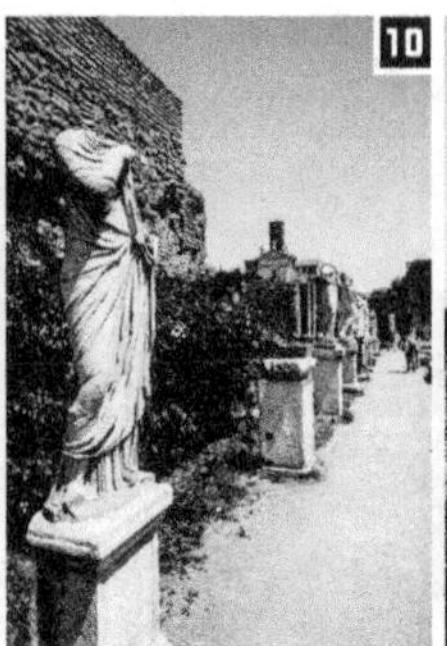

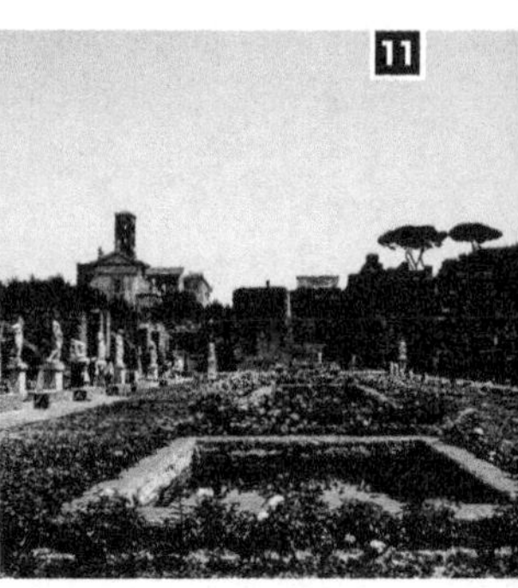

It is clearly visible they are carrying a seven-branched menorah, silver trumpets and other holy objects from the Temple of Jerusalem. **9**

This is the reason why Jews do not walk under the Arch even to this day. Ever since Pope Paul IV (1555–1559), every new Pope forced the Roman Jews to walk under this arch.

② The Vestal Virgins ★★ **10**

The House of the Vestals on the Roman Forum was a luxurious residential building for priestesses of the goddess Vesta, protectress of the holy fire and hearth. It was a three-story house with around fifty rooms.

It had an inner courtyard with two pools that still have fish and water lilies. **11**

At the end of the courtyard, there are parts of statues on pedestals dedicated to the most distinguished Vestals.

The best preserved statues can be found at the Palazzo Massimo alle Terme. [p.208]

The statue which stands the furthest to the east, towards the Colosseum, represents Numa Pompilius (715–673 BC), king of Rome and legendary founder of the Vestal cult.

③ Temple of Vesta ★ **12**

Six Vestal priestesses guarded the holy fire day and night in this ancient temple from the 7th century BC.

The fire had to keep burning. If it went out, the guilty Vestal would be flogged and dishonorably discharged from the order.

If a Vestal broke her virginal vow, she would be buried alive. A man responsible for such a blasphemy would be flogged to death.

In the history of Rome, around ten such cases have been recorded.

How to become a Vestal Virgin

A girl could join the order of the Vestals under two conditions: first, she had to be from an aristocratic Roman family. Second, she had to be a virgin. Vestal virgins were held in high esteem. **13**

They were accepted into the order before they turned ten years old and they were discharged after thirty years of loyal service to the goddess Vesta. After that, they could get married and lead a normal civil life.

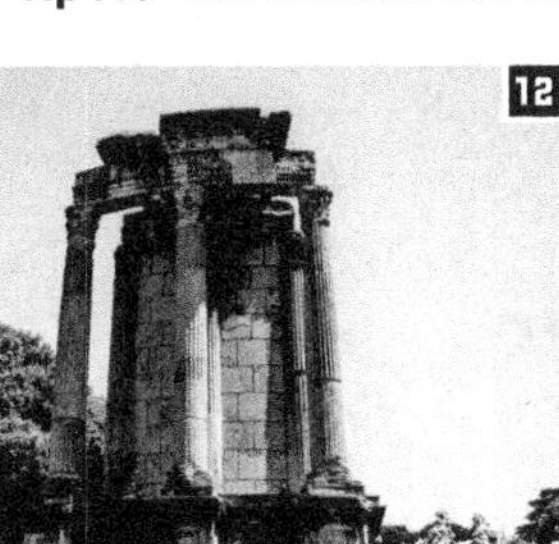
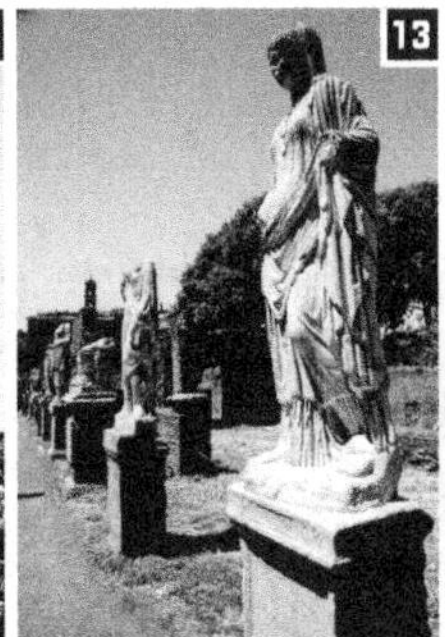
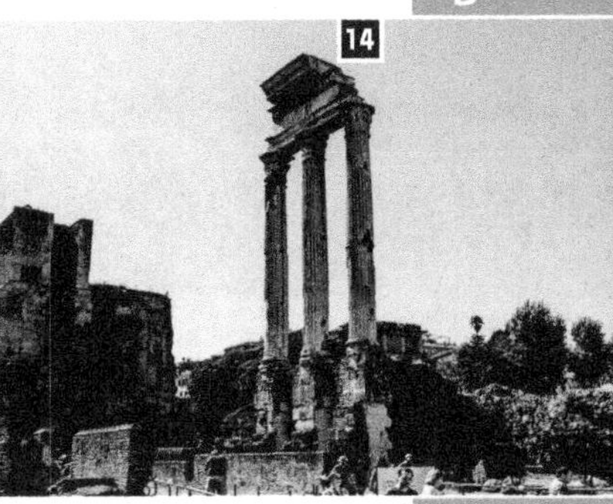

◇ ④ Regia ★

Regia was the oldest building on the Roman Forum, built in the eighth century BC. Regia was the official headquarters of the Pontifex Maximus, the highest priest among the college of Roman imperial priests.

Cicero notes that the Pontifex Maximus kept official records of all major religious and political events. Caesar's stepson Augustus declared himself Pontifex Maximus in 12 BC.

As the first Roman emperor, he declared himself Pontifex Maximus, which became standard practice afterwards. In case of dual reign, the ruler with a higher rank was Pontifex Maximus.

◇ ⑤ Castor and Pollux ★★ 14

This is one of the oldest temples on the Forum. It dates back to early 5th century BC. The columns and part of the architrave are from AD 6 when Emperor Augustus had it renovated.

Did you know?

The role of Pontifex Maximus

The Pontifex Maximus was also responsible for the calendar

Gaius Julius Caesar, Roman dictator and Pontifex Maximus, introduced the Julian calendar in 46 BC, solving the problem of leap year.

The Roman Senate named the months of July after Julius Caesar in 44 BC and August after Caesar's adopted son Augustus in 8 BC.

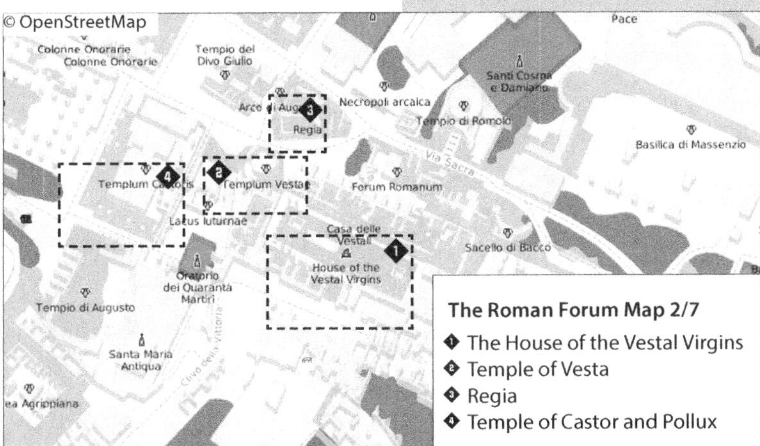

The Roman Forum Map 2/7
- ❶ The House of the Vestal Virgins
- ❷ Temple of Vesta
- ❸ Regia
- ❹ Temple of Castor and Pollux

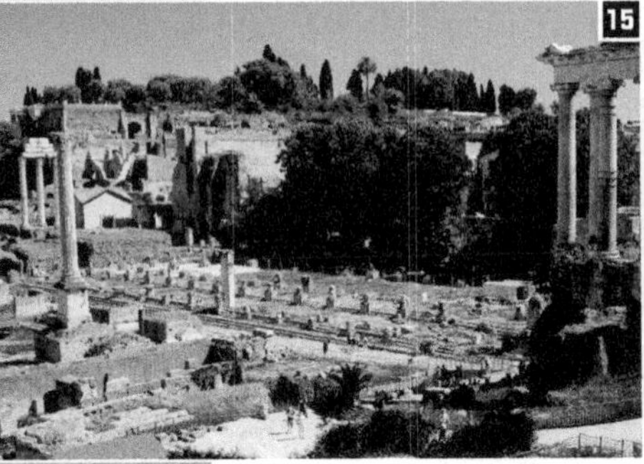

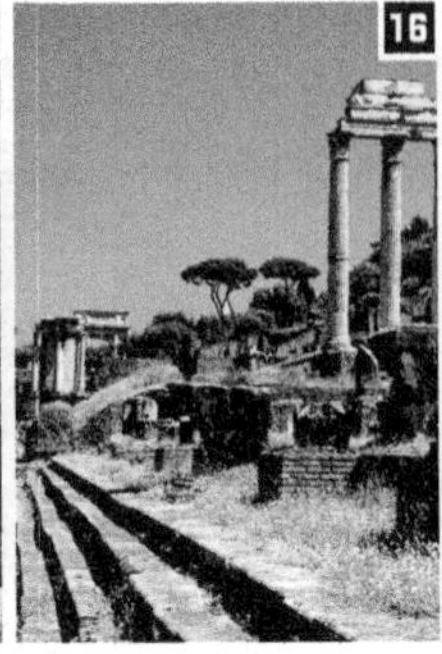

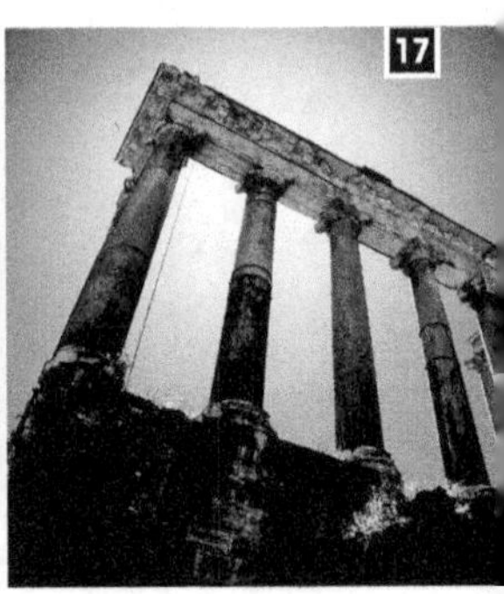

Castor and Pollux were Zeus's (Jupiter's) and Leda's twins. The cult of twins came to Rome through the Greek colonies, i.e., *Magna Graecia* (southern Italy). Sometimes, sessions of the Senate were organized in this temple during the Republican period.

Basilica Julia ★★

Behind the Temple of Castor and Pollux, there is the Basilica Julia, named after the person who ordered its construction in 54 BC, Julius Caesar.

It was the largest basilica of its time, 331 ft long and 161 ft wide or 101 m by 49 m. The main nave was divided with colonnades. The seat of the judge was in the apse. Basilica Julia was divided into several halls for hearings and sentencing. An audience could be present at the court. "The Court among a Hundred of Them" was the highest court with regard to inheritance claims.

Lawyers would pay the audience to clap after each argument in order to convince the judge they were making a valid point.

The entire Basilica Julia was unbelievably noisy, since hearings were scheduled simultaneously in different halls.

Did you know?

Board Games and Basilica Julia

On one of the thresholds in Basilica Julia on the side facing the Curia, there is still a drawing of an 8x8 square set in stone, similar to chess. This is a testament to how those who neither litigated nor passed sentences actually spent their time here.

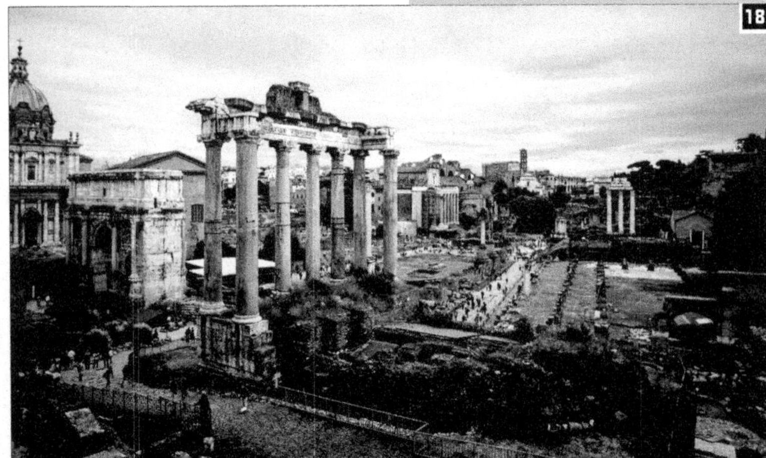

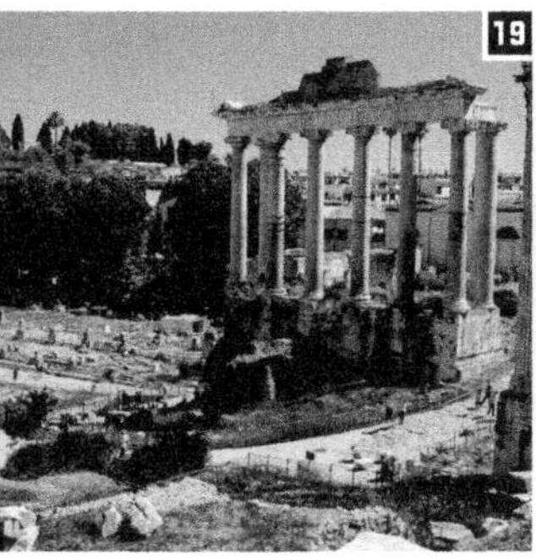
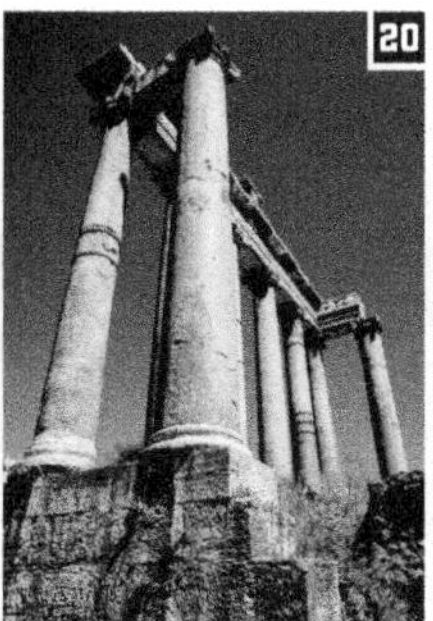
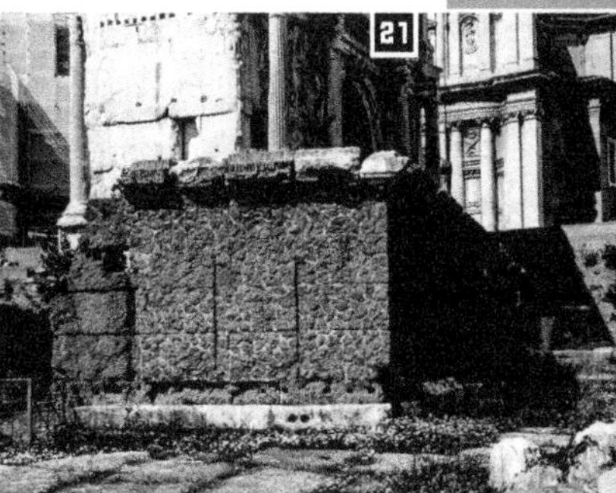

⑦ Temple of Saturn ★★ **17**

The Temple of Saturn has been situated at this very place since early fifth century BC. Saturn was the god of the mythical Golden Age on the Apennine Peninsula. **18**

According to legend, this was a time when there were no inequalities according to birth or wealth and wars and crimes did not exist. Today, only eight columns remain, the rest of the temple is gone. **19** Often, these columns are used as a symbol of Roman Forum and transiency. **20**

⑧ Rostra ★ **21**

Rostra means ship bows. After the Romans won in the Second Latin War (340–338 BC), they brought the bows of enemy ships to Rome and that is how this landmark got its name.

The platform was used for speeches after important battles. During the Roman Republic, Rostra was a venue for public court hearings.

Later on, it turned into a stage for displaying evidence after a political assassination.

Did you know?

The basis for Christmas celebrations

Roman slaves, servants and poor people were particularly fond of Saturn and worshiped his cult.

During the festivities, the social order would be reversed — masters served their servants and slaves, senators walked around the Forum not in their togas, but wearing wide tunics, same as poor citizens. Courts and schools would be closed.

Saturnalia were a family holiday — family members exchanged gifts, everyone gathered around the family table to eat, play games and light candles.

This became the basis for Christmas celebrations.

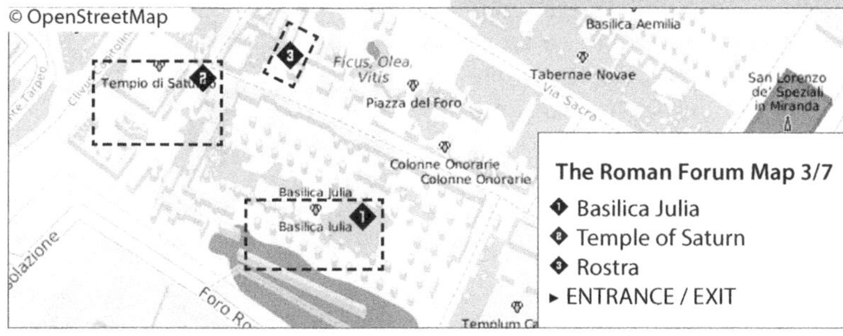

The Roman Forum Map 3/7
1. Basilica Julia
2. Temple of Saturn
3. Rostra
▶ ENTRANCE / EXIT

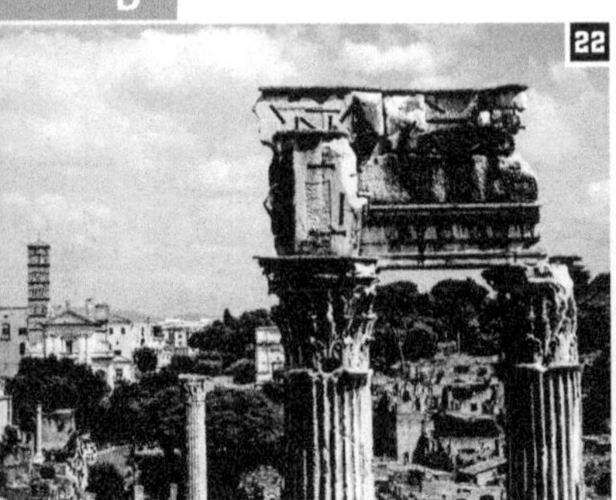

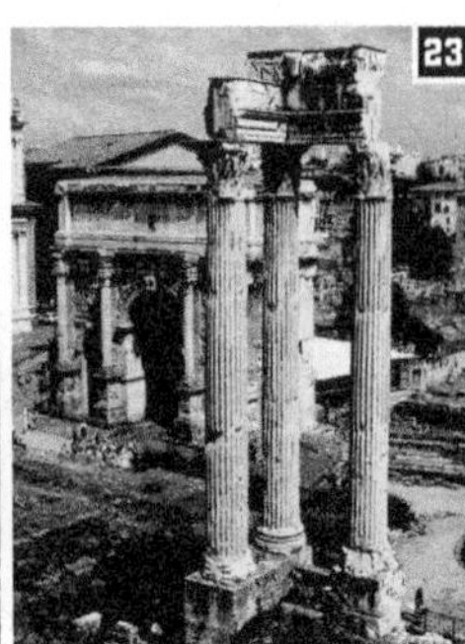

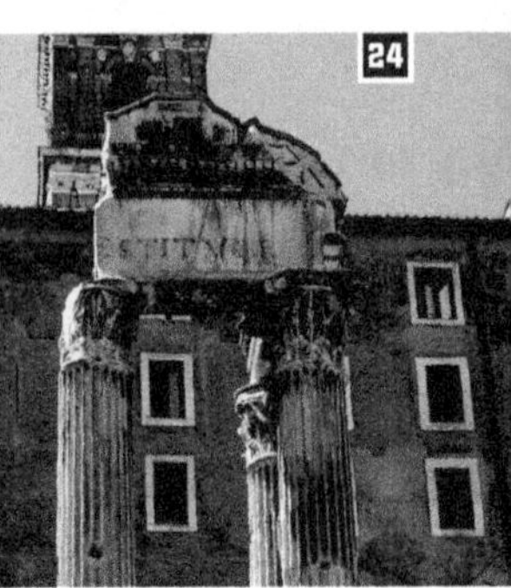

This is where Mark Antony presented the head and hand of Cicero after this great orator was executed under the Proscription Law from 43 BC. Brutus and Cassius gave their speech in front of a not-to-thrilled crowd after they had assassinated Caesar.

Rostra was known as the right place for handling political opponents. Julia the Elder, Augustus's daughter, allegedly prostituted herself around Rostra, which finally forced the emperor to throw his daughter into exile.

⑨ Milliarium Aureum ★

On the right side of the Rostra, there was a pillar called Milliarium Aureum, the central point of the Roman Empire.

Only a small portion of the pedestal remains with the inscription Milliarium Aureum. **1**

Milliarium Aureum was a bronze pillar covered in gold, erected by Emperor Augustus in AD 20. It is inscribed with capitals of Roman provinces and their distance from the column.

It was supposed to be a reminder of how enormous the empire was and represent Roman Forum as the central point.

The saying "All roads lead to Rome" came about because of this column.

Did you know?

The most brutal Roman law

The Proscription was the most brutal Roman law. Anyone could be declared an enemy of the state if their name was put on the notice board. In other words, Roman laws ceased to apply to that person and anyone could kill them, which sanctioned lynching, in essence. A hefty reward was offered to anyone who delivered the proscribed person's head. Aiding the convicted person was punished by death.

A convict's property and their family's assets were permanently taken away. In practice, this radical law was used to get rid of political enemies swiftly and efficiently.

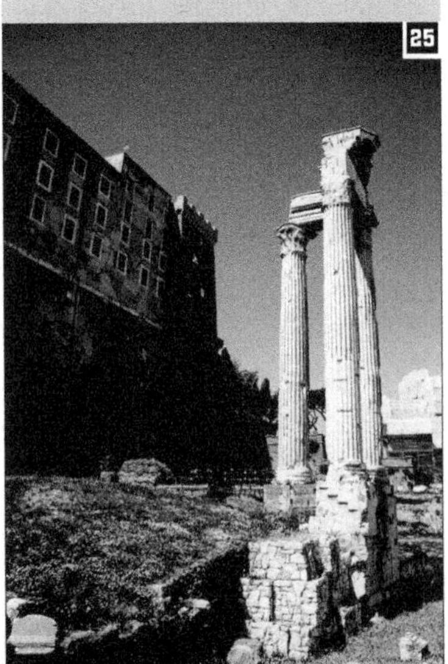

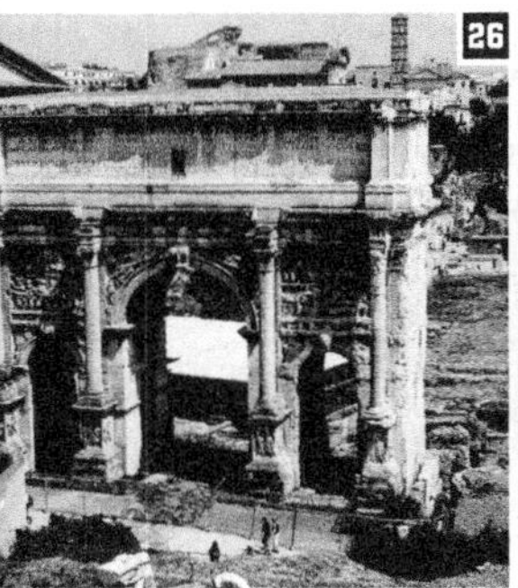

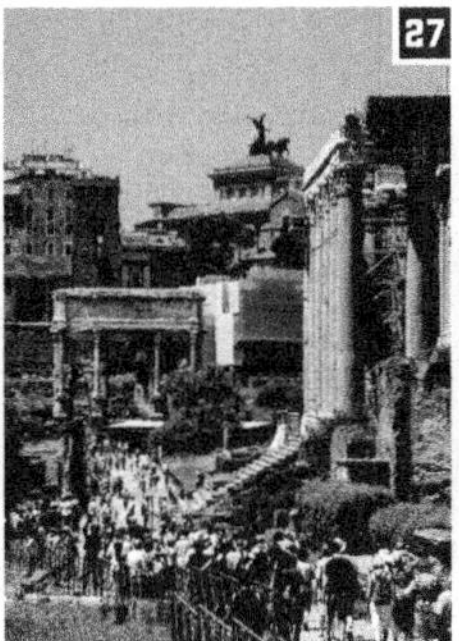

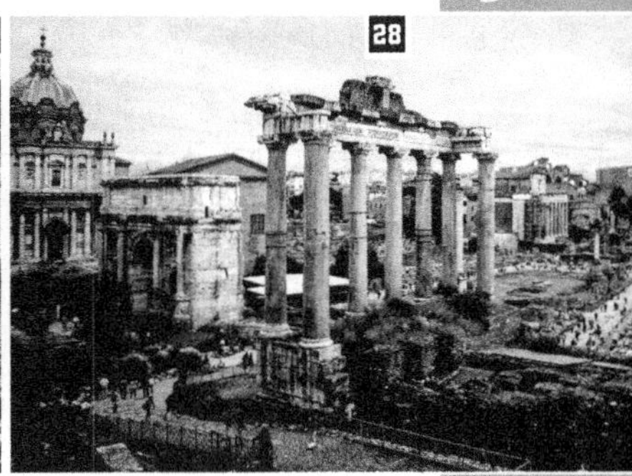

⑩ Temple of the Divine Vespasian and Titus ★★ 22

On the other side of the Temple of Saturn, there is the Temple of Vespasian and Titus. It is hard to miss — there are three Corinthian columns 50 ft or 15 m in height. 23

Once upon a time, these columns were part of an antechamber of a temple that stretched towards the Capitoline Hill.

It was built in AD 79. The temple was identified according to an inscription (now lost) copied by a pilgrim in the eighth century. 24

Behind this temple, there was a *Tabularium*, the state archives, now replaced by the Senate Palace on the Capitoline Hill. 25

Today it serves as the city hall for the mayor of Rome.

Part of the Tabularium can be viewed in an underground tunnel connecting Palazzo dei Conservatori Museum on the Capitoline Hill with the Palazzo Nuovo.

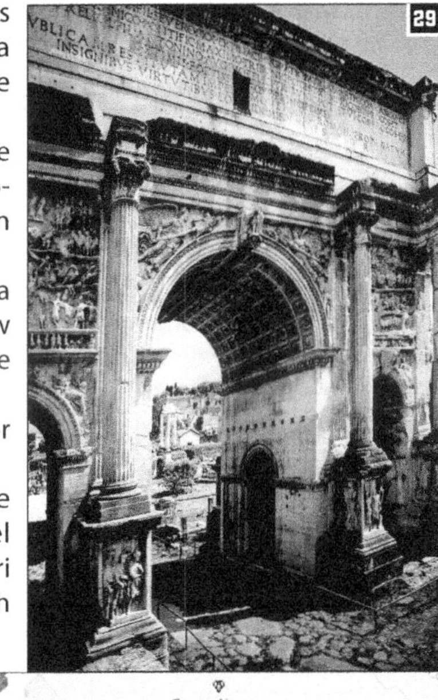

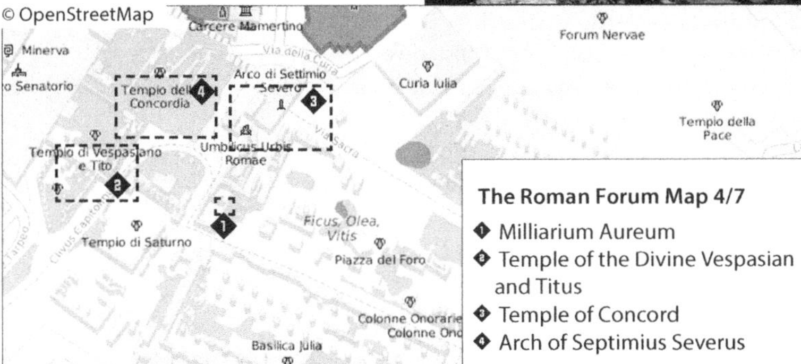

The Roman Forum Map 4/7

❶ Milliarium Aureum
❷ Temple of the Divine Vespasian and Titus
❸ Temple of Concord
❹ Arch of Septimius Severus

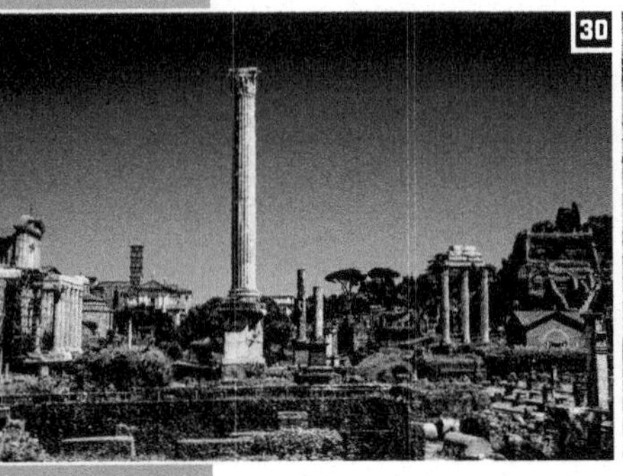

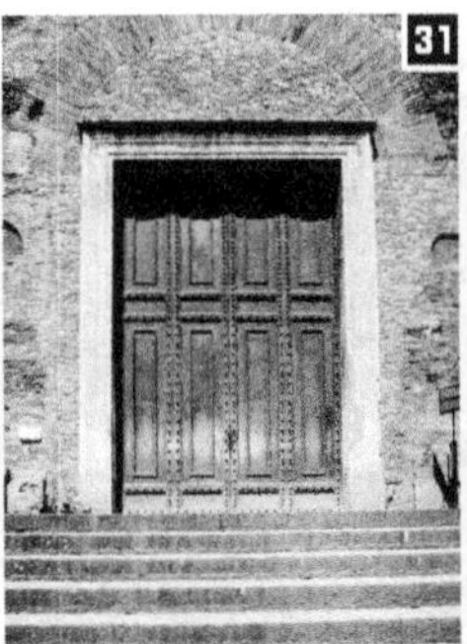

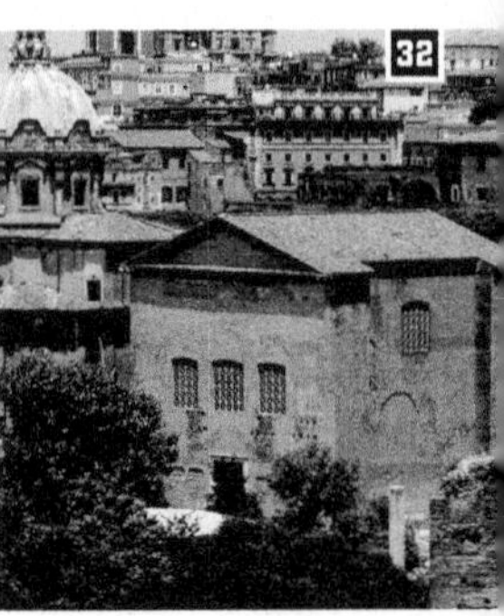

⑪ Temple of Concord ★

Going right from the Temple of Vespasian and Titus, there was a temple dedicated to the goddess of harmony, Concordia. The temple was meant to symbolize the end of fighting between patricians and plebeians in the fourth century BC. During the Republic, occasionally Senate was in session here and Cicero held his four famous "Speeches against Catilina". From what was once a 148 ft (45 meter) wide and 79 ft (24 m) long temple, there is only a podium left. It is likely that this temple served as a model for all the other Concordian temples throughout the empire. In 2002, in Merida, Spain, a reproduction of this building was found on the city forum.

⑫ Arch of Septimius Severus

★★★ 26 27 28 29

This arch was constructed to celebrate the tenth anniversary of Septimius Severus's rule (145–211), together with the victory of his sons and co-rulers from AD 209, Caracalla and Geta who defeated the Parthians (Iraq and Iran) and the Arab tribes in AD 203. After Severus died in AD 211, his sons respected their father's wish and shared the imperial title.

However, Caracalla had his younger brother Geta killed the following year, destroying any mention of him.

Did you know?

Caracalla's Massacre

According to the Roman consul and historian Cassius Dio, who witnessed the whole massacre, Caracalla did not stop at killing just his own brother.

Seeing an opportunity to get rid of political opponents, he ordered more than 20,000 men and women to be killed who had shown loyalty to his brother in one way or another.

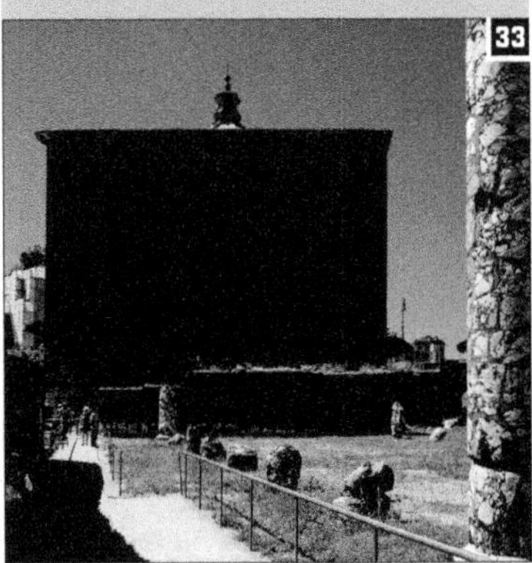

Did you know?

The deification of Julius Caesar

Caesar is the second Roman citizen, after Romulus, the founder of Rome, to be declared a god by the Senate.

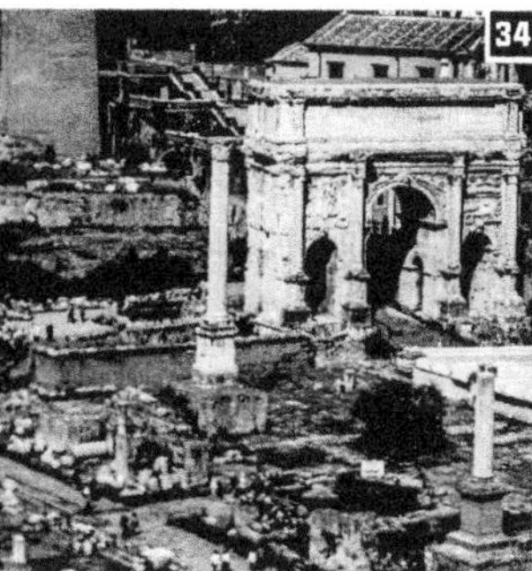
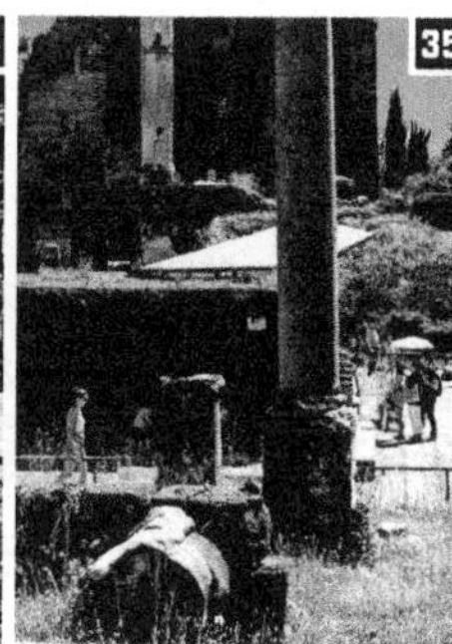
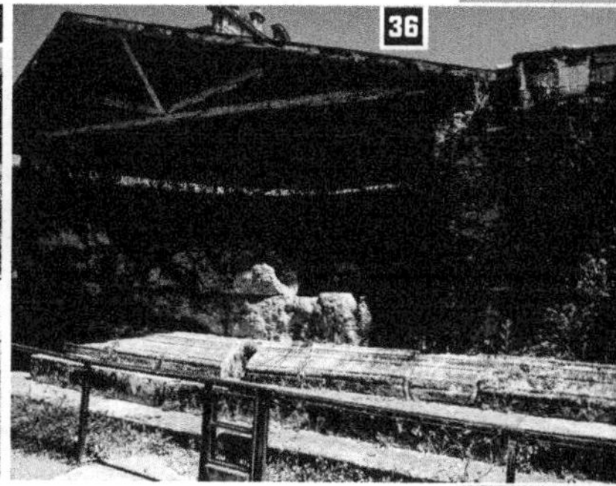

⑬ Column of Phocas ★★★ 30 34

The pillar was built in honor of the ruler of the Eastern Roman Empire, Phocas, on August 1, 608. To this day, it is considered as the last object ever to have been constructed on the Roman Forum. It is 45 ft or 13.6 m high and set on a square pedestal made of white marble.

⑭ Curia Julia ★★ 32

Curia Julia, the building of the Roman Senate was built in 44 BC by Gaius Julius Caesar. It was only one of many curias that were built on the same place. Emperor Diocletian built a new one in AD 283 after a great fire.

Pope Honorius I turned the Roman Senate into a church of Sant'Adriano al Foro in 630, which preserved it until the 1930's. This is when it was restored by removing all medieval additions. 33

The bronze doors are not from ancient Roman times. 31 The original doors of the Curia are in the Basilica di San Giovanni in Laterano (Basilica of St. John Lateran). [p.270]

The dimensions of the Curia accurately correspond to the architectural ideal supported by the ancient Roman architect and engineer Vitruvius (80–15 BC) in his work *De Architectura*.

This is why this Curia was established as the prototype for many later buildings. Even today, you can see the remarkable marble floor made of green serpentine and dark red porphyry. This floor was designed during Diocletian's restoration of the Curia.

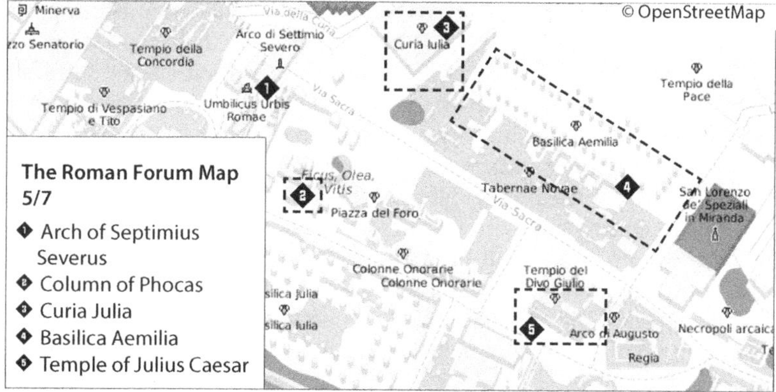

The Roman Forum Map
5/7

◆ Arch of Septimius Severus
◆ Column of Phocas
◆ Curia Julia
◆ Basilica Aemilia
◆ Temple of Julius Caesar

IMPERIAL ROME – Roman Forum ★★★★

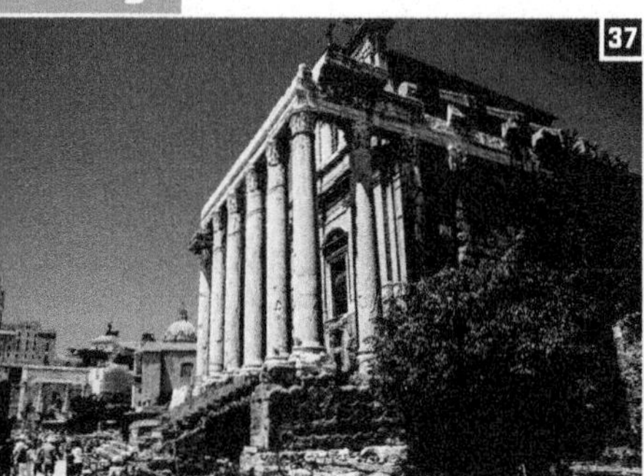

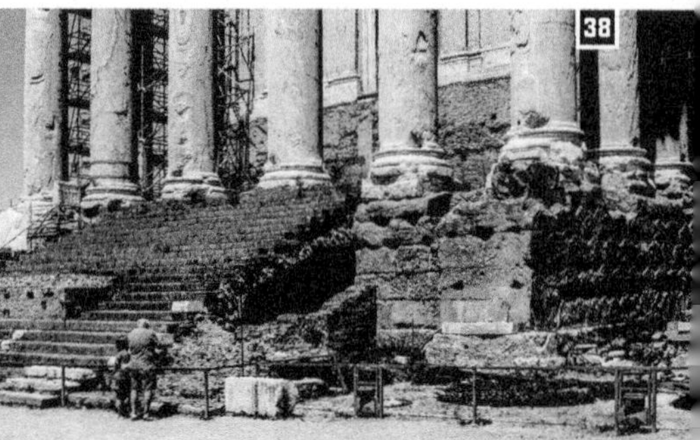

On each side, there are three wide steps that can seat around 300 senators. The chairman had a place on the wide podium.

⑮ Basilica Aemilia ★★

Next to the Curia, in the direction of the Colosseum, you can find the foundations of Basilica Aemilia, built in 179 BC. The basilica had three floors, it was 328 ft long and 98 ft wide (100×30 m). Longitudinally, there were two rows of columns with sixteen arches each. It functioned solely as a place of commerce and finance. This is where tax collectors, merchants, financial dealers (precursors to bankers) met and did business. When the Visigoth king Alaric broke into Rome in AD 410, Basilica Aemilia was burned to the ground.

⑯ Temple of Julius Caesar ★ 36

On the opposite side of Basilica Aemilia, crossing the Via della Salara Vecchia, there are remains of a temple dedicated to Julius Caesar. 35 It was erected by Augustus in 42 BC when the Senate declared Julius Caesar a god, two years after he was murdered. Octavian, also known as the first Roman Emperor Augustus, was Caesar's nephew and adopted son. The temple was built on the exact spot where Julius Caesar was cremated. There are fresh flowers on a semicircular altar in front of the temple, brought by Caesar's supporters even today.

⑰ Temple of Antoninus and Faustina ★★★ 41

The temple is situated next to the remains of Basilica Aemilia, opposite the Curia Julia. It was built in AD 141 during Antoninus Pius's reign. It is dedicated to his wife Faustina the Elder, who was declared a deity after she passed away. When the emperor died, the Senate also declared him a god, so the temple was renamed in honor of the couple. 38 In 11th century the temple was repurposed as a church of San Lorenzo in Miranda. According to legend, this is the precise place where St. Lawrence was sentenced to death. The church, as it is now, is mostly composed of Roman remains and additions from 1601. What has been preserved from old Roman days is the front of the temple with ten 56 ft (17 m) high Corinthian columns. The excavations are still underway. 37 On the main altar of the church, there is a painting of Martyrdom of St. Lawrence by Pietro da Cortona.

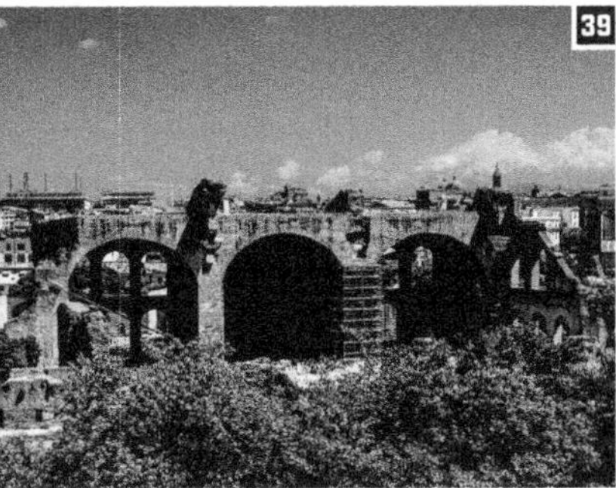

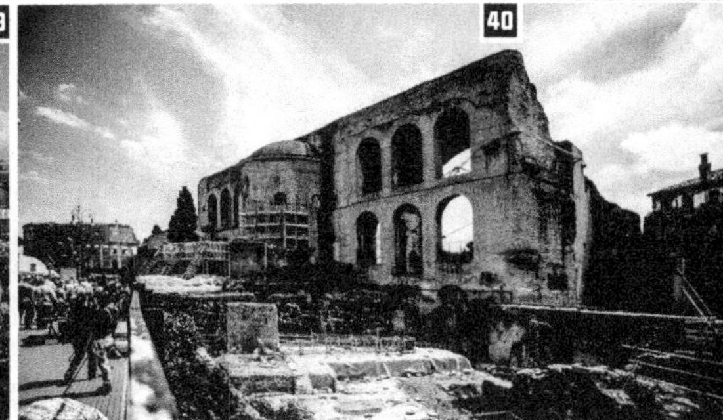

In the first chapel on the left, you can see the Madonna and Child with Saints (1626) by Domenichino.

(18) Basilica of Maxentius ★ 39

Emperor Maxentius (278–312) started building this basilica in AD 308. The construction was completed by Emperor Constantine the Great in AD 312, after he defeated Maxentius in the Battle at Milvian Bridge on October 28, 312. This is the last and largest basilica built on the Roman Forum. Its dimension are 230 ft by 328 ft or 70 m by 100 m.

It was precisely the layout of the Basilica of Maxentius that served as a model for St. Peter's Basilica in the early sixteen century. [p.136]

Instead of building a traditional basilica, Maxentius opted for a basilica that resembled a Roman bath, e.g., Diocletian's Baths in Rome. 40

Did you know?

Temple of Antoninus and Faustina

Each and every column was made from a single piece of stone. Due to the difference in height of nearly 20 ft (6 m), it is not possible today to go into the church from the Roman Forum. 41

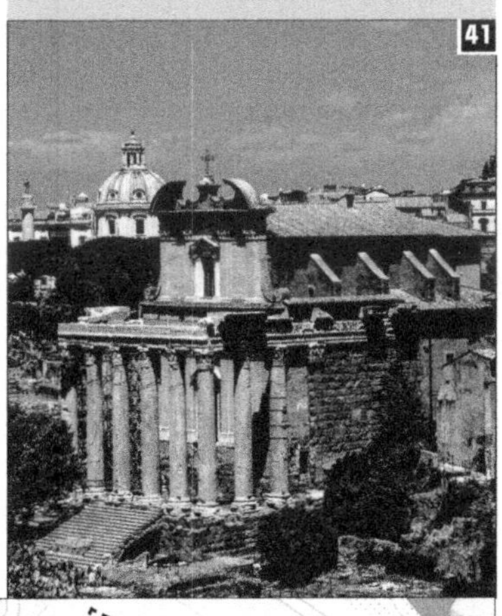

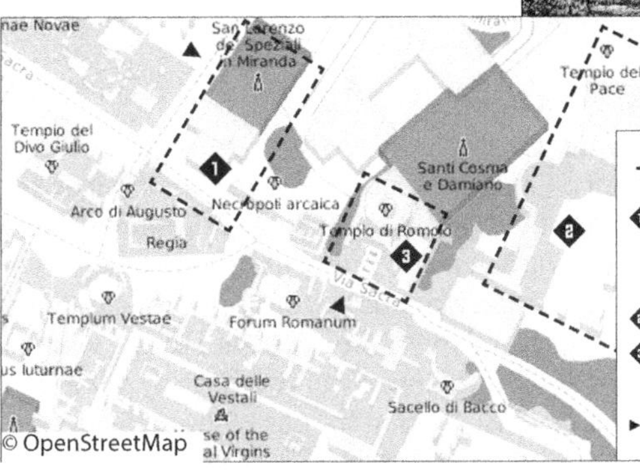

The Roman Forum Map 6/7

❶ Temple of Antoninus and Faustina or the Church of San Lorenzo in Miranda
❷ Basilica of Maxentius
❸ Temple of Romulus and Santi Cosma e Damiano
► ENTRANCE / EXIT

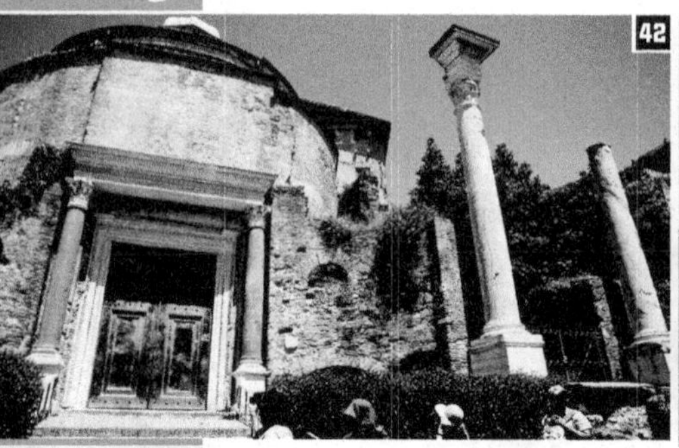

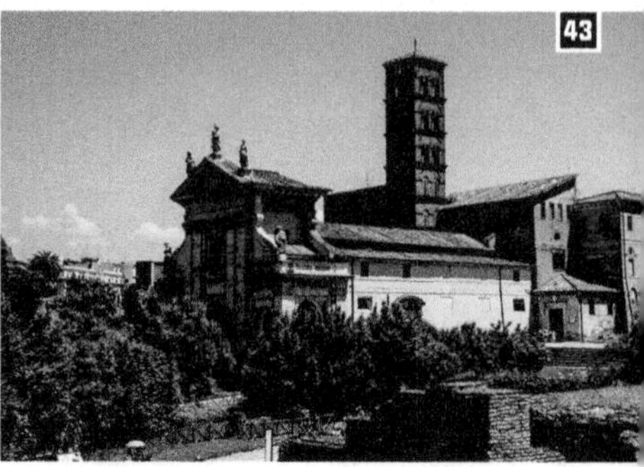

Constantine the Great finished the construction and put a statue of himself of colossal proportions in the central nave. Remains of this statue are kept in the Capitoline Museums. [p.81] The statue was made using the acrolith technique, a Greek manner of constructing gigantic statues which included making the naked parts of the human figure out of stone, while the parts covered with clothes were made of wood. The side aisles are 80 ft (24.5 m) high, which means the central hall must have been at least 115 ft (35 m) tall. It was only after a thousand years that this dome was outdone – when the Gothic cathedral in Cologne finally stood tall at 141 ft (43 m). What could not be taken was destroyed by earthquakes in 847 and 1349. Finally, in 1614, the remaining eight columns (66 ft or 20 m high) were ordered by Pope Paul V to be moved to the Piazza di Santa Maria Maggiore. The basilica was covered in gilded bricks until the seventh century when they were taken down to cover the roof old of St. Peter's Basilica.

19 Temple of Romulus ★★★ 42

The divine Emperor Maxentius built this temple on the Forum in honor of his deceased son Valerius Romulus, also declaring him a god. There are the original bronze doors at the entrance to Temple of Romulus with the original lock which still works. Together with the Pantheon, the Temple of Romulus is the best preserved temple in Rome from the imperial era. Temple of Romulus was attached to the Church of Santi Cosma e Damiano. The walls of this church are actually part of *Templum Pacis* or Temple of Peace, whose construction was commissioned by Emperor Vespasian after he won the Jewish War in AD 71. In the early 6th century king of Ostrogoths Theoderic gave this temple-turned-church to Pope Felix IV.

20 Church of Santa Francesca Romana ★ 43

The church has been through many additions from the ninth century to the early seventeenth century. Carlo Lombardi designed the final interior and façade. The belfry is from the twelfth century. The Church of Santa Francesca Romana or Santa Maria Nova was built on the exact spot where Pope Paul I located the death of Simon Magnus. According to legend, Simon Magnus wanted to compete with apostles Peter and Paul to see who had greater power, so he started levitating in front of them. They fell to their knees and started praying to God asking him to make Simon fall down.

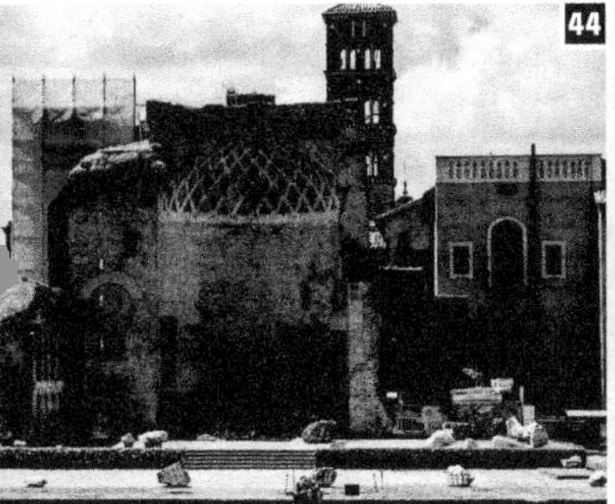

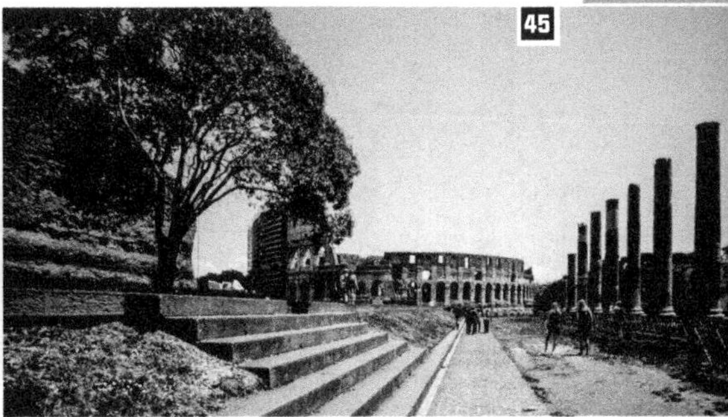

That is exactly what happened, Simon fell and the fall killed him. Basalt stone with the imprints of Peter and Paul's knees was built into the south transversal wall of the church, i.e., in the one closer to the Palatine. In the center of the church, there are medieval Cosmatesque mosaics, made with astonishing precision by inserting multicolored stones.

㉑ Temple of Venus and Rome ★★★ 44

This dual temple is situated on the back of the Church of Santa Francesca Romana. It was the biggest temple in ancient Rome (476 ft or 145 m long and 328 ft or 100 m wide). 45 The temple was dedicated to goddesses Venus Felix (serendipity) and Roma Aeterna (eternal Rome). Architect and the first builder of the temple was Emperor Hadrian himself (76–138), the most well-known engineer and architect among Roman emperors. After the official opening ceremony in 135, it was fully completed six years later by Emperor Antoninus Pius. A fire in 307 also meant that Emperor Maxentius had to renovate it. The Goddesses of Luck and Rome share another tie. Venus is the goddess of love. AMOR, Latin for love, reads ROMA in reverse.

Putting the two temples back to back reflects this verbal symmetry. Inside Venus's shrine, there was an altar where only married couples could bring sacrifices. Recently, the temple has been open to the public, after many years of restoration.

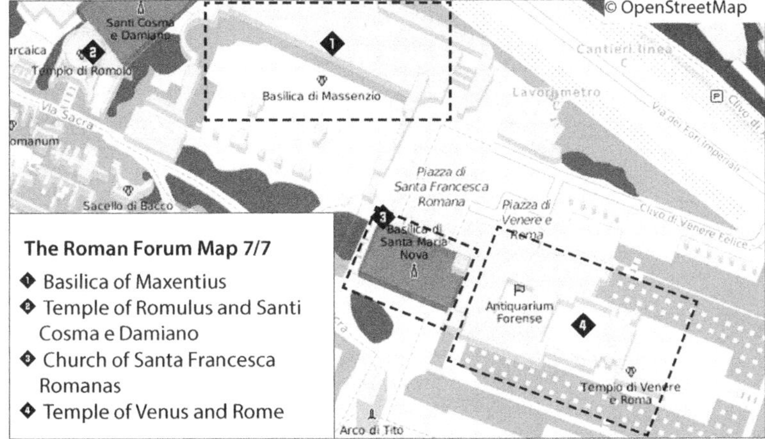

The Roman Forum Map 7/7

❶ Basilica of Maxentius
❷ Temple of Romulus and Santi Cosma e Damiano
❸ Church of Santa Francesca Romanas
❹ Temple of Venus and Rome

**Tip ::: ** THE PATH IS OFTEN UNEVEN, SO BE SURE TO HAVE A GOOD WALKING SHOES

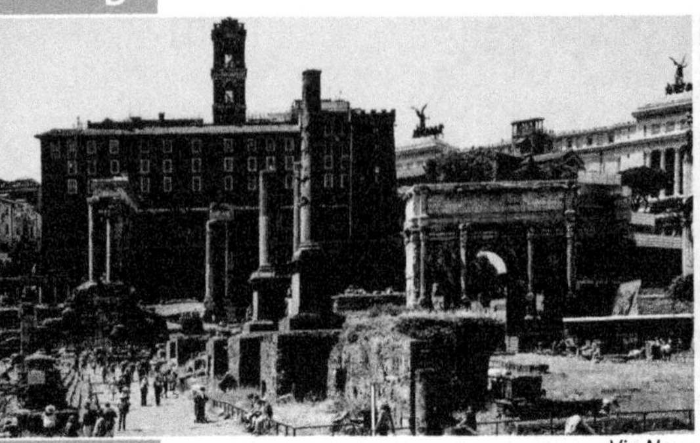
Via Nova

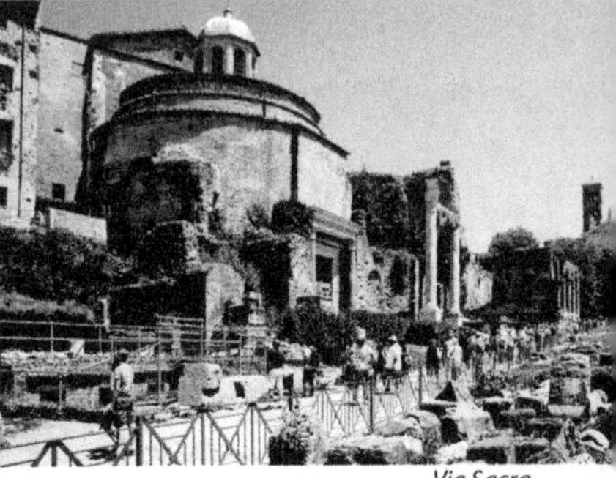
Via Sacra

Foro Romano | Roman Forum
Address: Via della Salara Vecchia, Roma
Online: www.coopculture.it/en

Public transportation: Metro B stop Colosseo | Bus stop Fori Imperiali or Colosseo: 51, 85, 87, 118

Accurate information about opening times: www.parcocolosseo.it/en

The Roman Forum All-In-One Map

❶ The Arch of Titus
❷ The House of the Vestal Virgins
❸ Temple of Vesta
❹ Regia
❺ Temple of Castor and Pollux
❻ Basilica Julia
❼ Temple of Saturn
❽ Rostra
❾ Milliarium Aureum
❿ Temple of the Divine Vespasian and Titus
⓫ Temple of Concord
⓬ Arch of Septimius Severus
⓭ Column of Phocas
⓮ Curia Julia
⓯ Basilica Aemilia
⓰ Temple of Julius Caesar
⓱ Temple of Antoninus and Faustina
⓲ Basilica of Maxentius
⓳ Temple of Romulus and Santi Cosma e Damiano
⓴ Church of Santa Francesca Romana
㉑ Temple of Venus and Rome
► ENTRANCE / EXIT

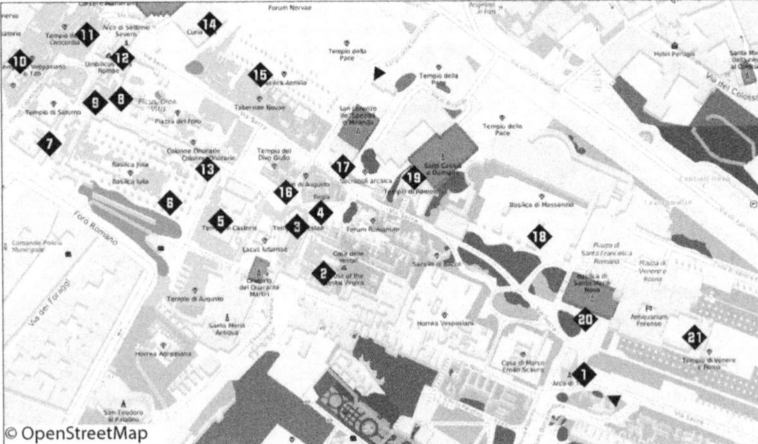

Trajan's Market – Museo dei Fori Imperiali

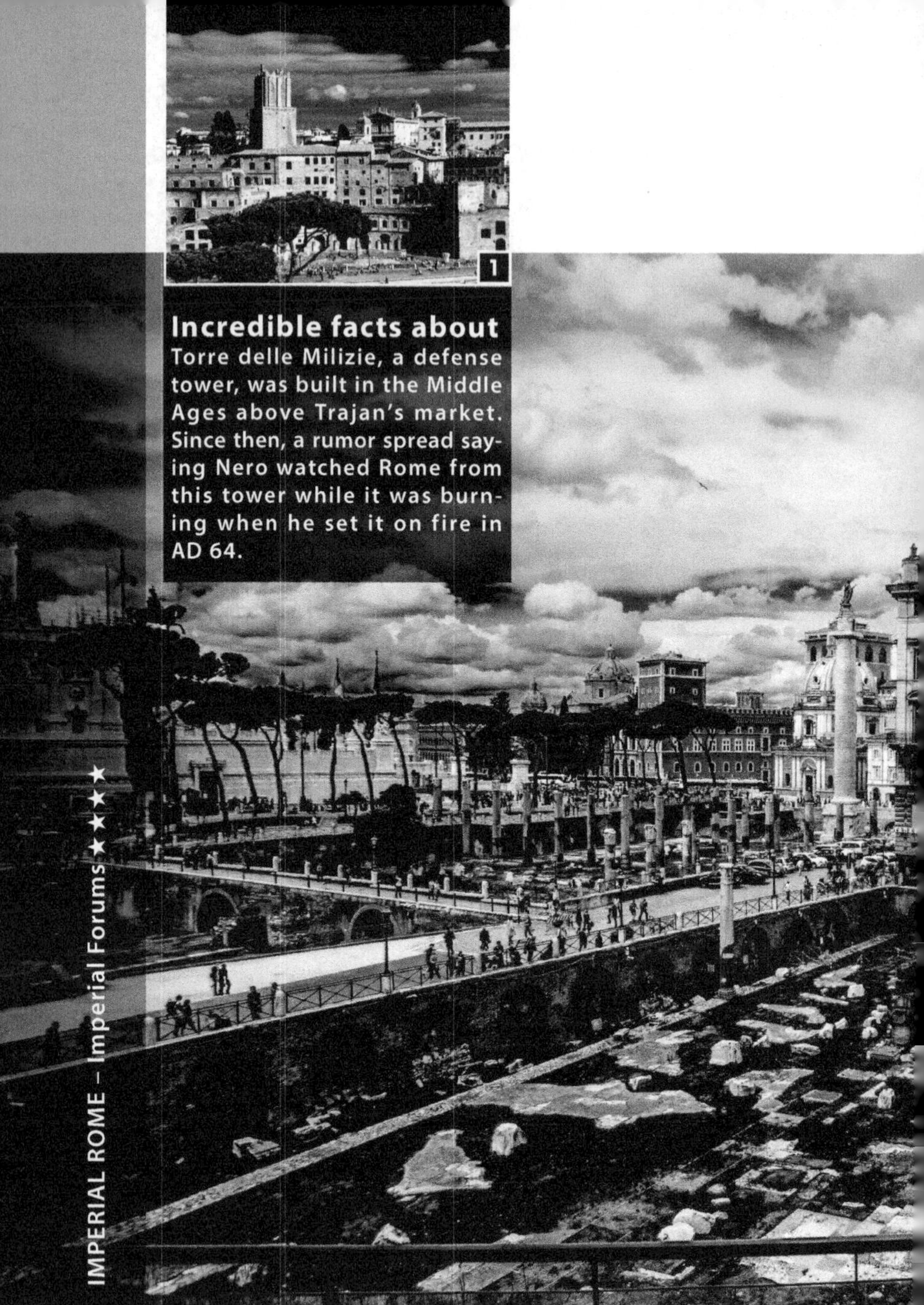

Incredible facts about
Torre delle Milizie, a defense tower, was built in the Middle Ages above Trajan's market. Since then, a rumor spread saying Nero watched Rome from this tower while it was burning when he set it on fire in AD 64.

Trajan's Market – Imperial Forums

Extra Tip : : :
There is a small but very interesting museum at the Trajan market with valuable fragments from the Imperial Forums. Don't miss out on the amazing view from the Belvedere in front of Trajan's market of the Capitoline Hill and Palazzo di Venezia.

Monumental public projects of Roman rulers

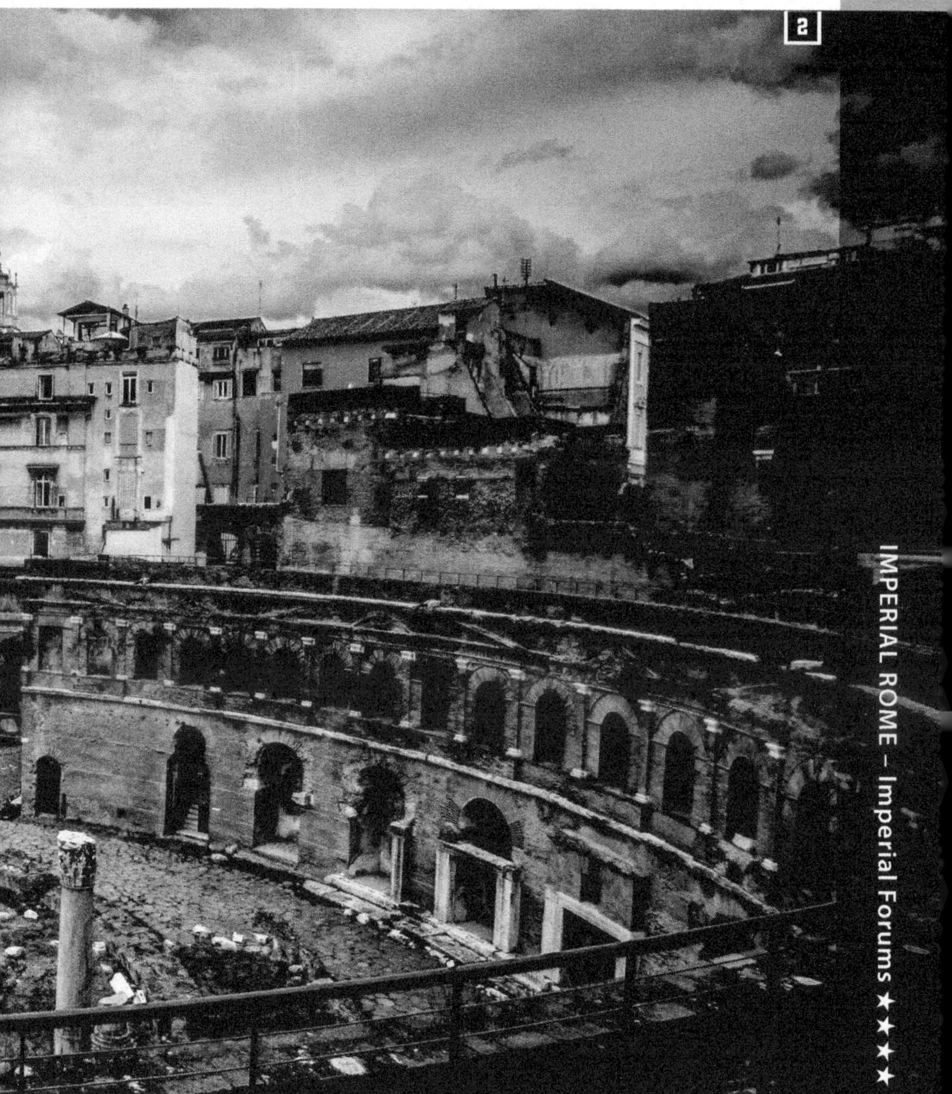

Museo dei Fori Imperiali | Museum of the Imperial Forums
Address: Via IV Novembre 94, Roma
Public transportation: Metro B stop Colosseo | Bus stop Fori Imperiali – Campido-glio 51, 85, 87
Opening hours and prices: www.mercatiditraiano.it/en

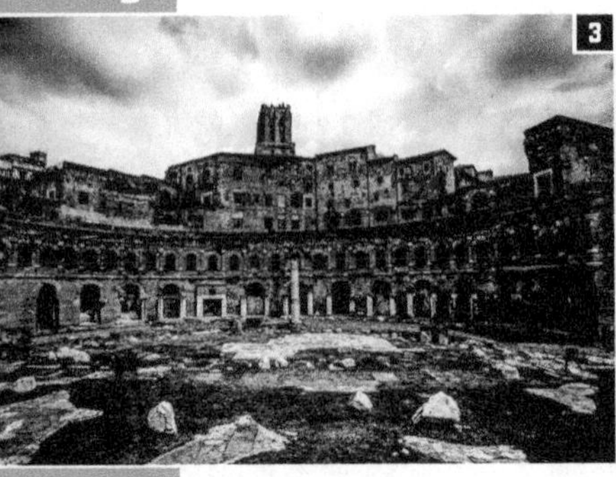 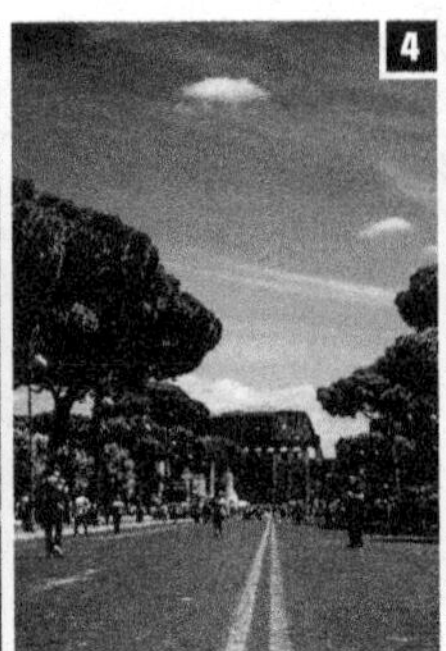 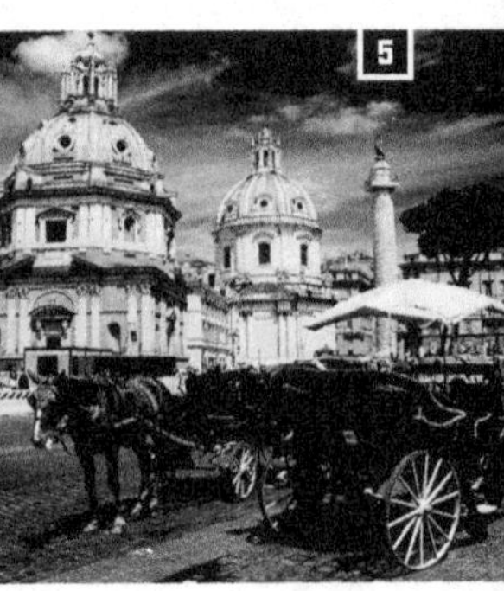

❶ Imperial Forums ★★★★

The Imperial forums were not part of the Roman Forum. Imperial forums were the centers of politics, religion and economy in the ancient Roman Empire.

① Via dei Fori Imperiali ★

The visible remnants of the forums constructed by Roman emperors start after the Via Cavour and Via dei Fori Imperiali intersection.

The wide avenue of Via dei Fori Imperiali on the Imperial Forums was built by the Italian fascist leader Benito Mussolini for representative purposes in the 1930s.

Not only were the Imperial Forums split in half by asphalt during the fascist regime, but Mussolini's government also took on an extensive excavation project that unearthed large portions of the Imperial Forums on the other side of Via dei Fori Imperiali.

② Forum of Vespasian and Nerva ★★

We will go towards Trajan's market to the Piazza Foro Traiano. The Forum of Vespasian, as well as the Forum of Nerva, are almost completely buried under the intersection of the streets Via Cavour and Via dei Fori Imperiali.

③ Augustus's Forum ★★

The first thing we will come across on our way to Piazza Foro Traiano is the Forum of Augustus. After the Battle at Philippi in 42 BC, Octavian, the future Augustus and the first Roman emperor, defeated Julius Caesar's assassins. [p.103]

In celebration, he built a temple dedicated to Mars Ultor, god of vengeance. In this way, Roman Forum was expanded by 410 ft (125 m) in length and 387 ft (118 m) in width. It was the second extension of the forum.

④ Caesar's Forum ★★

The first extension of Roman Forum happened while Julius Caesar was still alive, between what later became Forum of Augustus and Roman Forum. Today, most of Caesar's forum, completed during the Augustan period, is under Via dei Fori Imperiali.

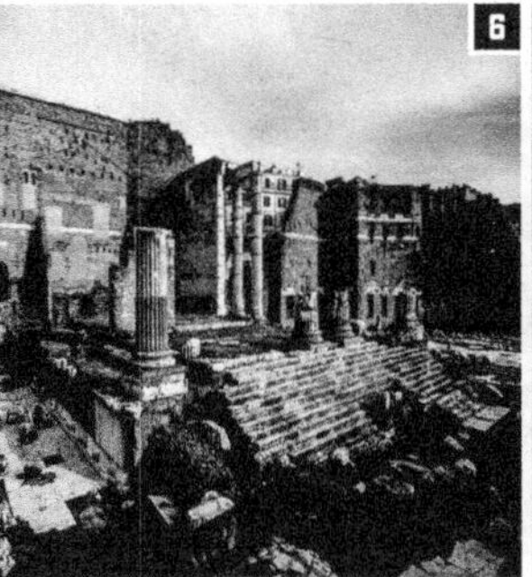
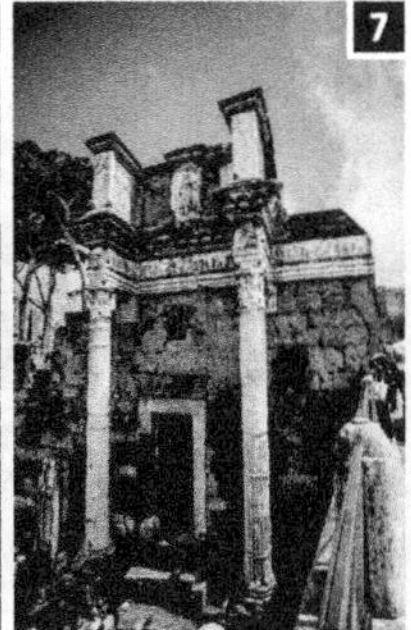
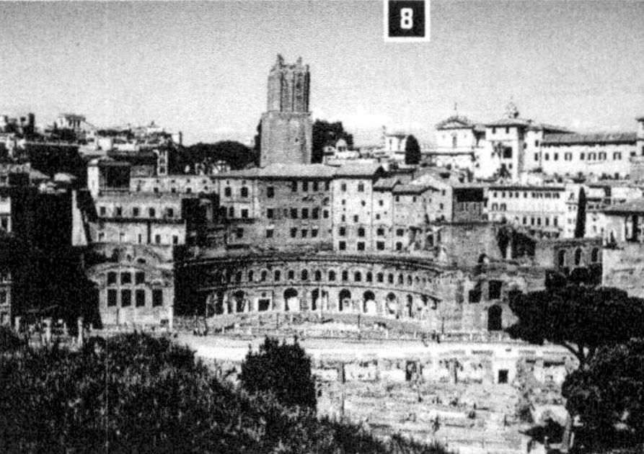

⬦ Trajan's Forum ★★★ **2**

This forum was the last and most memorable extension of the Imperial Forums. Trajan relied on one of the most gifted architects in ancient Rome, Apollodorus of Damascus, who built the Pantheon. Apollodorus designed Trajan's Forum as the center of Roman public life.

⬦ Main square on Trajan's Forum ★★ **9**

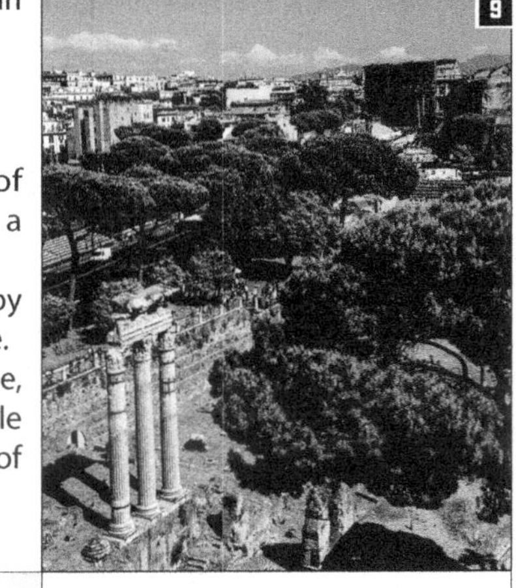

The clearing in the middle of Trajan's Forum was designed as a marble square.

It was 656 ft by 394 ft (200 m by 120 m), with an *exedra* on each side.

Exedra is a semi-circle, like a niche, overlooking the square. In the middle of the square, there was a statue of Trajan on a horse.

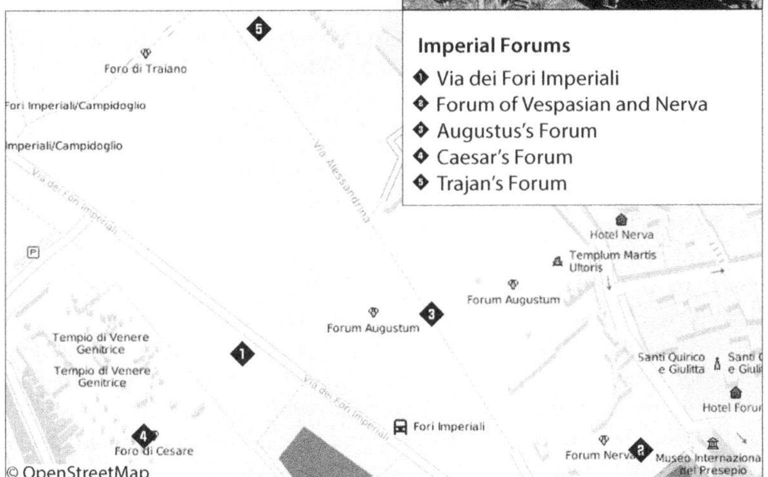

Imperial Forums
- ❶ Via dei Fori Imperiali
- ❷ Forum of Vespasian and Nerva
- ❸ Augustus's Forum
- ❹ Caesar's Forum
- ❺ Trajan's Forum

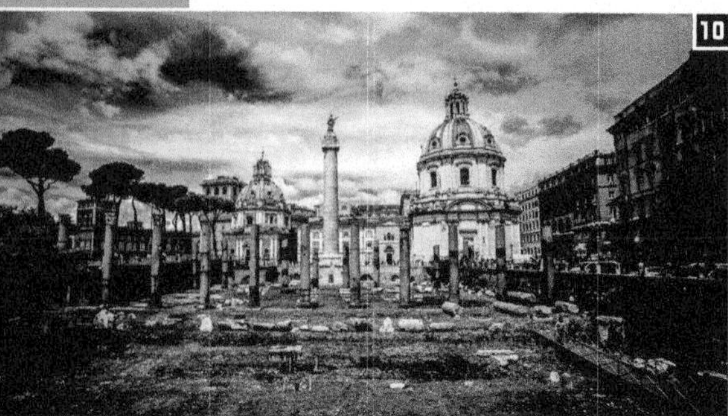
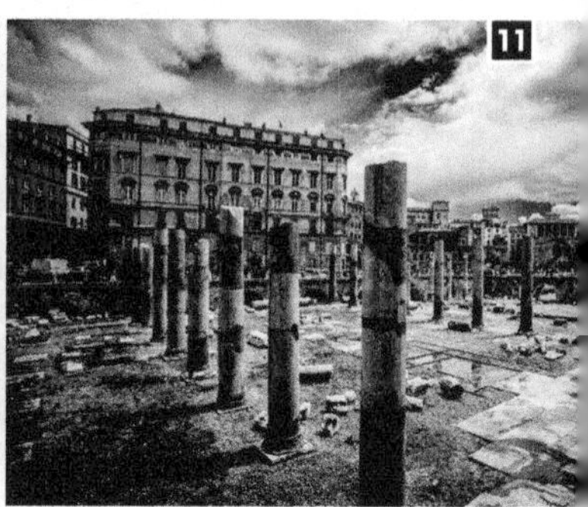

The entrance to the square was on the right, from Augustus's Forum, through Trajan's triumphal arch (AD 116) celebrating his Dacian victory of AD 106.

⑦ Trajan's Market ★★★

The first ancient shopping mall is located in the semicircular building at the end of the square, dating back to AD 110. Several stories high, it had shops, offices and warehouses where a large number of amphorae has been found. If you want to go in, you will have to come through 94 Via Quattro Novembre from the Piazza Madonna di Loreto. Via Biberatica 12, which used to have taverns and shops, splits the market in two. An identical building stood on the east side, the one closer to the Palatine Hill.

⑧ Basilica Ulpia ★★ 10 11

This is a very important basilica for the development of Christian sacral architecture. It was the biggest Roman basilica, 384 ft by 180 ft (117 by 55 m) and was called Ulpia after Emperor Trajan's middle name — Marcus Ulpius Traianus. Basilica Ulpia had five naves. The inner naves were divided by a colonnade. Walls and columns were made of the finest marble. There were two semicircular apses in the end. The building was three stories high, so that the roof was 164 ft (50 m) high. On the outside, the roof was covered in gilded bronze tiles. Indicators of the former glory of this basilica are the two rows of eight columns in the central area.

⑨ Trajan's Column ★★★ 13

Trajan's column was erected in AD 113. This free-standing column is probably the first monument of its kind in Roman history. There is a spiral relief with impressive representation of Trajan's success in the Dacian Wars (AD 101–102 and 105–106). It is likely that it was constructed by Apollodorus of Damascus at the order of the Roman Senate. Trajan's column is 98 ft or 30 m high, without the pedestal which adds 16.4 ft or 5-plus m. It is composed of twenty pieces of Carrara marble. Each of the disks weighs 32 tons and is 12 ft (3.7 m) wide. The frieze is 623 ft (190 m) long. There are detailed depictions of fights with complete battle gear. You can see *ballista* (a weapon transported on a carriage with a huge crossbow), catapults and other heavy weaponry. Around 2,500 people have been counted on the frieze, mostly Trajan's soldiers from the Dacian Wars.

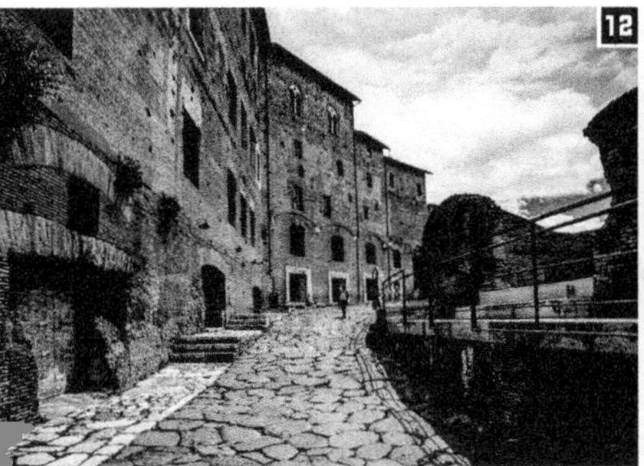

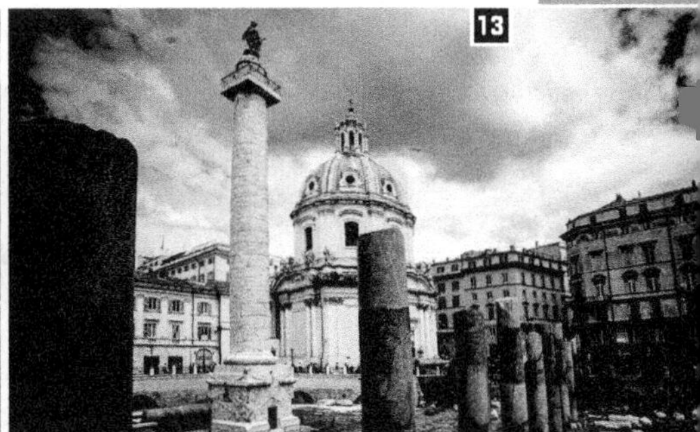

A pedestal holds the entire structure together (1100 tons). On top, there is a capital with a pedestal, weighing more than 53 tons. Inside the column, there is a stairway that goes all the way up to the platform. This is where Trajan's sculpture was originally placed. Trajan's column is as high as the hill that had to be moved to make room for Trajan's forum. After Trajan died, the Senate decided to put his ashes in a golden urn below the column. Today, we have a bronze statue of St. Peter, placed by Pope Sixtus V in 1587. Putting the statue of St. Peter on this spot was not a coincidence. According to Christianity, Peter and Paul were held in the Mamertine Prison before their execution.

⑩ Museo dei Fori Imperiali ★ ★ ★

There is a small but very interesting museum at the Trajan market with valuable fragments from the Imperial Forums. Don't miss out on the amazing view from the Belvedere in front of Trajan's market of the Capitoline Hill.

Museo dei Fori Imperiali | Museum of the Imperial Forums
Address: Via IV Novembre 94, Roma

Public transportation:
Bus stop Fori Imperiali – Campidoglio
51, 85, 87

Opening hours and prices:
http://www.mercatiditraiano.it/en

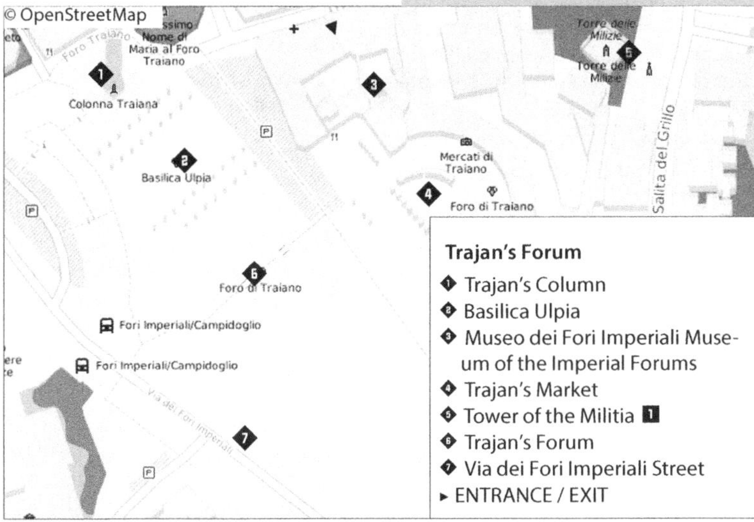

Trajan's Forum
1. Trajan's Column
2. Basilica Ulpia
3. Museo dei Fori Imperiali Museum of the Imperial Forums
4. Trajan's Market
5. Tower of the Militia
6. Trajan's Forum
7. Via dei Fori Imperiali Street
▶ ENTRANCE / EXIT

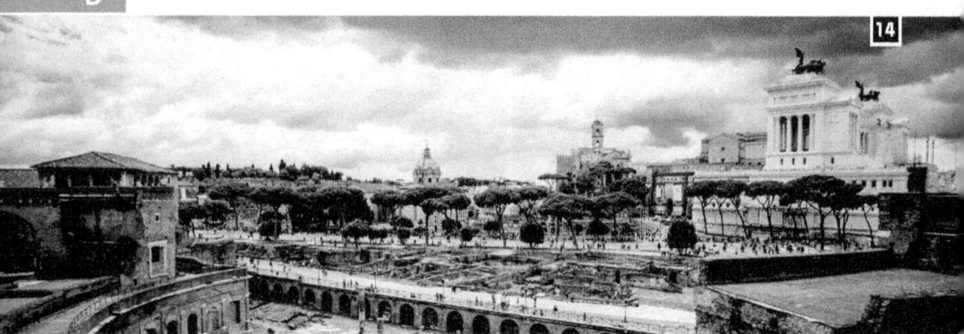

Walk around Imperial Forums

❷ Santa Maria di Loreto ★ 15

This is a sixteenth-century church, located just across the street from Trajan's Column, near the Piazza Venezia. The church was built atop an earlier fifteenth-century chapel, which contained an icon of the Virgin of Loreto. Santa Maria di Loreto was designed by Antonio da Sangallo the younger.

The interior decoration is best noted for a statue at the entrance by Andrea Sansovino and the very famous early Baroque statue of Santa Susanna by François Duquesnoy.

❸ Santissimo Nome di Maria al Foro Traiano ★ 17

This white church stands in front of the Column of Trajan, a few steps from the similarly domed Church of Santa Maria di Loreto. The interior is elliptical. There are seven small chapels, decorated in polychrome marble.

Did you know?

The largest archaeological park in the world

Today, Via dei Fori Imperiali is partially closed for traffic and the whole area is for pedestrians.

Soon, the Imperial Forums could shed their asphalt skin and reunite with the Roman Forum into a single archaeological park after eighty years.

When this idea, proposed by the Roman mayors, comes to life, this will be the largest archaeological park in the world.

Fori Imperiali | Imperial Forums
Address: Via dei Fori Imperiali, Roma

Public transportation: Bus stop Fori Imperiali – Campidoglio 51, 85, 87

Opening hours
Public place – always open

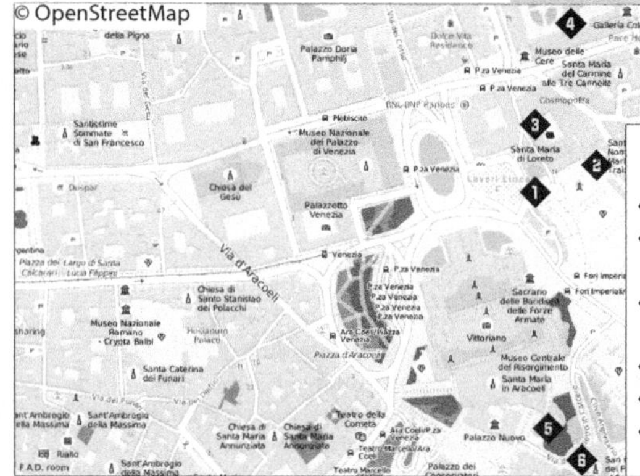

Around Imperial Forums

❶ Santa Maria di Loreto
❷ Santissimo Nome di Maria al Foro Traiano
❸ Le Domus Romane di Palazzo Valentini
❹ Palazzo Colonna
❺ Mamertine Prison
❻ Gemonian stairs

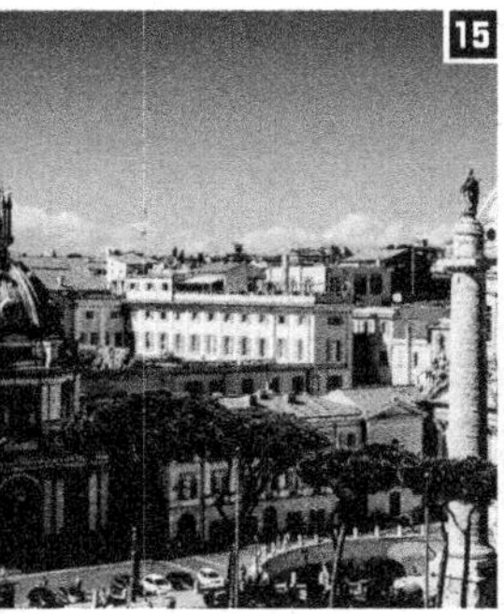
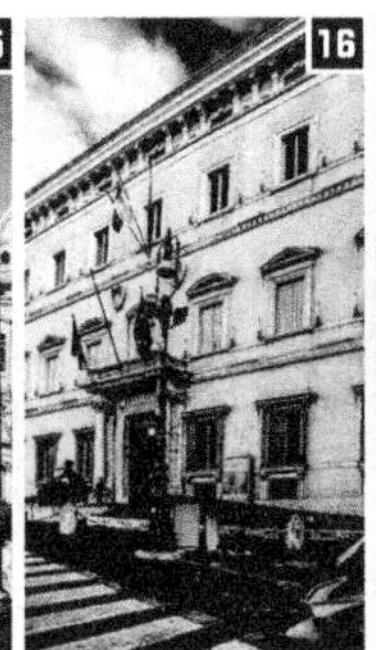
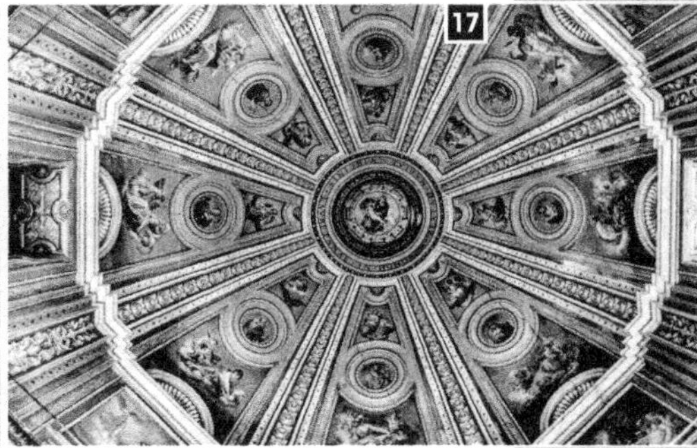

Le Domus Romane di Palazzo Valentini ★ ★

The excavations in the palazzo's basement have found, 23 ft or 7 m below street level, a small baths complex and a part of an adjacent residential complex. This multimedia exhibition in the Domus Romane brings ancient Rome to life. You learn about Roman life, and get to see an interesting excavation site through the glass floor. Booking in advance is recommended. The different tour hours run in different languages and it's impossible to enter without a tour.

❺ Palazzo Colonna ★ ★ ★

Palazzo Colonna is not only a Roman palace, it is also an entire city block, owned by the Colonna family for 23 generations. The influential Roman family raised 13 cardinals, a Pope Martin V (1417–1431), senators, military commander of the Papal Army (Prospero Colonna, 1452–1523), admiral Marcantonio Colonna (1535–1584), the winner of the naval battle at Lepanto and poets Vittoria Colonna (1490–1547). Almost all of them were patrons of art and most of the things they commissioned, adopted

or acquired are still in their palaces, more specifically, at the private museum called Galleria Colonna. Among many Roman antiques there are also paintings by **Lorenzo Monaco, Agnolo Bronzino, Domenico Ghirlandaio, Paolo Veronese, Palma il Vecchio, Jacopo and Domenico Tintoretto, Pietro da Cortona, Annibale Carracci, Francesco Albani, Guercino, Guido Reni, Carlo Maratta, Gaspard Poussin, Pompeo Batoni** and others.

The splendor of this private collection and the brilliant rooms of the Palazzo Colonna can only be compared to the private gallery at the Doria Pamphilj Palace. [p.101]

❻ Mamertine Prison ★ ★

Mamertine Prison or Tullianum was a dungeon since the third century BC. Primarily, it was a place for swift executions during political trials. The trials took place either in the basilicas at the forum or in the Senate. Whoever was put on trial, be they kings and leaders of subjugated peoples (Jugurtha, king of Numidia in AD 104, king of the Galls Vercingetorix in 46 BC) or prominent Roman politicians (Lucius Aelius Sejanus

Le Domus Romane di Palazzo Valentini
Address: Via IV Novembre 119/a, Roma
Online: www.palazzovalentini.it

Public transportation: Bus stop Piazza Venezia: 119 or Plebiscito: 30, 46, 62, 64, 70, 81, 87, 190F, 492, 628, 916, 916F

Opening hours: *see online*

Galleria Colonna in Palazzo Colonna
Address: Via della Pilotta 17, Roma
Online: www.galleriacolonna.it/en

Public transportation: Bus stop Piazza Venezia: 119 or Plebiscito: 30, 46, 62, 64, 70, 81, 87, 190F, 492, 628, 916, 916F

Opening hours: *see online*

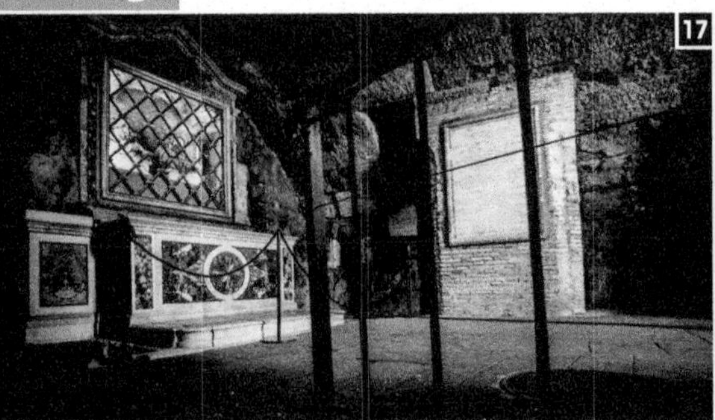

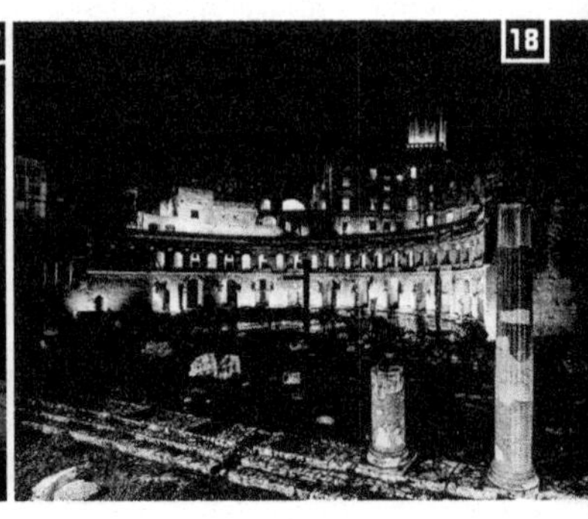

AD 31), the accused would be taken directly to the Tullianum and choked to death after a few days.

According to Christian tradition, Peter and Paul were held there before their executions.

It is located underneath a Church called San Giuseppe dei Falegnami. Dead bodies were sometimes brought to the Gemonian stairs. Other not-so-prominent inmates ended up in the Cloaca Maxima, the main sewer pipe, flowing right below the prison.

Today, the most horrid part of the prison is open to the public.

❼ Gemonian Stairs ★

The Gemonian Stairs were situated under what is now Via di San Pietro in Carcere. Publius Cornelius Lentulus Sura was executed here as the leader of Catiline's Conspiracy in 63 BC. Senator Lucius Sergius Catilina (108–62 BC) devised a plot that involved killing more than 400 senators in their sleep.

Catiline's Conspiracy was discovered by consul Cicero, who became a senator after that and the most famous Roman orator. This is where Titus Flavius Sabinus, Roman senator and brother of the future Emperor Vespasian, met his dishonorable death (AD 69).

This means that his body was put on display and dogs could drag bits and pieces of it around the streets. After an unsuccessful attempt to persuade Emperor Vitellius to give the city over to Vespasian, who was holding the whole town under siege, Titus and his followers retreated to the Capitoline Hill.

After a brief siege, Vitellius's men captured him, took him to the Tullianum and executed him on the Gemonian stairs. Emperor Vitellius himself met the same brutal end, when his own praetorian guard refused to take him out of the city under siege.

Vitellius was the third emperor during a year known as the Year of Four Emperors: Galba, Otho, Vitellius, Vespasian (AD 69).

Carcere Mamertino | Mamertine Prison
Address: Via Clivo Argentario 1, Roma
Online: www.omniavaticanrome.org/en/cards/carcer-tullianum

Public transportation: Bus stop Fori Imperiali – Campidoglio 51, 85, 87

Opening hours: *see online*

Did you know?

Cicero and Mark Antony

Publius Cornelius Lentulus, nicknamed Sura, although executed, was also Mark Antony's stepfather, which is why Cicero was executed twenty years later by Mark Antony. Cicero's head and right arm were put on display on the Rostra at the Roman Forum.

The bond of hatred between Cicero and Antony was so strong that Fulvia, Mark Antony's wife, pierced Cicero's dead tongue with a hairpin in front of everyone on the forum.

Capitoline Hill

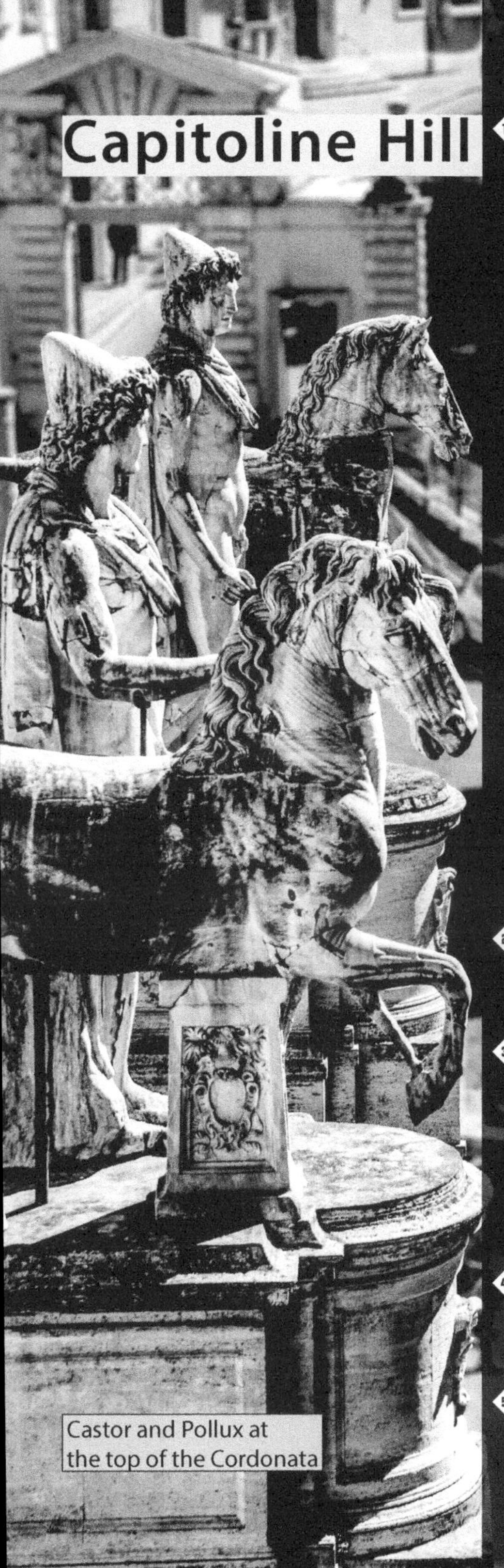

Castor and Pollux at the top of the Cordonata

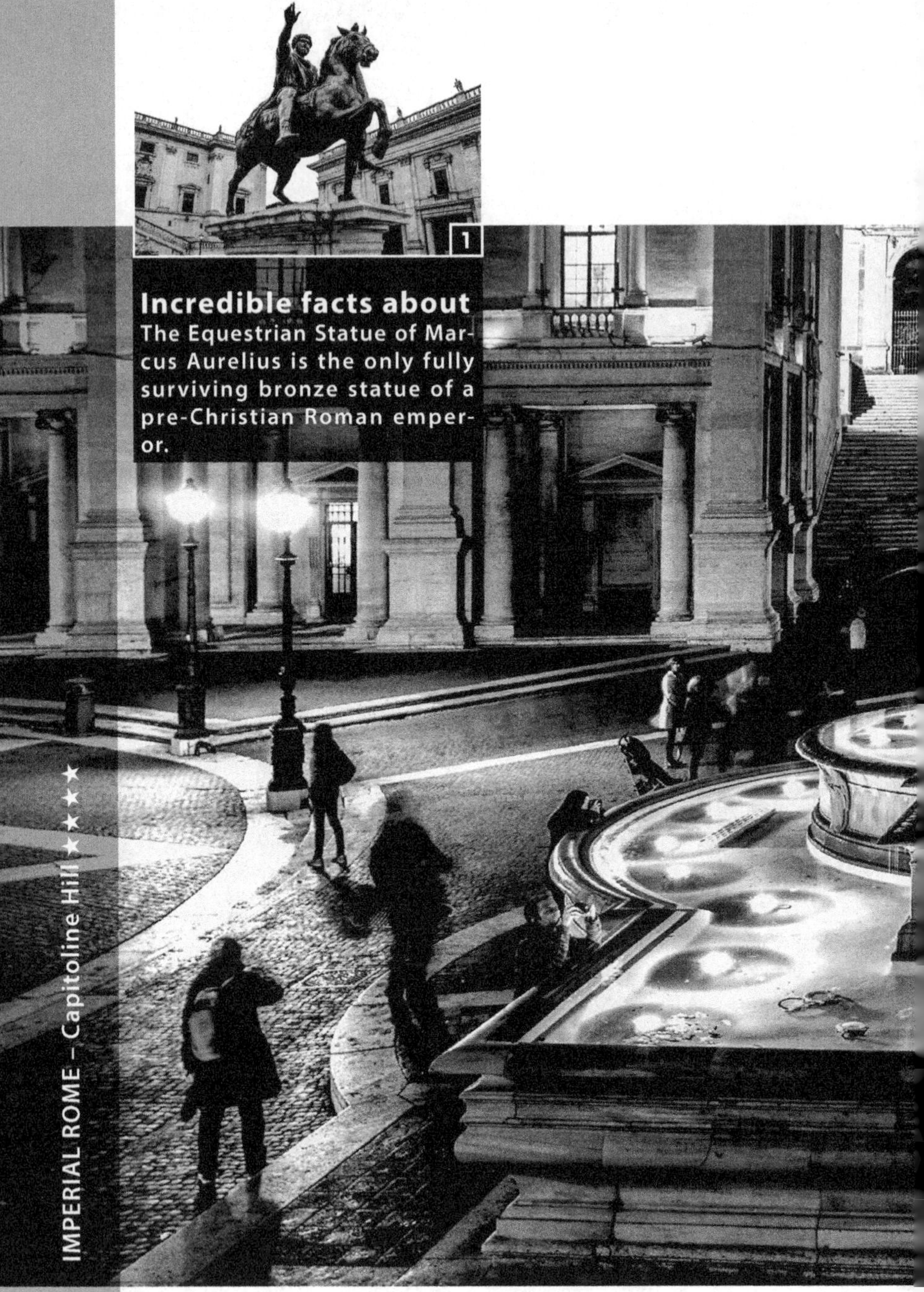

Incredible facts about
The Equestrian Statue of Marcus Aurelius is the only fully surviving bronze statue of a pre-Christian Roman emperor.

The fountain in front of the Senate Palace – Capitoline Hill

Extra Tip : : :
There is a panoramic view from the rooftop of Altar of the Fatherland, where you can climb for free or take the elevator for a fee.

A story of shifting the center of the world

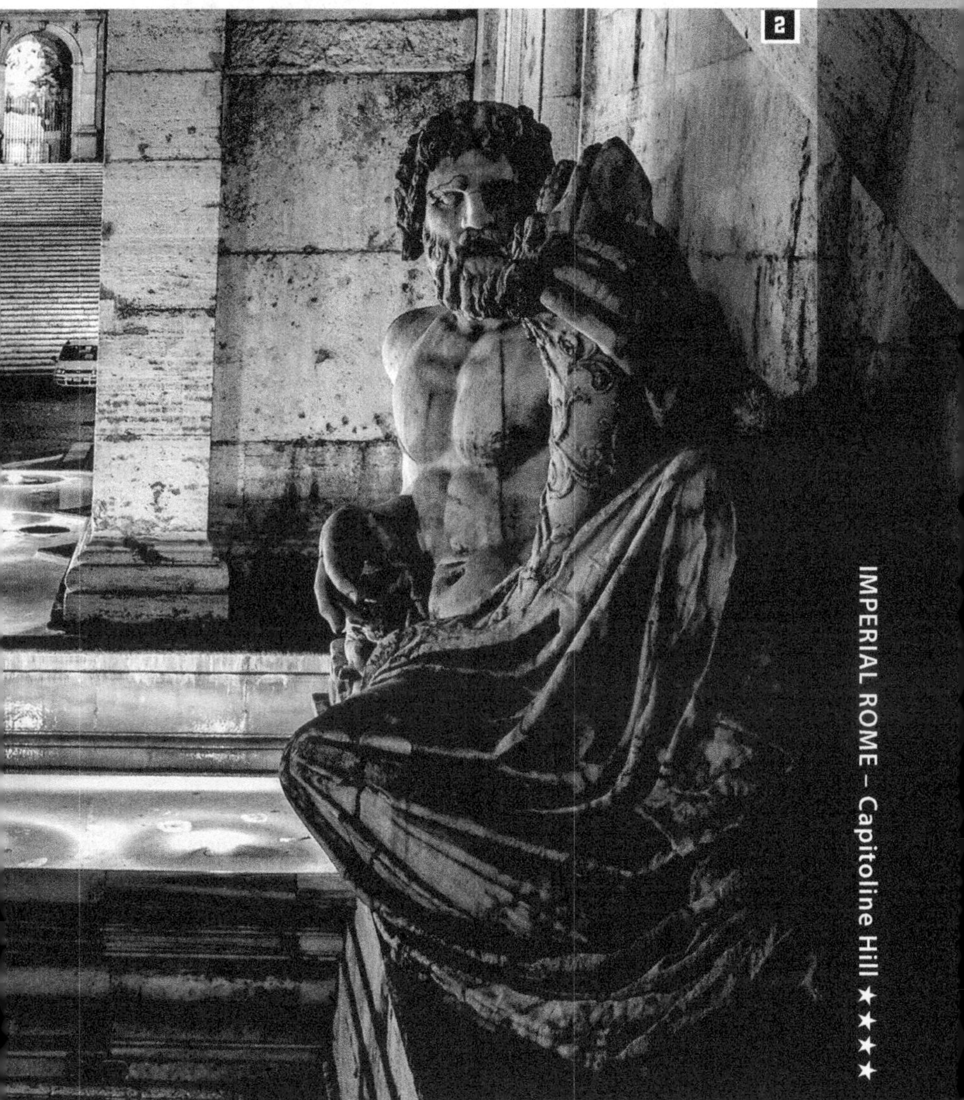

Musei Capitolini | Capitoline Museums
Address: Piazza del Campidoglio 1, Roma
Public transportation: Bus stop Piazza Venezia: 44, 46, 60, 80, 190F, 780, 781, 916, 916F | Tram stop Venezia: 8
Hours and tickets: www.museicapitolini.org/en

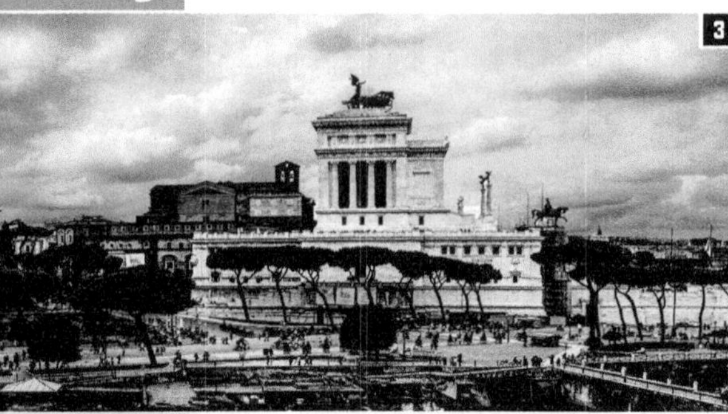

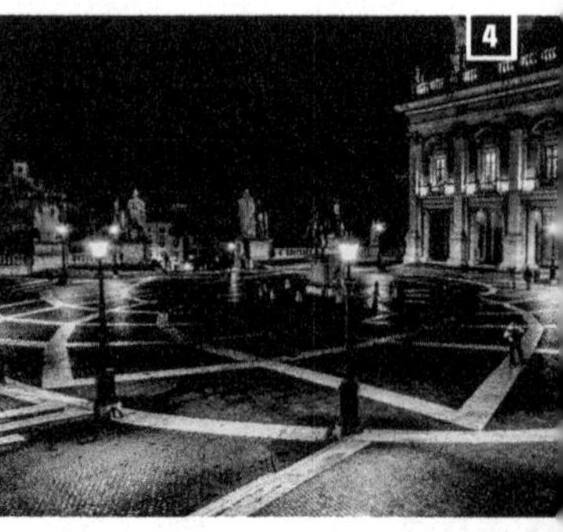

◆ Capitoline Hill ★★★★

The Capitoline Hill was the equivalent of the ancient Greek acropolis. Several important Roman temples are built on Capitoline Hill. **3** **16**

◇ Piazza del Campidoglio ★★★ **4** **15**

Michelangelo's vision is weaved into the design of Campidoglio Square and the surrounding buildings on the Capitoline Hill. Similar to most of Michelangelo's project, the commissioner was thrilled to accept artists' proposals which exceeded all expectations. The completion date was never really an issue and it was agreed that the artist was free to set the deadline for whenever he liked. It is an ancient Roman story of shifting the center of the world from Delphi to Rome. Pope Paul III liked the idea of Rome as *Caput Mundi*, Lat. for "Capital of the world". Such an ambitious project could not have happened over night. That it took four hundred years to be completed, would have been a great surprise even to the artist himself.

◇ Roman emperor on a horse ★★★ **1**

Michelangelo started designing Piazza del Campidoglio in 1536. Roman emperors used to end their triumphal marches at the Capitoline Hill, coming from Circus Maximus through Via Sacra. So, Michelangelo placed the only preserved equestrian statue on the new plateau, the future Piazza del Campidoglio. It was a gilded bronze statue of Marcus Aurelius on a horse from AD 165. When it was erected on the Piazza del Campidoglio, it was thought to represent Constantine the Great, the first Christian emperor in Rome. Michelangelo made a pedestal for the monument and decorated it with lilies and the Farnese coat of arms, the pope's family.

Did you know?

Where to see Michelangelo's architecture in Rome and Vatican?

► Piazza del Campidoglio complex Capitoline Hill (1536–1546)

► Palazzo Farnese (1546) [p.128]

► St. Peter's Basilica in Vatican City (1546–1564) [p.136]

► San Giovanni dei Fiorentini (1559–1560) [p.130]

► Sforza Chapel in the Basilica of Santa Maria Maggiore (1560) [p.277]

► Porta Pia (1561–1565) [p.249]

► Santa Maria degli Angeli e dei Martiri (1563–1564) [p.224]

► Michelangelo's Carthusian monastery (1561) [p.225]

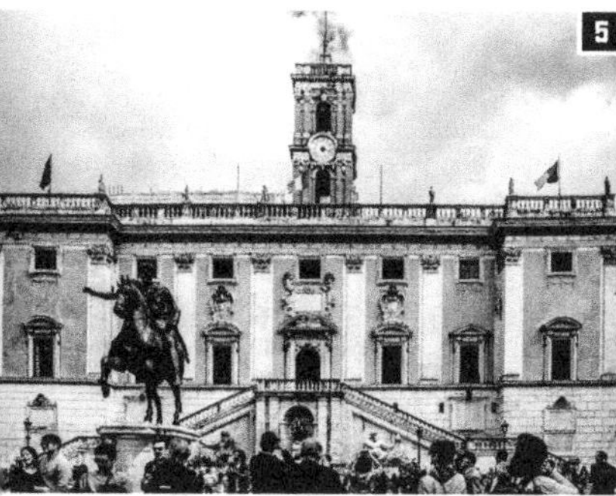

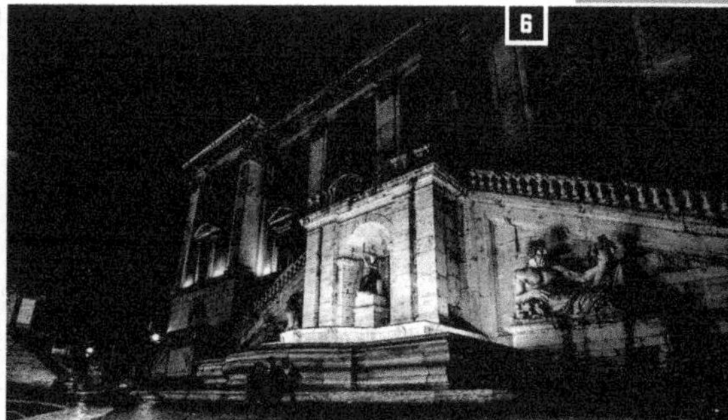

While the horseman alluded to Charles V as a visitor to the Holy Roman Empire, the location of the statue had to underline the emperor's dependence on the pope — the statue of the Roman emperor is facing St. Peter's Basilica. This could be interpreted in two ways.

First, the imperial horseman is turned to the Holy See, which means Charles V relies on the decision of the pope whose authority could not have been brought into question ever again.

Second, if the emperor thought the message was too direct, he could be reassured by the fact that Emperor Constantine the Great had considered himself to be an absolute leader whose decisions were the reflection of God's will.

Did you know?

Where is the original statue of Marcus Aurelius?

The statue of Marcus Aurelius was damaged in a bomb attack in 1979 and replaced with a copy.

The original statue is safe and sound at Palazzo dei Conservatori.

Did you know?

Michelangelo and Mussolini

It was only italian fascist leader Benito Mussolini who embraced Michelangelo's idea in 1940 when he wanted to restore the Roman Empire and ordered the twelve-pointed star designed by Michelangelo to be completed in its original form on the Piazza del Campidoglio.

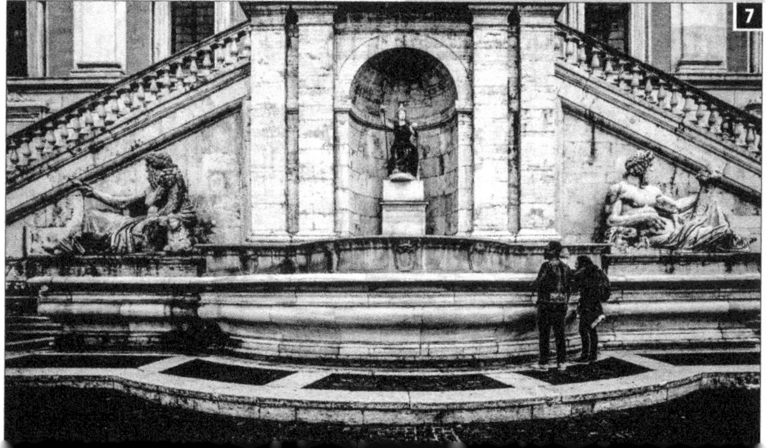

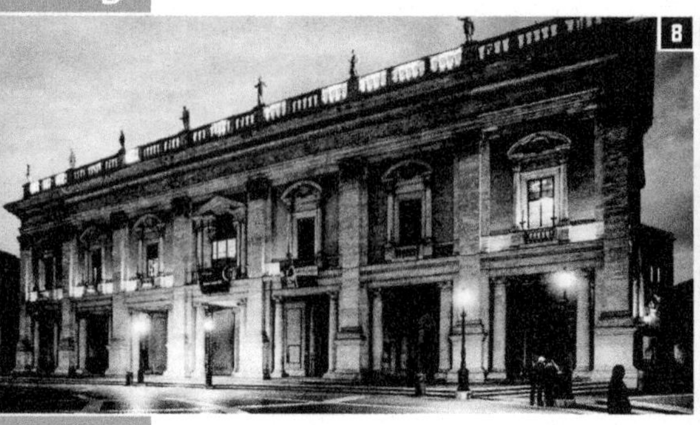

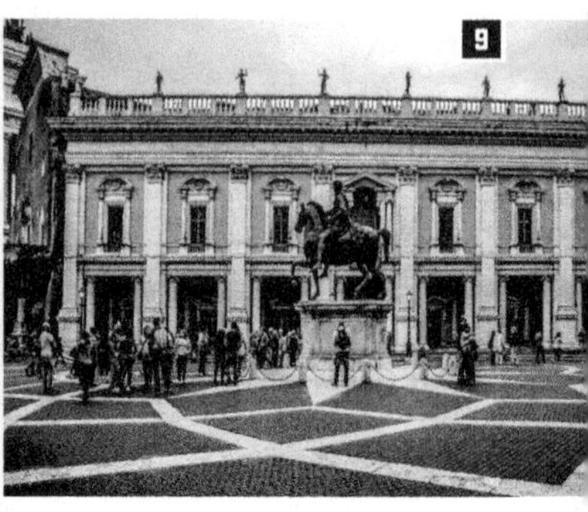

③ Palazzo Senatorio ★ ★ 5 13

Michelangelo added dual representative stairs to the Senate Palace. In front of the stairs, he placed a statue of Minerva above a fountain. 6

During the Renaissance, this statue was modified to represent goddess Roma. On each side, there is a statue from the second century. 7

The left one is the personification of the Nile, the one on the right is the Tiber. 2   A belfry was added to the Palace in 1582, following Martino Longhi the Elder's concept.

④ Palazzo dei Conservatori 8

Apart from the Senate Palace, Michelangelo also had to work on another existing palace, Palazzo dei Conservatori. 11

Conservatori were city magistrates in the Middle Ages. While the Senate Palace was founded on the remains of the city archive, the Tabularium, Palazzo dei Conservatori was built on the ruins of the most important and biggest Roman temple, dedicated to Jupiter.

Michelangelo intervened by adding Corinthian columns on the two upper floors, while Ionic columns support the lodge of the lower ground. Palazzo dei Conservatori was an administrative building for a long time,

Capitoline Hill

- ❶ Piazza del Campidoglio | Campidoglio Square
- ❷ Roman emperor on a horse
- ❸ Senate Palace
- ❹ Palazzo dei Conservatori & The Capitoline Museums
- ❺ Palazzo Nuovo & The Capitoline Museums
- ❻ Cordonata
- ❼ Basilica di Santa Maria in Ara Coeli al Campidoglio
- ❽ Altare della Patria | Altar of the Fatherland
- ❾ Piazza Venezia
- ❿ Trajan's Column

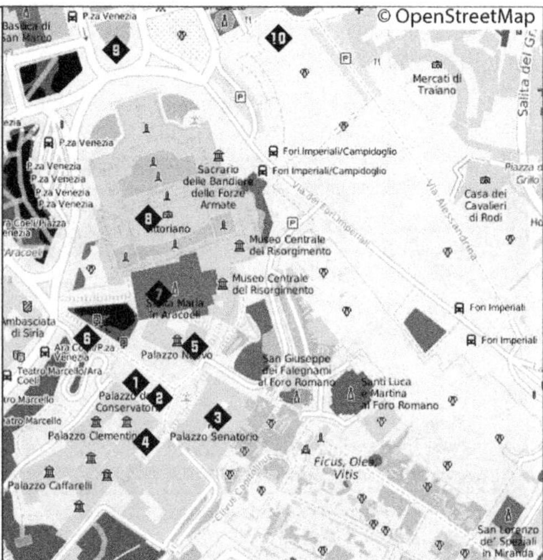

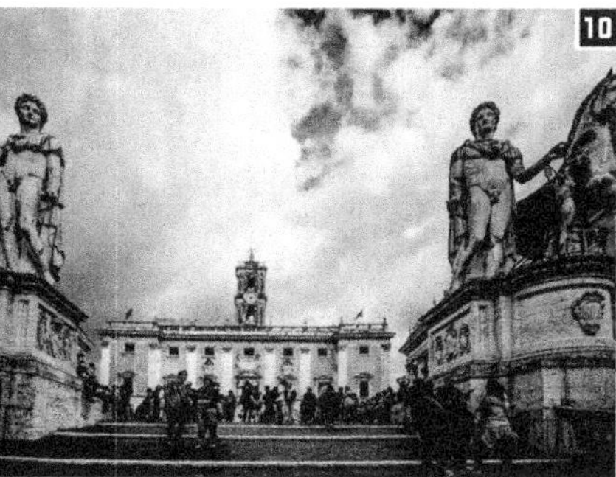

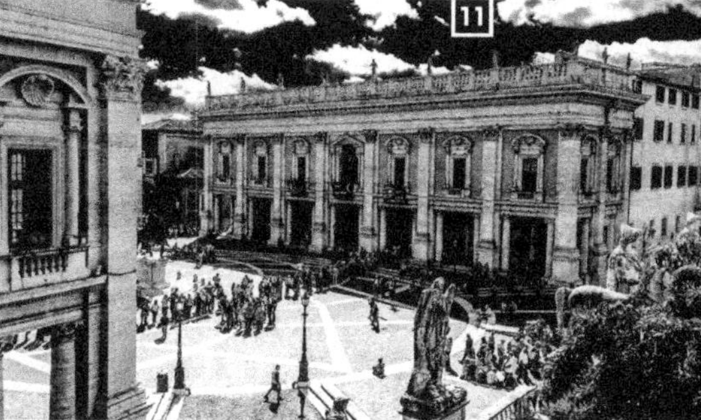

housing council sessions of the city government. Even today, some of the rooms in the palace are used for meetings of the city government. Palazzo Senatorio was and still is the office of the Roman mayor, i.e., the Roman City Hall.

⑤ Palazzo Nuovo 🟦

In order to balance everything out, Michelangelo designed Palazzo Nuovo, a palace that was supposed to be the mirror image of Palazzo dei Conservatori.

⑥ Cordonata 🔟

There is a balustrade leading to the Piazza del Campidoglio. The transition between the balustrade and the stairs is guarded by giant statues of Castor and Pollux holding their horses. The access ramp was designed by Michelangelo. The idea is that even horsemen could ride into Piazza del Campidoglio without dismounting. Michelangelo only lived long enough to see these stairs being built. Palazzo Nuovo was completed in 1654, and not opened to the public until 1734. 🔢

⑦ Musei Capitolini ★ ★ ★

The Capitoline Museums was the first public museum in the world. The Vatican Collection was the main reason for founding the Capitoline Museums. They were established by Pope Sixtus IV in 1471, when he donated a collection of statues of Greek and Roman gods to the city of Rome.

Then a larger donation arrived from the Vatican again, when Pope Pius V tried to purge the Vatican palaces of pagan statues. The collection was presented to the public for the first time in 1734. As the collection grew, the adjacent palaces on the Capitoline Hill were added to the complex.

Musei Capitolini | Capitoline Museums
Address: Piazza del Campidoglio 1, Roma
Online: www.museicapitolini.org/en

Terrazza Caffarelli
Online: https://www.terrazzacaffarelli.it/en/

Public transportation: Bus stop Piazza Venezia: 44, 46, 60, 80, 190F, 780, 781, 916, 916F | Tram stop Venezia: 8

Opening hours and tickets: see online

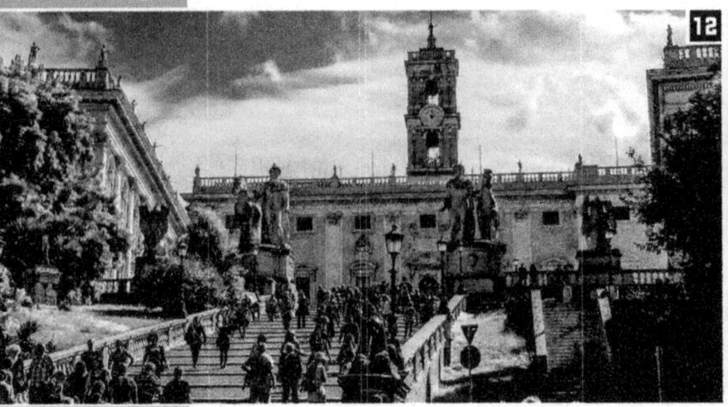

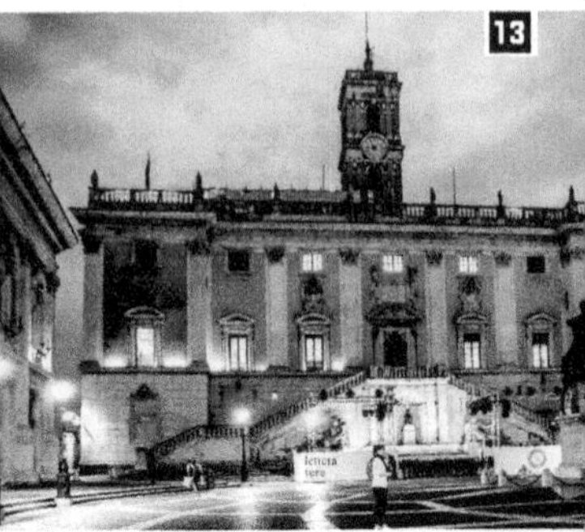

GROUND FLOOR – Palazzo dei Conservatori

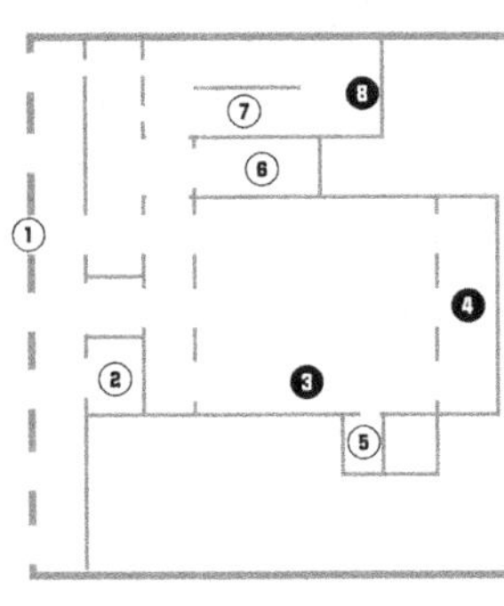

① Main Staircase

② Tickets

❸ Courtyard – Colossal statue of Constantine

❹ Remains of the Hadrian's Temple

⑤ Entrance to the Exhibition

⑥ Cloakroom

⑦ Stairs

❽ Reliefs from a triumphal arch shows the exploits of Marcus Aurelius

FIRST FLOOR – Palazzo dei Conservatori

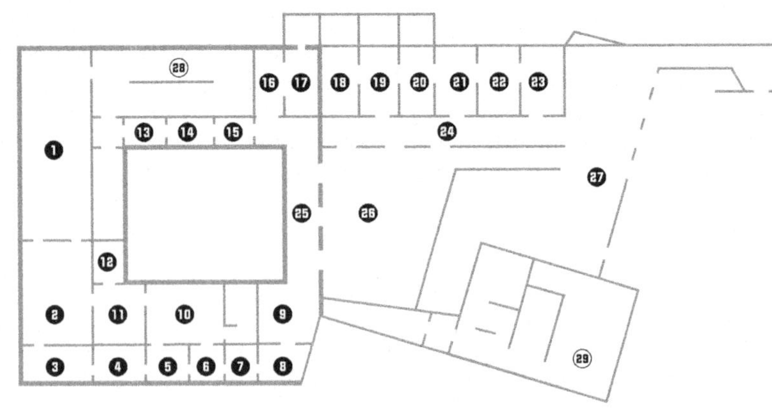

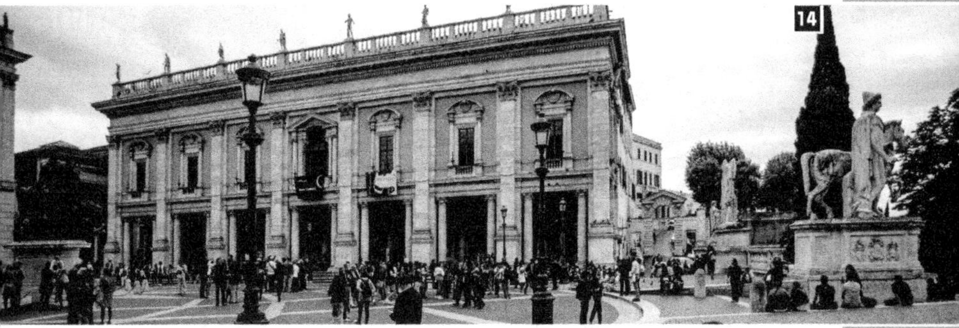

❶ Sala degli Orazi e Curiazi | Hall of the Horatii and Curiatii – Bernini's marble statue of Pope Urban VIII and Algardi's bronze statue of Pope Innocent X

❷ Sala dei Capitani | Hall of the Captains – *La Giustizia di Bruto*, painting by Tommaso Laureti (1530–1602)

❸ Sala dei Trionfi | Hall of the Triumphs – *Battle of Alexander versus Darius* by Pietro da Cortona (1650), The bronze statue of *Spinario, The Capitoline Brutus* (4th–3rd century BC)

❹ Sala della Lupa | Hall of the She-wolf – *She-wolf of Rome* (Wolf 11th/12th century) and *Twins* (15th century), *Fasti capitolini* and *Fasti triumphales*

❺ Sala delle Oche | Hall of the Geese – *Head of Medusa* by Bernini (1630)

❻ Sala delle Aquile | Hall of the Eagles Artemis of Ephesus (2nd century BC)

❼ Sala Castellani 1 – Castellani Hall 1 – Statues and bronzes from Magna Graecia and Etruscan civilization

❽ Sala Castellani 2 – Castellani Hall 2 – Statues and bronzes from Magna Graecia and Etruscan civilization

❾ Sala Castellani 3 – Castellani Hall 3 – Statues and bronzes from Magna Graecia and Etruscan civilizationing

❿ Sala degli Arazzi | Tapestry Hall – *Romulus and Remus* by Rubens

⓫ Sala di Anibale | Hall of Hannibal – *Fresco of Hannibal* by Jacopo Ripanda, 16th century

⓬ Cappella | Chapel

⓭ Sale dei fasti moderni | Halls of modern splendor – 19th century excavations from the various suburban Gardens (Esquiline, Quirinal and Viminal)

⓮ Sale dei fasti moderni | Halls of modern splendor – Sarcophagus that representing hunting wild boar of Calydon

⓯ ⓰ ⓱ ⓲ Sale degli Horti Lamiani | Halls of the Lamian Gardens – Excavations from the Esquiline Hill – todays area of the Piazza Vittorio Emanuele

⓳ Sale degli Horti Tauriani e Vettiani Caryatid Halls of the Taurian | Vetian gardens – *Portrait of Salonia Matidia* (1st century). Her maternal uncle was the Roman emperor Trajan.

⓴ Sale degli Horti Tauriani e Vettiani – *Portrait of the Roman Empress Vibia Sabina* (1st – 2nd century), the second wife of Hadrian

㉑ Sale degli Horti di Mecenate | Halls of the Gardens of Maecenas (Gardens on the top of the Esquiline Hill built by the Augustan era) – *Caryatid*

㉒ Sale degli Horti di Mecenate | Halls of the Gardens of Maecenas – *Eros and Thanatos*

㉓ Sale degli Horti di Mecenate | Halls of the Gardens of Maecenas – *Mosaic Orestes Iphigenia*

㉔ ㉕ Galleria degli Horti Lamiani – *Roman emperor Commodus dressed as Hercules* and *The Esquiline Venus*

㉖ *Esedra di Marco Aurelio* or A bronze equestrian statue of Marcus Aurelius

㉗ Aria del Tempio di Giove Capitolino | Great Temple of Jupiter Capitolinus is just below the Palazzo dei Conservatori (2nd century BC) – *The bronze Hercules*

㉘ Main Staircase to the Pinacoteca

㉙ Staircase to the Capitoline Cafe and the Terrace

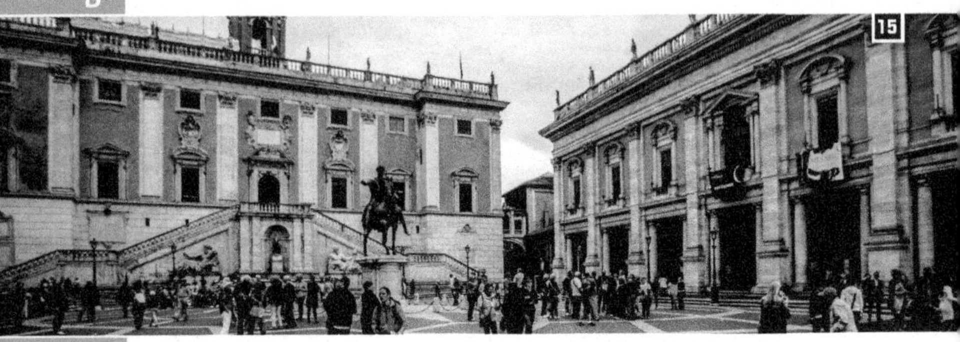

SECOND FLOOR – Palazzo dei Conservatoris

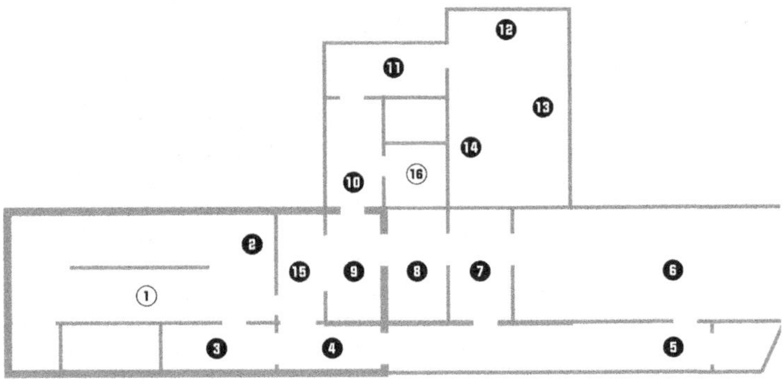

❶ Main Staircase

❷ *Tigres attacking a calf*, marble opus sectile (325–350) from the Basilica of Junius Bassus on the Esquiline Hill, Rome

❸ Cini Gallery

❹ Cini Gallery – *Portrait of the brothers Lucas and Cornelius de Wael* by Anthony van Dyck

❺ Cini Gallery

❻ Sala di Pietro da Cortona: *The Rape of the Sabine Women*

❼ Hall IV

❽ Hall III – Venetian painters: *Battesimo di Cristo* (Baptism of Christ) by Titian, *Il ratto di Europa* ("The Rape of Europa") by Veronese

❾ Hall II – Ferrarese painters: *Sacra Famiglia* (Holy Family) by Dosso Dossi

❿ Hall V

⓫ Hall VI – Bolognese painters: *San Sebastiano* by Guido Reni

⓬ *The Fortune Teller* by Caravaggio

⓭ *San Giovanni Battista* by Caravaggio

⓮ *Cumaean Sibyl* by Domenichino

⓯ Hall I

⓰ WC

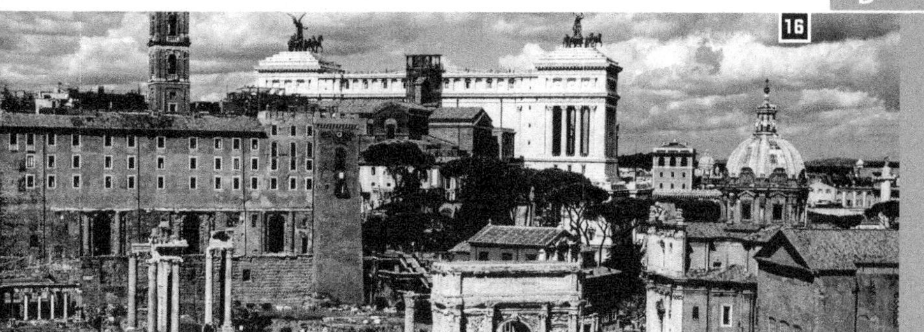

BASEMENT – Tabularium and Lapidarium

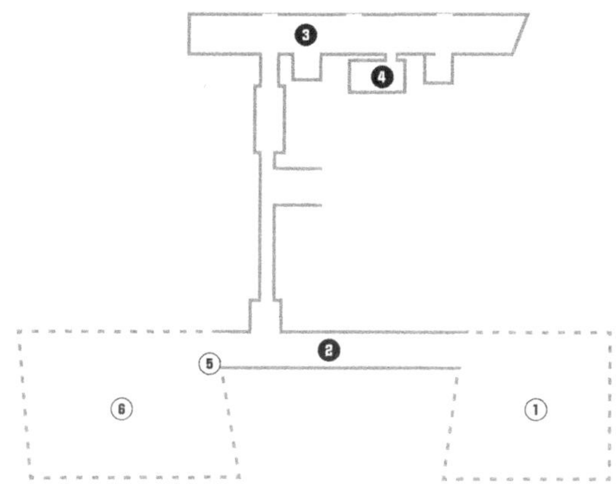

Roman Forum

① Palazzo dei Conservatori

❷ Galleria Lapidaria | Lapidarium –
Epigraphic collection

❸ Galleria del Tabularium | Tabularium

❹ Sala del Boia | Executioner's room

⑤ WC

⑥ Palazzo Nuovo

Palazzo Nuovo – GROUND FLOOR

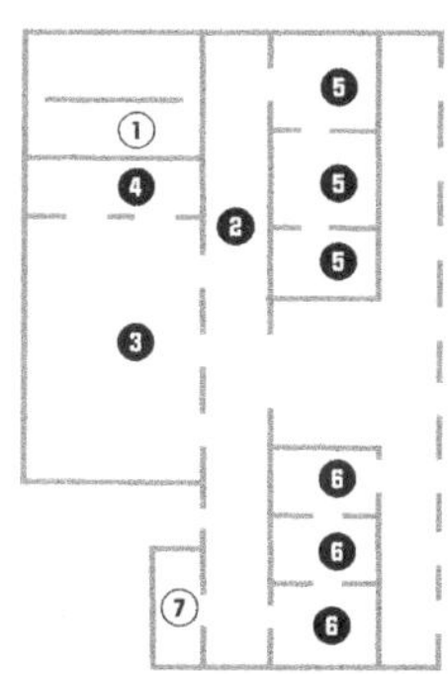

① Main Staircase

❷ Atrium – *Satua di Minerva*

❸ Courtyard – *Marforio*

❹ Collections of Egyptian antiquities

❺ Stanzette terrene I–III – Portraits of Roman private individuals, the epigraphic monuments and the fragments of post-Caesarian Roman calendars

❻ Temporary exhibitions

⑦ Elevator

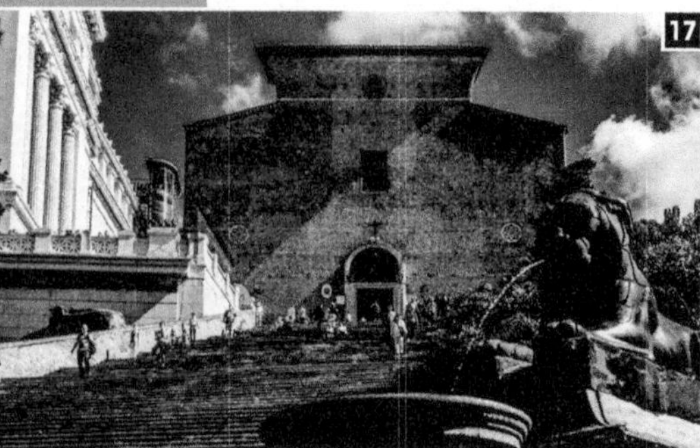

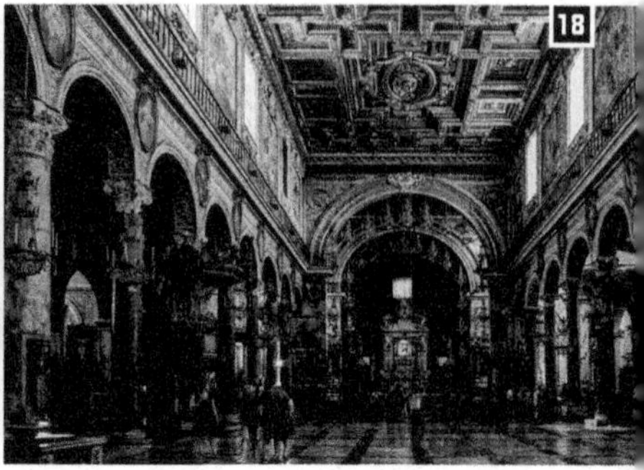

Palazzo Nuovo – FIRST FLOOR

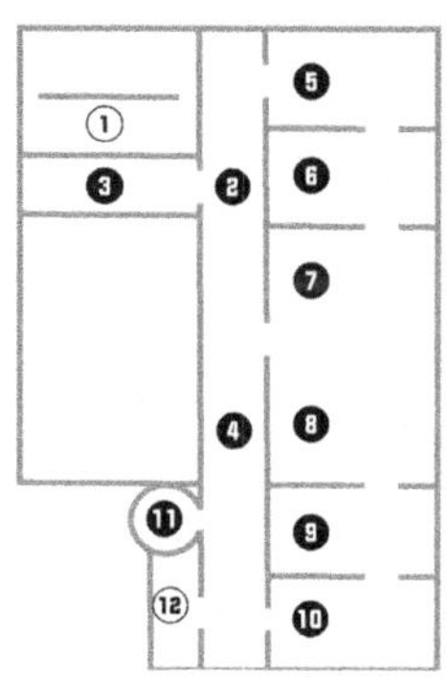

① Main Staircase
❷ Gallery – *Statue of Hercules, The Old Drunkard*
❸ Sala delle Colombe – *Mosaic of the Doves*
❹ *Jupiter*
❺ Sala del Galata – *Dying Galatian, Cupid, Psyche*
❻ Sala del Fauno – *The Faun*
❼ *Statue of the hunter with the hare*
❽ Il salone – *Apollos, Harpocrates, Centaurs*
❾ Sala dei Filosofi – Portraits of philosophers
❿ Sala degli Imperatori – Portraits of the Roman emperors and empresses
⓫ Venere Capitolina – *Statue of the Capitoline Venus*
⑫ Elevator

Musei Capitolini – Palazzo dei Conservatori 🔟

There is the Cortile dei Conservatori, an inner courtyard of the palace that holds pieces of the gigantic statue of Emperor Constantine the Great. This is the statue that used to stand in the main nave of the Basilica of Maxentius and Constantine on the Roman Forum.

Pinacoteca Capitolina – Picture Gallery

On the second floor of the Palazzo dei Conservatori, there is a gallery with works by Titian, Caravaggio and Rubens:

► Caravaggio's *St. John the Baptist* (1602)
► *Fortune Teller* by Caravaggio (1595)
► *The Holy Family* by Dosso Dossi (1528)
► *Romulus and Remus* by Rubens (1616)
► *Baptism of Christ* by Titian (1512)

Musei Capitolini – Tabularium

From the Palazzo dei Conservatori, there is an underground tunnel to the Palazzo Nuovo. Through a glass wall, you will get an amazing view of the Roman Forum.

Musei Capitolini – Palazzo Nuovo

The most famous hall in this palace is the one holding a big collection of canonized representations of philosophers, politicians and writers.

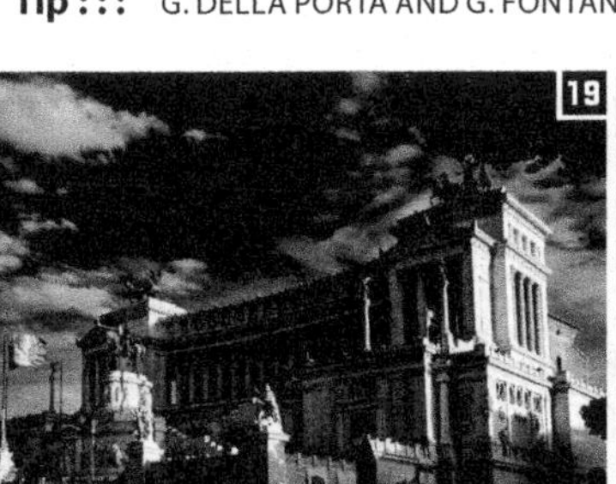

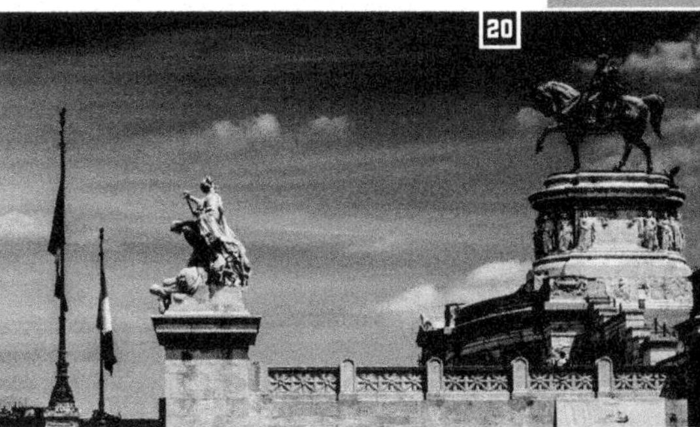

⑧ Basilica di Santa Maria in Ara Coeli al Campidoglio ★ ★ 🔟

The church is still the official church of the Roman City Council. It holds well-known relics, such as the relics of St. Helen. Pope Honorius IV (1210–1287), Queen Catherine of Bosnia (1425–1478), and the poet Giulio Salvadori (1862–1928) were buried in this church. The naves are divided by Roman pillars gathered from nearby Roman temples. 🔟 In the Middle Ages, death sentences were carried out at the bottom of the monumental staircase in front of the church. There are 124 stairs designed by Simone Andreozzi in 1348.

Highlights of Basilica di Santa Maria in Ara Coeli al Campidoglio:
- ► Pinturicchio's frescoes (15th century) of the *Life of Saint Bernardino of Siena*, the first chapel on the right
- ► *The tomb of Cecchino dei Bracci* by Michelangelo
- ► *The tombstone of Giovanni Crivelli* by Donatello
- ► The wooden ceiling
- ► The inlaid *Cosmatesque floor*

⑨ Altare della Patria ★ ★ 🔟

Construction of the monument to the newly-established parliamentary monarchy of Italy started in 1885 and was only entirely completed in 1925. It is made of white, Brescia marble, with oversized stairs, a fountain and an equine sculpture of the first Italian king Victor Emmanuell II. 🔟 In this extravagant Altar of the Fatherland, there is a temple to the unknown soldier with eternal fire, built after World War I. The Altare della Patria or Monumento Nazionale a Vittorio Emanuele II or Vittoriano building is 443 ft (135 m) wide and 230 ft (70 m) tall. The composition is 266 ft (81 m) high, including the goddess of victory.

Basilica di Santa Maria in Ara Coeli al Campidoglio
Address: Scala dell'Arcicapitolina 12, Roma

Public transportation: Bus stop Piazza Venezia: 44, 46, 60, 80, 190F, 780, 781, 916, 916F | Tram stop Venezia: 8

Opening hours:
Mon – Sun: 7.30 a.m. – 1 p.m.

Altare della Patria | Altar of the Fatherland
Address: Piazza Venezia, Roma
Online: https://vive.beniculturali.it/it/altare-della-patria/
Public transportation: Bus stop Piazza Venezia: 44, 46, 60, 80, 190F, 780, 781, 916, 916F | Tram stop Venezia: 8

Opening hours: *see online*

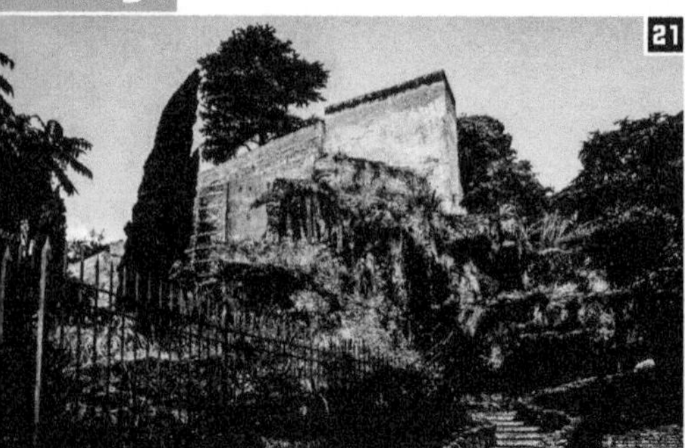

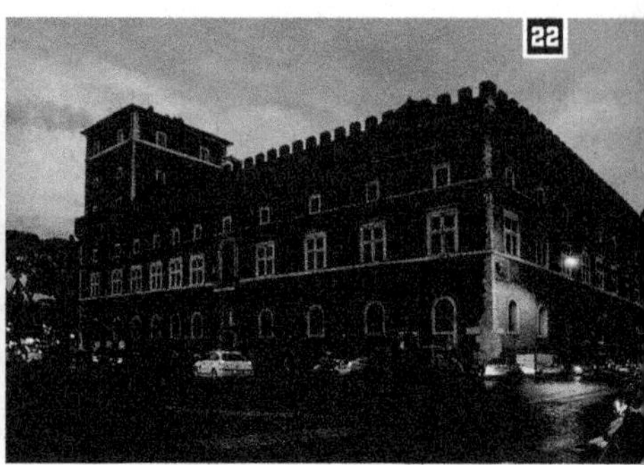

Walk around Capitoline Hill

❷ Tarpeian Rock ★

On the other side of the Capitoline Hill, you can see the Tarpeian Rock. During the Roman Republic (509–27 BC), prisoners accused of giving false oaths, incest or treason were thrown from this rock.

Getting thrown off the Tarpeian rock was the worst punishment, because the taboo was passed on to the prisoner's family.

Marcus Manlius Capitolinus (384 BC) was executed here because he attempted to establish a monarchy, as well as Simon bar Giora (AD 70), Jewish leader in the First Jewish-Roman War.

❸ Palazzo di Venezia ★★

If you are standing in front of Palazzo di Venezia, or better yet, at the Altar of the Fatherland, look at Basilica di San Marco Evangelista and the palace next to it. That is Palazzo di Venezia.

Palazzo di Venezia was built using the stones from the Colosseum, which functioned as a quarry until the nineteenth century. Pope Pius IV gave the palace to the Venetian Republic to be used as an embassy in 1564, which it was, until 1797, when it fell into Austrian hands due to secession. During the First World War, Italy fought against the Austro-Hungarian Empire, so the palace was nationalized in 1916. Benito Mussolini used Sala del Mappamondo in Palazzo di Venezia as his office. From the central balcony, above the main entrance, the fascist leader gave emo-

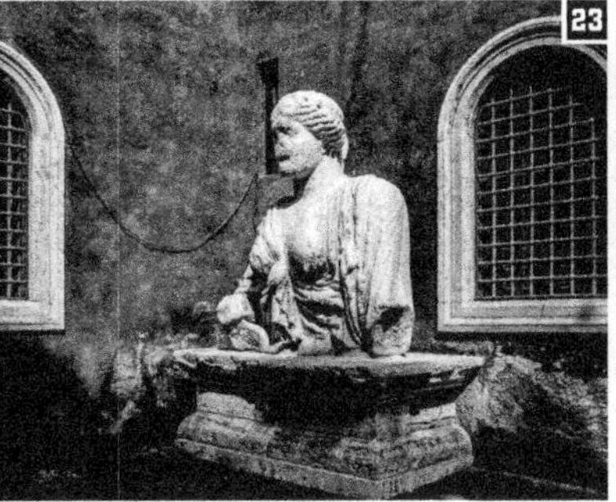

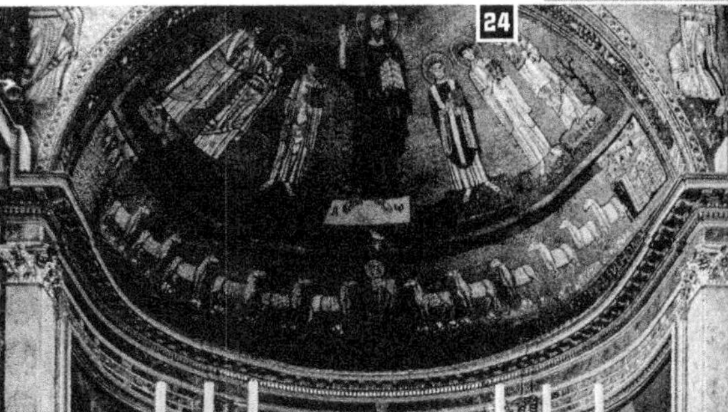

tional speeches to the crowd on Piazza Venezia. From the balcony, he oversaw military processions that marched down Via dei Fori Imperiali, built specifically for that purpose in the middle of the remains of the Roman Forum.

① National Museum of the Palazzo di Venezia ★★

In the National Museum of the Palazzo di Venezia you can see works by Carlo Maratta, Gian Lorenzo Bernini, Guido Reni, Pisanello, Giorgione and Giotto as well as tapestries, ceramics, Japanese and Chinese porcelain and weapons. In the Sala del Mappamondo and the Sala Regia you can see illusionistic architectural painting by Mantegna and Bramante.

④ Basilica di San Marco Evangelista al Campidoglio ★ 24

St. Mark's Basilica (324–1470) is placed on a small square called Piazza di San Marco. Next to the basilica entrance is the ancient bust of a statue of the Egyptian goddess Isis. 23

Museo Nazionale del Palazzo di Venezia | National Museum of the Palazzo di Venezia
Address: Via del Plebiscito 118, Roma
Online: https://vive.beniculturali.it/en/palazzo-venezia/

Public transportation: Bus stop Piazza Venezia: 44, 46, 60, 80, 190F, 780, 781, 916, 916F | Tram stop Venezia: 8

Opening hours: *see online*

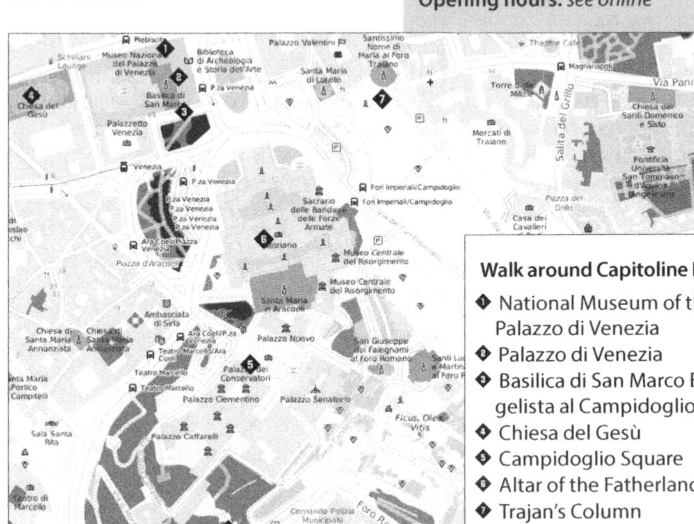

Walk around Capitoline HIll

❶ National Museum of the Palazzo di Venezia
❷ Palazzo di Venezia
❸ Basilica di San Marco Evangelista al Campidoglio
❹ Chiesa del Gesù
❺ Campidoglio Square
❻ Altar of the Fatherland
❼ Trajan's Column
❽ Tarpeian Rock

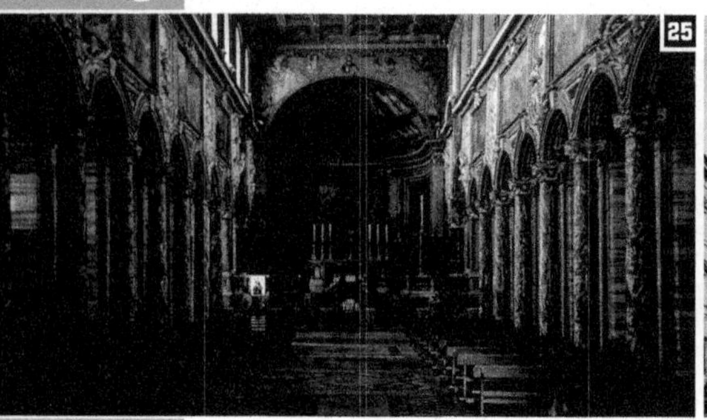

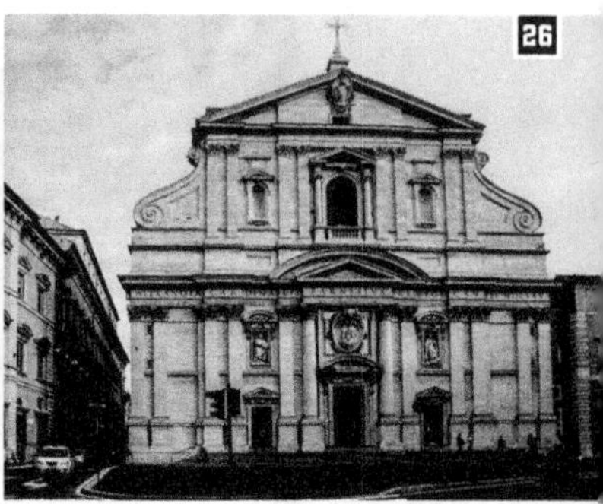

Traditionally, Basilica di San Marco Evangelista was the titular church of Venetian cardinals. Cardinal Pietro Barbo (Pope Paul II) commissioned a palace to be built next to the church in 1455, which was completed by Leon Battista Alberti in 1467. The wooden ceiling of the basilica with his emblem (15th century) is one of the two original wooden ceilings from this time in Rome. The other one is at Basilica di Santa Maria Maggiore. [p.276]

The apse mosaic (9th century) shows the Pope Gregory IV (827–844) with the squared halo, used for the living person.

⬥ Chiesa del Gesù ★ ★ ★

This church is the main Church of the Jesuits or the Society of Jesus. The façade is known as the first real Baroque façade. It was built by Giacomo Barozzi da Vignola and Giacomo della Porta, from 1568 to 1580.

Saint Ignatius of Loyola once prayed before the painting of the Holy Virgin, which can now be found at the Chapel of Ignatius, right of the altar. The elongated Saint Francis Xavier Chapel in the right transept was designed by Pietro da Cortona.

The last chapel on the right side of the high altar is called *Sacro Cuore*. The sacristy is on the right. There is Cardinal Robert Bellarmine's bust in the presbytery, made by Bernini. This church was visited by Bernini every day. The St. Ignatius Chapel, left of the transept was designed by Andrea Pozzo, from 1696 to 1700.

Basilica di San Marco Evangelista al Campidoglio | St. Mark's Basilica
Address: Piazza di San Marco 52, Roma
Online: www.sanmarcoevangelista.it
Public transportation: Bus stop Piazza Venezia: 44, 46, 60, 80, 190F, 780, 781, 916, 916F | Tram stop Venezia: 8

Opening hours: *see online*

Chiesa del Gesù
Address: Via degli Astalli 16, Roma
Online: www.chiesadelgesu.org

Public transportation: Bus stop Piazza Venezia: 44, 46, 60, 80, 190F, 780, 781, 916, 916F | Tram stop Venezia: 8

Opening hours: *see online*

Pantheon

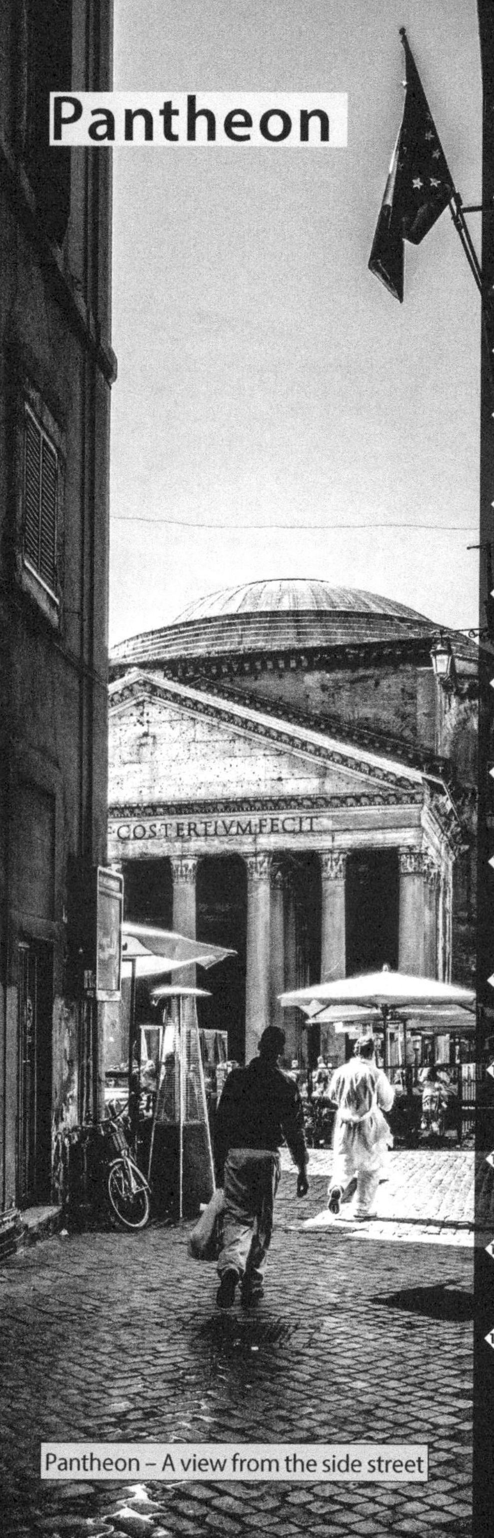

Pantheon – A view from the side street

① Pantheon
The best preserved building from the Roman Empire. *p. 94*

② Piazza della Rotonda
Ancient Egyptian obelisk in front of a Roman temple. *p. 97*

③ Tazza d'Oro
Coffee temple of Rome. *p. 97*

④ Giolitti
Gelato temple of Rome. *p. 97*

⑤ Palazzo Montecitorio
Italian Chamber of Deputies designed by Bernini. *p. 98*

⑥ Obelisk of Montecitorio
Originally used as the dial of the *Solarium Augusti*. *p. 98*

⑦ Palazzo Chigi
Residence of the Prime Minister of the Republic of Italy. *p. 98*

⑧ Piazza Colonna
Named for the marble column of Marcus Aurelius. *p. 98*

⑨ Palazzo Wedekind
With the monumental portico built with twelve columns of Veii. *p. 100*

⑩ Chiesa di Sant'Ignazio di Loyola in Campo Marzio
The perfect optical illusion of an unexisting dome. *p. 100*

⑪ Piazza di Pietra
Monumental façade of the Roman temple. *p. 101*

⑫ Galleria Doria Pamphilj
One of the largest private art collections in Rome. *p. 101*

⑬ Crypta Balbi
The little-known part of the National Roman Museum. *p. 102*

⑭ Largo di Torre Argentina
The spot where Julius Caesar was assassinated. *p. 103*

⑮ Santa Maria sopra Minerva
The only extant example of the Gothic church in Rome. *p. 104*

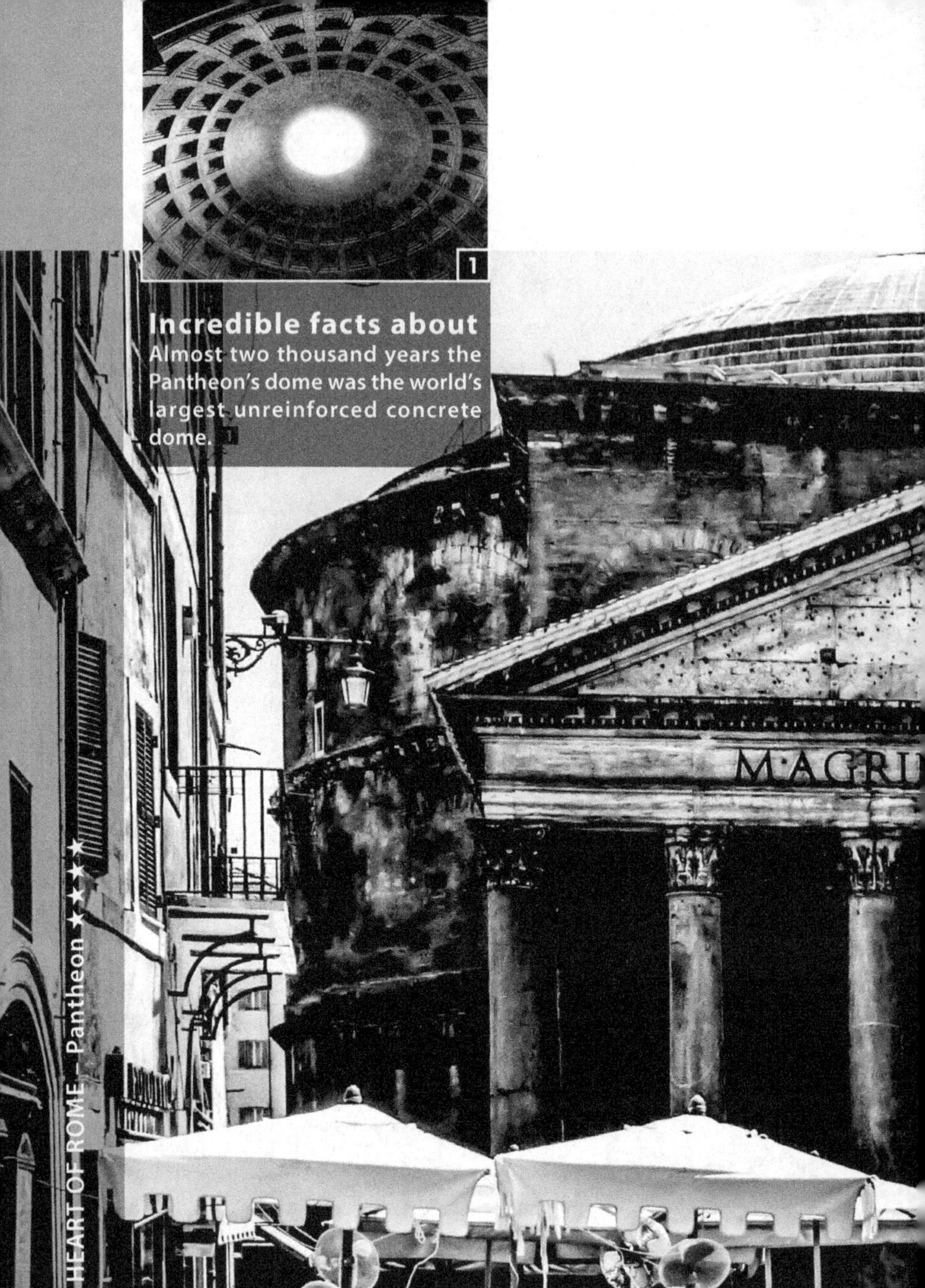

Incredible facts about
Almost two thousand years the Pantheon's dome was the world's largest unreinforced concrete dome.

Pantheon

Extra Tip : : :
In Gelateria Giolitti, you can have the best ice cream in Rome, only a few steps from the Pantheon. Special recipes are a carefully kept secret passed on from generation to generation for more than a hundred years.

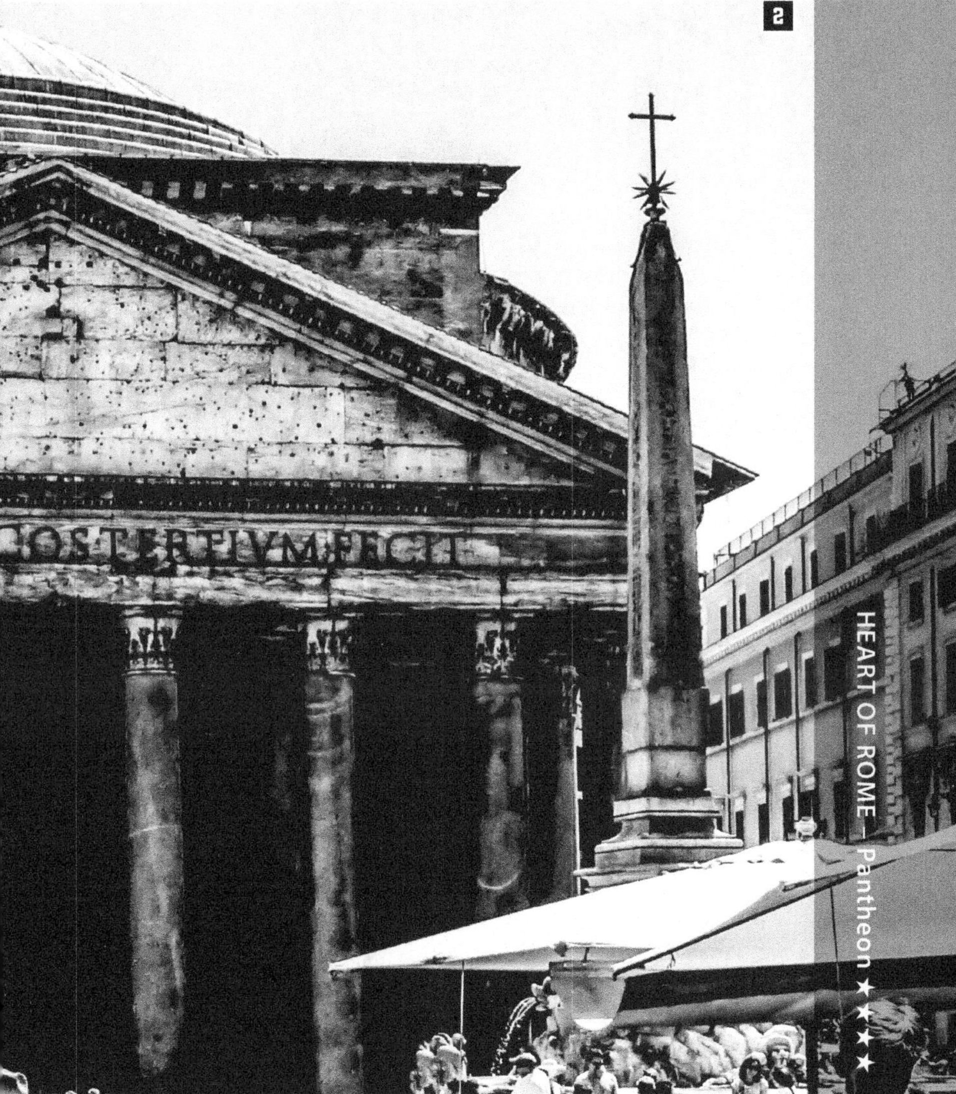

The perfect building in the heart of Rome

Pantheon
Address: Piazza della Rotonda, Roma
Public transportation: Bus stop Pie' Di Marmo: 116 or Largo Torre Argentina: 30, 40, 46, 62, 64, 70, 81, 87, 130F, 186, 190F, 492, 628, 916, 916F
Opening hours: 9 a.m. – 7 p.m.

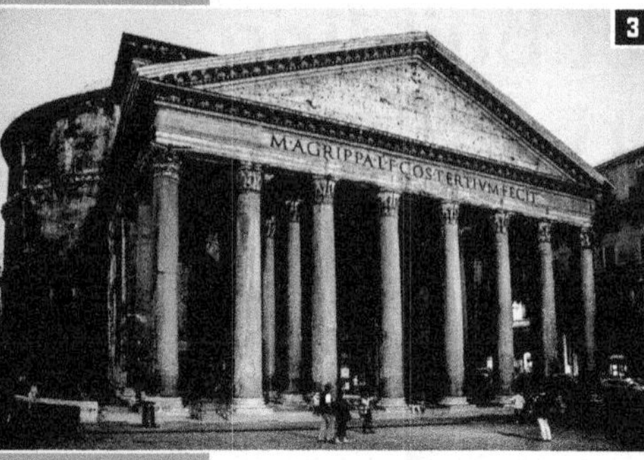
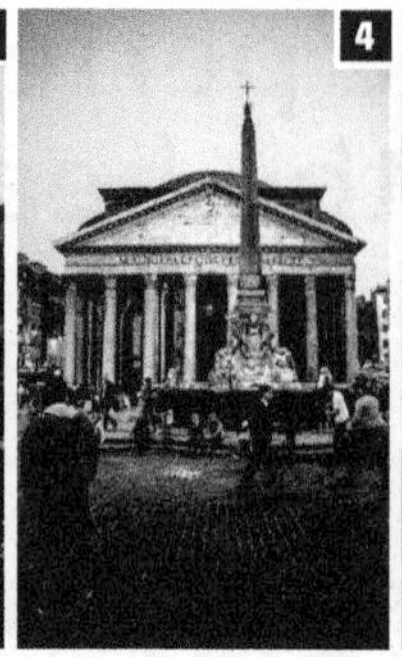
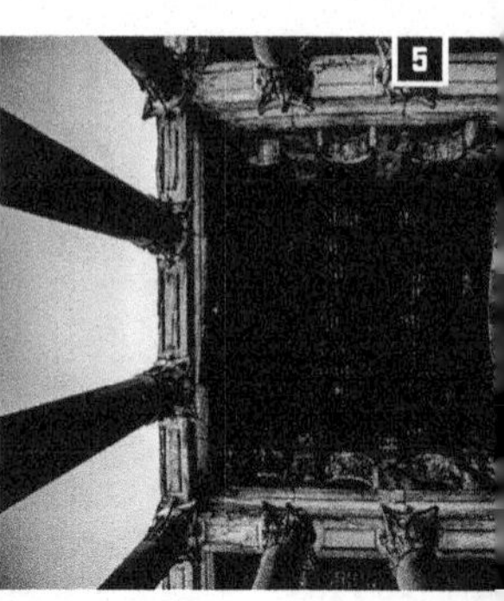

◆ Pantheon ★★★★ ▣

One of the most impressive and most popular buildings in the world, the Roman Pantheon, is on Piazza della Rotonda. ▣

The Pantheon is also the best preserved building from the Roman Empire. ▣

You are standing in front of a building which was completed in AD 126 during Emperor Hadrian. It was designed and planned by his predecessor, Emperor Trajan.

It is attributed to Apollodorus of Damascus. An even older building, built by Augustus's son-in-law Marcus Agrippa in 27 BC during his consulate, was burnt in a fire in AD 80. It served the same purpose as this building, clearly visible in the inscription on the front of the temple:

M AGRIPPA L F COS TERTIUM FECIT
M[arcus] Agrippa L[ucii] f[ilius] co[n] s[ul] tertium fecit

Marcus Agrippa, son of Lucius, made this building when he was consul for the third time.

Apollodorus designed the building as an expression of pure harmony and unity – it is the temple of all the gods. He used the sphere as the ideal geometrical body.

Vestibule ★★★ ▣

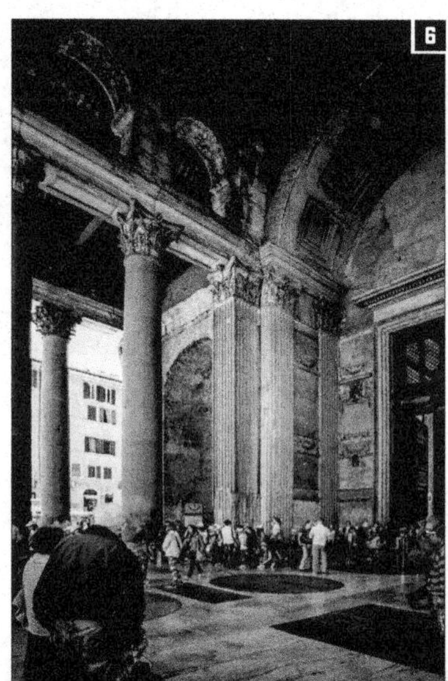

Let's go inside. First, we will pass through the monumental vestibule with three naves, built as a typical Roman podium temple.

It is a rectangle, 108×49 ft (33×15 m). The ceiling is supported by Corinthian columns, made of Egyptian granite on marble pedestals. ▣

The entrance is 20 ft high (6 m) and the door is made of bronze. These doors belong to the original temple, built by Agrippa.

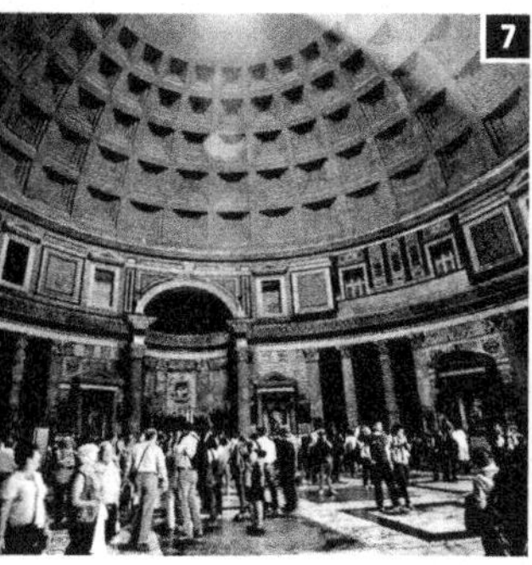
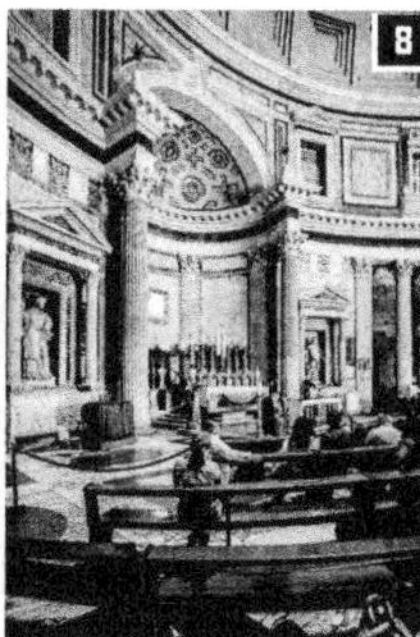
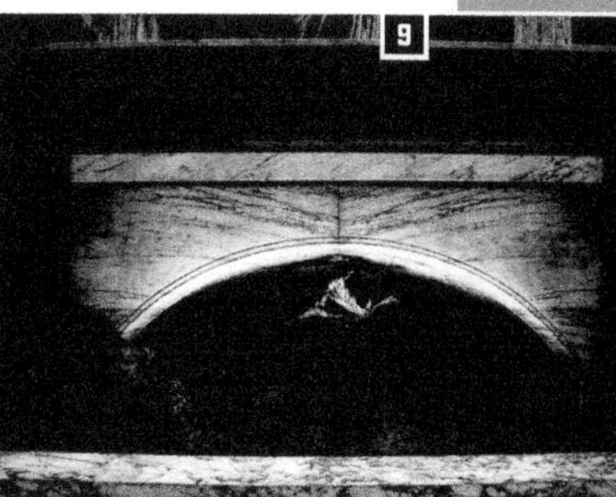

Rotunda ★★★ **7**

When you enter the gigantic spherical hall, you will probably experience a similar sensation as Emperor Hadrian when he first stepped inside — the feeling of harmony and unity induced by the proportions of this unique space. **8**

The dome's diameter is 150 Roman feet (145.67 ft or 44.4 m), and the hole in the middle, called oculus, is 30 Roman feet wide (28.9 ft or 8.5 m).

On the inside, the dome was covered in bronze, but the bronze was taken down by order of Pope Urban VIII Barberini, so that Bernini would have enough bronze to make the altar bronze canopy in St. Peter's Basilica.

The rest was used to make cannons for the Castel Sant'Angelo. This is why his fellow citizens invented the expression: "What the Barbarians did not do, the Barberini did."

The building material is Roman concrete with tuff, a light stone of consolidated volcanic ash.

This is still the largest unreinforced dome in the world. Never before or after did anyone have the courage to build a bigger dome in the same way.

The support walls are 21 ft wide (6.4 m) at the base of the dome, thinning upwards. At the oculus the walls are only 3.94 ft wide (1.11 m).

Did you know?

The Mystery of the Pantheon

The exact purpose of the building, about two thousand years after it had been completed, remained a mystery even to specialists.

The form and the inner shape of the dome suggested the name Pantheon (Greek: *pân* = all, *theós* = God).

Did you know?

Tombs of famous artists and politicians in the Pantheon

Since the Renaissance the Pantheon has been used as a tomb:

Painters
Raphael Sanzio da Urbino (1483–1520) **9**

Perino del Vaga (1501–1547),

Giovanni da Udine (1487–1564),

Taddeo Zuccari (1529–1566),

Annibale Carracci (1560–1609)

Composer
Arcangelo Corelli (1653–1713)

Architect
Baldassare Peruzzi (1481–1536)

Italian Kings
Victor Emmanuel II (1820–1878)

Umberto I (1844–1900) **12**

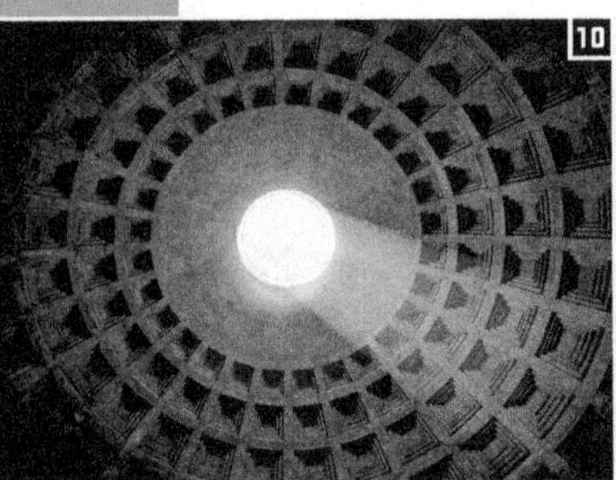

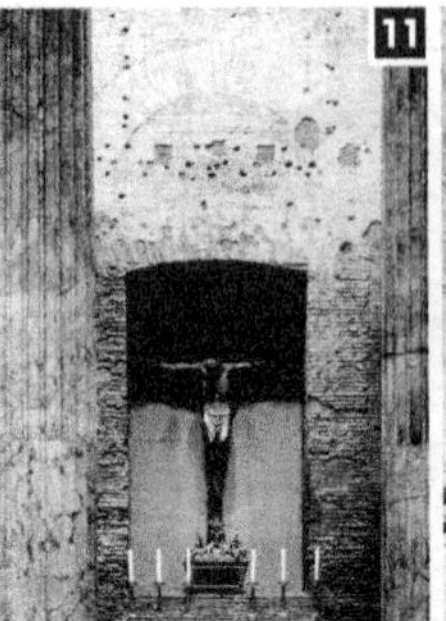

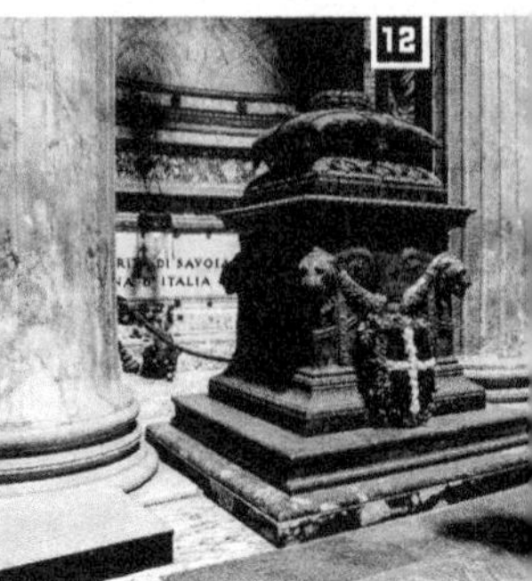

The walls are full of hidden crevices, probably amphorae, which was a frequent trick used by Roman engineers to redistribute the weight of the dome so that it would not collapse.

Dome ★ ★ ★

The dome is full of cassettes on the inside, organized in 5 rows of 28 cassettes. It is a decorative element, but also a static one, because it secures the dome. If we look at the dome from the outside, we can observe that it does not look like a perfect sphere. This is because the outer walls of the dome are higher that the inner ones.

This is probably due to the bronze gilded bricks that used to cover the dome and they were weighing it down.

Constantine the Great ordered the bricks to be taken off and moved to the new capital, Constantinople. In 609, Emperor Phocas donated the Pantheon to the Pope who immediately converted it into a church called Basilica di Santa Maria ad Martyres.

Masses are served in the church even today, on special Catholic holidays. From the Renaissance to the 20th century, Roman dignitaries were buried here.

Here is the final resting place of Raphael, one of the greatest Renaissance artists, and two 20th-century Italian kings.

Pantheon

Address: Piazza della Rotonda, Roma

Public transportation: Bus stop Pie' Di Marmo: 116 or Largo Torre Argentina: 30, 40, 46, 62, 64, 70, 81, 87, 130F, 186, 190F, 492, 628, 916, 916F

Opening hours:
Mon – Sat: 8:30 a.m. – 7:15 p.m.
Sun: 9 a.m. – 5:45 p.m.

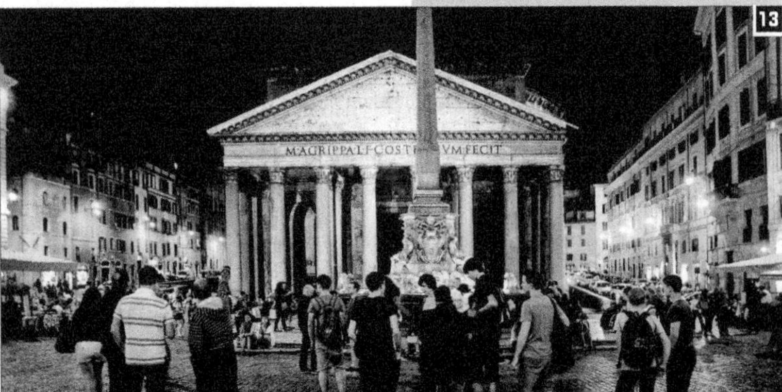

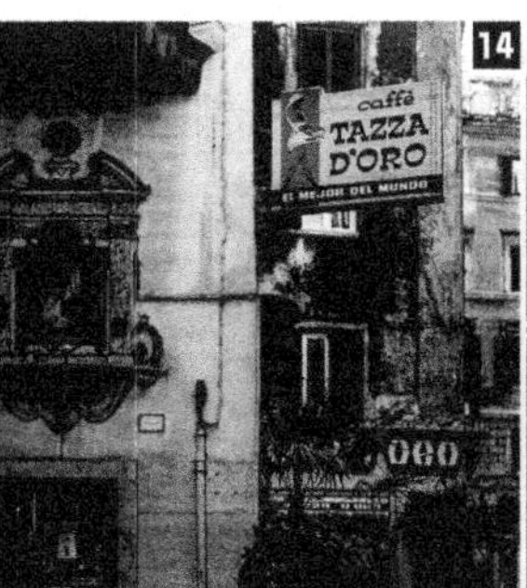

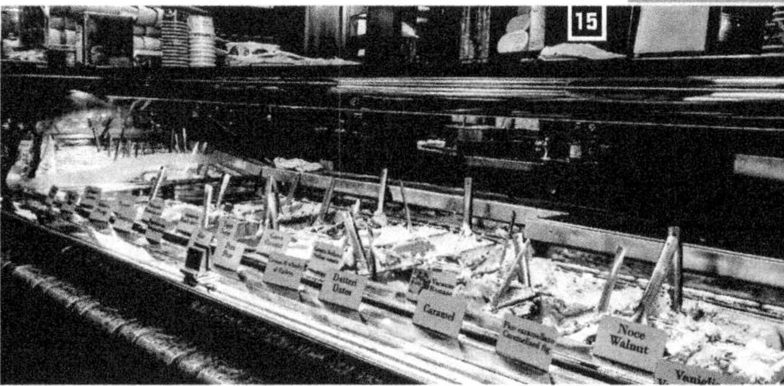

Walk around Pantheon

❷ Piazza della Rotonda ★★ 13

Piazza della Rotonda is in front of the Pantheon. It has a fountain with an obelisk called Macuteo. The obelisk dates back to the era of Ramesses II (1279–1213 BC) and it was brought to Rome from the Temple of the sun god Ra in Heliopolis, present-day suburb of Cairo. This is how a monument raised in honor of the main Ancient Egyptian god found itself in front of a Roman temple dedicated to all the gods, which has been a Christian church for 1400 years.

❸ Tazza d'Oro – The Coffee Temple

After visiting the Pantheon and delving into so much history, let's return to the present and have a look around. You can have the best coffee in Rome right next to the Pantheon, in Tazza d'Oro. You can enjoy the 1940's interior decoration while sipping on your espresso, cappuccino, or better yet, the house specialty – *granita di café*. It is a frozen espresso covered in cream. As in any other Italian coffee place, you order at the register, and then you take the receipt to get your order. 14

❹ Giolitti – The Gelato Temple

Ice cream is an Italian gastronomical landmark, just like spaghetti or pizza. You can choose between Florentine and Neapolitan ice cream. On Sicily, they have maybe the best version of their ice cream. But I will go even further and tell you where you can find the best ice cream in the world — only a few

La Casa Del Caffè Tazza d'Oro
Address: Via degli Orfani 84, Roma
Online:
www.tazzadorocoffeeshop.com
Public transportation: Bus stop Pie' Di Marmo: 116 or Largo Torre Argentina: 30, 40, 46, 62, 64, 70, 81, 87, 130F, 186, 190F, 492, 628, 916, 916F

Opening hours:
Mon – Sat: 7:00 a.m. – 7:00 p.m.
Sun: 10:30 a.m. – 7:30 p.m.

steps from the Pantheon, in Gelateria Giolitti. 15

Special recipes are a carefully kept secret passed on from generation to generation in the Giolitti family for more than a hundred years. It is also the oldest *gelateria* in Rome (since 1890). To get to this ice cream, you need to learn a few rules. First, you have to know which flavors you want, because the vendor does not have a lot of time for you to pick and choose once you get in line. The line frequently swerves around the corner, that's how popular the place is. So, go to the fridge first and pick your ice cream. Then get in line for the register.

Giolitti
Address: Via Uffici del Vicario 40, Roma
Online: www.giolitti.it

Public transportation: Bus stop Pie' Di Marmo: 116 or Largo Torre Argentina: 30, 40, 46, 62, 64, 70, 81, 87, 130F, 186, 190F, 492, 628, 916, 916F

Opening hours:
Mon – Sun: 7:00 a.m. – 11 p.m.

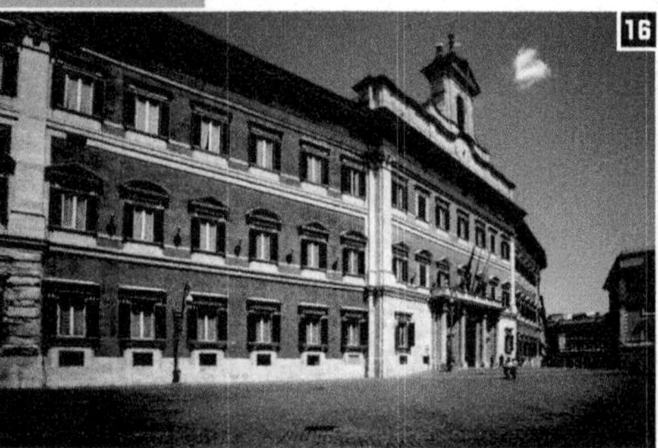

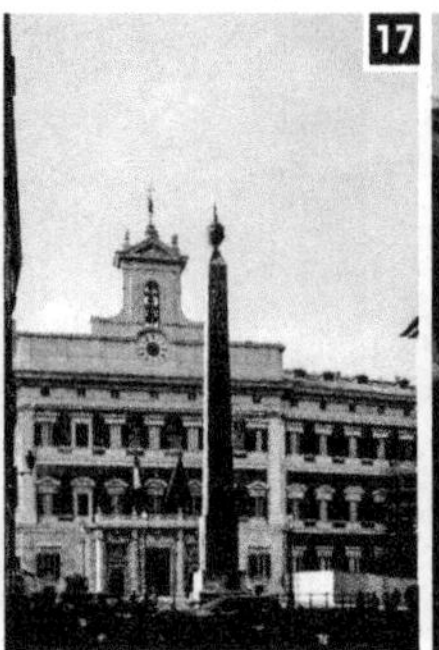

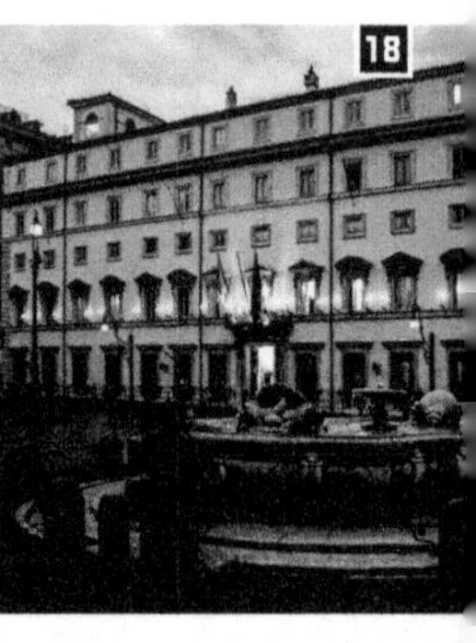

One of the Giolittis will give you a receipt according to the size of the ice cream you have chosen.

There are three standard sizes: small, medium and large. Only when you have the receipt, you get to the end of the line and wait to give it to the vendor behind the fridge.

When you say your flavors, he will ask you whether you want topping. It is on the house, of course. And that's it. Whatever you choose, you will be astonished by the rich flavor and texture. It is not easy to find your way among more than a hundred flavors. And the rice gelato is one of Giolitti originals.

If you find yourself in the E.U.R., the Giolitti family opened another store there. It is a lot less stressful and you can enjoy your ice cream in an idyllic atmosphere on a terrace by the lake.

◆ Palazzo Montecitorio ★ ★ 🔟

The Palazzo Montecitorio is located at the town center. It was built according to Gian Lorenzo Bernini's plans from 1650.

Carlo Fontana completed it in 1694. After the palace was allocated to Italy's parliamentarians in 1871, it was completely redone, so Bernini's idea has only been preserved in the façade. The whole of Italy's political power is concentrated in and around Palazzo Montecitorio.

◆ Obelisk of Montecitorio ★ 🔟

Right in the middle of Montecitorio Square, there is one of the most prominent obelisks in Rome. This is the Obelisk of Montecitorio, brought by the first Roman Emperor Augustus to decorate the *Solarium Augusti*, a sun clock whose dial was the obelisk.

It is 98 ft or 30 m high and made of red granite, brought in from the Egyptian town of Heliopolis.

On Augustus' birthday, September 23, the shadow of the obelisk fell directly onto the Ara Pacis, Altar of Peace.

At the Museo dell'Ara Pacis (Ara Pacis Museum), you can clearly see where the obelisk was situated during Augustus.

◆ Palazzo Chigi ★ 🔟

The palace has a turbulent history. The construction started under Giacomo della Porta in 1562, but it was finished by Carlo Maderno in 1580. It was commissioned by the Aldobrandini family.

The Chigi family bought it in 1659 and Cardinal Flavio Chigi ordered it to be redecorated by the architect Giovan Battista Contini.

In the 18th and 19th century this was the location of the Spanish and then the Austro-Hungarian embassy. The Chigi family sold the building in the 20th century to the Italian government to be the headquarters of the Ministry of the Colonies. After World War I all the way to 1961, this was the Ministry of Foreign Affairs.

After that, it became and has remained the Prime Minister's headquarters.

◆ Piazza Colonna ★ 🔟

The entire neighborhood is named after a column that has been here since AD 193.

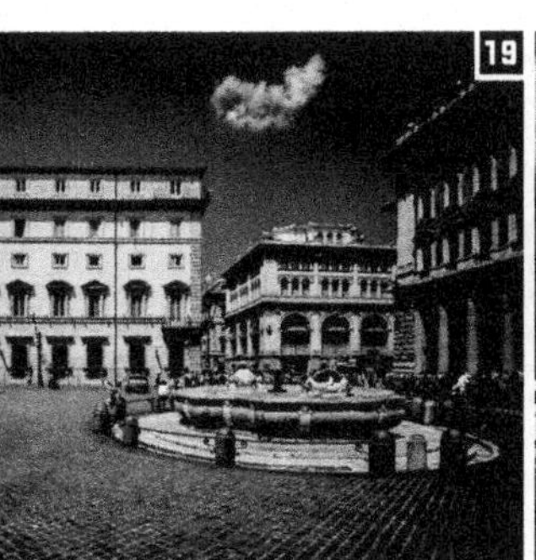
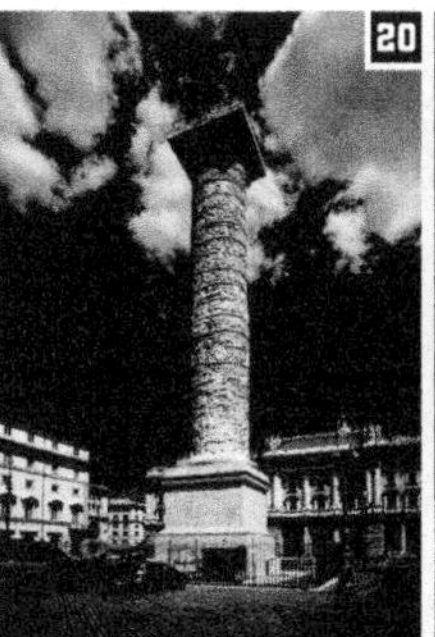
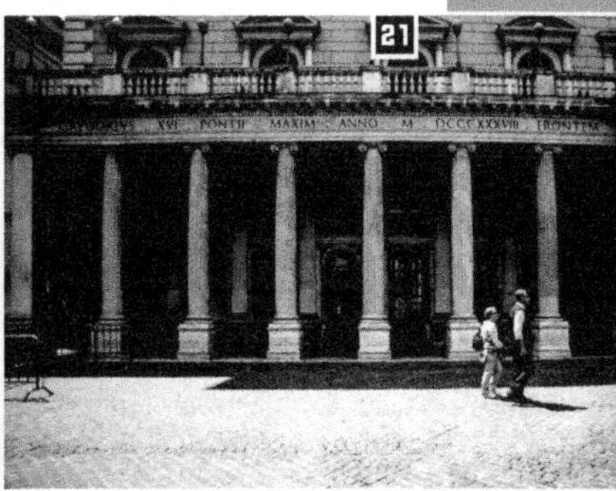

Column of Marcus Aurelius ★ ★

This Doric column was made in honor of Emperor Marcus Aurelius and modeled after Trajan's column. [20] It celebrates the military conquests over the Germanic tribes Marcomanni, Quadi and Sarmatians (172–175) on the Danube, near present-day Vienna. The column is around 30 ft or 9 m high. It was made of 27 blocks of Carrara marble and there are stairs in the middle all the way to the top. Peter the Apostle is on Trajan's column, so for this column, Pope Sixtus V ordered a statue of St. Paul holding a sword.

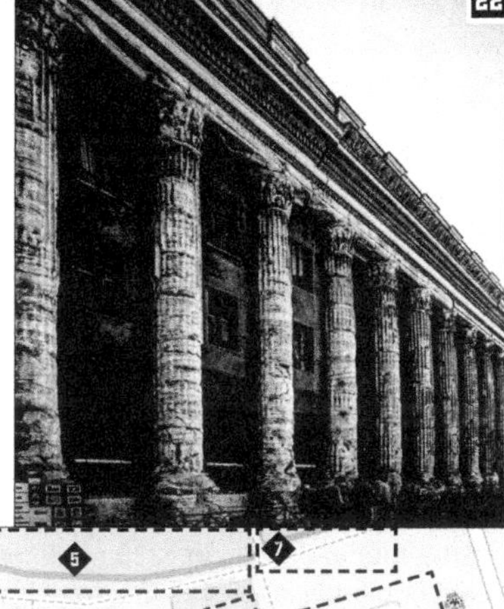

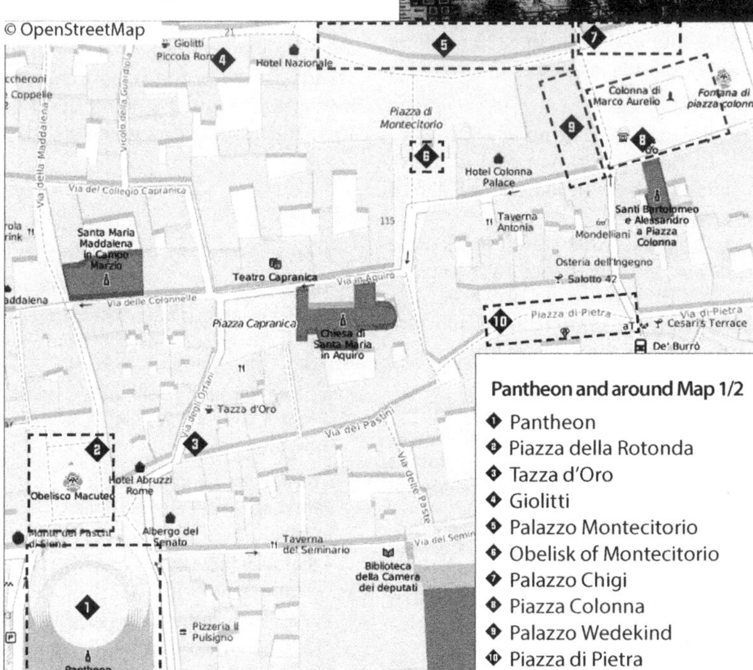

Pantheon and around Map 1/2

❶ Pantheon
❷ Piazza della Rotonda
❸ Tazza d'Oro
❹ Giolitti
❺ Palazzo Montecitorio
❻ Obelisk of Montecitorio
❼ Palazzo Chigi
❽ Piazza Colonna
❾ Palazzo Wedekind
❿ Piazza di Pietra

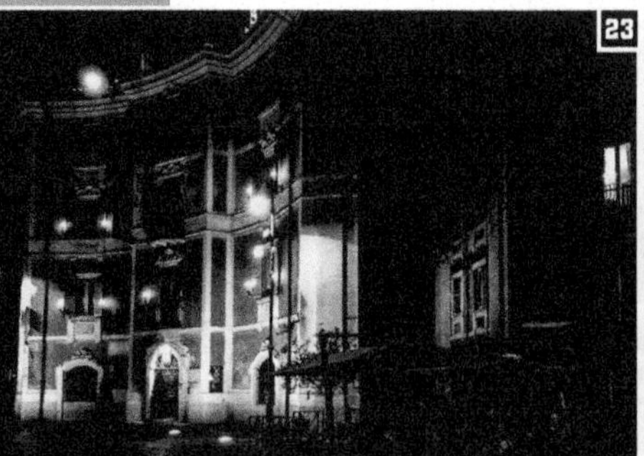
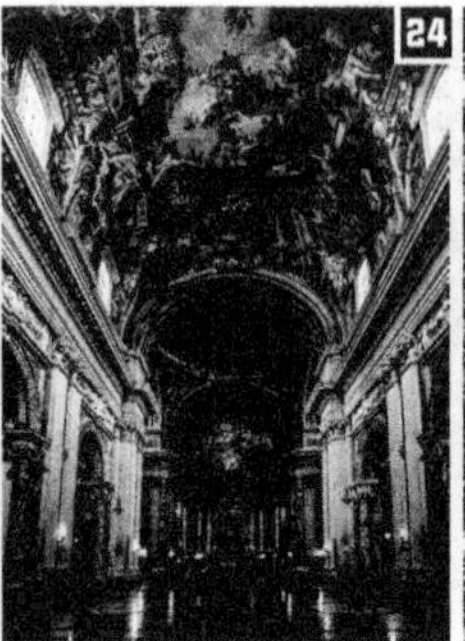
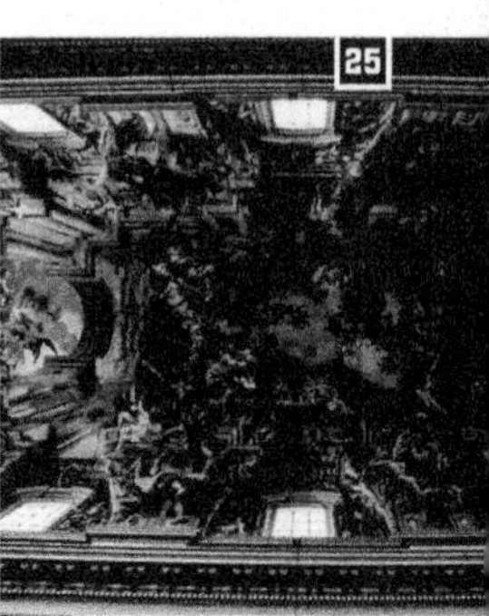

The interior staircase is not open for visitors.

Fontana di Piazza Colonna ★

The fountain at the Piazza Colonna has a history similar to Palazzo Chigi. The first version was designed by Giacomo della Porta in 1577, commissioned by Pope Gregory XIII.

Pink marble from a Greek island of Chios was used. Then the fountain was renovated by Bernini during Pope Alexander VII's pontificate, who was from the Chigi family. Pope Clement XI added his crest, the eight-pointed star, in 1702. Finally, Alessandro Stocchi put in the fountain basin in 1830 made of Carrara marble, as well as the dolphins on the side. **18**

❾ Palazzo Wedekind ★★ **21**

During the Roman period, there used to be a temple in honor of Marcus Aurelius.

The palace that stands in its place today owes its elegance to the colonnade with twelve antique columns, which were transported in the mid-19th century from the ruins of an Etruscan town of Veii.

Therefore, this is the last great Roman palace with original ancient structural elements. Only the two columns closest to the main entrance were not originally brought from Veii.

The palace was named after a German-Italian banker Karl Wedekind who bought it in 1852. Today, it is owned by the state.

❿ Chiesa di Sant'Ignazio di Loyola in Campo Marzio ★★ **23**

This church is located at the wonderful Piazza di Sant'Ignazio di Loyola, surrounded on three sides by the concave Rococo façades designed by Filippo Raguzzini in the 18th century. **24** The church was built in the 17th century, in honor of St. Ignatius of Loyola, who was sanctified in 1622. The façade, a typical Baroque one, was designed by Alessandro Algardi, the most distinguished Roman Baroque sculptor, alongside Bernini. The interior of the church is monumental. It is 262 ft (80 m) long and 141 ft (43 m) wide, and stands as one of the largest churches in Rome. The most striking thing has to be the frescoes on the ceiling, which

Did you know?

Alessandro Algardi's art in Rome

He was born in Bologna (1598), where he was educated at Lodovico Caracci's studio. Pope Innocent X from the Pamphilj family appointed him to replace Bernini in 1644 as the court sculptor. This is when he created his most famous work:

▸ Bust of the Olimpia Maidalchini Pamphilj (Doria Pamphili Gallery) [p.101]

▸ Statue of Pope Innozenz X (Palazzo dei Conservatori) [p.82]

▸ Magnificence and Religion (Chiesa di Sant'Ignazio di Loyola in Campo Marzio) [p.100]

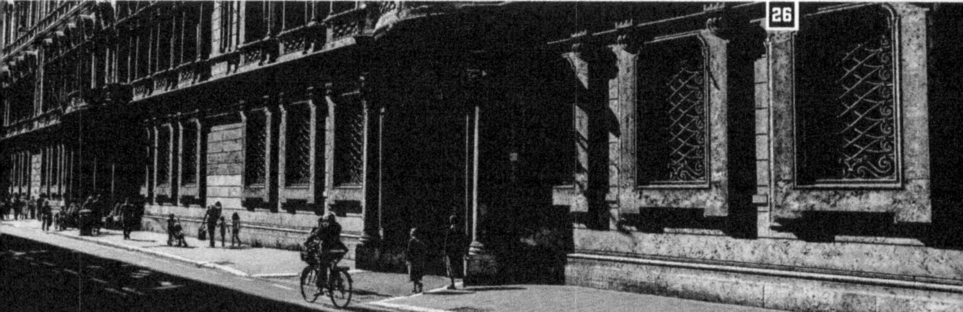

create an optical illusion, trompe-l'oeil, as if there is actual 3D space. This is the work of the Jesuit master of Baroque illusionist painting, Andrea Pozzo. Since the commissioners ran out of money to build an actual dome, it was painted on by Andrea Pozzo. **25**

⓫ Piazza di Pietra ★ ★ ★ **22**

Once you get to Piazza di Pietra, you will know immediately why you had to be there. The unmissable colonnade used to be part of Hadrian's temple built in his honor by his stepson Antoninus Pius in AD 145. Eleven Corinthian columns are 49 ft high (15 m) and placed on a pedestal which adds 13 more ft (4 m) of height. The colonnade used to consist of 15 columns, but four of them did not last until the 17th century when Carlo Fontana built the remaining 11 columns into the papal palace. Today, this is the building of the Roman stock market. While walking through Rome at night, you really should not miss Piazza di Pietra because the columns have amazing lighting.

⓬ Galleria Doria Pamphil ★ ★ ★

The history of this private gallery is inextricably linked with the history of the Doria Pamphilj family, a family that escapes a straightforward explanation. **26** The history of the Doria Pamphilj family reads like the who is who among the most influential Italian families. Marriages between members of various families, primarily, Doria, Pamphilj, Landi, Ludovisi and Aldobrandini, including several English families since the 19th century, created a powerful family of princes in the Papal State, which is in possession of this palace and the collection kept inside, one of the most remarkable private art collections in the world. The most well-known members of the family are Admiral Andrea Doria (1466–1560), who re-established the Genovese Republic and Olimpia Maidalchini Pamphilj (1591–1657), the most powerful person during Pope Innocent X. She is responsible for discovering Bernini, an honor which she shares with the Pope himself, Innocent

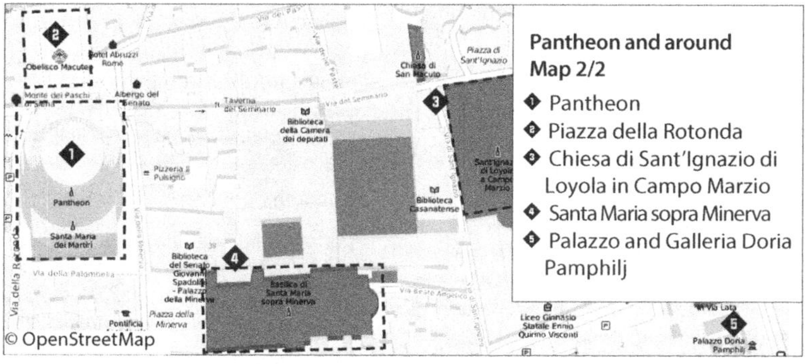

**Pantheon and around
Map 2/2**

❶ Pantheon
❷ Piazza della Rotonda
❸ Chiesa di Sant'Ignazio di Loyola in Campo Marzio
❹ Santa Maria sopra Minerva
❺ Palazzo and Galleria Doria Pamphilj

© OpenStreetMap

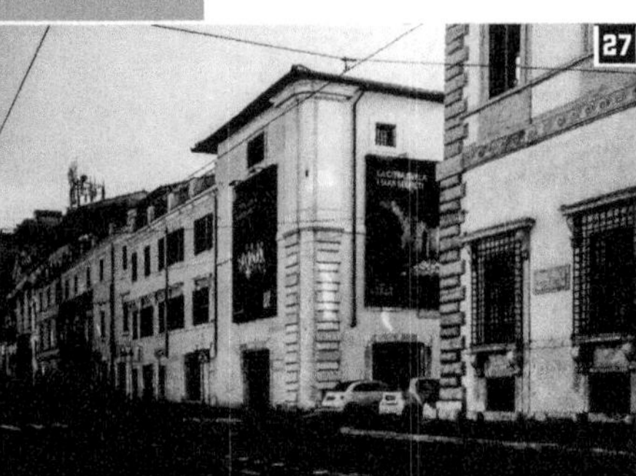

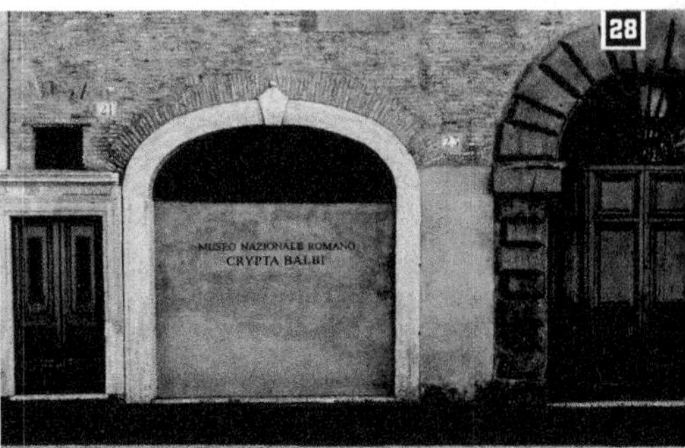

X (1574–1655), born Giovanni Battista Pamphilj. Apart from family portraits executed by some of the finest artist of their time, you can also visit the private chambers of individual family members, ballrooms, admire the walls full of closely stacked paintings made by famous artists, Roman sculptures, the family chapel with a holy mummy, carried around by the princesses of the family whenever they traveled. You certainly should not miss the audio tour narrated by Prince Jonathan Doria Pamphilj himself, an art historian who will guide you through all the rooms, point out each important detail while also casually retelling family anecdotes, peppered with great humor of a true English gentleman. When the British Queen visited Rome in 2000, she stayed at this palace, naturally. The list of painters and sculptors you can find here is almost unending. Here are some of the highlights: Alessandro Algardi, Gian Lorenzo Bernini, Pieter Bruegel the Elder, Caravaggio, Annibale Carracci, Domenichino, Filippo Lippi, Lorenzo Lotto, Jan Mabuse, Parmigianino, Sebastiano del Piombo, Raphael, Guido Reni, Titian, Diego Velázquez. These are mostly portraits commissioned by the family. And just when you think you have seen it all, you will walk past the wonderful and elegant Diana Baths which look absolutely surreal.

13 Crypta Balbi ★ 27

Crypta Balbi is one of four parts of the National Roman Museum. Others include Palazzo Massimo, Palazzo Altemps and Baths of Diocletian.

Doria Pamphilj Gallery
Address: Via del Corso 305, Roma
Online: www.doriapamphilj.it

Public transportation:
Bus stop Piazza Venezia: 119 or Plebiscito: 30, 46, 62, 64, 70, 81, 87, 190F, 492, 628, 916, 916F | Tram stop: Venezia 8

Opening hours: *see online*

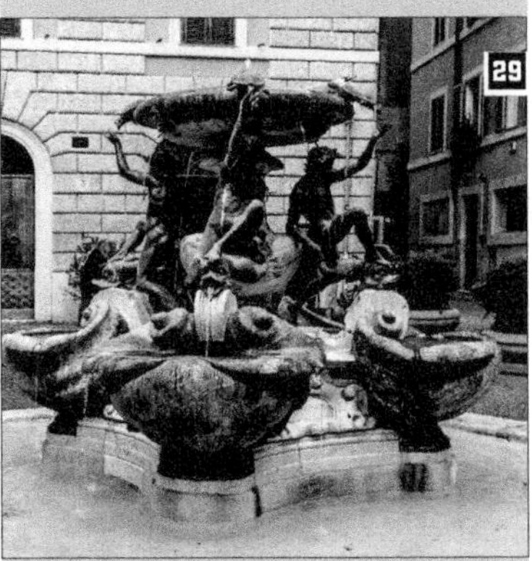

Crypta Balbi
Address: Via delle Botteghe Oscure 31, Roma
Online: www.museonazionaleromano.beniculturali.it/en

Public transportation:
Bus stop Largo Torre Argentina: 30, 40, 46, 62, 64, 70, 81, 87, 130F, 186, 190F, 492, 628, 916, 916F

Opening hours: *see online*

The combined ticket provide access to all four National Roman Museum's sites: Palazzo Massimo, Palazzo Altemps, Baths of Diocletian, Crypta Balbi.

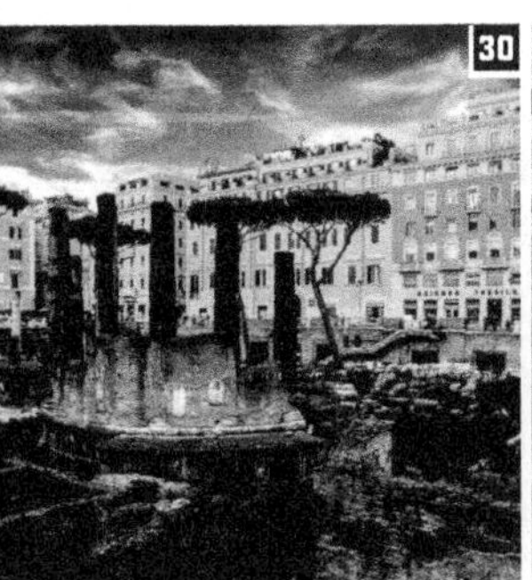
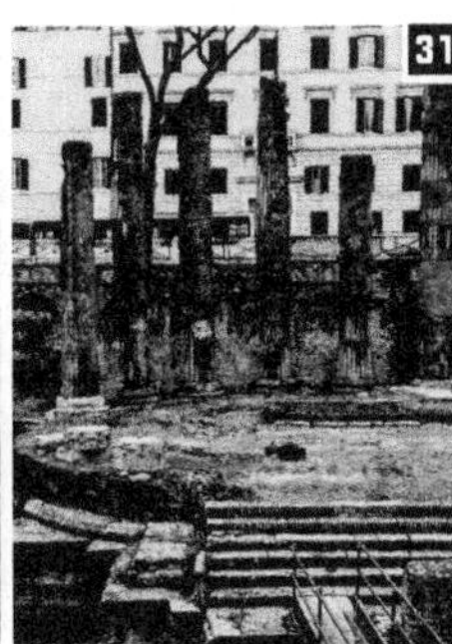
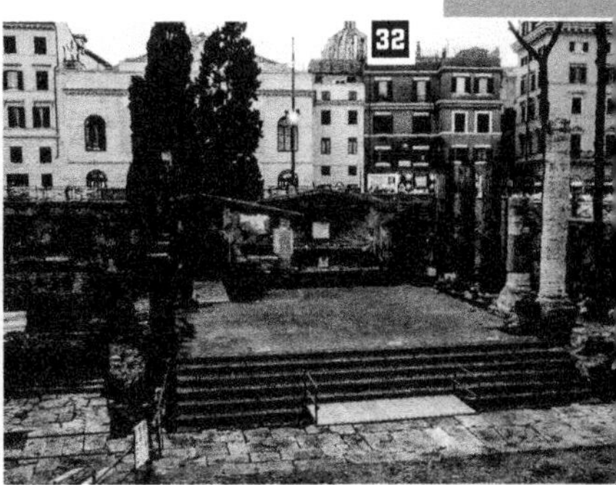

Crypta Balbi used to be part of the Theater of Balbus — at the Martian Field, built by the proconsul Lucius Cornelius Balbus the Younger in 13 BC. The theater was located between Theater of Marcellus and Theater of Pompey, and it was the smallest one. At the edge of a flat, D-shaped stage, there was a hall surrounded by columns on two floors. This is what you can tour at this museum. Apart from many amphorae and other Roman exhibits, there is also an interesting pottery collection from later periods, found during archaeological excavations. 28

14 Largo di Torre Argentina ★★

During the constructions works for the square in 1909, residential buildings and a church were removed and four temples dating back to the age of the Roman Republic were found in their place. Today, these temples are below street level and can be observed from all sides. In the 1st century BC, these temples were surrounded by newer buildings. The enormous Theater of Pompey was on the west towards Piazza de' Fiori. 30

Temple A

Temple A was built in 3rd century BC. Half of the original columns has been preserved at least in fragments. The temple had six columns on both the front and the back, while there were nine columns laterally. The temple was ordered by Gaius Lutatius Catulus after he won the First Punic War against Carthage in 241 BC. In the Middle Ages, the temple was converted into a church,

San Nicola dei Cesarini, whose crypt and partial apsis are still visible today. 31

Temple B

Temple B was a circular building surrounded by columns, six of which have been preserved. The temple was commissioned by Quintus Lutatius Catulus in 101 BC as a vow before the Battle of Vercellae. 32 The temple was raised in honor of the goddess Fortuna. The statue of the goddess Fortuna Huiusce Diei was made using the acrolithic technique — visible parts of the body were made of marble, while the covered parts

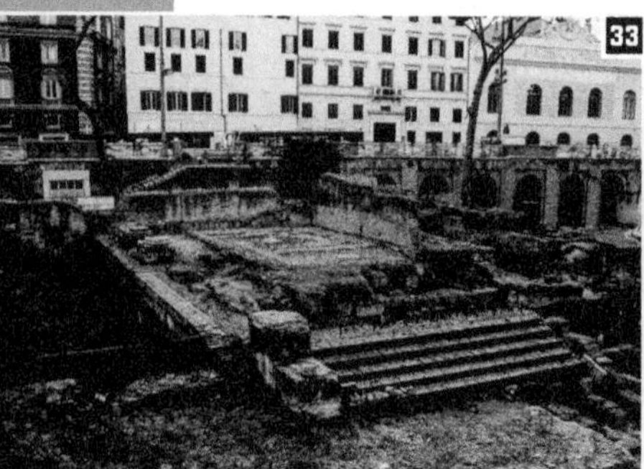
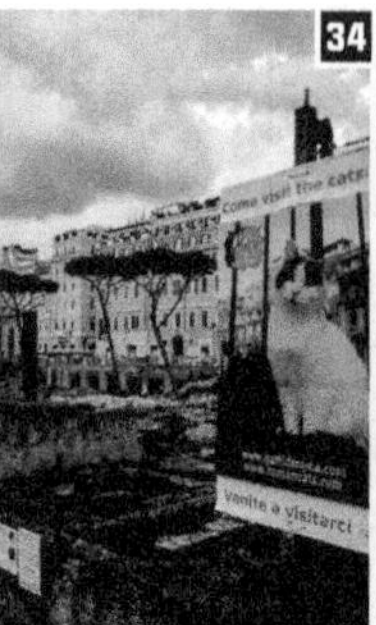
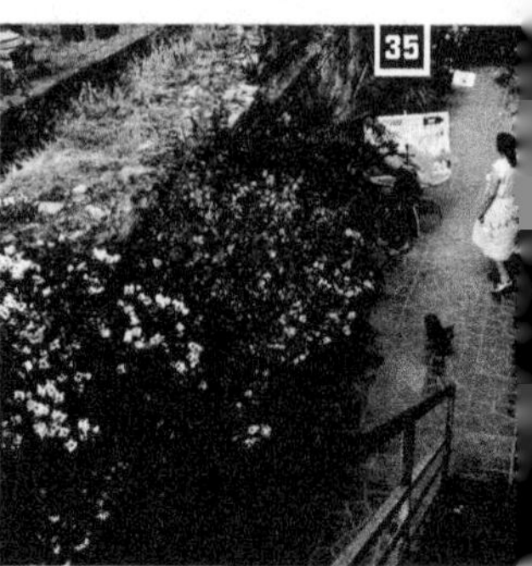

were made of wood. The marble parts are kept at the Capitoline Museums.

Temple C

Temple C is the smallest and also the oldest of the four temples. It is devoted to the goddess Feronia, pre-Roman goddess of the Earth.

Temple D

Temple D is the largest of the group, built in 2nd century BC. A significant portion of the temple is still under Via Florida. It was devoted to the spirit protectors of mariners.

Curia Pompeia

Behind the temples in the middle, B and C, there are parts of the Curia Pompeia, which was occasionally used for senatorial meetings. Julius Caesar was murdered in the curia of Theater of Pompey.

Torre Argentina Cat Sanctuary

This is where the most famous cat sanctuary in Rome is located. Cats walk around without a care in The world across the archaeological area. There is also a cat clinic with volunteers who take care of the feeding, sterilization and vaccination of street cats.

⑮ Santa Maria sopra Minerva
★★★

The Basilica Minor Santa Maria sopra Minerva is on Piazza della Minerva. This is the first and only Gothic church left in Rome. It is a convent, i.e. the main Dominican church. Sopra Minerva means "above Minerva", the Roman temple to goddess Minerva that used to be here before the church.

The construction of the church began in 1290 and it was adapted many times. In the 19th century, it was restored to its former Gothic glory.

The church is related to the Tuscan crème de la crème in other ways as well:

► Four Popes are buried here, including two from the Medici family, Leo X and Clement VII. The non-Florentine popes are Urban VII and Paul IV,

► The tomb of Fra Angelico, a Tuscan painter, is situated here,

► This is the final resting place of Saint Catherine of Siena, one of the most influential women in the history of the Catholic church. She is one of only four women who received the Doctor of the Church title from the Vatican. But, before we go into the church to admire the frescoes in the Carafa Chapel by the Tuscan master Filippino Lippi, Bernini's monument Maria Raggi and the biggest attraction, Risen Christ by Michelangelo, let's stay on Piazza della Minerva in front of the church. Look at the small obelisk on the elephant's back, which dominates the square.

Did you know?

The obelisk on the top of an elephant

Obelisks were placed in front of major Roman churches as traffic signs for pilgrims. When the Dominicans put this one in front of their church, they wanted to show their church was also relevant and worth a visit.

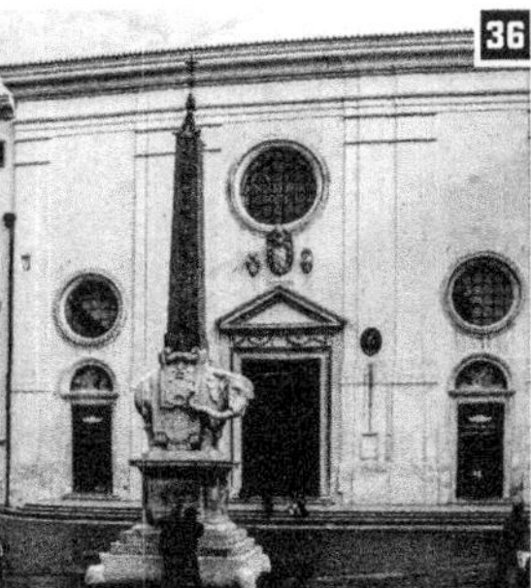
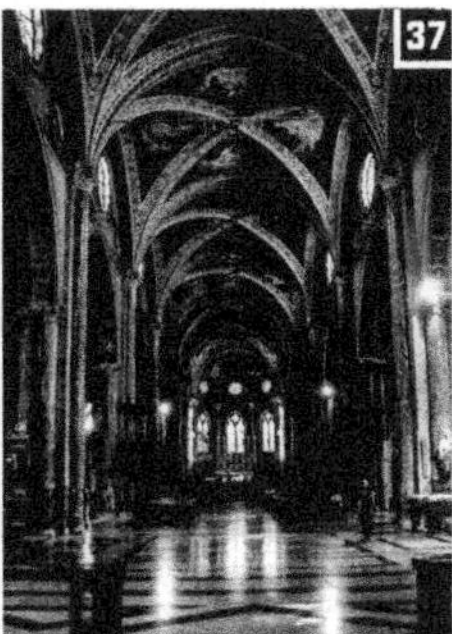
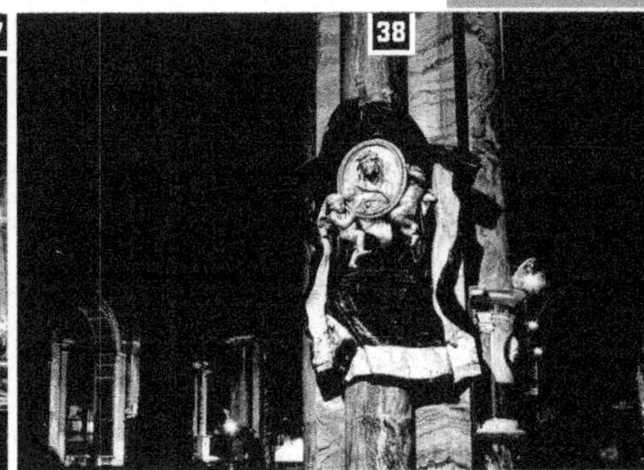

Obelisk ★ 36

It was found in the church courtyard in mid-17th century. It was part of the Temple of Minerva. In fact, the temple was originally dedicated to the goddess Isis. Greeks interpreted her as goddess Athena, while Romans called her Minerva. During Emperor Diocletian, the obelisk was transported from the Egyptian town of Sais, the center of the cult of Isis. It was actually paired up with an identical obelisk, which stands today in Urbino. The elephant was made by Bernini. More precisely, it was made by Ercole Ferrata in 1667, according to Bernini's designs. The saddle, however, was not Bernini's idea and was made on the insistence of the commissioners.

The elephant was meant to represent strength, wisdom and modesty, virtues upheld by Dominicans themselves — the elephant is also known as *porcino* or "piggy." This is because, allegedly, Bernini never saw a real elephant and based his sketch on a pig. Since the Temple of Minerva was located on the Martian Field, and the church is situated on one of the lowest points in Rome, it was frequently flooded. On the right wall of the church, you can find the records of the Tiber floods from 1442 to 1598.

Did you know?

This is where the Galileo Galilei trial took place

This church was also the inquisition headquarters. This is where the Galileo Galilei trial took place. The famous Florentine was forced to denounce his teachings, as well as Copernicus's and say that the Earth did not revolve around the Sun. He was sentenced to life imprisonment and then to a life-time of house arrest. He avoided being burnt at the stake, unlike his predecessor Giordano Bruno.

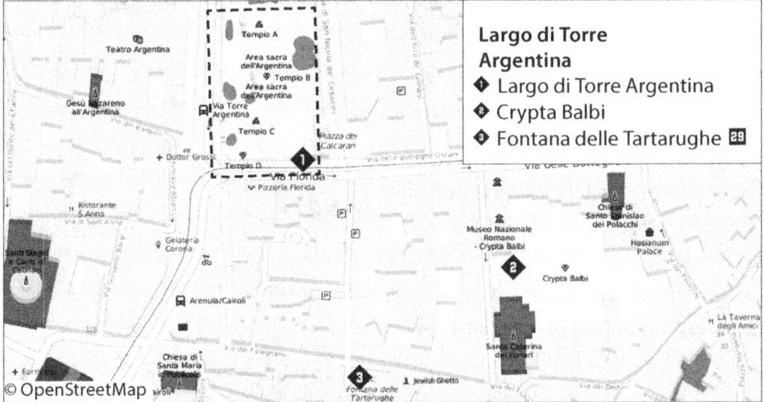

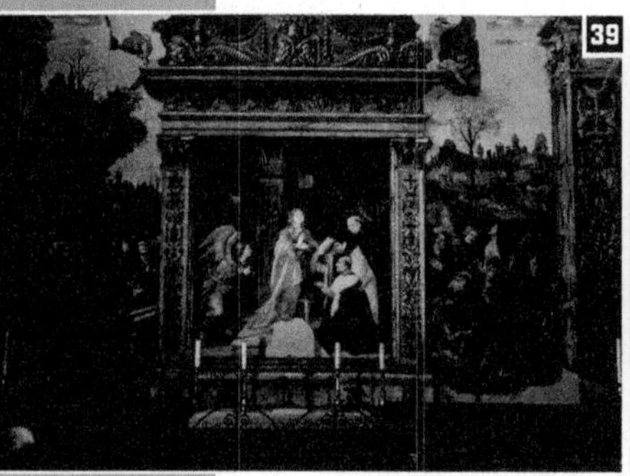
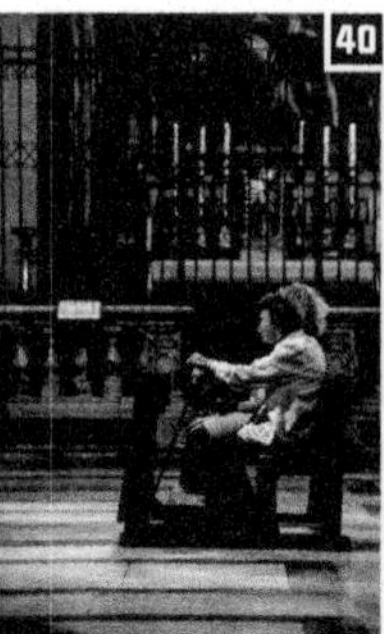
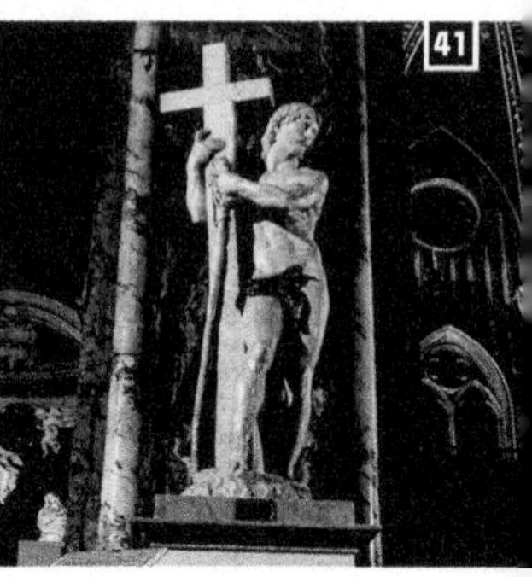

Memorial to Maria Raggi ★★

This is one of the first important monuments we will find inside. Memorial to Maria Raggi was made by Bernini, from 1647 to 1653. Maria Raggi was a nun from the Greek island of Chios. She was extremely devout and had epiphanies often. Her three cousins, Ottaviano, Tommaso and Loreno Raggi ordered the memorial from the famous artist who oversaw the construction of St. Peter's Basilica and put their names on the bottom part of the monument.

The statue is made of gilded bronze on a marble pedestal. It is inserted into one of the columns of the main nave. 38

Carafa Chapel ★★★

This is the most well-known chapel, painted by Filippino Lippi. It is on top of the right lateral nave. This chapel was dedicated to Cardinal Olivero Carafa in 1493 and it is also his tomb. Filippino Lippi painted it from 1488 to 1493. These are one of the most prominent Renaissance frescoes. By combining real and painted architectural elements, Lippi managed to create the illusion of space. Behind the altar, there is an open, spiritual world spreading out, while earthly scenes adorn the surfaces in front of the wall. Lively gestures and landscape are characteristic of early Renaissance. 39

The left side of the chapel is for the tomb of Pope Paul IV, but it all stays in the family. The Pope was Cardinal Carafa's nephew. The right wall has an interesting topographic detail. There is a painting of the Lateran Palace with the equestrian statue of Marcus Aurelius, which did stand there at the time of the frescoes. Today, the statue is kept at the Capitoline Museums.

Cristo della Minerva ★★★ 41

Left of the main altar, there is a statue of the Risen Christ, unveiled in 1521. Michelangelo found a black marble line in the stone while he was carving the statue. He was so disappointed that he left it unfinished. One of his pupils completed the statue making several mistakes. Afterwards, not even Michelangelo could correct them. Frustrated and deeply unhappy with his work, Michelangelo delivered the statue anyway. Despite everything, it is still one of his most valued works.

The painter Sebastiano del Piombo said the knees of this statue were more valuable than the whole of Rome. Michelangelo followed his own vision with this one as well.

Christ is holding a cross as something extremely precious, which demonstrates his unquestionable faith, since he was crucified of his own accord.

Santa Maria sopra Minerva | Saint Mary above Minerva 42
Address: Piazza della Minerva 42, Roma
Online:
www.santamariasopraminerva.it

Public transportation: Bus stop Pie' Di Marmo: 116 or Largo Torre Argentina: 30, 40, 46, 62, 64, 70, 81, 87, 130F, 186, 190F, 492, 628, 916, 916F

Opening hours: *see online*

Piazza Navona

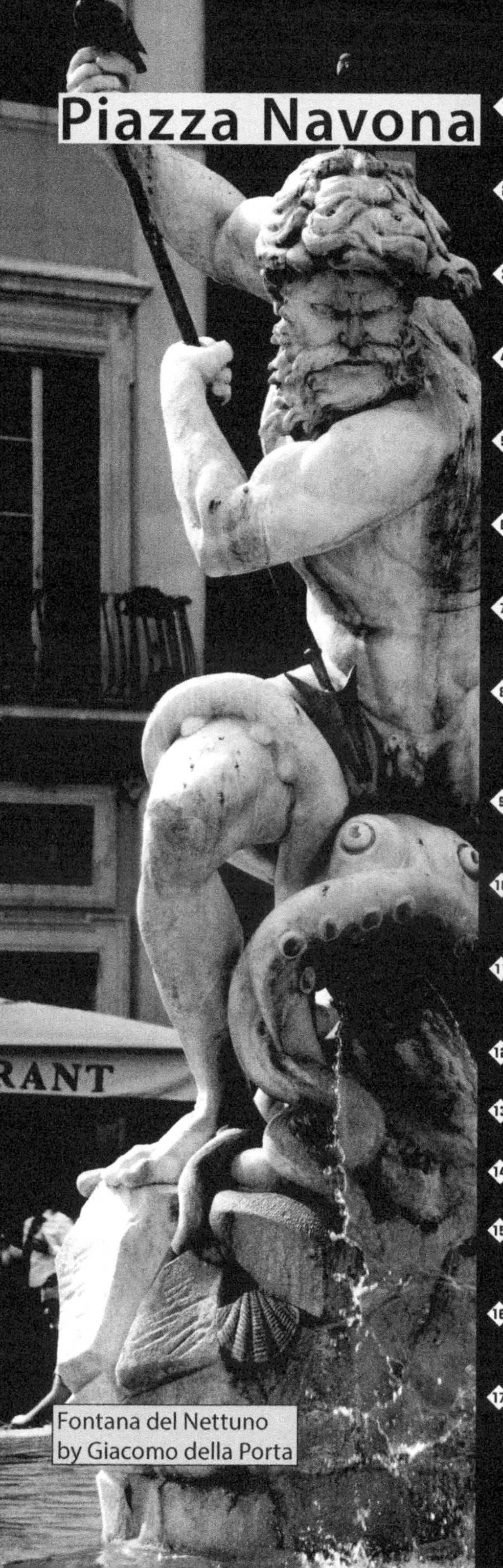

Fontana del Nettuno
by Giacomo della Porta

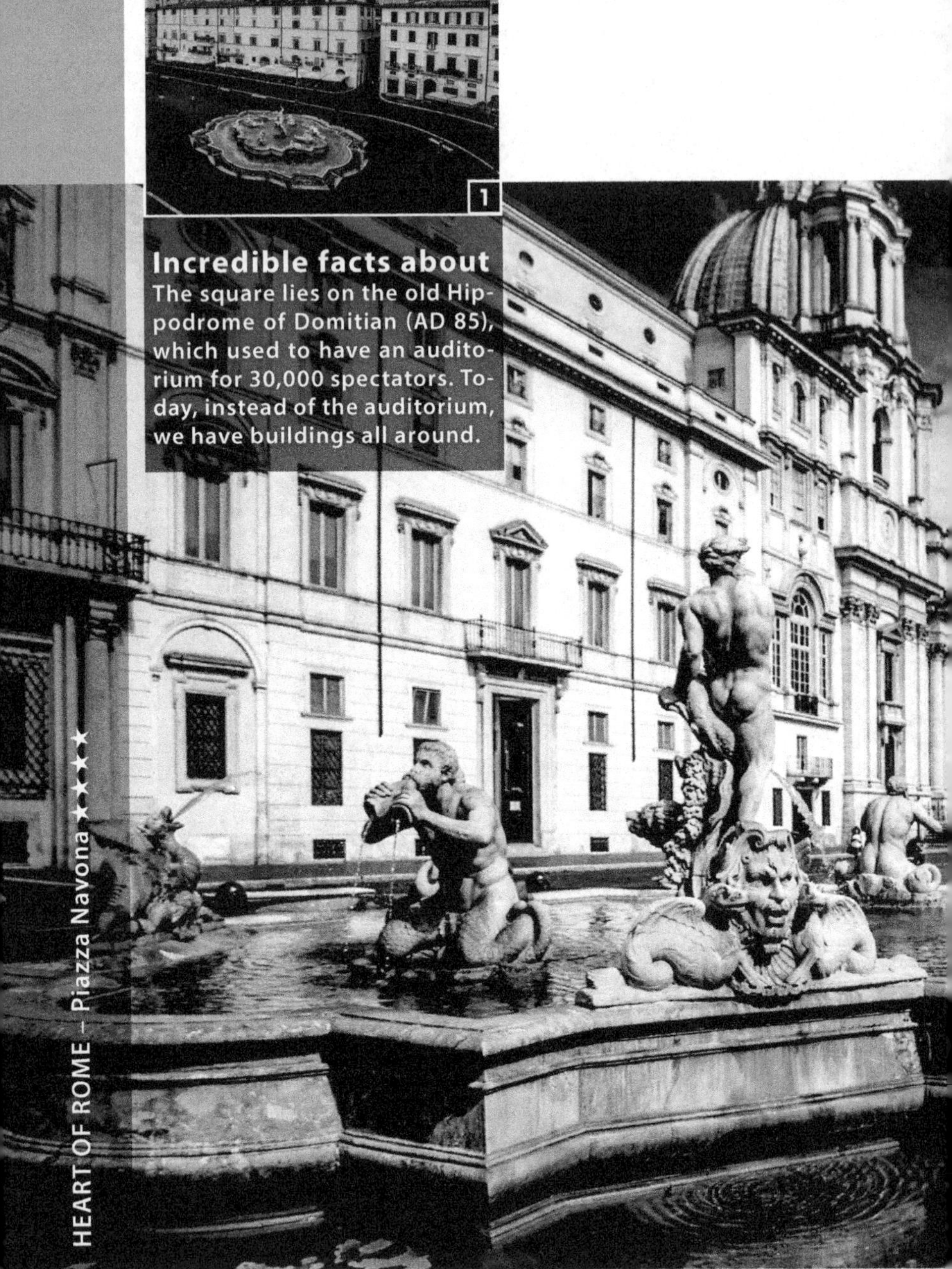

Incredible facts about
The square lies on the old Hippodrome of Domitian (AD 85), which used to have an auditorium for 30,000 spectators. Today, instead of the auditorium, we have buildings all around.

Fontana del Moro – Piazza Navona

Extra Tip : : :
Among the most beautiful and luxurious Roman fountains on it, Piazza Navona is one of the most visited Roman squares. If you want to take a walk along the square in peace, try and get there before 9 o'clock.

The most pleasant place to walk around

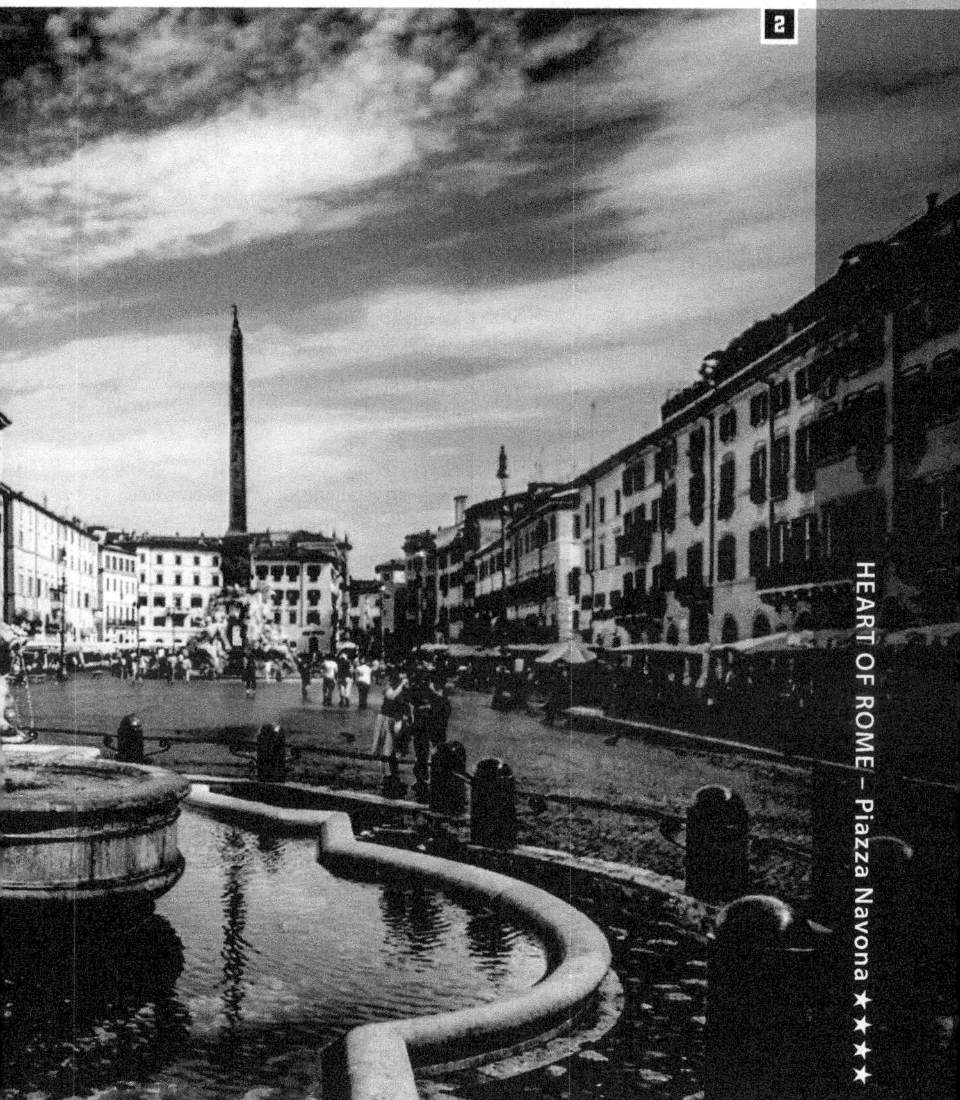

Piazza Navona
Address: Piazza Navona, Roma
Public transportation: Bus stop Senato and Corso Rinascimento: 30, 70, 81, 87, 116, 130F, 186, 492, 628, C3 or Corso Vittorio Emanuele – Navona: 46, 62, 64, 916, 916F

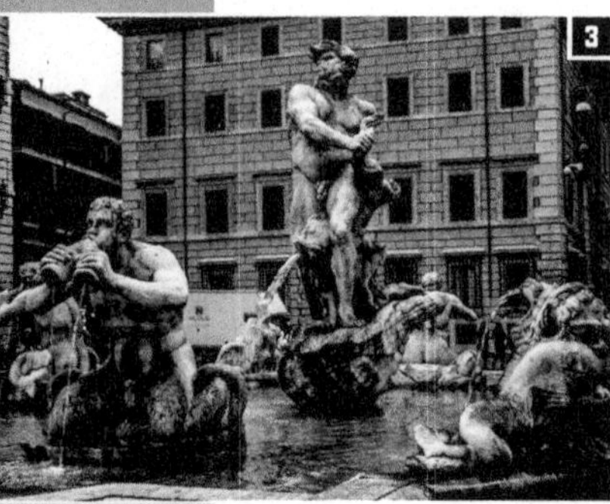
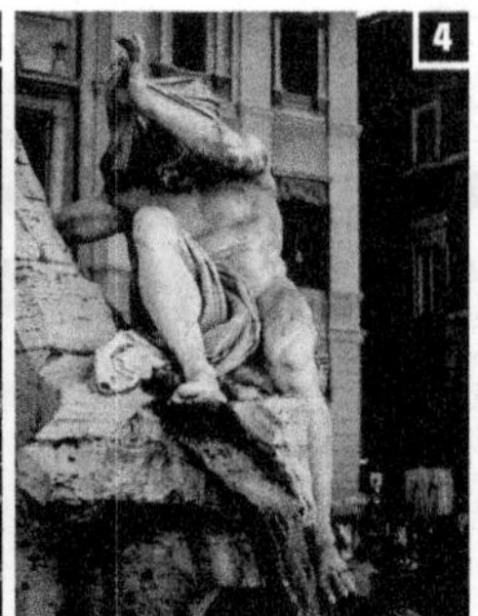
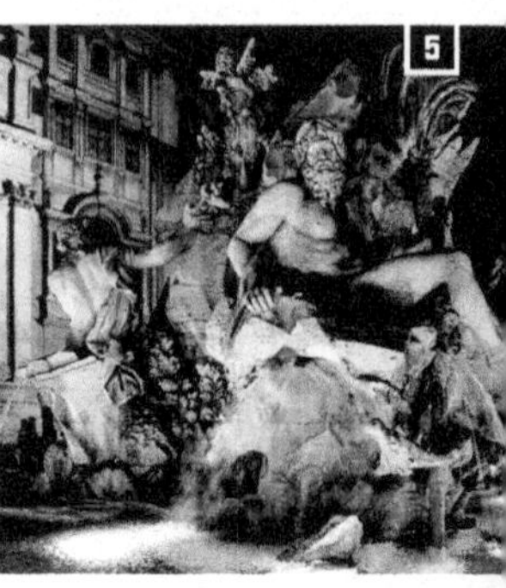

◆ Piazza Navona ★ ★ ★ ★

The Roman Stadium of Domitian used to be a venue for athletic events and equestrian competitions (Lat. Agones), so the stadium used be called *Circus Agonalis*. **1** Through the Middle Ages, the name changed from *agone* to *navone*, and later into *navona*. Pope Innocent X organized a tender for the construction of the fountain because Caracalla's obelisk required a proper setting when they dragged it from Via Appia. Bernini was not even part of the tender. His Roman projects revolved around the Barberini family, such as Fontana del Tritone (1642–1643) on Piazza Barberini. So, with the new Pope in town from the Pamphilij family, Bernini's options were limited, to say the least.

Prince Niccolò Albergati Ludovisi, husband of the Pope's niece, devised a cunning plan to include Bernini in the game. He asked the artist to make a model of the fountain and then secretly put it in Palazzo Pamphili, where the Pope was bound to see it.

Fontana del Moro ★ ★

Fontana del Moro was created 1575 by Giacomo della Porta.

In 1653, Bernini added the *Moor* or the *African* wrestling a dolphin to the statues on the Fontana del Moro.

Fontana dei Quattro Fiumi ★ ★ ★

Between the two fountains by Giacomo della Porta, Bernini designed Fontana dei Quattro Fiumi (1651). It represents an allegory of four rivers: the *Nile* **4**, the *Danube*, the *Ganges* **5** and *Rio de la Plata* which, in return, represent the four known continents: Africa, Europe, Asia and America.

Did you know?

Where to see Bernini's architecture and fountains in Rome and Vatican?

▸ St. Peter's Square and the Fountains of St. Peter's Square, by Carlo Maderno (1614) and Gian Lorenzo Bernini (1677) [p.134]

▸ Sant'Andrea al Quirinale (1658–1670) [p.231]

▸ Fontana del Tritone in the Piazza Barberini (1642) [p.227]

▸ Fontana delle Api in the Piazza Barberini (1642) [p.227]

▸ Fontana del Moro, a figure either of an African (1653), Piazza Navona [p.110]

▸ Fontana dei Quattro Fiumi (1651), Piazza Navona [p.110]

▸ Fontana della Barcaccia (1627) in Piazza di Spagna by Pietro Bernini and his son Gian Lorenzo Bernini [p.201]

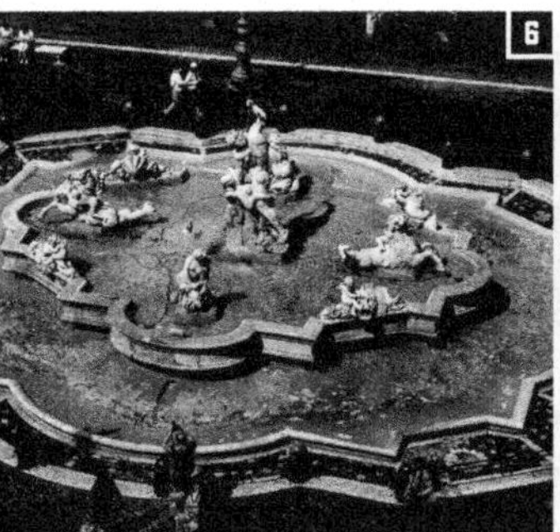
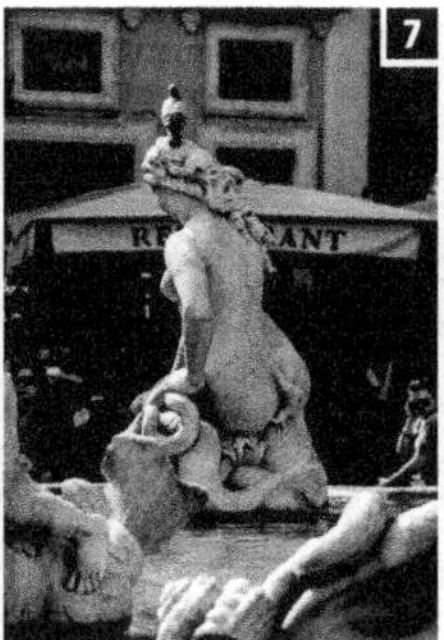
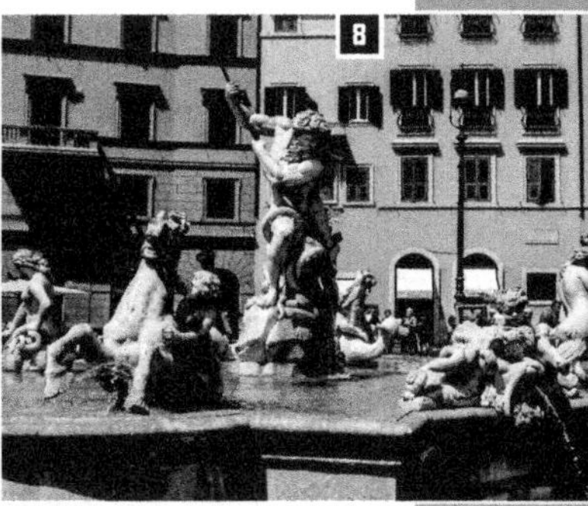

After the fountain saw the light of day, water flooded the whole square every weekend in August, the warmest month of the year. This refreshing tradition went on for more than two centuries. When the main market was transferred from Piazza Navona to the nearby Campo de' Fiori, the waterworks stopped. However, the Christmas fair is still held at Piazza Navona with toys as the great souvenir.

Fontana del Nettuno ★ ★ 6

The basin part of the Fontana del Nettuno was designed in 1574 by Giacomo della Porta. Antonio della Bitta added in 1878 the sculpture of *Neptune fighting with an octopus* 8 and Gregorio Zappalà created in the same year the other sculptures, based on the mythological theme of the Nereids, sea nymphs or female spirits of sea waters 7 with cupids and walruses.

Around Piazza Navona

- Piazza Navona
- Fontana del Moro
- Fontana dei Quattro Fiumi
- Fontana del Nettuno
- Sant'Agnese in Agone
- Palazzo Pamphili
- Santa Maria dell'Anima
- San Nicola dei Lorenesi
- Santa Maria della Pace
- Chiostro del Bramante
- Museum of the Stadium of Domitian
- Museo Palazzo Altemps
- Basilica di Sant'Agostino
- San Luigi dei Francesi
- Palazzo Madama – The seat of the Italian Senate
- Sant'Ivo alla Sapienza
- Sant'Eustachio Il Caffè
- Tourist Info Point (P.I.T.)
- Palazzo Braschi – Museo di Roma
- Pasquino

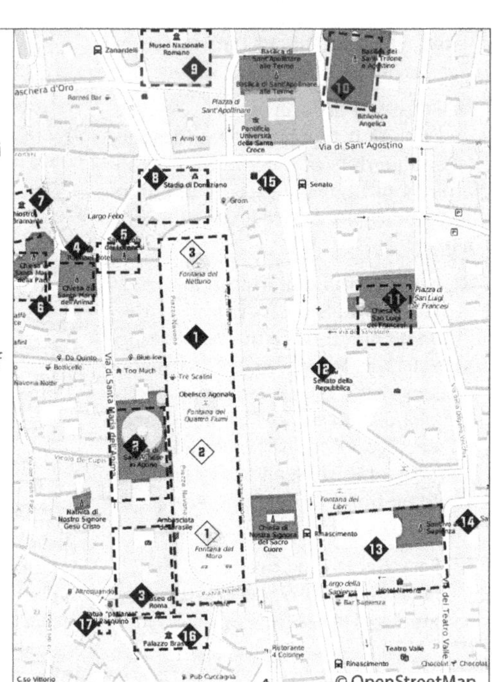

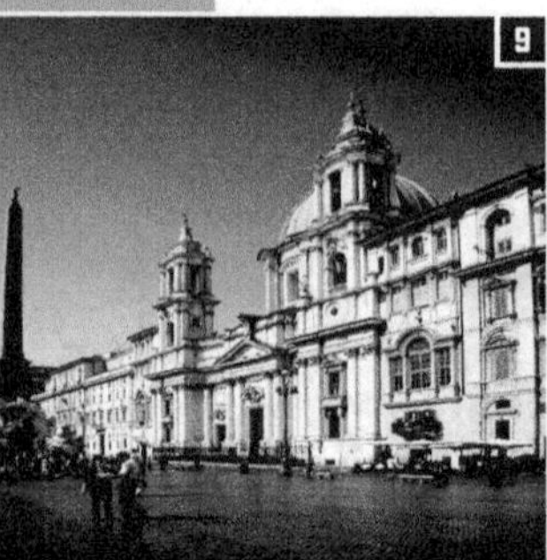
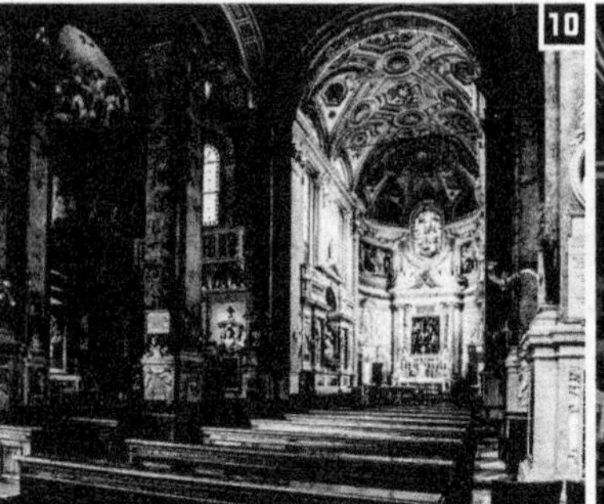
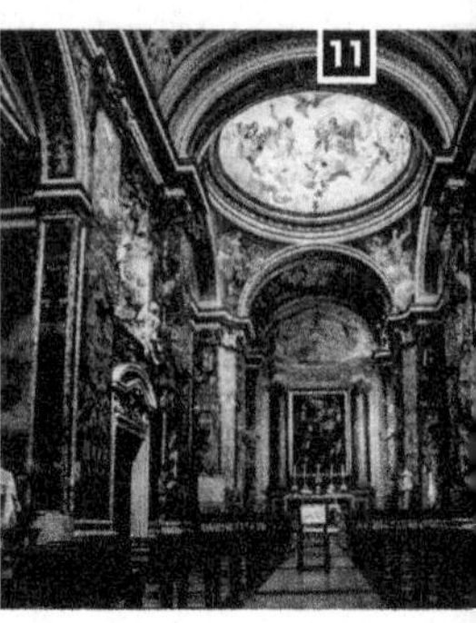

Walk around Piazza Navona

❷ Sant'Agnese in Agone ★★

The Roman origin of the place still lives on in the name of one of the churches. Sant'Agnese in Agone was built by Girolamo Rainaldi, Carlo Rainaldi and Francesco Borromini. It was the family chapel for the Pamphilj family. It dominates the central part of the west side of the square. The façade was made by Borromini. The church holds an important relic, the skull of St. Agnes. According to the legend, Agnes was brought in front of the crowd completely naked and her hair miraculously covered her intimate areas. ❾

❸ Palazzo Pamphili ★

On the left, there is Palazzo Pamphili, headquarters of a powerful Roman family, built by Girolamo Rianaldi in 1650. Today, the palace is the property of Brazil.

❹ Santa Maria dell'Anima ★★

This renaissance church is the national church of German-speaking Catholics in Rome. Apart from the frescoes made by Giovanni Francesco Grimaldi, altar paintings by Carlo Saraceni, Francesco Salviati and Giulio Romano, the most interesting part of this church would be the tomb of Pope Adrian VI, designed by Baldassare Peruzzi. ❿

❺ San Nicola dei Lorenesi ★ ⓫

This small baroque church was donated to France by Pope Gregory XV in 1622.

The paintings of *Saint Catherine* and *Visitatio* were painted by a Lorrain painter Nicolas de Bar. An Italian Rococo artist Corrado Giaquinto made the frescoes and the amazing dome called *The Paradise* (1731).

❻ Santa Maria della Pace ★★ ⓬

About a 330 ft or 100 m west of Piazza Navona, there is the renaissance church of Santa Maria della Pace, well-known for its baroque façade. Before this one, façades were usually flat and decorated in one way or another.

However, in 1656 Pietro da Cortona designed a convex entrance with Doric columns and Ionic architrave on the ground floor. Upper parts of the façade were concave, that is, curved like the inner surface of a round object, all executed in Ionic style.

Pietro da Cortona also designed the façades around the square where the church stands. The interior has a single nave and a particularly interesting dome — the structural elements were painted by Cortona himself, while the frescoes were done by Baladassare Peruzzi. The latter is better known for his architectural achievements, rather than painting, but that did not stop him to also paint the Ponzetti Chapel, first one on the left.

The most famous work in this church is above the Capella Chigi, that's the first chapel on the right. ⓰ The arch was painted by none other than Raphael in 1514 and the fresco is called *Four Sibyls Receiving Angelic Instruction*. The main altar was made by Carlo Maderno, from 1611 to1614.

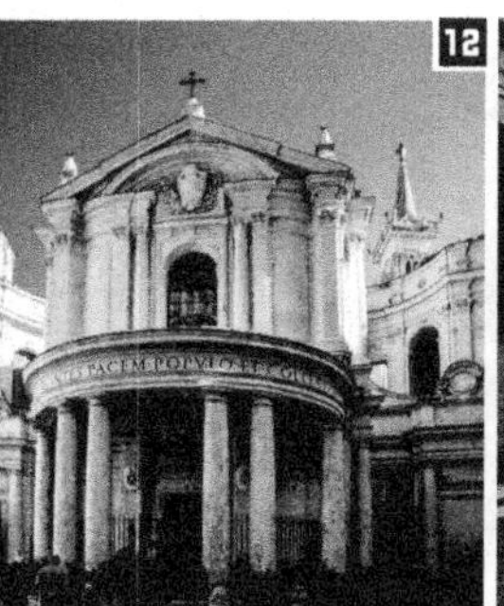
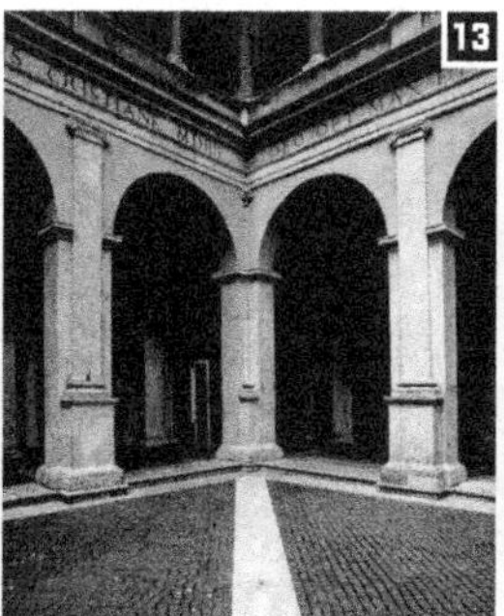
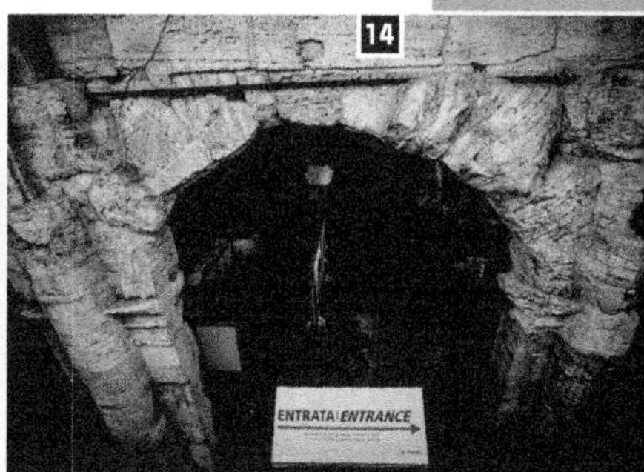

❼ Chiostro del Bramante ★★ 13

Bramante's cloister is his first work in Rome, executed from 1500 to 1504. His contemporaries were extremely critical of it. Today, there is a coffee shop on the first floor and it is a good place to view Bramante's solution for the courtyard of the monastery. You can come across interesting exhibitions throughout the year.

❽ Museum of the Stadium of Domitian ★

This small museum has been opened recently. It is not easy to find because the whole museum is under Piazza Navona. In order to visit it, you have to go to Piazza di Tor Sanguigna and turn towards the buildings organized in a semicircle towards Piazza Navona. 14 When you see the arcades of stadium from the street at the basement of the building, go back towards Via di Tor Sanguigna.

At the beginning of the street, the entrance to the museum should be on your left. You can see parts of Domitian's Stadium, with stadium stairs that have been extremely well preserved, a model of the stadium and other fascinating Roman remains. 1

❾ Museo Palazzo Altemps ★★★

Palazzo Altemps is the second largest location of the Museo Nazionale Romano. Some of the most important Roman and Greek artifacts are kept in this Renaissance palace.   Moreover, the building itself is a piece of art. It has well-preserved frescoes from the late 15th century, Roman art, a theater and a private church, as well as a beautiful courtyard designed by Martino Longhi the Elder in the second half of the 16th century.

In Palazzo Altemps, you can browse through the collections of Antique art just as enlightened Renaissance noblemen and collectors organized them. Affluent patrons of art, Ludovico Ludovisi and Cardinal Altemps, filled their town palaces feverishly with new treasures excavated on the Martian Field, every time a new well had to be dug out in the courtyard. Ludovisi sculptures are on the ground floor and the first floor of the Museo Palazzo Altemps. 15

After walking through a beautiful courtyard from the late Renaissance, you enter the world of Cardinal Ludovico Ludovisi.

Gaul Killing Himself and His Wife

The sculpture is also known by far more suggestive title, *The Galatian Suicide*. It is a Roman copy (2nd century) of a Hellenistic sculpture (230–20 BC) from Pergamon. What we see is a barbaric general who chooses death over slavery. After killing his own wife, he stabs himself with a sword, as a final act of free will.

Blood gushing across his chest, his wife's lethal wound under her left armpit and her lifeless stare, everything in the final moment shared between the two is utterly dramatic.

This sculpture is from the same group as the *Dying Gaul* from the Capitoline Hill Museums.

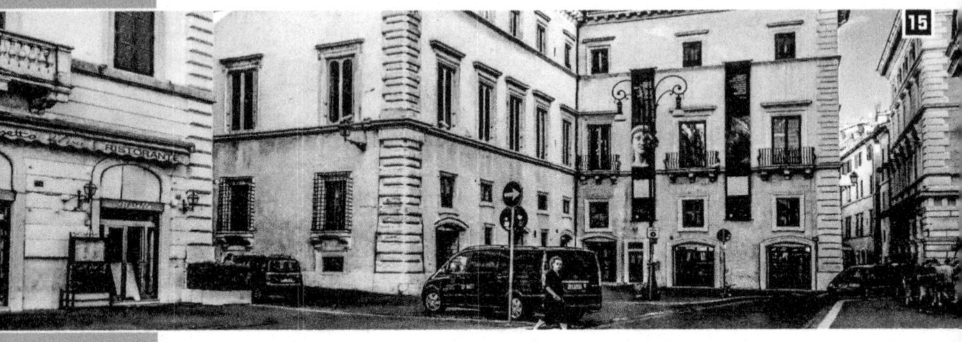

Palazzo Altemps – FIRST FLOOR

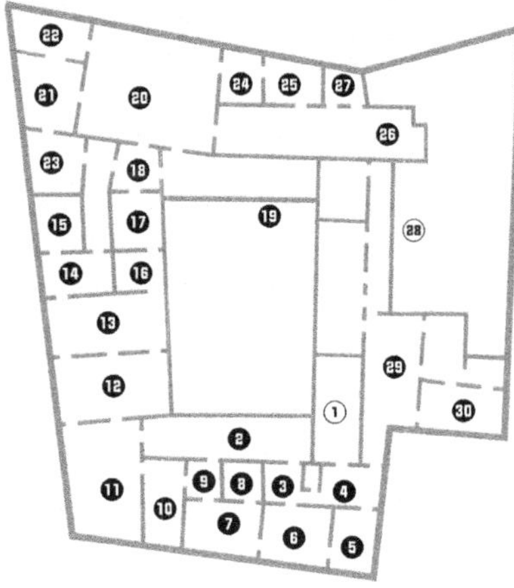

① Main stairs
❷ South Gallery
❸ Isiac Room
❹ Room of Serapis
❺ Room of the Great Gods
❻ Room of the Iseum and Serapeum

❼ Room of the Brancaccio Bull
❽ Room of the God of Janiculum
❾ Passageway of Aphordite
❿ Room of the Bacchants
⓫ Room of the Painted Views
⓬ Room of the Ludovisi Ares
⓭ Room of the Ludovisi Throne
⓮ Entrance to the Room
of the Duchess
⓯ Room of the Duchess
⓰ Entrance of the Cardinal's
Apartments
⓱ The Cardinal's Bedroom
⓲ Study
⓳ Painted Gallery
⓴ Great Room of Galata
㉑ Room of the Obelisks
㉒ Room of the Battles and
Triumphal Processions
㉓ Passageway of the Dadophorus
㉔ Chapel of San Carlo Borromeo
㉕ Sacristy
㉖ Church of Saint Ancetus
㉗ Octagonal Chapel
㉘ Stairs
㉙ Mattei Room
㉚ Apartment of the Stove

Ludovisi Ares

This is a marble statue of the Roman god Mars, a refined copy of the Greek original from the 330's BC. It is associated with the Greek master Lysippos and named after the Greek god of war, Ares. This is the most beautiful work by Lysippos. Ares or Mars is portrayed in an intimate moment. He is not belligerent at all. On the contrary, he is laying down his weapons before goddess of love, Aphrodite. At first, Ares seems relaxed. His sword is tucked in its sheath, he has stretched out his right leg, leaning on his left leg with both arms.

Museo Nazionale romano di palazzo Altemps | National Roman Museum — Palazzo Altemps
Address: Via Sant'Apollinare 46, Roma
Online: www.museonazionaleromano.beniculturali.it/en/

Public transportation: Bus stop Senato 30, 70, 81, 87, 130F, 186, 492, 628

Opening hours: *see online*

The combined ticket provide access to all four National Roman Museum's sites: Palazzo Massimo, Palazzo Altemps, Baths of Diocletian, Crypta Balbi.

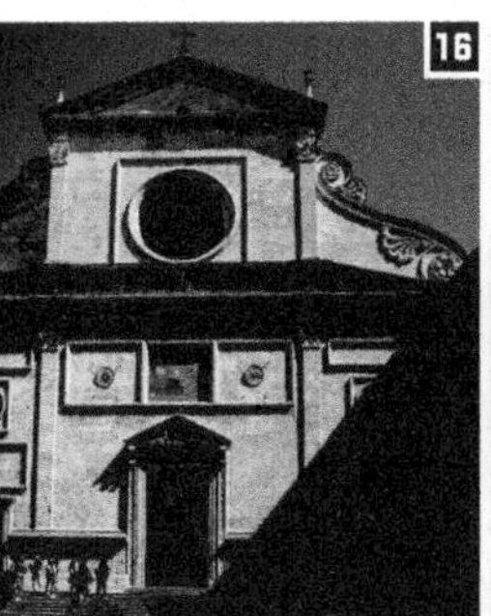
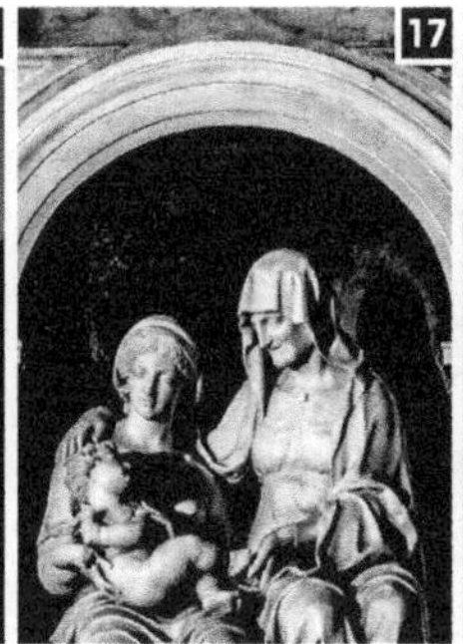
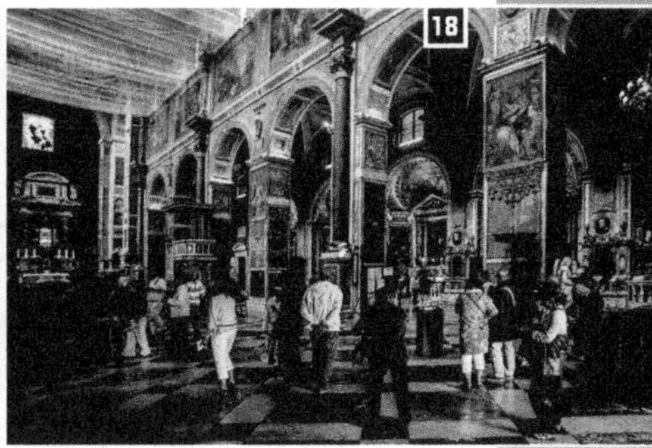

There is a robe over his arm and his head is slightly tilted. However, if you look more closely, you will see he is not relaxed at all. His body is tense and ready for a fight, but of a different kind, a love fight. Eros, meant to symbolize Aphrodite, was probably added under Ares's right foot by the Roman copyist. The sculpture was found in 1622 and restored by Bernini. You can find it on the first floor of Museum Altemps.

Ludovisi Dionysus

The statue was discovered during the construction of Palazzo Mattei at Quattro Fontane. It is a larger-than-life figure from 2nd century. There are grapes in his left hand, which point to the fact that he is the god of wine. Hands, chest, upper legs and the satyr are part of the original find, while everything else was added during the restoration in the 16th century.

Ludovisi Throne

This relief was also found on Ludovico Ludovisi's estate. It was probably an altar piece from the Temple of Aphrodite from Magna Graecia. It was made in mid-5th century BC. Goddess Aphrodite emerges from water. This is probably the birth of the goddess. According to Greek mythology, she came out of the water in Paphos, Cyprus. She is carried by Horas, goddesses of the seasons. A naked female playing the flute also belongs in this group, who was likely one of the temple staff. On the other side, there is priestess bringing a sacrifice of raisin in front of a *thymiaterion*, a ritual bowl for lighting incense.

Ludovisi Battle Sarcophagus

This astonishingly well-preserved sarcophagus was found near Porta Tiburtina in Rome. It shows an interesting battle between Romans and Goths, full of emotion on both sides. The style is characteristic of 3rd century. This is one of 25 sarcophagi with motives inspired by Pergamon, a Hellenistic masterpiece. The focus is on the young Roman general who is holding his hand high. The sarcophagus is probably dedicated to him. If you move closer, you can see an X on his forehead. This means he was under god's protection. The cult of Mithras was a widespread cult among Roman soldiers. Since the general died, the X also signifies his triumph over death. The relief is of such high quality that it was thought the artist must have been commissioned by a Roman emperor.

This led to various theories — some thought this was Hostilian, Emperor Decius's son. However, Hostilian died of a plague, so the theory fell short. Interestingly enough, Roman propaganda here still supports a ludicrous reality, barbarians are still portrayed as mere extras at the mercy of Roman troops.

The truth was quite the opposite. The Romans were losing against the barbarian warriors, which resulted in the fall of the Western Roman Empire.

Juno Ludovisi

This is a head of a statue from 1st century, an idealized portrait of Antonia Minor, niece to Emperor Augustus and mother to Emperor Claudius.

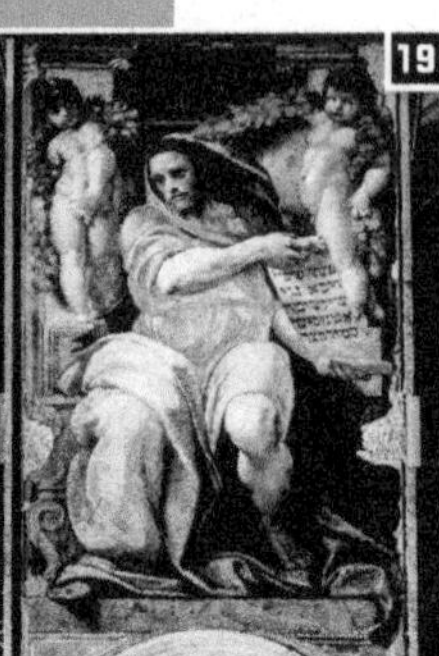

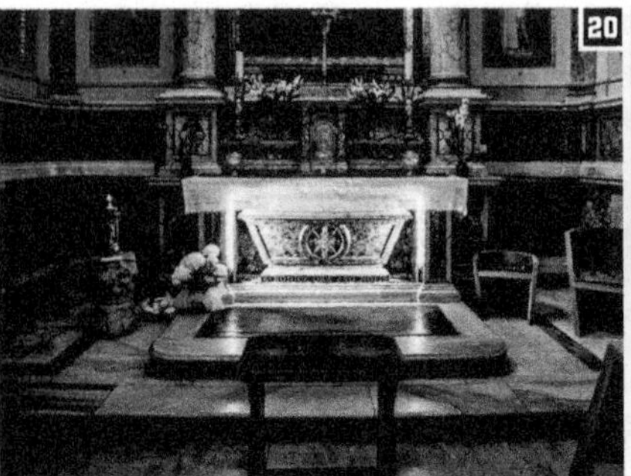

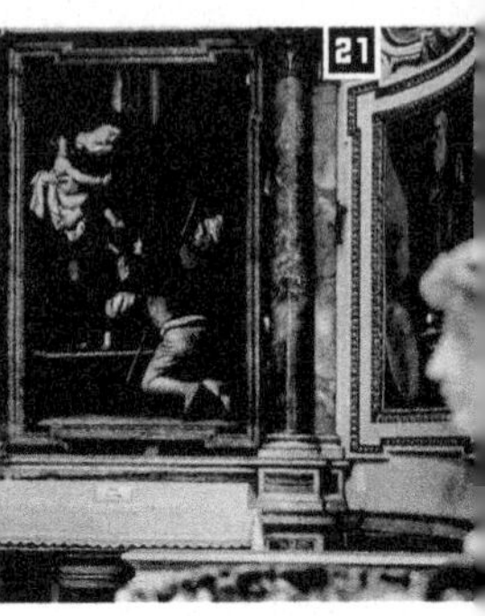

She looks like the Roman goddess of marriage, Juno. While traveling through Italy, Johann Wolfgang von Goethe saw Juno Ludovisi and was so impressed by her beauty that he wrote how he had finally found the love of his life.

⑩ Basilica di Sant'Agostino ★★★

This basilica was one of the first renaissance churches built in Rome. Instead of a Gothic Augustine church (1286), a new church was made from 1479 to 1483 according to Sebastiano Fiorentino's plans, with the façade made of travertine stone from the Colosseum by Giacomo di Pietrasanta. **16** In mid-18th century Luigi Vanvitelli designed the baptistery and the dome. The same architect also remodeled the Augustine buildings, made their main library called Biblioteca Angelica, situated at Piazza di Sant'Agostino. The interior of the library, where all the books banished by the Holy See were kept, was designed by Francesco Borromini. Basilica di Sant'Agostino in Campo Marzio is a three-nave church in the shape of the Latin cross. There are six chapels on each side. **18** There are several masterpieces as well. Right of the main altar there is the sculpture of *Madonna del Parto* or "Our Lady of Childbirth" by Jacopo Sansovino (1518–1521).

A fresco called *Prophet Isaiah* was painted by Raphael (1511–1512) and you can find it on the third column of the main nave. **19** The sculpture of "Anna and Virgin with Child" (1512) by Andrea Sansovino is directly below. **17** It is believed that the sculpture works miracles.

In the right transverse nave, there is a painting of *St. Augustine of Hippo, John the Evangelist and Jerome*, by Guercino. In the same nave, next to the main altar, there is Saint Monica's tombstone, the mother of St. Augustine. Her relics were transported form Ostia in 1430. **20**

The main altar was made by Gian Lorenzo Bernini. The painting which is definitely worth the visit to the church is in the first chapel left of the entrance. It is *Madonna di Loreto* by Caravaggio (1604–1606). This famous baroque painting has been the source of gossip for nearly four centuries. **21** Some managed to find similarities between the Holy Mary and a well-known courtesan of the time. Sant'Eustachio, the neighborhood in which this church is located, was a well known residential area of Roman prostitutes. Apart from her earthly charms, the gossip was also fueled by the fact that both the pilgrims and the Madonna have dirty feet. In any case, the woman who modeled for Caravaggio for this painting did it again for the "Madonna and Child with St. Anne" or *Dei Palafrenieri* (1605), currently kept at the Galleria Borghese.

⑪ Church of San Luigi dei Francesi ★★★★

No matter how many times you visit Rome, you will always get the feeling you are missing out on something. There are more than 900 churches in Rome, and this one should be included in the top ten. It is located in Via Santa Giovanna d'Arco, approximately half way between the Pantheon and Piazza Navona.

The construction went on during most of the 16th century, all the way to 1589. The façade is the work of Giacomo della Porta. 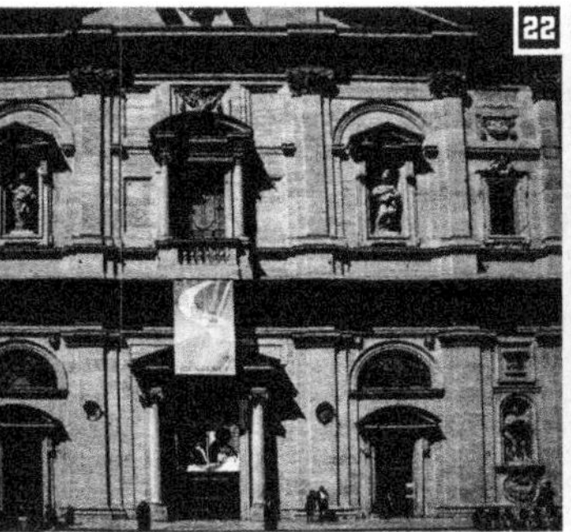

This versatile artist was among the busiest in 16th-century Rome. He often collaborated with Domenico Fontana on papal commissions. The two of them finished building Michelangelo's dome of St. Peter's Basilica while working on this church simultaneously. Since the Church of San Luigi dei Francesi is a French church, Giacomo della Porta incorporated a few historical French figures, such as, Charles the Great or Charlemagne, St. Louis, St. Clotilde and St. Jeanne of Valois. Even today, this church is reserved for the cardinal who is also the Parisian bishop. The architectural layout was designed by Domenico Fontana. After you have feasted your eyes on the shiny decorations on the ceiling 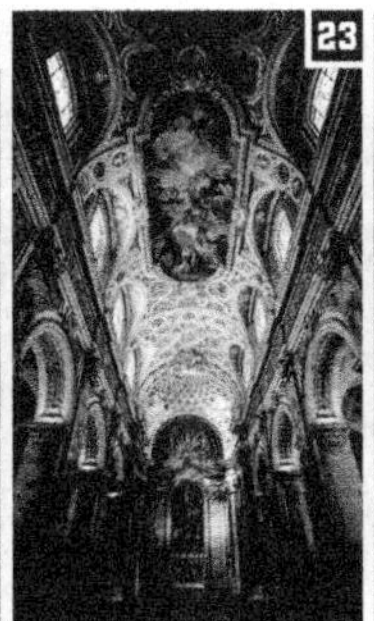, made in the Rococo manner by Charles-Joseph Natoire (1754–1756), direct your attention to the main attraction. It is the Contarelli Chapel with three famous paintings by the Baroque master Caravaggio, around 1600. 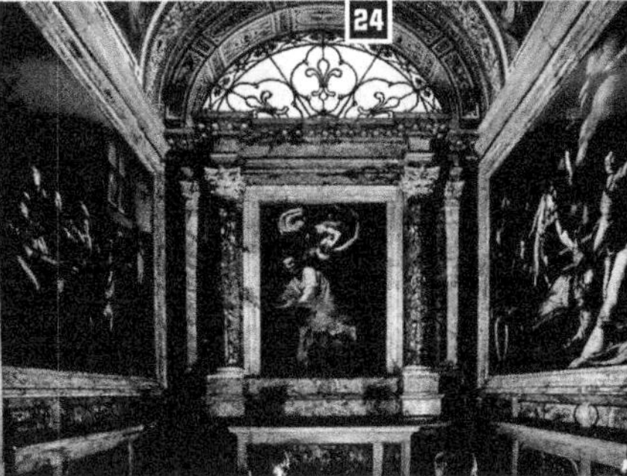 They are all dedicated to the life of Matthew, a Roman tax collector, who discovered faith with the help of Jesus Christ. The chapel is on the left from the main altar. Caravaggio insisted on juxtaposing light and dark in his work, the so-called *chiaroscuro*.

The Calling of Saint Matthew

The painting focuses on a moment of inspiration, when Jesus Christ convinces Matthew to follow him.

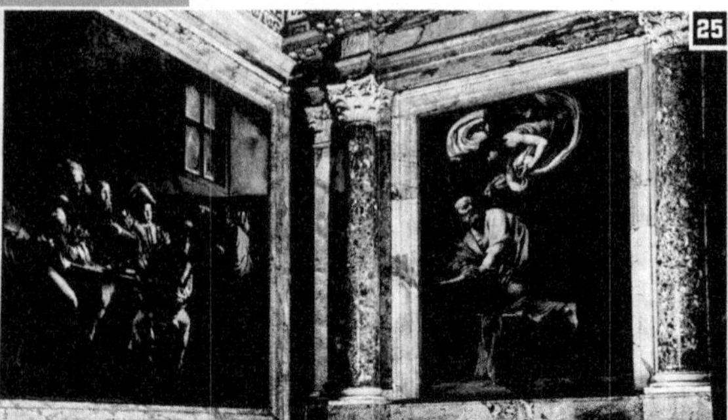

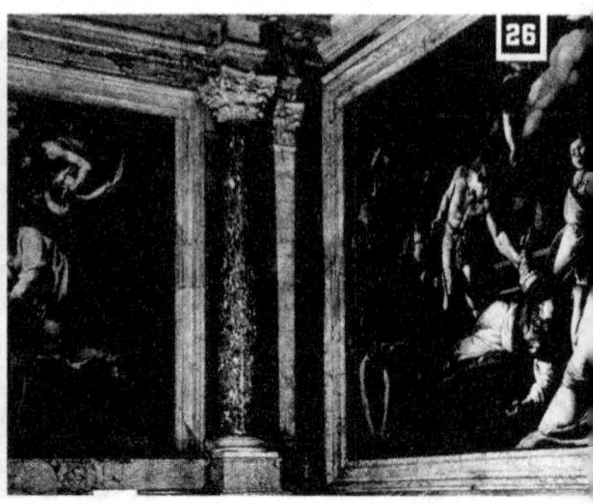

This is the first painting Caravaggio completed for the chapel (1600). We see Matthew sitting at a table with four other men. Jesus Christ and St. Peter come into the room, and Jesus is pointing to Matthew. Matthew has a big beard, a symbol of wisdom since antiquity. The divine light shines on him, coming from the direction of Jesus Christ and St. Peter. According to another interpretation, the bearded man at the table does not point to himself asking in disbelief "Me?" In fact, he may be pointing at the young man with his head bowed down, asking Jesus and St. Peter "Him?" If this theory is true, then Matthew would be the young man battling a hangover on the head of the table. Perhaps both young and old Matthew are in this painting, because the old man is present in all three paintings. Whatever the interpretation, the painting is deliberately ambiguous. 25

The Inspiration of Saint Matthew

The painting is at the Contarelli family altar and it was the last one from the program (1602). The reason it took longer to paint was because the artist had to follow the commissioner's instructions, Cardinal Francesco Maria del Monte's. Matthew is taking dictation from an angel. The entire scene looks as if it was set on a stage and the light only spots the main event. Everything else is in the dark. 25 26

The Martyrdom of Saint Matthew

Narratively speaking, this is the last painting, but it was painted first. 26 It has been here since 1600. Traditionally, the Ethiopian king ordered St. Matthew to be killed because he celebrated mass. The painting polarized the Roman art world of the time. Established Mannerist painters thought it was meaningless, while younger artists adored it. One of the novelties was omission of architectural elements. The figures emerge from the dark of a poorly lit church.

Did you know?

Where to see Caravaggio's paintings in Rome and Vatican City?

▶ San Luigi dei Francesi: *The Calling of St. Matthew, The Martyrdom of St. Matthew, St. Matthew and the Angel* **[p.116]**

▶ Galleria Borghese: *Madonna of the Serpent, David with the Head of Goliath, Young Bacchus and many others* **[p.188]**

▶ Capitoline Museum: *St. John the Baptist* **[p.81]**

▶ Palazzo Barberini: *Narcissus, Judith beheading Holofernes, St. Francis in Meditation* **[p.229]**

▶ Galleria Doria Pamphilj: *Mary Magdalene, Rest on the Flight into Egypt, Young St. John the Baptist* **[p.101]**

▶ Santa Maria del Popolo: *The Conversion of St. Paul, The Crucifixion of St. Peter* **[p.195]**

▶ Basilica di Sant'Agostino in Campo Marzio: *Madonna di Loreto* **[p.116]**

▶ Vatican Pinacoteca in Vatican Museums: *Deposition from the Cross* **[p.142]**

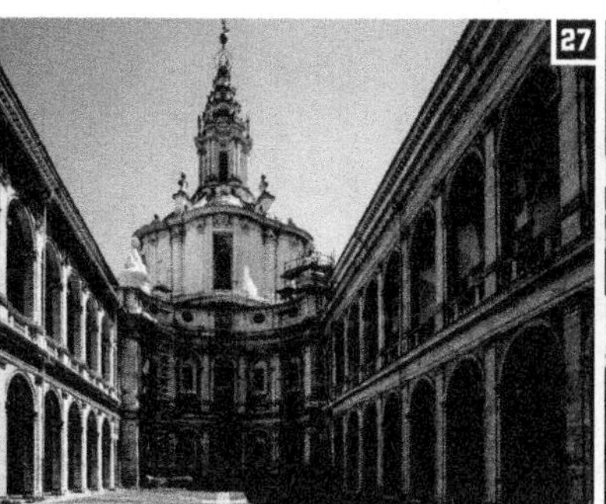

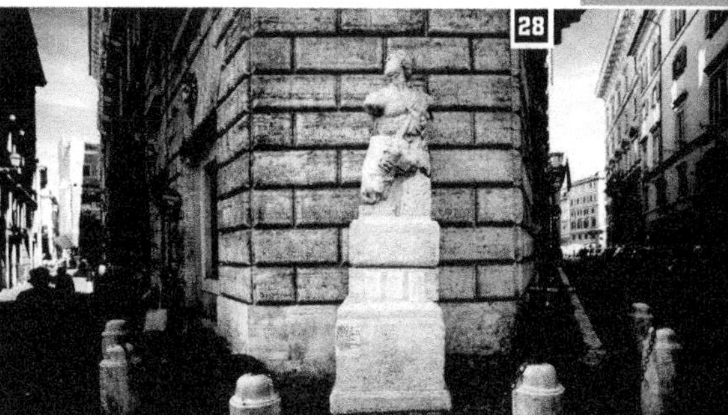

This was a radical approach in relation to the depiction of martyrdom in Italian painting. Up to that moment, it had always been portrayed as a moment of rapture. However, this painting relates all the terror and fear of such a situation.

The farthest figure, a little left from the middle of the painting, in line with the right shoulder of St. Matthew's killer, is Caravaggio's self-portrait.

Sant'Ivo alla Sapienza ★★★

This Baroque church (1642–1664) is one of Francesco Borromini's masterpieces. Today, it is the building of the Roman City Archives. The interplay between the convex and concave elements of the dome and the façade, a unique inner courtyard with arcades on two floors is a precious oasis of peace and harmony that you can enjoy in this noisy and crowded part of Rome.

Sant'Eustachio Il Caffè

Behind Saint Ivo Alla Sapienza, there is another Roman coffee temple. It is called Caffè Sant'Eustacchio. You can order your espresso *al vetro*, which means it is going to be served in a small glass cup.

Palazzo Braschi – Museo di Roma ★

The palace is a beautiful example of Classicist architecture. After Napoleon's demise, Duke Luigi Braschi presided there as mayor. The Braschi family sold the palace to the state in 1871 after which it became the Ministry of Internal Affairs.

Palazzo Braschi – Museo di Roma
Address: Piazza di San Pantaleo 10, Roma
Online: http://museodiroma.it/en/sede/palazzo_braschi
Public transportation: Bus stop Corso Rinascimento: 30, 70, 81, 87, 116, 130F, 186, 492, 628, C3 or Corso Vittorio Emanuele – Navona: 46, 62, 64, 916, 916F

Opening hours: *see online*

During the Fascist regime these were the fascist headquarters. Today, Palazzo Braschi is the Museum of Rome.

If you are interested in history, furniture and art of Italian bourgeois from 18th to 20th century, you are at the right place.

Pasquino ★

Pasquino can be found near Palazzo Braschi, on Piazza Pasquino. This is the only remaining "talking statue" in Rome.

It is called the talking statue because satirical verses about the people in power have somehow appeared under

Sant'Eustachio Il Caffè
Address: Piazza di Sant'Eustacchio 82, Roma
Online: www.caffesanteustachio.com

Public transportation: Bus stop Corso Rinascimento: 30, 70, 81, 87, 116, 130F, 186, 492, 628, C3

Opening hours: *see online*

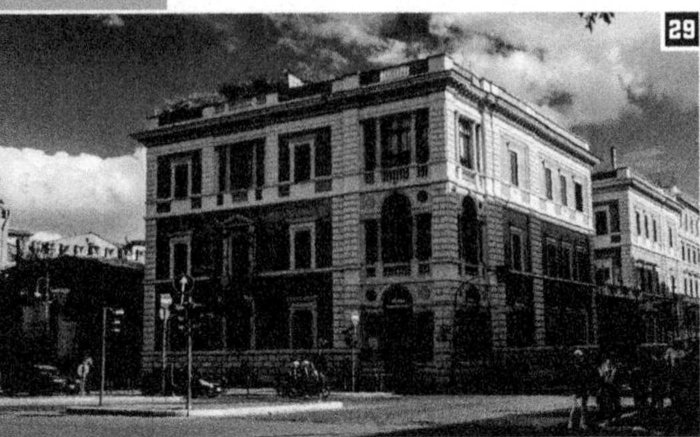

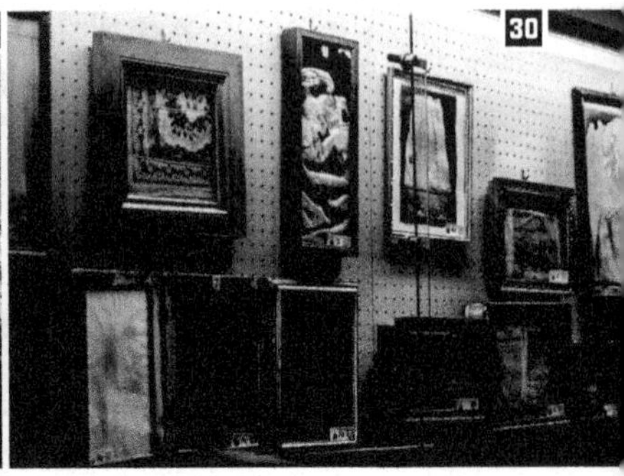

Museo Napoleonico | Napoleonic Museum
Address: Piazza di Ponte Umberto I 1, Roma
Online:
www.museonapoleonico.it/en

Public transportation: Bus stop Zanardelli: 30, 70, 81, 87, 130F, 492, 628

Opening hours: *see online*
Free entry to the permanent collection

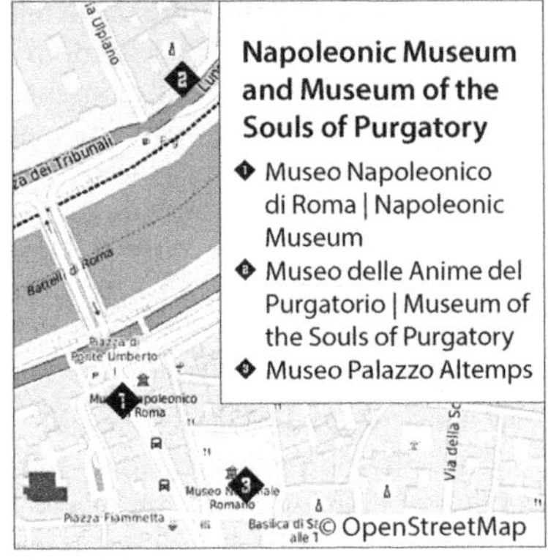

Napoleonic Museum and Museum of the Souls of Purgatory
❶ Museo Napoleonico di Roma | Napoleonic Museum
❷ Museo delle Anime del Purgatorio | Museum of the Souls of Purgatory
❸ Museo Palazzo Altemps

the statue, a common practice for over five centuries (1501 – today).

During the Papal State, satirical poems about the Pope and his government were published here. This is where the verse *Quod non fecerunt barbari, fecerunt Barberini*, meaning "What barbarians failed to do, Barberini actually did" was published.

Even today, the figure, what it represents and the writing around it has been an unruly sight for many important and powerful people.

⓰ Museo Napoleonico di Roma ★

The son of Count Pietro Primoli and Princess Charlotte Bonaparte Gabrielli, the daughter of Napoleon's younger brother Luciano, donated this remarkable collection of Napoleon's legacy to the city of Rome, together with the house so you can walk around Count Giuseppe Primoli's home (1851–1927) as if he himself had invited you over for tea. ⧆

⓱ Museo delle Anime del Purgatorio ★ ⧆

A Jesuit missionary Victor Jouët built the Neo-Gothic church of Sacro Cuore del Suffragio at the Tiber bank in the late 19th century, thanks to a lot of donations. It has a museum with handprints and soulprints of the unfortunate people stuck in purgatory who are trying to connect with the living. For years, Jouët collected these items going around Europe and recording confessions of those who had been contacted by the dead. Even though the museum consists of just one room, it is so memorable that it is worth a visit.

Sacro Cuore del Suffragio | Museum of the Souls of Purgatory
Address: Via Ulpiano 29, Roma
Online: www.romasegreta.it/prati/sacro-cuore-del-suffragio.html

Public transportation: Bus stop Zanardelli 30, 70, 81, 87, 130F, 492

Opening hours: *see online*

Campo de' Fiori

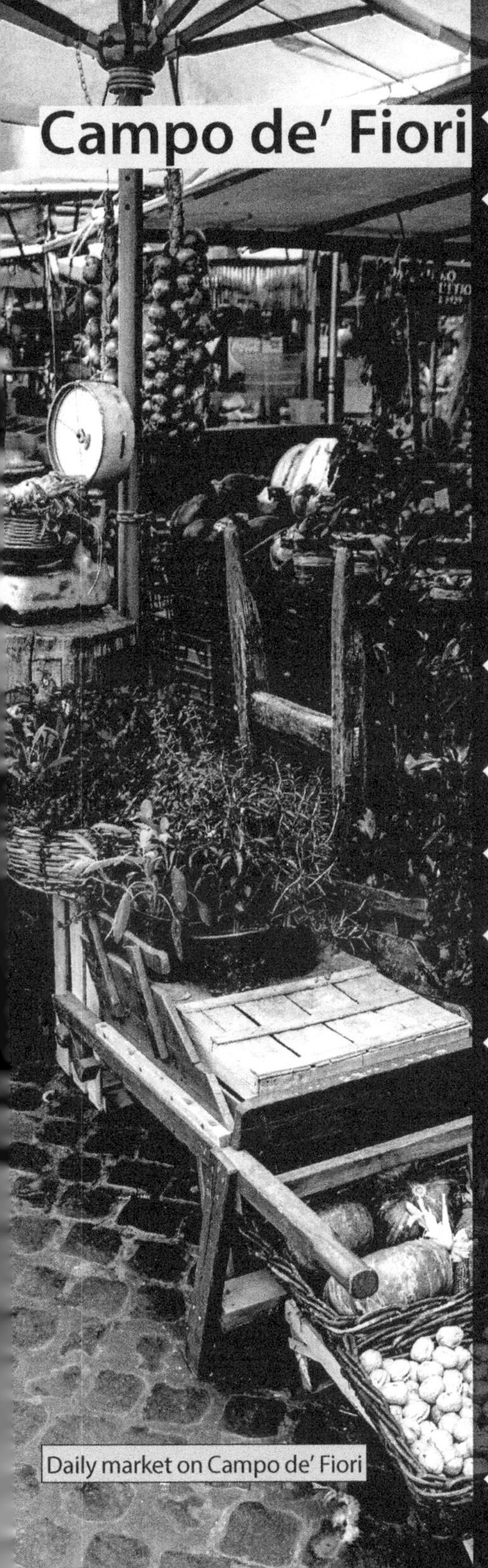

Daily market on Campo de' Fiori

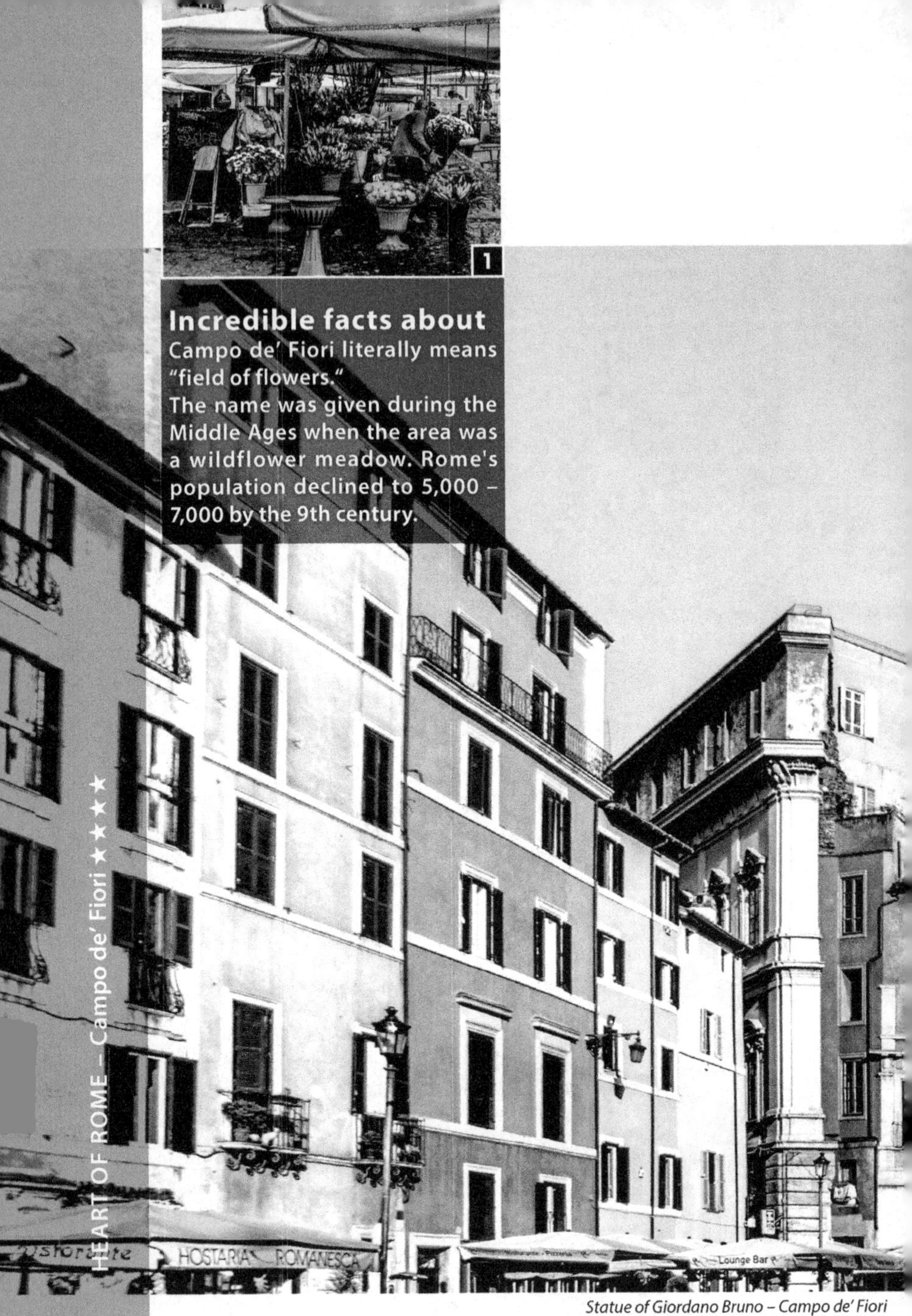

Incredible facts about

Campo de' Fiori literally means "field of flowers." The name was given during the Middle Ages when the area was a wildflower meadow. Rome's population declined to 5,000 – 7,000 by the 9th century.

Statue of Giordano Bruno – Campo de' Fiori

Extra Tip : : :
If you can hold for a little while longer, drink your cappuccino in the Bar del Cappuccino, the cappuccino temple of Rome, which is a little further away. [p.130]

Breakfast area away from the traffic noise

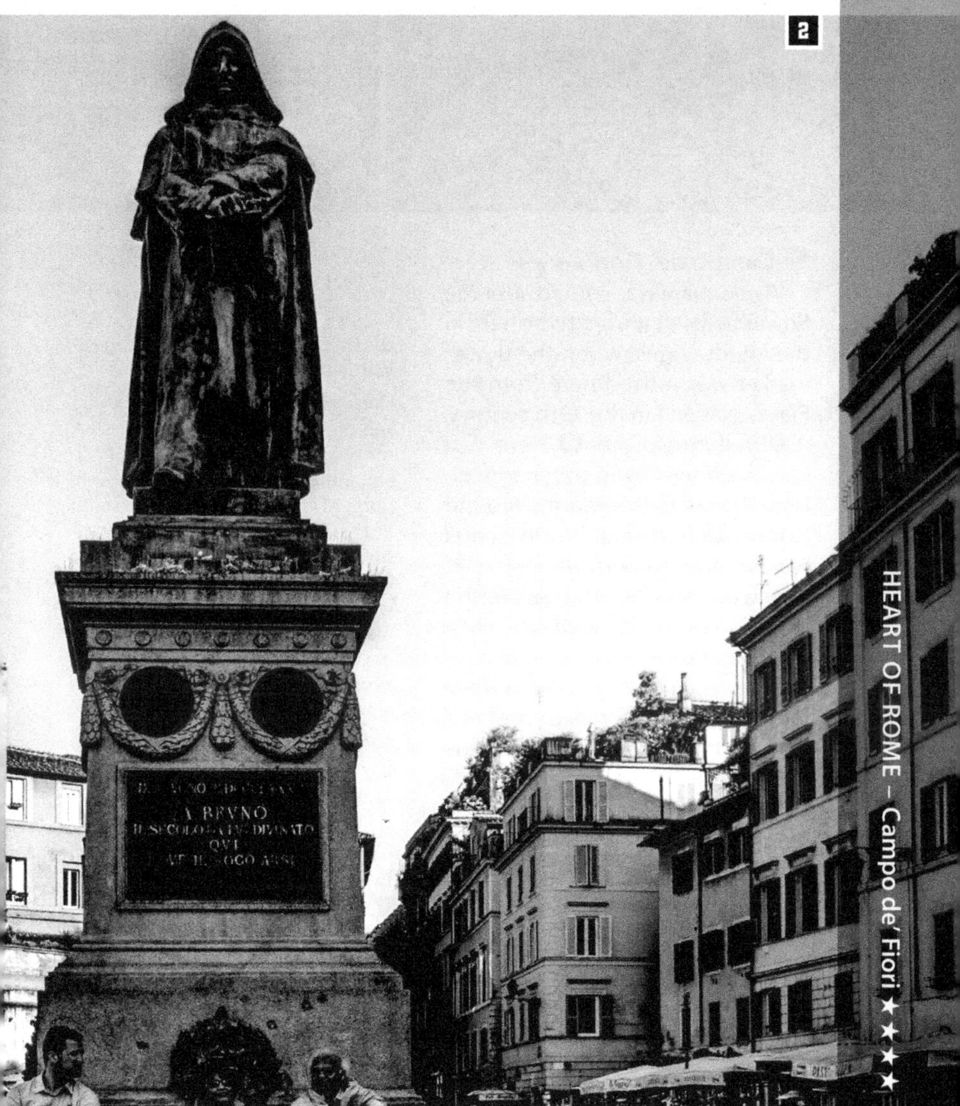

Piazza Campo de' Fiori
Address: Piazza Campo de' Fiori, Roma
Public transportation: Bus stop Corso Vittorio Emanuele – Sant'Andrea della Valle or Corso Vittorio Emanuele – Navona: 46, 62, 64, 916, 916F

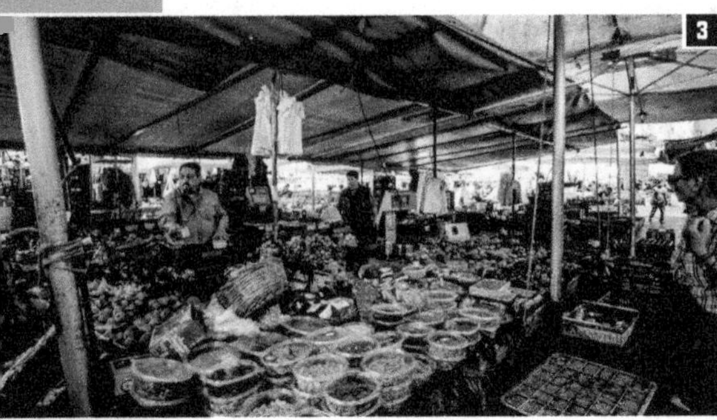

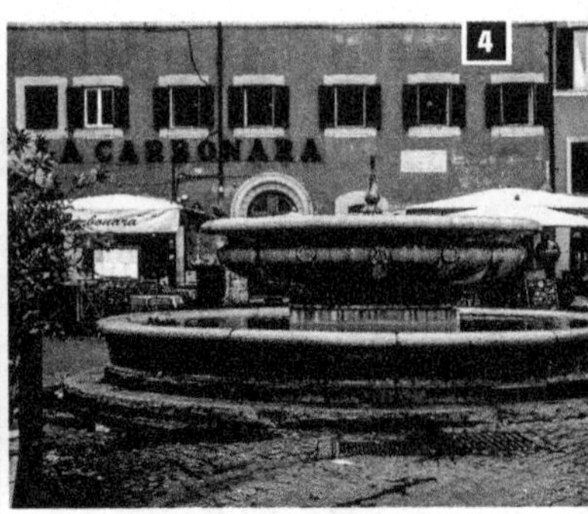

① Campo de' Fiori ★ ★ ★ ★

The square was named after the flower fields that used to be here in the Middle Ages. When the flower market was moved here from the Piazza Navona in the 19th century, it all fell into place. ③ Here you can buy flowers and other agricultural products from farms around Rome. ① There are numerous restaurants and cafés with terraces. Sitting and watching people passing by on a sunny day is practically a national sport.

If you can hold for a little while longer, do not have your coffee here. You will drink your cappuccino in the Bar del Cappuccino. Besides, people in Italy drink coffee after breakfast. On and around Campo de' Fiori there are plenty of opportunities to grab your morning snack. ⑤

This square has never had a strict architectural structure. Since the Middle Ages, Via dei Balestrari (Crossbow Maker Street), Via dei Baullari (Luggage Maker Street), Via dei Cappellari (Hatter Street), Via dei Chiavari (Locksmith Street) and Via dei Giubbonari (Tailor Street) have converged onto this square.

A copy of an antique fountain called Fontana *La Terrina* (Soupbowl) is also on this square. ④

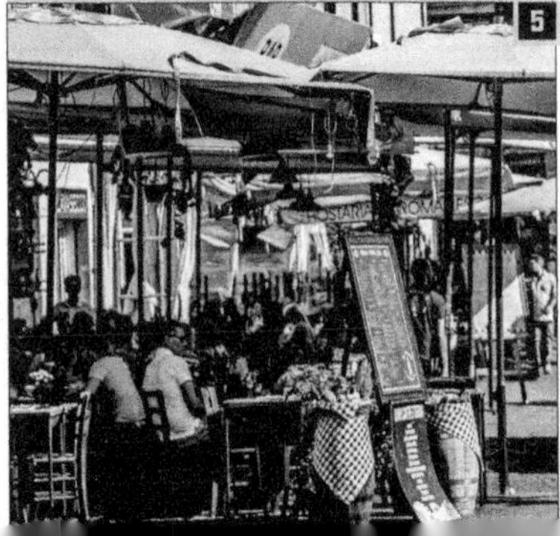

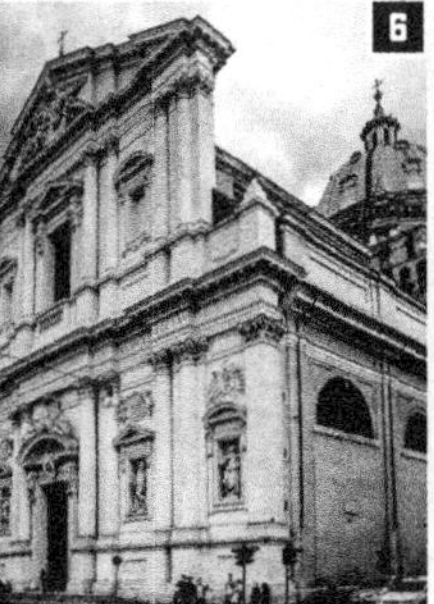

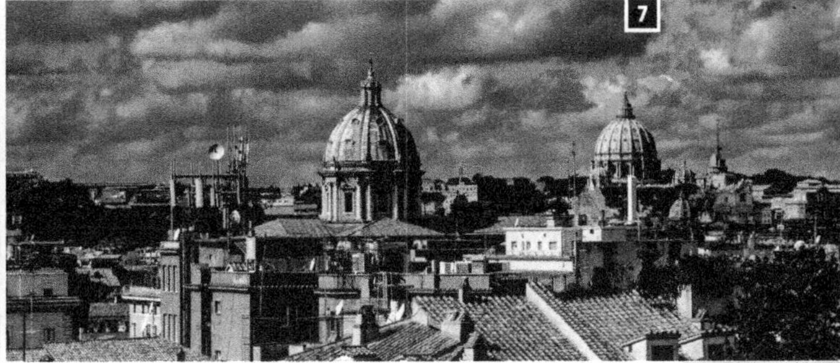

Walk around Campo de' Fiori

❷ **Sant'Andrea della Valle ★★**

If you come to the Campo de' Fiori from Largo di Torre Argentina, do not miss the chance to go to the monumental Sant'Andrea della Valle Church, which was an inspiration for Giacomo Puccini's first act of Tosca. In the second act, the story takes place at Palazzo Farnese [p.128], while the third act occurs at the upper levels of Castel Sant'Angelo [p.168]. Besides, the dome of this church is the second highest dome, after Michelangelo's dome of St. Peter's Basilica. The church was started during early Baroque and finished in the late baroque period, 1590–1650. Initially, the architects were Giacomo della Porta and Giovanni Francesco Grimaldi, followed by Carlo Maderno and Carlo Rainaldi.

Sant'Andrea della Valle
Address: Corso Vittorio Emanuele II 6, Roma
Online: www.vicariatusurbis.org

Public transportation: Bus stop Corso Vittorio Emanuelle - Sant'Andrea della Valle: 46, 62, 64, 916, 916F

Opening hours: daily 7:30 a.m. – 12:30 p.m., 4:30 – 8 p.m.

6 **7** **9**

◇ **The dom of the church**

Two of Caracci's pupils, Giovanni Lanfranco and Domenichino, painted the frescoes on the dome. The dome itself was painted by Lanfranco using the "Glory of paradise" motive, while Domenichino painted the four evangelists, directly below the dome.

Campo de' Fiori

❶ Campo de' Fiori
❷ Sant'Andrea della Valle
❸ Museo di Scultura Antica Giovanni Barracco
❹ Palazzo della Cancelleria
❺ Palazzo Farnese
❻ Via Giulia
❼ Bakery and pizzeria Antico Forno Roscioli
❽ Restaurant Da Pancrazio

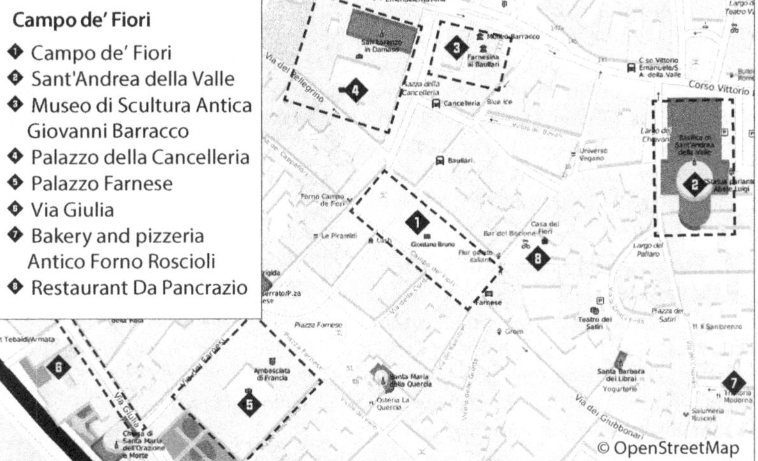

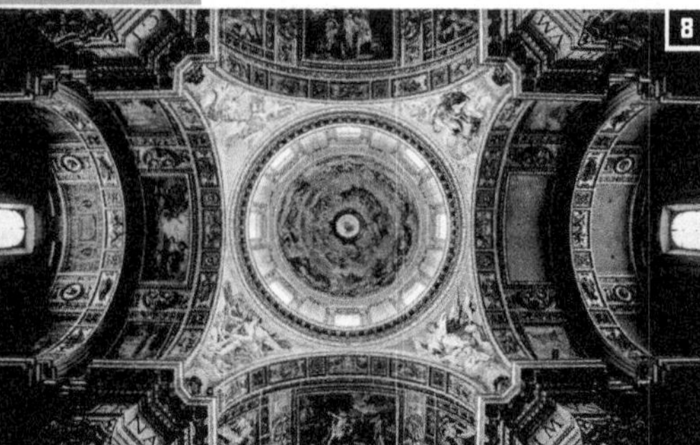

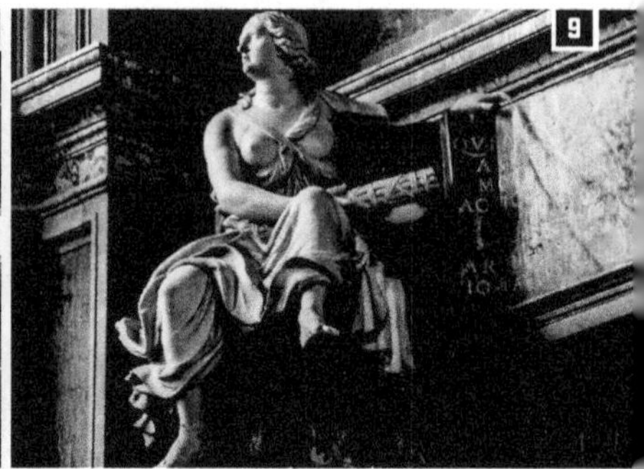

There are several chapels worth visiting:

② Ginetti Chapel

It is the first chapel on the right, designed by Carlo Fontana in 1670. Antonio Raggi, Bernini's pupil, made the relief of *Angel urges sacred family to flee to Egypt* (1675).

③ Strozzi Chapel

The second chapel on the right, designed by Michelangelo and executed by Leone Strozzi.

④ Chapel Barberini

It is the last chapel on the left. It was designed by Matteo Castelli according to soon-to-be Pope Urban VIII's wishes, from the Barberini family. The chapel is a crucial transitional point in art history from Mannerism to early Baroque. On the left, furthest away from visitors, there is Pietro Bernini's sculpture of Saint John the Baptist (1616). The artist was Lorenzo Bernini's father. There is also a pair of putti, also made by Bernini senior. Tombstones belonging to both popes from the Piccolomini family, Pius II and Pius III can be found at the end of the main nave. The building of the church was largely financed by the Piccolomini family trust.

⑤ Fontana di Piazza Sant'Andrea della Valle ★

On the little square opposite the church, there is a fountain made by Carlo Maderno, by the commission of Pope Paul V in 1614. Until the 20th century the fountain was in the Borgo district and supplied water to the local community and pilgrims. It has been here since 1958. The marble basin was replaced by a concrete one, but the pedestal is still original. 🗓

◆ Museo di Scultura Antica Giovanni Barracco ★★★ 🔟

This is certainly one of the most beautiful small museums in Rome.

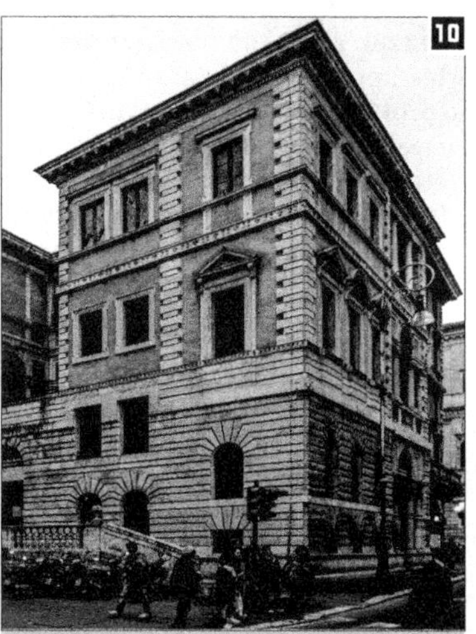

Museo di Scultura Antica Giovanni Barracco
Address: Corso Vittorio Emanuele 166/A, Roma
Online: http://museobarracco.it/en

Public transportation:
Bus stop Corso Vittorio Emanuele – Navona: 46, 62, 64, 916, 916F

Opening hours: *see online*

Free entry to the permanent collection

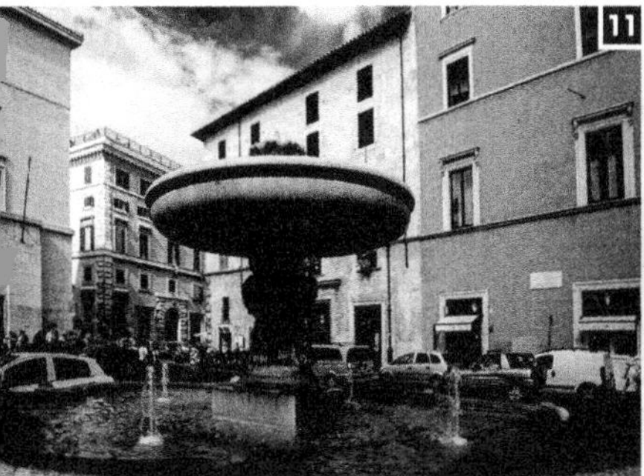

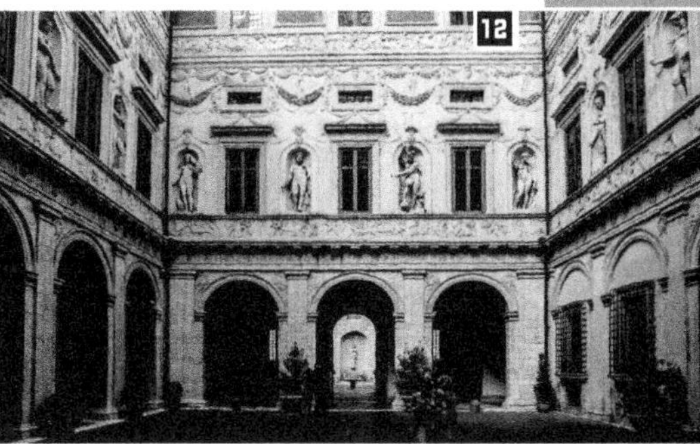

The collection may be small in size, but it features exquisite exhibits. There are some of the most wonderful artifacts from Old Egypt, Assyria, Etruria, Phoenicia and Classical Greece, as well as Roman sculptures and early medieval mosaics. The museum itself is a Renaissance palace from 1523 with many original decorative elements from the time when the French prelate Thomas Le Roy had it built. Apart from French royal lilies which are everywhere, you will have the unique opportunity of walking on amazing tiles from that period.

❹ Palazzo della Cancelleria ★ ★ ★

This palace made history as the first Roman palace constructed according to Renaissance principles from the ground up (1489–1513). The name, Palazzo della Cancelleria, refers to the Papal Chancellery, that is, the office of the Roman Curia that it used to accommodate.

Even today, the palace still belongs to the Holy See, as one of its ex-territorial properties, meaning outside the Vatican itself. The architects of this palace are listed as Donato Bramante, Andrea Bregno and Baccio Pontelli. Apart from the façade, which was divided according to the golden ratio and became a model for later renaissance façades, there are several other elements worth a look.

First of all, Bramante's inner courtyard with arches supported by 44 original columns taken from the Theater of Pompey. The columns, made of Egyptian granite, used to support the arches of the auditorium.

In general, most of the stones used for making the palace were harvested from the ruins of the Theater of Pompey.

This palace has also taken a whole church under its wings and that is the church of San Lorenzo in Damaso, one of the first early Christian churches in Rome (380).

In the 5th century it used to be located on the Martian Field, next to another church called San Lorenzo in Lucina. You can access the Church of San Lorenzo in Damaso through a door on the right. There is also a museum with faithful reproductions of machines designed by Leonardo da Vinci, made of wood. In the hall of *Salone dei Cento Giorni* or the "Hall of a hundred days", there is a giant fresco painted in a hundred days by the Tuscan architect and the first art historian Giorgio Vasari, with the help of his assistants in 1546.

When he proudly presented it to his friend and fellow countryman Michelangelo and pointed out that it was painted in only a hundred days, Michelangelo briefly replied by saying *si vede bene*, meaning, that's what it looks like.

Palazzo Spada & Galleria Spada
Address: Vicolo del Polverone 15B, Roma
Online: www.galleriaspada.beniculturali.it

Public transportation:
Bus stop Corso Vittorio - Sant'Andrea della Valle: 46, 62, 64, 916, 916F

Opening hours: *see online*

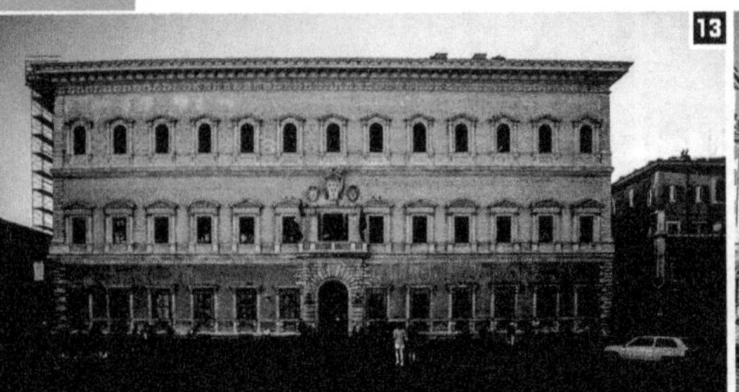

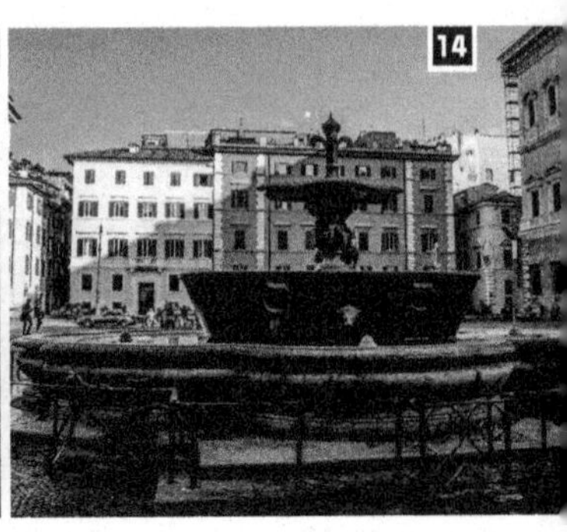

⑤ Palazzo Spada ★ ★ 🔟

The Renaissance palace Palazzo Spada was passed on to Cardinal Bernandino Spada in 1623 and the new owner ordered it to be redecorated by Borromini. Francesco Borromini reimagined the façade and created the most well-known optical illusion from the Mannerist period. When you walk into the palace courtyard, look to the left and you will see a long hallway with columns. Although the colonnade is only 26 ft (8 m) long, to the viewer it looks as if it is 121 ft (37 m) long. The sculpture at the end of the hall is only 2 ft (0.6 m) tall. To execute this optical illusion, Borromini hired a mathematician who calculated the exact proportions. This palace also has an interesting and valuable collection of ancient statues and paintings from the 16th and 17th century, including works by Andrea del Sarto, Guido Reni, Titian, Jan Brueghel the Elder, Guercino, Rubens, Dürer, Caravaggio, Domenichino, Carracci, Parmigianino and others.

⑥ Palazzo Farnese ★ ★ ★ 🔟

This is one of the most opulent and relevant renaissance palaces in Rome. Cardinal Alessandro Farnese ordered it in 1514 from Antonio da Sangallo the Younger.

This was exactly 20 years before the cardinal would become Pope Paul III. When the architect died, he was replaced by Michelangelo. Accentuating the balconies above the entrance, the large crest of Pope Paul III and the *piano nobile*, the floor above the one at street level, were all Michelangelo's ideas. He also added another floor. After Michelangelo, the palace was placed in the hands of Jacopo da Vignola, and the façade overlooking the Tiber was completed by Giacomo della Porta in 1589. Extraordinary frescoes that covered the entire palace cannot be seen today. In 1936, Benito Mussolini rented the palace to France for 99 years, for a symbolic amount. France is still a reliable lessee. The rent has risen to 1€ a month and this is the building of the French Embassy in Italy. There are two tubs from the Baths of Caracalla on the square in front of the palace. They were brought here while the palace was being built and then turned into fountains. 🔟 Michelangelo's plan was to open the Palazzo Farnese through the gardens towards the Tiber and link it via bridge with the other palace in possession of the Farnese family on the other side of the river. That plan was never executed. All that we have is a bridge arching over Via Giulia. 🔟

⑦ Via Giulia ★ ★ ★

Via Giulia, named after Pope Julius II or Giulio II in Italian, is a street designed in 1508.

Palazzo Farnese
Address: Piazza Farnese 67, Roma
Online: www.ambafrance-it.org

Public transportation: Bus stop Corso Vittorio Emanuele – Navona 46, 62, 64, 916, 916F

Opening hours: *see online*

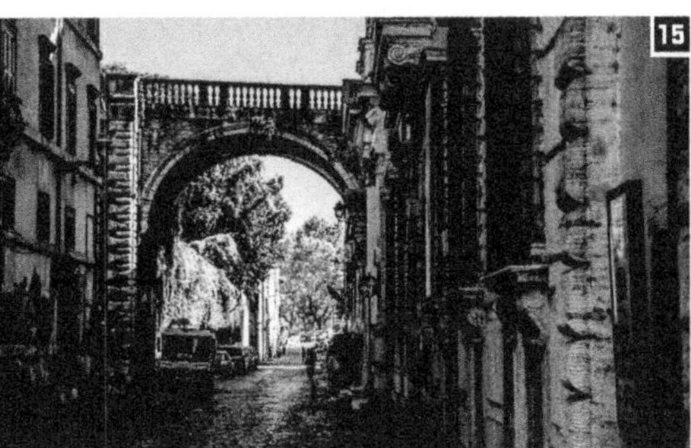

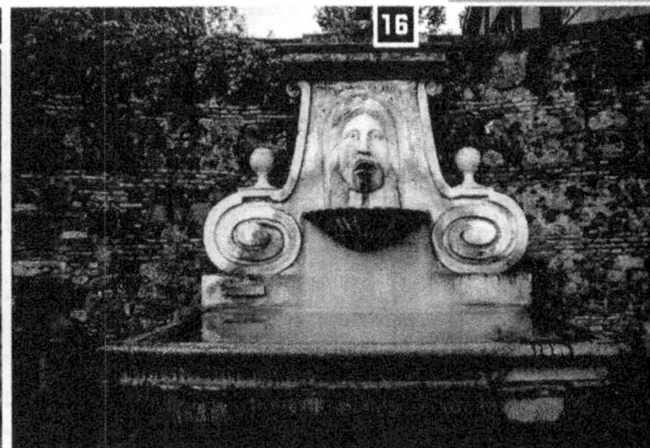

The Pope from the della Rovere family consulted the main architect of the new St. Peter's Basilica, Donato Bramante. In this street, there are several churches of once sovereign states: Florence, Siena, Spain and Armenia, among others. Do not be surprised if you notice members of the special police forces on the street. What used to be a medieval prison in Via Giulia is now the headquarters of the anti-mafia commission for entire Italy. There are several interesting antique stores as well. Also, Via Giulia is one of the most exclusive residential addresses in Rome.

① La Fontana del Mascherone ★

Left of Michelangelo's bridge, there is Fontana del Mascherone or the Mask Fountain. It has a lily, symbol of the Farnese family. During grand celebrations, such as announcing the Head of the Maltese Order in 1720, there would be wine flowing instead of water all night long from the mouth of the mask. 🔟

② Santa Maria dell'Orazione e Morte

Right next to Michelangelo's bridge, there is the Church of Saint Mary of the Prayer and Death, built in late 16th and early 17th century. The shape provides a feeling of harmony and calm, but this church has some other interesting features. First of all, there is a chapel decorated with human bones. A large number of skulls were used as decoration — there is a big, skull-encrusted cross, and even the candelabra are made of bones. The chapel is left of the main altar and if you are lucky, it should be open to visitors when you are around. It's always worth a try.

③ Palazzo Falconieri ★ 🔟

Next to the Church of Santa Maria dell'Orazione e Morte, there is a white palace called Falconieri from the 16th century, presently the Hungarian Academy. It was adapted by Borromini in the 17th century. There are entrances both from Via Giulia and Lungotevere dei Vallati, the latter separates the palace from the Tiber. It is on this side that Borromini added a baroque façade and a belvedere with a magnificent view over the Tiber and Trastevere.

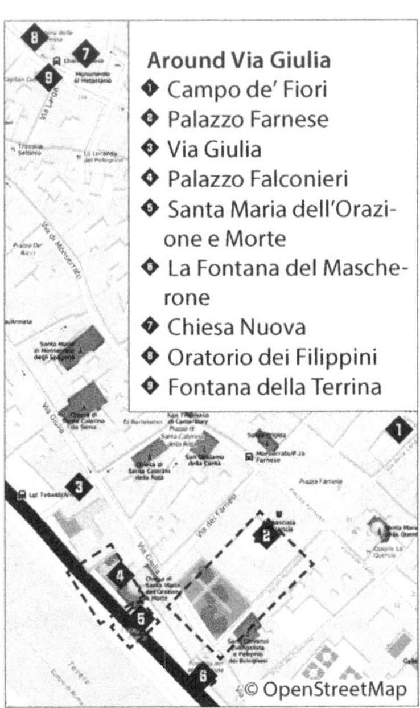

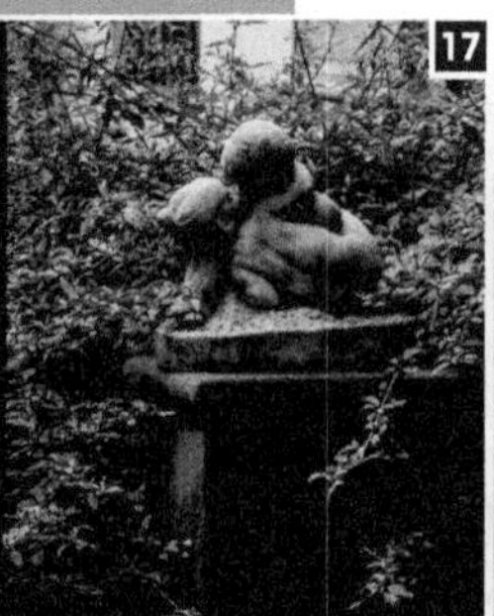

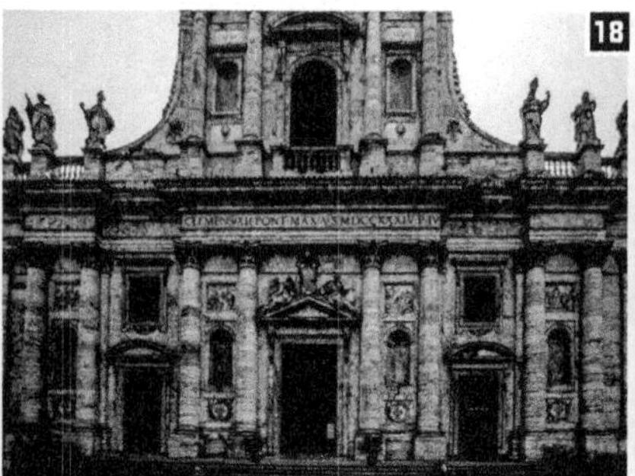

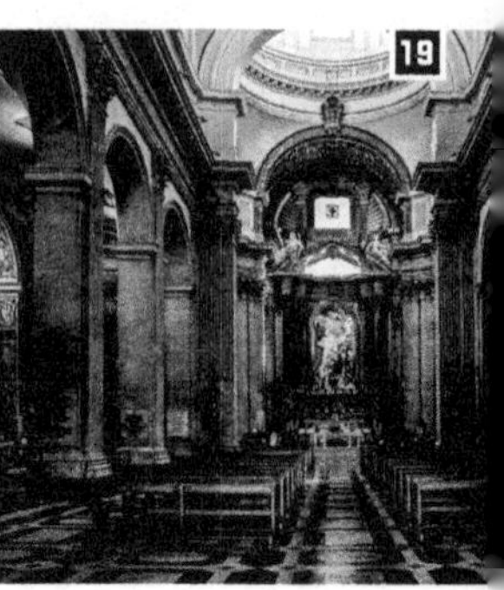

④ San Giovanni Battista dei Fiorentini ★★ 18

The most relevant one is San Giovanni dei Fiorentini, where Via Giulia meets Via del Consolato. There were several attempts at building the church in the 16th century, most notably by Jacopo Sansovino, Vignola and Michelangelo.

The project only came to life when it was taken over by Giacomo della Porta in late 16th century and completed in the 17th century, hence the baroque appearance. The aside was made by Pietro da Cortona, while the altar is the work of Francecso Borromini. He is buried under the dome of this church. 19

❽ Bar del Cappuccino ★★★ 20

From Via Giulia, you will go to Ponte Sisto in Lungotevere dei Vallati. Keep going until you reach Ponte Garibaldi. Turn to Via Arenula, just following the tram tracks. At Via Arenula 50, which you would probably miss in any other case, you will find the best cappuccino in Rome. Romans would probably add in the world, too. Bar del Cappuccino is run by a family, a father, mother and daughter.

It is unpretentious, as if the walls were not full of news clippings and pictures for one reason and one reason only — their unique cappuccino.

The coffee here is strong and rich. The milk is creamy and appears on the surface in the shape of a fan, apple or whatever the owner prefers.

Service is unostentatious and relaxed. You can combine cappuccino perfectly with a *croissant con crema*. Naturally, the croissants are also dangerously delicious.

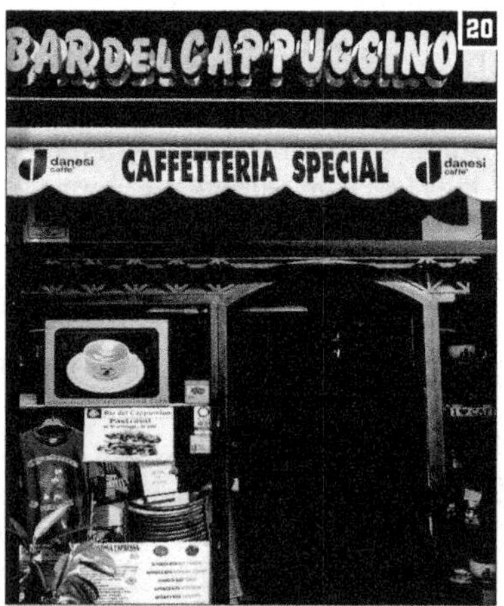

San Giovanni Battista dei Fiorentini
Address: Piazza dell'Oro 1, Roma
Online: www.sangiovannibattistade-ifiorentini.it

Public transportation:
Bus stop Ponte Vittorio Emanuele: 34, 40, 46, 62, 64, 190F, 916, 916F, 982

Opening hours: *see online*

Bar del Cappuccino
Address: Via Arenula 50, Roma

Public transportation: Tram stop Arenula – Ministero Grazia E Giustizia 8 | Bus stop Lungotevere de' Cenci – Arenula 23, 63, 280, 810

Opening hours:
Mon – Sun: 6 a.m. – 5 p.m.

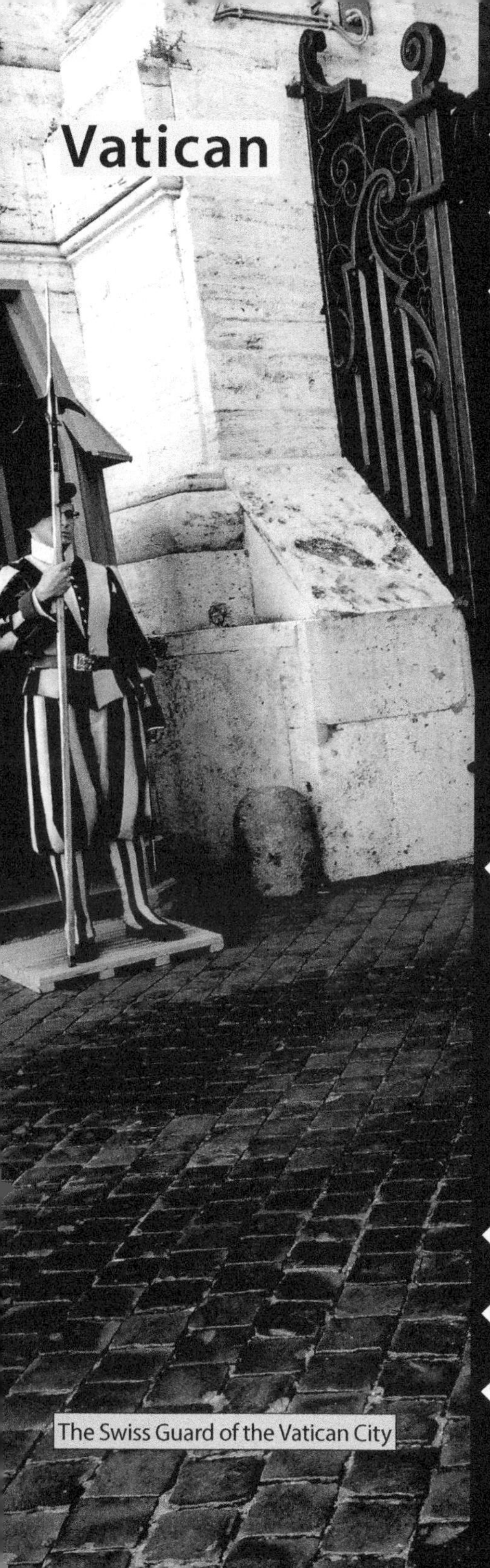

Vatican

The Swiss Guard of the Vatican City

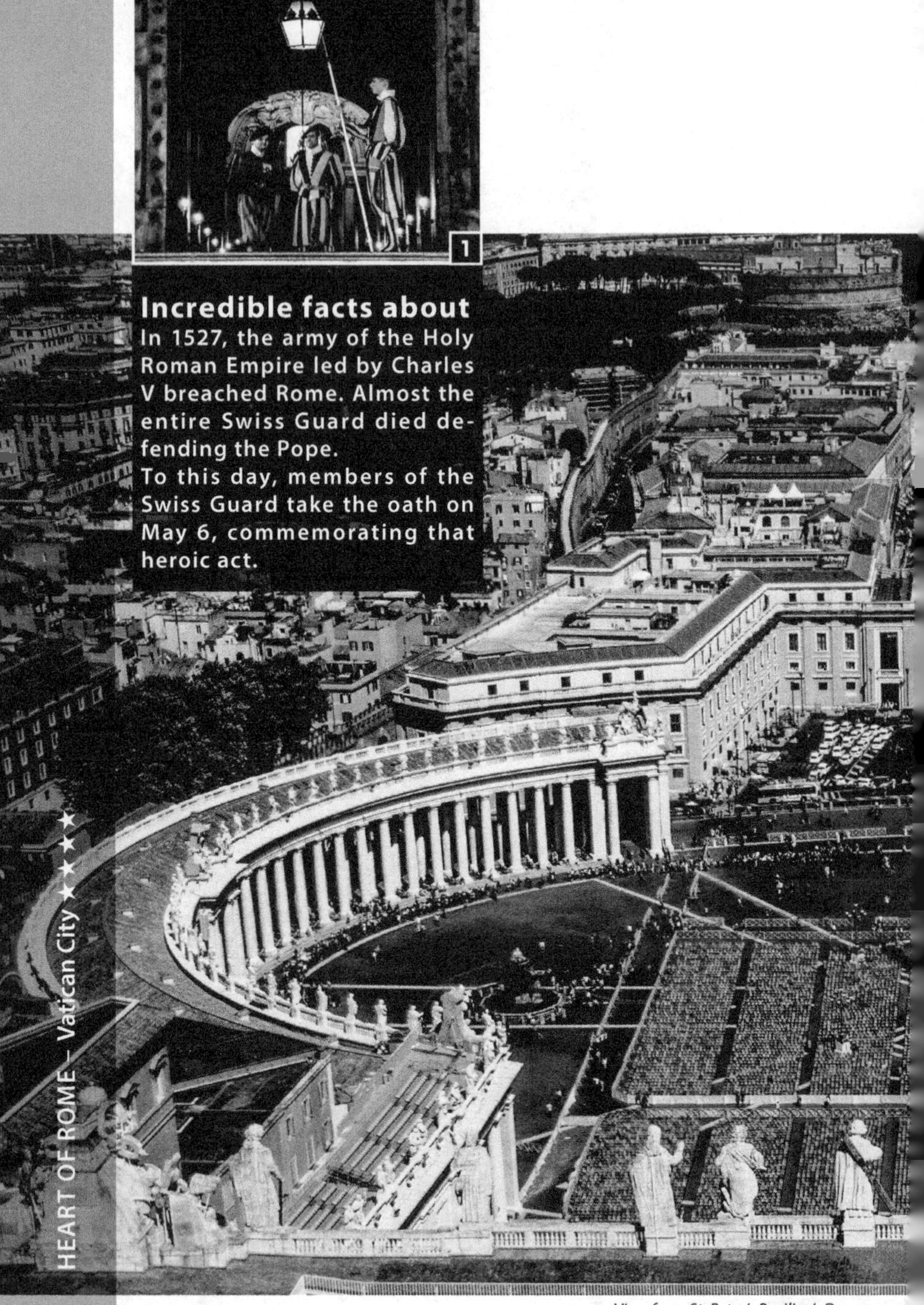

Incredible facts about
In 1527, the army of the Holy Roman Empire led by Charles V breached Rome. Almost the entire Swiss Guard died defending the Pope.
To this day, members of the Swiss Guard take the oath on May 6, commemorating that heroic act.

View from St. Peter's Basilica's Dome

Extra Tip : : :
From the roof of St. Peter's Basilica, there is a panoramic view of the Vatican. Next to the porch is the entrance to the roof. You have two options for climbing. There are 551 steps to climb or you can take the elevator and then you have 320 steps left.

Art of miracles and and miracle of arts

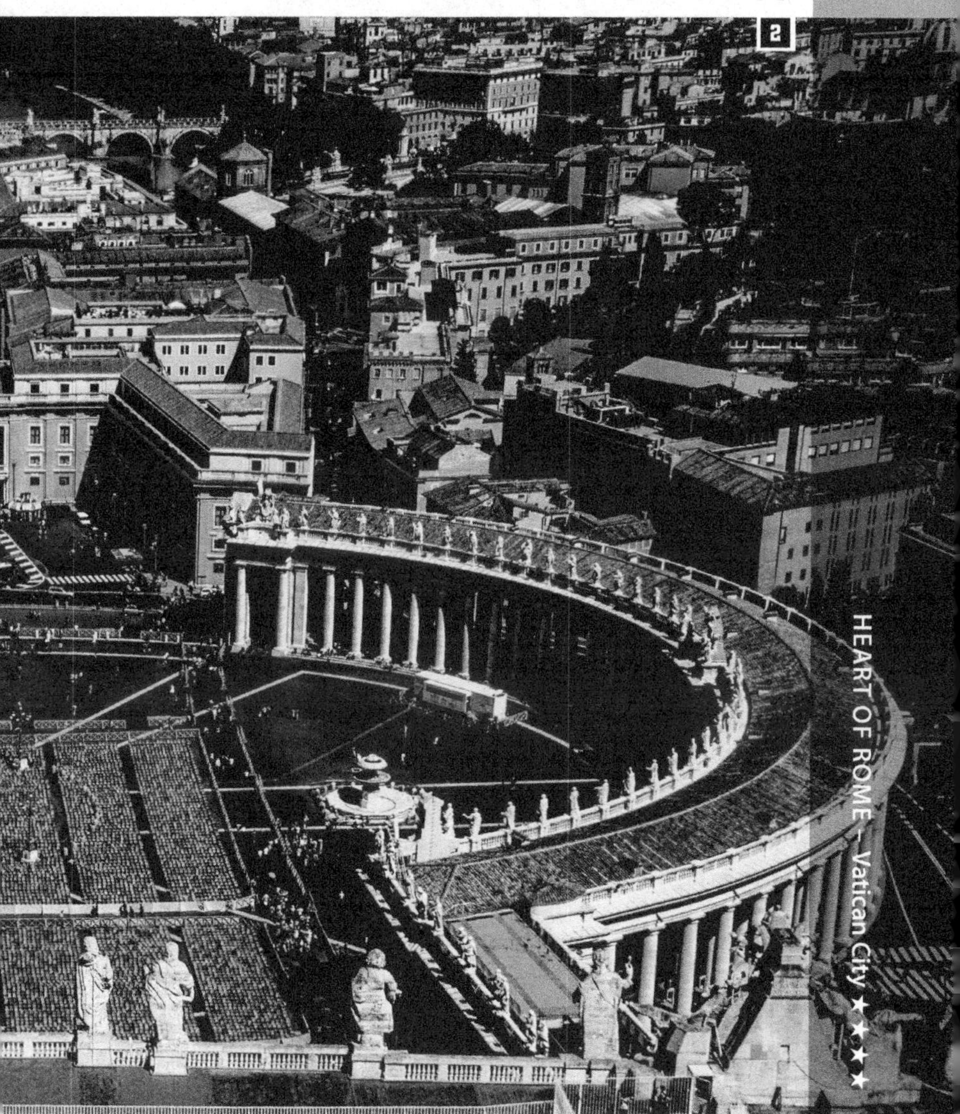

Vatican City

Address: Vatican City

Public transportation: Metro A stop Ottaviano | Bus stop Largo Di Porta Cavalleg-geri – Fornaci: 64 or stop Porta Pinciana: 116 | Tram stop Risorgimento – San Pietro: 19

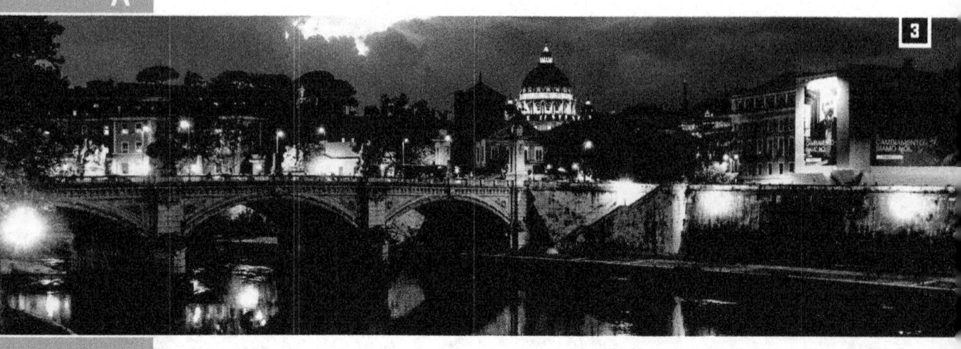

◆ Vatican City ★★★★ 4

In the middle of Rome is Vatican City. The Vatican is the smallest internationally recognized country. It covers 109 acres or 44 hectares.

For the most part, it is separated by a tall wall from the rest of Rome.

◆ St. Peter's Square ★★★★

This is one of the most monumental squares in Europe. The square is 787 ft (240 m) wide and 1,115 ft (340 m) long. 3 It is an example of baroque design and symmetry. 6

It was made by a great Baroque artist and architect, Gian Lorenzo Bernini. Pope Alexander VII asked Bernini to design a monumental square in front of St. Peter's Basilica in 1656, taking into account the already existing structures. We are talking about two things.

First, a fountain made by Domenico Fontana in 1586 and an obelisk, which was brought to the square that same year and has not been moved since. 9 Besides, pilgrims needed to have a clear view of the Benedictine Lodge, where the pope gives his blessing *urbi et orbi* or "to the City [of Rome] and to the World". 8

Obelisk

Keeping the obelisk on St. Peter's Square was also theologically relevant. 10

Did you know?

History of Vatican City (1929 – today)

After 59 years of captivity, since popes claimed the Papal State to be non-existent from 1870 to 1929, the Vatican City was established on February 11, 1929 under the Lateran Treaty and exists to this day. 2

Vatican citizenship is reserved for a little over 800 people and only half of them actually live in the Vatican. Diplomats, cardinals who live in Rome, as well as members of the Swiss Guard automatically become citizens of the Vatican, but they stop being citizens once they leave the service. Citizenship is not hereditary, and being born in the Vatican is not a criterion for obtaining citizenship. Every day, around 800 people live and work in the Vatican, either with a residential permit or as citizens.

The Vatican hasn't had it own army since 1970. Approximately 130 members of the Vatican Police protect the law and order in the Vatican. In addition, there are 111 members of the Swiss Guard in charge of pope's protection who oversee major points in the Vatican. 1

According to the Lateran Treaty, if a person loses Vatican citizenship, and has no other citizenship, they automatically become Italian citizens. Extraterritorial areas of the Vatican are also regulated by this treaty.

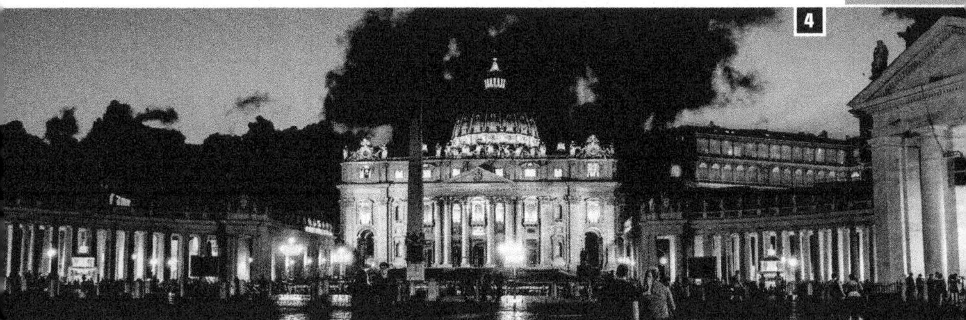

It used to be in the center of Nero's Circus, where Peter the Apostle was killed. The point of execution for Christian martyrs was *inter duas metas*, which means "between the two farthest points" of the stadium.

Originally, that is where this obelisk was placed.

In his book, *Della transportatione dell' obelisco Vaticano e delle fabriche di Sisto V* (Rome, 1590), Domenico Fontana describes this delicate engineering feat, which required 150 horses and 900 people. With the utmost synchronization, they pulled the obelisk which was hooked to forty-seven wires. For thirteen months – day in and day out.

On the base of the obelisk, there is a Latin inscription *Dominicus Fontana ex pago Mili agri Novocomenis transtulit et erexit* or "Domenico Fontana, from Melida county, New Como, transported and erected this obelisk at this location." This is the only obelisk in Rome that has never been torn down.

The gilded ball which used to be on top, allegedly containing Caesar's ashes, was removed and opened by Fontana. When he looked inside, there was nothing but dust. The ball is on display at the Capitoline Hill Museum. The legend of Caesar's ashes spread in the Middle Ages, thanks to the inscription on the pedestal:

DIVO CAESARI DIVI IULII F AUGUSTO

To the divine Caesar Augustus, son of the divine Gaius Julius Caesar

TI CAESARI DIVI AUGUSTI F AUGUSTO SACRUM

To Tiberius Caesar Augustus, son of the divine Augustus (this obelisk) is dedicated.

The largest sundial in the world

On the square, there are markings and circles with special meaning. In the nineteenth century, round stone signs were put on the ground and the shadow of the obelisk moves across them at noon depending on the season. So, this square is also the largest sundial in the world. **11**

Bernini's colonnades

According to Bernini's plans, there are two colonnades on the edges of the square. They frame the elliptical square. **14**

There are four rows of Doric columns in each colonnade. **17** **18** Bernini explained they are meant to look like hands reaching out to embrace the pilgrims in the middle of the square, just like the Church embraces its congregation. There is a fountain on each side of the obelisk. **15**

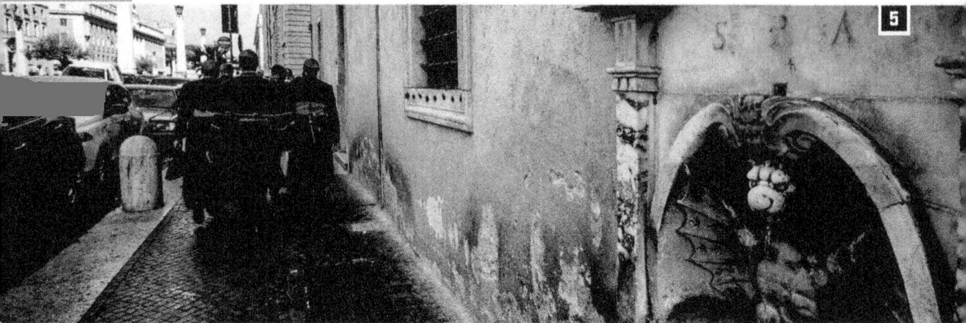

Two white stones mark the points from which you can observe Bernini's masterpiece. If you step on one of these stones, the illusion will be complete. From that point, the quadruple colonnade looks like a single row of columns, because the other rows are perfectly hidden behind the front row. 🔟

You can access the square or leave it going through Via della Conciliazione, which is connected to the Castle St. Angelo. 🔟 🔟 When the Vatican signed the Lateran Treaty with Italy in 1929, Bernini's colonnades became the state border between the Vatican City and Italy.

◆ ❸ St. Peter's Basilica ★★★★ 🔟

St. Peter's Basilica is the largest and also the longest church in the world. It was built on the foundations of the old St. Peter's Church from 326, while Constantine the Great was the emperor.

Allegedly, this is also the location of St. Peter's grave, which is why this spot was chosen in the first place. The construction lasted from 1506 to 1626. It was built by the most prominent architects and artists of the time. Chief architects and interior designers were employed, including Donato Bramante, Raphael Santi, Michelangelo Buonarroti, Giacomo Vignola, Carlo Maderno, Francesco Borromini and Lorenzo Bernini.

Pope Julius II placed the foundation stone in 1506 below what was to become the base of Veronica's Column. The most valuable relic of the Catholic Church was meant to be stored in it, Veronica's veil. According to a legend, Veronica gave Jesus her veil and he wiped his face during the Way of Cross and his face was imprinted on the veil.

Each new architect, as well as the pope, had their own vision of the main Catholic church. Bramante, for instance, designed a church shaped like a Greek cross, i.e., with all the arms of equal length. Michelangelo kept the Greek cross, adding an antechamber in front of the square. 🔟 🔟

Carlo Maderno added more length to the antechamber, creating a longitudinal nave and a monumental baroque façade, which we can see today. Five doors lead into the basilica. 🔟

The doors on the very right are called the Holy Door and they are only open during the Holy Years. 🔟

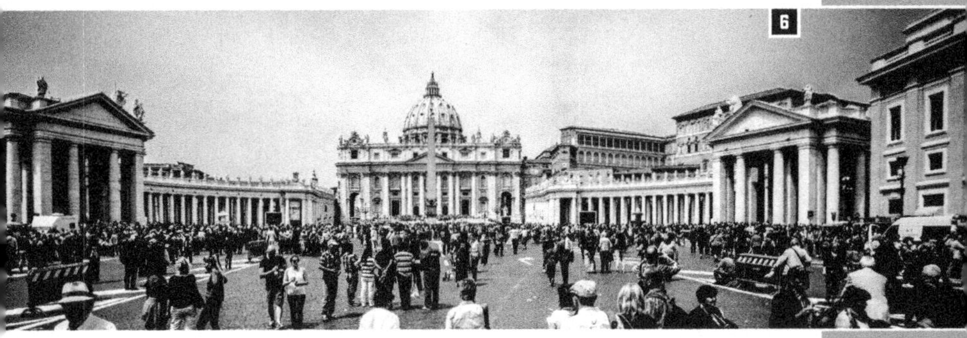

On the inside, this 692 ft (211 m) long and 433 ft (132 m) tall building can hold up to 20,000 people. The nave is 452 ft (138 m) long and 88 ft (27 m) wide. **23**

The lateral nave is also 452 ft (138 m) long. There are forty-five altars. Even though the proportions are gigantic, they are meant to be impressive, rather than intimidating. **24**

The interior is full of marble reliefs and sculptures. **26 27** There are over a hundred graves, ninety-one of which belong to the popes. Apart from that, there are many sculptures in the niches and chapels all over the basilica. **46**

① Pietà ★★★★ **30**

After stepping into the basilica, there is Michelangelo's Pietà on the right, which he sculptured when he was twenty-five years old.

During Michelangelo's first visit to Rome (1496–1501), French Cardinal Jean de Billheres contacted him and requested a marble Pietà for his grave. Marble Pietàs had not been made in Italy until then, so Michelangelo accepted the challenge.

The contract clearly stipulated that the statue should contain the Virgin Mary in clothes, holding the dying Christ in her hands. The contract also stated that the monument should be the most beautiful statue in Rome.

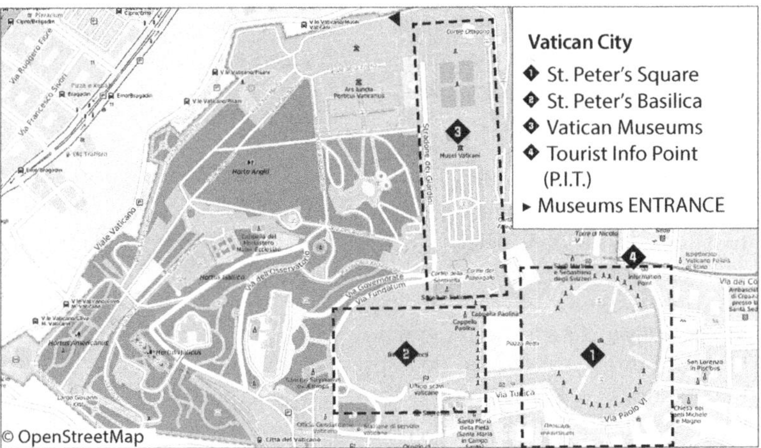

HEART OF ROME – Vatican City ★★★★

137

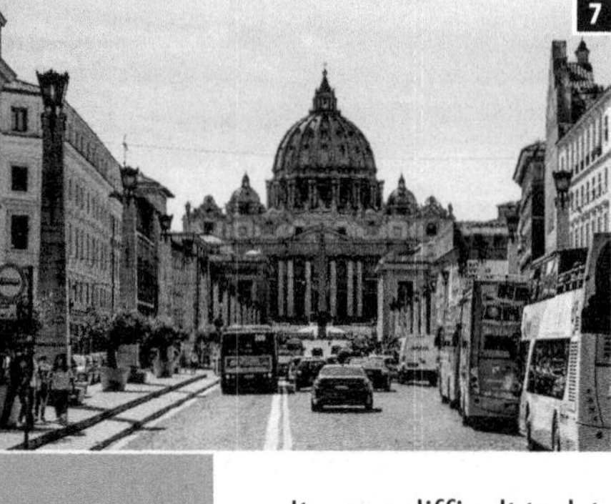

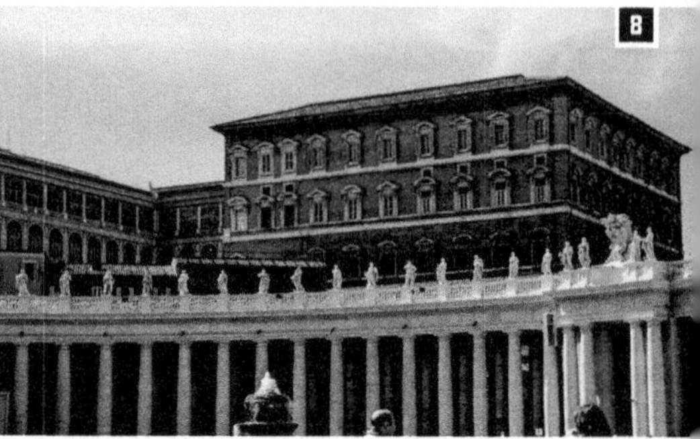

It was a difficult task to fulfill in a city packed with ancient masterpieces. After completion, the artist would receive the rest of the total sum (450 florins in total, more than $65,000). Michelangelo went to Carrara to pick out the marble himself and oversaw the transport personally. He made the sculpture in less than two years. In the meantime, the cardinal who commissioned the statue passed away. However, since the church in which he was buried was demolished to build the new St. Peter's Basilica, the Pietà was placed in the old St. Peter's Basilica. It has been at this location since 1749, in the so-called "Chapel of Pietà."

Controversial proportions

Michelangelo shortened Christ's body and made it smaller than Mary's, so that it does not seem too heavy.

Composition and perspective play an important part in covering up this trick, along with rich drapery flowing from the Virgin Mary. All this contributes to the effect of lightness while she is holding the body of Christ.

According to humanist principles of the renaissance, Christ looks like he is sleeping and practically all the signs of martyrdom are absent. There is no stigma on his left foot, and the wounds from the thorn crown are also gone.

Controversy of the age difference

There is another controversy that draws attention after watching these two figures for a while. **31**

The Virgin Mary is very young. Not only is she nowhere near fifty, she actually looks a lot younger than her thirty-three-year-old son. Perhaps Michelangelo was inspired by the first verses of Canto 33 of Dante's

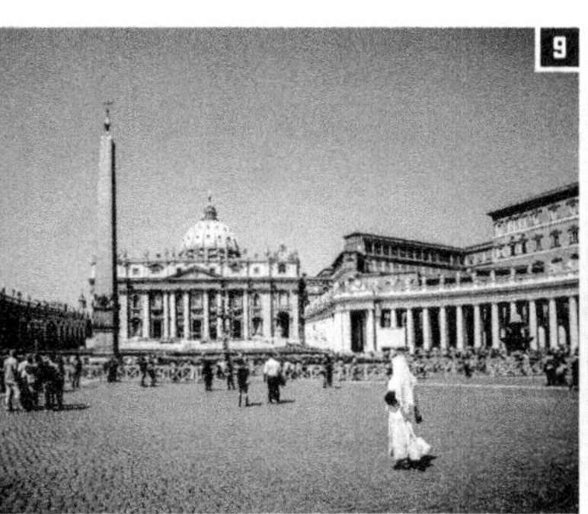

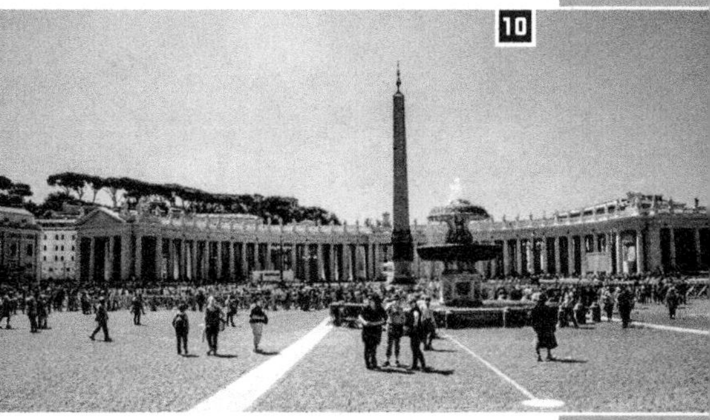

Paradise in *The Divine Comedy*, where the poet refers to Mary as: "Thou Virgin Mother, Daughter of Thy Son." Either Dante and Michelangelo's idea of virgin beauty was a woman who aged incredibly slowly, or there was some other kind of Tuscan superstition involved. Ascanio Candivi, Michelangelo's first biographer marked his master's words: "Do you not know that chaste women retain their fresh looks much longer than those who are not chaste? How much more, therefore, a Virgin in whom not even the least unchaste desire ever arose?" The Pietà is the only statue signed by Michelangelo. The Virgin Mary carries his signature across her chest like a ribbon. Roman Antiqua font reads:

MICHEL.A[N]GELVS BONAROTVS FLORENT[INVS] FACIEBA[T].

Michelangelo Buonarroti from Florence made this.

Michelangelo's Pietà has been an overwhelming sight for centuries. Its contemporaries regarded it as perfection and it certainly catapulted Michelangelo to stardom overnight. Because the Pietà was deliberately damaged by a visitor in 1972, it has since been placed behind bulletproof glass.

② St. Peter ★★★ 32

The most famous statue of St. Peter can be found in the main nave. The foot of this bronze statue has been replaced several times over the centuries because visitors keep touching it. Behind and above St. Peter, who is sitting, there is a mosaic which supports a brocade drapery. This was made by Virginio Vespignani in 1871. Above the stone canopy, an inscription and a medallion of Pope Pius IX (1846–1878) were made that same year, held by two putti. Pope Pius IX had a monument set up in honor of his own pontificate, the longest one up to that point.

③ Porphyry disc ★★ 33

In the central nave, there is a round surface made of red porphyry, a stone that was always directly linked to Roman emperors, whether as a material for making sarcophagi, thrones or a coronation site, which is the case here. This is where Pope Leo III crowned Charles the Great or Charlemagne in 800 as the first emperor of the Holy Roman Empire. The plate was located in front of the altar of the old St. Peter's Basilica.

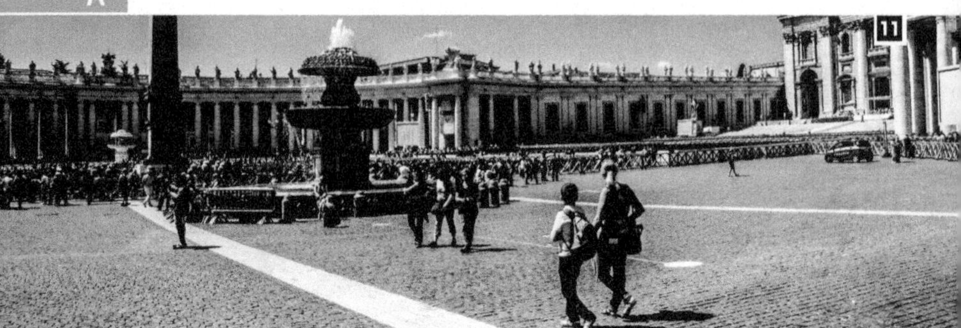

④ Baldacchino ★ ★ ★ ★ 34

Above the papal altar, which is, in fact, a marble plate from Nero's Circus, there is a monumental canopy made of gilded bronze. 35 That much bronze was difficult to come by in the seventeenth century, so Pope Urban VIII ordered the bronze to be taken down from the Pantheon. Soon after, an inscription, *Quod non fecerunt barbari, fecerunt Barberini* emerged at the Piazza Navona, meaning "What barbarians failed to do, Barberini actually did." [p.119] 36 Four bronze columns support the canopy. They are 66 ft or 20 m high, made according to Solomon's columns. Traditionally, the latter were transported from Jerusalem's Temple of Solomon by Constantine the Great. Twisting columns appear as vines and they were part of the old St. Peter's Basilica. Today, nine of them remain, out of twelve in total. The ninth column is in the Basilica Treasury. Notice two monumental tombstones on both sides of the apside: Pope Paul II's grave, made by Guglielmo della Porta in 1575 and Pope Urban VIII's, made by Bernini in 1647.

⑤ Saints' Niches ★ ★ ★

Next to the columns supporting the dome, there are four marble statues, each of them 14.8 ft or 4.5 m in height. The figures indicate important relics, some of which are still stored here:

▸ Bernini's *St. Longinus* – he has a spear that he used to stab Jesus, 37

▸ *St. Apostle Andreas* by François Duquesnoy – in 1964, the apostle's skull was returned to Patras, 38

▸ *St. Veronica* by Francesco Mochi – she offered her veil to Jesus and his face was imprinted on it – allegedly, the veil is kept right here, 39

▸ *St. Helena* by Andrea Bolgi – mother of Constantine the Great, who, according to tradition, found the cross on which Jesus Christ was crucified. 40

The basilica holds many other monuments, the most prominent ones being, artistically speaking:

▸ *Christina of Sweden* by Carlo Fontana (1702), 25

▸ *Matilda from Canossa* by Bernini (1635),

▸ *Tomb of Pope Alexander VII* by Bernini (1678), 41

▸ *Pope Urban VIII* by Bernini (1647),

▸ *Baptistery Chapel* by Carlo Fontana (1698) with a reused rich red porphyry basin, the lid of a funerary urn of Emperor Hadrian from the

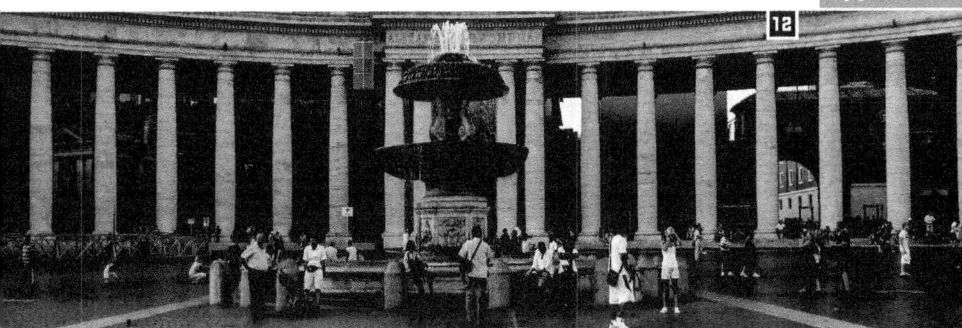

Castel Sant'Angelo, used to cover the sarcophagus of Emperor Otto II. Emperor Otto II died in Rome in 983,

▸ *Pope Clement XIII* by Canova (1792),

▸ *Tomb of the Last Stuarts* by Canova (1829). **42**

⑥ St. Peter's Chair ★★★ 43

St. Peter's Chair is actually a huge reliquary made by Bernini. It is made of bronze and holds a wooden chair thought to have belonged to Simon Petrus while he was preaching Christianity. Above the throne, there is a baroque representation of heaven. In the middle, there is a pigeon between rays as the symbol of the Holy Spirit. The upper part of Bernini's masterpiece is gilded. The gold represents the Divine Principle. There are angels around the heaven. Below, there are four fathers holding the throne, which appears to be floating. Two of the fathers come from the Greek East, St. John Chrysostom and St. Athanasius, while the other two belong to the Latin West, St. Augustine of Hippo and St. Ambrose.

⑦ Dome ★★★★

The dome of St. Peter's Basilica is the largest free-standing brick construction in the world. With 138.91 ft or 42.34 m in diameter, it is more narrow than the Pantheon by only 2.82 ft or 0.86 m.

History of the Papal State (756–1870)

While fighting with the Langobards over Northern Italy, King of the Franks, Pepin the Short asked the pope to crown him, which was exactly what Pope Stephen II did in 754, in Paris.

Pepin the Short earned the title of Patricius Romanorum (Patrician of the Romans), which was the first time the pope crowned a civil ruler. In return, the pope was given the Exarchate of Ravenna and surrounding places along the Adriatic coast, such as Rimini, Pesaro, Fano, Senigallia and Ancona. This gift was recorded in history as Pepin's donation. The Papal State officially came to be with Pepin's donation.

By taking over the Exarchate Ravenna, the Holy See publicly turned its back on the Eastern Roman Empire, once and for all. Pepin the Short's son, Charles the Great (742–814), also known as Charlemagne, confirmed his father's donation.

In 800, he was crowned in St. Peter's Basilica in Rome by the pope, as the first emperor of the Holy Roman Empire. The Empire lasted until 1806. Along with the Papal State, its end was abrupt due to the Napoleonic Wars.

The new, united Kingdom of Italy annexed the Papal State in 1870.

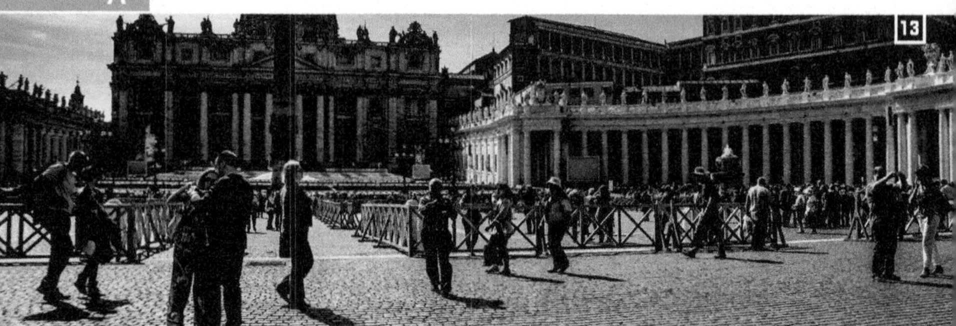

It has a greater diameter by approximately 30 ft or 9.1 m than Constantinople's Hagia Sophia church (Istanbul, Turkey). It is 141 ft or 43 m high, and from the floor of the basilica to the top of the external cross is 448 ft or 136.6 m. Inside, on the edge of the dome, there are 6.56 ft or 2 m tall letters that say:

> TV ES PETRVS ET SVPER HANC PETRAM: AEDIFICABO ECCLESIAM MEAM. TIBI DABO CLAVES REGNI CAELORVM
>
> *... you are Peter, and on this rock I will build my church. ... I will give you the keys of the kingdom of heaven...*
>
> Matthew 16:18 – 19.

After the plans of Bramante (1506) and Sangallo (1513), Michelangelo redesigned the dome (1547). 50 After his death (1564) the work was continued under Michelangelo's assistant Jacopo Barozzi da Vignola. At this time, Giorgio Vasari was appointed as architectural supervisor by Pope Pius V, to make sure that Michelangelo's plans were carried out exactly. 51 52 53 54 Giacomo della Porta (1895), assisted by Domenico Fontana, brought the dome to completion in 1590. 55 56 57 59

◆ **Vatican Museums** ★ ★ ★ ★ 58

Renaissance Pope Julius II was the founder of the Vatican Museums. He was the same Pope who decided to demolish Constantine's St. Peter's Basilica and build a new one.

Basilica di San Pietro in Vaticano | St. Peter's Basilica in Vatikan City
Address: Piazza San Pietro, Vatican City
Online: www.vaticanstate.va

Public transportation: Metro A stop Ottaviano | Bus stop Largo Di Porta Cavalleggeri – Fornaci: 64 or stop Porta Pinciana: 116 or stop Piazza Della Rovere: 34, 46, 64, 98, 881, 916, 916F, 982 or stop Piazza Pia – Castel Sant'Angelo: 23, 34, 40, 62, 280, 982 | Tram stop Risorgimento – San Pietro: 19 | Train stop Roma S. Pietro Station: Pisa–Livorno–Grosseto: FL3, FL5

Opening hours:
April to September: Mon – Sun: 7:00 a.m. – 7:00 p.m.
October to March: Mon – Sun: 7:00 a.m. – 6:00 p.m.

Closed: Easter Sunday, the 29th of June (St. Peter and Paul), 25th and 26th of December (Christmas and St. Stephen)

Saint Peter's Dome 48 49 51 53 55
Opening hours:
April to September: Mon – Sun: 8:00 a.m. – 6:00 p.m.
October to March: Mon – Sun: 8:00 a.m. – 5:00 p.m.

Saint Peter's Treasury
Opening hours:
April to September: Mon – Sun: 9:00 a.m. – 6:15 p.m.
October to March: Mon – Sun: 9:00 a.m. – 7:15 p.m.

The entrance to the Saint Peter's Treasury is from inside St. Peter's Basilica and the ticket will be charged.

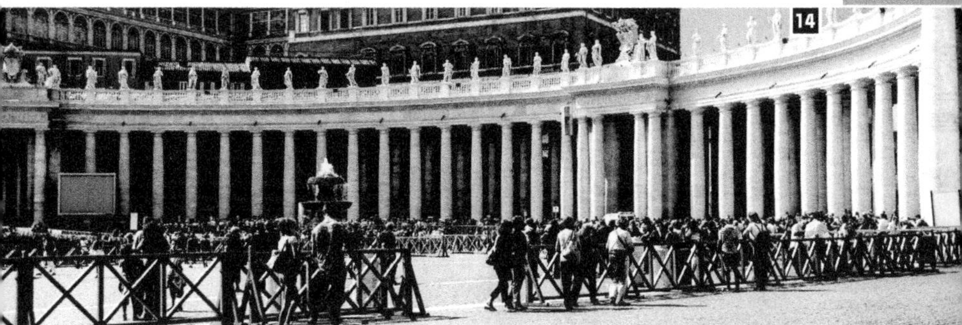

He was also the first pope to employ the Swiss Guard. **15** In the eighteenth century, the Vatican Museums were opened to the general public. In sixty galleries, also called *salas*, there is a plethora of famous works of art from different periods. The galleries are divided into museums. The Vatican Museums followed not only art trends, but also paid attention to public demand. Immediately after Napoleon's campaign in Egypt (1798–1801), the whole of Europe was crazy about Egyptian artifacts. This was facilitated by more than a hundred scientists who accompanied Napoleon and recorded his conquests on both banks of the Nile.

Moreover, a new style in art was formed based on Ancient Egyptian motives, the so-called "Empire style". The popes were not immune to the Egyptomania, so Pope Gregory XVI opened the Gregorian Egyptian Museum in 1839. Apart from many priceless sculptures, sarcophagi, reliefs and mosaics from Italy, Greece, Egypt and the Middle East, there is also an imposing number of art commissioned by the popes themselves.

First of all, there are *Stanze* (rooms) by Raphael, ordered by Pope Julius II. Raphael worked on them until his death in 1520. The painting 5,511 sq. ft. (512 sq. m.) of the ceiling in the Sistine Chapel was placed in the hands of Michelangelo, who managed to paint the whole surface in only four years (1508–1512).

Along with Raphael's "Stanze", it is considered as the finest masterpiece of the Italian High Renaissance. Usually, while strolling through this type of classical museum, the collection ends with the nineteenth century.

This is not the case in the Vatican. Here, there is also a Museum of Modern Art, with artworks that correspond to spiritual themes. Many famous artists donated their works to this museum. The Vatican Museum got a new attraction in 1932 — the

Musei Vaticani | Vatican Museums

Address: Viale Vaticano, Roma

Online: www.museivaticani.va

Public transportation:

Metro A stop Ottaviano | Bus stop Viale Vaticano – Musei Vaticani: 49 or Risorgimento: 32, 81, 590 | Tram stop Risorgimento – San Pietro Station: 19

Opening hours:

Mon – Sat: 9:00 a.m. – 6:00 p.m.

Last admission: 2 hours before closing time

Free admission:

The last Sunday of every month: 9:00 a.m. – 2:00 p.m.

Last admission: 12:30 p.m.

Closed: Easter Sunday, the 29th of June (St. Peter and Paul), 25th and 26th of December (Christmas and St. Stephen)

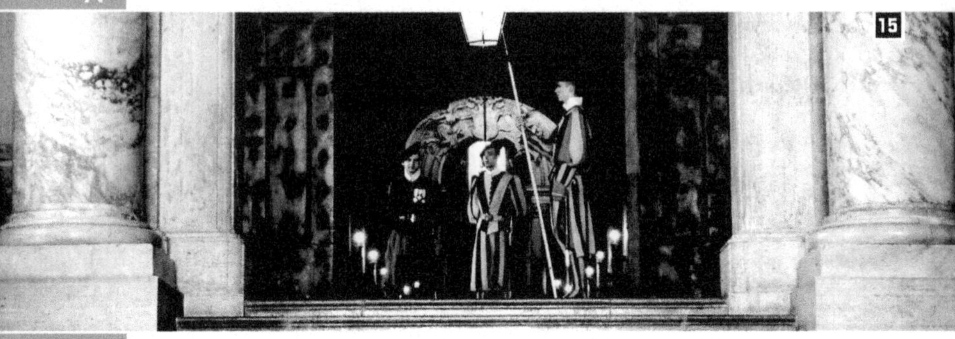

St. Peter's Basilica – FLOOR PLAN

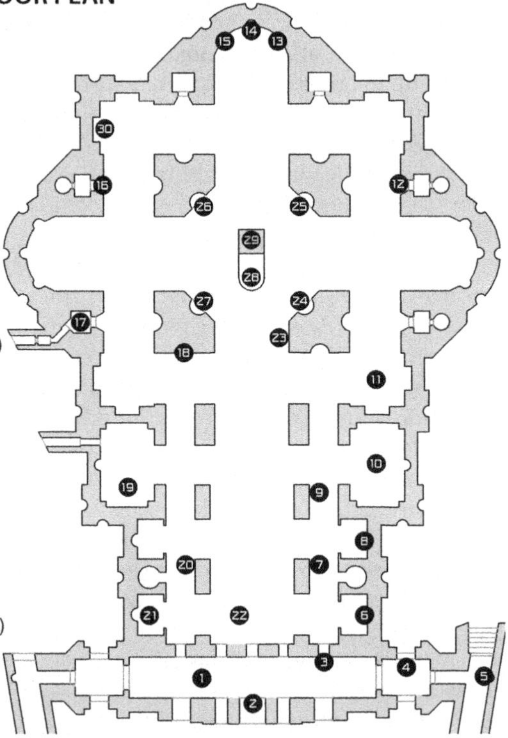

❶ Atrium
❷ *Navicella mosaic* by Giotto
❸ Holy Door
❹ Grottoes & Cupola entrance
❺ *Equestrian statue of Constantine* by Bernini (1670)
❻ *Pietà* by Michelangelo (1498–1499)
❼ *Christina of Sweden* by Carlo Fontana (1702)
❽ *Altarpiece* painting by Domenichino (1628–1631)
❾ *Matilda of Canossa* by Bernini (1633–1637)
❿ *Blessed Sacrament Chapel* and *Tabernacle* by Bernini (1674)
⓫ *Gregorian Chapel* by Michelangelo and Giacomo della Porta
⓬ *Clement XIII* by Canova (1792)
⓭ *Urban VIII* by Bernini (1647)
⓮ *Cathedra Petri* by Bernini (1666)
⓯ *Paul III* by Giacomo della Porta (1533–1602)
⓰ *Alexander VII* by Bernini (1678)
⓱ Sacristy and Treasury Museum
⓲ *Altar of Transfiguration* painting by Raphael (1520)
⓳ *Chapel of the Choir* by Maderno, Bianchi and Borromini
⓴ *Monument to the Stuarts* by Canova (1829)
㉑ *Baptistery Chapel* by Carlo Fontana with the lid of a funerary urn of Emperor Hadrian
㉒ *Porphyry plate* — Coronation site of an emperor
㉓ *St. Peter* by Arnolfo di Cambio, (1300)
㉔ *St. Longinus* by Bernini (1635)
㉕ *Statue of St. Helena*
㉖ *Statue of St. Veronica*
㉗ *Statue of St. Andrew*
㉘ Confessio — Tomb of St. Peter
㉙ *Papal Altar and Baldacchino* by Bernini (1633)
㉚ *Altar of St. Leo the Great* by Alessandro Algardi (1645–53)

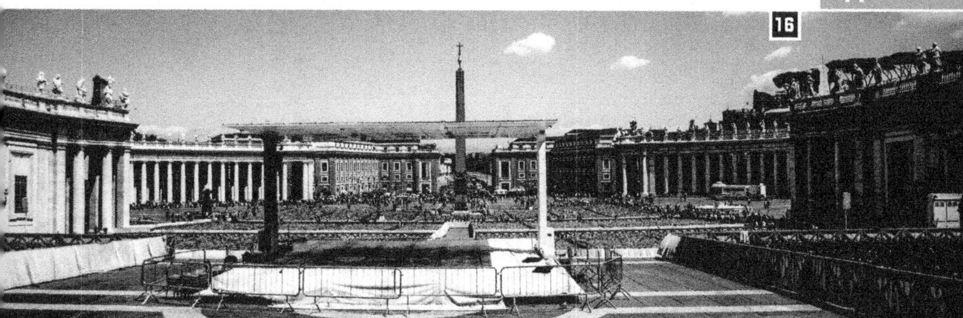

Scale Vaticani, a double spiral staircase in Cortile delle Corazze designed by the architect Giuseppe Momo. The same architect was also in charge of designing the Palazzo del Governatorato in the Vatican State (1931). While we are going through the Vatican Museums, we will also pass through the Apostolic Palace, we will see rooms, halls, galleries, stairways, corridors, chapels, courtyards, gardens and libraries. What is accessible to the public nowadays, can be divided into two parts:

> ▶ There are museums and collections grouped according to content,
> ▶ There are galleries, rooms and chapels situated in the Vatican Palace itself.

Museo Pio-Clementino

Here are some of the most important Greek and Roman artifacts, mostly sculptures: *Apoxyomenos, Laocoön Group, Apollo Belvedere, River god (Arno), The triumphant Perseus, The Belvedere Torso, Sarcophagus of Helena, Discobolus, Sleeping Ariadne, Dorifor, Pericles* and many others.

Vestibolo Quadrato | Square Vestibule

Pope Clemente XIV was in charge of decorating the museum in mid-eighteen century. Here, you will find headstones from the Scipio family tomb on the Via Appia. Further, there is the monumental sarcophagus of Lucius Cornelius Scipio Barbatus (280 BC). It dates to the Roman Republic. Its importance lies in the fact that some of the oldest Latin verses have been preserved on it:

Cornelius Lucius Scipio Barbatus Gnaivod Patre
Prognatus Fortis Vir Sapiensque
Quoius Forma Virtutei Parisuma
Fuit Consol Censor Aidilis Quei Fuit Apud Vos
Taurasia Cisauna
Samnio Cepit Subigit Omne Loucana Opsidesque Abdoucit

Lucius Cornelius Scipio, son of Gnaeus, a valiant gentleman and wise,
whose fine form matched his bravery surpassing well, was aedile,
consul and censor among you; he took Taurasia and Cisauna, in fact Samnium;
he overcame all the Lucanian land and brought hostages therefrom.

Originally, the letters were painted red. Below the inscription, there is a plate in Doric style.

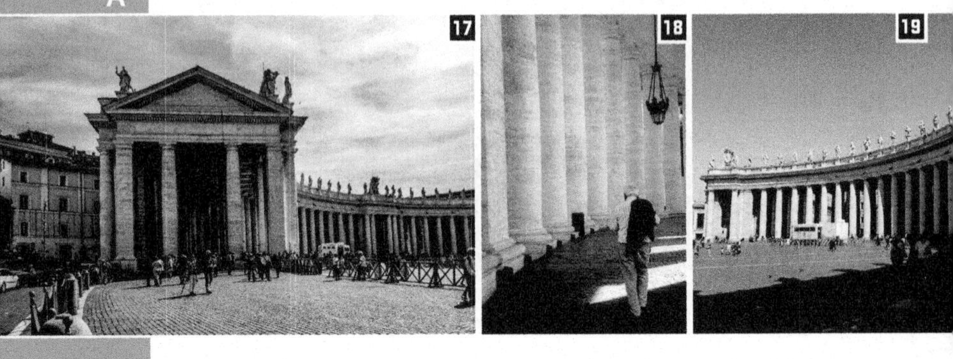
17
18
19

Viale Vaticano
EXIT

EXIT
St. Peter's Basilica

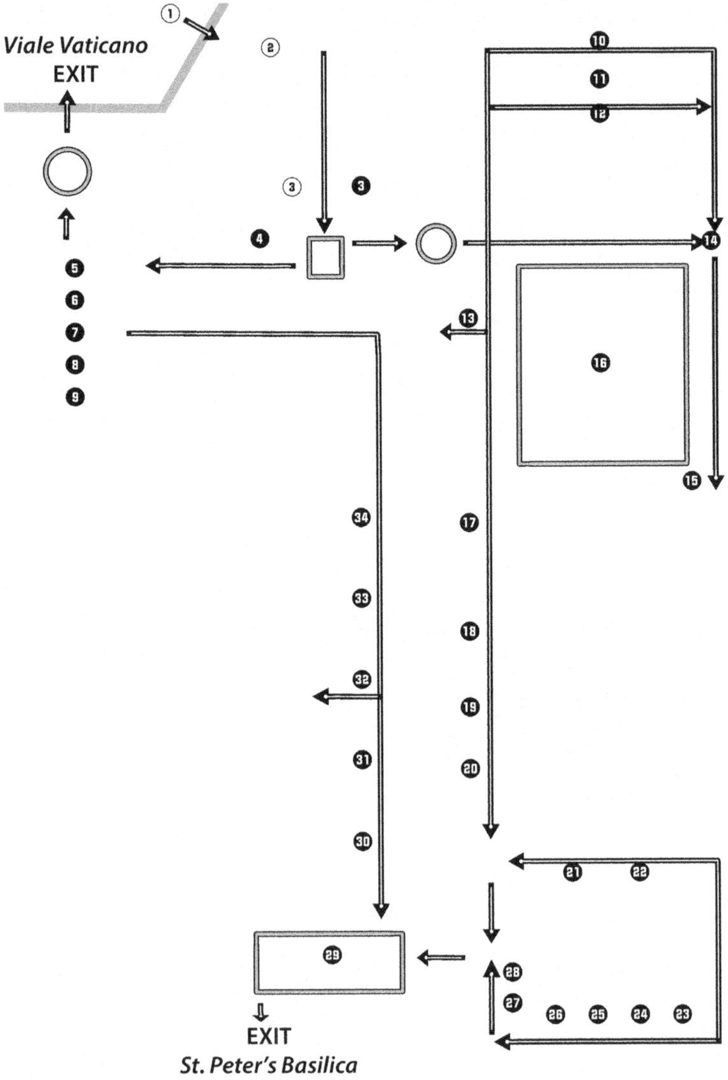

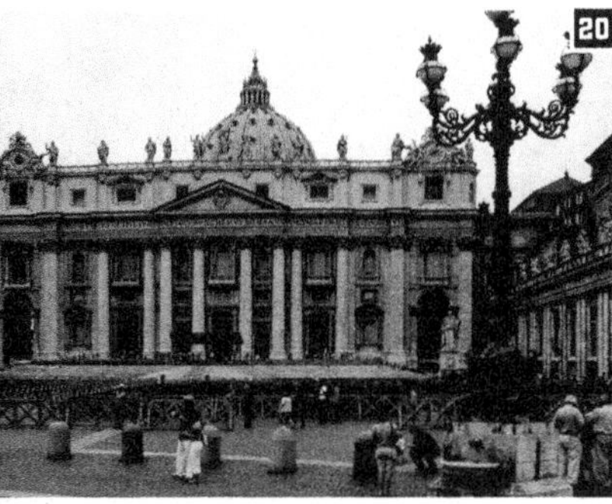

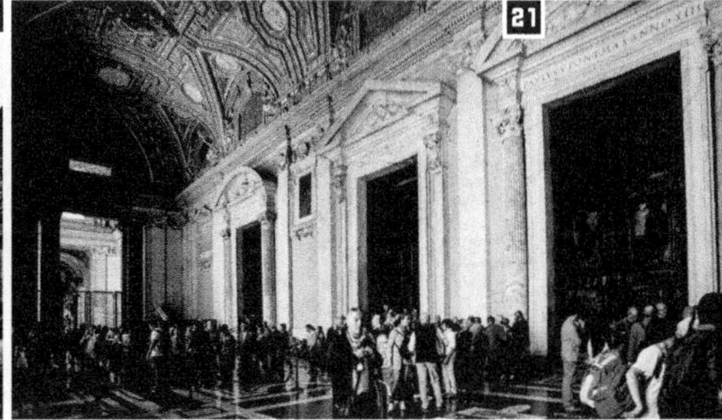

Vatican Museums Map

① Entrance
② Tickets | Wardrobe | WC
③ Double spiral staircase
❸ Cortile delle Corazze | Courtyard of the "Corazze"
❹ Giardino Quadrato | Square Garden
❺ Pinacoteca Vaticana | The Vatican Pinacoteca
❻ Museo Etnologico | Ethnological Museum
❼ Museo Gregoriano Profano | Gregorian Profane Museum
❽ Museo Pio-Cristiano | Pio Cristiano Museum
❾ Museo Filatelico e Numismatico | Philatelic and Numismatic Museum
❿ Museo Pio-Clementino | Pio Clementino Museum
⓫ Museo Gregoriano Etrusco | Gregorian Etruscan Museum
⓬ Museo Gregoriano Egizio | Gregorian Egyptian Museum
⓭ Sala Della Biga | Hall of the Chariot
⓮ Museo Chiaramonti | Chiaramonti Museum
⓯ Braccio Nuovo | New Wing Gallery
⓰ Cortile della Pigna | Courtyard of the "Pigna"
⓱ Galleria dei Candelabri | Gallery of the Candelabra
⓲ Galleria degli Arazzi | Gallery of Tapestries
⓳ Galleria delle Carte Geografiche | Gallery of Maps
⓴ Appartamento di San Pio V | Apartment of Pius V
㉑ Sala Sobieski | Sobieski Hall
㉒ Sala dell'immacolata | The Immaculate Conception Hall
㉓ Sala di Cosstantino | Hall of Constantine
㉔ Stanza di Eliodoro | Room of Heliodorus
㉕ Stanza della Segnatura | Room of the Signatura
㉖ Stanza dell'incendio del Borgo | Room of the Fire in the Borgo
㉗ Cappella Niccolina | Chapel of Nicholas V
㉘ Appartamento Borgia | Borgia Apartments
㉙ Cappella Sistina | The Sistine Chapel
㉚ Cappella di San Pietro Martire | Chapel of St. Peter Martyr
㉛ Sala degli Indirizzi | Hall of Addresses
㉜ Sala delle Nozze Aldobrandine | Hall of Aldobrandini Wedding
㉝ Sala dei Papiri | Hall of the Papyri
㉞ Sala del Museo Cristiano | Hall of the Christian Museum

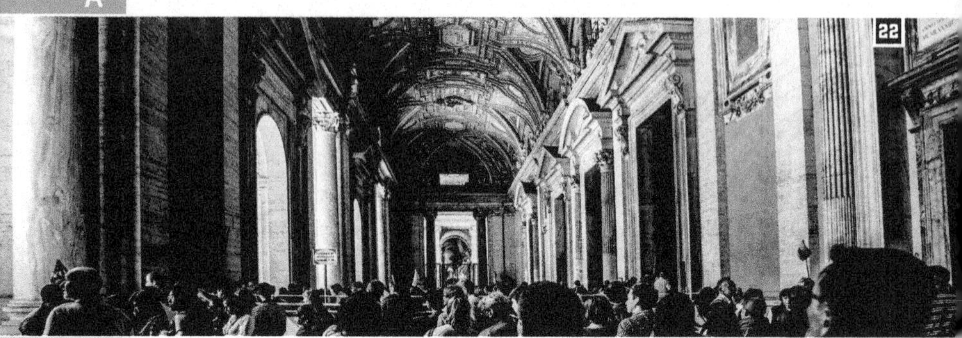

Cabinet of Apoxyomenos

Let's move on through the Vestibolo Rotondo to the Cabinet of Apoxyomenos. This is where you will find the marble copy of the famous bronze statue made by Lysippos, a Greek artist.

He was a sculptor at the court of Alexander the Great. It is a statue of Apoxyomenos, one of the favorite motives in Hellenic times. The athlete is shown scraping dirt and sweat of his oiled body after the race. For this, Greek athletes used a curvy scraper.

This statue is a copy from the first century, while the original was made by Lysippos around 320 BC. In mid-nineteenth century, it was found during excavation in the Trastevere, a part of Rome on the other bank of the Tiber.

Head of Ennius

Now, look for the head of a young man wearing a laurel wreath. The so-called "Head of Ennius" was found at the Scapio family tomb. Supposedly, it dates back to 2nd century BC.

It is an example of Roman art developed under Etruscan influence. The head is tilted, so presumably, it was a part of a larger statue with a body.

Cortile delle Statue | Courtyard of Statues

All the original exhibits that allowed Pope Julius II to establish the Vatican Museums are here, including Apollo Belvedere and Laocoön.

Apollo Belvedere

Apollo Belvedere is a marble copy of a bronze original. The original dates from around 350 BC.

It shows the Greek god Apollo as he is just about to fire one of his deadly arrows. The sculpture is 7.3 ft or 2.23 m high. His right forearm, as well as the left arm, do not belong to the original – they were replaced by Giovanni Montorsoli, one of Michelangelo's pupils.

For centuries, the sculpture was considered as an example of classical beauty. It was found in late 15th century in a former Roman colony of Terracina, a 62 miles or 100 kilometers south of Rome.

First, it was placed on a private property owned by Giuliano della Rovere, future Pope Julius II.

It served as inspiration for many artists, first of all Dürer and Michelangelo.

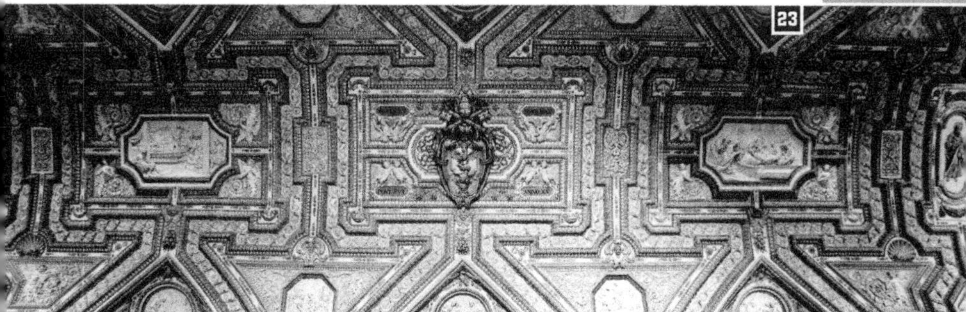

Laocoön Group

Immediately after it was discovered in 1506, the Laocoön Group was identified as such.

Pliny the Elder documented it as the masterpiece of Agesander, Polydorus and Athenodorus from Rhodes. A marble copy from 1st century BC stands before us. The original was probably made of bronze, but lost.This mythological group had an enormous impact on generations of renaissance artists from the moment it was discovered.

When Michelangelo set his eyes on it, he found the Hellenistic proportions of the male body particularly impressive.

Other artists flocked to this statue in order to fully comprehend the secrets of Greek art and the expressive movement frozen in stone. This is especially the case with Laocoön's twisted torso. Even today, the statue enjoys cult status among artists and art historians.

The statue shows the Apollonic priest, Laocoön of Troy, who contradicted his fellow citizens when they wanted to accept the Trojan horse as a gift from the Greek army. Athena and Poseidon sent two giant sea serpents to murder Laocoön and his two sons.

The Romans, however, had their own reason for loving this motive. The death of Laocoön and his sons marked the beginning of the Eagean exile and their emigration to the Apennine peninsula, related to the foundation of Rome.

River god (Arno)

The lying figure of the River god originates from Hadrian's period (117–138). The emperor was well known for his love of anything Greek. The sculpture probably follows a Hellenistic template. It is located in front of a sarcophagus which has been turned into a fountain.

The sarcophagus dates from AD 170 and it features battle scenes between the Greeks and the Amazons. Some alternations were made during the Renaissance. The head was reshaped so that the face would be more expressive. A small lion head was inserted on the vase that the god is holding, probably in honor of Pope Leo X Medici. This is why the statue is called the River god of Arno, since the Arno passes through Florence, Pope Medici's hometown. Others interpreted it as a wild cat, perhaps a tiger, which would allude to the River god of the Tigris.

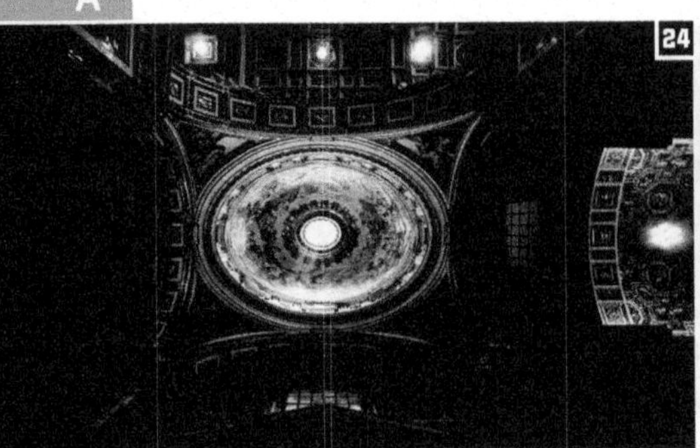

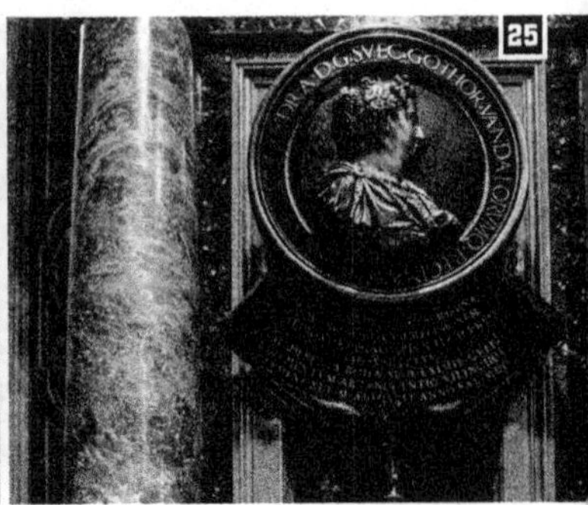

The Belvedere Hermes

This Hermes is probably a copy of a bronze statue from the period of Hadrian, originally made by the Greek sculptor Praxiteles or his pupils. The marble statue is of Hermes, Greek god and companion of the deceased to the other world. He is looking down and waiting for the deceased. The artwork was found in 1540 in the garden of Hadrian's Mausoleum, present-day Castel Sant'Angelo.

The triumphant Perseus

In the Octagonal Court there is more than just antique sculptures. An early 19th-century artist managed to grab the attention of popes with his works, following the tradition of Roman copyists.

His name was Antonio Canova. He was from Venice and belonged to the Classicist movement. Everything about Canova's Perseus points to his source of inspiration, the Belvedere Apollo – the expressiveness, proportions and balance.

Sala degli Animali | Hall of Animals

When you step into the Hall of Animals, which actually consists of two rooms, you will find something completely different.

Mythical and hunting scenes are organized thematically.

Movement and animal instinct were the most challenging parts of creating animals from ancient Rome.

Did you know?

Art patronage of Julius II

Pope Julius II spared no expense to buy off the Laocoön Group from the vineyard owner, whose property included Nero's Golden Villa and the sculpture.

The wine-grower Felice de Fredis certainly knew how to close a great deal. He managed to squeeze out travel expenses from Porta San Giovanni, 1,500 florins and a tomb at the Basilica di Santa Maria in Ara Coeli on the Capitoline Hill.

All this speaks volumes on how much Pope Julius II appreciated ancient art.

His commissions include:
- ► 1503–1512 – The Cortile del Belvedere in (Vatican City)
- ► 1505–1545 – Julius' tomb in San Pietro in Vincoli
- ► 1505–1626 – St. Peter's Basilica (Vatican City)
- ► 1508–1512 – The Sistine Chapel ceiling (Vatican City)
- ► 1509–1516 – Raphael's Stanze in the Vatican Palace
- ► 1511 – Raphael's Portrait of the Pope Julius II (National Gallery, London and Uffizi version in Florence)

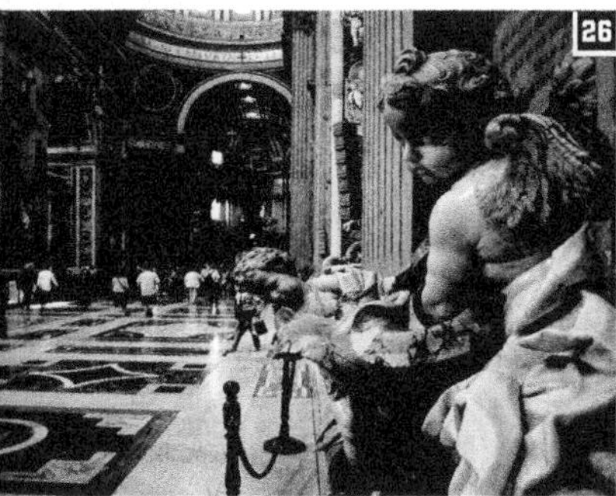

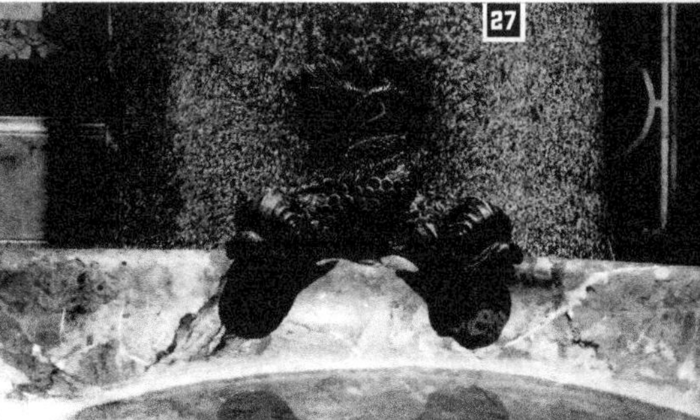

Galleria delle Statue e Sala dei Busti | Gallery of the Statues and Hall of Busts

Ariadne

This sculpture is a Roman copy of a Hellenic original from 2nd century BC, attributed to Pergamon's school. We have Ariadne, princess of Crete and daughter of king Minos, who helped Theseus in the Minotaur's labyrinth by unraveling a bobbin so he could find his way out.

She is in an impossible sleeping position, napping before Dionysius shows up and marries her. The sculpture was procured by Pope Julius II in 1512 and placed as an ornament on a fountain.

The Chiaramonti Caesar

The face of the dictator has some individual features, which is a rarity among portraits of rulers. Still, this is no exception. It is assumed that the Roman artist allowed for some individualism by using idealized features of a Hellenic ruler. Something like this could have happened after Caesar's death (44 BC), when his adopted son Augustus introduced the cult of Caesar.

Since the sculpture was kept in the Chiaramonti Museum for a long time, it still bears its name.

Gabinetto delle Maschere | Cabinet of Masks

Mosaics on the central part of the floor were brought from Hadrian's Villa in Tivoli. There are several female statues, including Nymph (especially admired by German poet Goethe) and Aphrodite.

Sala delle Muse | Hall of the Muses

Here are statues found in the Villa di Cassio near Tivoli. All of them date to Hadrian's times, which means they were strongly influenced by Greek art.

The Belvedere Torso

The famous marble torso found in Rome in the 15th century is also here. It has been the source of admiration for many people, especially artists, even today. Allegedly, Pope Julius II asked Michelangelo to make the lost pieces, which Michelangelo refused by saying that the torso was too perfect and did not need any alterations.

Most of the figures in the Sistine Chapel have been modeled according to this torso. The sculpture still has the author's signature — Apollonios, son of Nestor Athenian.

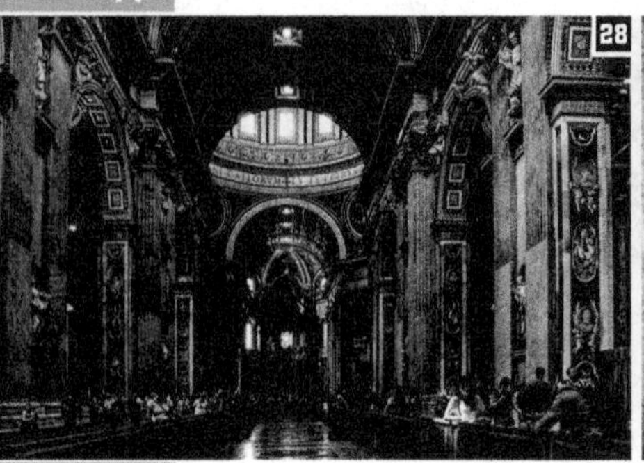
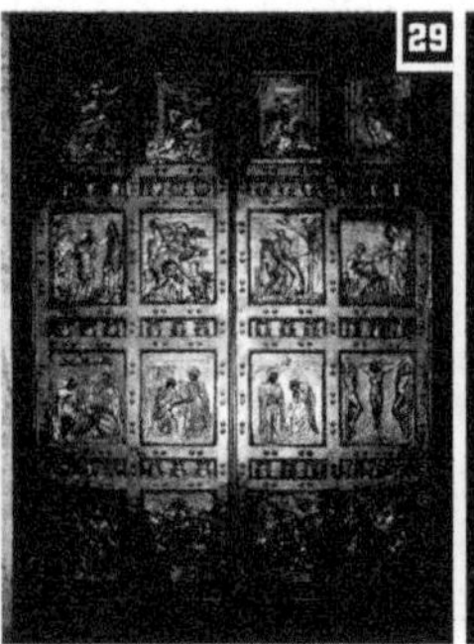
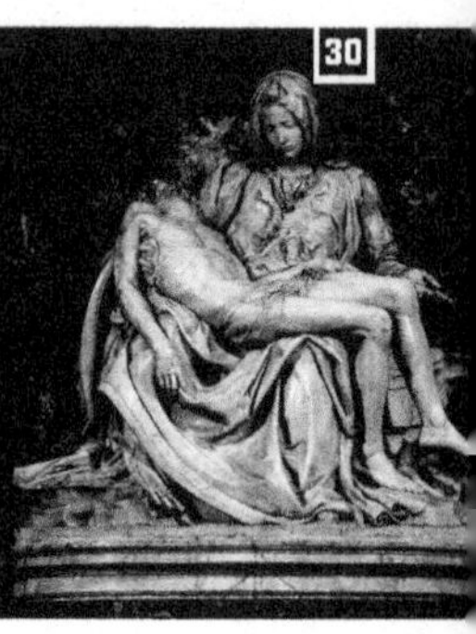

Pericles with the Corinthian helmet

In the Hall of the Muses, immediately before the Sala della Rotonda, there is the most famous statue of the Athenian politician Pericles, on the right. It is a Roman copy from Hadrian's era.

The original was made by a Greek sculptor called Kresilas in 5th century BC. On the bottom part, there is an inscription which reads: "Pericles, son of Xanthippus, Athenian."

Sala della Rotonda | Round Hall

Gigantic marble and bronze figures are placed in the Round Hall. Its ceiling was made in imitation of the Pantheon.

Monolithic Porphyry Basin

In the middle of the room, there is one of the most impressive objects in the Vatican Museums, a large porphyry basin, the largest such basin that has been preserved. The inner diameter is around 13 ft or 4 m. It was an ornament in Nero's Golden House, Domus Aurea.

Mosaics from Otricoli and Sacrofano

The mosaics on the floor date from 3rd century. They were found in Otricoli, Roman town of Otriculum, present-day village in Umbria, about 25 mi (40 km) north of Rome.

Also, the head of Claudius and Zeus are from Otriculum. The mosaics have been built into the floor together with the mosaics from Sacrofano, 18.5 mi or 30 km outside Rome, also on the Via Flaminia.

Heracles

A gilded bronze statue of Heracles is in one of the niches and you will not miss it for sure. This gigantic piece was found under the courtyard of the Palazzo Orsini Pio Righetti, near Campo de' Fiori. Originally, it was part of the sculptural exposition around Teatro di Pompeo. The statue is from 2nd century. In terms of proportions, it could be attributed to the Greek sculptor Lysippos. Therefore, it can be assumed it was modeled after a Greek original.

The so-called *contrapposto*, the uneven distribution of weight resting on one leg, is a typical feature of Lysippos's work.

Heracles is leaning on a cudgel, and the fur of the Nemean lion is draped comfortably over his long arm.

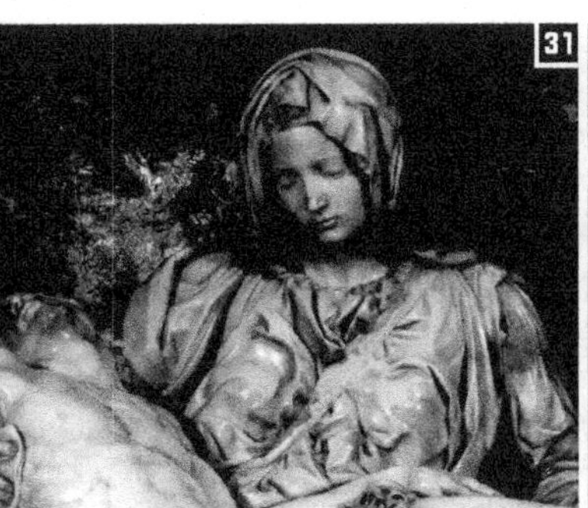

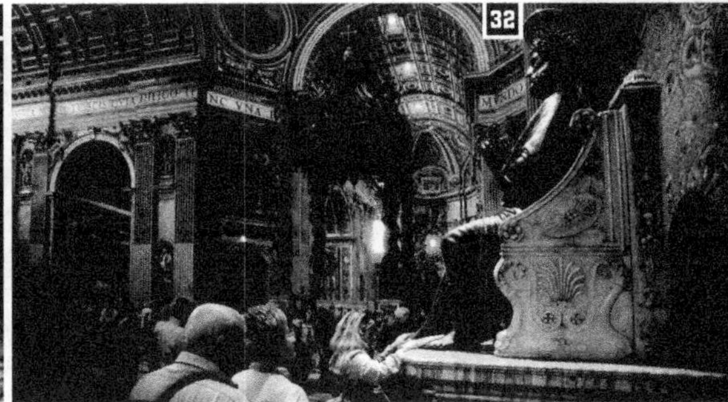

Antinous – Bacchus

Further, there is a monumental statue of Antinous, Emperor Hadrian's lover. After he drowned in Egypt, Antinous was deified and worshiped across the empire.

In Sala della Rotonda, he is portrayed as the Roman Bacchus, a fertility god. This marble statue was discovered in late 18th century in one of Hadrian's villas near Palestrina, 25 mi (40 km) east of Rome.

Sala a Croce Greca | Greek Cross Hall

This hall is all about the people from the Emperor Constantine the Great's inner circle.

Here we have two enormous sarcophagi made of red porphyry, the most expensive stone in the ancient world, shipped from the Egyptian desert, only to be used for emperors and their families. The sarcophagi of Costanza, daughter of Constantine, and his mother Helena can be found here.

They are so monumental and precious that it is almost impossible to divert your eyes from them.

Still, if you manage to do exactly that, you will also come across a posthumous portrait of Emperor Augustus as hero, accompanied by a statue of Gaius Caesar, his great-uncle and adoptive father.

Sarcophagus of Helena

In the Sala a Croce Greca there is a large sarcophagus of St. Helena made of red porphyry. St. Helena died in 355.

She was buried in this sarcophagus in a niche facing the entrance to the Mausoleum of Helena, whose remains still stand in Via Casilina, in an eastern suburb of Rome. The proportions of the sarcophagus are monumental – it is 8.86 ft long (2.7 m) and 5.91 ft (1.8 m) high.

Battle themes testify to the possible original use of the sarcophagus. It may have been made for Emperor Constantine the Great himself.

However, when the emperor moved his residence to Constantinople, the sarcophagus stayed behind as the final resting place for his mother.

Until 11th century, the sarcophagus was placed in the mausoleum and then moved to the Basilica di San Giovanni in Laterano. The saint had to concede her place to Pope Anastasius IV.

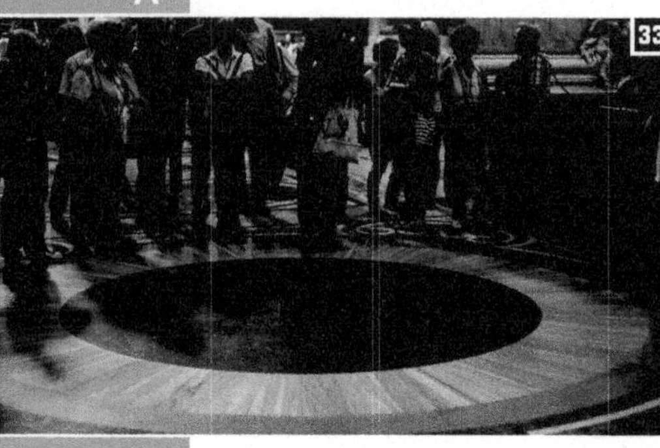

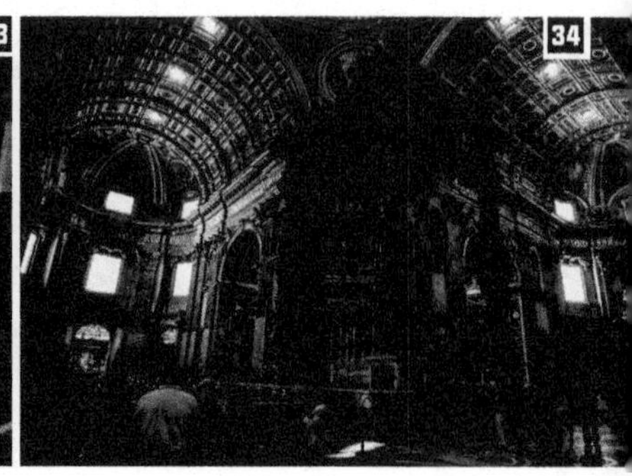

Sarcophagus of Costanza

Opposite Helena's sarcophagus, there is another one, dedicated to Constantine the Great's daughter who died in 354. The sarcophagus was kept in the Church of Santa Costanza until mid-15th century.

The church itself was built as a mausoleum for the emperor's daughter around her grave. The sarcophagus is 4.2 ft (1.28 m) tall and 7.64 ft (2.33 m) long. Dionysian scenes are depicted, with grape vines and cupids.

Galleria dei Candelabri | Gallery of the Candelabra

The name comes from enormous marble lamps situated in the niches. Pay attention to the statues of the old Roman man and Artemis from Ephesus, the Greek goddess with three rows of breasts and vertical bulls painted all over her body, found in Hadrian's Villa.

The Persian Warrior

The warrior is wearing a Phrygian cap. He is frozen in a desperate last gesture of resistance, aware of his own defeat. Humiliation and defeat can be seen not only in the position of his body, but also read on his expressive face. Supposedly, the statue was part of a larger group made in bronze.

This is a Roman copy from AD 110–120, found in early 16th century during the construction of the Medici Palace, present-day Palazzo Madama, near Piazza Navona. In Roman times, this used be the location of the Stadium of Domitian (Circus Agonalis). It is entirely plausible that the statue belonged to the Domitian Stadium.

Galleria degli Arazzi | Gallery of Tapestries

This gallery holds the Flemish tapestries made in Brussels in the 16th century according to the designs created by the pupils of Raphael.

Galleria delle Carte Geografiche | Gallery of Maps

The gallery contains 40 map panels exhibited in a 394 feet or 120 meter-long line (1580–1583). The maps are based on Ignazio Danti's drawings, who was a 16th-century Italian geographer. The panels show maps of Italy and major cities in the area. Decoration and lavish stucco on the ceiling were made by the Mannerist masters Cesare Nebbia and Girolamo Muziano.

Appartamento di San Pio V | Apartment of Pius V

The apartments consist of a gallery, two rooms and a chapel. Pope Pius V commissioned Giorgio Vasari and Federico Zuccari to paint them.

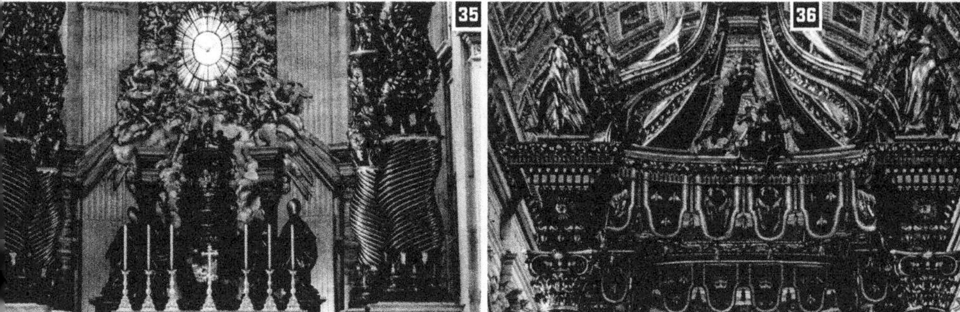

Apart from Flemish tapestries from the 15th and 16th century, there is also medieval and Renaissance pottery and mosaics from the 18th and 19th century.

Sala Sobieski | Sobieski Hall

The gallery was named after a 19th-century painting of a Polish king who defeated the Ottoman army in the Battle of Vienna in 1683.

Sala dell'immacolata | The Immaculate Conception Hall

The books on display were a present for Pope Pius IX from the French bishops and diocese when he proclaimed the dogma of the Immaculate Conception in 1854. There are four frescoes celebrating the Immaculate Conception, as well as the reveal of the dogma to Pope Pius IX. The six octagonal frescoes on the ceiling are particularly interesting, with allegories and stories from the Old Testament.

Cappella di San Pietro Martire | Chapel of St. Peter Martyr

The chapel is located in a tower corner in the Vatican Palace, commissioned by Pope Pius V. As with the apartments, Giorgio Vasari and Federico Zuccari were told to do the stucco and frescoes (1570). The glass-fronted cabinet holds "the most holy of relics" or *Sancta Sanctorum* from the former Papal Lateran Palace.

Sala degli Indirizzi | Hall of Addresses

This is a gallery with a magnificent collection of fine art made of ivory, enamel and precious metals. These are all gifts sent to the pope by heads of state from every corner of the world. One of the gifts is a cross which the French King Louis XVI wore his whole life. It is the last thing he gave to the executioner at the guillotine in 1793.

Sala delle Nozze Aldobrandine | Hall of Aldobrandini Wedding

Close to the Church of Santa Maria Maggiore, in the former Maecenas Gardens, an Antique Roman fresco from the Augustan period was found, named by its original owner, Cardinal Cinzio Passeri Aldobrandini.

Sala dei Papiri | Hall of Papyri

The documents from the Ravenna Church (6th to 9th century) used to be kept in this room, but they have been replaced by photographs. The frescoes date back to Pope Pius VI, painted by several artists among which Anton Raphael Mengs stands out (1772–73). There are also valuable pottery pieces by Gian Lorenzo Bernini and Alessandro Algardi.

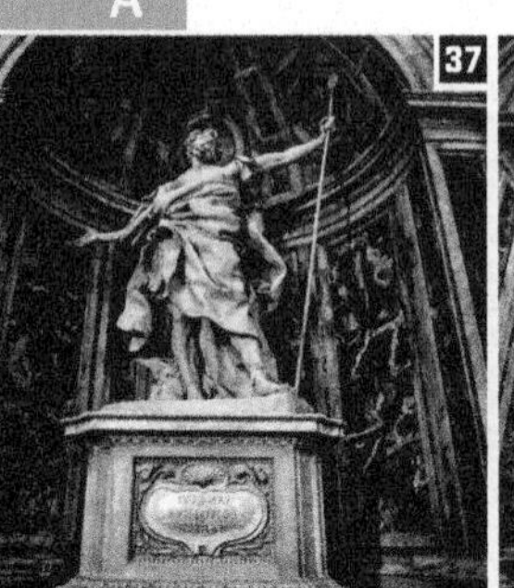
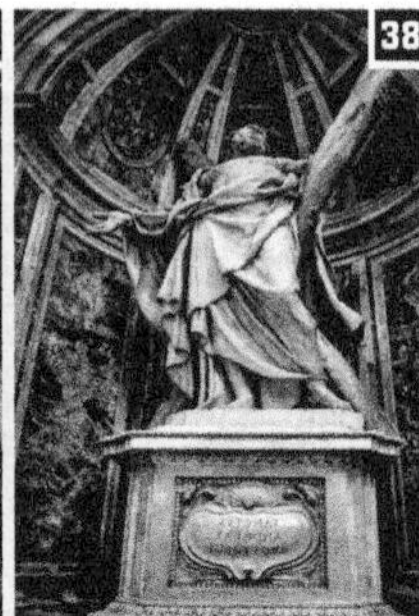
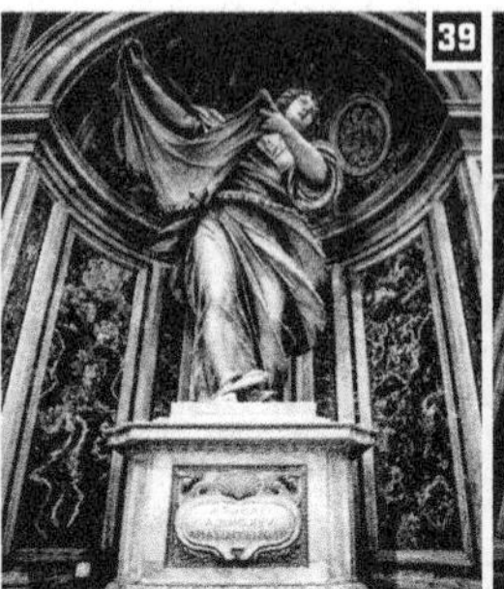
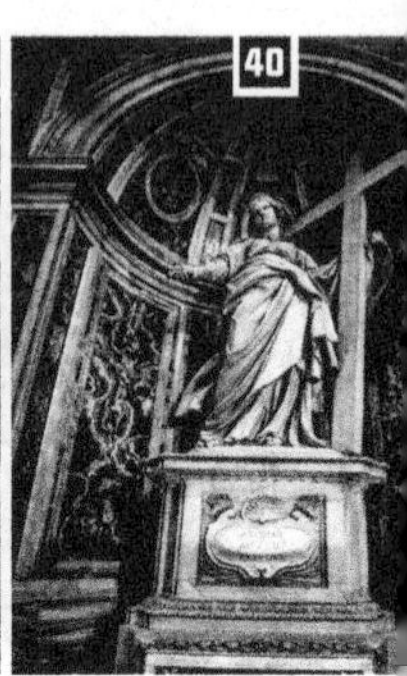

Sala del Museo Cristiano | Hall of the Christian Museum

This is here you can find Early Christian fine art from the Late Roman period.

The collection features not only specimens from the heart of the Roman Empire, but also from the Roman provinces: clay lamps, decorated glass and crystal objects which used be in the Vatican Library.

Museo Chiaramonti

This museum was commissioned by Pope Pius VII, whose last name was Chiaramonti. It was built in 1807, to house newly purchased ancient artifacts. The pope was in a buying frenzy, trying to replace the ancient statues taken to Paris from the Vatican Museums by Napoleon.

Most objects confiscated by Napoleon have been returned to Italy, thanks to Antonio Canova, the Vatican representative at the Viennese Congress (1815). Three sisterly arts are represented here: sculpture, architecture and frescoes. There are hundreds of portraits and pieces of sarcophagi.

When the statues stolen by Napoleon were returned, the museum was expanded. A new wing was added fifteen years later, Braccio Nuovo, for exhibiting important statues, Roman copies of Greek originals, as well as original Roman statues and mosaics built into the floor.

Galleria Lapidaria

With more than 3,000 inscribed stone tablets, is the largest such collection in the world. Unfortunately, it is only accessible to experts who obtain a special permit. You can peek inside through an iron fence at the other end of the hall filled with statues.

Braccio Nuovo | New Wing Gallery

Augustus Prima Porta

This statue was discovered in 1863 in Livia's Villa in Prima Porta near Rome, where Augustus's wife lived after she was widowed. This is a copy of a bronze original, ordered by the Roman Senate in 20 BC. We see Augustus addressing the soldiers. He is wearing an armor and drapery around his thighs. During the Augustan period, this was a very common type of representation of the emperor.

The composition is very similar to Doryphoros, a masterpiece attributed to the Greek sculptor Polykleitos. The copy of that sculpture is also displayed in the Braccio Nuovo.

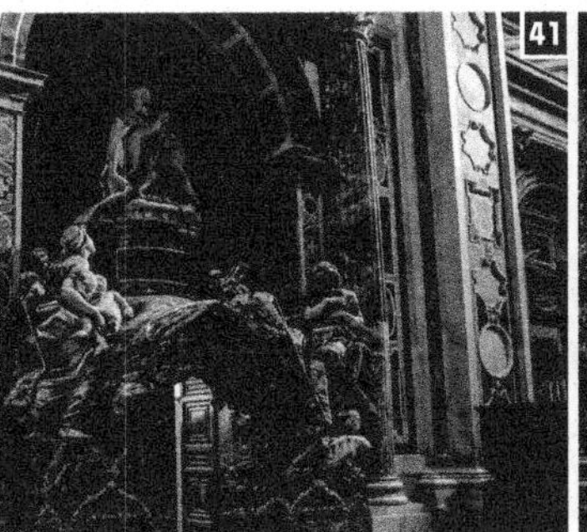
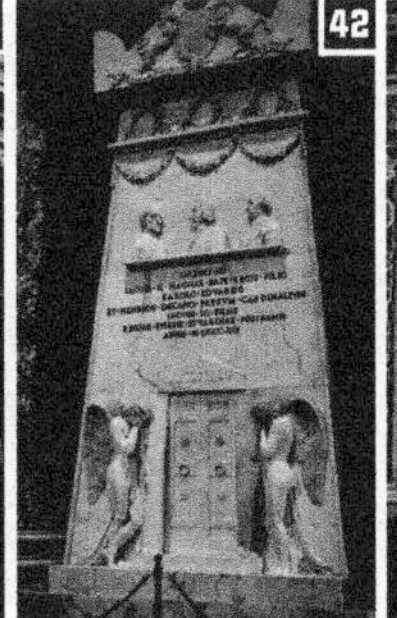
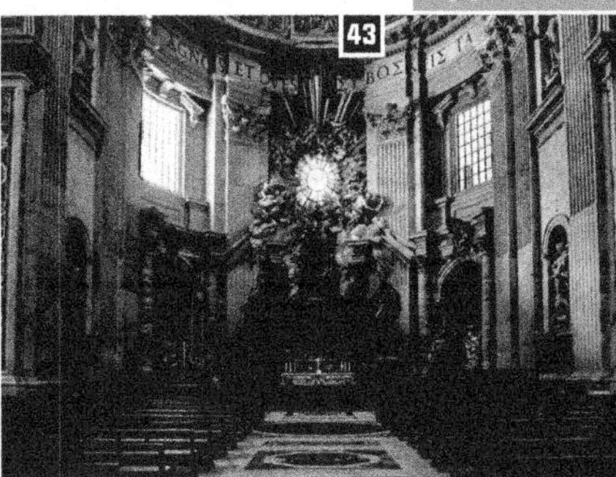

Sala Della Biga | Hall of the Chariot

In the Chariot Room, there are statues and sarcophagi associated with athletes and the Roman Circus. In the middle, there is a marble statue of a *biga*, a chariot with two horses.

Discobolus

One of the best preserved Roman copies of the Greek Discobolus is in this hall. Discobolus was a Greek bronze statue, made by Myron in 460–450 BC. This copy dates to Hadrian's period. The head is not original and it has been badly positioned. According to the original, the head should be turned towards the disk. Of course, the fig leaf does not belong to the original either. Discobolus is suspended in time, as he is just about to throw the disk. The muscles on his arms are tight, his torso is twisted, the toes on his left foot – everything is about the movement and the swing. The other two copies in Rome can be found in Palazzo Massimo alle Terme. [p.208]

Museo Gregoriano Profano | Gregorian Profane Museum

The Museum contains artifacts from Ancient Greece all the way to the Late Roman period. The works are displayed in chronological order, starting from original Greek sculptures. There are funeral stelas, votive reliefs and pieces of architecture, such as, three marble fragments from the Parthenon in Athens. After that, there are Roman copies of Greek sculptures, mostly portraits and idealized Roman emperors. In addition, you will also find amazing art on urns, sarcophagi and altars.

Marble fragments from the Parthenon

These are extremely partial, so the origin is more relevant than the fragments themselves. There are fragments of a horse's head, one of the horses from Athena's chariot. The head of a young man has been identified as one of the bread bearers in an Athenian procession. Head of a bearded man belongs to a metope from a temple with the representation of Centauromachy, Battle with Centaurs.

Chiaramonti Niobide

This is one of Niobe's daughters, running away from arrows thrown by Apollo and Artemis. Niobe, Queen of Thebes, had 14 children. She bragged about how she was the best mother, not only in Greece, but also compared to gods, especially when compared to Leto, who only gave birth to Zeus's twins, Apollo and Artemis.

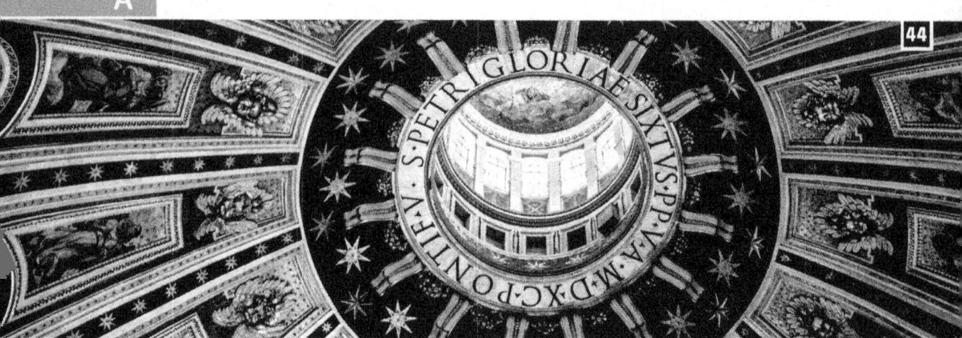

Children of the goddess Leto, Apollo and Artemis wanted to avenge their mother and started killing Niobe's children. Apollo killed the boys, and Artemis took the girls. This sculpture probably belonged to a larger group. It is a copy from Hadrian's period of an unknown Greek original, found in the 16th century in Hadrian's Villa in Tivoli.

Cancelleria Reliefs

They were found in the Palazzo della Cancelleria, so this is where their name comes from. Both reliefs belonged to some sort of public monument from Domitian's era. Only one plate, out of four in total, has been preserved.

It shows the *adventus*, i.e. arrival of Emperor Vespasian to Rome. He is greeted by a young general in a toga, supposedly his son Domitian. Genie, the spirit guardians of the Roman Senate and the Genie of the Roman people are also present.

To the left the goddess of Rome with a spear and a Vestal Virgins. Another relief, which is better preserved, shows profection, i.e., going on a military campaign. Minerva and Mars are opposite the emperor, and the emperor is escorted by goddess Rome, the Genie of the Senate with a sceptre and the Genie of the Roman people holding a *cornucopia*, the horn of plenty. The scene is completed by Roman soldiers.

Emperor Nerva is shown here. However, this was not originally on the relief. After Domitian was killed in AD 96, the Roman Senate declared *damnatio memoriae*, erasing all memory of Emperor Domitian by systematically destroying any traces of his presence.

In this case, it meant replacing Domitian's head with Nerva's. Although this was skillfully done, the interventions are still visible. If you look closer, you will see his eyes are uneven, and his neck is too long.

Museo Gregoriano Egizio | Gregorian Egyptian Museum

Pope Gregory XVI opened the Museo Gregoriano Egizio to the public in 1839, the Museum of Ancient Egyptian art in the Vatican.

The exhibits mostly concentrate on Ancient Egyptian artefacts found in Rome, as well as the ones discovered in Hadrain's Villa in Tivoli.

The pope opened this museum to justify his interest for Egyptian funerary artefacts. This polytheistic culture had a huge influence on shaping the Bible and Christianity.

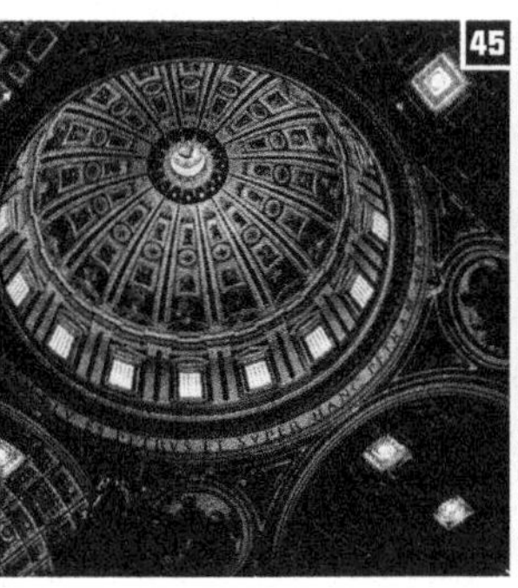
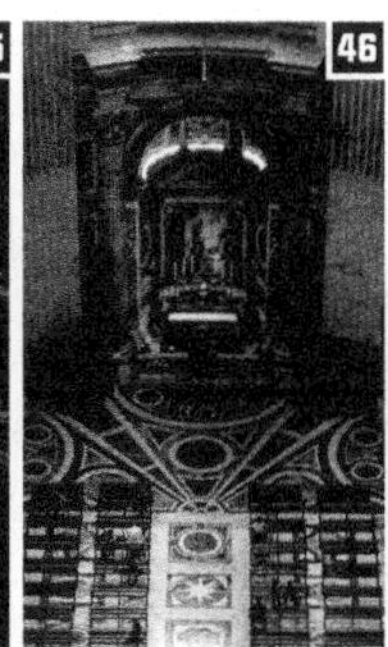
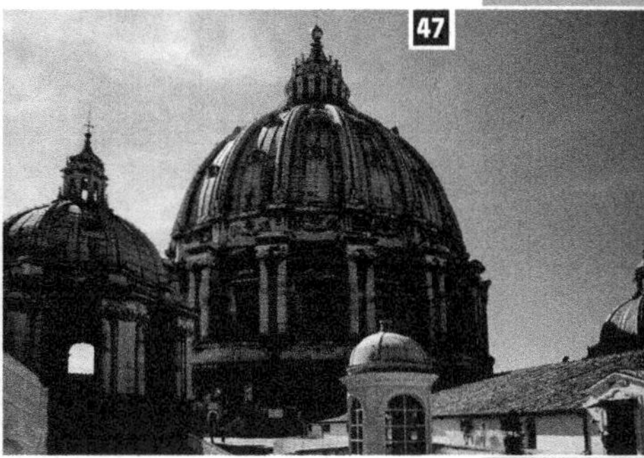

The concept also supported Mesopotamian and Middle Eastern art, which can be found near the end of the museum.

Room I. Stelas and statues from Ancient Egypt, 2600 BC – AD 600
Room II. Funerary cult in Ancient Egypt, 2600 BC – AD 200
Room III. Reconstruction of Serapeions from Hadrian's Villa in Tivoli, AD 131
Room IV. Egypt according to Roman interpretation, 1st and 2nd century
Semicircular Hall V. Pharaoh, sculpture, 2000 BC – AD 100
Room VI. Votive bronze objects from the 1st millennium BC
Room VII. Bronze and clay figures from Hellenic and Roman era in Egypt
Room VIII. Tablets with cuneiform, Mesopotamian seals, 3rd – 1st millennium BC, bronze pots from the Middle East and the Palmira relief from 1st – 3rd century
Room IX. Relief with an inscription from the Assyrian Palestina, 883 –612 BC

Museo Etnologico | Ethnological Museum

For centuries, Catholic missionaries collected interesting artefacts from different cultures.

More than 100,000 objects have been collected in this way. From plaster portraits of Native Americans, Prehistoric archaeological finds from Jerusalem to the collection of Chinese coins.

Museo Gregoriano Etrusco | Gregorian Etruscan Museum

Museo Gregoriano Etrusco spans across eight galleries. Etruscan vases, sarcophagi and bronze pieces are on display, including artefacts from south Italy, both Hellenic and Roman.

Mars from Todi

One of the most prominent exhibits from this collection is a unique, almost life-size sculpture of the Etruscan warrior made of bronze (5th – 4th century BC). It was found in Todi, ancient Tuder. It is a representation of the Etruscan god of war Laran.

Etruscans came into contact with the Greek colonists quite early on Sicily and the south of Italy, calling it *Magna Graecia*. While trading with them, they were introduced to Greek art and craft, which they copied religiously.

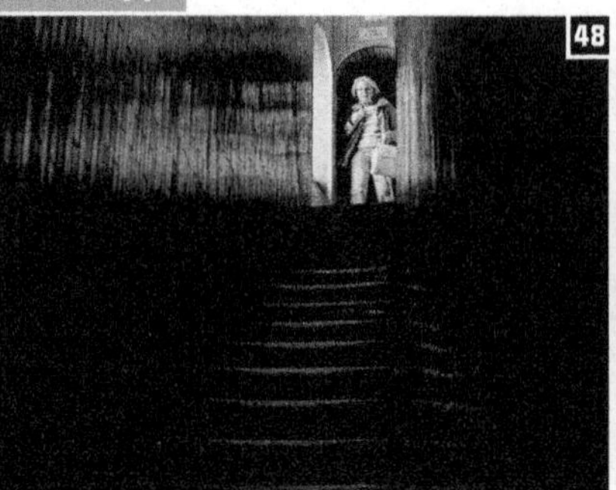

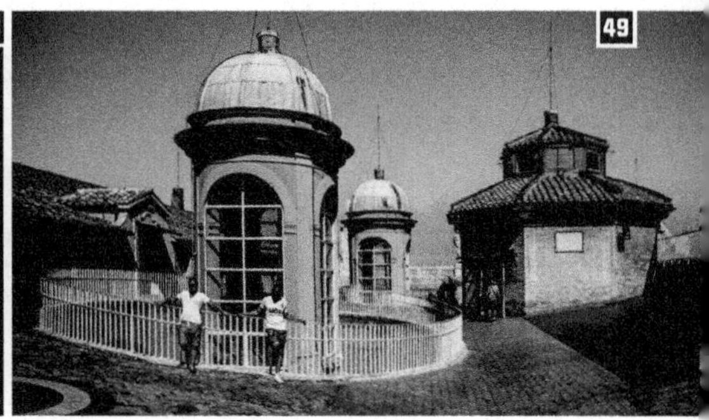

This sculpture is a good example of the strong influence classic Greek art, especially in the position of the legs, the so-called *Greek contrapposto*. Even though the face is rather lifeless, the eyes enliven it.

Pinacoteca Vaticana | The Vatican Pinacoteca (ART Gallery)

It is safe to say that the Vatican Pinacoteca can be considered as one of the most important museums in the history of Western European painting. Majority of great Italian painters are represented in 18 rooms. Some of the highlights are: Giotto's *Stefaneschi Triptych*, Olivuccio di Ciccarello's *Opere di Misericordia*, Raphael's *Madonna of Foligno*, Oddi *Altarpiece* and *Transfiguration*, Leonardo da Vinci's *St. Jerome in the Wilderness*, Caravaggio's *Entombment*, Perugino's *Madonna and Child with Saints* and San Francesco al Prato *Resurrection*, Filippo Lippi's *Marsuppini Coronation*.

Room I. 12th – 15th century (Nicolò e Giovanni Pisano)
Room II. 13th – 15th century (Giotto di Bondone)
Room III. 15th century (Beato Angelico)
Room IV. 15th – 16th century (Melozzo da Forlì)
Room V. 15th century (Ercole de' Roberti)
Room VI. 15th – century (Winged altars)
Room VII. 15th – 16th century (Perugino)
Room VIII. 16th century (Raphael)
Room IX. 15th – 16th century (Leonardo da Vinci)
Room X. 16th century (Raphael's School and Venetian art)
Room XI. 16th century (Federico Barocci)
Room XII. 17th century (Caravaggio)
Room XIII. 17th century (Pietro da Cortona)
Room XIV. 17th century (Carlo Maratta)
Room XV. 18th century (Giovanni Battista Crespi)
Room XVI. 19th century (Wenzel Peter)
Room XVII. 17th century (Gian Lorenzo Bernini)
Room XVIII. 15th – 16th century (Icons)

Unfortunately, most of the rooms are very poorly lit, which rather ruins the chance to actually observe the paintings.

Museo Pio-Cristiano | Pio Cristiano Museum

The museum was established by Pope Pius IV in 1854 and moved to the Lateran Palace in the Vatican in 1963.

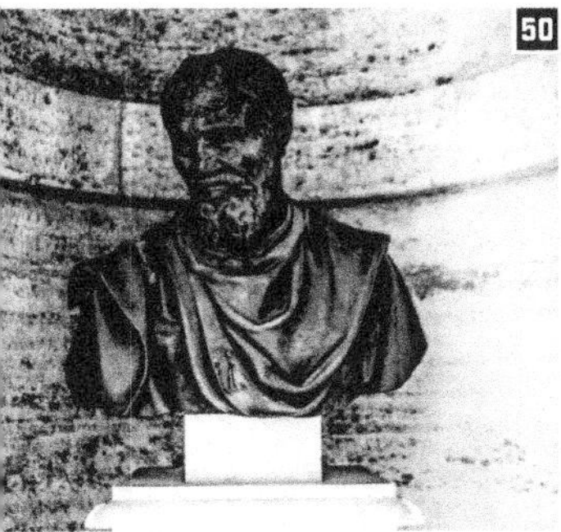

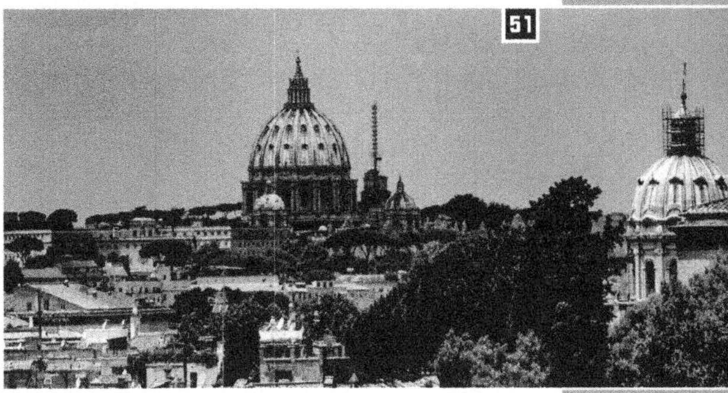

It features archaeological exhibits from the Early Christian period. Stone sarcophagi with scenes from the 6th century onward are particularly interesting. The epigraphic section of the museum is not open to the public.

Museo Filatelico e Numismatico | Philatelic and Numismatic Museum

The museum is perfect for a comprehensive overview of philatelist and numismatic editions of the Vatican State since 1929. In addition, there are postal seals, sketches and printing plates illustrating various stages in the making of stamps and coins.

① Stanze di Raffaello | Raphael Rooms ★★★★

After visiting all the museums, it is time to go to the part of the Vatican Palace open to the public. First of all, this is where you can find some of the most famous Italian frescoes.

A hardcore patron of the arts, Pope Julius II, decided to decorate his chambers at the other end of the Vatican Palace. For this task, he hired Raphael, the most esteemed painter of his generation.

There are four rooms or *stanze*, painted by Raphael and his assistants from top to bottom until the artist died in 1520.

The work continued even after his death, until 1524. The rooms are named according to themes on the frescoes. We have Hall of Constantine, Heliodorus's Room, Room of the Signatura and Room of the Fire in the Borgo.

Sala di Costantino | Hall of Constantine

In the first room, Sala di Costantino, there are four scenes depicting the life of the Roman Emperor Constantine the Great, the first Roman Christian emperor. An underlying theme in all the scenes is triumph of true faith, victory of Christianity over polytheism.

Apparition of the Cross, Battle at the Milvian Bridge, Baptism of Constantine and his Charter – these are accompanied by allegories of virtue, as well as popes. The scenes go clockwise.

Apparition of the Cross

Constantine the Great saw the Cross immediately before his battle against Maxentius. Constantine decided to throw away the Roman eagle and put the cross to lead his army. Traditionally, it was precisely when he fought under the cross that he secured his victory.

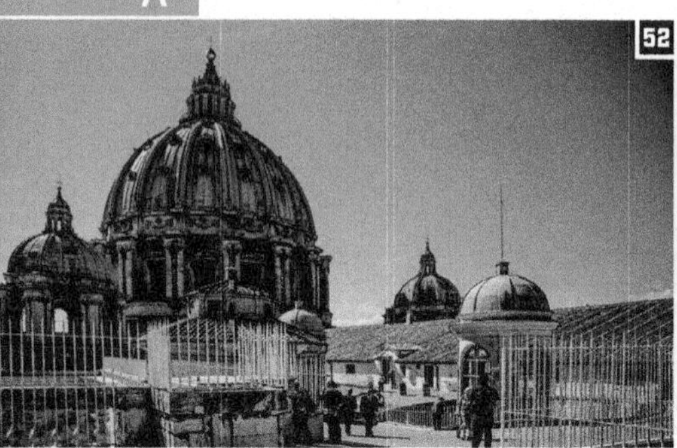

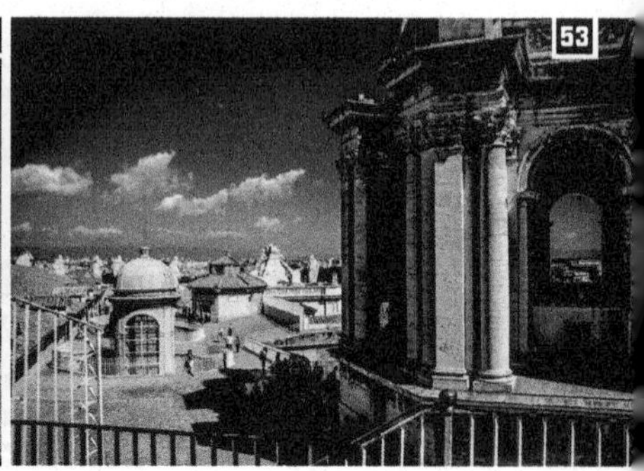

The Battle of the Milvian Bridge

In northern Rome, there was a battle between Constantine and Maxentius in 312. Under the protection of the cross, Constantine's army killed Maxentius and won.

Baptism of Constantine

After bearing witness to the power of the cross and true faith on the Milvian Bridge, Constantine took up Christianity. In this scene, he is being baptized by Pope Sylvester I.

The pope, however, has the face of another pope, Clement VII, because he took over the Holy See while the fresco was being completed. This was after Raphael's death and the fresco was completed by his pupil, Giovanni Penni.

Constantine's Charter

Since Constantine's state power was subjugated to God, the last fresco also aims to confirm papal authority. Even though it was later discovered that the Charter was a fake, the show still had to go on as far as this room was concerned. In matters of faith, material evidence did not always play a crucial role.

Pope Sylvester's face was also replaced by Pope Clement VII's in this scene. On the ceiling, there is the Triumph of Christianity, a fresco by Tommaso Laureti.

Stanza di Eliodoro | Room of Heliodorus

During Julius II's papacy, this room was used for private audiences. The character of the frescoes is also political and religious. They promote the independence of the pope with regard to profane rulers, in light of usurping tendencies shown by the French king charging on the Apennine peninsula. The visual program was designed to restore papal authority, both morally and politically.

This seemed to be very important to Pope Julius II, after the popes of Avignon and counter-popes in the 14th century, followed by the moral decay of the church under the Borgias in the 15th century.

The Syrian officer Heliodorus is banished from the Jewish Temple in Jerusalem, which he was ordered to pillage by the Syrian king.

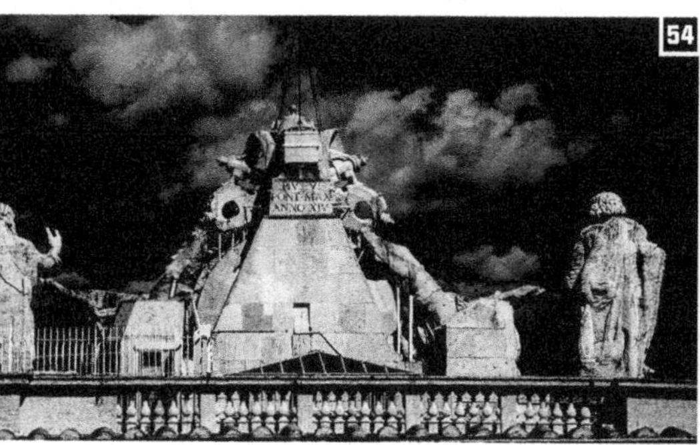

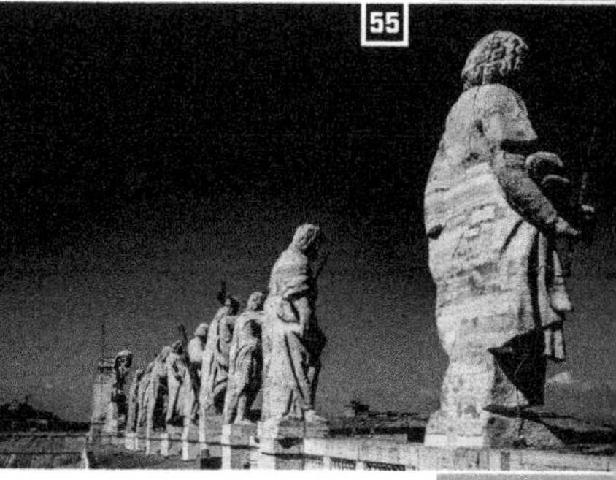

A horseman and his assistants, sent by God himself, chase away Heliodorus and his army. The pope is sitting on the other side, on a carrying chair, the so-called *sedia gestatoria*. Raphael is among the carriers.

Mass of Bolsena

Here, a miracle from 1263 is shown. The blood of Jesus started dripping from a wafer. Since that day, the Christians celebrate Chorpus Christi and the Church in Orvieto was built on the site of this miracle.

Liberation of St. Peter

An angel sets Peter free from prison. The first Roman bishop, Peter, is cleverly linked to the French occupation of the Papal State and its liberation by Pope Julius II, when he was just a cardinal in San Pietro in Vincoli.

Encounter of Leo the Great with Attila

Chronologically speaking, the last fresco in this room is this one, because Pope Julius II was no longer alive when it was made.

Pope Leo I is shown with a holy army, headed by Peter and Paul with swords in their hands, managing to convince Attila the Hun to leave the Apennine peninsula.

Once again, political elements are abundant.

This time they are aimed against the Habsburgs — an army led by the Spanish Habsburg Charles V will pillage Rome and jeopardize pope's existence in 1527.

The pope barely made it alive, escaping through a secret tunnel connecting the Vatican to the Castel Sant'Angelo.

Did you know?

Where to see Raphael's paintings and frescoes in Rome and Vatican?

▸ *Portrait of a Man*, Galleria Borghese (1502)

▸ *Lady with a Unicorn*, Galleria Borghese (1506)

▸ *The Deposition*, Galleria Borghese (1507)

▸ *La Fornarina*, Galleria Borghese (1520)

▸ *The Prophet Isaiah*, Basilica of Sant'Agostino, (1511–1512)

▸ *The Triumph of Galatea*, Villa Farnesina (1511–1513)

▸ *The Sibyls*, Santa Maria della Pace (1514)

▸ *Double Portrait*, Doria Pamphilj Gallery (1516)

▸ *The Transfiguration*, Vatican Museums (1516–1520)

▸ *Stanze di Raffaello*, Vatican (1508–1520)

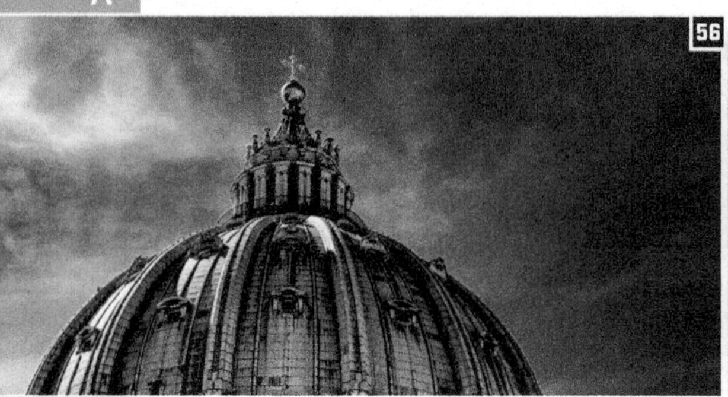 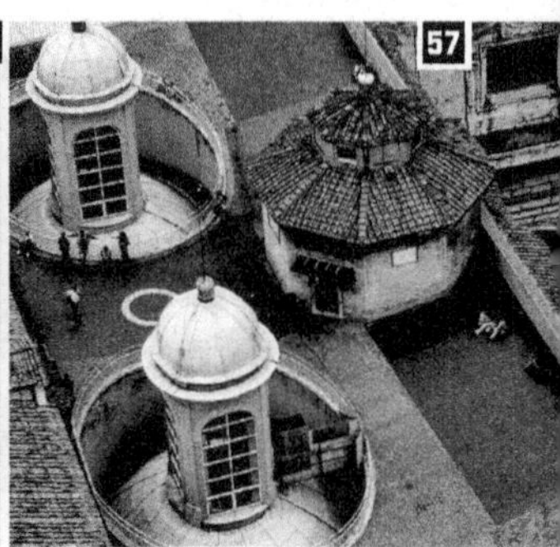

Stanza della Segnatura | Room of the Segnatura

This room, perhaps the most beautiful of all four, was the first room painted by Raphael (1508–1511). Today, it is considered as the defining work of the High Renaissance. Also, the year of Raphael's death, 1524, is considered as the end of the High Renaissance. Here, the pope is the head of the highest judiciary body of the Holy See, the *Segnatura Gratiae et Lustitiae*, where he brought important verdicts. The topics in this room pertain to the three highest principles of the mind: Truth, Goodness and Beauty.

School of Athens

The most impressive fresco is the School of Athens, painted by Raphael in 1510–11. This is an allegory of ancient philosophy as a precursor of Christian wisdom. We can see Plato, Aristotle, Pythagoras, Diogenes, Heraclitus, Euclid, Zoroaster and Ptolemy, among others. Some of the faces were replaced by contemporary figures, such as Bramante (Archimedes with students), Michelangelo (Heraclitus), Leonardo da Vinci (Parmenides).

The setting is also contemporary, they find themselves surrounded by renaissance architecture, more precisely, Bramante's version of the new St. Peter's Church.

Disputation over the Most Holy Sacrament

On the opposite wall, there is a fresco with heavenly and earthly figures. Among the earthlings, there is Adam, Moses, Jacob, while Christ, Mary and John the Baptist are above them.

In the lower half of the fresco, there are popes and holy church fathers, accompanied by Dante Alighieri on the right with a laurel wreath on his head, and Bramante, Raphael's mentor, shown as an old man with no hair, holding a book while resting on a balustrade.

Parnassus

This is a depiction of a mythical place where Apollo and the Muses lived. This is also the home of poets. Many poets are represented, from Homer and Ovid, to Petrarch, Ariosto and Dante.

Stanza dell'incendio del Borgo | Room of the Fire in the Borgo

This room was also used for judiciary purposes. The ceiling painting is dedicated to the room's original function.

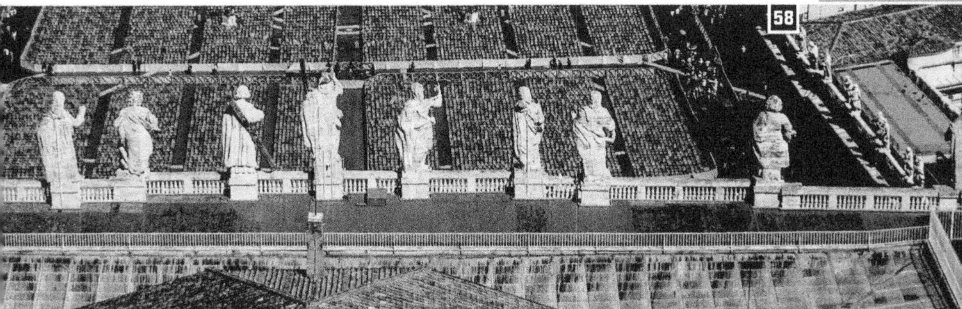

The fresco on the ceiling was made by Perugino in 1508. Pope Leo X repurposed it into a dining room. The room was painted by Raphael from 1514 to 1517. Papal authority is still in focus.

Coronation of Charles the Great or Charlemagne

The fresco emphasizes political dependence on the will of the Pope. In this case, it is the first emperor of the Holy Roman Empire Charles the Great being crowned by Pope Leo III in 800.

Justification of Leo III

This is an episode in which the Pope refuses to answer charges made by the nephew of Pope's predecessor, Hadrian I.

It was the day before Pope Leo III would crown Charlemagne as the first emperor of the Holy Roman Empire in St. Peter's Basilica.

The statement behind the piece is that the Pope is only responsible to God as His representative in this world, so he is infallible.

Fire in the Borgo

This was probably painted by Raphael's student Giulio Romano. According to *Liber Pontificalis*, there was a fire in the Borgo in 847, a neighborhood in front of St. Peter's Basilica.

Pope Leo IV blessed the neighborhood, after which the fire was miraculously extinguished. This is a strong message on how the church is the savior of people.

Maritime Battle at Ostia

A maritime battle from 849 when soldiers of the Papal League (Papal, Neapolitan and Gaetano armies), led by Pope Leo IV, fought against the Saracen ships.

Papal soldiers defeated the pagans, which is clear message sent by Pope Leo X in support of the Crusades.

⌾ Cappella Niccolina | Chapel of Nicholas V ★★★

In this chapel, you will find amazing frescoes by Fra Angelico, a Dominican painter and the holiest of all Italian painters.

③ Borgia Apartments ★★

In the apartments of Pope Alexander VI Borgia, there are frescoes with Biblical scenes by Pinturicchio of Umbria. Most of the five-room apartment is used today as the Vatican Museum of Modern Art.

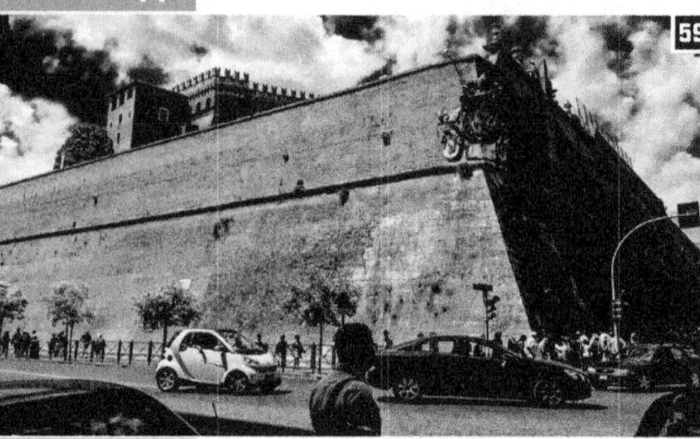

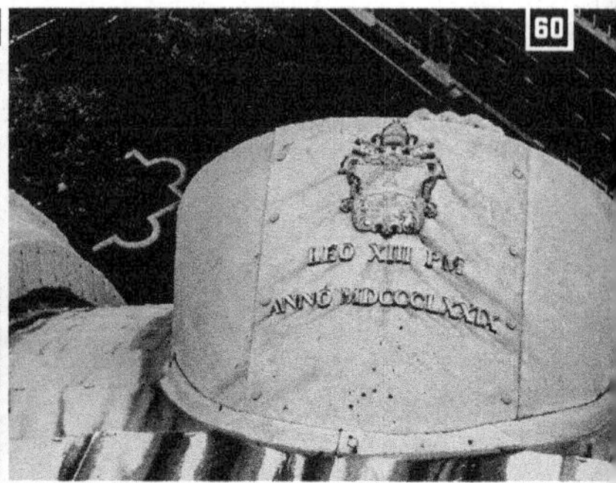

Here, you will find about 600 paintings, sculptures and graphic works, by some of the most famous artists of the 20th century.

The entry requirement for art works is to depict a theme of spiritual nature.

④ The Sistine Chapel ★★★★

The Sistine Chapel contains some of the most famous images in the world. Even today, the Papal Conclave takes place here to elect the new Pope.

The Chapel was designed and built by Baccio Pontelli (1475–1483), a Florentine architect, characterized by Vasari as the court architect of Pope Sixtus IV. The Chapel is 131 ft (40 m) long, 43 ft (13 m) wide and 66 ft (20 m) high. It was made according to the proportions of the Temple of Solomon, which means it is twice as long as it is high and thrice as wide.

The visual repertoire on the walls examines the life of Moses and Jesus, protagonists of the Old and the New Testament, respectively. The scenes were painted by Sandro Botticelli and Pietro Perugino, among others.

The Last Judgement

Out of all these paintings, the most famous one is at the altar. The Last Judgement covers an entire side of the chapel above the altar. Michelangelo began working on it in 1536, 20 years after he had finished painting the ceiling. He completed it in 1541, when he was 66 years old. It spans across 2,152 sq. ft. (200 sq. m.) and contains around 390 figures, painted by the great master himself, without any help from his pupils.

The painting is interesting because it was a huge bone of contention between Michelangelo and Cardinal Oliviero Carafa who thought the imagery was amoral and obscene. Michelangelo even inserted a self-portrait — you can see him in the skin peeled off from the martyred Bartholomew.

Since you only have 15 minutes to visit the Sistine Chapel, let's move on to the most astonishing part – the ceiling.

The ceiling of the Sistine Chapel

Michelangelo painted the ceiling in four years, from 1508 to 1512.

There are 115 over-life sized figures across 5,511 sq. ft. (512 sq. m.). Contrary to popular belief, which holds the artist had to paint while lying on his back, Vasari reports that the artist was standing with his head and hand high.

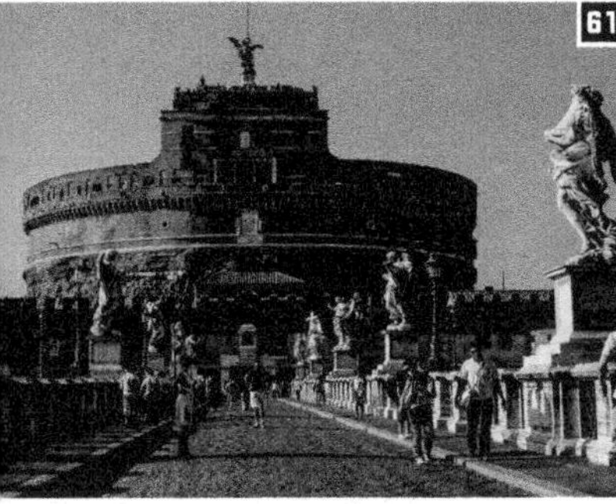

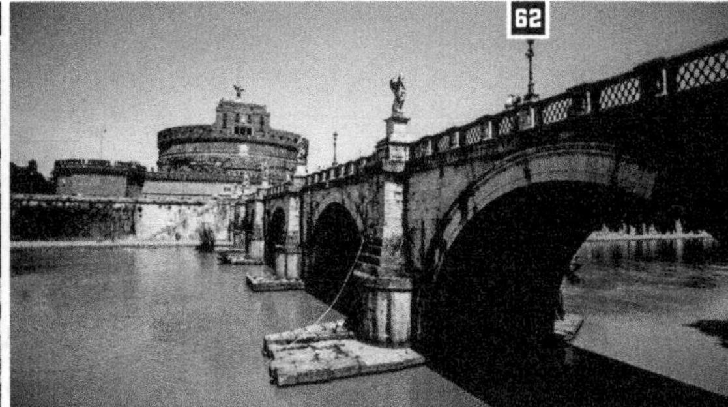

The repertoire from the altar to the main entrance is as follows:

- The Separation of Light and Darkness
- The Creation of the Sun, Moon and Earth
- The Separation of Land and Water
- The Creation of Adam
- The Creation of Eve
- The Temptation and Expulsion
- The Sacrifice of Noah
- The Great Flood
- The Drunkenness of Noah

◆ Vatican Courtyards ★★

There are three courtyards, with two of them open to the public.

Cortile della Pigna

Here you can find the famous Fontana della Pigna. Both the fountain and the courtyard were named after the large Roman pine cone that once belonged to a Roman fountain.

The cone was 13 ft or 4 m high and stood somewhere near the Pantheon, next to the Temple of Isis.

Bronze peacocks were placed on both sides of the cone, and were, in fact, copies of the peacocks that decorated Hadrian's Mausoleum, present-day Castel Sant'Angelo. The original peacocks are kept at the Vatican Braccio Nuovo.

Cortile della Pigna is part of an enormous courtyard called Cortile del Belvedere, designed by Donato Bramante.

Cortile del Belvedere was divided into two areas when the Vatican Library was built. There is a bronze sculpture in the middle of the courtyard called Sphere Within Sphere, by a contemporary Italian sculptor Arnaldo Pomodoro.

Giardino Quadrato

Until recently, this garden was secret and now it is open to visitors. Giardino Quadrato is in front of the Vatican Pinacoteca. Initially, it was reserved for papal guests only.

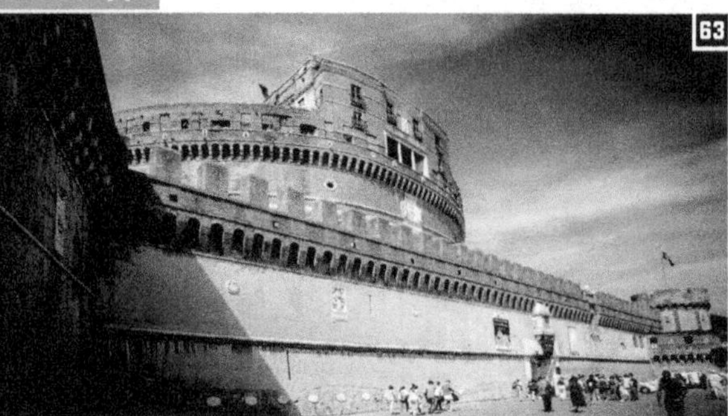

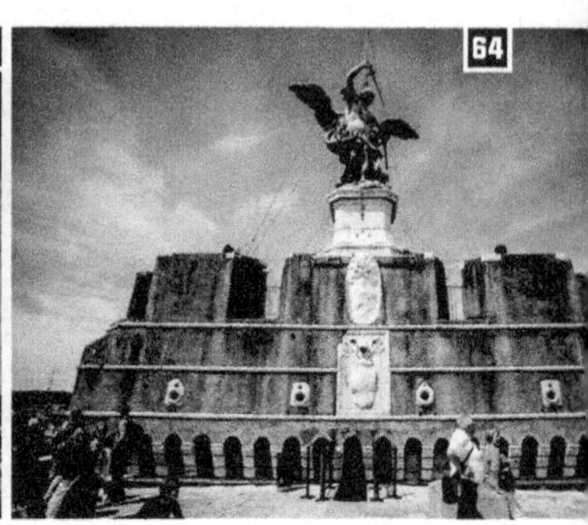

Walk around Vatican City

❻ Ponte Sant'Angelo ★★★ 🟥

Crossing the Tiber over Hadrian's Bridge, Pons Aelius (AD 134) will get you to the Castle of the Holy Angel. During the Inquisition, bodies of the prisoners executed in the Honor Courtyard were displayed on this bridge. Pope Clement VII placed statues of St. Peter and St. Paul in 1535. 🟥 Pope Paul III employed Bernini to make ten angels for the bridge, to welcome the visitors.

Bernini managed to complete only two of them. They have the inscription I.N.R.I. and thorny crowns. Bernini's statues were replaced by copies, while the originals are in the Church of Sant'Andrea delle Fratte. 🟥 **[p.204]**

Angels on Ponte Sant'Angelo

▸ Angel with the Column by Antonio Raggi: *Tronus meus in columna | My throne is upon a column,*

▸ Angel with the Whips by Lazzaro Morelli: *In flagella paratus sum | I am ready for the whip,*

▸ Angel with the Crown of Thorns by Bernini and his son Paolo Valentino: *ZIn aerumna mea dum configitur spina | In my affliction, whilst the thorn is fastened upon me,* 🟥

Original is in church of Sant'Andrea delle Fratte,

▸ Angel with the Sudarium or Veronica's Veil by Cosimo Fancelli: *Respice faciem Christi tui | Look upon the face of thy Christ,*

▸ Angel with the Garment and Dice by Paolo Naldini:

Super vestimentum meum miserunt sortem | Upon my vesture they cast lots,

▸ Angel with the Nail by Girolamo Lucenti: *Aspicient ad me quem confixerunt | They shall look upon me whom they have pierced,*

▸ Angel with the Cross by Ercole Ferrata: *Cuius principatus super humerum eius | Whose government shall be upon His shoulder,*

▸ Angel with the Superscription by Bernini and his son Paolo Valentino: *Regnavit a ligno deus | God has reigned from the Tree.* Original is in church of Sant'Andrea delle Fratte,

▸ Angel with the Sponge or with vinegar by Antonio Giorgetti: *Potaverunt me aceto | They gave me vinegar to drink,*

▸ Angel with the Lance by Domenico Guidi: *Vulnerasti cor meum | Thou hast ravished my heart.*

❼ Castel Sant'Angelo ★★★★

Castle of the Holy Angel was built around AD 138 as a mausoleum for Emperor Hadrian and his family. Roman emperors were buried here until 217. Urns were placed in the present-day Treasury Room. Urns belonging to seven Roman emperors were kept here: Hadrian, Antoninus Pius, Lucius Verus, Marcus Aurelius, Commodus, Septimius Severus and Caracalla. During the great plague of Rome in 590, Pope Gregory I saw an angel laying down its sword, which was interpreted as a sign that the epidemic was going to end. As a symbol of gratitude, the Pope ordered an angel to be placed on top of the mausoleum.

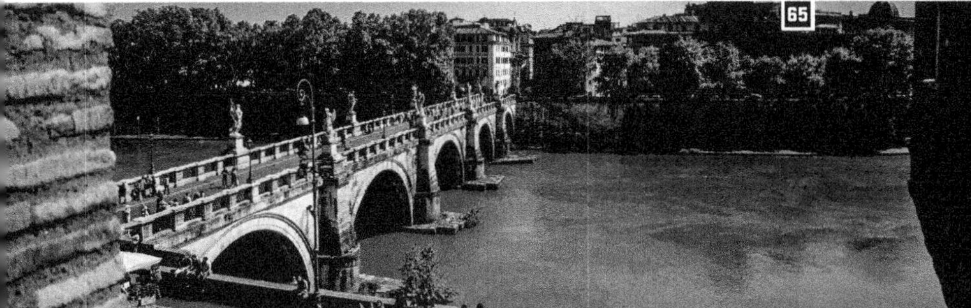

This is how Hadrian's Mausoleum became Castle of the Holy Angel. Another version says that Romans were so desperate during the plague that they pleaded with the ancient Roman gods and brought them sacrifices in front of Hadrian's Mausoleum. The Pope organized a procession to the Mausoleum. In the middle of all this, archangel Michael appeared in front of the Pope, putting his bloodied sword back into the sheath. Mausoleum was deconsecrated in 401 when Emperor Honorius decided to insert it in the Aurelian Wall as a citadel, due to the threat of Germanic invasion. In 410, the Visigoths lead by Alaric sacked Rome, pillaging anything they could get their hands on, including Hadrian's Mausoleum. Bronze plates and stone statues were destroyed. Whatever remained was used during the construction of St. Peter's Basilica in the 16th century. In 847, Pope Leo IV redecorated Hadrian's Mausoleum and turned it into a papal fortress. Pope Nicholas III joined the Vatican and the Castle via a corridor. The secret passage is called *Passetto di Borgo*. On more than one occasion, it was used as a spectacular getaway from St. Peter's Basilica by the Popes. Passetto di Borgo is located within the defense walls leading from the Basilica, parallel to Bernini's Baroque colonnade all the way to the Castle of the Holy Angel. The most spectacular escape through the Passetto di Borgo can be credited to Pope Clement VII in 1527, when the Army of the Holy Roman Empire lead by Charles V breached Rome.

Did you know?

How to visit the Passetto di Borgo

Visits to the Passetto di Borgo Galleries can be organized for smaller groups, if you buy a ticket to the Castle of the Holy Angel.

For security reasons, a visit to the Passetto di Borgo is only available with advanced booking: www.tosc.it/en

It is usually open only in summer in the framework of the event *Notti d'Estate a Castel Sant'Angelo* (Summer Nights in Castel Sant'Angel)

Opening hours: see online

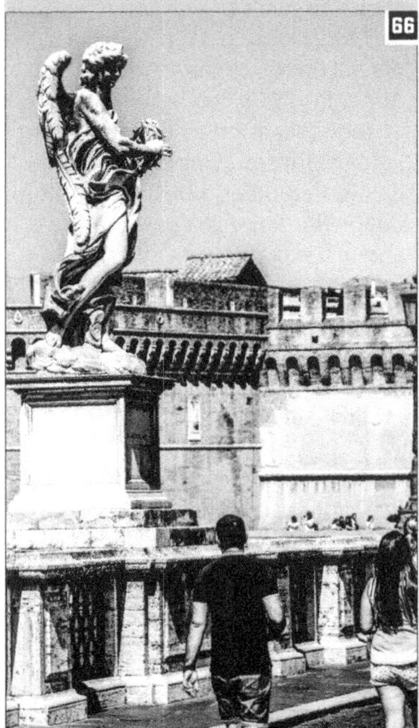

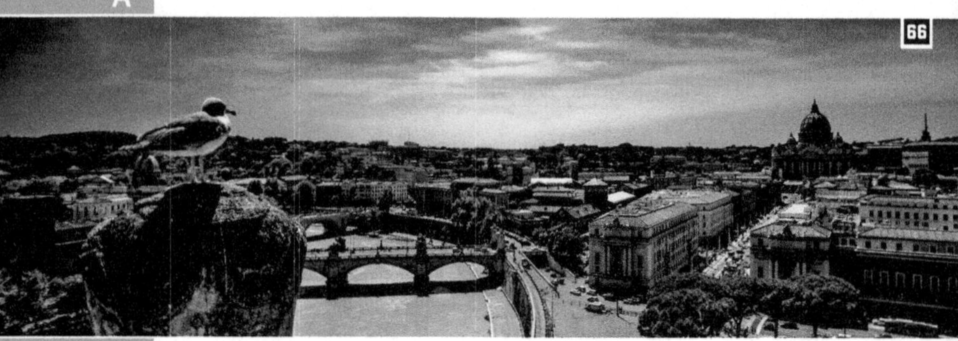

In this decisive moment for the Papal State, almost the entire Swiss Guard died defending the Pope. To this day, members of the Swiss Guard take the oath on May 6, commemorating that heroic act.

During the Renaissance, the Castle was also used as a prison by the Inquisition. Many historical figures were held captive here, including Giordano Bruno for six years, Galileo Galilei, Caravaggio and Benvenuto Cellini. In the so-called "Honor Courtyard", swift executions of less respectable prisoners took place. **63**

Cortile del' Angelo

When you climb to the courtyard, you will come across an angel sculpture, which is how the courtyard got its name. The angel was made by one of Michelangelo's busier pupils, Raffaello da Montelupo in 1536. Initially, it was placed on top of the Castle of the Holy Angel. In 1753, it was replaced by another angel, sculpted by the Flemish artist Peter Anton von Verschaffelt. Raffaello da Montelupo also built the Madonna Chapel for Pope Leo X at the opposite end of the courtyard.

However, the façade and the chapel (1514–1521) are attributed to Michelangelo. The Castle of the Holy Angel has five levels:

▶ The lowest level is the ramp from Roman times,

▶ The Renaissance prison cells are one level up,

▶ On the third level, there is the Angel Courtyard with the Chapel of Leo X,

▶ Papal apartments are on the fourth level, including the Sala Paolina and the Treasury. The Court Library is also worth exploring,

▶ On the last level, there is a refreshment shop and a terrace with an amazing view of the city. **66**

Castel Sant'Angelo
Address: Lungotevere Castello 50, Roma
Online:
www.castelsantangelo.beniculturali.it

Public transportation: Metro A stop Ottaviano or stop Lepanto

Opening hours: *see online*

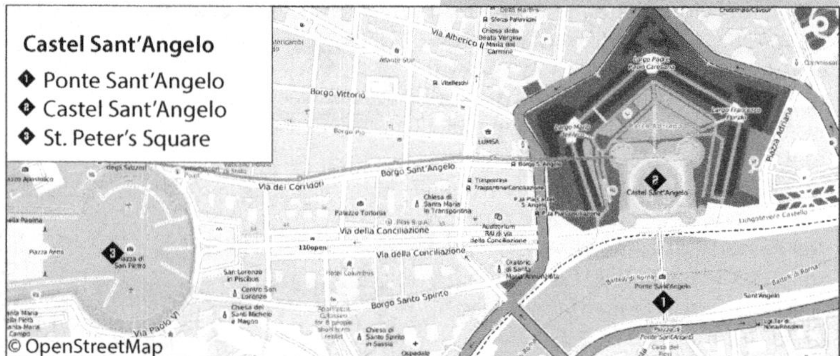

Along the Tiber

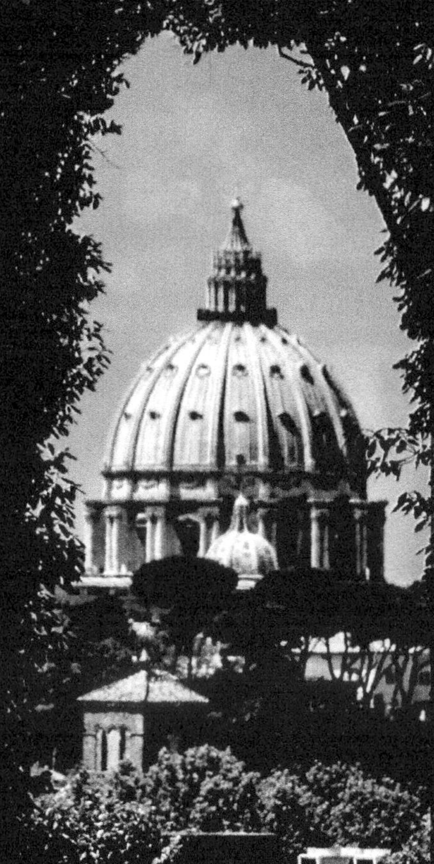

The secret keyhole view of St. Peter's Basilica

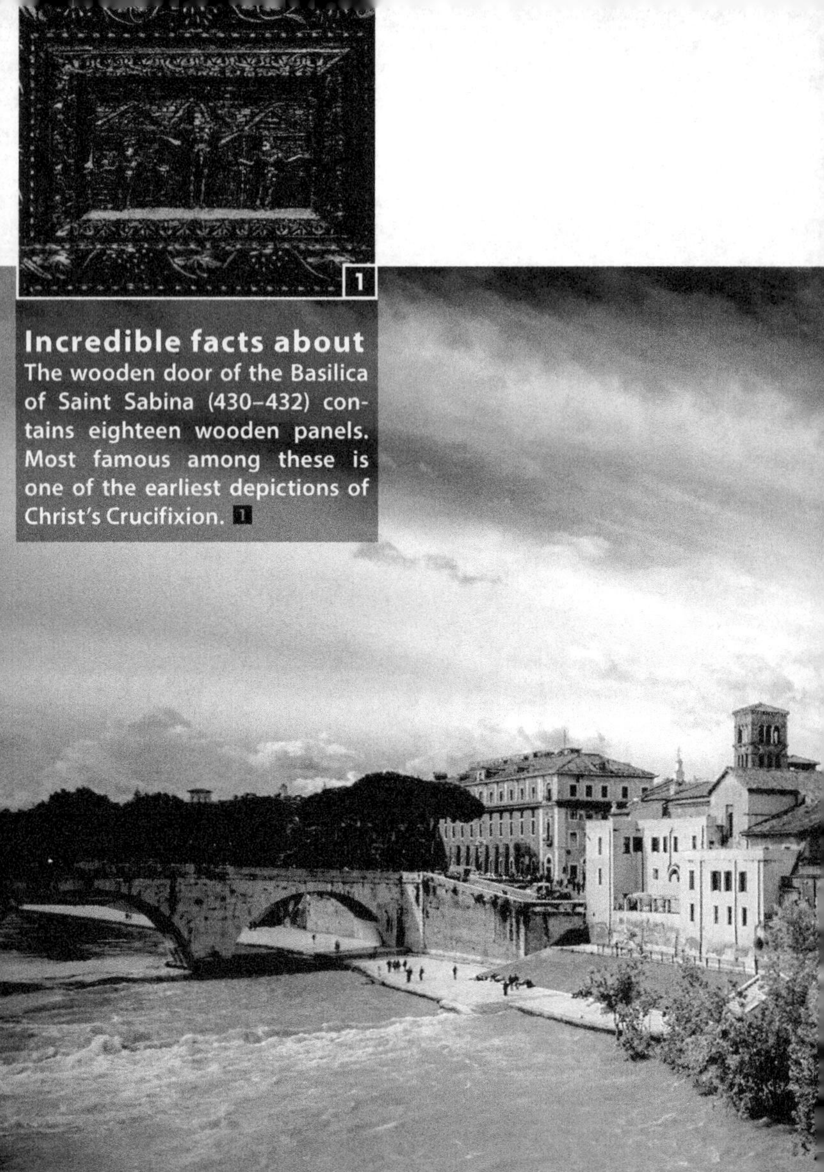

Incredible facts about
The wooden door of the Basilica of Saint Sabina (430–432) contains eighteen wooden panels. Most famous among these is one of the earliest depictions of Christ's Crucifixion. **1**

Tiber Island

Extra Tip : : :
If you visit Rome in the summer or early fall, make sure to walk to the Tiber Island when it gets dark. The river banks are full of cafés and people. There is also *Isola del Cinema*, an open air summer film festival.

Twists and turns through the history

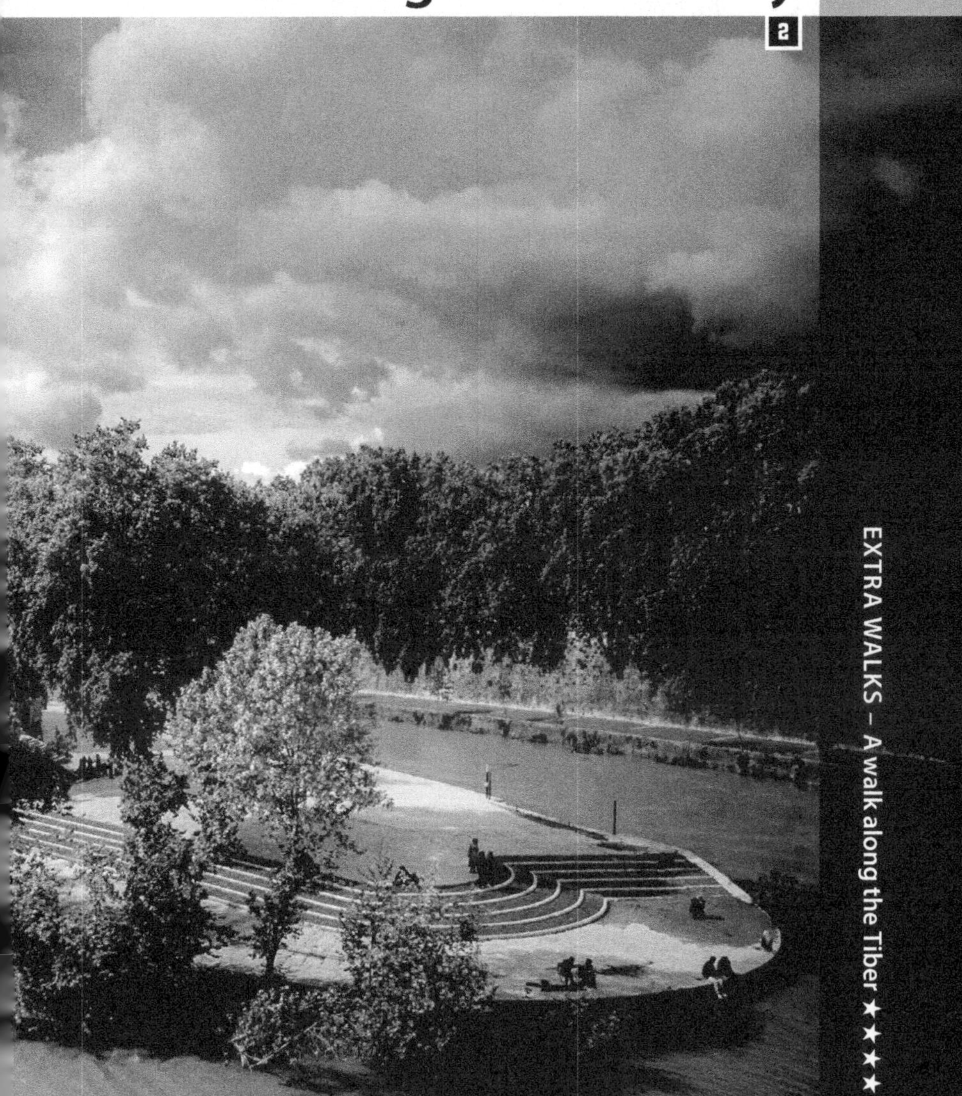

Isola Tiberina | Tiber Island
Address: Isola Tiberina, Roma
Public transportation: Bus stop Piazza Monte Savello: 23, 63, 280, 810 | Tram stop Arenula – Ministero Grazia E Giustizia: 8

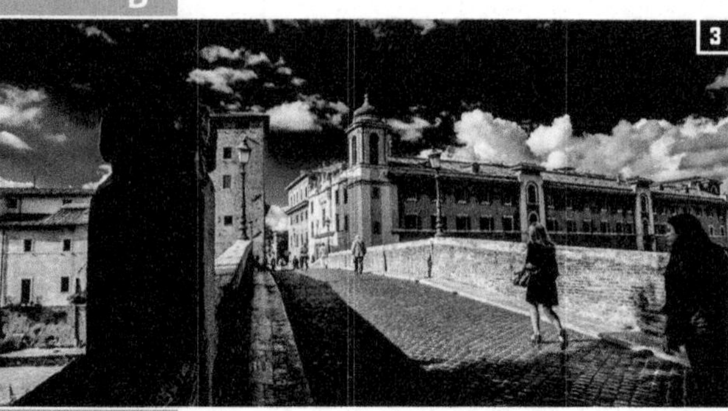

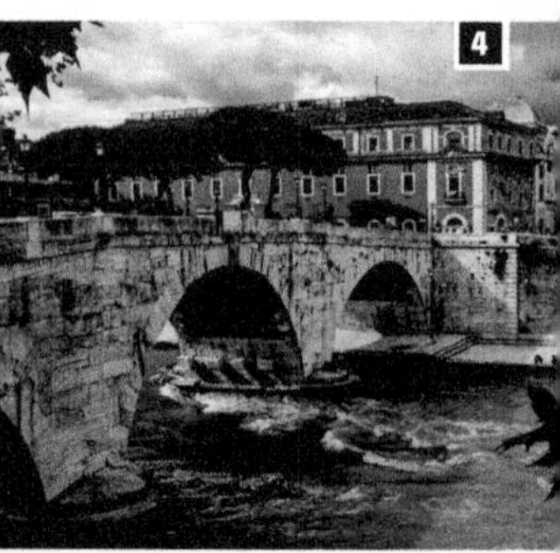

◆ Tiber Island ★★★★ 2

Isola Tiberina is the only island on the Roman Tiber. It was very important for the progress of Rome, because it was easier to join the riversides by using the landmass in the middle of the river. Not only was the island relevant for traffic, but it also has extraordinary history. The first hospital was built here in 289 BC. Healing houses and temples dedicated to the gods of healing found their place here. In Christian Rome, temples were replaced with churches dedicated to healer saints. The hospital that we have today was built in 1584. Most of the employees come from the *Fatebenefratelli* or the Hospital Order of St. John of God. In Roman times, it was called *Insula Inter Duos Pontes* or "The Island between two bridges." Even today, those same old bridges connect the left bank with the right one via the island. They are two short, pedestrian bridges that lean on the island. 3

◇ Ponte Cestio ★★ 4

The second bridge, the one from the direction of Trastevere, is called Ponte Cestio or Pons Cestius in Latin. It was built by Lucius Cestius circa 50 BC. Lucius Cestius was the brother of Caius Cestius, who built the only preserved Roman pyramid. [p.254] Originally, the bridge had two arches, just like Ponte Fabricio. However, in late 19th century, the bridge was completely "renovated" to have three arches. The one in the middle is mostly from the Roman period.

◇ Ponte Fabricio ★★ 5

The ancient bridge of Pons Fabricius connects the banks in front of the Roman Ghetto with the Tiber Island. It is the oldest fully preserved bridge in Rome, built by Lucius Fabricius, a Roman street curator in 62 BC. This has been recorded in a stone arch, the one closer to the Roman shore:

Did you know?

Tiber Island during the Roman Empire

During the Roman Empire, it was common for masters to get rid of slaves who were terminally ill. In other words, they just left them on this island.

The ones who miraculously survived were automatically freed by the emperor.

Those slaves were few, so we can guess more people died on this island than anywhere else in Rome, even the Colosseum.

EXTRA WALKS – A walk along the Tiber ★★★★

174

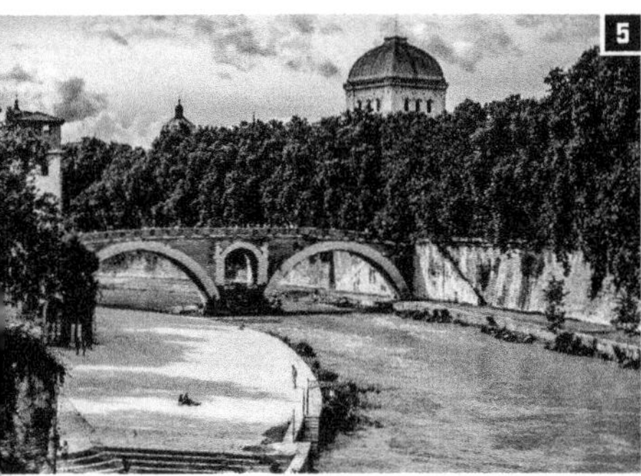

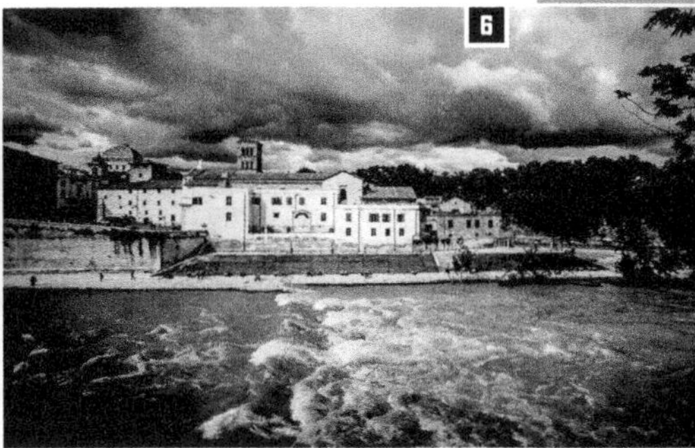

L . FABRICIVS . C . F . CVR . VIAR | FACIVNDVM . COERAVIT | IDEMQVE | PROBAVIT

Lucius Fabricius, Son of Gaius, Head Road Curator, ensured the building of this bridge

Underneath the ancient inscription, there is another sign in Latin, informing us that Pope Innocent XI restored the bridge in the 17th century. Ponte Fabricio is sometimes called *Ponte dei Quattro Capi*, due to two Roman stelas at the foot of the bridge. Heads of Janus and Hercules look at opposites sides of the world. **3**

③ San Bartolomeo all'Isola ★★ **6**

The Basilica of St. Bartholomew on the Island is a church right in the middle of the Tiber Island. It was built in 1000 by Emperor Otto III. The baroque façade that you can see today was designed by Orazio Torriani (1624). The oldest elements of the church are 14 columns and two medieval lions.

The nearby tower called Torre dei Caetani, was part of a medieval fort erected by the Pierleoni family. The island also has a hospital, which has been there since Roman times, called *Ospedale Fatebenefratelli*, and run by Brothers Hospitallers of St. John of God.

④ Ponte Aemilius ★★ **7**

If you look down the river, you will notice the remains of another Roman bridge. This was Pons Aemilius. There is only the middle arch, so Romans also call it Ponte Rotto or Broken Bridge.

This was the oldest stone bridge in Rome, built way back in 174 BC. It had six arches, connecting Rome with the main road to Ostia. It was named after the consul who ordered it — Marcus Aemilius Lepidus.

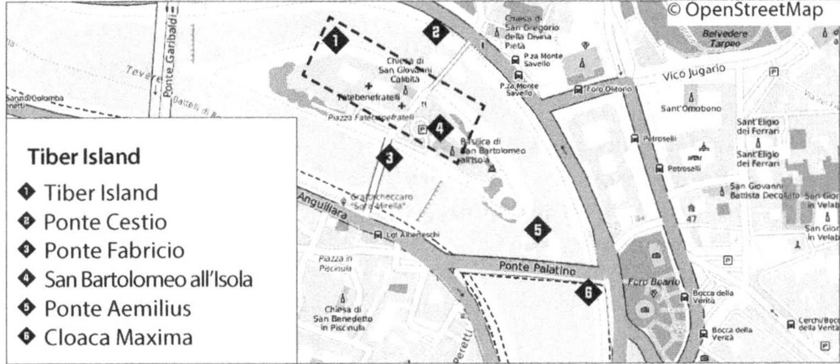

Tiber Island

❶ Tiber Island
❷ Ponte Cestio
❸ Ponte Fabricio
❹ San Bartolomeo all'Isola
❺ Ponte Aemilius
❻ Cloaca Maxima

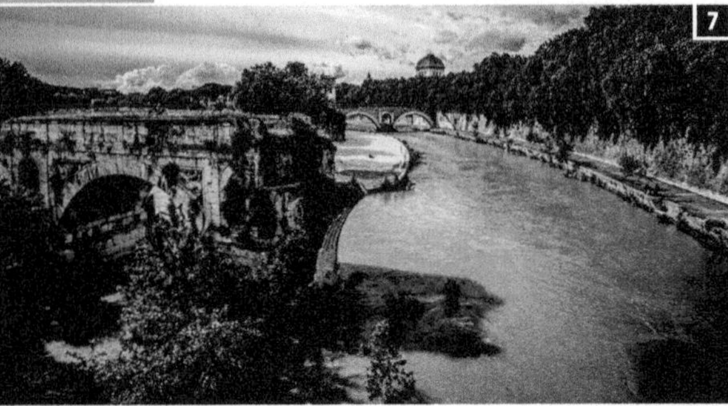

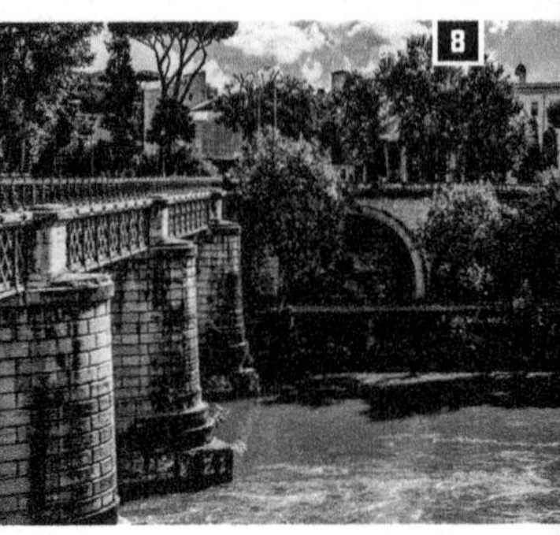

The bridge was later restored by Emperor Augustus, who was in charge of bridges as Pontifex Maximus, the main Roman priest. The bridge was named Pons Maximus, as the largest of Roman bridges at the time.

Artificial additions to the island caused the river to expand as well. This, in turn, caused the collapse of the bridge on both sides.

The last restoration was undertaken in 1598. Unfortunately, the decrepit pillars could not withstand the water pressure and they collapsed.

Not far from this bridge, under Ponte Palatino, there is Cloaca Maxima, the main sewer pipe. You can still see the tunnel under the bridge.

⑤ Cloaca Maxima ★ 8

Romans knew that the basis of survival and progress of a civilization is not in the water pipes, but in an efficient sewage system. Cloaca Maxima is one of the first sewage systems in the world.

Apparently, the fifth Roman King Tarquinius Priscus (600 BC) ordered the construction of a sewage network with a natural fall between the Palatine and Capitoline Hill.

The most important duct was Cloaca Maxima which is the prototype of all ancient drain pipes. It was 10 ft (3 m) wide and 13 ft (4 m) high.

Proof of how much Romans appreciated this duct was is the Venus Cloacina, the goddess of the Cloaca, with a shrine on the Roman Forum.

All eleven of Roman aqueducts from early 1st century were connected to this sewage system.

Cloaca Maxima exited in the Tiber and the ancient duct can still be seen next to Ponte Palatino, a modern bridge that replaced the crumbled bridge Ponte Aemilius.

Did you know?

Cosmati mosaics in Rome

► Santa Maria in Trastevere [p.238]

► Basilica di San Giovanni in Laterano [p.270]

► San Lorenzo fuori le Mura [p.282]

► Basilica di San Saba [p.184]

► San Paolo fuori le Mura [p.274]

► Basilica di Santa Maria in Ara coel [p.87]

► Santa Maria in Cosmedin [p.181]

► Santa Maria Maggiore [p.277]

►Basilica di San Clemente [p.33]

► Santa Croce in Gerusalemme [p.284]

► Sistine Chapel, Vatican [p.166]

► Stanza della Segnatura, Vatican [p.161]

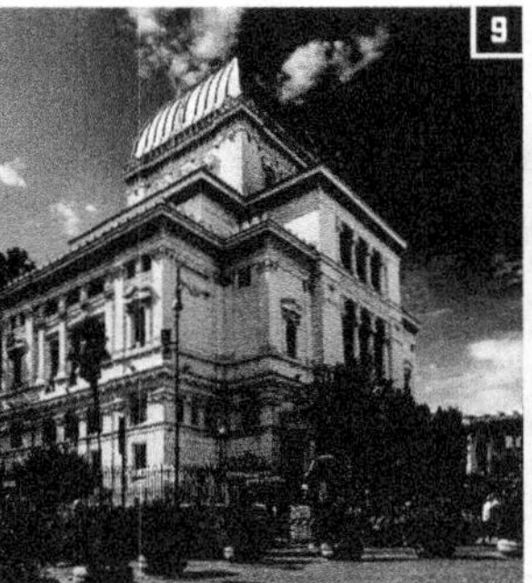

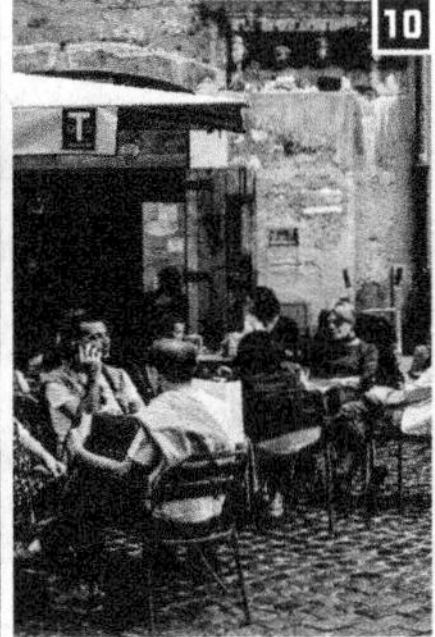

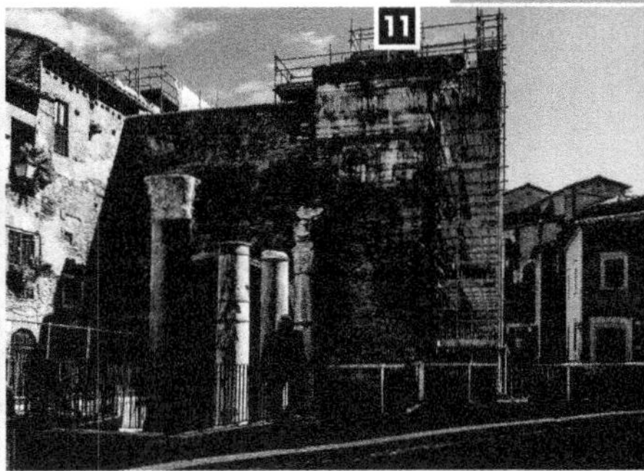

Walk around Tiber Island

❷ Roman-Jewish Quarter ★★★

The Roman ghetto or Ghetto di Roma, used to be a Jewish ghetto established by Pope Paul IV in 1555. It was closed off by walls, it had three gates which closed it off entirely during the night. This went on until 1870, when the unification army joined Rome and the Kingdom of Italy. Presently, this is where the Roman synagogue is, the Jewish Museum and some of the best restaurants in Rome, with special and very tasty Jewish-Roman cuisine, alongside the inevitable Roman antiques. 🔟

① Portico di Ottavia ★ 11

In order to get to our next spot, we have to go back to the Lungotevere and walk parallel to the Tiber Island. At the next bridge, Pons Fabricius, that cuts the Tiber Island in half, turn left onto Via del Portico d'Ottavia. Walk to the Portico, the only empty house with no windows and doors that nevertheless has Roman columns. This used to be a representative building ordered by Augustus in honor of his sister Octavia the Younger soon after 27 BC. It was an open hall framed by columns, 390 ft (119 m) wide and 433 ft (132 m) long. It was used to show 34 bronze statues of Alexander the Great by Lysippos. This is also where the only female bust was ever put on display in public. This was Cornelia (190–100 BC), mother of the Gracchi brothers. The Portico is an important symbol for Roman Jews. This was their ghetto since 1555, when they were exiled from Trastevere. There is the largest Roman synagogue nearby called Tempio Maggiore di Roma, as well as the Jewish Museum. On the right side of the Portico di Ottavia, there is a passage. Walk there and then turn right. You should be on a clearing where a couple of Roman columns are still holding together.

② Synagogue of Rome ★★ 9

The present building was raised only after the unification of Italy, when the Roman ghetto was destroyed and Jews were given equal civil rights. It was designed by Vincenzo Costa and Osvaldo Armanni. There is a four-sided aluminum dome on top, the only four-sided dome in Rome.

③ Jewish Museum ★★

This collection dating back to the years of the Ghetto (1555–1870) and the visit includes also two synagogues: The Great Synagogue and the Spanish Synagogue. A new virtual tour through the Jewish Old Ghetto allows visitors to walk down the streets of the ancient Jewish ghetto as they were centuries years ago (Room 2).

Museo Eebraico di Roma | Jewish Museum
Address: Lungotevere De' Cenci, Roma
Online:
www.museoebraico.roma.it/en
Public transportation:
Bus stop Lungotevere de' Cenci – Arenula or stop Piazza Monte Savello: 23, 63, 280, 810
Opening hours: *see online*

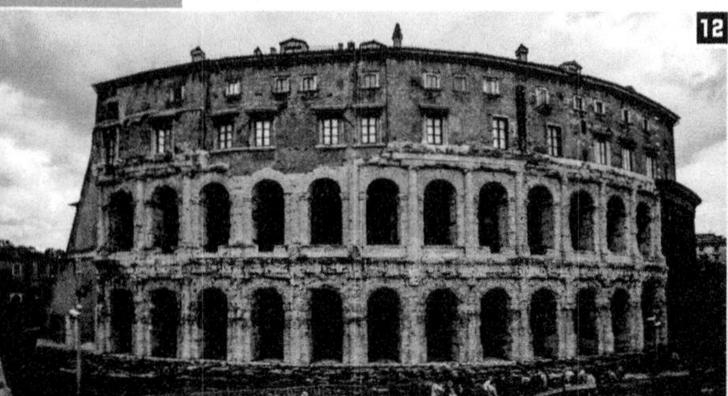

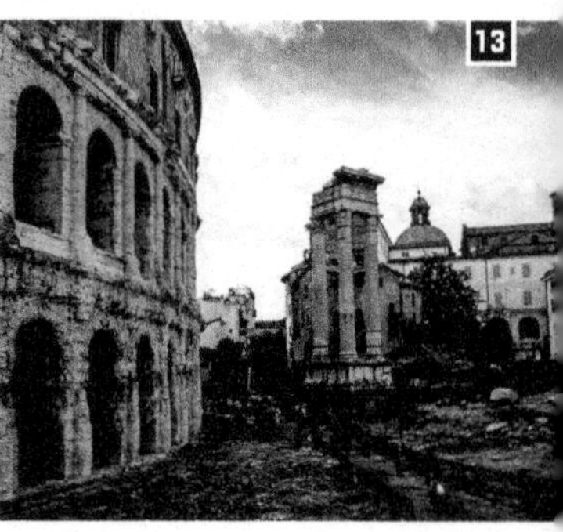

◇ Temple of Apollo Sosianus ★

This temple was located between, or better to say behind Portico di Ottavia and the Theater of Marcellus. Titus Livius claimed the temple had been in that place since 431 BC. Today, the most conspicuous remains are the ones of three Corinthian columns (46 ft or 14 m high), linked by an architrave with a frieze. The temple is dedicated to the Greek god Apollo Sosianus, who was believed to protect people from epidemics. The temple could not be built in the center of Rome because it honored a non-Roman god. 13

❸ Theater of Marcellus ★★ 12

Do a 180 turn and you will see the most remarkable blend of ancient Roman architecture and modern on one of the semi-circular walls. Theater of Marcellus was named after Augustus's nephew Marcellus, who died prematurely. It was completed in 13 BC. Performances took place here until 4th century. Two rows of arcades are still visible, incorporated into the renaissance structure of the Orsini family palace by Baldassare Peruzzi. Theater of Marcellus had a diameter of 364 ft (111 m), enough to accommodate ten to fifteen thousand spectators. The stage has not been preserved. The structure of this largest theater in Rome was an inspiration for the Colosseum.

◆ San Nicola in Carcere ★★

Church of San Nicola in Carcere was built on the ruins of three Roman temples. There are three ancient temples underneath, one next to the other. On the left side of the church, you can see six columns with the architrave, once part of the Janus Temple from 90 BC.

San Nicola in Carcere | Church of St. Nicholas in Prison
Address: Via del Teatro di Marcello 46, Roma

Public transportation: Bus stop Foro Olitorio: 780, H or stop Petroselli: 30, 44, 44F, 51, 81, 83, 85, 87, 118, 130F 160, 170, 628, 715, 716, 781, C3

Opening hours: *see on Google Maps*

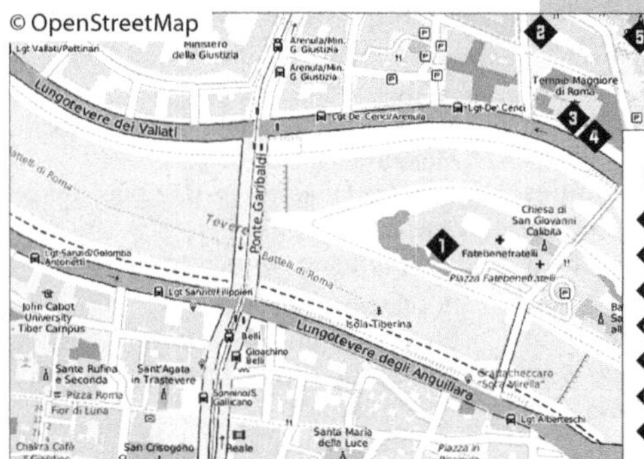

Roman-Jewish Quarter

❶ Tiber Island
❷ Roman-Jewish Quarter
❸ Synagogue of Rome
❹ Jewish Museum
❺ Portico di Ottavia
❻ Theater of Marcellus
❼ Temple of Apollo Sosianus

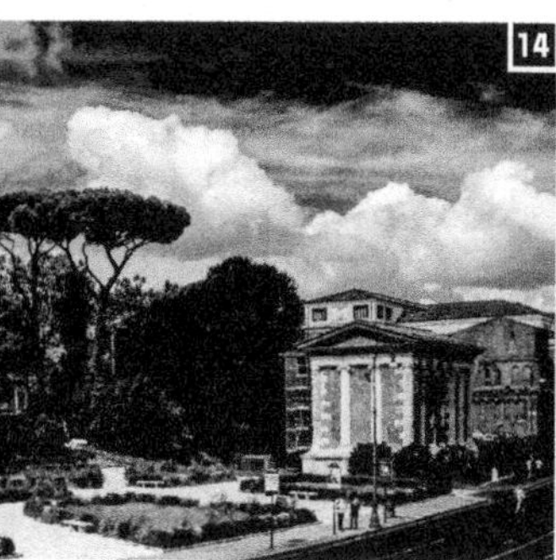
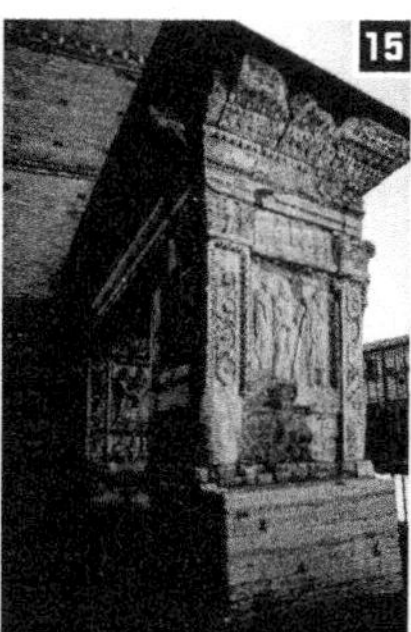
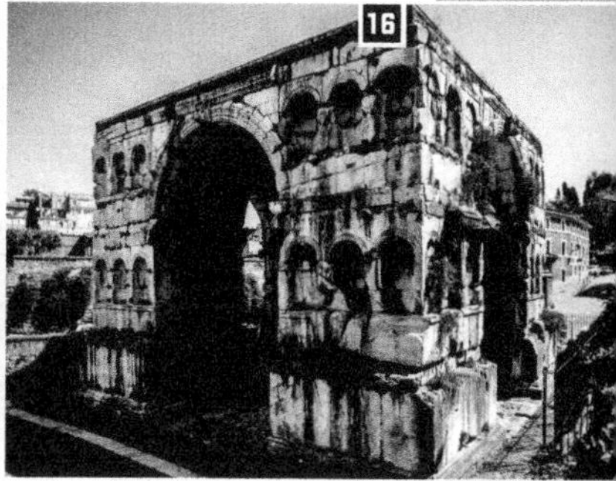

Inside the church, the remains of the two other temples are visible: Ionic columns from the Temple of Spes and the Doric columns from Temple of Juno. The Church of St. Nicholas in Prison is dedicated to a Greek saint because in Roman times this was part of the Greek quarter, and more specifically, a prison in early Christian and Byzantine period.

Piazza Bocca della Verità ★★

To get from Theater of Marcellus to Forum Boarium or todays Piazza Bocca della Verità, go downhill on Via del Teatro di Marcello and continue on Via Luigi Petroselli until you get to a big intersection called Piazza Bocca della Verità. This is the beginning of what used to be Forum Boarium that had several different functions over the centuries. It was a cattle market — cattle was brought into the city across a bridge from Trastevere. Also, roads from north and south Italy converged here. There are two almost fully preserved temples on the Forum Boarium: the square one is the Temple of Portunus, and the circular temple with a colonnade is the Temple of Hercules Victor. The Arch of Janus is nearby.

Arch of Janus ★★★

Arch of Janus is the only arch in Rome that is open on all four sides. Constantine II erected it to honor Emperor Constantine in 4th century. It was located on a very important intersection. The Frangipani family turned it into a fort in the Middle Ages, a fate also shared by the Colosseum and Theater of Marcellus.

Arcus Argentariorum ★

Behind the four-sided arch there is the so-called "Arcus Argentariorum", seemingly protruding from the wall of the San Giorgio al Velabro church. The arch was dedicated to Emperor Septimius Severus and his family. This was not the official state arch, but a private donation. It was commissioned by the *arentarii* or money handlers, precursors to bankers. On the architrave, the upper part of the arch connecting the sides, there is a representation of Hercules. On the inner sides, there are well-preserved reliefs that show Emperor Septimius Severus, his wife Julia Domna and Caracalla, emperor's son and heir. Some of the figures have been damaged beyond recognition. Supposedly, they were removed on purpose: they represented Caracalla's brother Geta, his wife Plautilla and her father Plautianus. After Geta's death, Caracalla declared *damnatio memoriae* against his brother. It meant wiping any memory of him, chiefly any mention of his name on public buildings and monuments across the Empire. The outer reliefs feature soldiers, prisoners and military banners.

San Giorgio al Velabro ★★

This three-nave church from the 9th century is captivating in its archaic simplicity, with Roman columns and a pleasant, cool shade. The church used to be surrounded by the Greek quarter full of Greek merchants, and even Pope Zachary (741–752) was of Greek origin from Cappadocia. So, when relics of St. George were moved from Cappadocia,

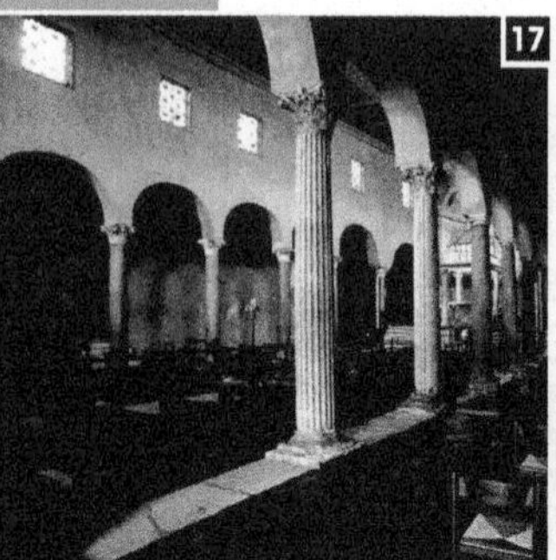
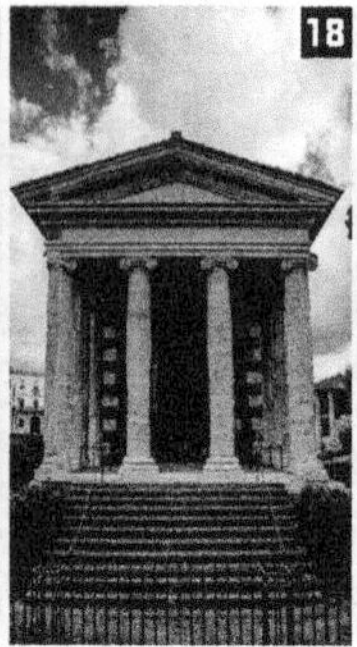
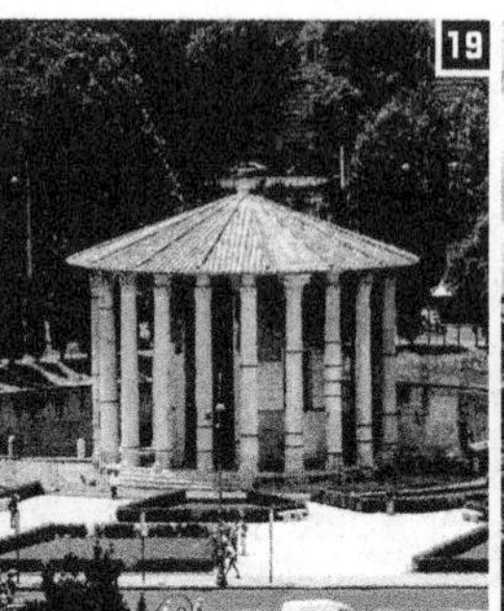
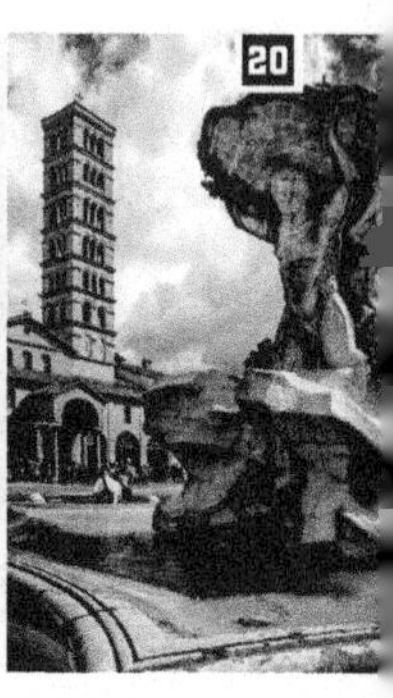

he decided to bestow the honor of keeping the relics in this church. They are still kept under the altar. The tabernacle was made in the Cosmati family workshop (12th to 14th century). **17**

④ Temple of Portunus ★★ **18**

This square temple is dedicated to the god of ports. The city port used to be on the Tiber right underneath this temple. This was the final destination for goods that landed in Ostia Antica. The temple has an antechamber (portico) with free-standing Ionic columns and a cult hall with four walls (cella) with half-columns. Inside, there was the statue of Portunus. The temple was built in 1st century BC, although remains from previous temples dating back to the 4th century BC were also found. The temple was converted into a church in the 9th century.

⑤ Temple of Hercules Victor ★★

This is the oldest preserved temple in Rome. It is also the oldest ancient marble building. **19** The temple dates back to 120 BC. The *cella* is 49 ft (15 m) in diameter, with a marble colonnade of 20 pillars, each 33 ft (10 m) in height. The temple was ordered by an olive oil merchant by the name of Marcus Octavius Herrenus and dedicated to Hercules because he was the protector of oil merchants. It was believed that no flee or dog would come into the temple – an important feature for a building situated so close to the cattle market. The temple has been preserved almost in its entirety because it was also turned into a church in 1132.

If you have visited the church of San Pietro in Montorio and Tempietto, then you will know where Donato Bramante drew his inspiration from. **[p.241]**

⑥ Fontana dei Tritoni ★ **20**

There are two fountains in Rome with almost identical names. Fontana del Tritone is on Piazza Barberini and this one, Fontana dei Tritoni on Piazza Bocca della Verità, in front of the of Church Santa Maria in Cosmedin. It took quite a long time to build this fountain, from 1610 to 1715. After the great success of Bernini's Fontana dei Quattro Fiumi on Piazza Navona, this fountain should also have a pedestal made of rocks. Water is pouring out of an oyster shell supported by two kneeling Tritons. Between them, there is an eight-pointed star, Pope Clement XI's coat of arms.

⑦ La Bocca della Verità ★ **21**

The Mouth of Truth has been in the lobby of Santa Maria in Cosmedin for almost four centuries. This round marble relief from 1stcentury is 5.74 ft or 1.75 m wide and weighs 2866 lbs or 1300 kg. We can only guess its original purpose. There are various hypotheses — some say it was part of a fountain or a manhole lid, since it was found near the sewers of Cloaca Maxima. Also, it could be a representation of Oceanus, Jupiter or the River god of the Tiber. What is certain is that it has been known as a lie detector since the Middle Ages. The legend has it that whoever puts their hand in the mouth of the beast shown on the relief has to tell the truth. Otherwise, the monster will bite off their arm.

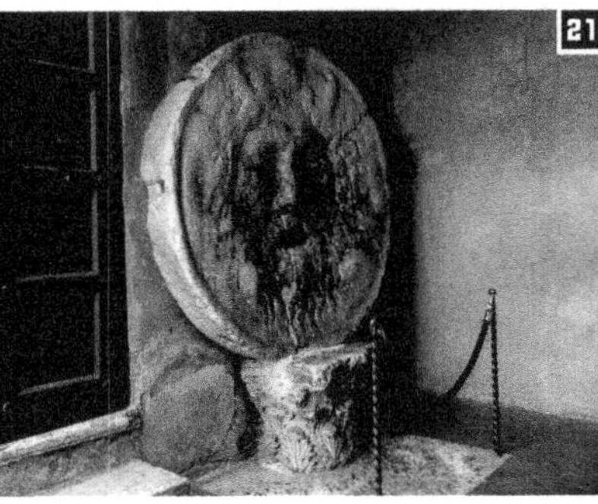

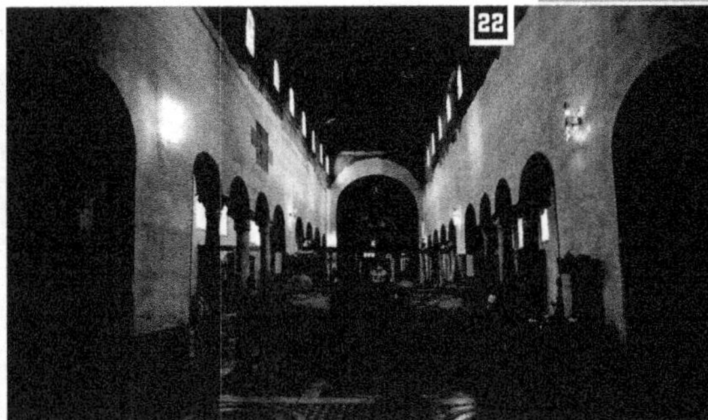

⑧ Santa Maria in Cosmedin ★ ★ ★

Church was built on the remains of Temple of Hercule Pompeiani and Statio Annonae, a wheat distribution center from 1st century. In fact, the Statio Annonae building was completely incorporated into the church. 🖪 Since it was founded in 6th century, the church was Greek Orthodox. During the great Byzantine civil war that broke out between supporters and opponent of icons, many Greek supporters of icons found refuge in Rome. Pope Hadrian expanded this church in 772 and has been named Santa Maria in Cosmedin ever since. It was expanded and adapted several times until 1200. In the interior, we can still see Statio Annonae's 18 Corinthian columns. There is a beautiful Cosmati mosaic from late 13th century. The altar is not in the apse, but in front of it, which is typical for an Early Christian church. The apse was meant for the bishop's throne – the same way a judge used to sit in the courtroom basilica. The bishop's throne is decorated with two ancient lion heads.

Santa Maria in Cosmedin
Address: Piazza Bocca della Verità 18, Roma

Public transportation:
Bus stop Bocca Della Verita: 44, 44F, 83, 160, 160F, 170, 176, 781, C3

Opening hours: *see on Google Maps*

San Giorgio al Velabro
Address: Via del Velabro 19, Roma
Online: www.sangiorgioinvelabro.org
Public transportation:
Bus stop Bocca Della Verita: 44, 44F, 83, 160, 160F, 170, 176, 781, C3

Opening hours: *see online*

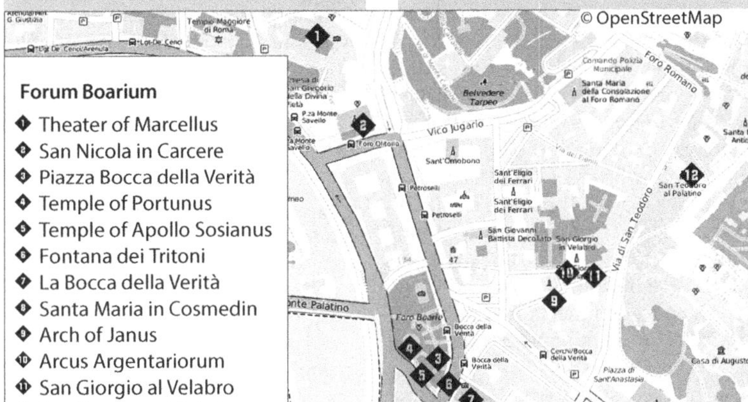

Forum Boarium

1. Theater of Marcellus
2. San Nicola in Carcere
3. Piazza Bocca della Verità
4. Temple of Portunus
5. Temple of Apollo Sosianus
6. Fontana dei Tritoni
7. La Bocca della Verità
8. Santa Maria in Cosmedin
9. Arch of Janus
10. Arcus Argentariorum
11. San Giorgio al Velabro
12. San Teodoro al Palatino

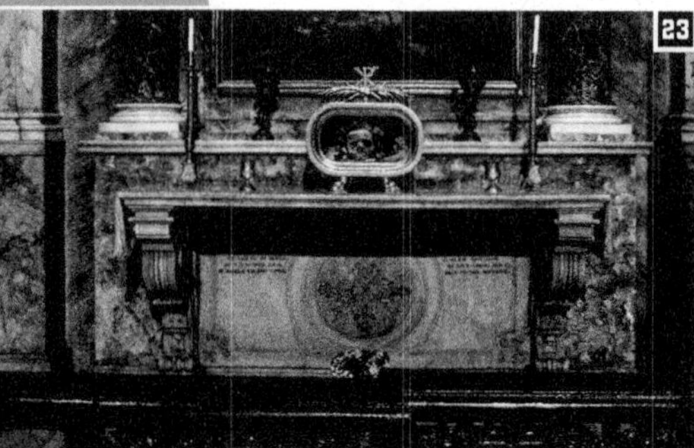

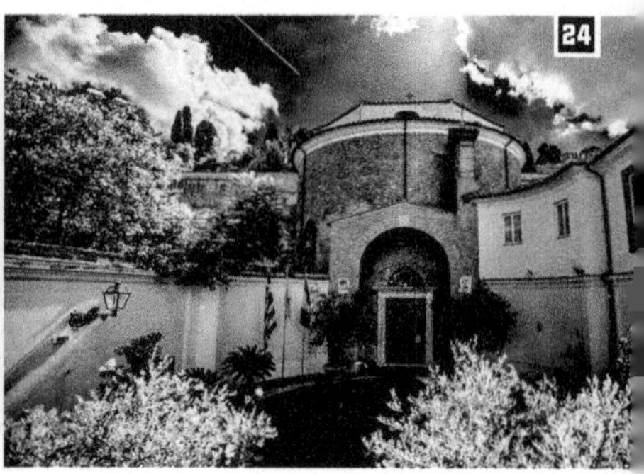

The altar is made of a single granite block from the 13th century. There is a relic with fresh flowers which always seem to be in front of it. It is the skull of St. Valentine, the bishop of Terni (Region of Umbria) and protector of lovers. He performed wedding ceremonies according to Christian rituals, even though this was strictly forbidden by Emperor Claudius II. Valentine was executed on February 14, 269.

❻ San Teodoro al Palatino ★ ★

This church was built in the 6th century next to an ancient road that used to connect Forum Boarium and Roman Forum. The shape suggests it may have been built on the remains of an older building, presumably, the Temple of Minerva Medica. In the atrium in front of the church, there is still an ancient altar. The last renovation took place in the 18th century under Carlo Fontana (1703–1705). He made the baroque courtyard as well as the interior of the church, keeping the top of the apse from the 6th century. It shows Jesus sitting on a sphere which represents heaven. He is surrounded by Peter and Paul and martyrs Theodore and Cleonicus. The church may have been dedicated to the Greek martyr Theodore in the 9th century, due to the strong Byzantine influence in Rome at the time. This was probably a deciding factor when John Paul II conceded the church to the Patriarch of Constantinople and the Greek Orthodox Church.

You can also buy wonderful Orthodox icons in the church, made inside the church by the artists themselves. Until 1471, the Capitoline she-wolf was kept in this church, the most important symbol of old Rome, probably made somewhere between 9th and 13th century, and not in the 5th century in Etruria, as it was previously assumed.

❼ Aventine Hill ★ ★ ★ ★

During the Roman Republic, this was an important stronghold of the plebeians or the *populares*, the opposition against the independent rule of the aristocratic senators. In 121 BC, Gaius Sempronius Gracchus and his plebeian supporters were surrounded and the rebellion squashed on the Aventine Hill. During the Roman Empire, the Aventine was a great place for elite and luxury buildings, a tradition that has been upheld to this day. In order to get to the Basilica di Santa Sabina, you need to go from the Church of Santa Maria in Cosmedin down Largo Amerigo Petrucci street. At the corner near Circus Maximus, turn right to Clivo dei Publicii. Head on to Via di Santa Sabina. On your right, the square called Piazza Pietro D'Illiria should appear soon along with the Basilica of Santa Sabina all'Aventino.

San Teodoro al Palatino
Address: Via di San Teodoro 7, Roma
Online (only in Greek):
www.chiesaortodossa-roma.org

Public transportation:
Bus stop Bocca Della Verita: 44, 44F, 83, 160, 160F, 170, 176, 781, C3

Opening hours: *see on Google Maps*

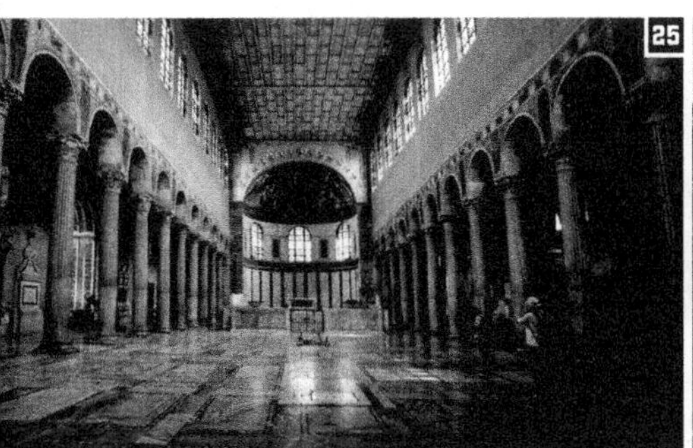

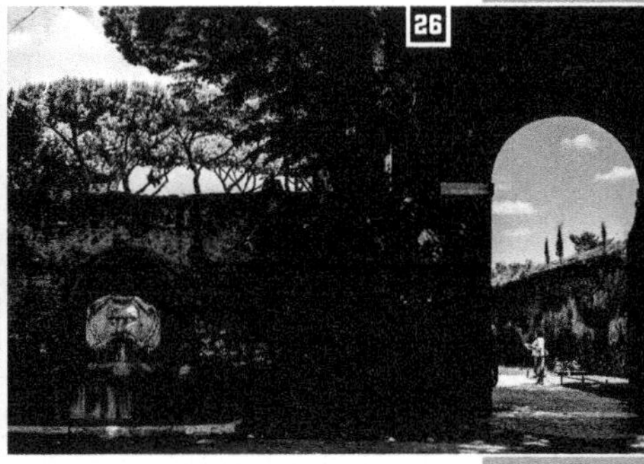

① Basilica of Santa Sabina ★ ★

Basilica di Santa Sabina all'Aventino is an early Christian basilica from the 4th century, with classical rectangular layout and massive ancient columns. It is practically without ornaments, and thanks to the light which comes in through giant windows, it is one of the most airy churches in Rome. Due to its simplicity, it marks a transitional point in church building from the Roman curia to more traditional Christian churches. The church was ordered by Peter of Illyria, a Dalmatian priest (423), to be built close to the Temple of Juno. The interior of the church was renovated by artists such as Domenico Fontana (1587) and Francesco Borromini (1643). The Basilica of Saint Sabina is the main church of the Dominican Order.

On the wooden entrance door, the Crucifixion is represented in the upper left corner, one of the oldest representations of this key event from the New Testament. The cedar door itself is the oldest preserved church door in history (AD 432). The church is also relevant to the history of the Church because Pope Honorius offered it to St. Dominic and his order in 1219. A monastery was also built here, and even St. Augustine of Hippo himself taught in it. One of the highlights definitely includes the Roman name Rufenus, etched at the base of one of 24 Corinthian columns which separate the main nave from the lateral naves. Supposedly, this is the name of the merchant from whom these columns were bought.

② Giardino degli Aranci ★

If you go right at the church entrance, you will find a park called the Giardino degli Aranci (The Orange Garden). From the terrace, you can enjoy one of the most spectacular vistas of Rome. The park is full of sour oranges and Roman pines. Before you go into the park, you can cool down in the shade in front of a fountain made of pools from the Roman Baths and a marble mask with water running out of it.

③ Secret keyhole ★

If you continue down Via di Santa Sabina, it will only take you a couple of minutes to get to the park entrance of Santa Maria del Priorato, the main church of the Maltese knights. Although you cannot go into the church without a special permit which you have to arrange in advance, the locked doors are still worth the visit. If you look through the keyhole, you will get the most beautiful view of Michelangelo's dome of St. Peter's Basilica, which will surely be etched in your memory forever.

The Order of the Maltese knights is a sovereign entity, with other words, this view take you through three different

Basilica di Santa Sabina all'Aventino | The Basilica of Saint Sabina
Address: Piazza Pietro D'Illiria 1, Roma

Public transportation:
Bus stop Bocca Della Verita: 44, 44F, 83, 160, 160F, 170, 176, 781, C3

Opening hours: *see on Google Maps*

EXTRA WALKS – A walk along the Tiber ★ ★ ★ ★

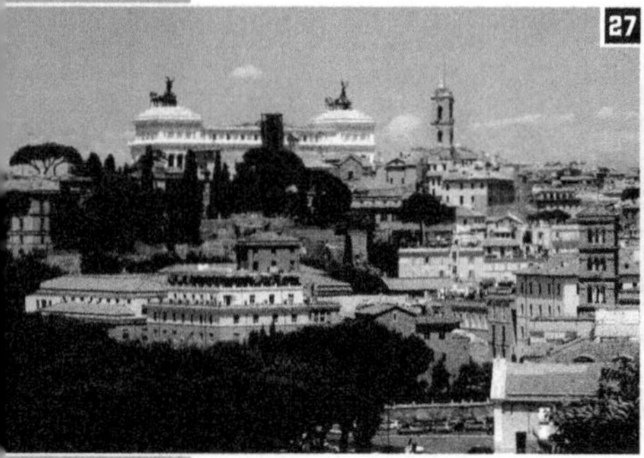

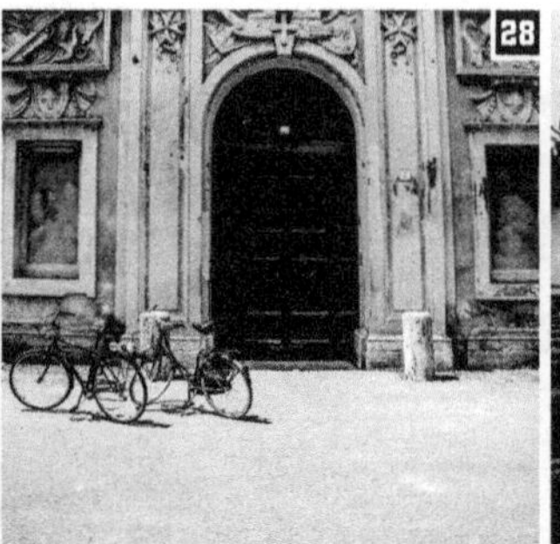

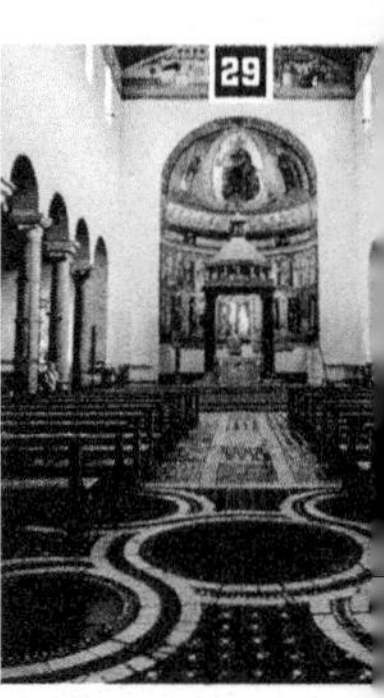

countries – Order of the Maltese knights, Italy and Vatican City. 28

❽ Basilica di San Saba★ ★ ★

This church is located on the Piccolo Aventino hill, across the Aventine Hill. As with most Roman churches, legends and history are intertwined. On the foundations of the Fourth Cohort Vigiles' barracks, that is, the imperial Roman fire brigade, a house was built in the Late Antique, which allegedly belonged to Saint Silvia, mother to Pope Gregory I.

Saint Silvia first built an oratory, on the basis of which a church was erected to shelter the prosecuted monks from Jerusalem. This is how the church was named after Sabbas the Sanctified, a monk who served in Jerusalem before coming to Rome. The façade is from the 15th century.

There are many statues from the Roman period in the vaulted antechamber, as well as a well-preserved Roman sarcophagus under glass. While you are in the church, pay attention to the floor, made by the Cosmati family in the 13th century.

In the middle of the left nave there is a fresco with an unusual representation of Saint Nicholas who is giving a bag of money to three naked girls, trying to save them from prostitution. 29

Basilica di San Saba | San Saba
Address: Piazza Gian Lorenzo Bernini 20, Roma

Public transportation:
Bus stop San Saba – Ponzio Flaminio: 715, Tram stop Albania: 8

Opening hours: *see on Google Maps*

EXTRA WALKS – A walk along the Tiber ★ ★ ★

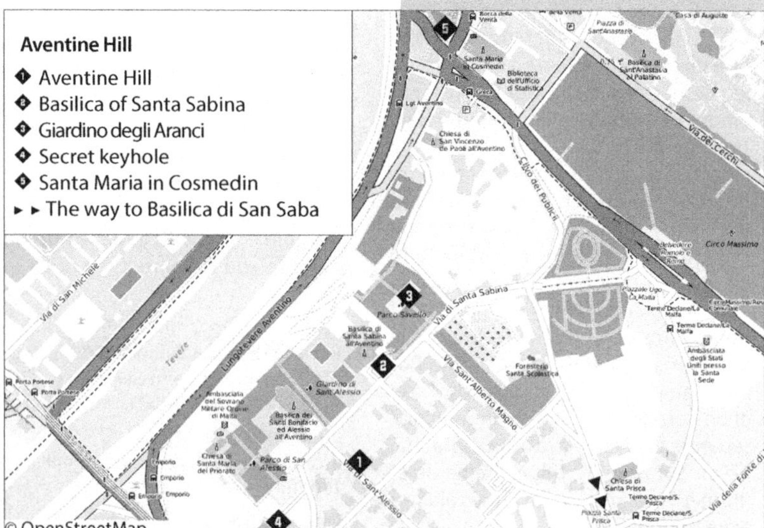

From Galleria Borghese to Trevi Fountain

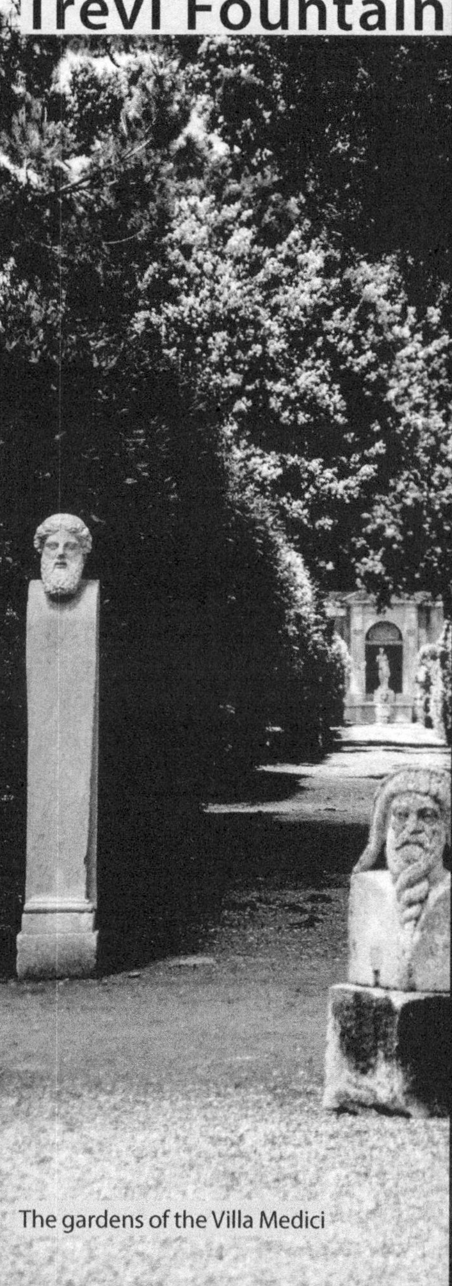

The gardens of the Villa Medici

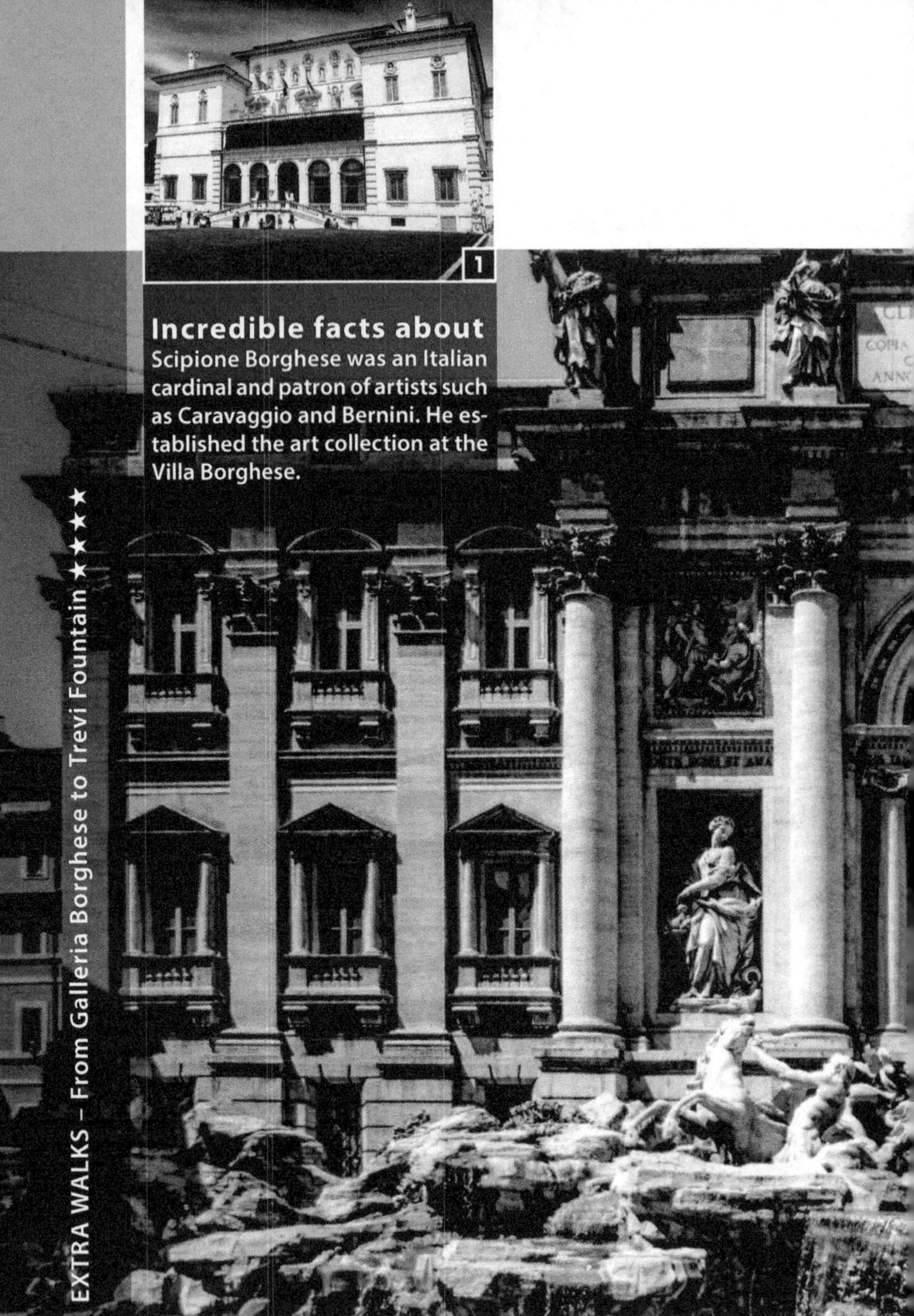

Incredible facts about

Scipione Borghese was an Italian cardinal and patron of artists such as Caravaggio and Bernini. He established the art collection at the Villa Borghese.

Trevi Fountain

Extra Tip : : :

One of the highlights of Golden Age Roman culture is Ara Pacis temple. The new glass building of the Museo dell'Ara Pacis was designed by Richard Meier. The museum is airy and has a lot of natural light, as a worthy dedication to Augustus's idea of peace.

Museums and parks, fountains and squares

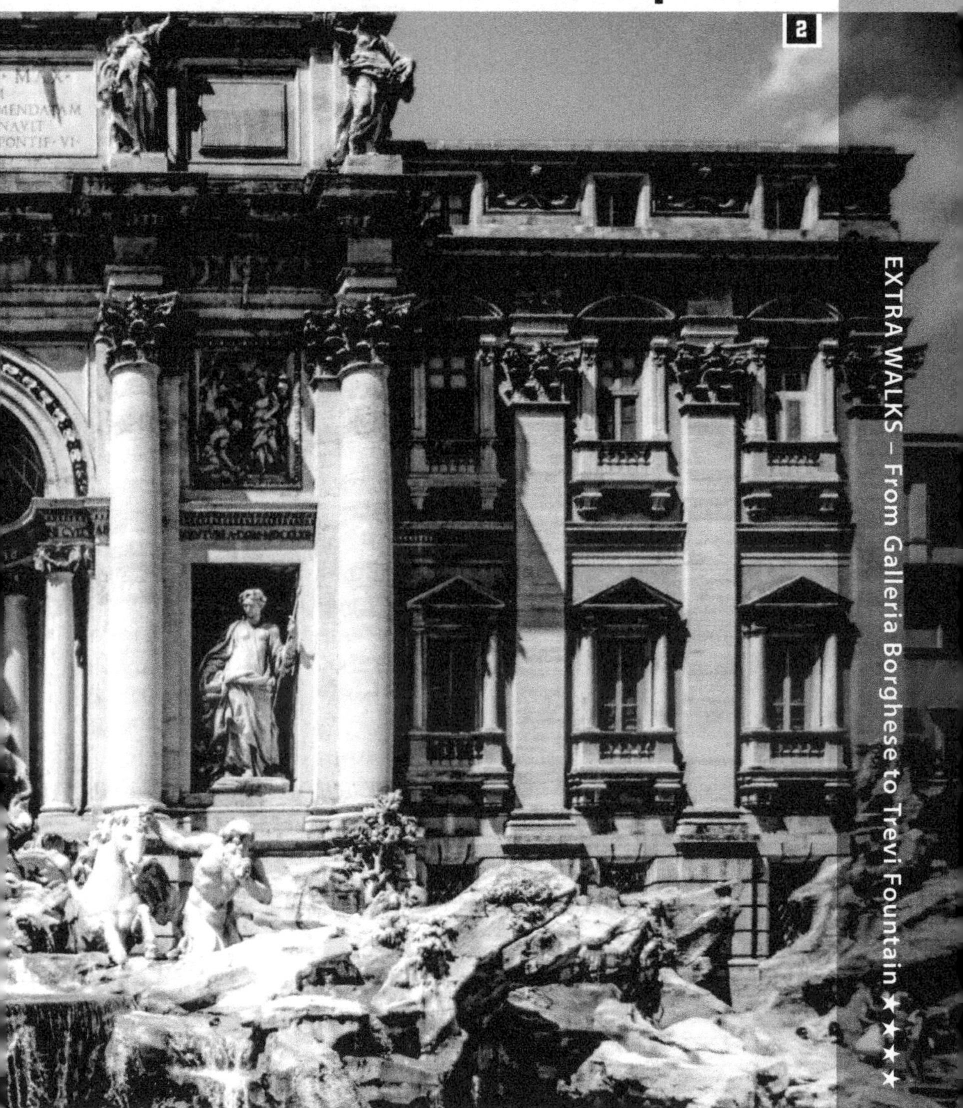

Museo dell'Ara Pacis | Ara Pacis Museum
Address: Lungotevere in Augusta, Roma
Public transportation: Bus stop Augusto Imperatore – Ara Pacis: 81, 628, C33
Opening hours: Daily 9:30 a.m. – 7:30 p.m.

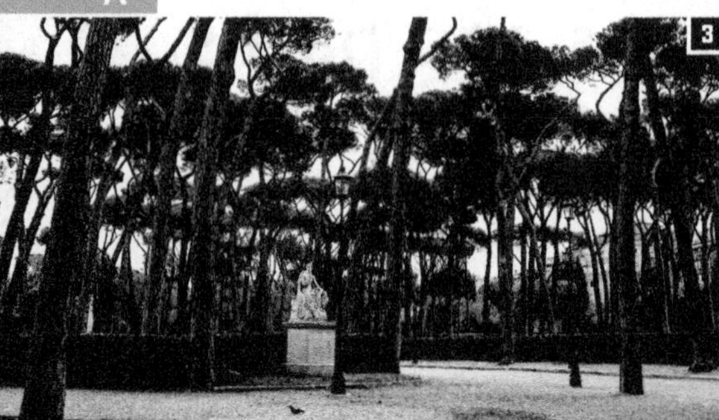

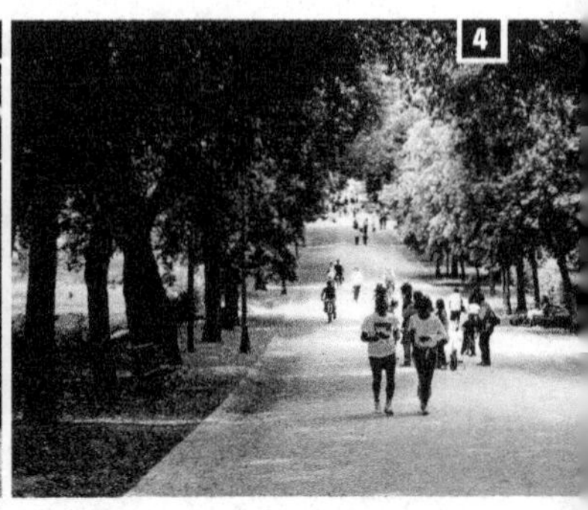

❶ Villa Borghese Gardens ★★★★ 🖪

Villa Borghese Gardens is a park situated close to the Flaminia Metro Station. There are many museums and palaces hidden in the greenery, the most famous certainly being Galleria Borghese. 🖪 The park stretches across 2 square miles or 5 square kilometers. 🖪 🖪

◇ Museo Borghese e Galleria Borghese | Borghese Museum and Gallery Borghese ★★★★

The villa was built by Pope Paul V's nephew, Cardinal Scipione Borghese in 1616. Scipione Borghese was a passionate art collector and patron of artists such as Caravaggio and Bernini. Apart from renaissance and baroque sculptures, there are also valuable sculptures from ancient Rome. The museum is divided into Museo Borghese and Galleria Borghese. Museo Borghese holds sculptures on the ground floor, while Galleria Borghese is on the first floor with all the paintings. 🖪 Some of the highlights:

▸ Caravaggio: *Boy with a Basket of Fruit* (1593), *St. John the Baptist* (1610), *St. Jerome* (1606), *Bacchus* (1593), *Madonna with Child and Serpent* (1605–1606), *David with the Head of Goliath* (1609),

▸ Bernini: *Self Portrait* (1623), *The Goat Amalthea with the Infant Jupiter and a Faun* (1615), *Apollo and Daphne* (1622), *David* (1623–1624), *Bust of Pope Paul V* (1618), *Truth Unveiled by Time* (1645–1652), *Rape of Proserpina* (1621–1622), *Two Busts of Cardinal Scipione Borghese* (1632),

▸ Raphael: *Portrait of a Young Man* (1502), *Deposition* (1507), *Lady with a Unicorn* (1505),

▸ Titian: *Sacred and Profane Love* (1514), *The Scourging of Christ* (1560), *St. Dominic* (1565), *Venus Blindfolding Cupid* (1565),

▸ *Madonna and Child* (1510) by Giovanni Bellini,

▸ *St. John the Baptist* (1562) by Paolo Veronese,

▸ *Portrait of a Man* (1528) by Parmigianino,

▸ *Pauline Bonaparte or Venus Victrix* (1805 – 1808) by Canova.

Museo Borghese e Galleria Borghese | Borghese Museum and Gallery Borghese
Address: Piazzale del Museo Borghese 5, Roma
Online: www.galleriaborghese.it

Public transportation:
Metro A stop Flaminio | Bus stop Pinciana – Museo Borghese: 53, 63, 83, 92, 223, 360, 910
Opening hours: *see online*

Ticket reservations must be made in advance!

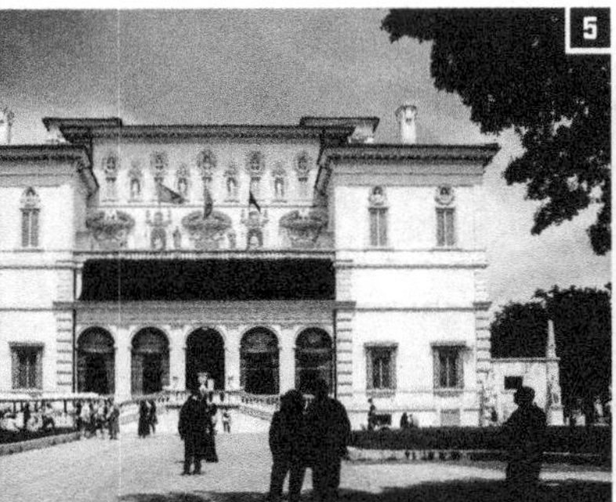

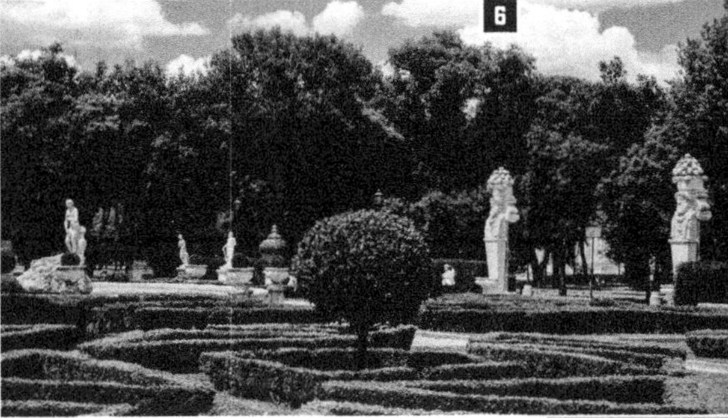

Museo Borghese (Sculptures) – GROUND FLOOR

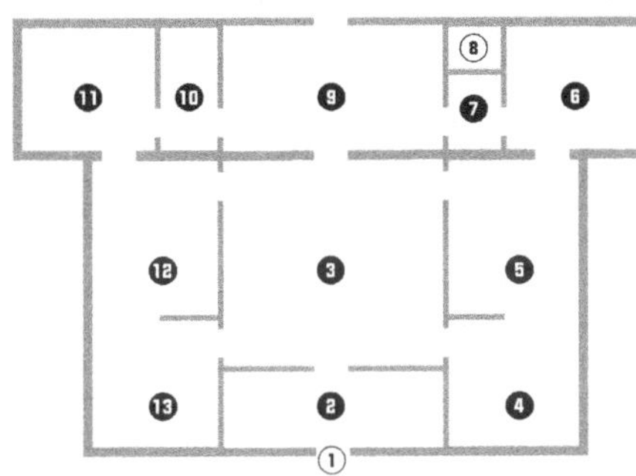

① Entrance
❷ Portico
❸ Salone d'ingresso | Entrance Hall
❹ Sala della Paolina, *Paolina Borghese* by Canova

❺ Sala del Davide, *David* by Bernini
❻ Sala dell' Apollo e Dafne, *Apollo and Daphne* by Bernini
❼ Cappella
⑧ Elevator
❾ Galleria degli Imperatori, *Rape of Proserpina* by Bernini
⑬ Sala del Fauno Danzante, *The Goat Amalthea with the Infant Jupiter* and a *Faun* by Bernini
⑩ Sala dell' Ermafrodito | Hall of Hermaphrodite
⑪ Sala dell' Enea e Anchise, *Aeneas, Anchises, and Ascanius* by Bernini
⑫ Sala Egizia | Egyptian Hall

Galleria Borghese (Paintings) – FIRST FLOOR

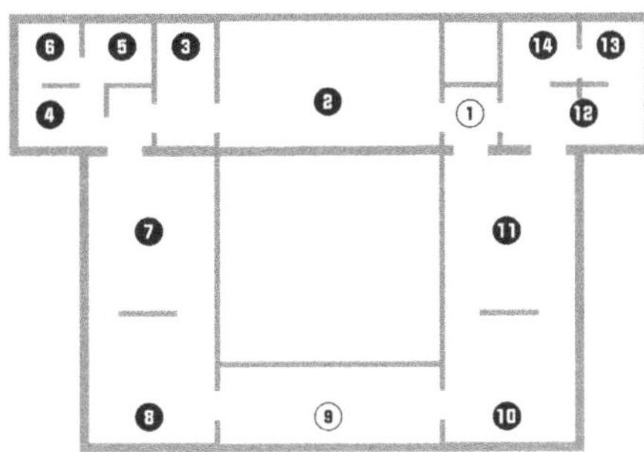

① Entrance
❷ Gallery of Lanfranco, 17th century
❸ Ferrara, Veneto and Brescia Schools, 16th century

❹ Florentine Mannerism, 16th century
❺ 17th and 18th century
❻ 17th century
❼ 17th century
❽ Veneto School, 16th century
⑨ Terazzo | Terrace
⑩ Italian Mannerism, 16th century
⑪ Florentine School, 16th century
⑫ Ferrara School, 16th century
⑬ Siena, Lombardy and Veneto Schools, 16th century
⑭ Florentine School, 16th century

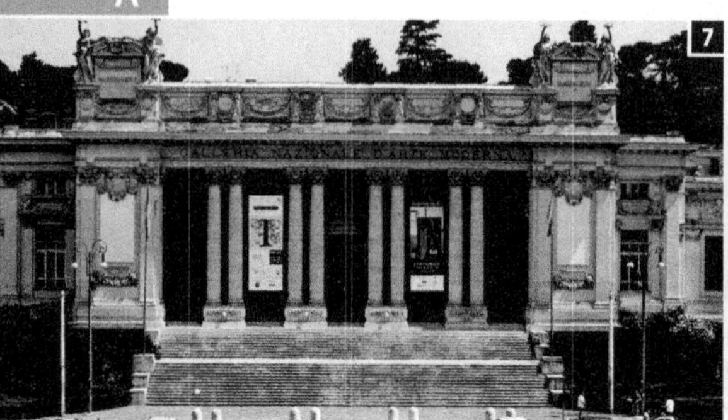

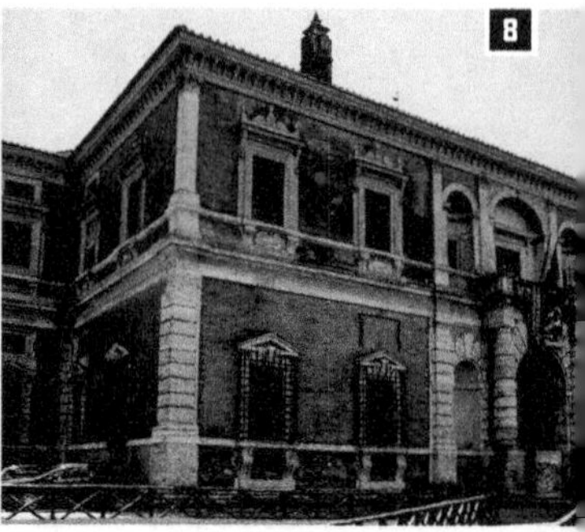

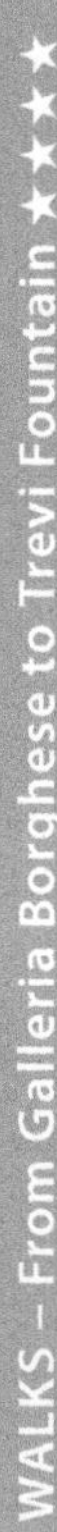

② Galleria Nazionale d'Arte Moderna e Contemporanea | National Gallery of Modern and Contemporary Art ★★★ 7

The modern art museum is situated between Villa Borghese and Villa Giulia, in a lavish late 19th-century historicist palace. It holds more than 5,000 sculptures and paintings from the 19th and 20th century. The emphasis is on Italian art, but the collection is still versatile: there is Giorgio de Chirico, Cézanne, Duchamp, Amedeo Modigliani, Giacometti, Braque, Giorgio Morandi, Degas, Wassily Kandinsky, Mondrian, Monet, Jackson Pollock, Rodin, Van Gogh and so many others.

③ Villa Giulia ★★★ 8

This renaissance villa was built by Pope Julius III in 1553 as his summer residence. The construction was put in the safe hands of Giacomo da Vignola. Nymphaeum and other garden buildings were done by Bartolomeo Ammanati, Giorgo Vasari and Michelangelo. Today, the villa is the Etruscan Museum or Museo Nazionale Etrusco di Villa Giulia with the largest collection of Etruscan monuments in the world.

④ Villa Medici ★★★ 9

Villa Medici was built in 1544 on the remains of an old Roman villa. Today, it is owned by France. Since 1804, these are the headquarters of the French Academy in Rome.

Galleria Nazionale d'Arte Moderna e Contemporanea | National Gallery of Modern and Contemporary Art
Address: Viale delle Belle Arti 131, Roma
Online: www.lagallerianazionale.com

Public transportation:
Metro A stop Flaminio | Bus stop Pinciana – Museo Borghese: 53, 63, 83, 92, 223, 360, 910 | Tram stop Galleria Arte Moderna: 2, 19
Opening hours: *see online*

Museo Nazionale Etrusco di Villa Giulia | National Etruscan Museum of Villa Giulia
Address: Piazzale di Villa Giulia 9, Roma
Online: www.museoetru.it/en

Public transportation:
Metro A stop Flaminio | Bus stop Pinciana – Museo Borghese: 53, 63, 83, 92, 223, 360, 910 | Tram stop Galleria Arte Moderna: 2, 19 or Museo Etrusco Villa Giulia: 2, 19

Opening hours: see online

Villa Medici
Address: Viale della Trinità dei Monti 1, Roma
Online: www.villamedici.it/en

Public transportation:
Metro A stop Spagna

Opening hours: see online

The ticket includes the guided tour of the Villa, the gardens and the temporary exhibition.

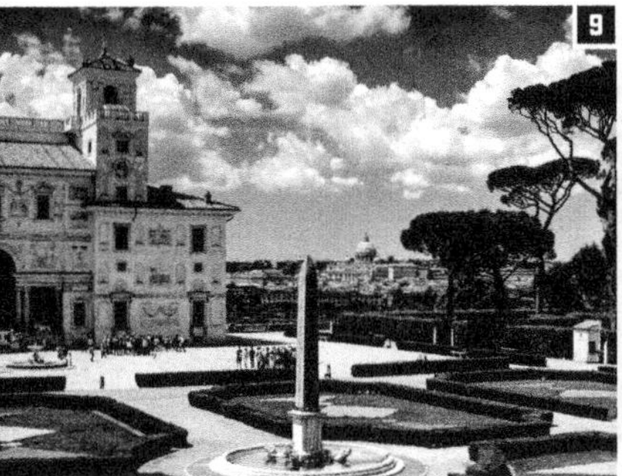

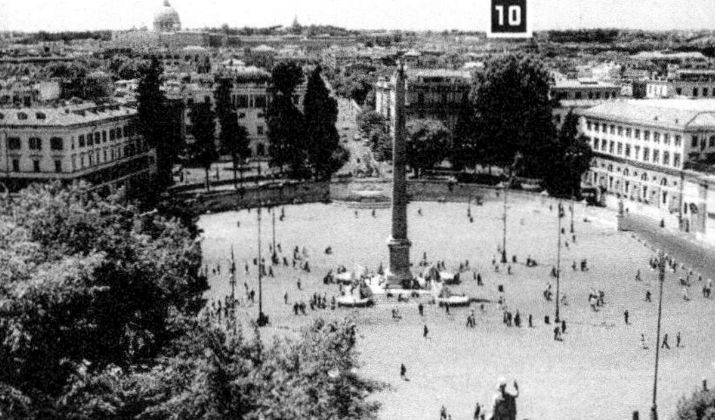

The villa was named after Cardinal Ferdinando I de' Medici, who bought it in 1576. This is where Galileo Galilei was held captive in 1633.

⑤ Museo Pietro Canonica ★

It is a small but lovely museum and an interesting example of the museums based on artist's house. The Pietro Canonica Museum consists primarily of works by the Italian sculptor, painter and opera composer Pietro Canonica (1869–1959).

⑥ Museo Carlo Bilotti ★★

The Carlo Bilotti Museum consists primarily collection of 18 works by Giorgio de Chirico (1888–1978). He was one of the most influential artists of the 20th century. If you want to see more de Chirico's works, Giorgio De Chirico House is the right place for you [p.202].

Museo Pietro Canonica | Pietro Canonica Museum
Address: Viale Pietro Canonica (Piazza di Siena) 2, Roma
Online: www.museocanonica.it/en

Public transportation: Bus stop Canonica – Piazza Di Siena: 116

Opening hours: *see online*

Free entry to the permanent collection

Museo Carlo Bilotti | Carlo Bilotti Museum
Address: Viale Pietro Canonica (Piazza di Siena) 2, Roma
Online: www.museocarlobilotti.it/en

Public transportation: Bus stop Canonica – Piazza Di Siena: 116

Opening hours:
Oct to May: 10:00 a.m. – 4:00 p.m.
June to Sept: 1:00 p.m. – 7:00 p.m.

Free entry to the permanent collection

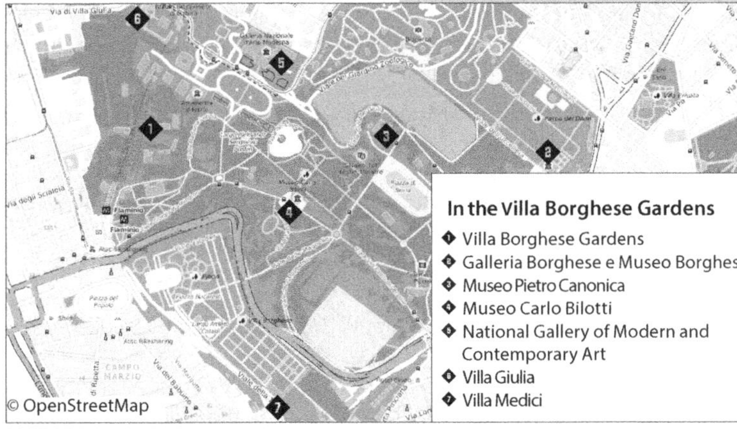

In the Villa Borghese Gardens

- Villa Borghese Gardens
- Galleria Borghese e Museo Borghese
- Museo Pietro Canonica
- Museo Carlo Bilotti
- National Gallery of Modern and Contemporary Art
- Villa Giulia
- Villa Medici

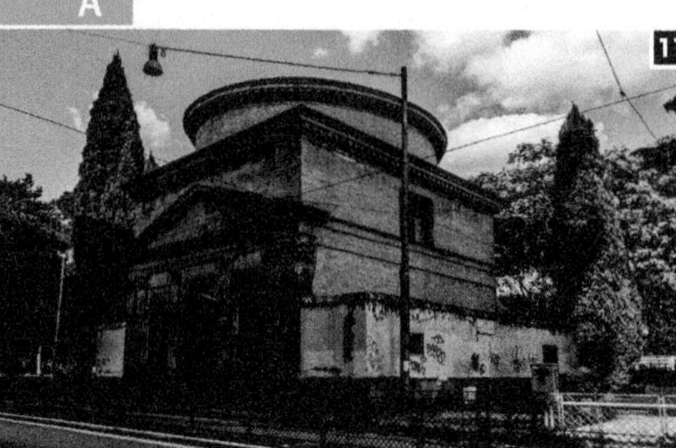

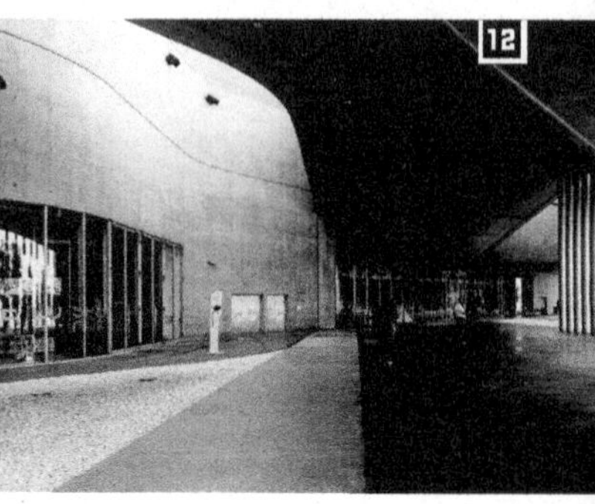

❷ Sant'Andrea in Via Flaminia ★

On the way to the MAXXI (designed by Zaha Hadid) and MUSA (designed by Renzo Piano), every architecture aficionado has to get off on the Flaminia – Belle Arti station and pay their respects to the famous architect from a small town Vignola near Modena, Giacomo Barozzi da Vignola and the first sacral building he built in Rome. ⑪ In 1550, Pope Julius III commissioned Barozzi to build this small church. Since the building is just the size of an average chapel, the architect experimented and actually came up with something that put a stamp on an entire period. He designed an oval dome, which became one of the main components of Baroque architecture. After his initial success, Vignola went on to design Villa Giulia (1551–1553). Apart from Villa Giulia, he also made Chiesa del Gesù, whose façade is considered to be the first real Baroque façade in general. After working with Michelangelo on St. Peter's Basilica, Vignola completed Michelangelo's mission when the great artist passed away in 1564. Da Vignola died in 1573 in Rome. His grave is located at the Pantheon.

❸ Museo Nazionale delle arti del XXI secolo ★★ ⑫

MAXXI or National Museum of the 21st Century Arts is a contemporary art and architecture museum designed by Zaha Hadid. Apart from the permanent exhibition, there are many and frequent temporary exhibitions. Even if you did not plan to visit a museum of contemporary art, you should check this one out, especially because of its architectural concept. The easiest way to get to this museum is by Tram – No. 2 from Piazzale Flaminio, right next to Piazza del Popolo.

❹ Auditorium Parco della Musica ★★

The large complex is an example of the extraordinary avant-garde contemporary architecture (2002) designed by one of the most famous contemporary Italian architects, Renzo Piano. Auditorium Parco della Musica is a music complex with:

- ► A three large concert halls,
- ► A theater,
- ► A small museum with the artifacts that were discovered during construction of the auditorium,
- ► The Accademia Nazionale di Santa Cecilia or National Academy of St. Cecilia is one of the oldest musical institutions in the world (1585),

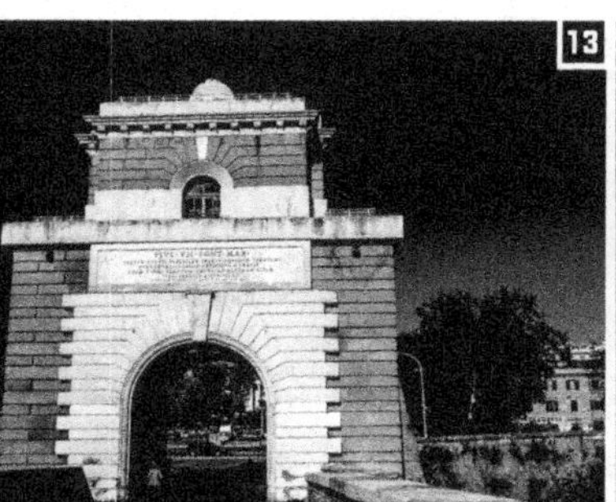

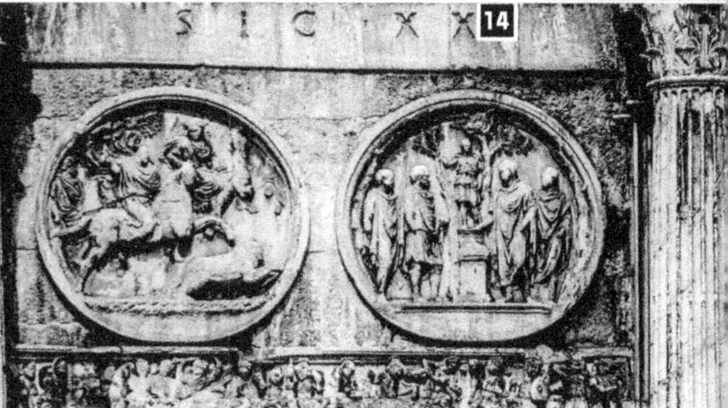

▶ The Museum of Musical Instruments (MUSA) is a part of the National Academy of St. Cecilia.

◆ Ponte Milvio ★ 13

The Milvian Bridge is a Roman bridge (115 BC) related to the famous Battle of the Milvian Bridge (AD 312). This is when Constantine the Great defeated Maxentius and became the only ruler in the Western Roman Empire. Later on, according to Christian oral tradition, Constantine the Great attributed his victory at the Milvian Bridge to the miraculous intervention of the Christian God, so it became an important battle for Christians. A scene from the battle is featured on the Constantine's Arch near the Colosseum, showing Constantine's soldiers chasing Maxentius' troops in the Tiber. 14 Emperor Maxentius drowned in the Tiber in front of Constantine's army.

Sant'Andrea in Via Flaminia | Chiesa di Sant'Andrea del Vignola
Address: Via Flaminia 194, Roma

Public transportation:
Tram stop Flaminia – Belle Arti: 2

Opening hours: *permanently closed*

Auditorium Parco della Musica
Address: Via Pietro de Coubertin 30, Roma
Online: https://en.auditorium.com/

Public transportation:
Tram stop Piazza Mancini: 2

Opening hours: *see online*

Museo Nazionale delle arti del XXI secolo (MAXXI) | National Museum of the 21st Century Arts
Address: Via Guido Reni 4a, Roma
Online: www.maxxi.art/en

Public transportation:
Tram stop Piazza Mancini: 2

Opening hours: *see online*

MAXXI – Auditorium – Ponte Milvio

◆ MAXXI or National Museum of the 21st Century Arts
◆ Auditorium Parco della Musica
◆ Ponte Milvio

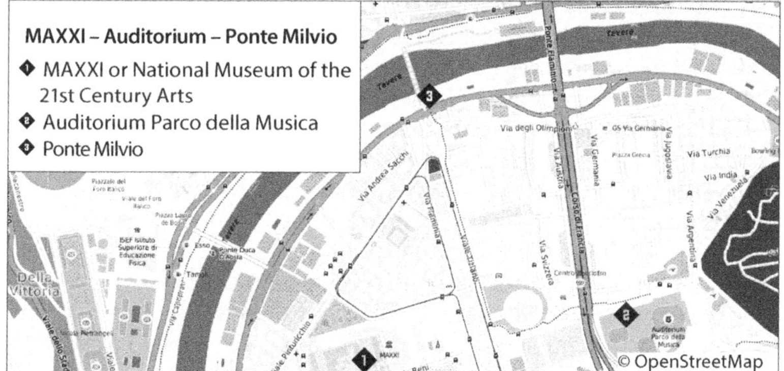

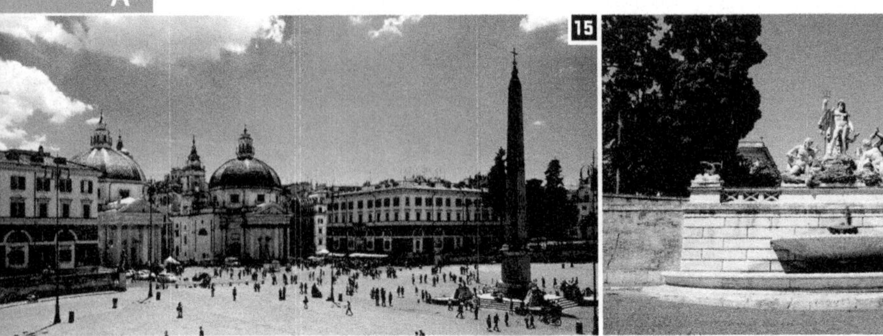

⬥ Piazza del Popolo ★★★ 🔟

Piazza del Popolo has been a Roman square since ancient times. For centuries, it was the first thing visitors saw when entering Rome through Via Flaminia. Besides, all the way to the 19th century, this was the square for public executions, the most popular folk entertainments in Rome. Since the 16th century, three streets connect to the square:

▸ Via del Babuino leading to the Piazza di Spagna and beyond, to the Santa Maria Maggiore Basilica,

▸ Via di Ripetta that goes all the way to the Vatican,

▸ Via del Corso is the oldest and also the only street parallel to Via Flaminia. It ends at Piazza Venezia, right before the Capitoline Hill.

The square was completed in 1822 by a Classicist architect Giuseppe Valadier. The most fascinating sight are the twin churches on either side of Via del Corso – Santa Maria dei Miracoli and Santa Maria in Montesanto. 🔢

Porta del Popolo 🔢

They gate are called Porta del Popolo and date back to the Aurelian era when the emperor was fortifying the city (271–275). The gates, as well as the square, used to be called Flaminio, because the most important road north of Rome started here (Via Flaminia) and went all the way to Ariminium, present-day Rimini on the Adriatic coast. The inner façade (1655) of Porta del Popolo was designed by Bernini.

Obelisk and Fountains

Fountains came and went for centuries. The square is dominated by an Egyptian obelisk. Three sides of the obelisk are dedicated to Seti I, while the remaining side is dedicated to his son Ramesses II (1279–1213 BC). The latter erected the obelisk to honor his father in Heliopolis, present-day suburb of Cairo. It was brought to Rome in 10 BC by Augustus's order and put in the center of Circus Maximus. After the fall of the Roman Empire, the obelisk was found in 1587, lying in the ground broken in half. Pope Sixtus V placed it on Piazza del Popolo in 1589. Fontana dell' Obelisco has four lion sculptures that were added in 1818. Fountains at the edges of the square were designed by Giovanni Ceccarini in 1823. Fontana del Nettuno shows Neptune and two dolphins. 🔢 On the other side of the square, the goddess Roma is holding a spear and wearing a helmet. In front of her, she-wolf suckling Romulus and Remus.

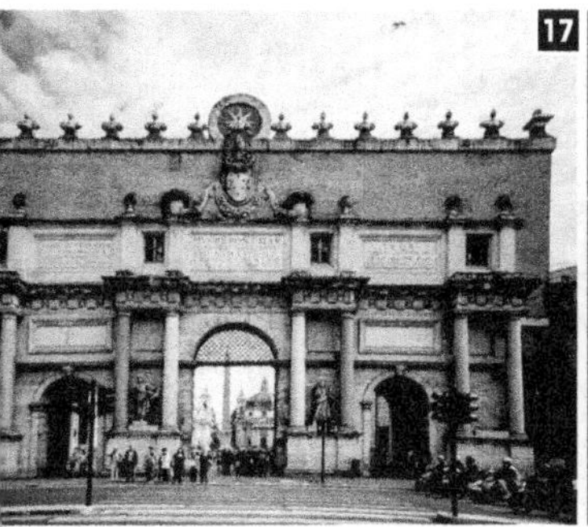

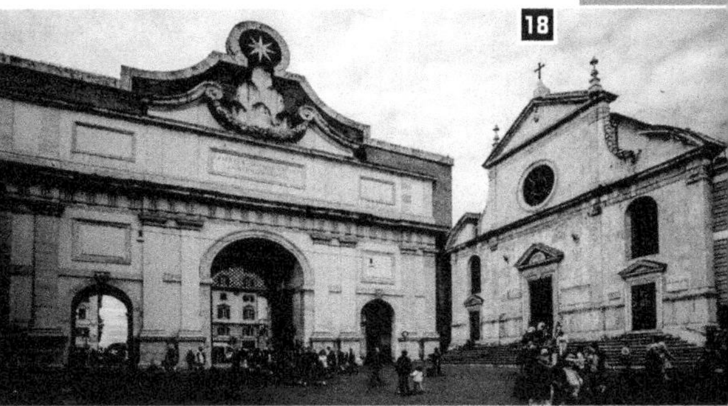

Behind this fountain, there is Pincio, a green hill with the gardens of the Villa Borghese.

① Santa Maria del Popolo ★★★★ 18

After you pass through Porta del Popolo, you will have an amazing view of Piazza del Popolo, with several fountains and a big obelisk in the middle. On the left, next to the Aurelian wall, there is Santa Maria del Popolo, a church from 1099. It is lavishly decorated and full of paintings, sculptures and architectural wonders by Raphael, Bernini, Caravaggio, Carlo Fontana, Pinturicchio, Bramante and many more. The façade is baroque. It is the work of Bernini (1655–1660). The three-nave church has plenty of chapels dedicated to respectable Roman families. It can be said they represent the Who is Who of 15th and 16th-century Rome. The rich and powerful Romans had to compete even after death, outdoing each other by designing extravagant tombs. 24 We can start with the first chapel in the right nave and then work our way forward until we finish where we started, at the entrance.

Della Rovere Chapel

The first chapel on the right belongs to the della Rovere family. Many cardinals and two influential Renaissance popes came from this family: Sixtus IV, responsible for the Sistine

Santa Maria del Popolo
Address: Piazza del Popolo 12, Roma

Public transportation:
Metro A stop Flaminio

Opening hours: *see on Google Maps*

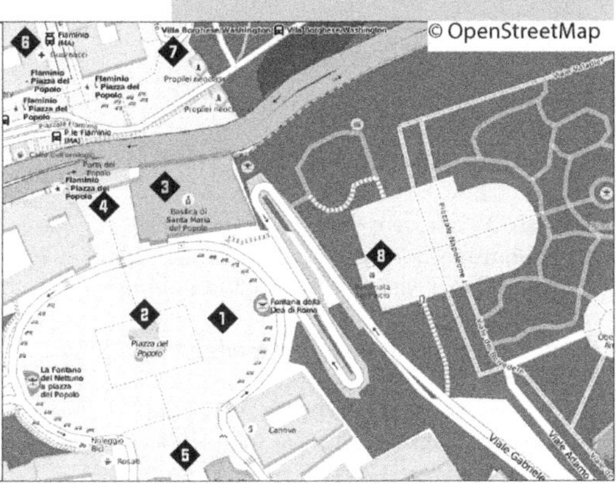

Piazza del Popolo

◆ Piazza del Popolo
◆ Obelisk and Fountains
◆ Santa Maria del Popolo
◆ Porta del Popolo
◆ Santa Maria dei Miracoli and Santa Maria in Montesanto
◆ Tram stop Piazzale Flaminio to stop Apollodoro (MAXXI and Ponte Milvio)
◆ Metro A stop Flaminio
◆ Il Pincio or the Pincian Hill

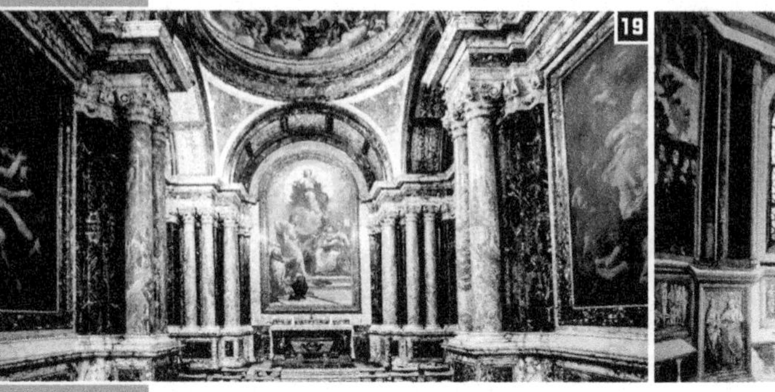

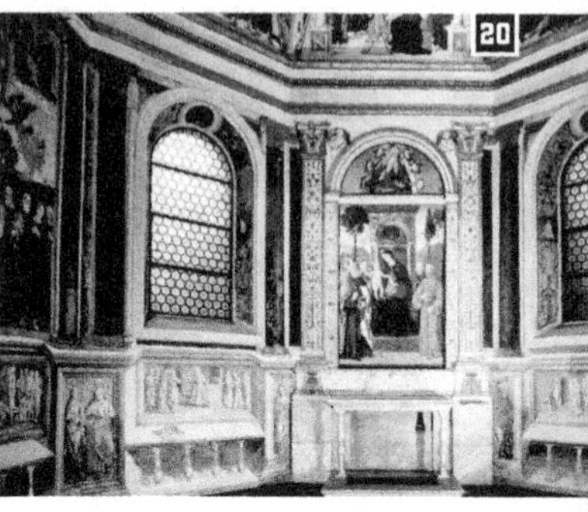

Santa Maria del Popolo

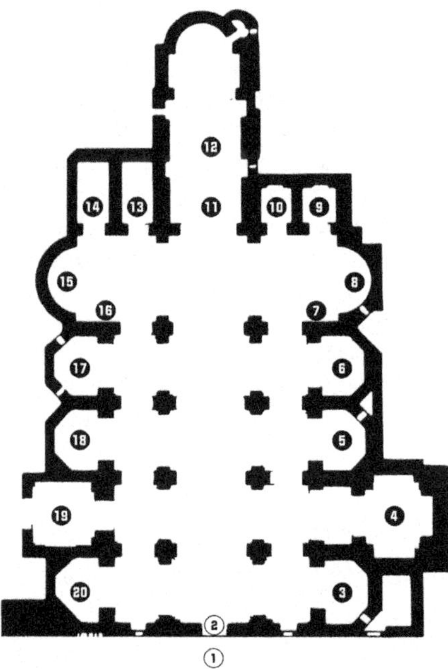

① Stairs
② Main entrance
❸ Della Rovere Chapel with the paintings of Pinturicchio and his pupils
❹ Cybo Chapel was designed by Carlo Fontana
❺ Basso Della Rovere Chapel with the paintings of Pinturicchio and his pupils
❻ Costa Chapel with the paintings of Pinturicchio and his pupils
❼ *The funeral monument of cardinal Ludovico Prodocator*
❽ *Angel* on the right side by Ercole Ferrata
❾ Chapel of Saint Rita with *The tomb of Odoardo Cicada* made by Guglielmo della Porta

❿ The Chapel of Saint Thomas of Villanova with the painting by Fabrizio Chiari
⓫ High altar by Andrea Bregno
⓬ Chor ceiling by Pinturicchio
⓭ Cerasi Chapel – *Assumption of the Virgin* by Annibale Carracci (Altarpiece), *Crucifixion of St. Peter* by Caravaggio (left side wall), *Conversion of Saint Paul* by Caravaggio (right side wall)
⓮ Theodoli Chapel is a major Roman Mannerism work by Giulio Mazzoni (1575)
⓯ *Angel* on the right by Antonio Raggi and on the left by Giovanni Antonio Mari
⓰ *The funeral monument of cardinal Bernardino Lonati* by Andrea Bregno (1493)
⓱ Cybo-Soderini Chapel with the frescoes of a Flemish artist Pieter van Lint (1636–40)
⓲ Mellini Chapel with the tombs of Cardinal Giovanni Garzia Mellini (1638) and Urbano Mellini (1652) by Alessandro Algardi
⓳ Chigi Chapel designed by Raphael (1513) and completed by Bernini (1656), *Statues of Habakkuk and the Angel* (1661) and *Daniel* by Bernini (1657), *Statues of Elijah and Jonah* by Lorenzetto, *The mosaics of the ceiling* by Raphael, *The Birth of the Virgin* by Sebastiano del Piombo.
⓴ Montemirabile Chapel (Baptistery)

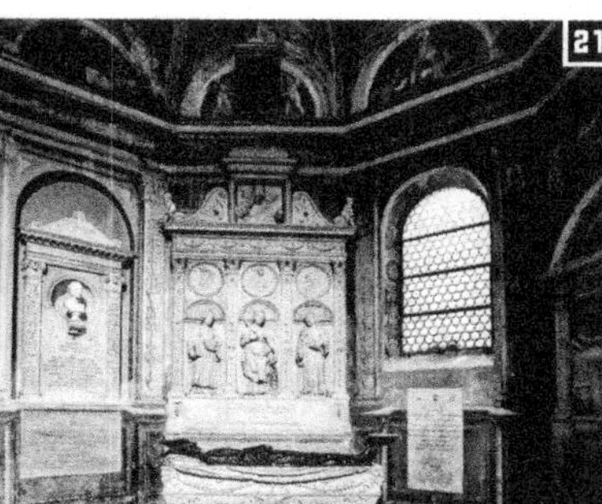

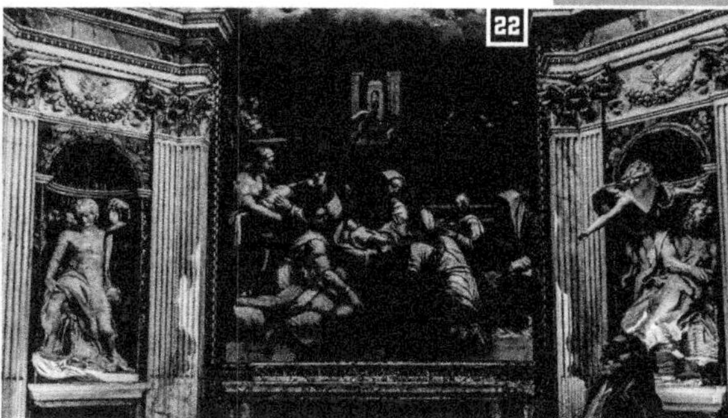

Chapel, and Sixtus's nephew Pope Julius II, who built St. Peter's Basilica, founded the Vatican Museums and established the Swiss Guard.

This is the tomb of Domenico della Rovere and his brother Cristoforo, another one of Pope Sixtus's nephews. The altar painting is by Bernardino di Betto, called Pinturicchio, with scenes from the life of St. Hieronymus.

Cybo Chapel 🔟

The second chapel on the right is for the Cybo family, designed by Carlo Fontana, Roman architect and city planner.

Basso Della Rovere Chapel 🔟

The third chapel is the Basso della Rovere Chapel, dedicated by Cardinal Girolamo Basso della Rovere in 1484 and donated to the church. The paintings are the work of Pinturicchio's pupil.

Costa Chapel 🔟

The fourth chapel is called the Costa Chapel. It was covered in frescoes by Pinturicchio in 1489.

Although it was commissioned by the della Roveres, it was sold to the Portuguese Cardinal Giorgio Costa even before it had been completed, so the cardinal was buried here.

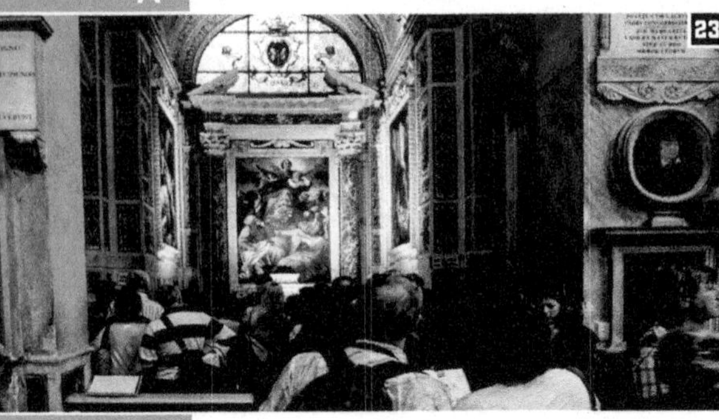

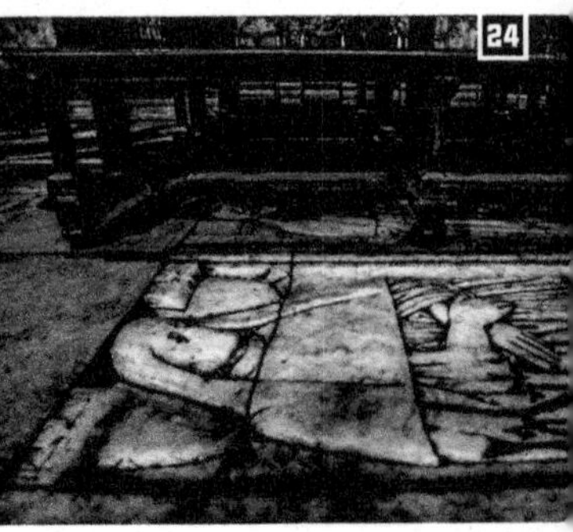

Capella Maggiore

The big chapel behind the altar in the back of the main nave is the Capella Maggiore with the tomb of Cardinal Ascanio Maria Sforza. The chapel was made by the order of Pope Julius II at the Andrea Sansovino's workshop. Pope Julius II, from the della Rovere family, maintained a rivalry with the most powerful Milanese family Sforza. Since he required allies in his fight against the French troops in Northern Italy, he ordered this chapel as a symbol of reconciliation for one of the Sforzas. There is fresco of Mary's coronation in the arch by Pinturicchio.

Cerasi Chapel 23

The first chapel left of the altar is the Cerasi Chapel with two famous paintings by Caravaggio: Crucifixion of St. Peter (1600) and Conversion on the Way to Damascus (1601). Caravaggio's grotesque and extremely realistic compositions caused a lot of public controversy. He was equally admired and hated. In the Conversion on the Way to Damascus, he deliberately did not disperse the Divine Light on a specific character for symbolic value. On the contrary, the light shines on the horse and the recumbent Roman soldier. In the Crucifixion of St. Peter, the feet of one of the crucifier are very dirty, the nails in the hands and feet of St. Peter look absolutely real. In the forefront, the back and filthy feet of an anonymous crucifier come into full view.

Cybo-Soderini Chapel

In the Chapel of the Crucifixion, in the middle of the left nave, there is a cross with Jesus Christ from the 14th century.

Cappella Chigi 22

This is the second chapel on the left to the entrance. It was commissioned by the papal banker Agostino Chigi in 1511 from Raphael. The artist was responsible not only for painting, but also the entire architectural design. However, in 1520, both the artist and the banker died, so the chapel was never completed. In any case, Raphael managed to build the chapel, as well as the gilded dome with cassettes and a lantern mosaic. We can see God the Creator, surrounded with symbols of the Sun and the seven planets which are all aligned to the date of the birth of Jesus Christ. The rest of the decor was done by others after Raphael's death. Conceptually, the scenes

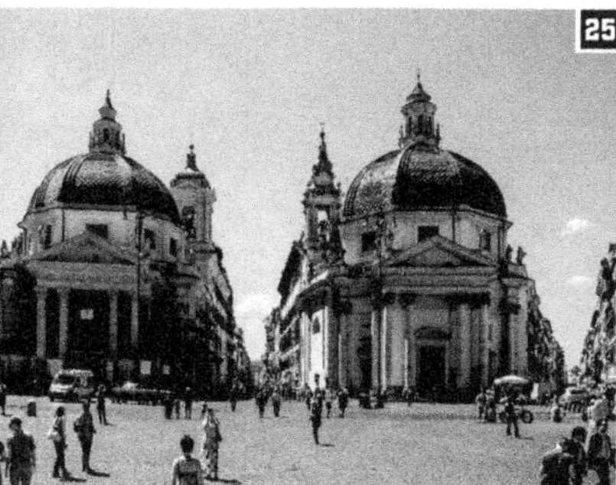

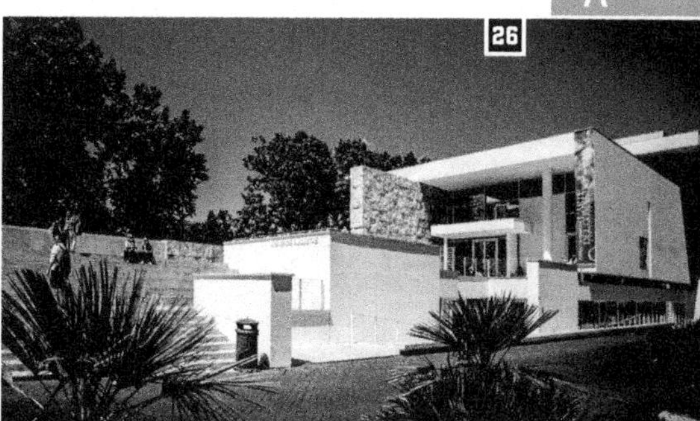

are united under the slogan written on the floor: *Mors aD CaeLos Iter* or "Death is the way to heaven." The altar painting was made by Sebastiano del Piombo in 1534. A pope from the Chigi family, Alexander VII, ordered Bernini to finish the family tomb. Bernini made two sculptures, the prophets Daniel and Habakkuk, as portrait medallions.

Montemirabile Chapel

The last chapel on our tour of this church is the first one left of the entrance. The Montemirabile Chapel was built by Bishop Giovanni Montemirabile in 1479 and later adapted into a baptistery.

Santa Maria dei Miracoli and Santa Maria in Montesanto ★★

Both baroque churches next to Via del Corso were ordered by Pope Alexander VII in the 17th century. The project was redesigned by Bernini and the final touches were applied by Carlo Fontana in 1675. From the mid-20th century, there are Sunday sermons in Santa Maria dei Miracoli, from the last Sunday in October to June 29, dedicated to artists and held by artists.

Ara Pacis Augustus ★★★★

Pacis was the Roman goddess of peace and Augustus claimed her as his protectress. It suited his political agenda, called *Pax Romana* or Roman

Santa Maria dei Miracoli 🗓25
Address: Via del Corso 528, Roma
Online: www.chiesadegliartisti.it

Public transportation:
Metro A stop Flaminio

Opening hours: *see online*

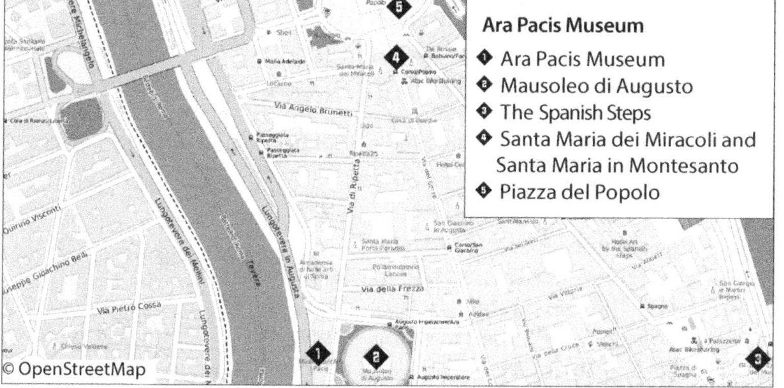

Ara Pacis Museum

❶ Ara Pacis Museum
❷ Mausoleo di Augusto
❸ The Spanish Steps
❹ Santa Maria dei Miracoli and Santa Maria in Montesanto
❺ Piazza del Popolo

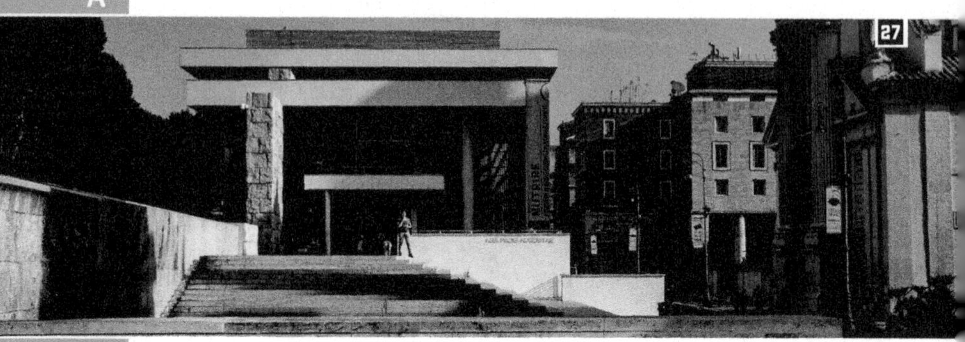

Peace, carried out under the rule of the first Roman emperor. Hence another name for it, Pax Augusta. It is a peace altar entirely made of Carrara marble, situated close to the Mausoleum of Augustus.

It was officially commissioned by the Roman Senate in 13 BC consecrated in 9 BC to honor Augustus's return from Hispania and Gaul after a three-year campaign. The Tiber flooded this altar for years, covering it in layers and layers of mud until it was 13 ft or 4 m underground. The first fragments of the temple, mentioned in ancient literature many times, were discovered in the 16th century, underneath San Lorenzo in Lucina, a basilica behind Palazzo Montecitorio or present-day Italian Parliament. In Augustus's heyday, this is where Solarium Augusti stood, an enormous sun clock that used an obelisk instead of a hand.

Every year on September 23, on Augustus's birthday, the shadow of the obelisk covered Ara Pacis. Due to the fact that the figures are of incredibly high quality, it is believed that they were made by Greek artists. Once a year, a sacrifice was brought to the altar of peace. Ara Pacis is the most important sculptural specimen from the Augustan era. The new glass building of the Museo dell'Ara Pacis was designed by Richard Meier in 2006. **27** The museum is airy and has a lot of natural light, as a worthy dedication to Augustus's idea of peace. The space in front of the museum, with lots of water and light, is one of the most pleasant places to take a short break in the middle of the city.

◆ 8 Mausoleo di Augusto ★★

After his victory over Mark Antony and Cleopatra, which allowed him to join Egypt to the Roman state, Octavian (later Augustus) returned to Rome in 29 BC, at the age of 34.

Museo dell'Ara Pacis | Ara Pacis Museum
Address: Lungotevere in Augusta, Roma
Online: www.arapacis.it/en

Public transportation: Bus stop Augusto Imperatore – Ara Pacis: 81, 628, C3 or stop Augusto Imperatore: 913 or Tomacelli: 81, 301, 628, 913, C3

Opening hours: *see online*

Mausoleo di Augusto | Mausoleum of Augustus
Address: Piazza Augusto Imperatore, Roma
Online: www.mausoleodiaugusto.it/en

Public transportation: Bus stop Augusto Imperatore – Ara Pacis: 81, 628, C3 or stop Augusto Imperatore: 913 or Tomacelli: 81, 301, 628, 913, C3

Opening hours: *see online*

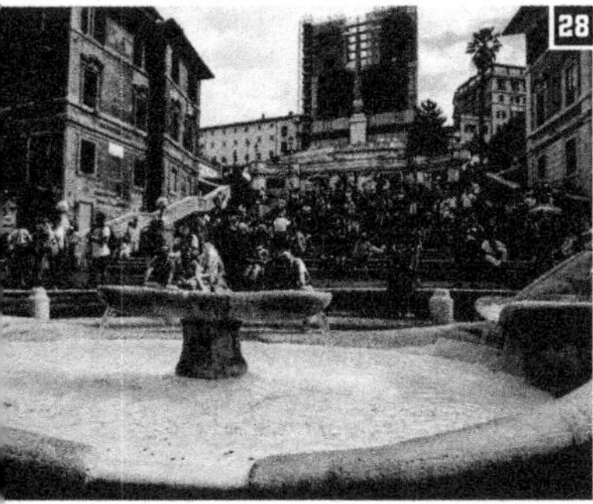

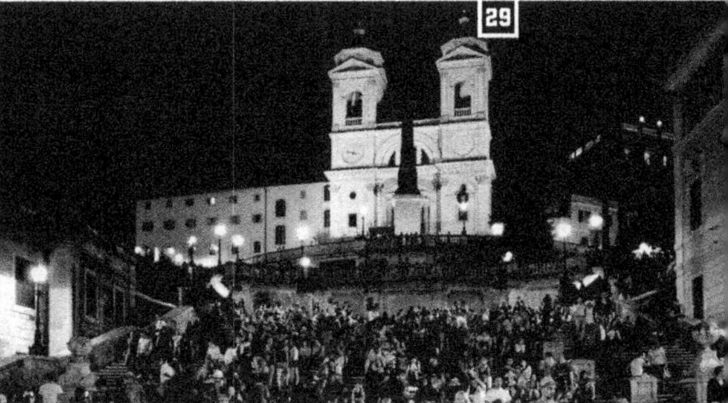

He began building a mausoleum for himself and his family at the Martian Field. Mausoleum of Augustus was constructed according to the mausoleum of Alexander the Great, which Augustus visited in Alexandria. Apart from numerous members of Augustus's family, almost every emperor from the Julio-Claudian dynasty was buried here: Augustus (AD 14), Tiberius (AD 37), Caligula (AD 41) and Claudius (AD 54). Nero from the Julian dynasty was not buried here, but Emperor Nerva was buried here in AD 94. When Visigoth king Alaric sacked Rome in 410, his soldiers stormed the mausoleum, stealing the golden urns and throwing away the ashes.

◆ Spanish Steps ★★ 28

The Spanish Steps connect Piazza di Spagna and Piazza Trinità dei Monti, so their name in Italian is Scalinata della Trinità dei Monti. This monumental staircase is the largest one in Europe, commissioned by a French diplomat Étienne Gueffier in 1725. He wanted to link the Spanish Burbon Embassy of the Holy See in Palazzo Monaldeschi with the French church of Trinità dei Monti. The stairs were designed by Francesco de Sanctis and Alessandro Specchi. 29

◇ Fontana della Barcaccia ★★

There is an unusual fountain in front of the Spanish Steps called Fontana della Barcaccia or "Fountain of the Ugly Boat", by Pietro Bernini, father to the famous Gian Lorenzo Bernini. The fountain was erected in 1729. The story goes that Pope Urban VIII wanted a fountain exactly like this one because he was impressed by a sinking ship when the Tiber flooded this area. 30

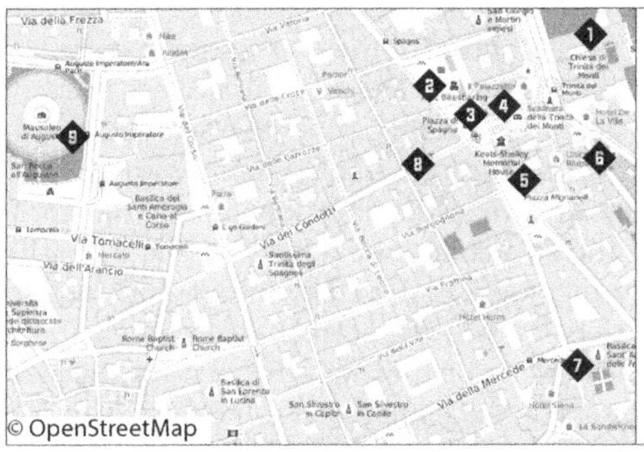

The Spanish Steps

- ◆ Church of the Santissima Trinità dei Monti
- ◆ The Spanish Steps
- ◆ Fontana della Barcaccia
- ◆ Keats-Shelley Memorial House
- ◆ Giorgio De Chirico House
- ◆ Palazzo Zuccari
- ◆ Sant'Andrea delle Fratte
- ◆ Via Condotti
- ◆ Mausoleo di Augusto

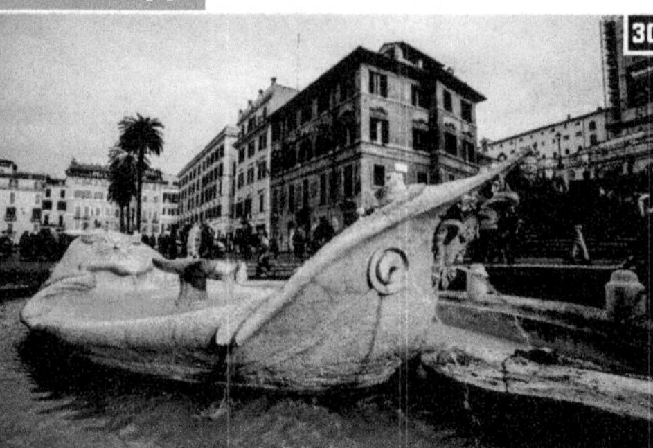
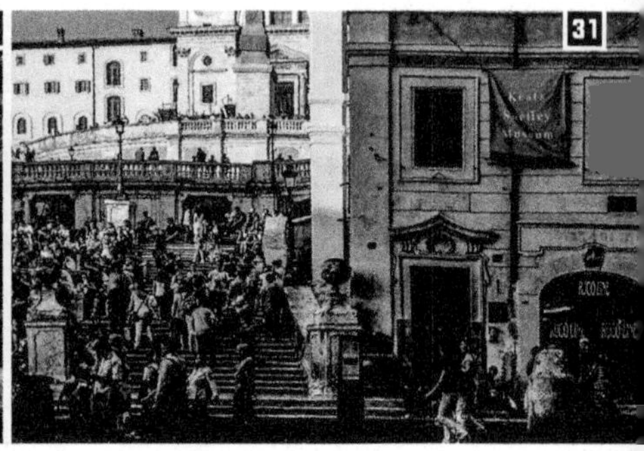

② Keats-Shelley Memorial House ★

Some of the most interesting poets and painters lived in Rome and chose a home in the immediate vicinity of the Spanish Steps. **31**

The English Romantic poet, Percy Bysshe Shelley, lived in the yellow building on the right, which is also where another romantic poet felt at home, and that was John Keats. On the second floor of the Keats-Shelley Memorial House, there are items related to Keats, Shelley, Lord Byron, Robert Browning, as well as the Irish poet Oscar Wilde. Shelley died soon after Keats. His friends, lead by Lord Byron, burnt Shelley's body and buried the remains at the Protestant cemetery next to the John Keats.

③ Giorgio De Chirico House ★★★

Giorgio de Chirico lived at 31 Piazza di Spagna in Palazzetto del Borgognoni until his death in 1978. This museum is run by the foundation established in his honor for around twenty of his works. **32**

Giorgio de Chirico had a huge influence on the surrealist movement, more than any other artist. His metaphysical paintings were inspired by Nietzsche and Schopenhauer. If you visit E.U.R., a modern part of Rome built in the 1940's, you will feel like you are walking through 3D representations of his paintings with long shadows, surreal buildings and avenues. [p.258] In any way, Giorgio de Chirico was not the supporter of the Italian fascism. Before you go to E.U.R., the best thing to do is to visit de Chirico's home. His grave is in the church San Francesco a Ripa in Trastevere [p.237].

④ Palazzo Zuccari ★ **33**

If you get tired of watching people on the Spanish Steps, go up to the church of Santissima Trinità dei Monti with the two towers overlooking the steps. If you go right, down Via Gregoriana, you will arrive in front of a façade whose windows and doors come from the mouth of a monster – that is Palazzo Zuccari. These so-called *mascarons*, ornaments with distorted faces, were meant to prevent the evil spirits from coming into the house. Frederico Zuccari, a painter and an architect, built this house for himself in the late 16th century. Today, the house is owned by the German research institute the Max Planck Society for the Advancement of Science with the famous Hertziana library. The frescoes on the ground floor were also made by the artist and former owner Frederico Zuccari.

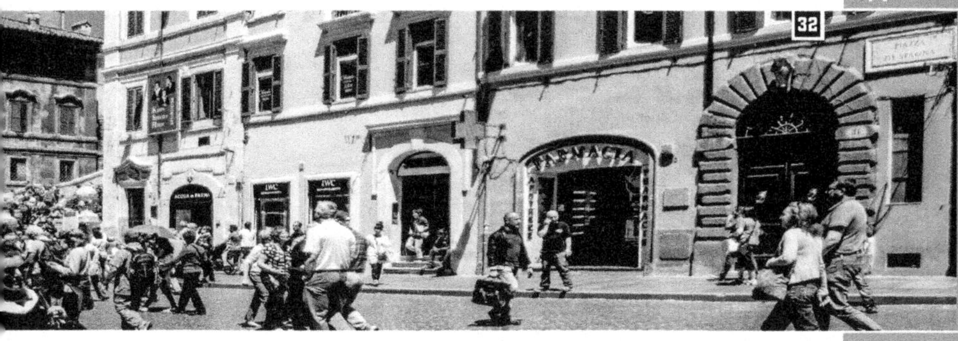

⑩ Fontana di Trevi | Trevi Fountain ★★★★ ②

Fontana di Trevi is the most famous and largest fountain in a city of fountains. Trevi fountain is Nicola Salvi's masterpiece. When Pope Clement XII organized a tender for this fountain, no one thought that the young and inexperienced Nicola Salvi would have a chance to turn his vision into reality. Pope chose him and the young Salvi started working in 1732, a process that would last 30 years. In the background, there is a three-piece triumphal arch. ㉞

The central figure is Oceanus, god of the sea, made by Pietro Bracci. Oceanus is standing on a carriage made of seashells. There are seahorses dragging the carriage, attended by Tritons, half-people, half-fish from the Greek mythology. This monumental baroque composition is 164 by 82 ft or 50 by 25 m. In the lateral niches, there are personifications of wealth and healing. These figures are the work of Filippo della Vale. Reliefs above these statues illustrate real and imaginary events relating to the construction of the Aqua Virgo aqueduct. Trevi Fountain was built on the end of this aqueduct. The legend goes that if you throw a coin with your left hand over your right shoulder, that means you will return to Rome for sure.

Keats-Shelley Memorial House
Address: Piazza di Spagna 26, Roma
Online: www.ksh.roma.it

Public transportation: Metro A stop Spagna | Bus stop Trinita' Dei Monti: 117

Opening hours: *see online*

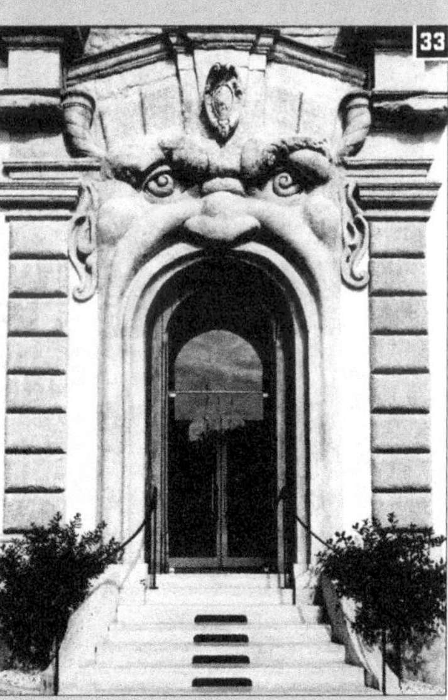

Casa-museo Giorgio de Chirico | Giorgio De Chirico House Museum
Address: Piazza di Spagna 31, Roma
Online: www.fondazionedechirico.org/en

Public transportation: Metro A stop Spagna | Bus stop Trinita' Dei Monti: 117

The ticket reservation must be made in advance!

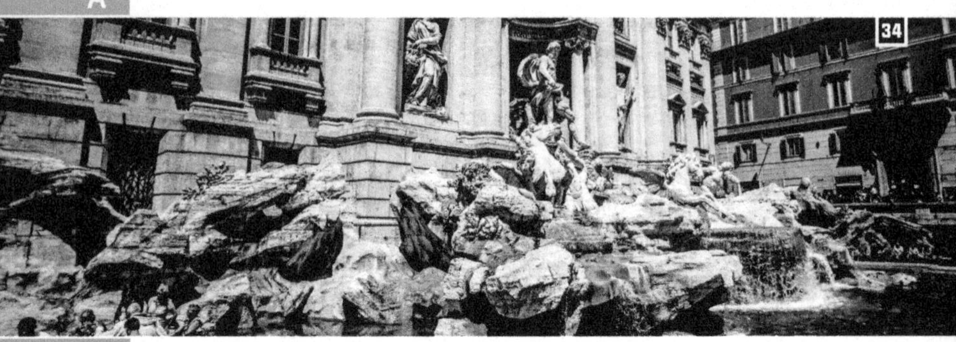

Until that wish comes true, you can rest in the knowledge that you have done a good deed — over a million Euro in coins is thrown in the Trevi fountain every year and all the money goes to Caritas, the social mission of the Catholic Church.

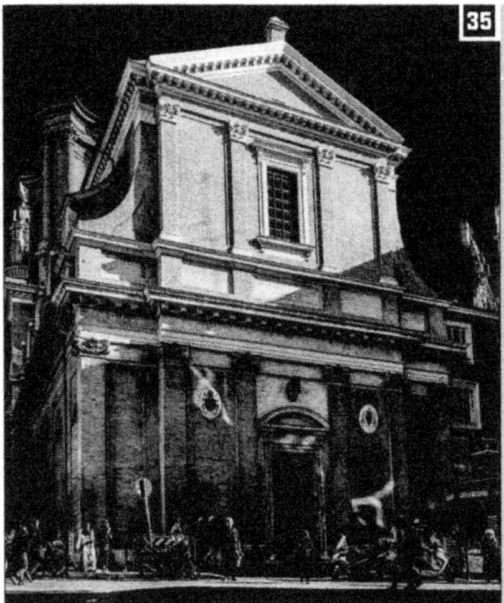

Did you know?

Aqua Virgo Aqueduct

This aqueduct was built by Augustus and Agrippa, his friend and general. In 19 BC, a virgin showed Agrippa the source which was used to supply the baths with water.

Agrippa's baths were fully functional for over 400 years. Every day, 3531467 cubic feet or 100,000 cubic meters of water were supplied from the Aqua Virgo aqueduct.

Then, the baths were closed for 300 years and restored in the 8th century thanks to Pope Adrian I.

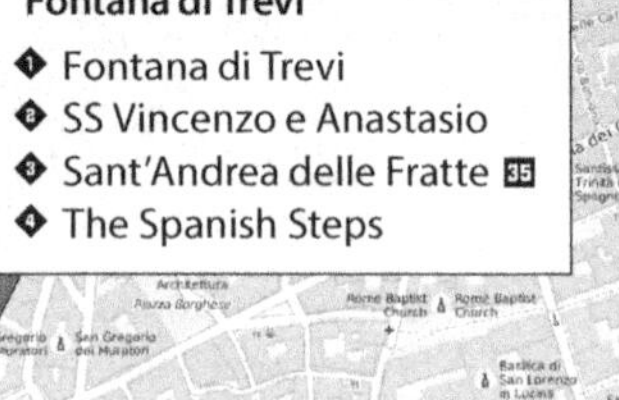

Fontana di Trevi

❶ Fontana di Trevi
❷ SS Vincenzo e Anastasio
❸ Sant'Andrea delle Fratte 35
❹ The Spanish Steps

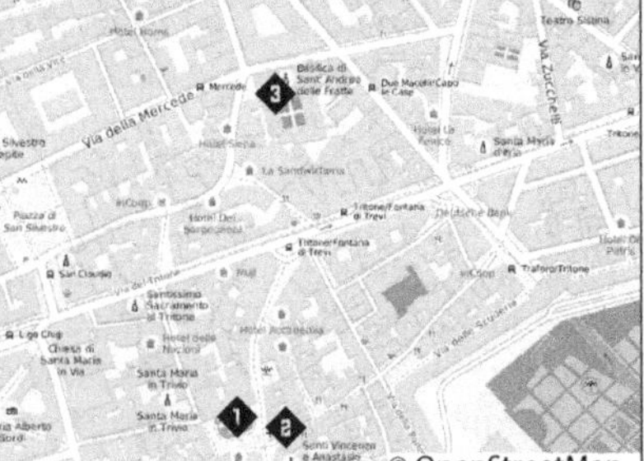

From Baths of Diocletian to the Piazza del Quirinale

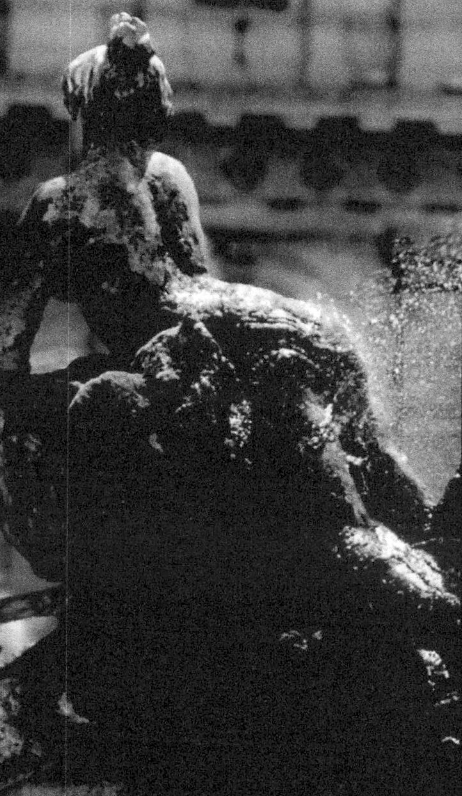

A Naiad on the Fontanza delle Naiadi

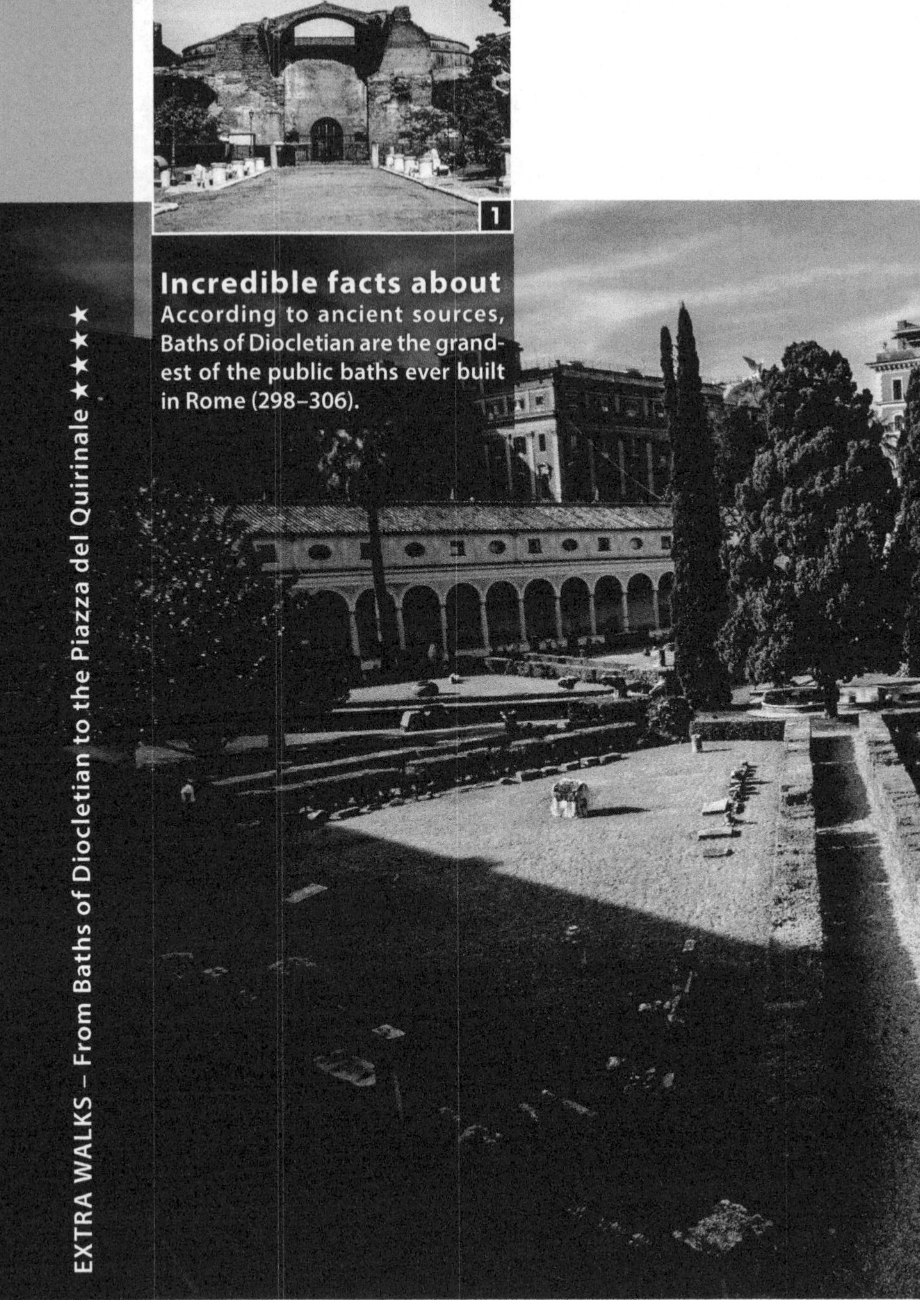

Incredible facts about

According to ancient sources, Baths of Diocletian are the grandest of the public baths ever built in Rome (298–306).

Michelangelo's Carthusian monastery, Baths of Diocletian

Extra Tip : : :
Single ticket for the National Roman Museum is valid for 7 days at 4 sites: Palazzo Massimo alle Terme, Palazzo Altemps, Crypta Balbi and Baths of Diocletian. The ticket prices are more than reasonable.

Ancient and Baroque Rome in one afternoon

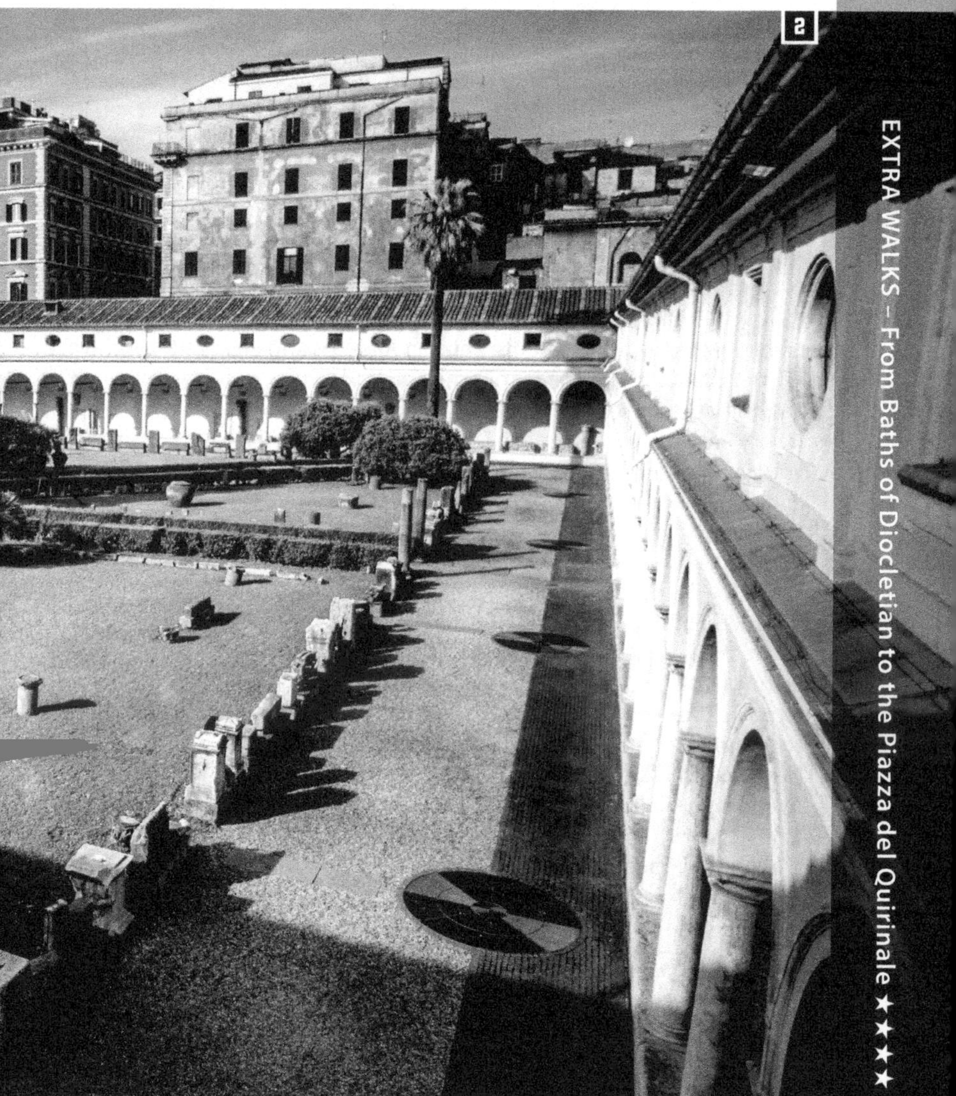

National Roman Museum – Baths of Diocletian
Address: Viale Enrico de Nicola 79, Roma
Public transportation: Metro A and B stop Termini | Bus stop Termini: 16, 75, 150F, 360, 590, 649, 717, C3 | Tram stop Termini: 5, 14

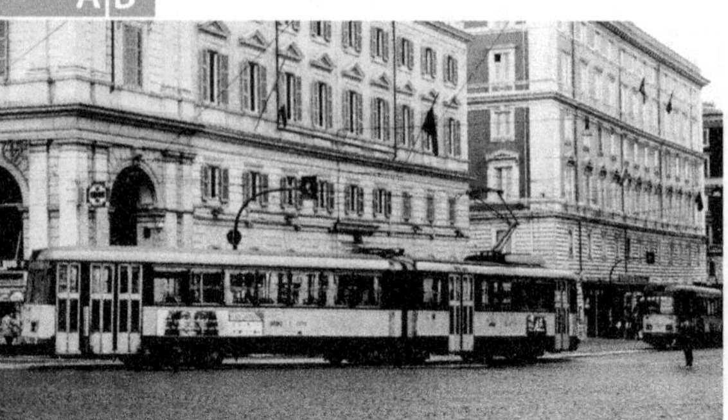

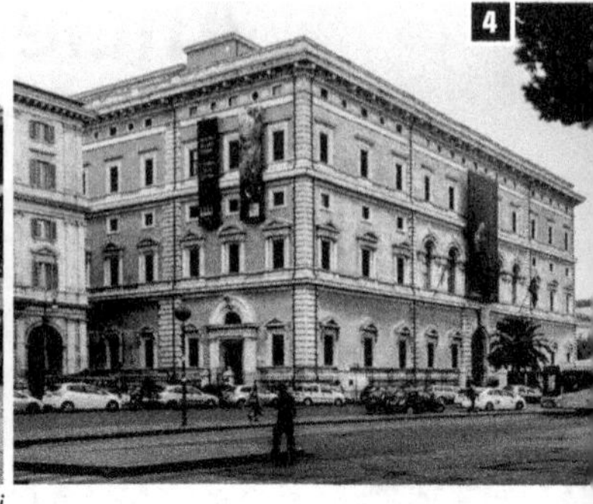

Piazza di Termini

❶ National Roman Museum – Palazzo Massimo alle Terme ★ ★ ★ ★

The main museum of the largest museum of Roman antiquities is in the Palazzo Massimo alle Terme. The museum itself is on four locations: the Balbi Crypt, Diocletian's Baths, Palazzo Altemps and Palazzo Massimo alle Terme. If I did not have a lot of time and had to pick only one museum of antiquity to visit in Rome, I would choose Palazzo Massimo alle Terme. It is very easy to get to because it is right next to the Termini Station, which you can reach by two underground lines (A and B), many buses and two train lines (5 and 14). Unlike the Vatican Museum, you will not have to wait for hours to get in.

The exhibition is brand new and artefacts are explained in such way as to please both art lovers and experts. It took more than thirty years to adapt the palace into a museum. Here, you will find the most complete overview of Roman history, from the Late Republic (2nd century BC) to the end of the Empire (5th century). Moreover, you will come across some of the

Museo Nazionale Romano – Palazzo Massimo | National Roman Museum – Palazzo Massimo alle Terme

Address: Piazza dei Cinquecento 67, Roma
Online: www.museonazionaleromano.beniculturali.it/en

Public transportation: Metro A and B stop Termini | Bus stop Termini: 16, 75, 150F, 360, 590, 649, 717, C3 | Tram stop Termini: 5, 14

Opening hours: *see online*

The combined ticket provide access to all four National Roman Museum's sites: Palazzo Massimo, Palazzo Altemps, Baths of Diocletian, Crypta Balbi.

Piazza della Repubblica

- ❶ Museum Palazzo Massimo alle Terme
- ❷ Piazza della Repubblica
- ❸ Baths of Diocletian
- ❹ Santa Maria degli Angeli e dei Martiri
- ❺ Museum in the Baths of Diocletian
- ❻ Michelangelo's Carthusian monastery
- ❼ Fontana dell'Acqua Felice
- ❽ Santa Maria della Vittoria
- ❾ San Bernardo alle Terme
- ❿ Santa Susanna Church

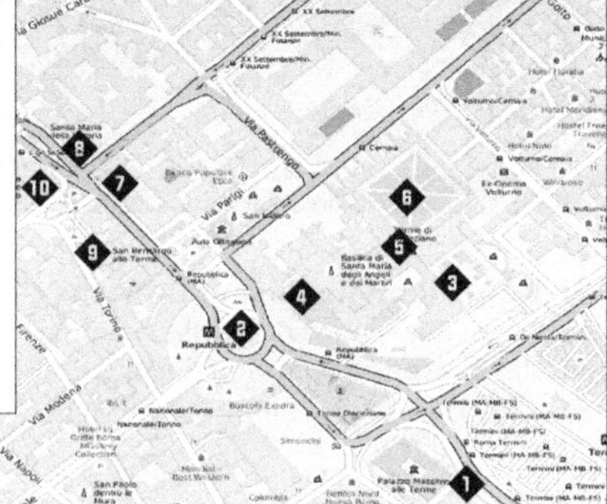

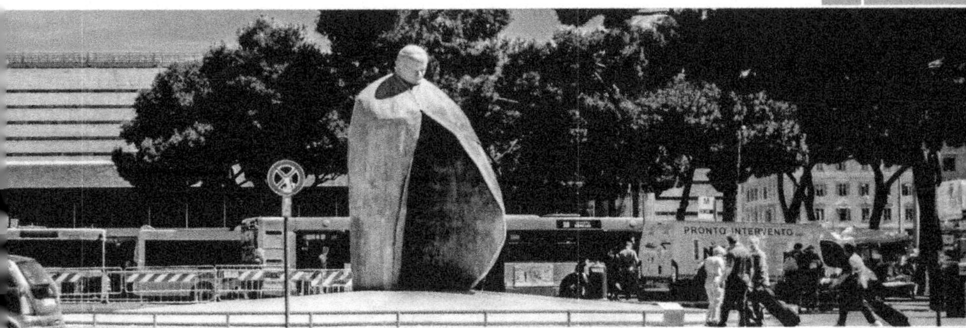

Pope John Paul II Statue at Piazza di Termini

most fascinating examples of Roman art. Highlights: *Augustus as Pontifex Maximus*, *Dying Niobid*, several versions of *Discobolus*, bronze *Dionysius, the Boxer, Sleeping Hermaphrodite, Sarcophagus Portonaccio*, Frescoes from Villa Farnesina, Frescoes from Villa Livia, bronze from two of Caligula's ships, so-called "Nemi ships", and many more. Also, this is the best place to browse through Roman portraits. ◢ [p.211]

Palazzo Massimo – GROUND FLOOR

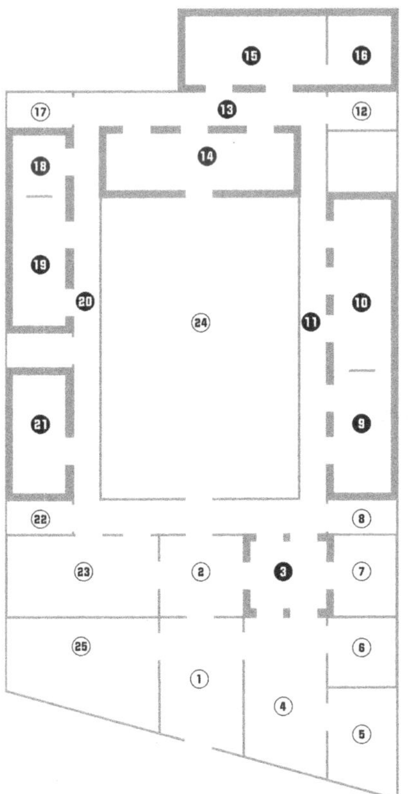

① Entrance
② Info point
❸ Minerva Room
④ Tickets
⑤ Wardrobe
⑥ WC
⑦ Elevator
⑧ Stairs
❾ The Calendar of Anzio
❿ Temporary exhibitions
⓫ Portraits from the Republican Era
⑫ Stairs
⓭ Portraits of the Julio-Claudian family
⓮ The representation of power and Calendar of Palestrina
⓯ Temporary exhibitions
⓰ Temporary exhibitions
⑰ WC
⓲ *Niobide Statue* from the Gardens of Sallust
⓳ *The Boxer* and *the Prince*
⓴ Portraits of the Roman era and Greek portraits
㉑ Works in the Neo-Attic Style from the 1st – 2nd century BC
㉒ Stairs
㉓ Main stairs
㉔ Inner court
㉕ Bookshop and gift shop

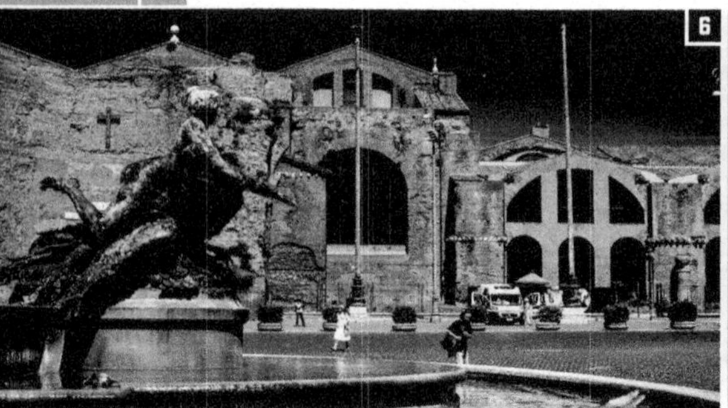

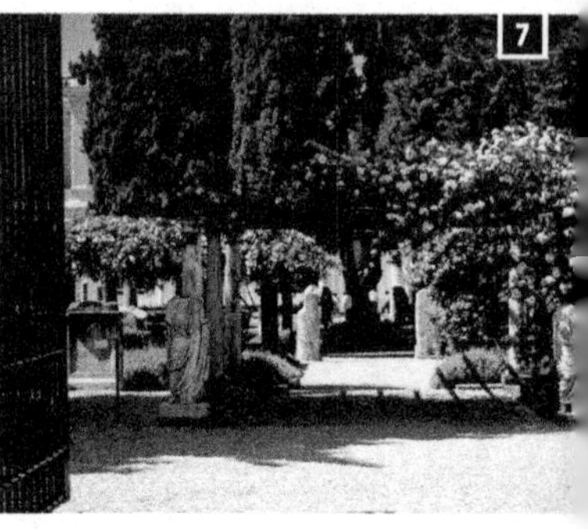

If you come in from the street, you will find yourself on the ground floor and this is the best place to start. We will go to the basement last, after we go through all the three floors above it. Although a vast majority of what is best in Rome has been kept in copies of bronze and marble Greek originals, there are several priceless Greek originals on the ground floor.

❸ *Minerva Room*

After you collect your ticket and go to the checkroom, there is an imposing larger-than-life statue of goddess Minerva from 1st century BC waiting in the first room.

❾ *Room 1 – Calendar of Anzio*

Fasti Antiates maiores is a wall calendar from the Roman Republican era. It is the oldest calendar of this kind before the reform of the Julian calendar.

⓫ *Gallery 1 – Portraits from the Republican Era*

Alongside the portraits in Room 1, Gallery 1 has an exceptional and rare collection of early Roman portraits.

⓭ *Gallery 2 – Portraits of the Julio-Claudian family*

Imperial and private portraits mainly differ in their purpose and the purpose dictated the extent of realism. The more public they were, the more idealized and canonic they became. Among the portraits of the imperial

Did you know?

Roman copies of Greek originals

Graecia capta ferum victorem cepit
Greece, although captured, took its wild conqueror captive.
Horatio

Distinguishing Greek originals from copies is not an easy task. Copies of Greek statues were not only made by Roman artists. If someone is a Roman artist, it says very little about their origin.

The Roman Empire span all the way to Egypt from 30 BC and included Greece from 27 BC onwards, so all the artists in those areas made copies of Greek originals from previous periods. The last free ruler of Egypt, Cleopatra, was the 20th ruler of the Ptolemy dynasty. They ruled Egypt for 275 years as a Greek dynasty, during the Hellenic period, that is to say, from the death of Alexander the Great in 323 BC to the Roman conquest of Egypt in 30 BC. Besides, distinguishing something Greek from something non-Greek is even more complex when it comes to art from *Magna Graecia*, Greek colonies in Southern Italy, established in 8th century BC. Due to the influence of art from Magna Graecia, Etruscan art was largely impacted by Greek art. Greek vases and sculptures were often copied by Etruscans without any original additions or interpretation.

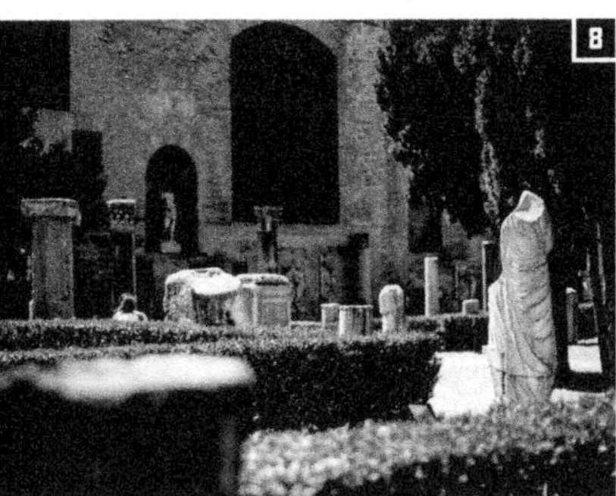

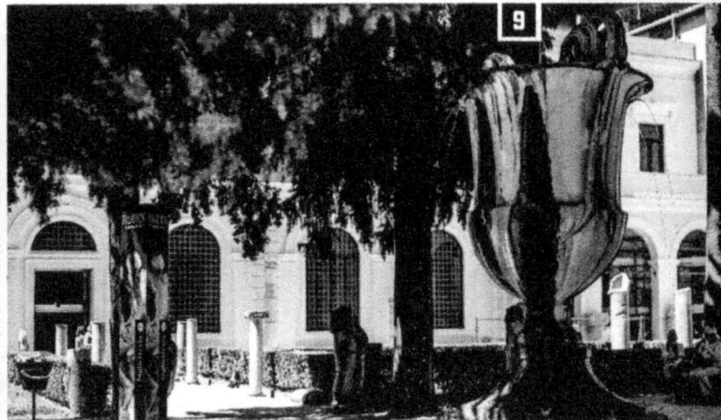

family, portraits of children were more individualized, especially if they were not immediate successors to the throne.

⑩ ⑮ ⑯ *Rooms 2, 3, 4*

This is where usually temporary exhibitions take place.

⑭ *Room 5 – The representation of power*

Pontifex Maximus

This is also one of the portraits of Augustus as Pontifex Maximus, the highest Roman priest, that was frozen in its ideal form for decades and distributed across the vast empire. When it comes to Augustus, there are only a few types of portraits: as warrior, civil administrator or priest with a face of a young man all the way to AD 14, when he died at the age of 76. This portrait from 12 BC was discovered in Villa Labicana in 1910. There is a veil over Augustus's head, which is a mark of a priest or it points to sacrificing at the altar — both included wearing a toga over your head.

Fasti Praenestini | Calendar of Palestrina

This calendar was made by Marcus Verrius Flaccus, a freed slave, excellent grammarian and teacher to Augustus's grandchildren. Marcus Terentius Varro referred to Flaccus as the "most learned of all the Romans. The calendar was on display in Praenestina,

Roman portrait art

This is probably the most important contribution of Roman art to art in general. Unlike Greek portraits where the artist was constantly looking for ideal and universal forms, consciously avoiding any hint of individuality, Roman portraits are characterized by realism. They depict real human beings in works of extraordinary quality. Portraits were usually marble because bronze was more expensive. Very few portraits from the Republican period have been preserved. They can usually be linked to real historical figures. Imperial portraits were only partly individualized. Once it was made, it was copied endlessly as part of political propaganda, representing the central authority. For example, Emperor Augustus's portraits (27 BC – AD 14), even though he ruled for quite a long time, always depicted him in his thirties. However, one thing remained constant — until the last days of the Western Roman Empire, in most cases, the best artists, either copyists or original artists, came from Greece. Generally speaking, the prevailing opinion is that if a Roman artefacts is perfect, there is a good chance it was produced by a Greek artist. This is the case with Ara Pacis, for instance, an altar from the Augustan period. [p.199]

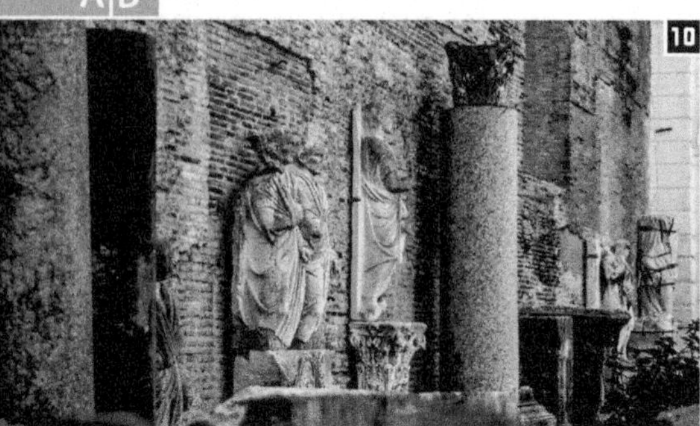

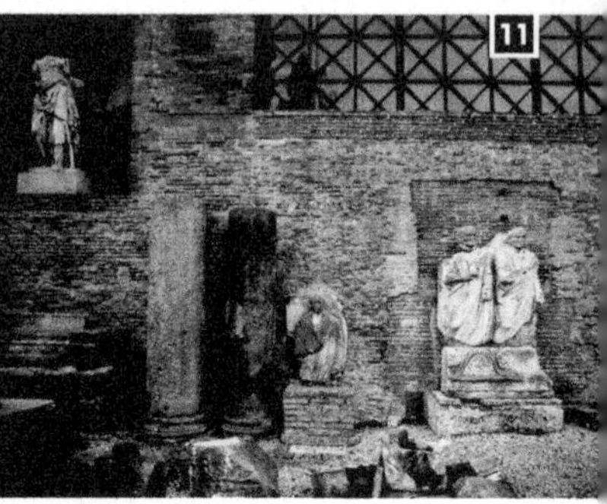

a town near Rome. This calendar is also featured in Gaius Suetonius Tranquillus's notes, a Roman historian (69–130): *His (Flaccus's) calendar is set up on the upper part of the forum in Praeneste (Palestrina) near the hemicycle (semicircular debating chamber), with a calendar inscribed into the marble pedestal.*

㉒ *Gallery 3 – Portraits of the Roman era and Greek portraits*

Roman and Greek portraits can be found in the third gallery. Here, you can compare and contrast the characteristics of both types of portraits.

⑱ *Room 6 – Niobide Statue from the Gardens of Sallust*

According to Greek mythology, Niobids were the children of Amphion from Thebes and Niobe, who was killed by Apollo and Artemis. Niobe was bragging how she had more children than this divine couple, which caused a grave insult to the gods. The statue represents one of Niobe's daughters in fatal terror while she is trying to pull out one of Artemis's arrow from her body. The statue was probably part of a group from a Greek temple. It dates to 440 BC.

⑲ *Room 7 – The Boxer and the Prince*

The Boxer

This is one of the most well-known Greek sculptures. It was found in 1885 in Rome, dated back to 4th century BC. It is a statue of a boxer who is resting. His entire body and face are covered in wounds and scars — look at the ears, swelling under his eyes, his deformed nose, cuts and bruises with clots all over his body. The wounds and mouth were accentuated with red copper. Although he is bruised and beaten, his eyes are clear and sharp, there is tension in his muscly body, and he still has not taken the leather bandages off his hands after the fight. Supposedly, the statue was made by Lysippos. There are only a few bronze Greek sculptures left in the world. Two are in this room.

The Hellenistic prince

This is a statue of a naked ruler, found close to the Boxer in 1885. It is possible it was originally placed in the Diocletian's Baths. The statue is from 180 to 160 BC. The way the statue is positioned suggests the person is a ruler.

Proportions indicate that the author followed Lysippos's scale. Since the figure does not have a crown, nor a beard, it is likely this man was intended for the throne. This is why he is called a prince. It is 6.69 ft or 2.04 m high.

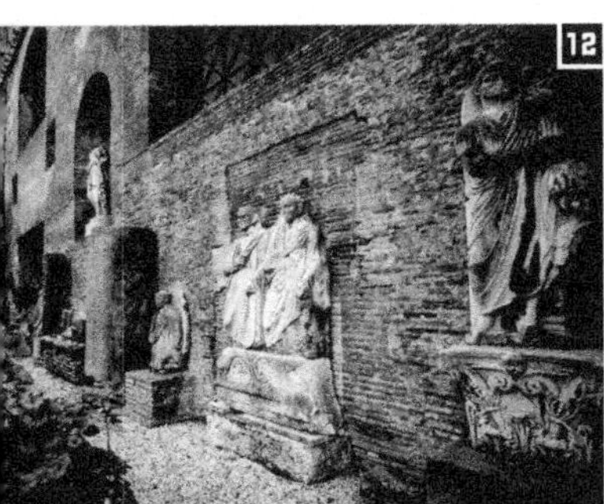

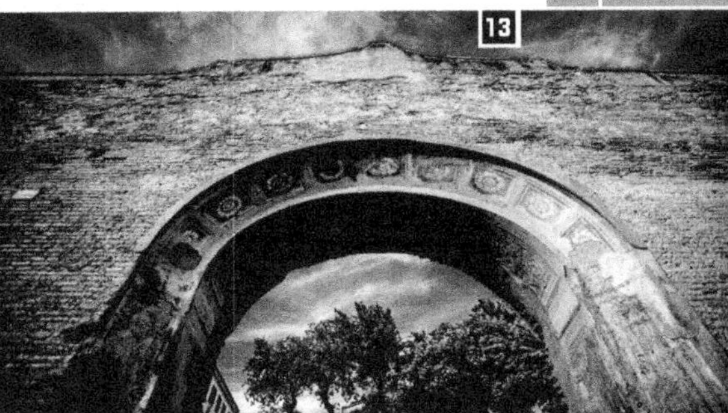

❷❶ *Room 8 – Works in the Neo-Attic Style from the 1st – 2nd century BC*

Neo-Attic sculptures from this room are relevant to the history art because they represent one of the first instances of the Neoclassical style, suggesting an imitation of a previous i.e. classical period in art. When it comes to sculptures and vases, this style, which originated in 2nd century BC and went on to 2nd century, imitated the reliefs and statues from the Classical period (5th – 4th century BC) and even the Archaic period of Greek art (6th century BC). Neo-Attic workshops started in Athens at first, and moved to the Apennine peninsula due to their extreme popularity. There is a beautiful Maenad relief here. Meanad were female followers of Dionysius. One of them is dancing in a see-through dress and her body is exposed completely. The marble relief is a copy of a 5th-century Greek original.

❷ *Room 1 – The Charioteers of the Sacellum of Hercules*

❸ *Room 2 – Trajan's and Hadrian's imperial portraits*

Hadrian wanted to distance himself from his predecessor Trajan, and one of the ways to do it was through portraits. The biggest difference is in hair and beard.

Did you know?

Gardens of Sallust

Given the quantity and quality of the sculptures, the Gardens of Sallust are the richest location of Roman art in general. The property of the *Horti Sallustiani* belonged to a Roman historian and politician Gaius Sallustius Crispus, anglicised as Sallust (86–35 BC). Initially, the land was owned by Caesar, then Octavian and then it was bought by Sallust. After Tiberius, the property was taken over again by Roman rulers: Nero, Diocletian and Constantine the Great all resided in the palaces around the gardens. The gardens were frequently visited by both Vespasian and Aurelian, and Emperor Nerva died there. During the sack of Rome by the Visigoths in 410, the gardens were destroyed. The statues, however, were unharmed, they were just left to rot for centuries in flood after flood, sinking deeper and deeper into the ground. The remains of Hadrian's Villa in these gardens are 46 ft or 14 m below street level. Cardinal Ludovico Ludovisi bought the land to build his villa, an elaborate residence that he only lived in for two years (1621–1623). Ludovico Ludovisi was Pope Gregory XV's nephew. During construction, so many sculptures were found in a period of only two years, that the Cardinal soon became the proud owner of the largest and most valuable collection of Roman art. [p.113]

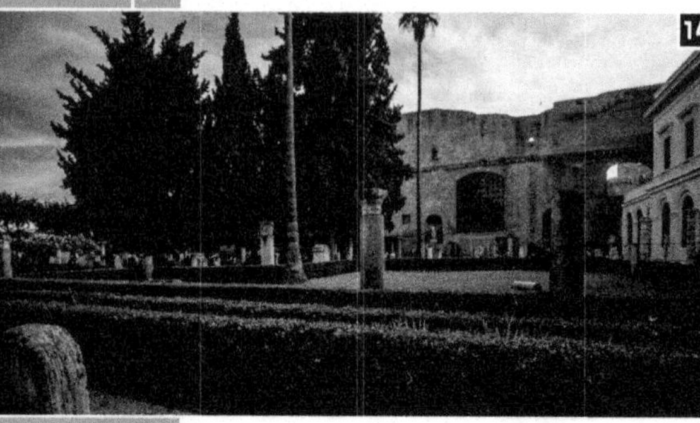

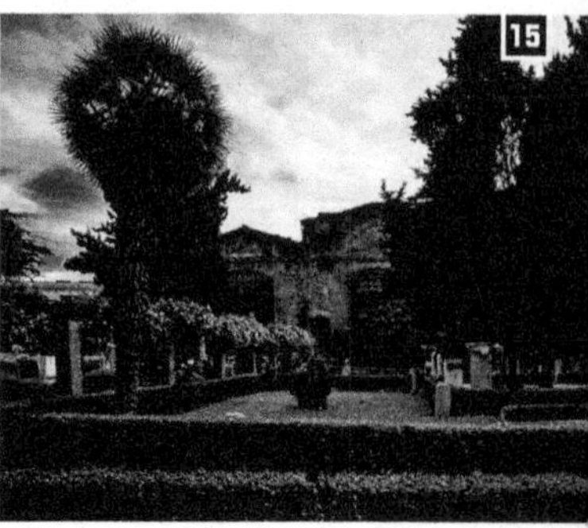

Hadrian has curly hair falling over his forehead, which is a contrast to Trajan who has a neat haircut with a fringe and a parting. The beards are even more dissimilar. Hadrian's beard is reminiscent of Greek philosophers' and this influenced fashion for a whole century. This is how Hadrian tried to underline his loyalty to Greek tradition. He was also often portrayed wearing Greek clothes.

Palazzo Massimo – FIRST FLOOR

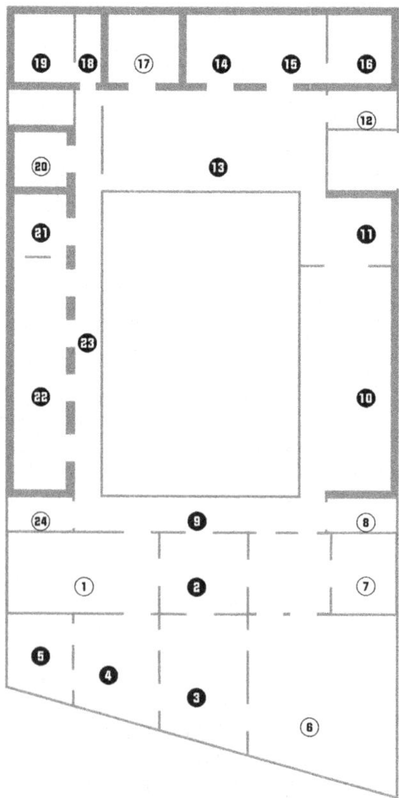

① Main stairs
❷ The Charioteers of the Sacellum of Hercules
❸ Trajan's and Hadrian's imperial portraits
❹ Portraits from the age of Emperor Antoninus
❺ Portraits from the age of Emperor Antoninus
⑥ Conference Room
⑦ Elevator
⑧ Stairs
❾ Portraits of Flavian and Antoninian emperors
❿ *Maiden of Antium* or *Girl of Anzio* and other sculptures
⓫ *Discobolus* and other sculptures
⑫ Stairs
⓭ *The Sleeping Hermaphrodite*
⓮ Nemi Ships
⓯ Gods and mythology
⓰ Gods and mythology
⑰ Stairs
⓲ Representations of military exploits
⓳ *Portonaccio Sarcophagus*
⑳ WC
㉑ ㉒ Soldier emperors (235–284 AD)
㉓ Portraits of women (2nd – 4th century)
㉔ WC

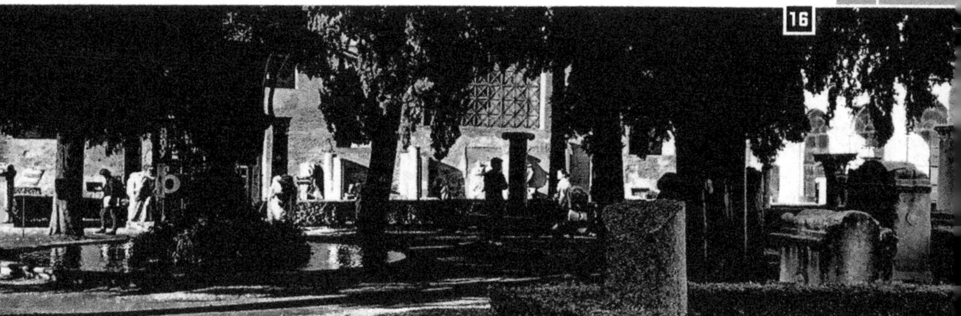

Did you know?

Two enlightened emperors: Trajan & Hadrian

Trajan Optimus (53–117)

Trajan was the first Roman emperor (98–117) born in one of the provinces.

After he released the senators imprisoned by Emperor Domitian and other rulers of the Flavian Dynasty who confiscated their possessions, Trajan was unanimously deemed *Optimus* in all senatorial records — simply the best Roman ruler.

He conquered Armenia, Mesopotamia and Dacia (present-day Romania) and expanded the Roman Empire like no one before. Trajan's markets, Trajan's Forum and Trajan's Column in Rome are only a few projects executed during his reign.

Trajan was born in Italica, a Roman town 9 km outside Seville in Spain. His successor and adopted son Hadrian, was also born there. Trajan as well as Hadrian after him, ruled during a time of unbelievable prosperity.

Hadrian (76–138)

After Trajan's conquest, Hadrian (117–138) tried to incorporate a sense of longevity into the Roman Empire.

He relinquished Armenia and Mesopotamia and concentrated on consolidation, rather than military campaigning. He managed to bring peace and prosperity. As a huge lover of Greek art and anything Greek, he influenced the re-establishment of Greek style in Roman art.

He was the first Hellenophile among Roman emperors. This is most obvious when you look at the sculptures from Hadrian's Villa (Italian: Villa Adriana) in Tivoli.

The best preserved monument in Rome dates back precisely to his time: Castel Sant'Angelo, build as a mausoleum for himself and his family; the Pantheon was also his project; Temple of Rome and Venus on the Roman Forum.

Emperor Trajan was the only one who was declared a deity during Hadrian's rule, but also his Greek favorite Antinous, after he drowned in the Nile. After Antinous's death, Hadrian established the city of Antinoupolis. Antinous's busts represent him in many ways — as Osiris, imperial priest, Dionysius or Hermes. They were present across the Empire. The divine Antinous is the timeless ideal of classic male beauty — his bust has been a model for artistic reproduction since the Renaissance.

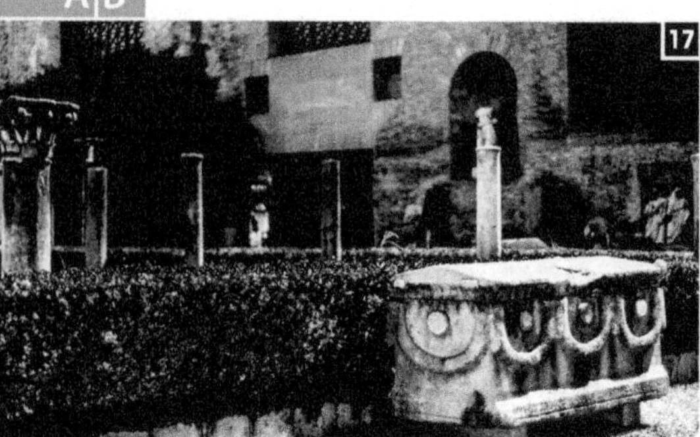

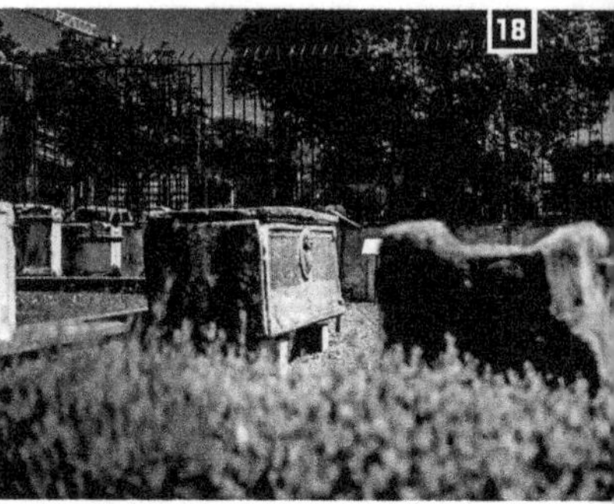

❹ ❺ *Rooms 3, 4 – Portraits from the age of Emperor Antoninus*

Antoninus Pius's portrait is similar to that of Emperor Hadrian, with a strong, Greek beard. Unlike Hadrian, Antoninus Pius was more frequently represented as a Greek god, often completely naked, with a toga draped across his arm. Since Hadrian was not among Senate's favorites, the senators only agreed to declare him a deity when Antoninus insisted on it. This is how he got his nickname Pius, which means "dutiful in affection" or loyal.

❾ *Gallery 1*

Various portraits of Flavian and Antoninian emperors are in the first gallery on the first floor.

❿ ⓫ *Rooms 5, 6*

One of the highlights of the whole museum is the Room 5. It is full of exemplary sculptures of ideal Greek proportions admired so much by the Romans.

The Maiden of Antium – Fanciulla D'anzio or The Girl of Anzio

This sculpture is right in the middle of Room 5 as its central and most interesting exhibit. The girl is looking at a sacrificial plate she is holding in her hands. There is a scroll, a laurel branch, a lion claw and a partial bowl of some kind for lighting incense on the plate. She does not mind that her clothes are rather disheveled, as well as her hair, tied in a messy bun. Her body is relaxed, which only emphasizes the fact that she is absent-minded — she is entirely concentrated on the sacrificial ritual. The torsion of her body and head distinguish this sculpture from the Classical style. It is safe to assume it dates back to around 250 BC.

Did you know?

Antoninus Pius (86–161) and Faustina the Elder (100–140)
During Antoninus Pius's reign, Rome was going through its last phase of prolonged peace. His successor, Marcus Aurelius had nothing but kind words to say about his predecessor.
Faustina the Elder, Antoninus Pius's wife, also deserves to be mentioned. Roman history remembers her as an extremely beautiful and wise woman. She dedicated her life to charity, working with the poor and educating Roman children, especially girls.

After she died, Emperor Antoninus built a temple in her honor on the Imperial Forums.
After his death, the temple was consecrated by the Senate as the Temple of Antoninus and Faustina the Elder. It is one of the best kept Roman temples on the whole. [p.60]

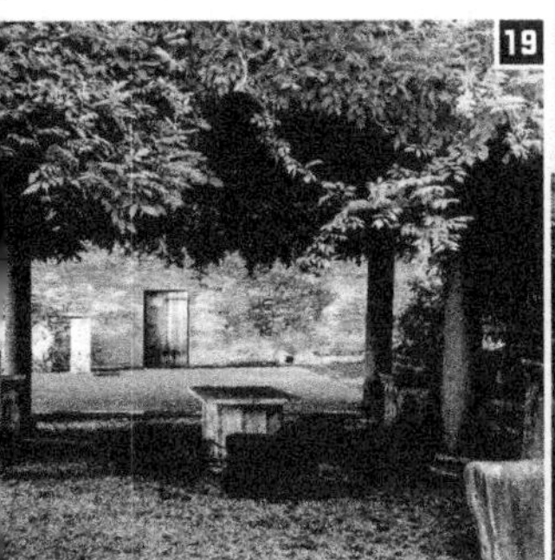

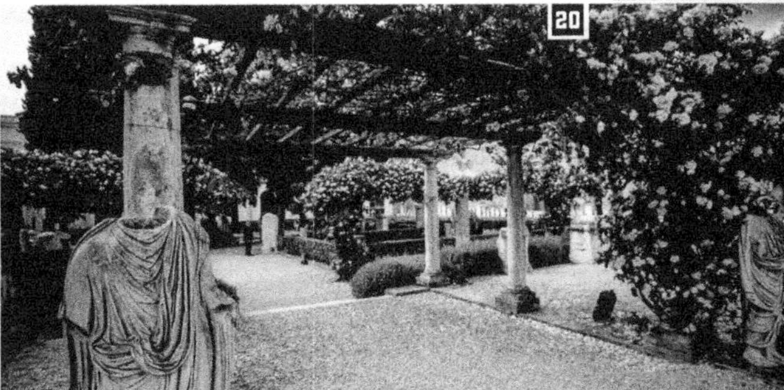

Discoboli or Discus Thrower

There are two disk throwers in the same room. These are marble copies of the original Greek Discobolus made of bronze from 450 BC by Myron, a Greek sculptor. The Roman copies always had a tree next to the athlete, because it was impossible for the heavy, marble statue to stand without support of some kind. There is a well-preserved copy in the Vatican Museums as well, whose head was added later. This is obvious because the thrower does not follow the disc with his eyes, whereas the original one does. So far, six Roman copies of Discobolus have been discovered. The Greek original has been lost.

⓭ ⓯ ⓰ Rooms 7, 8, 9 – Gods and mythology in Roman sculpture

Room 7 is no less sensational than Room 5. It features sculptures of gods and other mythological creatures.

The Sleeping Hermaphrodite

A mythical creature that represents the ideal of female beauty, apart from having male genitalia. Ovid described Hermaphrodite in his Metamorphoses as the son of Aphrodite and Hermes. He was seduced by the nymph Salmacis. She hugged him unexpectedly and that is when he became a hermaphrodite.

Dionysius with Thyrsus

This is a bronze Dionysius from Hadrian's period. It was discovered on the island in the Tiber in late 19th century. Expressive limestone eyes still make him seem very alive.

⓮ Room 10 – The Nemi Ships

This is the room with the Nemi ships, one of the most exciting discoveries of the 20th century. Nemi ships are two ships commissioned by Caligula (37–41) as a floating temple of Diana to honor the goddess. They were launched at Lake Nemi, 18 miles or 29 kilometers outside Rome. Both ships are a little over 230 ft (70 m) long and 66 ft (20 m) wide. Even as early as the 15th century, it was a well-known fact that the ships were on the bottom of the lake. Leon Battista Alberti was the first person who tried to pull them out. It was only in 1928 that one of numerous attempts was finally successful. The ships were taken out, but only after the whole lake was drained. A museum was built near the lake. Unfortunately, during the German retreat in 1944, the museum caught fire and the ships were burned.

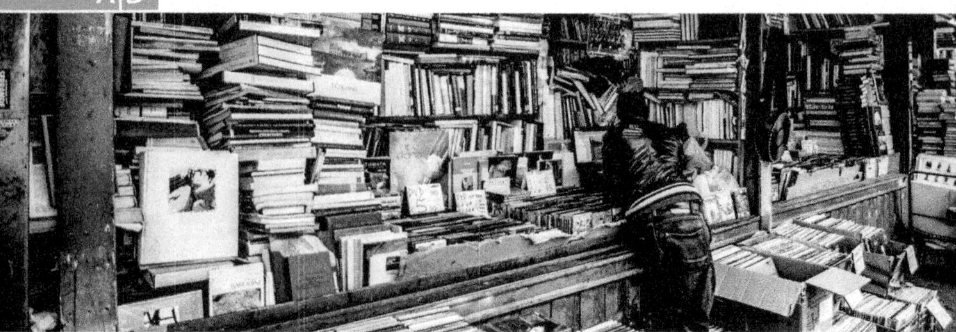

Street Bookshop at Palazzo Massimo alle Terme

Only metal parts remained and they are kept here, in Room 10. There is a computer animation that enables us to get an idea of what the ships actually looked like while sailing on Lake Nemi.

⑱ ⑲ *Rooms 11, 12 – Representations of military exploits*
Portonaccio Sarcophagus

This is one of 25 sarcophagi made for military commanders between AD 170 and 210. This one is similar to the Ludovisi sarcophagus from Palazzo Altemps, another one of the museums belonging to the National Museum of Rome. The head of the commander is unfinished. This could mean the artist was waiting for him.

This is true not only for the central figure, but also for the figures on both front sides of the sarcophagus, where a man and a woman are holding hands. According to the inscription, we know this was made for one of Marcus Aurelius's generals who fought with the emperor against German tribes of Marcomanni and Quadi on the Danube.

This is also where Emperor Marcus Aurelius himself died in AD 180, in Vindobona, i.e. present-day Vienna.

㉑ ㉒ *Rooms 13, 14 – Portraits from the era between the emperors Severi and Constantine*
Soldier emperors

Barracks emperors or soldier emperors were the ones who completely ignored the Roman Senate and came to power using brutal military force. Background or education played no part on the way to the throne.

Did you know?

The List of the Soldier Emperors

► Maximinus the Thracian (235–238)
► Gordian I and Gordian II (238)
► Balbinus & Pupienus Maximus (238)
► Gordian III (238–244)
► Philip I the Arab (244–249)
► Philip II (247–249)
► Decius (249–251)
► Trebonianus Gallus (251–253)
► Aemilian (253)
► Valerian (253–260)
► Gallienus (253–268)
► Claudius II Gothicus (268–270)
► Aurelian (270–275)
► Tacitus (275–276)
► Florian (276)
► Probus (276–282)
► Carus (282–283)
► Carinus (283–285)
► Numerian (283–284)

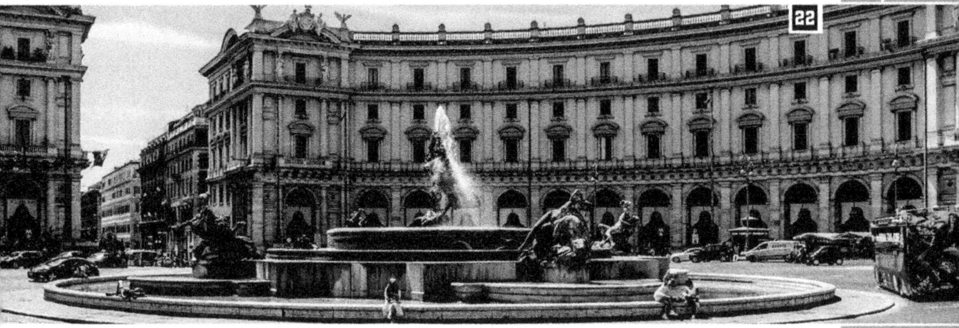

Their era started with the murder of the last Severi emperor, Severus Alexander, succeeded by a military commander by the name of Maximinus Thrax, a man despised by all the senators. Not only was Maximinus Thrax a soldier of low birth, but he was also from Thrace, practically a barbarian, as far as the Senate was concerned. This is also the beginning of the Third Century Roman Crisis, during which the Roman Empire was on a full scale defensive against the Germanic tribes from the north, Skyths and Sasanians from the east. Meanwhile, the Empire was being torn apart on the inside by a civil war. Military violence ceased and civil state was restored by Emperor Diocletian (284–305) with radical economic and administrative reforms. This provided stability within the Empire, which was reflected on its borders as well.

㉓ Gallery 2 – Portraits of women from the 2nd – 4th century

Female Roman portraits can be dated to specific periods according to hairstyles. During the Flavian dynasty, sculptors used augers to mold the hair, which is how the so-called "corkscrew hairstyle" was created. This was always an important element of the female portrait. Moreover, according to one of the portraits of a lady on the Tomb of Hilarus Fuscus on Via Appia Antica, we can date an entire building to precisely 30 BC.

Did you know?

Museums of Antiquity in Rome

The largest and perhaps the most important museum of Roman antiquity in the world is the National Roman Museum. If you have plenty of time on your hands, go to the Vatican Museums, Capitoline Hill Museums and at least two museums of the National Roman Museum:

▸ More than half a day for the Vatican Museum [p.142]

▸ Musei Capitolini (three or more hours) [p.81]

▸ Massimo alle Terme (three or more hours) [p.208]

▸ Palazzo Altemps (around two hours) [p.113]

▸ Baths of Diocletian (around two hours) [p.225]

▸ Museo Centrale Montemartini (two or more hours) [p.256]

▸ The Etruscan Museum in Villa Giulia is also worth a visit (an hour) [p.190]

▸ Ara Pacis Augustus (an hour) [p.199]

▸ Museo di Scultura Antica Giovanni Barracco (an hour) [p.126]

▸ Museo dei Fori Imperiali (an hour) [p.71]

▸ Crypta Balbi Museum (an hour) [p.102]

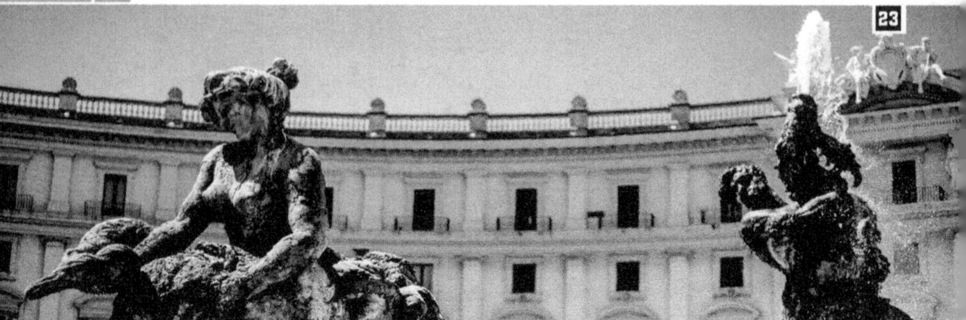

❸ ❹ *Gallery 1 and Room 1 – Columbarium of Villa Pamphili*

Columbarium is a repository for urns. The name comes from *columba*, Latin for dove, because the shape reminded Romans of dovecotes. Each urn had its own niche, framed by frescoes depicting the life of the deceased.

Here, we have highly suggestive frescoes from the columbarium of Villa Pamphili from 1st century BC.

Palazzo Massimo – SECOND FLOOR

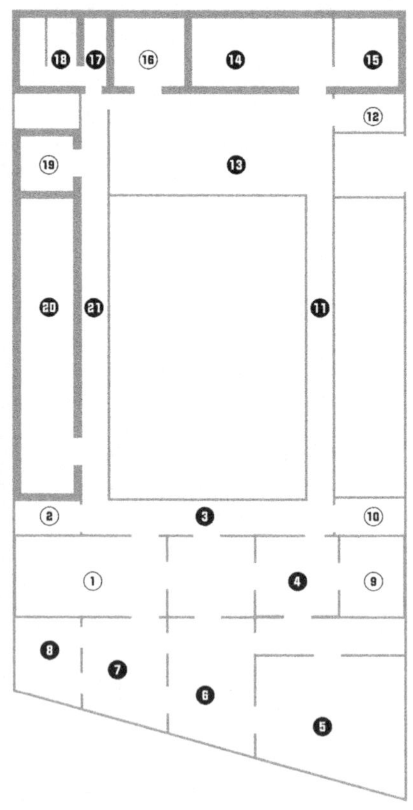

① Main stairs
② WC
❸ Columbarium of Villa Pamphili
❹ Columbarium of Villa Pamphili
❺ The painted garden of the Villa of Livia at Prima Porta
❻ Mosaics from Villa di Baccano
❼ Paintings from the Late Imperial Period
❽ Paintings from the Late Imperial Period
⑨ Elevator
⑩ Stairs
⑪ Frescoes, stuccoes and mosaics from the Villa Farnesina
⑫ Stairs
⑬ Frescoes, stuccoes and mosaics from the Villa Farnesina
⑭ Frescoes, stuccoes and mosaics from the Villa Farnesina
⑮ Frescoes, stuccoes and mosaics from the Villa Farnesina
⑯ Stairs
⑰ Villa of Castel di Guido
⑱ Villa of Castel di Guido
⑲ WC
⑳ Frescoes and mosaics found under the Termini Station
㉑ Floor mosaics (1st century BC – AD 5th century)

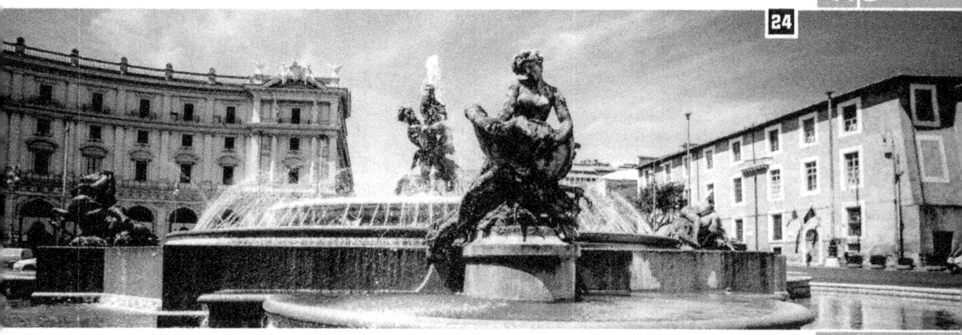

❺ Room 2 – *The painted garden of the Villa of Livia at Prima Porta*
This is a mosaic from 30–20 BC. It was situated in a dining room of Livia Drusilla's Villa. Livia Drusilla was Augustus's wife. The mosaic is full of flora and fauna, as an ideal garden spreading on all four walls. There are pines, melons, apples, pomegranate, myrtle, oleander, dates, laurel, oak, cypress, ivy and other fruits and trees. The meadows are full of roses, poppy, oxeye, violets and chamomile, just like today.

⓫ ⓭ ⓮ ⓯ *Gallery 2 and Rooms 3, 4, 5*
Frescoes, stuccoes and mosaics from the Villa Farnesina
Villa Farnesina or Casa della Farnesina is a luxurious palace from the Augustan era, discovered on the Trastevere while trying to regulate the flow of the Tiber. After it was partially explored, the villa was destroyed. What has remained, mosaics and frescoes, can be attributed to the so-called "Second Style" of Roman painting.

Many Egyptian motives in the decoration of the villa can be interpreted as celebration after the conquest of Egypt. The villa belonged to Marcus Vipsanius Agrippa (63–12 BC), Octavian's general who beat Mark Antony and Cleopatra in the Battle of Actium in 31 BC. The frescoes from the bedroom are particularly interesting, featuring a lot of architecture in order to create the illusion of space. The center is occupied by Dionysius with a nymph, the left panel has Aphrodite with Eros.

⓱ ⓲ *Rooms 6, 7 – Frescoes and mosaics from the Villa of Castel di Guido*
Frescoes and mosaics from Villa of Castel di Guido are interesting because they have tiny figures decorating the architectural elements. They are from the first half of the 1st century.

㉑ *Gallery 3*
Floor mosaics from 1st century BC to the 5th century.

⓴ *Room 8*
Frescoes and mosaics found during the extension of the Termini Station.

❻ Room 9 – *Mosaics from Villa di Baccano*
Mosaics uncovered in Villa di Baccano on the Via Cassia are the finest Roman mosaics. They represent half-bull, half-fish beings and other fantastical creatures.

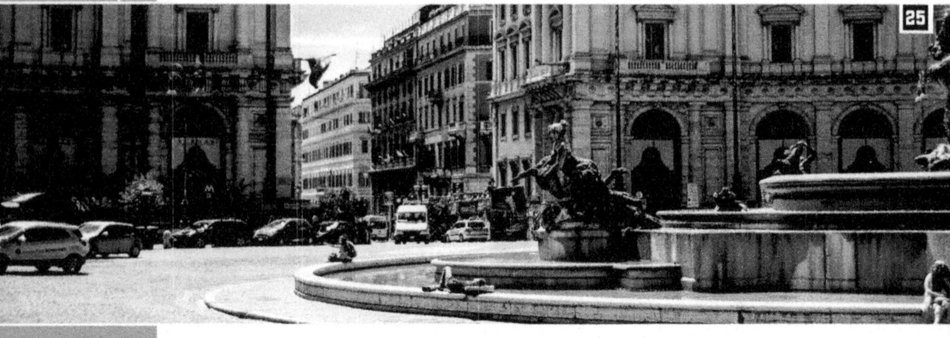

❼ ❽ *Rooms 10, 11 – Paintings from the Late Imperial Period*

In the last room on the second floor, you will find paintings from the Late Imperial Period. There is a famous fresco of Venus as personification of Rome. This is the so-called "Dea Barberini", i.e. the Barberini goddess from the 1st half of the 4th century.

❷ *Room 1 – Coins and prices in Rome*

Everyday objects from ancient Rome.

❹ *Room 2 – Grottarossa mummy*

Grottarossa mummy is a mummy of an eight-year old girl found in 1964 in Rome. It was wrapped in scented fabric and bandages covered with resin, the same as in Egypt. The girl is wearing a tunic of Chinese silk, a golden necklace with sapphires, golden earrings and a golden ring. The ring was engraved with a figure of god of victory. Further, an amber amulet was also found, alongside an ivory puppet.

Palazzo Massimo – BASEMENT

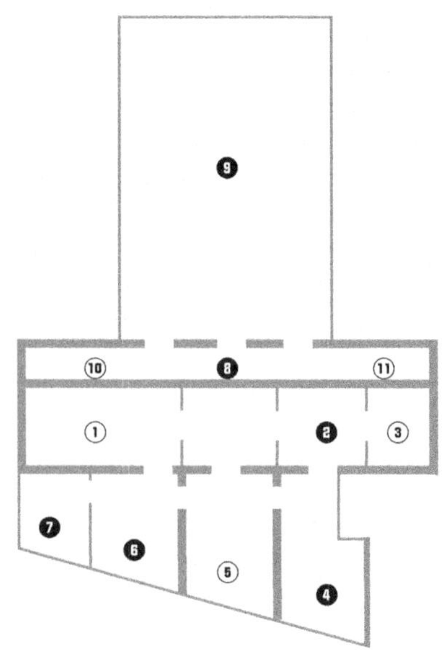

① Main stairs
❷ Coins and prices in Rome
③ Elevator
❹ Grottarossa mummy
⑤ WC
❻ Imperial insignia from the Palatine Hill
❼ Everyday life through artifacts
❽ Everyday life through artifacts
❾ The numismatic collection
⑩ Stairs
⑪ Stairs

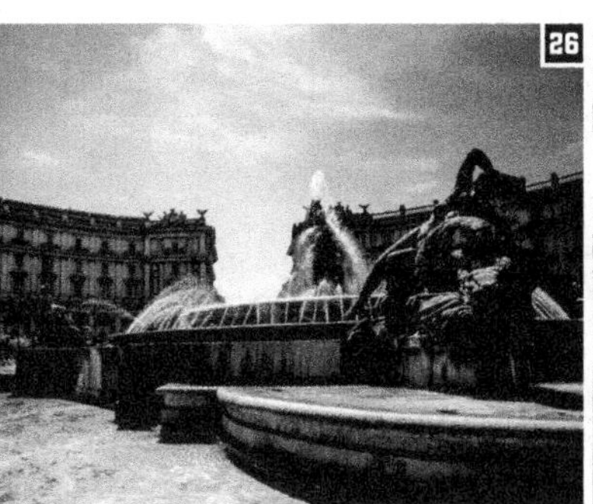

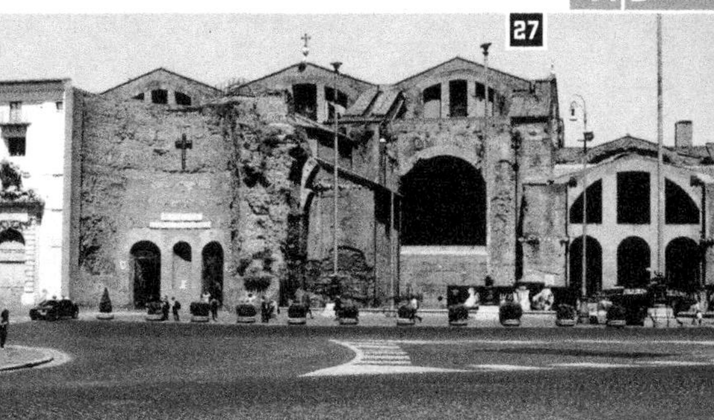

The girl was found in a marble sarcophagus, also on display in this room. The sarcophagus is decorated with hunting scenes. The girl supposedly died of tuberculosis. According to the funerary gifts and the style of the sarcophagus, she could have died sometime in mid-2nd century AD.

❾ Room 3 – *The numismatic collection*

What you see here is only a small part of the largest Roman numismatic collection in the world. This collection is also unique due to the way it is presented. Each glass case has a magnifier, so feel free to take a closer look.

❻ Room 4 – *Imperial insignia from the Palatine Hill*

These are the only imperial Roman insignia ever found. They were found on the Palatine Hill in 2006 and attributed to emperor Maxentius. They were wrapped in silk and carefully stored in a wooden chest. Up to that moment, Roman insignia could only be seen on coins. We can assume that the insignia were hidden by Maxentius's supporters to honor his memory after he was defeated by Constantine the Great in the Battle of Milvian Bridge in AD 312.

❷ Piazza della Repubblica ★★

There is a fountain here from 1898 called Fontana delle Naiadi ili Fontana delle Naiadi. There are four Naiads, Ancient Greek nymphs: the ocean Naiad riding a horse, the Naiad of underground waters next to a dragon, the lake Naiad holding a swan and the river Naiad stretching on a river monster. 🖪

The playful water nymphs and animals are a 20th-century masterpiece by Mario Rutelli. 🖪 When the fountain was revealed in 1901, the naked nymphs caused quite a scandal in Rome. 🖪 🖪

❸ Terme di Diocleziano | Baths of Diocletian ★ ★ ★ 🖪

The remains are located 0.2 miles or 300 m from Termini Train Station.

Museo Nazionale Romano – Terme di Diocleziano | National Roman Museum – Baths of Diocletian

Address: Viale Enrico de Nicola 79, Roma

Online: www.museonazionaleroma-no.beniculturali.it/en

Public transportation: Metro A and B stop Termini | Bus stop Termini: 16, 75, 150F, 360, 590, 649, 717, C3 | Tram stop Termini: 5, 14

Opening hours: see online

The combined ticket provide access to all four National Roman Museum's sites: Palazzo Massimo, Palazzo Altemps, Baths of Diocletian, Crypta Balbi.

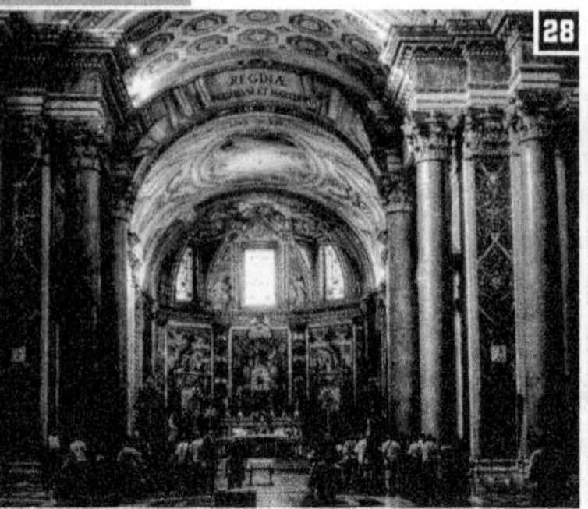

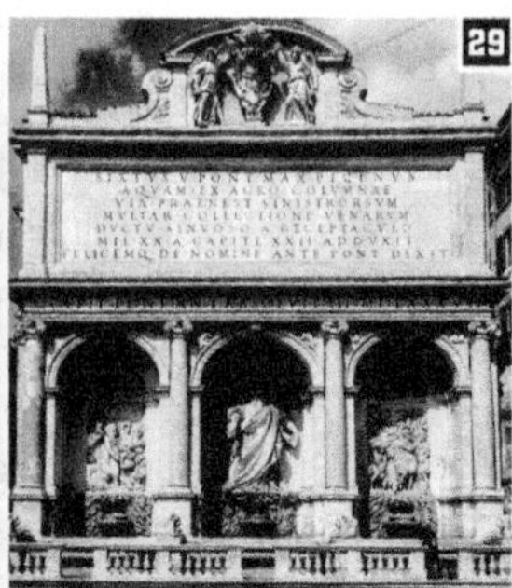

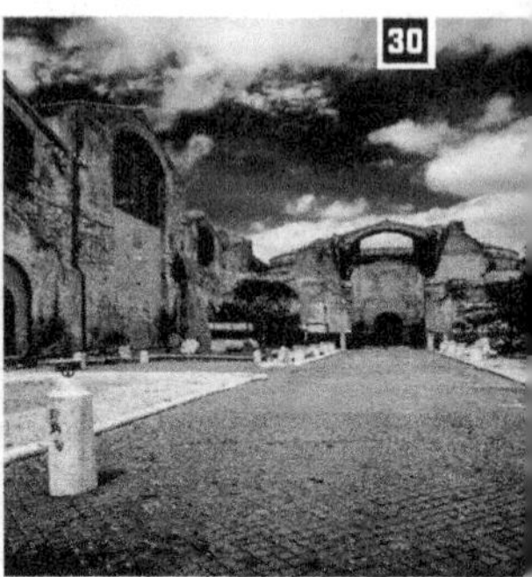

The Latin for baths is *termae*, so that is how the station got its name. According to ancient sources, Terme di Diocleziano were the biggest ones in old Rome. They were 1,233×1,184 ft or 376×361 m, which means that they could accommodate roughly 3,000 bathers. **6 20**

They were built by 40,000 slaves from 298 to 306. As all other public baths, they closed its doors after the Goths destroyed the aqueducts in 537, including the Aqua Marcia which supplied this facility. Since then, the baths were used as a quarry. However, what has remained is still extraordinary.

① Santa Maria degli Angeli e dei Martiri ★ ★ ★ **27**

This monumental church was designed by Michelangelo in 1561. It is 295 ft (90 m) long and 89 ft (27 m) wide, rising 98 ft (30 m) in the air. It could have been even higher, if Michelangelo had not leveled the floor with the street — the difference would have been 6.56 ft (2 m).

Both the main and transverse nave were incorporated in the halls of Diocletian's baths, *caldarium*, a hot plunge bath and *tepidarium*, warm bathroom. The two halls served Michelangelo to make a church in the shape of a Greek cross. Giant, red granite pillars belong to the 1700-year old building. Appropriately enough, given that Pope Pius IV commissioned this church, he was buried in it as well. **28**

The meridian line

In 1700, Pope Clement XI established a commission to verify the Gregorian calendar. This is why the meridian line appeared on the floor of the church, in order for astronomers and mathematicians to calculate the calendar.

This precise clock mechanism for determining the solar noon is still on the floor of the church, 12° 30′. The meridian line counts the solar hours with extreme precision, as well as noon of each day. Rays of sunlight pass through a small hole in the wall and fall exactly down the middle of the line at noon. The line is 147.6 ft or 45 m long:

Santa Maria degli Angeli e dei Martiri | Basilica of St. Mary of the Angels and the Martyrs
Address: Piazza della Repubblica, Roma
Online: www.santamariadegliangeliroma.it

Public transportation:
Metro A stop Repubblica | Bus stop Termini: 16, 75, 150F, 360, 590, 649, 717, C3 | Tram stop Termini 5, 14

Opening hours: *see on Google Maps*

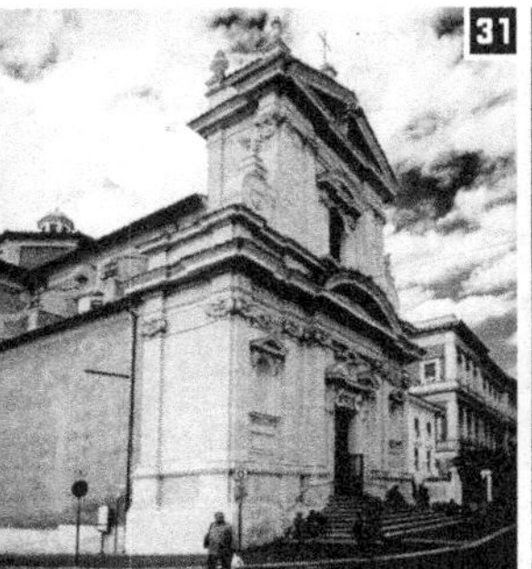
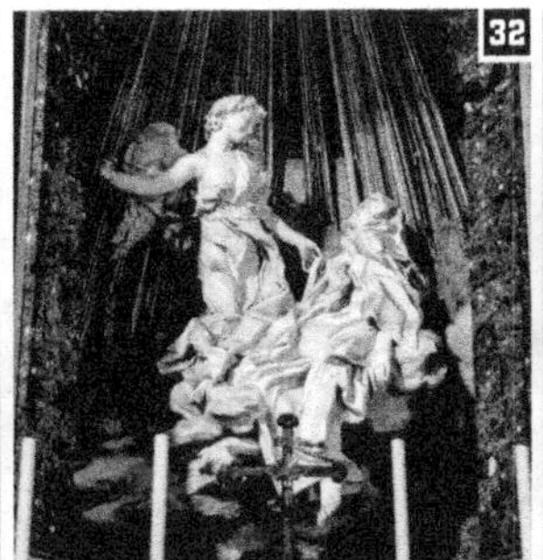
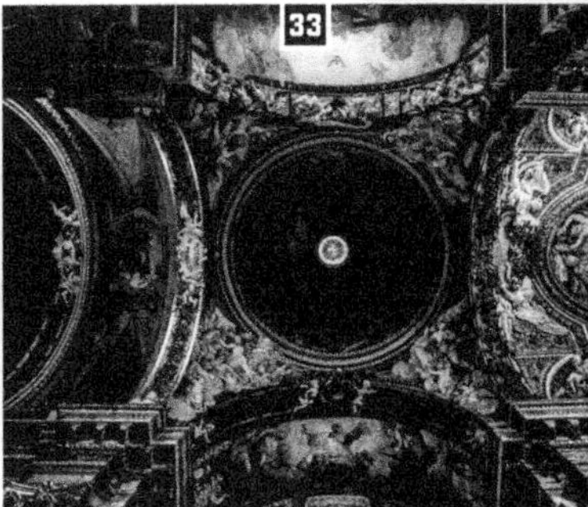

▸ During the winter solstice, around December 21, the rays hit the line on the floor furthest from the wall,

▸ During the summer solstice, around June 21, the beam crosses on the other end of the line,

▸ During both equinoxes, March 20 and September 22, the sun beam will stay exactly half way between the solstice points.

② National Roman Museum in the Baths of Diocletian ★ ★ ★

The entrance from Piazza Cinquecento leads straight into the garden, a nice and shady place on a summer's day, with climbing roses, benches, small ancient monuments and fountains. **30**

This is where one of four branches of Museo Nazionale Romano is situated. Apart from more than 400 statues, reliefs, altars and sarcophagi on display in the courtyard, the museum also holds a prehistoric collection and a Roman epigraphic collection. **7**

③ Michelangelo's Carthusian monastery★ ★ **2**

Michelangelo planned a Carthusian monastery here (1561). Only the courtyard has remained. With its 107,639 square feet (10,000 square meters) and its wings of 328 ft or 100 m, the Cloister of Michelangelo is one of the largest in Italy.

④ Fontana dell'Acqua Felice ★ ★ **29**

Fontana dell'Acqua Felice or Fountain of Moses was designed by Domenico Fontana (1588), next to the Church of Santa Maria della Vittoria. In the central arch is a large statue of Moses.

To the left is Aaron and to the right Joshua. The statue of Moses was criticized at the time for its large size but the most confusing are his horns.

These are the result of a translation error of the Old Testament from Hebrew. Hebrew writing omits vowels, so the word in question was spelt *krn*. The translator added two E's between the consonants.

Krn turned into *keren*, which means "with horns." The translation was also in use while Michelangelo was working on his Moses for San Pietro in Vincoli. [p.36]

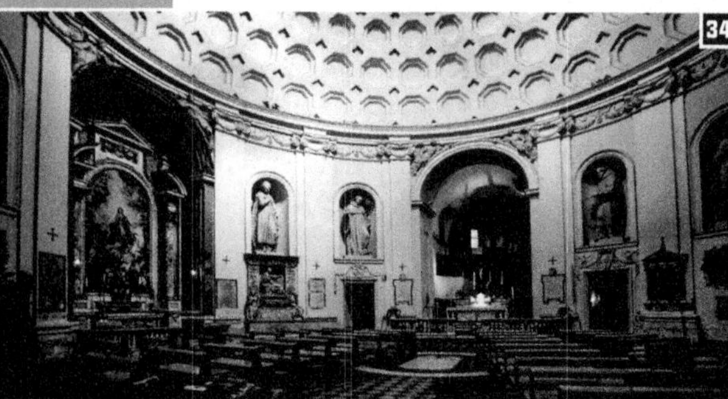

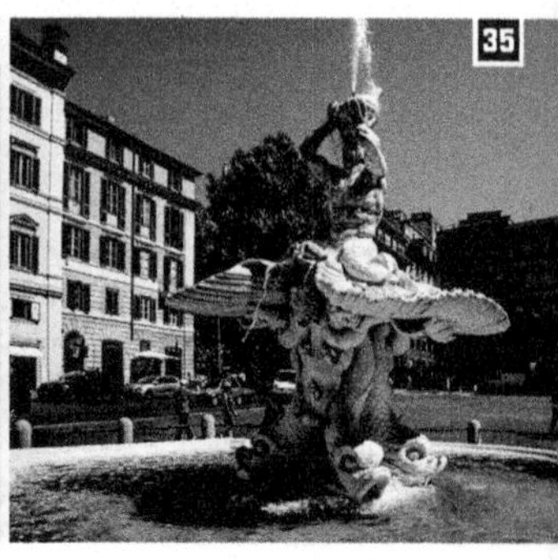

◆ Santa Maria della Vittoria ★★★

The church is designed by the Baroque architect Carlo Maderno (1605–1620). **31** **33**

Ecstasy of Saint Teresa **32**

In his depiction of the Ecstasy of Saint Teresa, Bernini fuses baroque expressiveness with counter-reformist mysticism in an extremely suggestive manner. There has always been criticism from the Church about too much eroticism. At the same time, Bernini did not stray from what Saint Teresa herself described in her autobiography. The artist showed more than just the saint's vision. Bernini chose to illustrate the moment when the angel's arrow stabs her in the heart. This is when she feels pain and pleasure simultaneously. Angel's clothes are still fluttering, as if he has just landed. Saint Teresa is in ecstasy, her mouth is slightly open, eyes closed and she is writhing with pleasure. Golden rays behind the figures represent the divine light which frames the whole scene.

The Cornaro Chapel

The Cornaro Chapel (1647–1652) was ordered by Cardinal Federico Cornaro of Venice for his tomb. On the right, cardinals from the Cornaro family observe the scene from a balcony, as if they were in a theater.

Battle of White Mountain

The church bears a battle title due to the Discalced (Barefoot) Carmelites who viewed themselves as fearless defenders of Catholicism in a time when it was oppressed by Protestantism and Islam in Central Europe. Therefore, the main altar has the "Victorious Painting", allegedly carried by one of the members of the order into the Battle of White Mountain in 1620.

◆ San Bernardo alle Terme ★ **34**

There is a church that occupies a round tower in one of the corners of the baths. It is called San Bernardo alle Terme, built in 1598. This octagonal building has an *oculus*, a hole in the dome, just like the Pantheon, which provides light. Another tower, identical to this one, used to be at the other end of the baths, with a library and a lecture hall.

Today, between this two octagonal building we can find semi-circular buildings on Piazza della Repubblica, which follow the outlines of the Diocletian's baths. **22**

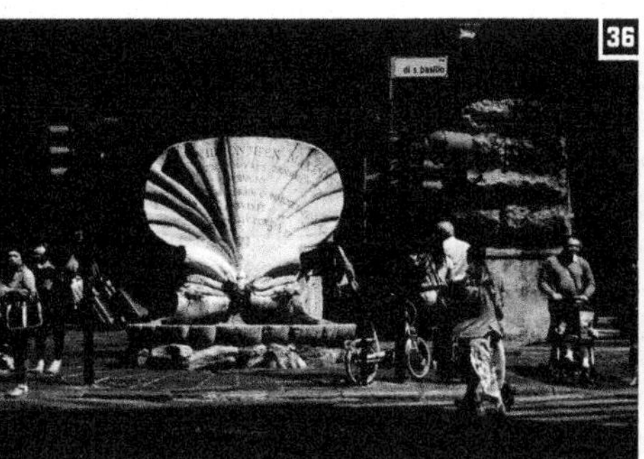

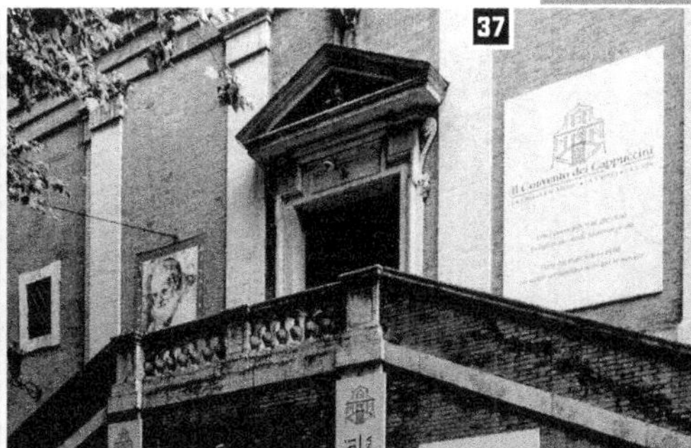

❼ Piazza Barberini ★★

Only wealthy Romans lived here in ancient times. After the fall of the Roman Empire, the area was abandoned and turned into vineyards in the Middle Ages. When Pope Urban VIII initiated extensive construction in the 17th century, the area started attracting well-to-do Romans again.

Fontana del Tritone ★★★ 35

Immediately after Palazzo Barberini was built, Bernini also made two fountains, presently part of the Piazza Barberini. Fontana del Tritone is composed of four dolphins carrying a large seashell on their tails. This is where the sea god Triton sits, half-man, half-fish. He is holding a big sea snail and blowing into it to make the water come out. There is a bee crest between the dolphins, a symbol of the Barberini family. Bernini made this fountain in 1643.

Fontana delle Api | Fountain of the Bees ★ 36

Where Via Veneto meets Piazza Barberini, there is the Fontana delle Api (1644).

Santa Maria della Vittoria | Our Lady of Victory
Address: Via 20 Settembre 17, Roma

Public transportation: Metro A stop Repubblica | Bus stop Largo Santa Susanna: 61, 62, 85, 150F, 492

Opening hours: *see on Google Maps*

San Bernardo alle Terme
Address: Via Torino, 94, Roma

Public transportation:
Metro A stop Repubblica | Bus stop Largo Santa Susanna: 61, 62, 85, 150F, 492

Opening hours: *see on Google Maps*

Piazza Barberini – Quirinale

❶ Fontana dell'Acqua Felice
❷ Santa Maria della Vittoria
❸ Piazza Barberini
❹ Fontana del Tritone
❺ Fontana delle Api
❻ The Capuchin Crypt
❼ Via Veneto
❽ Palazzo Barberini
❾ Quattro Fontane
❿ San Carlo alle Quattro Fontane
⓫ Sant'Andrea al Quirinale
⓬ Palazzo del Quirinale

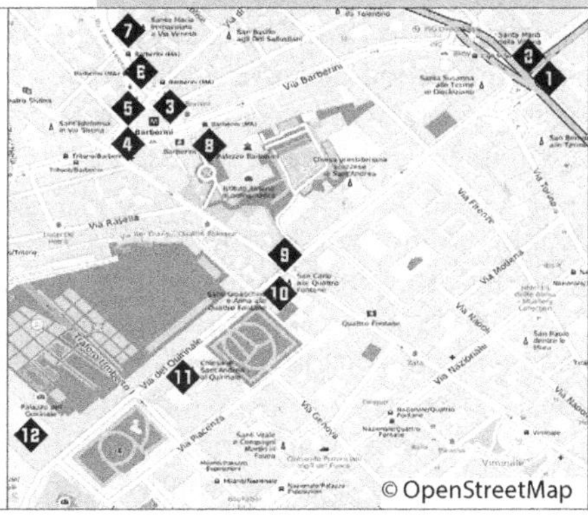

© OpenStreetMap

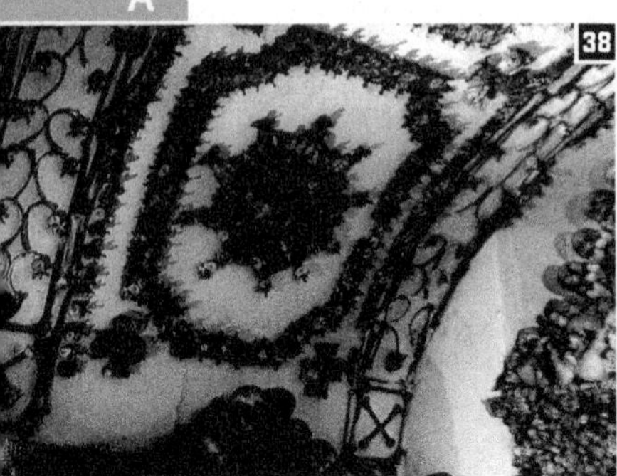

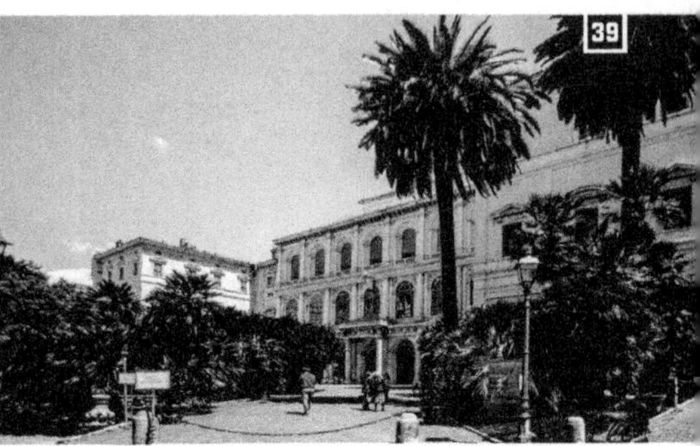

However, unlike the Fountain del Tritone, it is considered one of Bernini's lesser accomplishments.

◆ Santa Maria della Concezione dei Cappuccini ★★

This church was built by the order of Pope Urban VIII in 1626. Pope's older brother, Cardinal Antonio Barberini was in the Capuchin order, so the church was conveniently placed near the Palazzo Barberini. In terms of architecture and art, this church does not belong on the must-see list.

However, among the 900 plus churches in Rome, the abject horror displayed in the decor of the Crypt is definitely worth your visit.

The Capuchin Crypt

In fact, this is a series of crypts linked by a hallway. It contains the bones of 3,700 Capuchins who died between 1528 and 1870. This creepy practice was banned by the new Italian State in 1870. The composition is so grotesque because bones were used as part of the decor — skulls as wallpaper, vertebrae as stucco, nothing was off limits for the anonymous Capuchin interior decorators. If you are interested in stylistic features of a Renaissance or Baroque interior made of bones, you are in the right place. There is a *memento mori* in six languages as a reminder: "What you are now, we once were; what we are

Did you know?

The dark side of Rome
- ► Colosseum [p.30]
- ► Mamertine Prison [p.73]
- ► Gemonian stairs [p.74]
- ► Tarpeian Rock [p.88]
- ► The Capuchin Crypt [p.228]
- ► Santa Maria dell'Orazione e Morte [p.129]
- ► Catacombs on Via Appia Antica [p.294]
- ► Catacombs of Marcellinus and Peter [p.282]
- ► The inquisition headquarter [p.104]
- ► Castel Sant'Angelo [p.168]
- ► Piazza del Popolo [p.194]
- ► Museo delle Anime del Purgatorio [p.120]
- ► Villa Torlonia [p.247]
- ► Villa Paganini [p.249]
- ► Mausoleo di Santa Costanza [p.246]

Santa Maria della Concezione dei Cappuccini | Our Lady of the Conception of the Capuchins
Address: Via Vittorio Veneto 27, Roma
Online: www.cappucciniviaveneto.it

Public transportation:
Metro A stop Barberini

Opening hours: *see online*

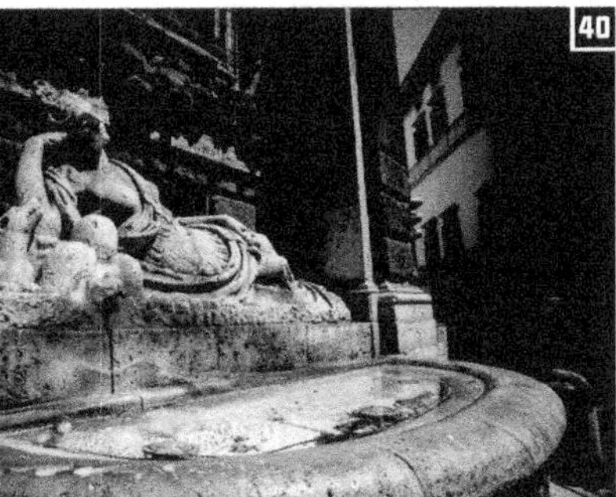

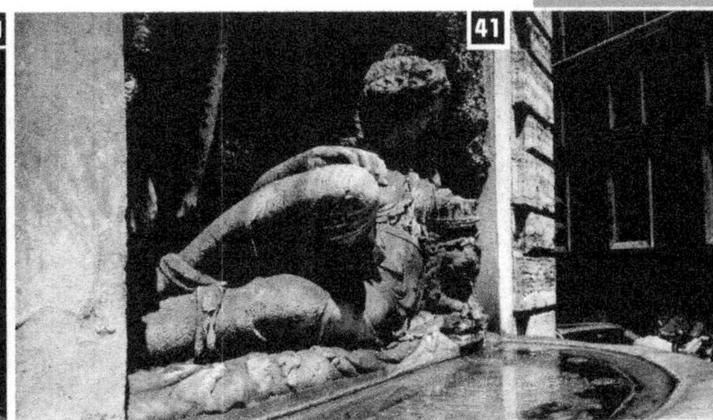

now, you shall be." After visiting the Crypt in 1775, even Marquis de Sade said that it was the most impressive thing he had ever seen. Every once in a while, a visitor gets sick, so it should be avoided by the faint of heart.

Palazzo Barberini ★★★

Maffeo Barberini, soon to become Pope Urban VIII, bought a vineyard from Cardinal Alessandro Sforza with a smallish palace in 1625. He employed architect Carlo Maderno to design a majestic palace for the Barberini family. Carlo Maderno took on Gian Lorenzo Bernini, Pietro da Cortona and Francesco Borromini as assistants, who would later become the leading baroque architects of Rome.

Encouraged by the Pope, they built some of the most beautiful fountains and churches. When Maderno passed away soon after he had agreed to the project, Bernini continued his work on Palazzo Barberini. Instead of using the usual layout of a Roman villa, consisting of a square with four interconnected wings and a courtyard, Maderno decided to design an elongated main wing and two lateral ones, as an H-shape building. This idea was executed by Bernini.

The façade is also original. It was inspired by the Colosseum, with arches on all three floors: the ground floor has Doric, first floor Ionic and the second floor has Corinthian semi-columns, i.e. pilasters.

Galleria Nazionale d'Arte Antica | National Gallery of Ancient Art

There is a Museum called Galleria Nazionale d'Arte Antica in the left wing, with various artworks from the 13th to the 18th century. Some of the highlights of Palazzo Barberini and the museum are:

- ► Borromini's spiral staircase in the right wing,
- ► Bernini's staircase in the left wing,
- ► *Judith Beheading Holofernes* by Caravaggio (1598–1599),
- ► *John the Baptist in the Wilderness* by Caravaggio (1604),
- ► *Narcissus* by Caravaggio (1597–1599),
- ► *The Portrait of a Young Woman (La Fornarina)* by Raphael (1518–1519),
- ► *Venus and Adonis* by Titian (1560).

Mithraeum of Palazzo Barberini (3rd century AD)
Reservation is mandatory:
www.coopculture.it/en/poi/mithraeum-of-palazzo-barberini/

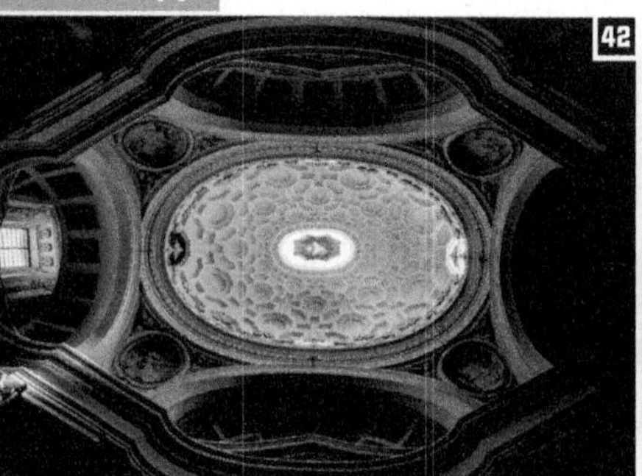
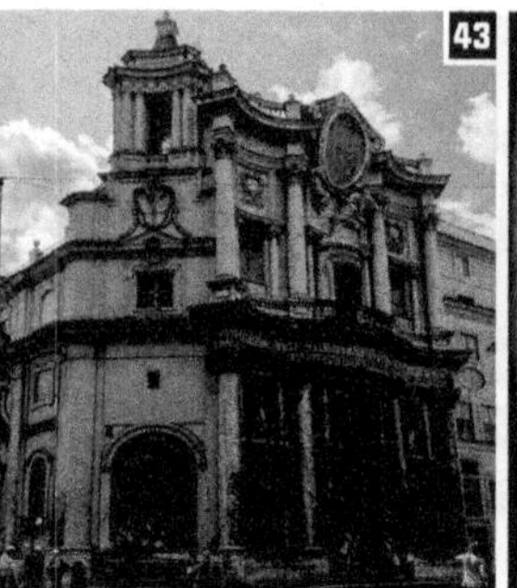
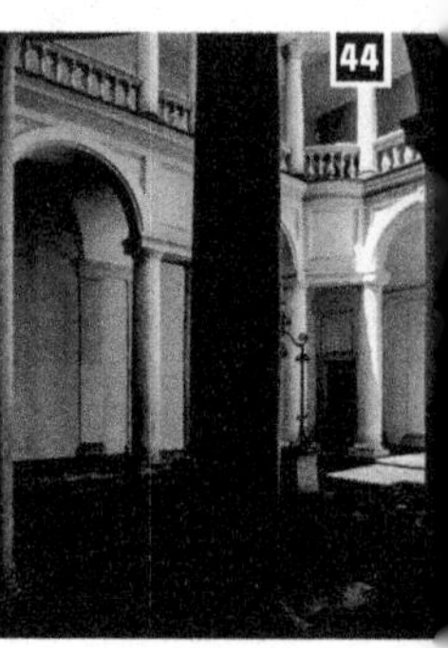

⑩ Quattro Fontane ★★

The four fountains were planned by the Mannerist architect Domenico Fontana. They were ordered by Pope Sixtus V. From the middle of the crossing you can see the four focal points of Rome: obelisk on the Piazza del Quirinale and Porta Pia, the city gate opposite, then the obelisk above the Spanish Steps and the one in front of Santa Maria Maggiore on the opposite end. Nevertheless, do not even try this, because the traffic is crazy. The four fountains, each occupying one of the corners, were erected between 1588 and 1593. Each of them has a main figure that is leaning on one hand with symbolic scenes in the background. The two male figures are river gods Tiber and Arno. The goddesses are Diana ⑩ and Juno ⑪. They were all made by Domenico Fontana, except Diana's Fountain, which was made by Pietro da Cortona.

⑪ San Carlo alle Quattro Fontane ★★★ ㊸

Church of San Carlo alle Quattro Fontane was the work of Francesco Borromini, ordered by Cardinal Francesco Barberini and built between 1638 and 1641. ㊹ Borromini managed to create one of the most interesting architectural works of the Italian Baroque. This was Borromini's first independent project in Rome. Due to its proximity to the Four Fountains, they were inserted into the name of the church itself. San Carlo relates to St. Charles Borromeo, to whom the church is dedicated. Relying upon the protection of this saint, the architect changed his own last name Castelli to Borromini. There is a huge medallion with an image of St. Charles Borromeo held by angels on the façade. The façade is divided in two levels that have niches with saints. The interplay between convex and concave elements continues inside the church as well. In the oval dome, polygonal cassettes interchange with cross-shaped ones. ㊷

They get progressively smaller towards the center, just like the cassettes on the dome of the Pantheon. This increases the sense of depth and space. Sunlight shines on the edge of the oval, so the dome appears to be floating.

Galleria Nazionale d'Arte Antica a Palazzo Barberini | National Gallery of Ancient Art in Barberini Palace
Address: Via delle Quattro Fontane 13, Roma
Online: www.barberinicorsini.org/en

Public transportation:
Metro A stop Barberini

Opening hours: *see online*

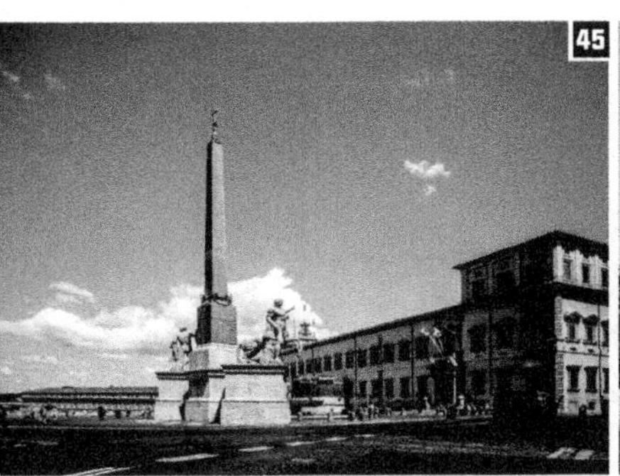

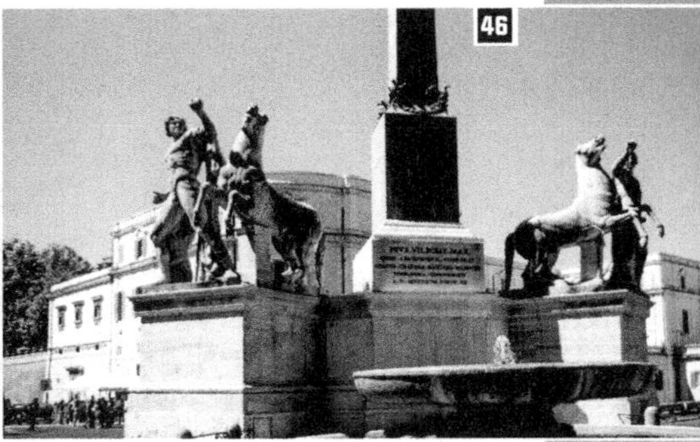

On the left, there are winding steps to an underground chapel also designed by Borromini.

It includes a tomb that the artist made for himself. In fact, Borromini was never buried in it because he committed suicide. His uncle was Carlo Maderno, so Borromini was laid to rest in Maderno's tomb in the church of San Giovanni dei Fiorentini in Rome. [p.130]

Sant'Andrea al Quirinale ★ ★ ★

Only a few steps away from Quattro Fontane, there is Sant'Andrea al Quirinale in Via del Quirinale.

The church was made by Bernini who finished it in 1661. He considered it one of his best works. According to his son Domenico, Bernini used to spend hours sitting in the church and admiring the harmony of his own masterpiece.

The church was commissioned by Camillo Pamphili, Pope Innocent X's nephew.

Since the building site was wide, but not deep enough, Bernini opted for an oval shape. The view in the semicircle goes to the door with the altar opposite.

Piazza del Quirinale ★ ★

There is the eponymous square in front with the Dioscuri Fountain.

Francesco Borromini (1599–1667) and his works in Rome

After studying to be sculptor in Milan, he came to Rome in 1619 to his uncle Carlo Maderno, the leading Roman architect at the time. Borromini and his mentor worked on St. Peter's Basilica and Palazzo Barberini (1627–1638), the headquarters of Pope Urban VIII (1623–1644). After Maderno died in 1629, the construction of St. Peter's Church and Palazzo Barberini was taken over by Gian Lorenzo Bernini. Pretty soon, Bernini and Borromini started to fight and developed a rivalry. Innocent X (1644–1655) from the Pamphilj family named Borromini the main Roman architect. Alexander VII (1655–1667) gave all major state projects to Bernini. In 1667, Borromini committed suicide.

Borromini's works in Rome:

▸ San Carlo alle Quattro Fontane [p.230]

▸ Sant'Ivo alla Sapienza [p.119]

▸ Oratorio dei Filippini [p.129]

▸ Sant'Agnese in Agone [p.112]

▸ Palazzo Barberini (oval staircase) [p.229]

▸ Basilica di San Giovanni in Laterano (Interior) [p.270]

▸ Palazzo Falconieri (façade) [p.129]

▸ Palazzo Spada (forced perspective gallery) [p.128]

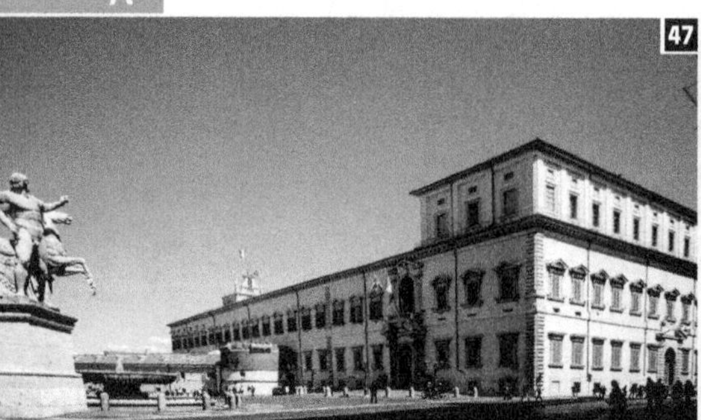

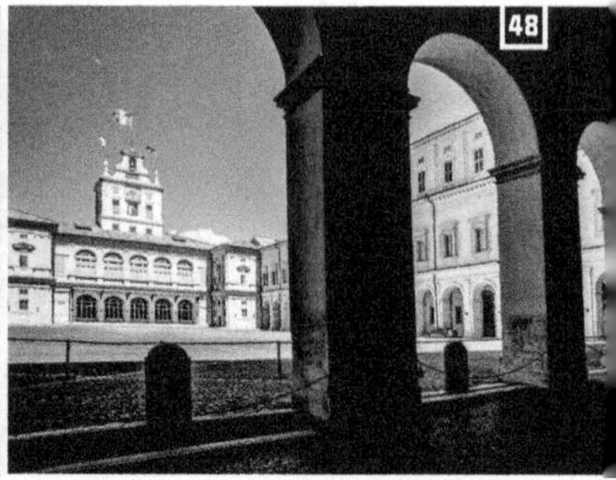

It has an obelisk (46 ft or 14 m) that used to be in front of the Mausoleum of Augustus.

On each side, there are giant sculptures of Castor and Pollux (18 ft or 5.5 m). **45** **46**

These are Roman copies of the Greek originals, placed by Domenico Fontana. They used to belong to Baths of Constantine on the Quirinal Hill.

14 Palazzo del Quirinale ★★★

It is still one of the largest palaces in the world.

It has been a representative building of the highest level since 1583. Initially, it was used as a summer residence by thirty popes.

After 1870, it became the royal residence of all four Italian kings. Since 1946, it has been the official residence of the Italian president. **47**. **48**

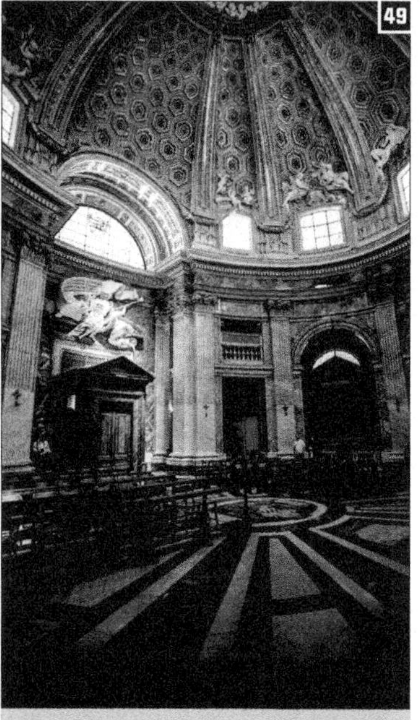

Palazzo del Quirinale
Address: Piazza del Quirinale, Roma
Online: https://palazzo.quirinale.it/

Public transportation:
Metro A stop Barberini

How to visit:
Reservation is mandatory and may be made at least 5 days prior to the tour:
http://palazzo.quirinale.it

Tel. +39 639 967 557

At the Infopoint: Palazzo Sant'Andrea, Via del Quirinale 30

San Carlo alle Quattro Fontane
Address: Via del Quirinale 23, Roma
Online address: *unknown*

Public transportation:
Metro A stop Barberini

Opening hours: *see on Google Maps*

Sant'Andrea al Quirinale
Address: Via del Quirinale 28, Roma
Online: https://santandrea.gesuiti.it

Public transportation:
Metro A stop Barberini

Opening hours: *see on Google Maps*

Trastevere and Gianicolo

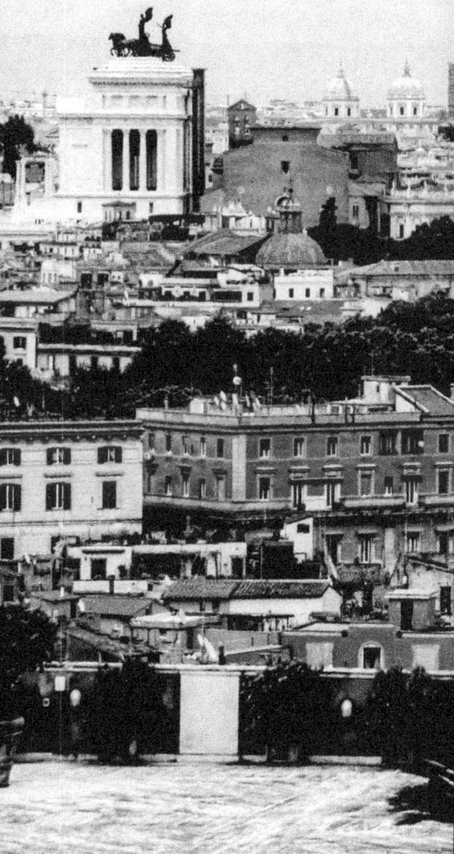

Views from Fontana dell'Acqua Paola

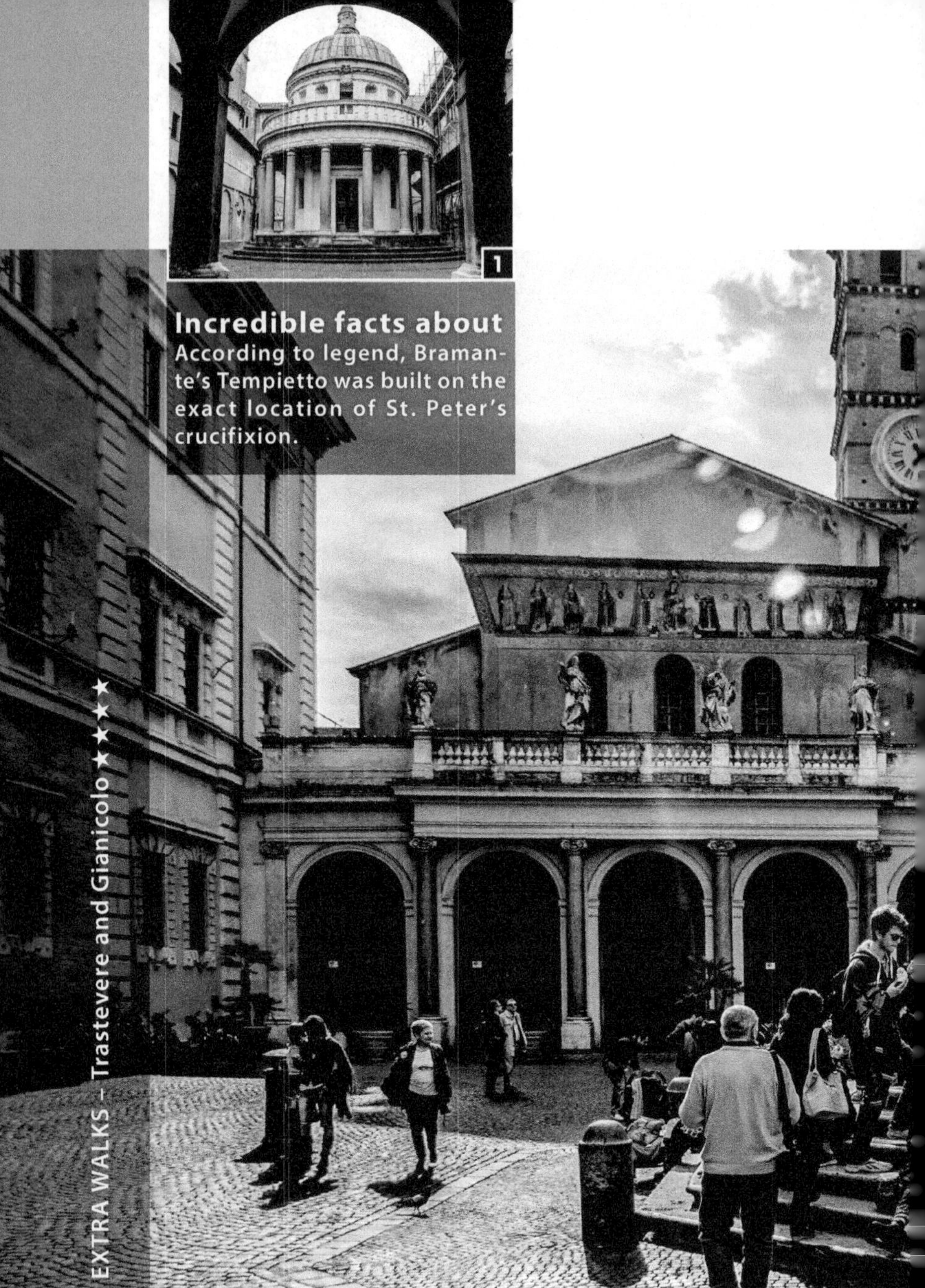

Incredible facts about

According to legend, Bramante's Tempietto was built on the exact location of St. Peter's crucifixion.

Basilica di Santa Maria in Trastevere

Extra Tip :::

The cause for building the church Santa Maria in Trastevere at this location was due to a belief that in 38 BC oil was pouring out of the earth. Jews believed this was a sign of the arrival of Messiah and Christians saw it as the Annunciation of Jesus Christ.

Outside the main tourist routes but still international

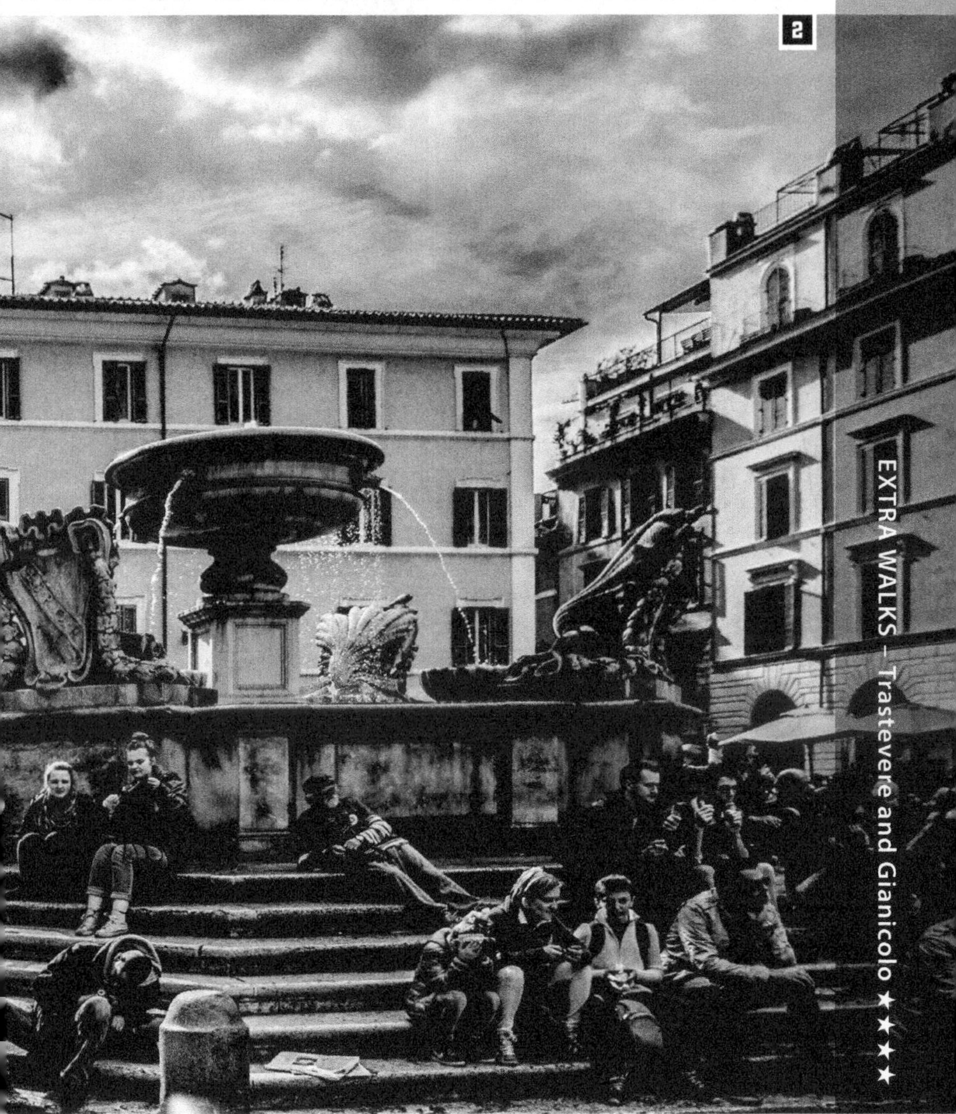

Santa Maria in Trastevere | The Basilica of Our Lady
Address: Piazza di Santa Maria in Trastevere, Roma
Public transportation: Bus stop Sonnino – San Gallicano: 780, H |
Tram stop Trastevere – Mastai: 8

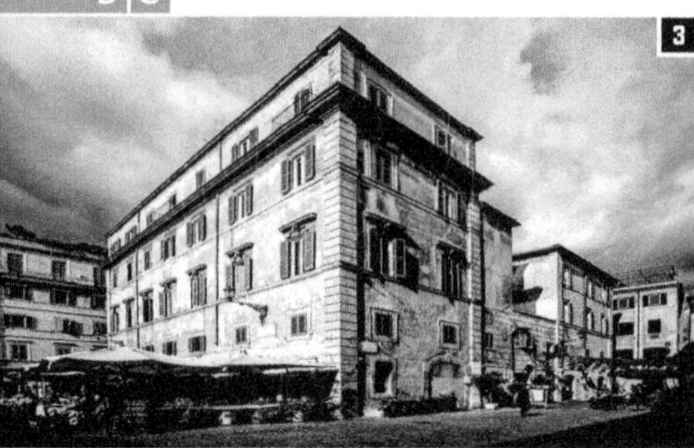

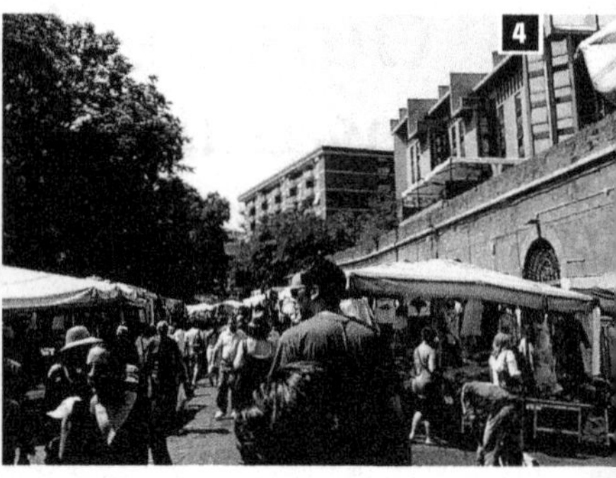

❶ Trastevere ★★★★

A great number of medieval streets and buildings, and several exceptional churches are also what makes Trastevere special and unique. **3** All this attracts a lot of tourists, although Trastevere is not only a tourist attraction — this is also one of the most popular hangouts for the locals. Many international scientific institutions are located here, such as, the American University of Rome, John Cabot University, the American Academy in Rome, the Rome campus of the Thomas More College of Liberal Arts, the Canadian University of Waterloo School of Architecture and the American Pratt Institute School of Architecture.

The rich atmosphere was appealing to the making of *Spaghetti westerns*: Sergio Leone, the director who became famous by making Italian westerns with Clint Eastwood, went to the same private Catholic school in Trastevere as the legendary movie composer Ennio Morricone.

① Santa Cecilia in Trastevere ★★

In order to get to this church, you will walk on charming medieval streets.

Notice the old warehouse gates along the way. The church was constructed in 5th century, in honor of St. Cecilia.

Santa Cecilia in Trastevere
Address: Piazza di S. Cecilia 22, Roma
Online:
www.benedettinesantacecilia.it

Public transportation:
Bus stop Sonnino – San Gallicano: 780, H | Tram stop Belli: 8

Opening hours: *see on Google Maps*

Trastevere

❶ Santa Cecilia in Trastevere
❷ San Francesco a Ripa
❸ Santa Maria in Trastevere

© OpenStreetMap

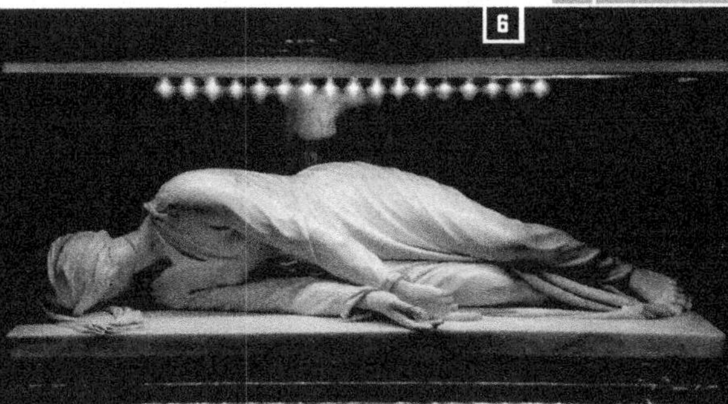

She is an early Christian martyr. Legend says she used to live on the location of the church with her husband Valerianus. There are remains of a house entrance from ancient times, partially visible on the floor of the crypt. Cecilia was tortured for being Christian. First, they boiled her and since that did not kill her, they severed her head. 5 6

Pope Paschalis renovated the church in the 9th century after finding Cecilia's body in the Catacombe di San Callisto. Her remains were transferred to this church.

In 1600, Stefano Maderno created a beautiful statue of the saint, according to the position she was found in, so she is lying on her back peacefully. The sculpture is under the altar.

◈ San Francesco a Ripa ★★ 8

St. Francis of Assisi lived in a hospice here in 1219.

Blessed Ludovica Albertoni 7

Bernini's Blessed Ludovica Albertoni can be found in the Paluzzi-Albertoni Chapel. It was made in 1674, only three years after this Franciscan monk was declared a saint. This was almost 30 years after the controversial Ecstasy of St. Theresa, whose ecstasy was considered to be of a much more profane origin. The truth is in the eye of the beholder. In any case, Bernini stayed true to his interpretation of divine bliss.

Giorgio de Chirico's grave

The grave of he greatest Italian painter of the 20th century, Giorgio de Chirico, is in the room next to the Chapel of Mary's Immaculate Conception.

San Francesco a Ripa
Address: Piazza di San Francesco D'Assisi 88, Roma
Online: www.sanfrancescoaripa.com

Public transportation:
Bus stop Porta Portese: 3B, 44, 44F, 75 | Tram stop Porta Portese: 8

Opening hours: *see on Google Maps*

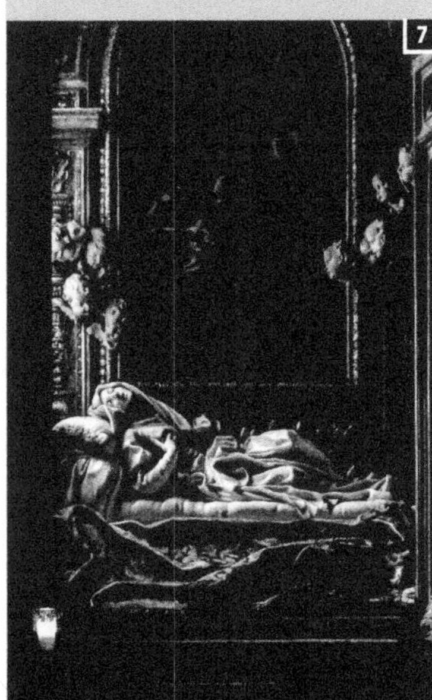

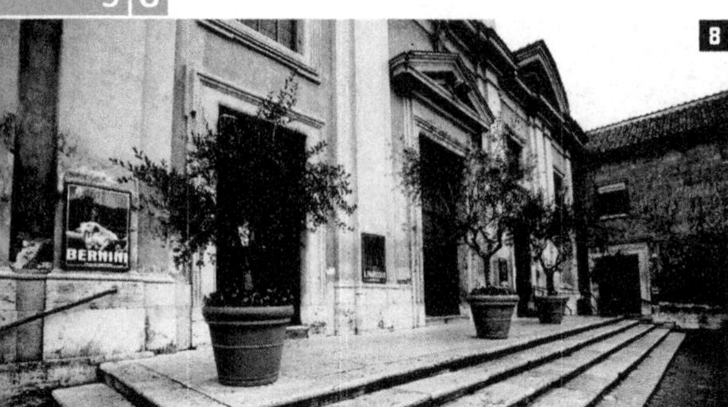

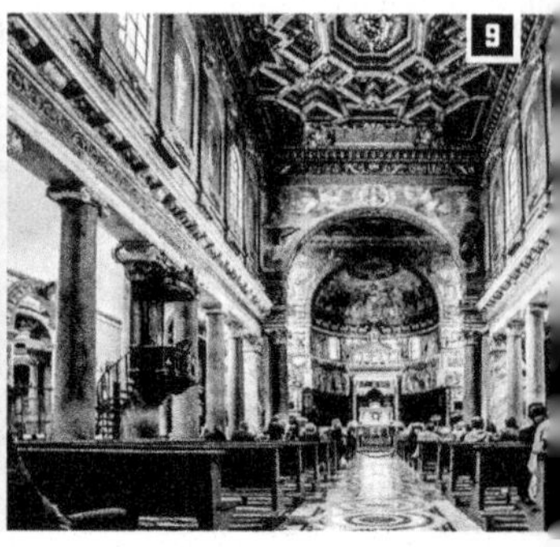

③ Santa Maria in Trastevere ★★★

The Basilica of Our Lady is the oldest church in Rome dedicated to the Marian cult. **1** The cause for building the church at this location as early as 3rd century was due to a belief that in 38 BC, oil was pouring out of the earth.

Jews, many of whom lived around here until the Ghetto was created, believed this was a sign of the arrival of Messiah. Christians saw it as the Annunciation of Jesus Christ.

In mid-4th century Pope Julius I erected a basilica. In 1140, the church was expanded and a belfry added by Pope Innocent II. Even though there were further additions in the baroque period, it still looks like a medieval building.

The central nave is supported by 22 antique columns with Ionic and Corinthian capitals. Supposedly, these were brought in from the Baths of Caracalla. **9**

The triumphal arch of the main nave was painted by Pietro Cavallini in the 13th century. The entire Life of the Virgin from 1291 is also one of his works. You can admire these frescoes in the lower half of the semicircular apse. Mosaics in the upper half of the apse belong to the old church. The baroque façade and the fountain on the square were made by Carlo Fontana in early 18th century.

④ Porta Settimiana ★ **10**

Porta Settimiana was built in 1498 after Pope Alexander VI's orders to construct new, bigger gates on the Aurelian Wall.

Out of three city gates, these are the only ones that remained on the right bank of the Tiber.

This is also the beginning of the Trastevere area, famous for its nightlife, restaurants and bars. **13**

Santa Maria in Trastevere
Address: Piazza di Santa Maria in Trastevere, Roma
Online: www.santamariaintrastevere.it

Public transportation:
Bus stop Sonnino – San Gallicano: 780, H | Tram stop Belli: 8
Opening hours: *see online*

Galleria Nazionale d'Arte Antica – Galleria Corsini | National Gallery of Ancient Art – Galleria Corsini
Address: Via della Lungara 10, Roma
Online: www.barberinicorsini.org/en

Public transportation:
Bus stop Lungara – Orto Botanico: 125
Opening hours: *see online*

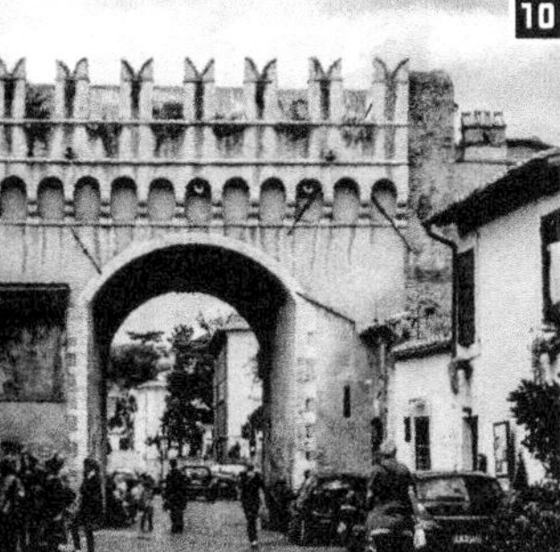
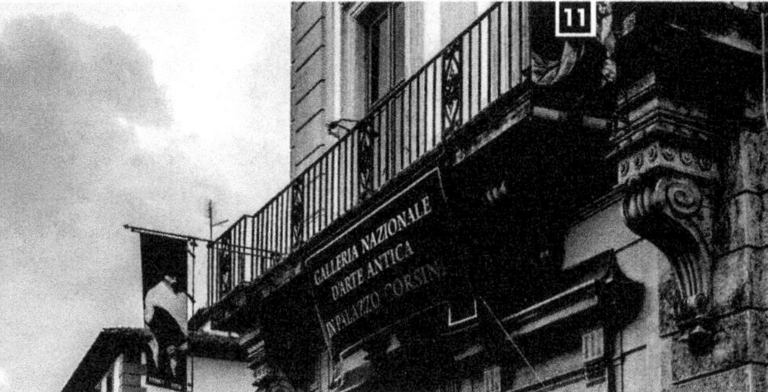

⬦ Palazzo Corsini Gallery ★★

National Gallery of Ancient Art is actually on two locations: in Palazzo Barberini, and the other one is here, in Palazzo Corsini.

This 18th-century Baroque palace features a lot of artworks donated by the Corsini family and Pope Clement XII (1730–1740) to the state. On the first floor, there are Baroque works by Carlo Maratta, Guido Reni, Annibale Carracci, Caravaggio, Jacopo Bassano, Rubens and others. What really makes this palace extraordinary is the park that stretches behind it all the way to Gianicolo Hill. These are also the Botanical Gardens of Rome.

⬦ Orto Botanico di Roma ★★

The Botanical Gardens were based in the park of the Palazzo Corsini in 1883, as the successor to the botanical gardens whose history goes back to the Renaissance.

With over 3,000 plants, a Japanese garden, a bamboo forest and an herbal plant garden, these botanical gardens are a wonderful place to relax and walk around.

Orto Botanico di Roma | Botanical Garden of Rome
Address: Largo Cristina di Svezia 24, Roma
Online: https://web.uniroma1.it/ortobotanico/en
Public transportation:
Bus stop Lungara – Orto Botanico: 125

Opening hours: *see online*

Villa Farnesina
Address: Via della Lungara 230, Roma
Online: www.villafarnesina.it
Public transportation:
Bus stop Lungara – Orto Botanico: 125

Opening hours: see online

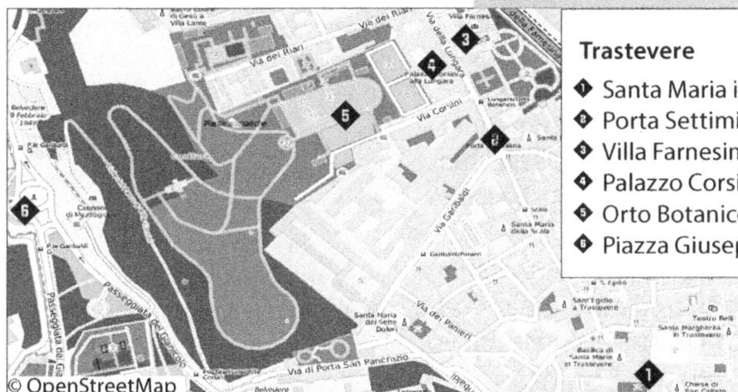
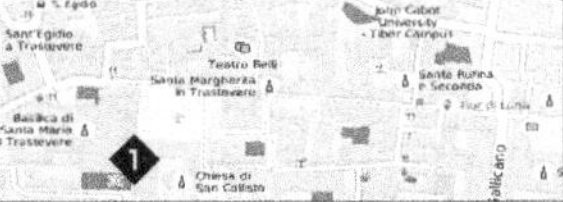

Trastevere
1. Santa Maria in Trastevere
2. Porta Settimiana
3. Villa Farnesina
4. Palazzo Corsini
5. Orto Botanico di Roma
6. Piazza Giuseppe Garibaldi

EXTRA WALKS – Trastevere and Gianicolo ★★★★★

239

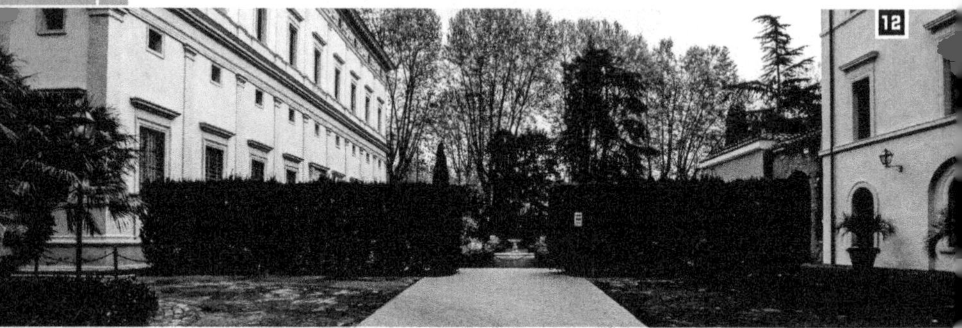

⑦ **Villa Farnesina ★★★**

The luxurious Renaissance villa was built to reflect Roman *villa suburbana* (suburban villa). A banker from Tuscany, Agostino Chigi put his fellow Tuscan Baldassare Peruzzi in charge of building it (1508–1511).

The interior was decorated with frescoes by Raphael, Sebastiano del Piombo, Giulio Romano, and Il Sodoma. The whole complex, not just the villa, but also the park, was meant to display the humanistic worldview of the owner. In 1577, the ownership of the villa was passed on to the Farnese family and it bears their name to this day. An unfinished bridge by Michelangelo, just above Via Giulia, was designed to go over the Tiber and connect Palazzo Farnese to Villa Farnesina.

Casa della Farnesina, the only *antique villa urbana*, was discovered in the Villa Farnesina gardens in 1880 during construction works to fortify the bank of the Tiber. This villa may have actually been Villa Iulia, a house from 20 BC, owned by Marcus Vipsanius Agrippa, a military commander and politician who also ordered the construction of the Pantheon. His wife Julia was the daughter of the first Roman Emperor Augustus. Remarkable frescoes from this villa can be found at the National Roman Museum – Palazzo Massimo alle Terme.

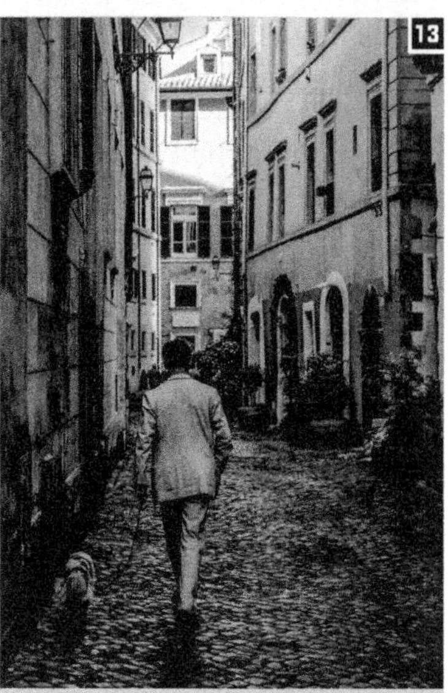

Did you know?

The best scenic walking areas

▸ From Piazza Navona to Ponte Sant'Angelo, [p.110]

▸ Campo de' Fiori – Palazzo Farnese – Via Giulia and around, [p.124]

▸ Villa Borghese Garden [p.188]

▸ Trastevere, [p.236]

▸ Palatine – Roman Forum – Imperial Forums – Hills of Capitol, [p.40]

▸ Via Appia Antica, [p.290]

▸ Tiber Island – Former Jewish Ghetto – Forum Boarium, [p.174]

▸ Esposizione Universale di Roma – E.U.R., [p.258]

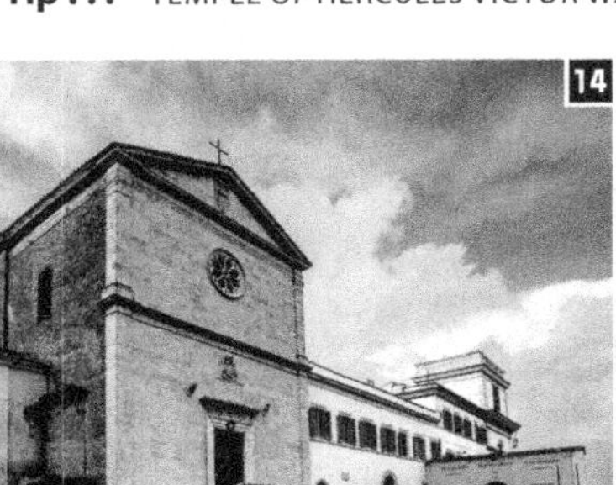

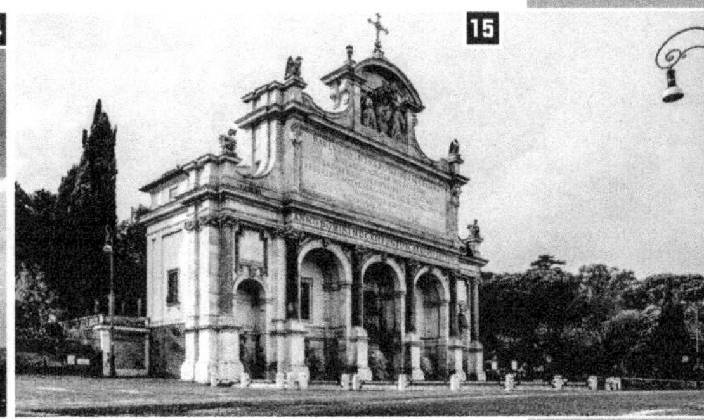

❖ Gianicolo or Janiculum ★ ★ ★ ★

Due to its strategic position, this hill was an integral part of the city's defense. Garibaldi's troops fought against the French here in 1849. This is why Gianicolo is full of monuments dedicated to Garibaldi and heroes who fought for Italian independence.

① Piazza Giuseppe Garibaldi ★

The most beautiful view of Rome can be enjoyed from this hill. However, Janiculum, just like the Pincio Hill near Piazza del Popolo, does not count as one of the seven Roman hills. 18

② Tempietto ★ ★ ★ 2

The masterpiece of High Renaissance architecture was achieved by Donato Bramante. Bramante's Tempietto was built on the exact location of St. Peter's crucifixion, according to legend.

Tempietto in the Franciscan monastery courtyard, as well as the nearby church of San Pietro in Montorio were commissioned by Ferdinand and Isabella of Spain around 1500. 14

Consequently, at the Great Jubilee of 2000, Spanish King Juan Carlos I, financed the restoration of Tempietto. The Doric colonnade was modeled after the Theater of Marcellus. Tempietto is one of the most harmonious renaissance buildings ever made.

Did you know?

The best scenic views of Rome

► Altare della Patria | Altar of the Fatherland – View from the rooftop, 16 [p.87]

► The keyhole of the embassy of the Order of Malta – Great view of St. Peter's Basilica, [p.179]

► Musei Capitolini – View from Terrazza Caffarelli, [p.81]

► Terrazza del Gianicolo – One of the most famous panoramic views of Rome, 17 [p.241]

► Campidoglio – View from the Capitoline Hill on Roman Forum, [p.78]

► The Dom of the Basilica di San Pietro, [p.141]

► Giardino degli Aranci [p.183]

► View from Palatino | the Palatine Hill on the Roman Forum. [p.44]

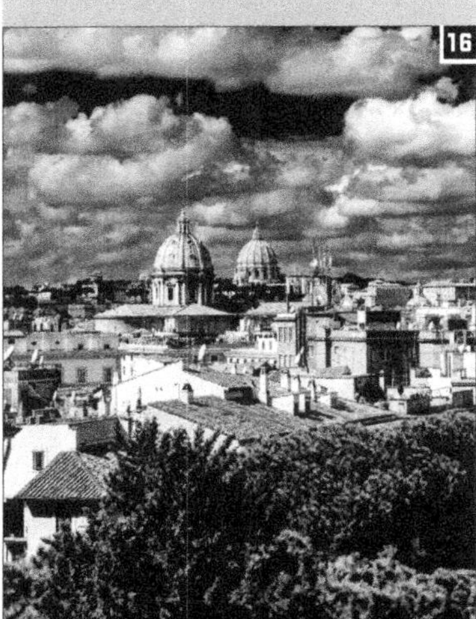

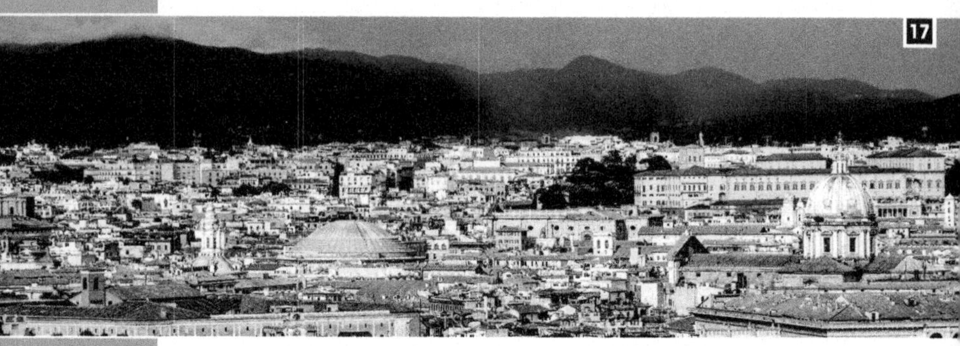

17

In other words, the perfect Tempietto, built on the exact spot of St. Peter's crucifixion, was the best reference Bramante could hope for while applying to become the chief architect of the new St. Peter's Basilica. Pope Julius II gave him the job in 1506.

③ Fontana dell'Acqua ★★★

The monumental baroque fountain was the first fountain on the left bank of the Tiber. It was supposedly built by Flaminio Ponzio and Giovanni Fontana (1610–1612) by orders of Pope Paul V, who wanted to mark the end of Aqua Traiana Aqueduct.

The aqueduct was renovated by the Pope himself to provide drinkable water to the residents of Gianicolo. This fountain was inspiration for Fontana di Trevi. **14**

Tempietto
Address: Via di San Pietro in Montorio, Roma
Online: www.sanpietroinmontorio.it

Public transportation:
Bus stop Garibaldi – Iacobucci: 115

Opening hours: see online

Museo della Repubblica Romana e della Memoria Garibaldina | Museum of the Roman Republic and the Memory of Garibaldi and his Followers
Address: Largo di Porta San Pancrazio, Roma

Online:
www.museodellarepubblicaromana.it/en

Public transportation: Bus stop Mura Gianicolens: 115, 870

Opening hours: *see online*

Free entry to the permanent collection

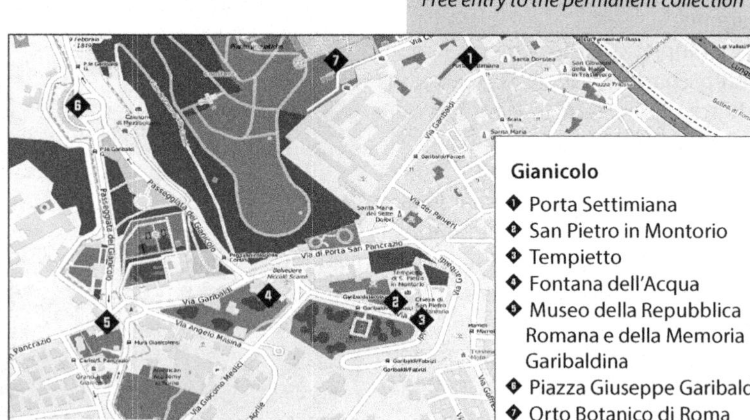

Gianicolo

❶ Porta Settimiana
❷ San Pietro in Montorio
❸ Tempietto
❹ Fontana dell'Acqua
❺ Museo della Repubblica Romana e della Memoria Garibaldina
❻ Piazza Giuseppe Garibaldi
❼ Orto Botanico di Roma

Via Nomentana

Porta Pia by Michelangelo

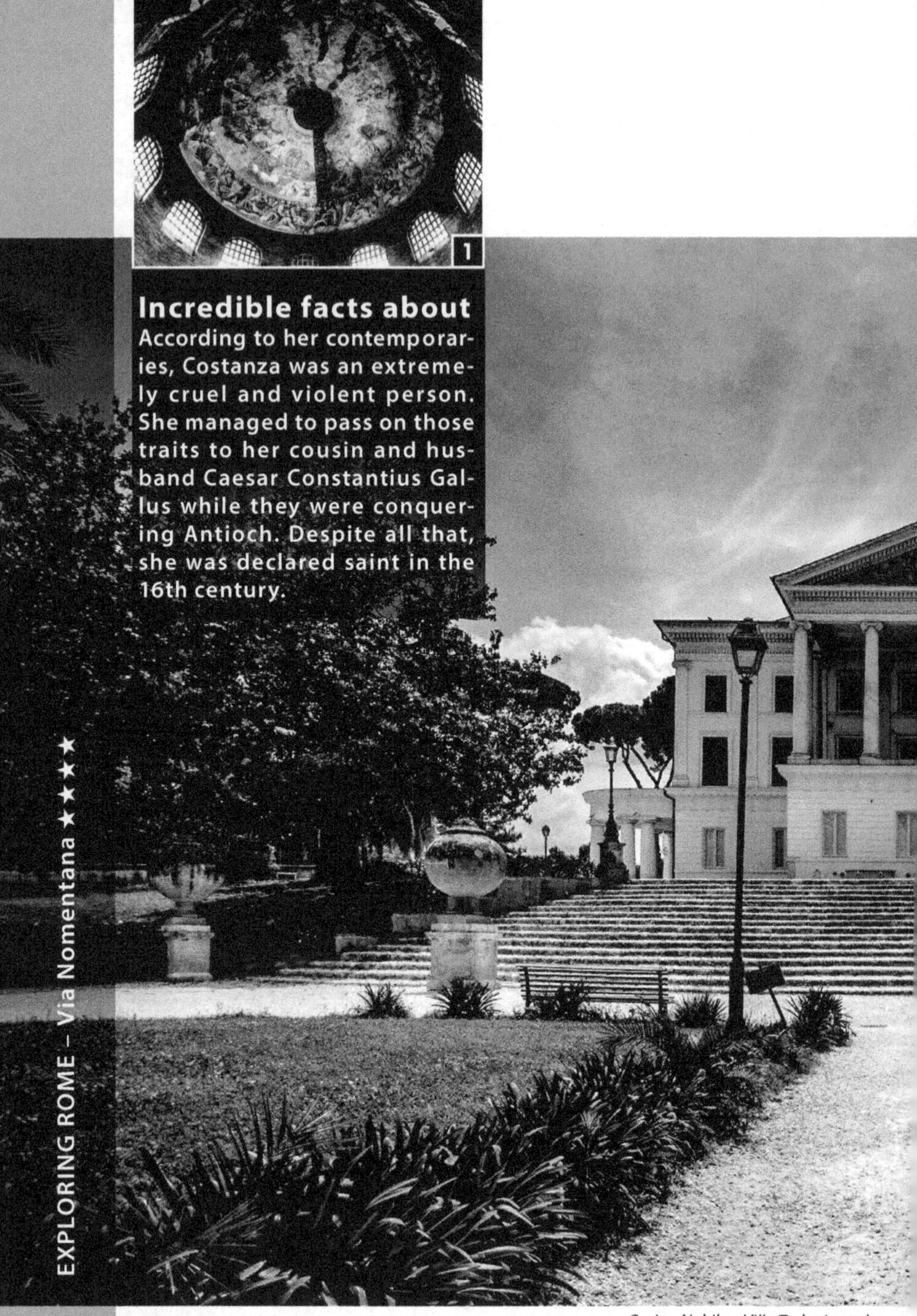

Incredible facts about

According to her contemporaries, Costanza was an extremely cruel and violent person. She managed to pass on those traits to her cousin and husband Caesar Constantius Gallus while they were conquering Antioch. Despite all that, she was declared saint in the 16th century.

Casino Nobile – Villa Torlonia park

Extra Tip : : :
The Mausoleo di Santa Costanzas is definitely worth a visit because of its frescoes and extremely well preserved Early Christian mosaics on the ceiling. These mosaics reflect the Antique repertoire with birds, floral motifs and everyday scenes. **7**

Along an (un)usual boulevard

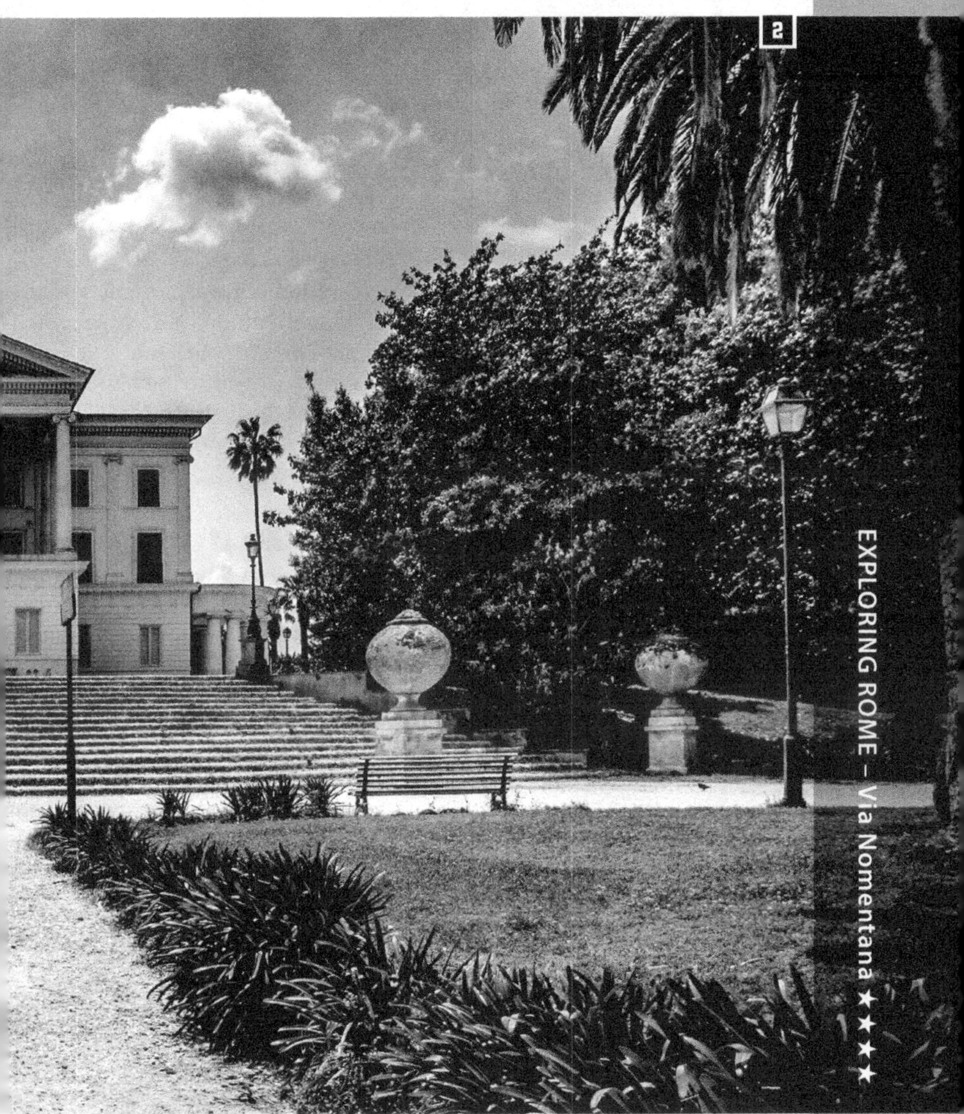

Villa Torlonia | Villa Torlonia park
Address: Via Nomentana 70, Roma
Public transportation: Metro B1stop S. Agnese | Bus stop Sant'agnese – Annibaliano:
38, 80, 88, 89
Opening hours: www.museivillatorlonia.it/en

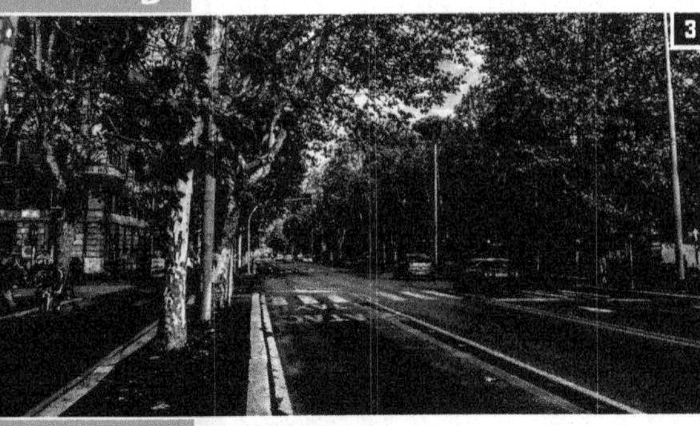

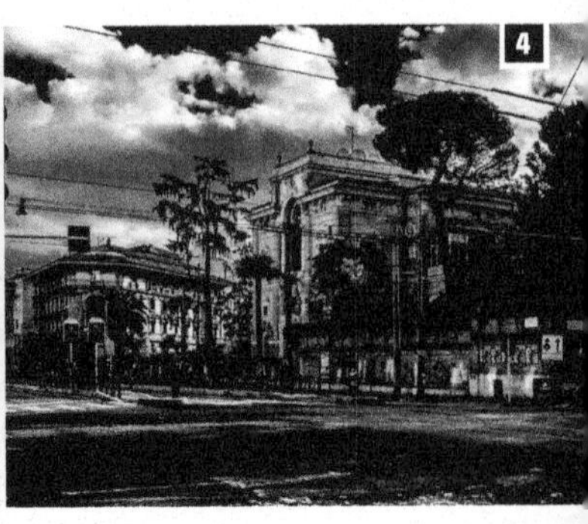

◈ Via Nomentana ★★★★

Via Nomentana is an avenue in North East Rome. It is an ancient Roman road which connected to Via Salaria. **3** Via Nomentana is lined up with palaces and luxurious gardens **4**, Antique churches and mausoleums, remains of old Roman city walls, Mussolini's residence and the Museum of Contemporary Art. A 30-minute stroll separates the first site, Mausoleo di Santa Costanza, from the last one — Michelangelo's Porta Pia.

◈ Mausoleo di Santa Costanza | Mausoleum of Santa Costanza ★★★

Basilica di Santa Costanza was built during Emperor Julian (361–363), who had it constructed for his wife, Costanza's sister. **5** Costanza was the eldest daughter of Emperor Constantine the Great. She was the wife of Caesar Constantius Gallus. As Augusta, a title given to women in the imperial family, Costanza wielded considerable political clout in the Empire.

The basilica was next to the Mausoleum which was originally an integral part of the complex, then it was turned into a baptistery. **1**

After the basilica turned to ruin, the Mausoleum was turned into the Church of Saint Costanza, which is what saved it from destruction. **6** **7** Costanza's monumental sarcophagus made of red porphyry is at the Vatican Museums, opposite an equally splendid sarcophagus of her grandmother, the mother of Emperor Constantine the Great, St. Helena. The mausoleum holds a copy of the sarcophagus in its original place. The church of Saint Agnes Outside the Walls also belongs to this complex, built 3 centuries after the Mausoleum.

◈ Sant'Agnese fuori le mura | Saint Agnes Outside the Walls ★★★

Church of Saint Agnes Outside the Walls is dedicated to St. Agnes of Rome, protector of virgins and couples. In terms of the iconography, she is always shown with a lamb by her side or something to that effect. **8**

The same saint also has a church on Piazza Navona, built by Borromini, the Church of Sant'Agnese in Agone, which was built on the same spot where she was tortured in AD 304 during Emperor Diocletian. Pope Honorius commissioned the Church of Saint Agnes Outside the Walls to be built above the catacombs where St. Agnes was buried. Those were one of the largest Roman catacombs, stretching for 6.2 miles or 10 kilometers. St. Agnes' grave is under the altar of this relatively small three-nave church.

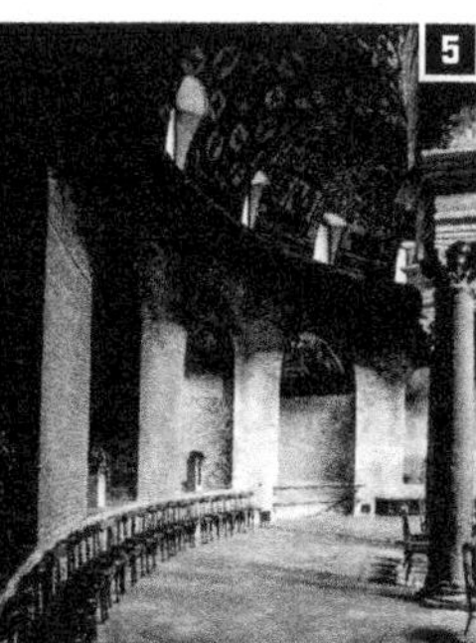
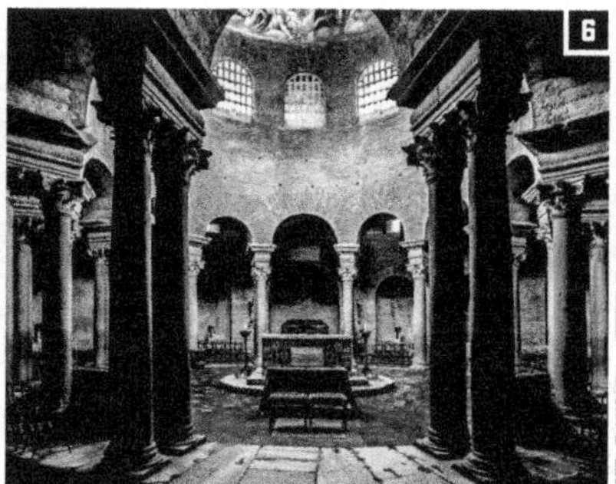
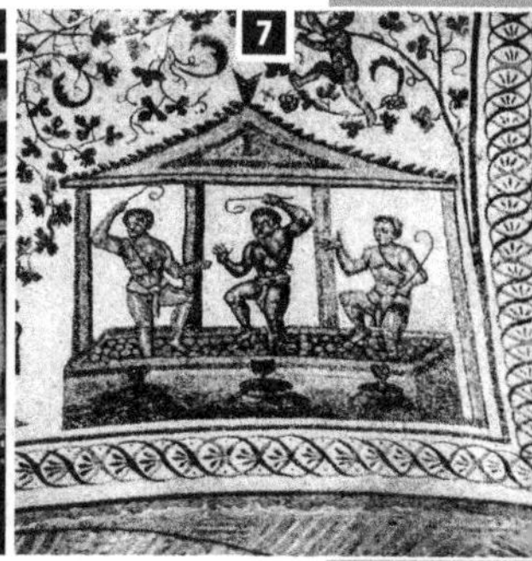

The naves are separated by arches supported by 16 ancient Roman columns. The original pieces include the bishop's chair and mosaics in the apside with St. Agnes sporting a royal Byzantine outfit. Symbols of martyrdom, fire and sword, are shown below, while St. Agnes herself is holding a lamb. Pope Honorius is right next to St. Agnes as a benefactor with a model of the church in his hands. Pope St. Symmachus is on the other side.

The monumental wooden decoration on the ceiling was executed in 1606. **9**

Marble lamps are from the 13th century. The upper gallery, known as the *matronaeum*, was for women only. The oldest part of the catacombs from the 2nd century can only be visited in the company of a guide, included in the price of admission.

◆ Villa Torlonia★★

The designer of the present-day Piazza del Popolo, the architect Giuseppe Valadier, took on the design of banker Giovanni Torlonia's lavish villa and estate in 1802.

① Casino Nobile **2**

The central palace in Villa Torlonia was the official residence of the Italian fascist leader Benito Mussolini from 1925 until he was ousted and had to flee Rome in 1943.

Sant'Agnese fuori le mura | Saint Agnes Outside the Walls
Address: Via Nomentana 349, Roma
Online: www.santagnese.com

Public transportation:
Metro B1 stop S. Agnese – Annibaliano | Bus stop Sant'agnese – Annibaliano: 38, 80, 88, 89 or stop Nomentana – Sant'Agnese: 66, 82

Opening hours: *see on Google Maps*

Catacombe di Sant'Agnese | Catacombs of Saint Agnes
For groups booking is mandatory: catacombe@santagnese.net

Mausoleo di Santa Costanza | Church of Santa Costanza
Address: Via Nomentana 349, Roma
Online:
www.santagnese.org/mausoleo.htm

Public transportation:
Metro B1 stop S. Agnese – Annibaliano | Bus stop Sant'agnese – Annibaliano: 38, 80, 88, 89 or stop Nomentana – Sant'Agnese: 66, 82

Opening hours: *see on Google Maps*

Casino Nobile & Casina delle Civette
Address: Via Nomentana 70, Roma
Online: www.museivillatorlonia.it/en

Public transportation:
Bus stop Nomentana – Villa Torlonia 60, 66, 82

Opening hours: *see online*

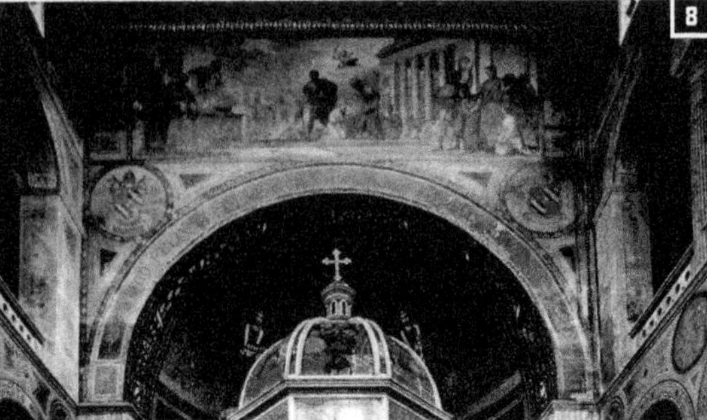

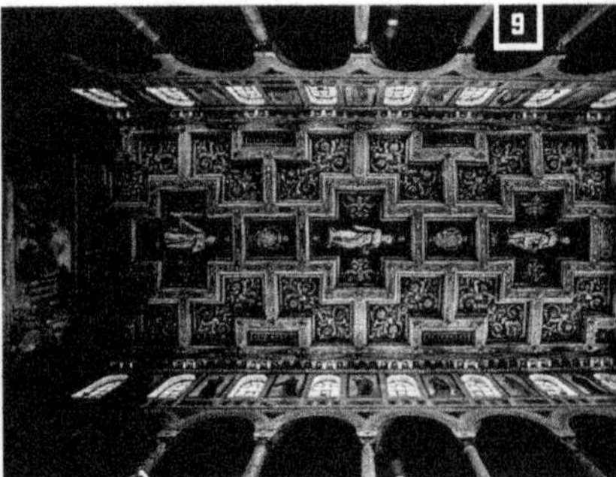

Today, the building is a museum with several works by Canova, certain elements from the grave monuments from Via Appia and parts of the original furniture used by the Italian dictator.

② Rifugio

Rifugio consists of two underground bunkers made by Mussolini as protection against air strikes in 1942. It is, in fact, a remodeled basement of the vila. Rifugio has recently been opened for visitors.

③ Jewish catacombs

Jewish catacombs date back to the 2nd and 3rd century, and there are even some parts from the 1st century. Frescoes and inscriptions are particularly interesting. Along with the Vigna Randanini, Via Appia Pignatelli 4, these are the only Jewish catacombs open for visitors. [p.295]

EXPLORING ROME – Via Nomentana ★ ★ ★ ★

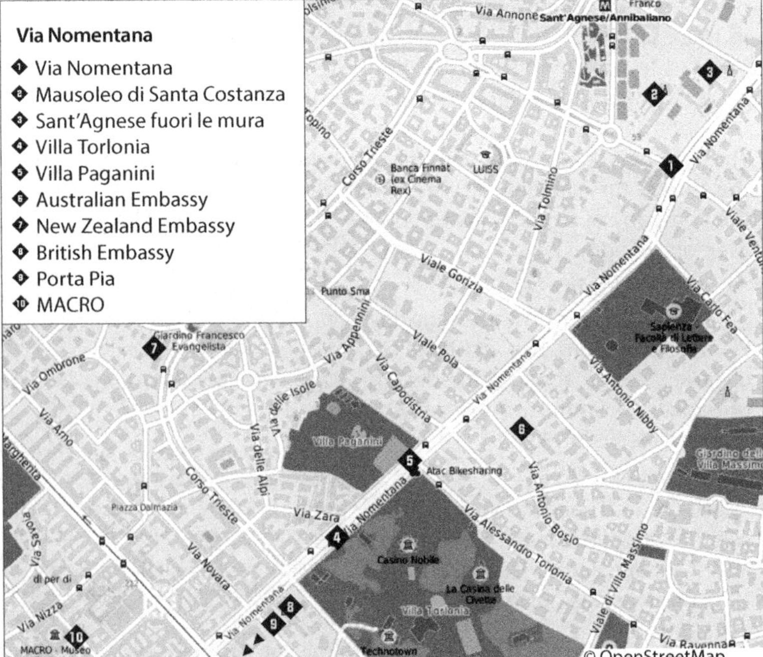

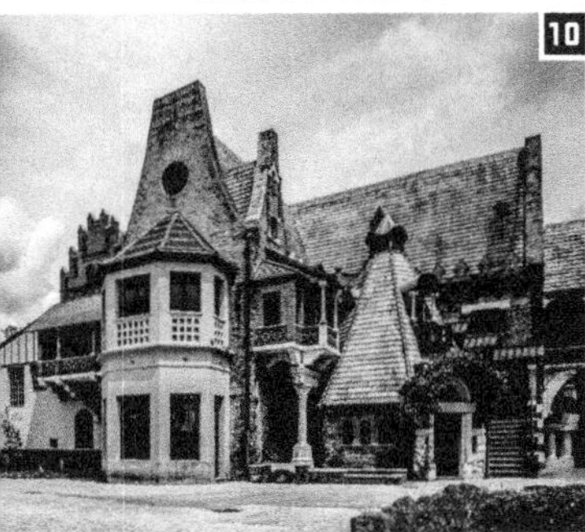
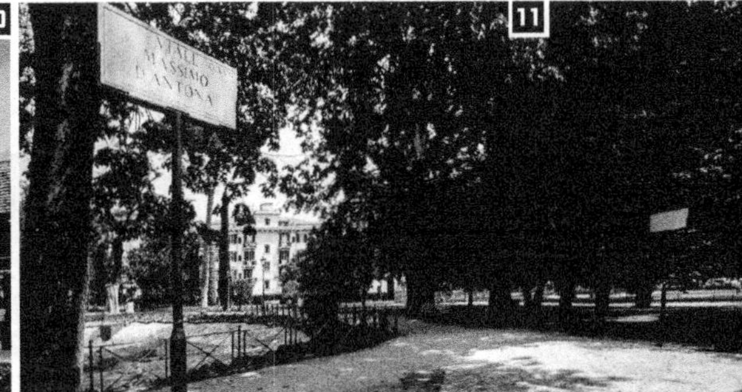

◈ Park Villa Torlonia

Once a private estate, this is now a public park full of colorful sites across 32 acres or 13 hectares. It has exotic vegetation, two artificial lakes, Neo-Classicist sculptures and many buildings and features, such as, obelisks, vases, sculptures, sphinxes, Temple of Saturn, a Moorish-styled greenhouse, a medieval tournament stadium, etc.

◈ Casina delle Civette

The Casina delle Civette or House of the Owls (1840–1909) is an unusual building designed and redesigned by different architects for almost 70 years.

The interior has maintained Art Nouveau features (1916–1920). Today, this is a museum of Art Nouveau glass with temporary exhibitions by contemporary artists who work with glass.

◆ Villa Paganini★

Villa Paganini is a park on Via Nomentana across the Villa Torlonia Park. It was named after Senator Roberto Paganini, who owned the park (1890–1913) which was originally commissioned by Cardinal Giulio Alberoni in the early 18th century. Since 1934, the park has been owned by the city of Rome.

What makes this park unique and unforgettable are the names of numerous footpaths zig-zagging through the park — each one was named after a mafia victim, including the dates of their birth and death.

◆ Museo d'Arte Contemporanea di Roma (MACRO) | Museum of Contemporary Art of Rome ★ ★

The museum offers a comprehensive overview of contemporary Italian artists from 1960 onwards, including Carla Accardi, Antonio Sanfilippo, Achille Perilli, Piero Dorazio, Leoncillo, Ettore Colla et al.

This museum also has an exhibition place in Testaccio district — MACRO Testaccio located in a former slaughterhouse.

◆ Porta Pia ★ ★

Porta Pia is a city gate on the Aurelian Wall, named after its commissioner Pope Pius IV and designed by Michelangelo (1561–1565). According to Vasari, Michelangelo had three proposals for the Pope, and the Pope decided on the cheapest option.

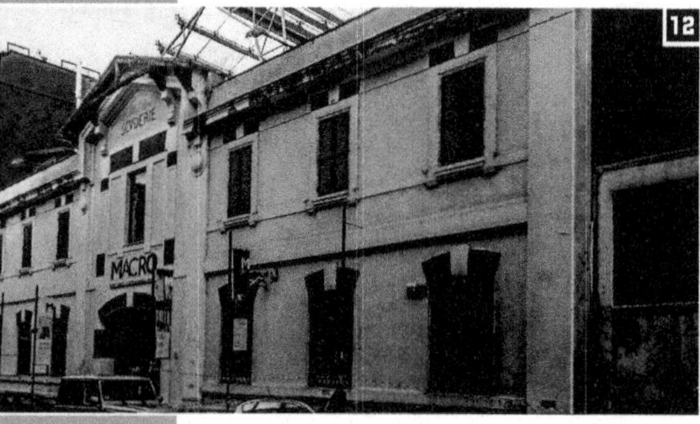

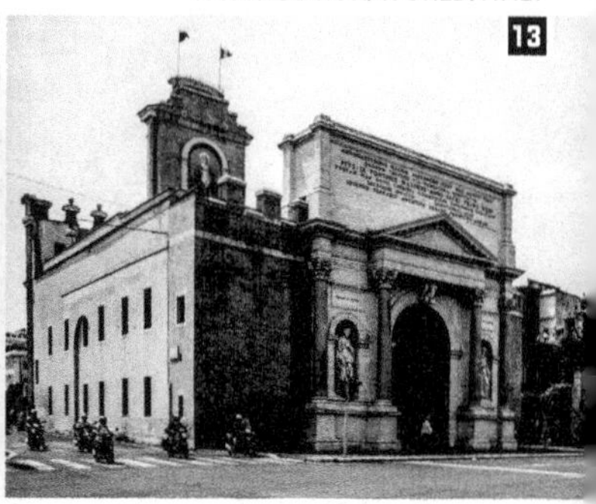

This is Michelangelo's final architectonic achievement. The city gate was commissioned to replace the Antique Porta Nomentana, approximately a 60 ft or 100 m south of Porta Pia. The Italian anti-fascist Gino Lucetti threw a bomb near Porta Pia against Benito Mussolini car on September 11 1926. The assassination failed, however.

◆ Museo Storico dei Bersaglieri | Historical Museum of the Bersaglieri ★

A 60 ft or 100 m north of Porta Pia, Bersaglieri, the elite corps of the Italian Army, breached the Aurelian Wall with their artillery on September 20, 1870, marking the end of the temporal power of the Papal State over Rome, which lasted for 56 years (1815–1871).

The defeated Pope Pius IX retreated into the Vatican calling himself "the Vatican prisoner."

Secular government was passed on to King Victor Emmanuel II (1870–1878) of the House of Savoy.

The monumental grave of the first Italian king is in the Pantheon. September 20, 1870 became the symbolic date of Italian unification. Almost every Italian town has a street called Via Venti Settembre.

This is also why the history museum, Museo Storico dei Bersaglieri (1932), is located at Porta Pia. Museo Storico dei Bersaglieri or

The Historical Museum of the Bersaglieri has documents and reports about Bersaglieri's endeavors. You can also have a look at their firearms, uniforms and medals.

Museo d'Arte Contemporanea di Roma (MACRO) | Museum of Contemporary Art of Rome
Address: Via Nizza 138, Roma
Online: www.museomacro.it

Public transportation:
Bus stop Nomentana – Regina Margherita: 60, 62, 66, 82, 90

Opening hours: *see online*

MACRO Testaccio
Address: Piazza Orazio Giustiniani 4, Roma
Online: www.museomacro.it

Public transportation:
Bus stop Ponte Testaccio: 170, 719, 781

Opening hours: *see online*

Museo Storico dei Bersaglieri | Historical Museum of the Bersaglieri
Address: Piazzale di Porta Pia, Roma

Public transport:
Metro B stop Castro Pretorio

Opening hours: *see on Google Maps*

Outside the City Walls

Colosseo Quadrato – E.U.R.

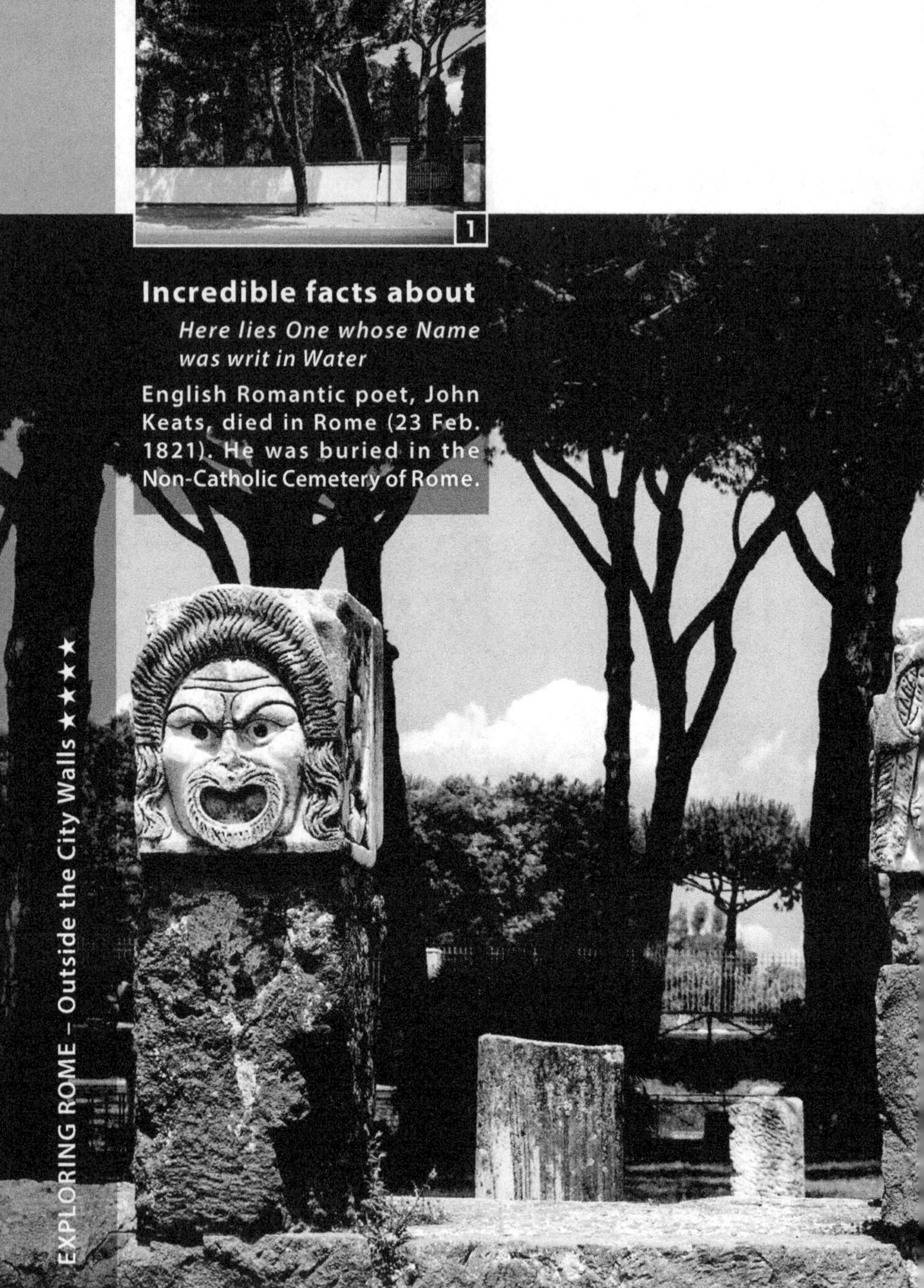

Incredible facts about

Here lies One whose Name was writ in Water

English Romantic poet, John Keats, died in Rome (23 Feb. 1821). He was buried in the Non-Catholic Cemetery of Rome.

Theatrical masks at theater in Ostia Antica

Extra Tip : : :

Ostia Antica has a simple layout. It is neither too big, nor too small. The buildings are in great condition, with the outer walls going as far as three floors – this is the best place to get a glimpse of everyday life in ancient Rome.

On the way to the sea

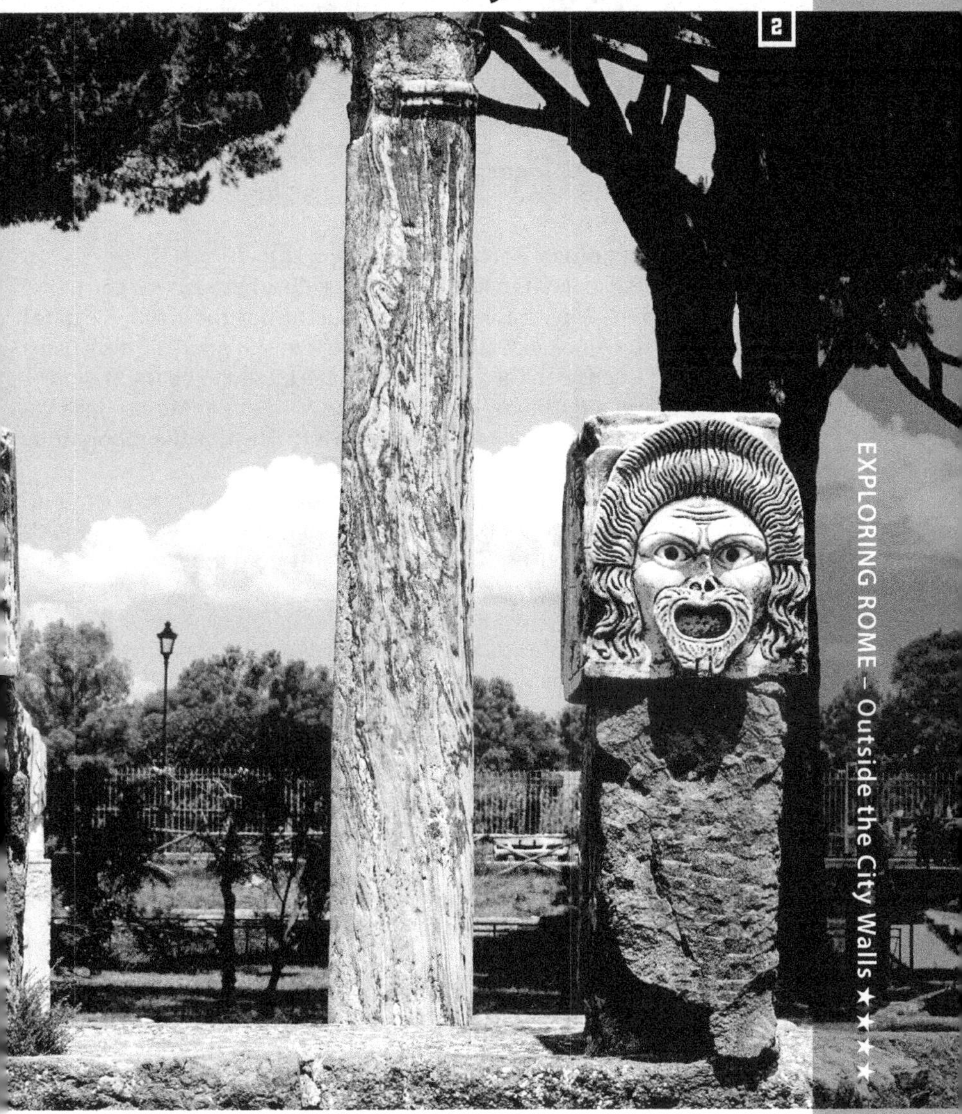

Ostia Antica
Address: Via Caio Cestio 6, Roma
Public transportation: Train FC2 from the Train Station Porta San Paolo to Ostia Antica [p.263]

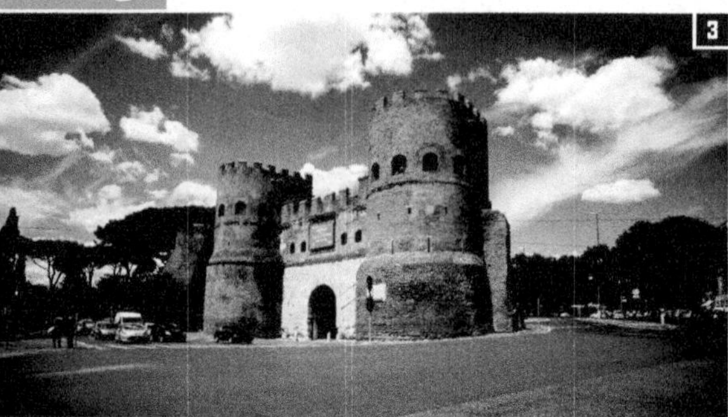

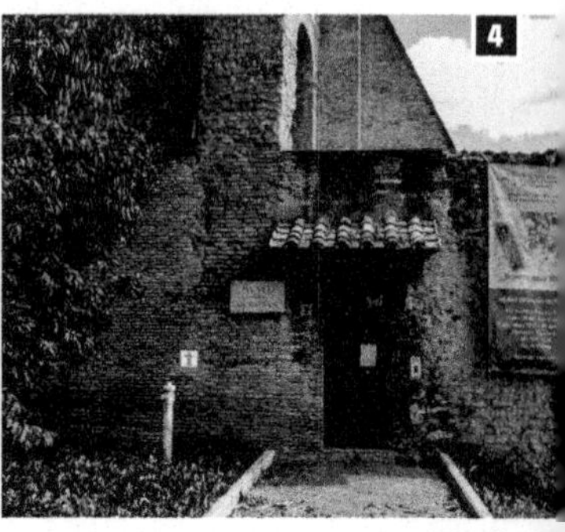

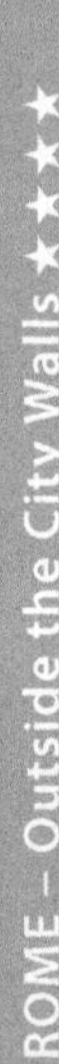

◆ Porta San Paolo or Porta Ostiensis ★ ★ 3

Porta San Paolo got its name in the 6th century because you can find it on the way to the Papal Basilica of Saint Paul Outside the Walls. The gates were part of the Aurelian Walls built around Rome in AD 275. These gates were on Via Ostiense on the way to Ostia, which used to be the city port.

There is also a museum — the Ostiense Museum or Museo della Via Ostiense. The primary goal of this museum is to illustrate the topography between Rome and ancient port of Ostia. 4

There are stone plates with inscriptions and Roman funerary monuments. On the first floor of the Porta San Paolo towers, there are models of ancient Ostia, as well as of the imperial port from the age of Emperor Claudius and Emperor Trajan.

The models are the work of Italo Gismondi, architect and director of Ostia excavations for many years. Another one of his famous models is in the Museum of the Roman Civilization, featuring Rome.

Until fairly recently, both Porta San Paolo and the Pyramid were part of the Aurelian Walls. During the bombardments in 1943, some of the Walls between these two landmarks were destroyed.

◆ Piramide di Caio Cestio | Pyramid of Cestius ★ ★ ★ 5

This is the only pyramid left in Rome, built by praetor and Roman priest Caius Cestius between 18 and 12 BC.

After the Romans conquered Egypt, turning it in one of the provinces in 30 BC, Egyptomania started across the Empire.

Museo della Via Ostiense – Porta San Paolo | St. Paul's Gate and Museum of the Ostian Way
Address: Via Raffaele Persichetti 3, Roma
Online:
www.soprintendenzaspecialeroma.it

Public transportation:
Metro B stop Piramide | Bus stop Piazzale Ostiense: 3B, 118, 769 | Tram stop San Paolo: 8

Opening hours: *see on Google Maps*

Piramide di Caio Cestio | Pyramid of Cestius
Address: Via Raffaele Persichetti, Roma
Online: www.coopculture.it/it/poi/piramide-cestia
Public transportation:
Metro B stop Piramide | Bus stop Piazzale Ostiense: 3B, 118, 769 | Tram stop San Paolo: 8

Opening hours: *see on Google Maps*

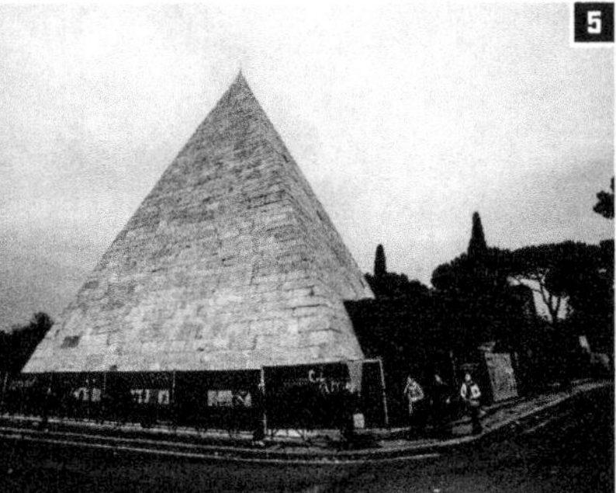

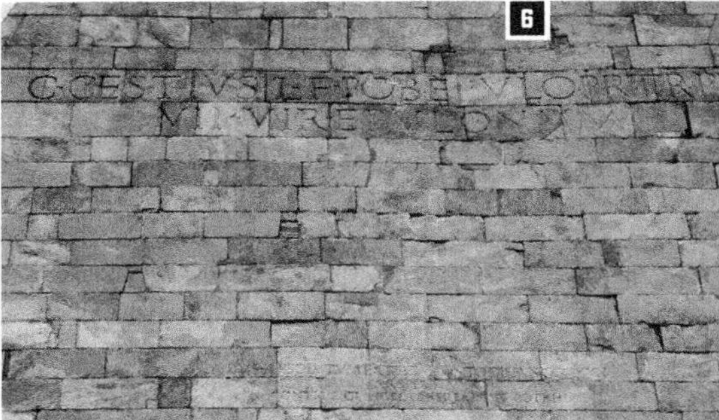

A similar trend occurred in 19th-century Europe after Napoleon's Egyptian campaign. The pyramid is made of brick and enveloped in Carrara marble.

It is 118 ft or 36 m high and 98 ft or 30 m long on each side. Also, there is a tomb inside (13×20 ft or 4×6 m and 16 ft or 5 m high). Fresco remains can also be found, made in the ornate style.

They are chronologically relevant for Roman painting, being the first frescoes of the Third Pompeiian Style. There is a text on the upper part, on the side that is facing the street 🟦6:

C(aius) CESTIUS L(ucii) F(ilius) POB(lilia) EPULO PR(aetor) TR(ibunus) PL(ebis)
VII VIR EPULONUM

G(aius) Cestius, son of L(ucius), of the gens Pob(ilia), member of the College of Epulones, pr(aetor), tr(ibune) of the pl(ebs), septemvir of the Epulones

OPUS APSOLUTUM EX TESTAMENTO DIEBus: CCCXXX ARBITRATU
PONTI P(ublii) F(ilii) CLA(audia) MELAE HEREDIS ET POTHI L(iberti)

The work was completed, in accordance with the will, in 330 days, by the decision of the heir Pontus Mela, son of P(ublius) of the Cla(udia) and Pothus, f(reedman)

Other texts are from the 17th century when the pyramid was restored.

❸ The Non-Catholic Cemetery of Rome ★ ★ 🟦7

The so-called "Protestant Cemetery" is called *Il Cimitero Acattolico di Roma* or The Non-Catholic Cemetery of Rome. All the way until the early 19th century, only Catholics could be buried in Rome, and Jews in certain parts of the city.

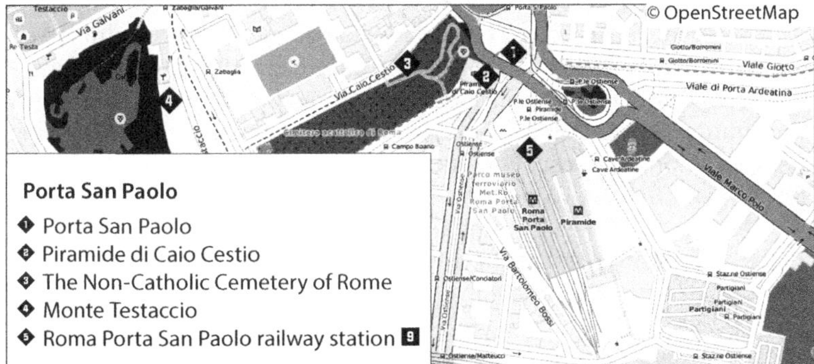

Porta San Paolo

❶ Porta San Paolo
❷ Piramide di Caio Cestio
❸ The Non-Catholic Cemetery of Rome
❹ Monte Testaccio
❺ Roma Porta San Paolo railway station 🟦9

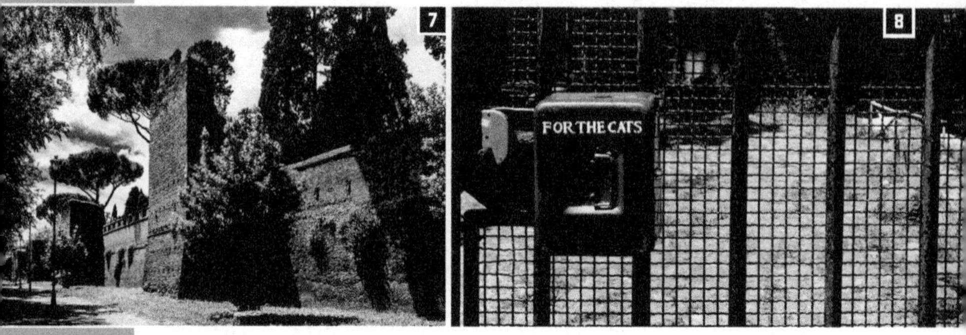

In 1821, this cemetery was opened to bury all the non-Catholics. Poets such as John Keats and Percy Shelley were among the first foreigners buried here. **1**

Many British, Russian, German, American and Italian poets, writers, sculptors, painters, diplomats and scientists were buried in this cemetery, sometimes in extravagantly decorated tombs.

Some say this is the area most densely populated by famous and relevant people in the world.

Others, for instance, Henry James, decided to bury their protagonists here, like he did with Daisy Miller. Oscar Wilde called it the most sacred place in Rome. There are a lot of cats around the cemetery, regularly fed by volunteers. **8**

◆ Monte Testaccio ★

This is an ancient artificial hill, made of 53 million amphorae used for transporting olive oil (140–250). They could hold 70 liters of olive oil and made of sturdy material, used as construction material. When they switched to different amphoras, the old ones were recycled and mixed into the concrete.

The hill is 114 ft or 35 m high, with a 0.6 mile or 1 kilometer diameter. Supposedly, this amphora dumping site was more than 148 ft or 45 m high. According to various oil makers' seals, archaeologists managed to recreate ancient distribution routes. Most of the seals are from Baetica, a Roman province on the south of Spain.

◆ Centrale Montemartini ★ ★ ★

One of the most recent and exciting Roman museums is Centrale Montemartini, which is actually part of the Capitoline Museums. It is located not that far from the Basilica Papale San Paolo fuori le Mura. The story of the strangest archaeological museum in the world started in 1997, when the exhibition "The machines and the gods" was organized in the former power plant Giovanni Montemartini. **10**

Between turbines and steam engines, workers and engineers were replaced by Roman statues from the Republican period, over 400 of them in total.

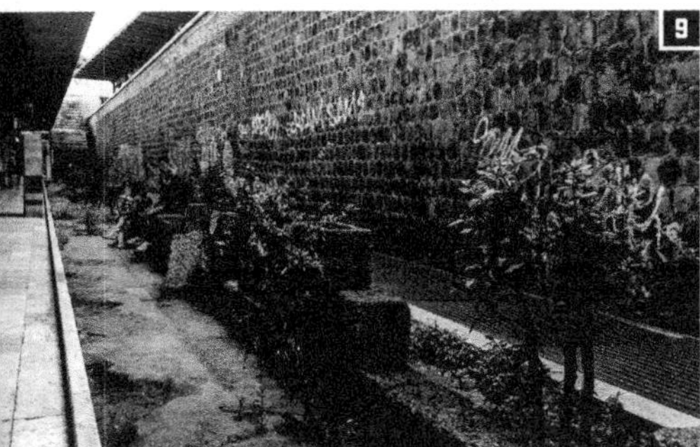

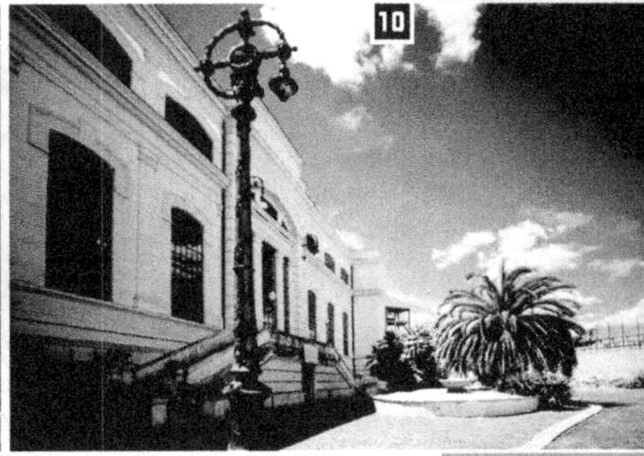

Archaeological artifacts are organized according to origin and grouped according to theme.

There are three main groups:

▸ "Column hall" with exhibits from the Roman Republic,

▸ Central hall or the "Machine room", with artifacts excavated in central Rome (Circus Flaminius, Temple of Apollo Sosianus, Capitoline Hill, Largo di Torre Argentina, Theater of Pompey),

▸ "Boiler-house" with various objects and mosaics from imperial residences, the Domus and gardens.

The impossible combination of dehumanizing industrial machinery and artistic masterpieces leaves everyone speechless.

◆ **Basilica Papale di San Paolo fuori le Mura | The Papal Basilica of Saint Paul Outside the Walls ★ ★ ★ ★ 11**

Since this basilica is situated outside Aurelian Walls, the toponym is part of its name.

The construction started under Emperor Constantine on the same place where, according to a legend, St. Paul was buried in AD 67.

You can read about this extraordinary basilica in the chapter Pilgrim's Rome [p.274].

Cimitero Acattolico di Roma | The Non-Catholic Cemetery of Rome (Protestant Cemetery)
Address: Via Caio Cestio, 6, Roma
Online: www.cemeteryrome.it

Public transportation:
Metro B stop Piramide | Bus stop Piazzale Ostiense: 3B, 118, 769 | Tram stop San Paolo: 8

Opening hours: *see online*

Did you know?

Centrale Montemartini

The powerplant's engine rooms with turbines and smell of grease and oil were left intact in 1963.

Ever since 1912, they were used to turn diesel fuel into electrical power.

The fascist regime acquired it in 1930 and Benito Mussolini opened it in 1933 as the focal point that was supposed to breathe life into his lifelong project — E.U.R., a modern settlement created for the World Expo in 1942, the highest example of an ideal fascist city of tomorrow.

Centrale Montemartini
Address: Via Ostiense 106, Roma
Online:
www.centralemontemartini.org/en

Public transportation:
Metro B stop Garbatella

Opening hours: *see online*

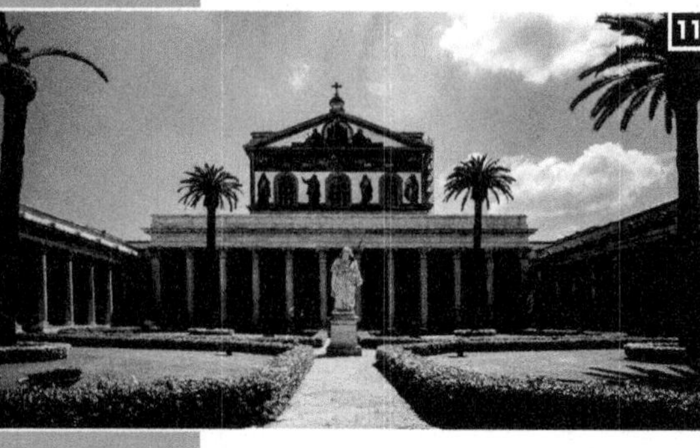

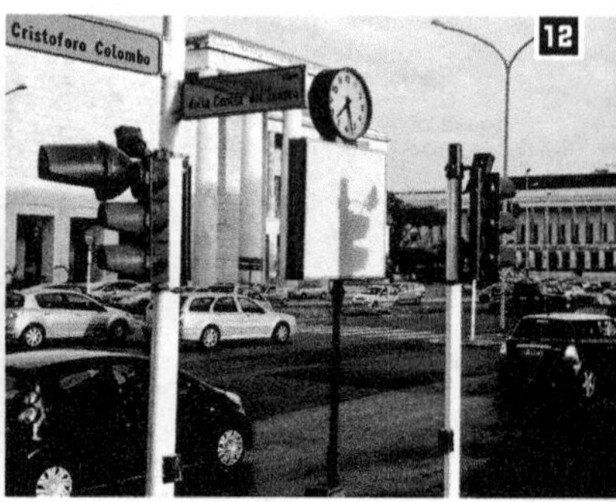

❼ E.U.R. ★★★

Esposizione **U**niversale di **R**oma is the only part of Rome that was built entirely during Mussolini's fascist regime (1922–1943).

The suburb was completed in 1942 to host the World Expo. However, due to World War II, the Expo never took place. E.U.R. is extremely interesting not only from a historical perspective, but also as a reflection of fascist ideology. Visions of fascist architecture collide with ancient Roman and early 20th-century Italian art. Of course, neither ancient Roman art nor the Metaphysical Movement headed by

Basilica Papale di San Paolo fuori le Mura | The Papal Basilica of Saint Paul Outside the Walls
Address: Piazzale San Paolo 1, Roma
Online:
www.basilicasanpaolo.org/en

Public transportation:
Metro B stop Basilica San Paolo | Bus stop Via Ostiense – San Paolo: 23, 769 | Train FC2 Station S. Paolo

Opening hours: *see online*

From Rome to the E.U.R.
Public transportation:
Metro B stop E.U.R. Fermi or stop E.U.R. Palasport | Train FC2 stop E.U.R. Magliana

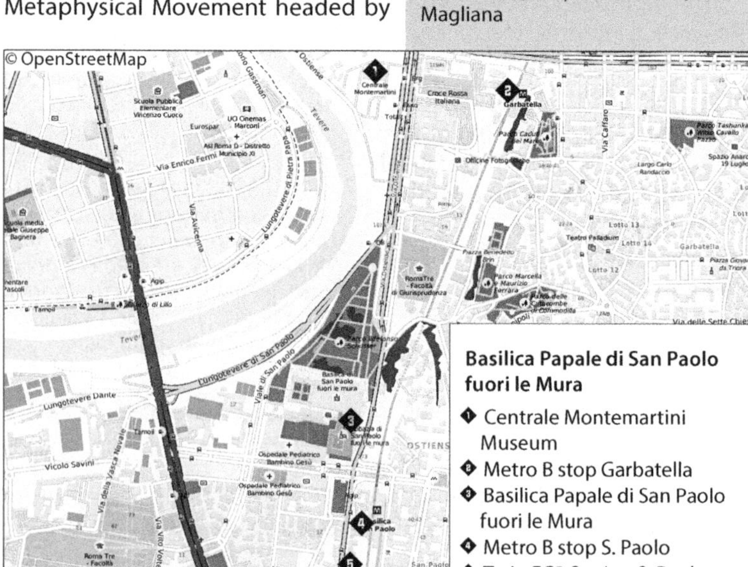

Basilica Papale di San Paolo fuori le Mura

❶ Centrale Montemartini Museum
❷ Metro B stop Garbatella
❸ Basilica Papale di San Paolo fuori le Mura
❹ Metro B stop S. Paolo
❺ Train FC2 Station S. Paolo

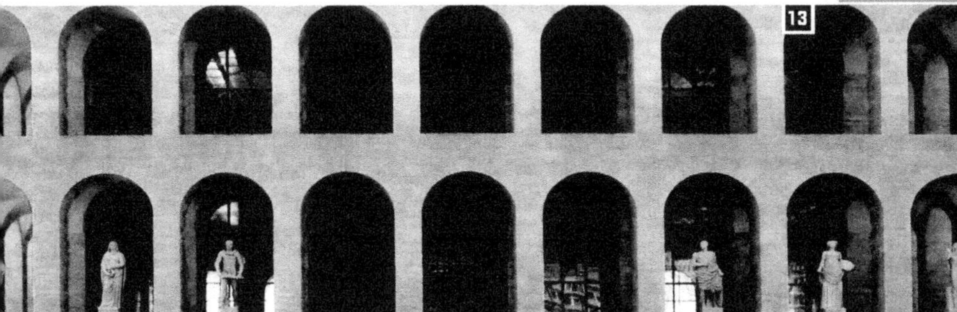

Giorgio de Chirico are in any way responsible for interpretations introduced by Mussolini's architects. E.U.R. has the layout of a Roman imperial settlement. It has two main orthogonal streets, just like any other main street in a new Roman city: *Cardo Maximus* and *Decumanus Maximus*. In E.U.R., Cardo Maximus as the principal traffic artery going from north to south is called Via Cristoforo Colombo. **12** This wide avenue goes to the Aurelian Walls, parallel to Via Ostiense, that goes all the way to the sea.

According to Mussolini's plans, Rome was supposed to expand towards the sea and the Mediterranean Sea was intended to become the internal sea of the new, Italian empire, as it once was during the Roman Empire. Under Mussolini's regime, Marcello Piacentini was what Albert Speer was to Hitler — the chief architect for megalomaniac ideas of the great leader.

Piacentini followed the fascist doctrine of mythological heroism to the last detail, interpreting Roman imperial architecture without any sensibility for human proportions or individualism. Roman columns turned into barren bars without capitals, base or curvatures, so tall that their shadows could cover enormous squares, while people seemed like ants in comparison.

This also happens to be one of the most striking visual effects of *Pittura metafisica*, a movement in Italian painting from the 1920's. Nevertheless, while the long shadows in Giorgio de Chirico's paintings depict loneliness of an individual, Piacentini and his architects celebrate the mythical grandeur of Italian nationalism. One way or another, when you walk through E.U.R., you will feel like you are walking through one of de Chirico's painting or at least as if you have stepped into the twilight zone on a summer afternoon.

Today, E.U.R. is an elite business and residential part of Rome. Buildings devoid of any need to accommodate people and express individualism have become ideal locations for global corporate headquarters. Spacious parks, as well as a large artificial lake as wide as E.U.R. itself, is populated by everything you could wish for while running away from the busy city — joggers, pedestrians and a lot of couples in love.

◇ **Palazzo della Civiltà Italiana or Colosseo Quadrato ★ ★ 13**

This surreal building is at the end of Viale della Civiltà del Lavoro. Originally, it was meant to host an all-encompassing exhibition of Italian civilization, with fascism as the high point.

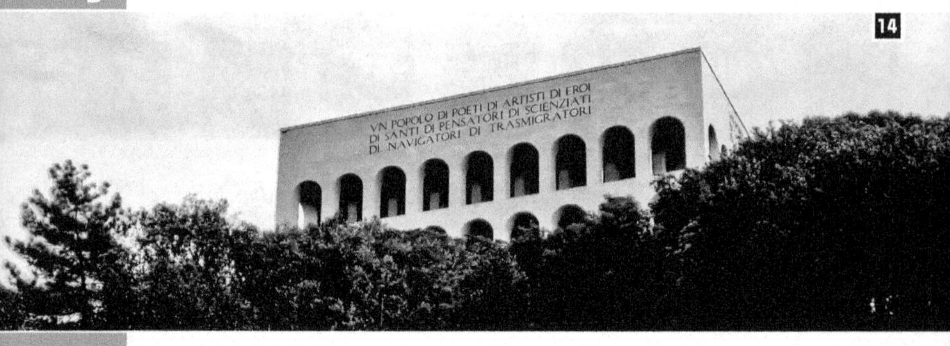

The palace is enveloped in travertine marble, like palaces from the Augustan period. Mussolini gladly identified himself with the first Roman emperor Augustus. Similar to the Colosseum, this imposing structure has a series of loggias, nine in each row and six in each column on every side.

In this way, they can also spell the great leader's name – Benito (6) Mussolini (9). The building is 223 ft or 68 m high. In front of the building, there is a huge mythological statue on each corner. They represent Castor and Pollux with their horses, Zeus and Leda. There are 28 statues above the base of the building, each being around 11.48 ft or 3.5 m high, made of Carrara marble.

They are illustrations of various human endeavors, a visual representation of the pamphlet written on top of the building, glorifying the Italian nation:

UN POPOLO DI POETI DI ARTISTI DI EROI
DI SANTI DI PENSATORI DI SCIENZIATI
DI NAVIGATORI DI TRASMIGRATORI

People of poets, artists, heroes,
saints, thinkers, scientists,
seamen, travelers

Basilica dei Santi Pietro e Paolo a Via Ostiense ★

Unlike German national-socialism, Italian fascism maintained good relations with the Catholic Church. This church was supposed to be the main symbol on the 1942 World Expo and to promote the Catholic Church around the world. The church was finished only after the war. The 236 ft or 72 m high dome of the church is the third largest in the city. To the left and right of the entrance are statues of Peter and Paul made by Domenico Ponzi and Francesco Nagni.

Museo della Civiltà Romana | Museum of Roman Civilization ★ ★

If you want to have a closer look at all 623 ft or 190 m of relief from Trajan's Column, you will have to go to the Museum of the Roman Civilization or Museo della Civiltà Romana. Not only will you see the complete casts from Trajan's Column, but also the most famous and precise model of Ancient Rome in 1:250 ratio, meticulously put together by Italo Gismondi over the period of 35 years.

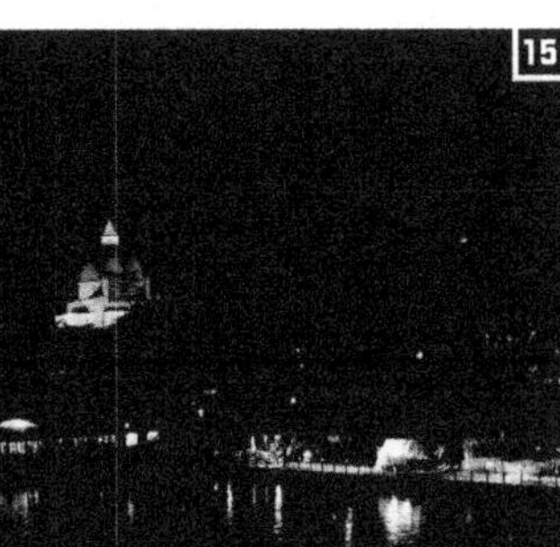

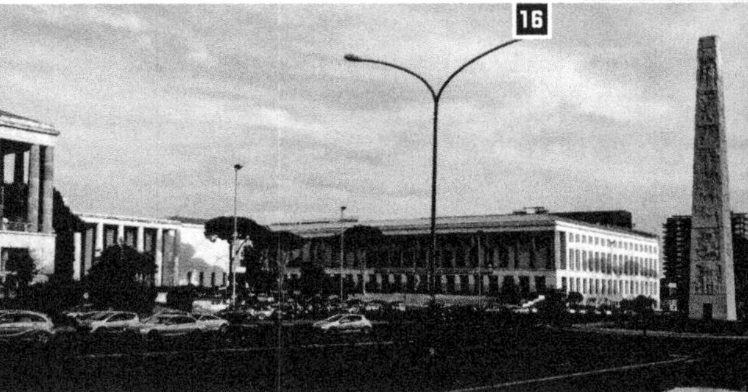

◇ Museo Nazionale dell'Alto Mediosevo | National Museum of the Early Middle Ages ★ ★ ★

Museo Nazionale dell'Alto Medioevo is dedicated to a period between 4th and 9th century, one of the most dramatic eras in Roman history. The grandiose *opus sectile* floor from Porta Marina (around AD 390) in Ostia Antica can be found here. Opus sectile is a technique used to combine multi-colored pieces of marble to create a visual effect. Unlike mosaic, the pieces are much larger. In the Middle Ages (12th – 13th century) members of the Cosmati family passed on this tradition from one generation to the next and managed to preserve it.

Basilica dei Santi Pietro e Paolo
Address: Piazzale dei Santi Pietro e Paolo a Via Ostiense 8, Roma
Online: www.santipietroepaoloroma.it

Public transportation: Bus stop Santi Pietro e Paolo – Europa 709

Opening hours: *see online*

Museo della Civiltà Romana | Museum of Roman Civilization
Address: Piazza Giovanni Agnelli 10, Roma
Online:
www.museociviltaromana.it/en

Public transportation: Metro B stop E.U.R. Fermi or stop E.U.R. Palasport | Bus stop Museo Civilta' Romana: 703, 703L, 707, 767, C8

Opening hours: *see online*

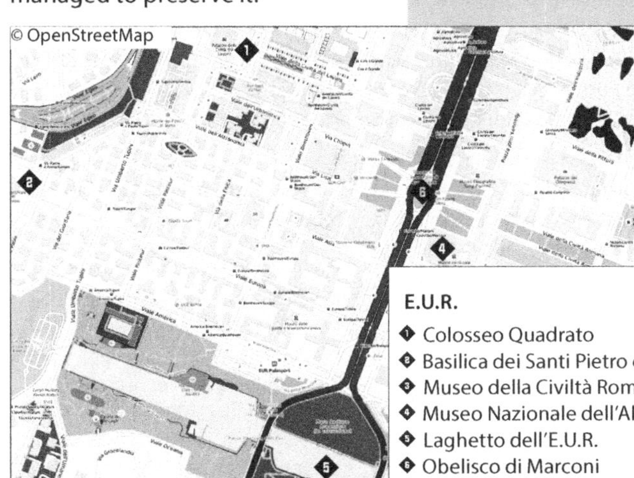

E.U.R.

- ❶ Colosseo Quadrato
- ❷ Basilica dei Santi Pietro e Paolo
- ❸ Museo della Civiltà Romana
- ❹ Museo Nazionale dell'Alto Medioevo
- ❺ Laghetto dell'E.U.R.
- ❻ Obelisco di Marconi

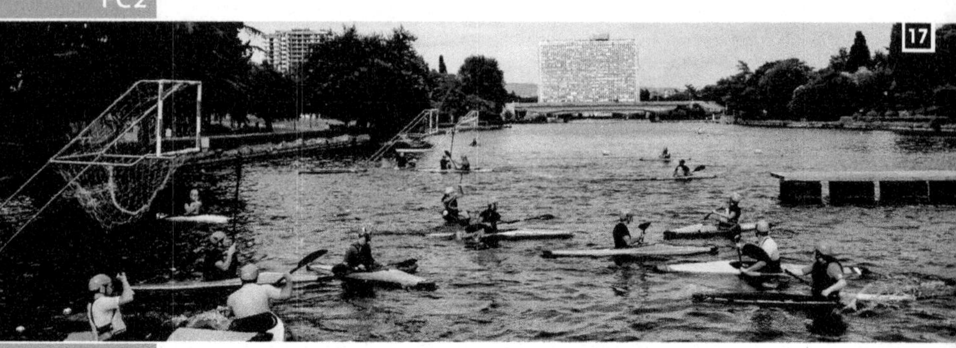

▸ **Room I** – Late Antique imperial portraits from 4th and 5th century, and a golden-leafed fibula.

▸ **Rooms II and III** – Finds from Lombardy from 166 graves in Nocera Umbra (Perugia) and 237 graves near Castel Trosino in Ascoli Piceno. Various and rich assortment of jewelry and everyday items from women's graves, weapons and horse gear from men's graves.

▸ **Rooms IV and V** – Marble and ceramic items from the Caroline era (8th and 9th century) found during excavation at the Roman Forum.

▸ **Rooms VI and VII** – Marble and ceramic finds from the surrounding Roman area with floor mosaics from the early Middle Ages.

▸ **Room VIII** – Coptic textiles and Egyptian reliefs (5th – 10th century), from the late Roman period all the way to the early Islamic era.

If you find yourself in E.U.R., this museum is definitely worth a visit.

⑤ Laghetto dell'E.U.R. ★ ★

There are two Metro stops in E.U.R. – E.U.R. Palasport and E.U.R. Fermi on the shore of this artificial lake, perfect for rowing and other recreational activities.

Pass Via Cristoforo Colombo to get to the other, greener side of E.U.R. Go to the lake shore and take a nice walk. **17** You will be accompanied by ducks, couples and other passersby. There is Salon Giolitti on the end of the lake, the only other ice cream store of the Giolitti family, the other one is next to the Pantheon. It is less crowded here, the terrace is gorgeous and the ice cream is just as delicious as the one next to the Pantheon. [p.94]

◆ Ostia Antica ★ ★ ★ ★ **2**

Ostia Antica is one of the best preserved Roman towns in general. Here, more than anywhere else, you can really grasp what life was like in a Roman town.

Houses for rent, stores, wheat warehouses, bakeries, baths, taverns, theater **19**, temples, brothels, public toilets, fishmonger's, everything has been preserved thanks to the swampy,

Museo Nazionale dell'Alto Medio-evo | National Museum of the Early Middle Ages

Address: Viale Lincoln 3, Roma

Online: https://museocivilta.cultura. gov.it/prepara-la-visita

Public transportation:
Metro B stop E.U.R. Fermi or stop E.U.R. Palasport | Bus stop Colombo – Marconi: 714, 791

Opening hours: *see on Google Maps*

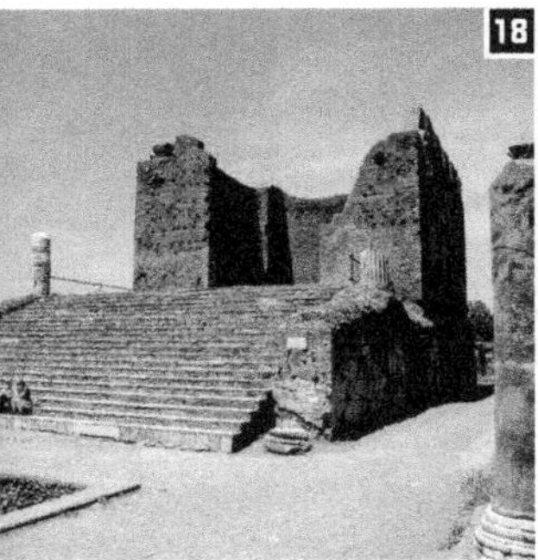

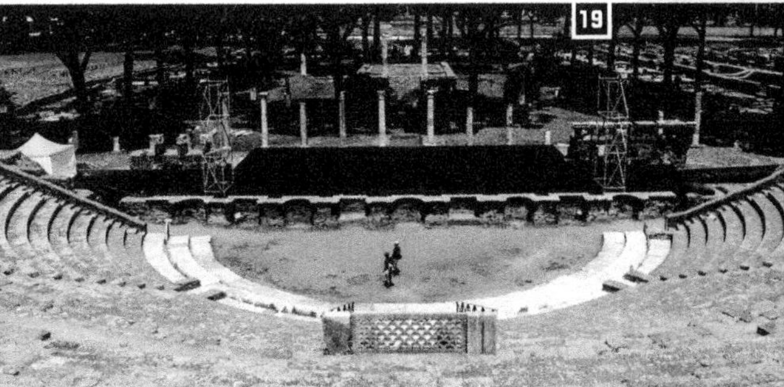

malaria-infested area, which kept everything just as it was. Today, it is no longer a swamp. Ostia Antica developed around the main Roman harbor. Its population in 2nd century was around 50,000 people and 17,000 of them were slaves. **23**

Ostia Antica is 14 mil or 23 km away from the center of Rome. Even though Ostia Antica was built on the mouth of the Tiber, sand and dirt alluviated the river mouth, so the sea was getting pulled further and further away from Ostia even in ancient days.

This is why a new Roman harbor started operating in AD 54 called Portus. The port authority was still based in Ostia until AD 314. It was only after AD 314 that Portus was raised to the status of *colonia*, and both settlements were joined to form Portus Romae.

As far as Christian tradition is concerned, Ostia had a bishop. Monica, St. Augustine's mother died in Ostia in 387 on her way to North Africa, mentioned by St. Augustine of Hippo in his *Confessiones*.

Did you know?

From Rome to the sea with FC2 train

▸ Piramide / Porta San Paolo (Metro B) **9**

▸ Basilica San Paolo (Metro B)

▸ E.U.R. Magliana (Metro B)

▸ Tor di Valle

▸ Vitinia

▸ Casal Bernocchi

▸ Acilia

▸ Ostia Antica

▸ Lido Nord

▸ Lido Centro

▸ Stella Polare

▸ Castel Fusano

▸ Cristoforo Colombo

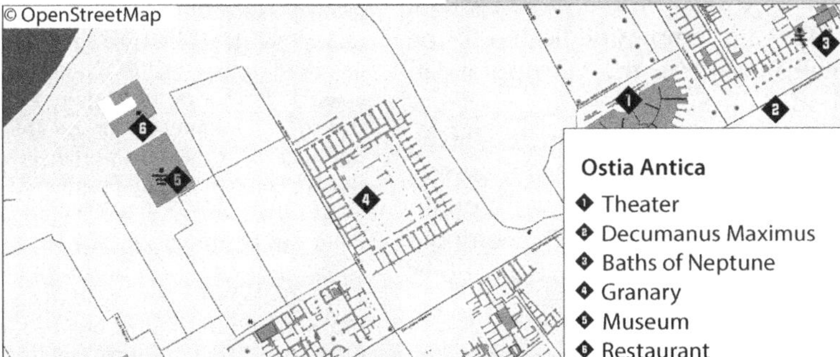

As Rome's population was decreasing, so was the relevance of Ostia. There were around 1.5 million people living in Rome in 3rd century BC. Two centuries later, the number shrank to 100,000, with only 15,000 people living in Rome in the Middle Ages.

The harbor became less and less relevant and the entire mouth of the Tiber was gradually turning into a swamp. This is why malaria broke out in the Ostia Antica area.

Ostia Antica was where foreigners from distant lands stepped on European soil for the first time. Commercial and naval associations from all over the empire gravitated towards this place. 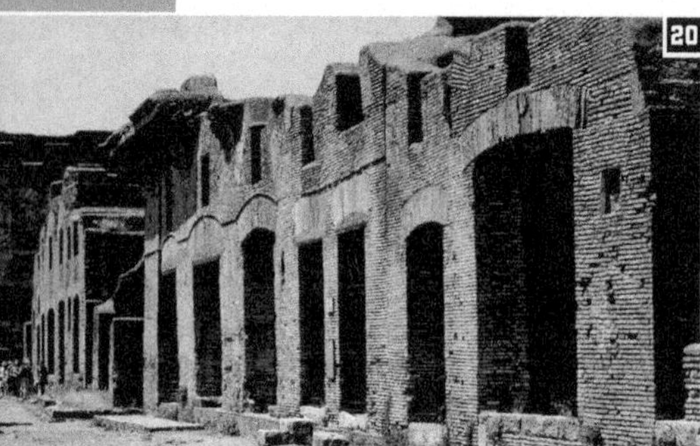 Merchants and seamen from the Black Sea, Mesopotamia, Asia Minor, the Middle East and Africa lived here for generations.

Among other temples, one of the first synagogues outside Palestine was discovered here, even before Titus pillaged the Temple of Jerusalem. There are temples dedicated to the cult of Mithras, the Mesopotamian god of the Sun.

After Octavian conquered Egypt, the largest wheat-producing country on the Mediterranean was brought under the Roman rule. They brought along their own gods, like Osiris, Horus and Isis.

Did you know?

Ostia was the harbour city of the Ancient Rome

During the Roman Empire, this was an extremely important port for Rome. Most of the wheat was imported from Egypt through this harbor. The second largest import was olive oil. 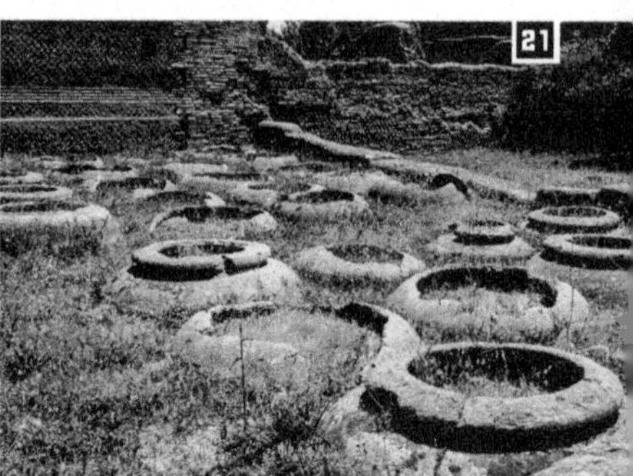 We know from the artificial hill of Monte Testaccio near Porta San Paolo the sort of vast quantities they were trading with.

Did you know?

Wheat as a key political issue

Giving away wheat to the people of Rome was a crucial thing, both socially and politically. An emperor that could not provide enough wheat for his citizens could face rebellions, civil unrest and be dethroned. Rome is well-known for its political cruelty. Prominent politicians, generals, their families and even distant relatives could be slaughtered for political gain. All this speaks volumes about the importance of the main city port in the Roman Empire. Caserma dei Vigili, Ostia City Guard and Fire Department was disproportionately large compared to the size of the city. This is because no one could risk a fire stopping the supply of wheat for the capital of the Roman Empire.

EXPLORING ROME – Outside the City Walls ★★★★

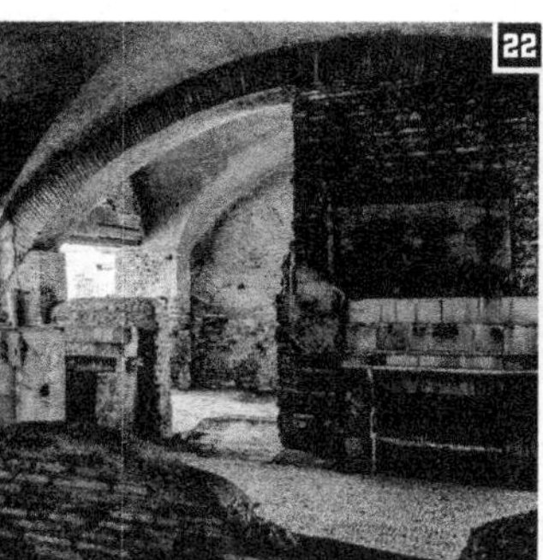

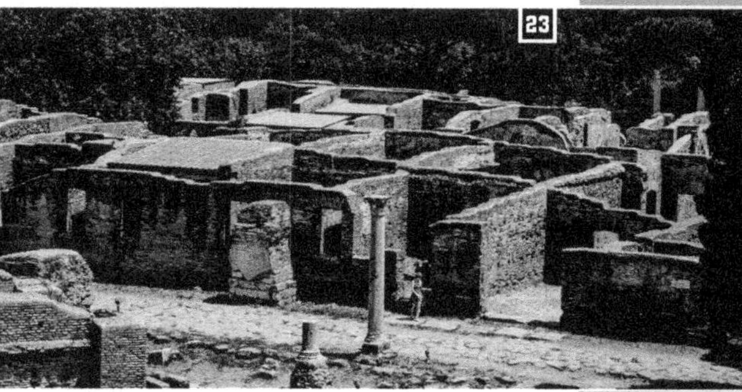

Some of the temples found in Ostia were dedicated to these gods who soon joined gods of the Greek and Roman pantheon. The most important temples in Ostia are on the Capitoline Hill.

They honor the official gods of the state: Jupiter, Juno, Minerva and the goddess Roma. As a large and wealthy Roman city, Ostia had many baths. They were encrusted with marble and decorated with mosaics and sculptures. Mosaics are especially beautiful, mostly black and white, that is, black figures on a white surface. They are still on their original location. The city theater takes central position on the Decumanus Maximus, one of two high streets. It was built during Emperor Augustus by his loyal associate Agrippa.

As a Roman port, Ostia flourished during the Augustan period, after Augustus conquered Egypt in 30 BC and solved the problem of wheat supply for centuries to come.

The city had a Forum, Curia, Basilica **18**, big grain tanks, a shopping mall, Piazzale delle Corporazioni, right next to the theater and a well-organized fire department.

Private palaces, rental houses, workshops, bakeries and restaurants **22** are all excellently preserved.

Ostia Antica vs Pompeii or Herculaneum

Apart from the fascinating streets, there is very little left in Pompeii. Anything of any value was taken away from Pompeii to the National Archaeological Museum in Naples or it is closed to the public. If you go to Pompeii anytime between May and October, the heat will definitely kill any enjoyment you may find while trying to decipher Italian names and Roman signs on the streets of Pompeii.

There are few places in the world with so many desperate people holding on to maps and looking utterly lost. Therefore, do not go to Pompeii without the proper clothes, shoes, hat or sunshade, a decent guidebook and lots of water. **25**

Ostia Antica
Address: Via Caio Cestio, 6, Roma
Online:
www.ostiaantica.beniculturali.it/en

Public transportation:
Metro B stop Piramide | Bus stop Piazzale Ostiense 3B, 118, 769 | Tram stop Piazzale Ostiense: 3 to Train FC2 Station Porta San Paolo to Station Ostia Antica (35 min)

Opening hours: *see online*

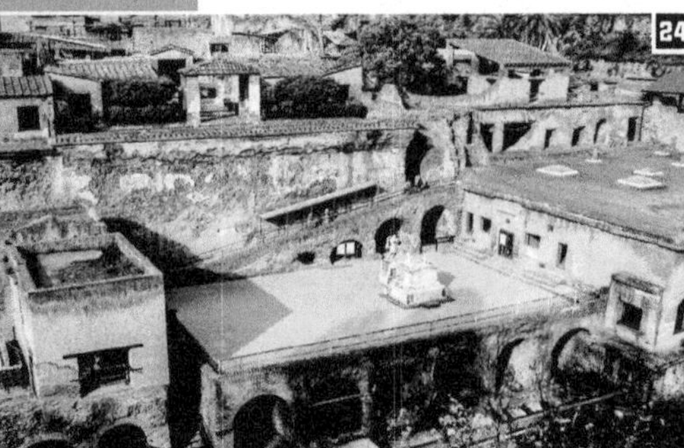

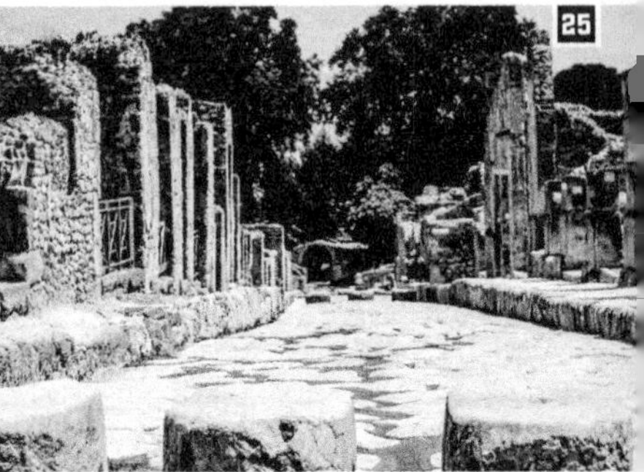

If you go to Herculaneum, the situation is looking up. There are original mosaics still in the houses and the houses are practically intact. Then again, the Neapolitan Commuter Trains with many pickpockets but without air conditioning is not everyone's cup of tea.

Ostia Antica has a simple layout. It is neither too big, nor too small. The buildings are in great condition, with the outer walls going as far as three floors. This is the best place to get a glimpse of everyday life in ancient Rome. Moreover, numerous pine trees will add a lovely flavor to the whole experience, making it quite unforgettable.

Castello di Giulio II ★ ★

There was a fort built by the order of Pope Julius II in the 15th century, and it is still here. It was meant to control the little traffic that occurred. However, in 1557 the Great Flood changed the flow of the Tiber, so the fort lost all purpose. At the roof top you will find a nice café and one of the best views of the St. Peter's Basilica.

Lido di Ostia ★ ★ ★

Beaches at Lido di Ostia are crowded during the summer months and are full of deck chairs and sunbeds that you have to rent. Stella Polare stop is the favorite one. With the station at your back, walk in a straight line for about 550 yd or 500 m, and you are at the see.

Castello di Giulio II or Rocca di Ostia
Address: Piazza della Rocca, 13, Roma
Online:
www.ostiaantica.beniculturali.it/en

Public transportation:
Train FC2 Station Porta San Paolo to Station Ostia Antica (35 min)

Opening hours: *see online*

EXPLORING ROME – Outside the City Walls ★ ★ ★

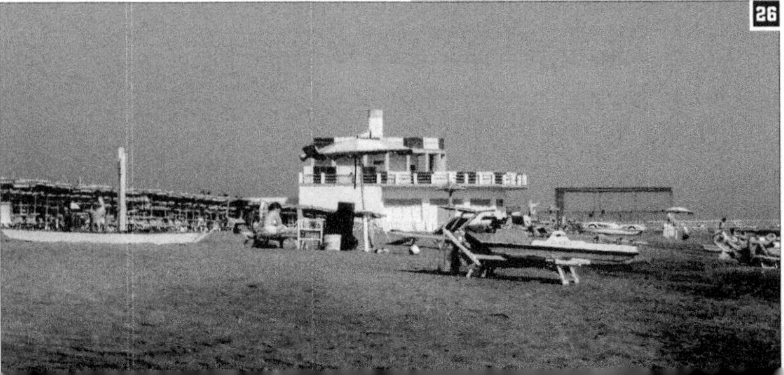

Pilgrim's Rome

Cloister of the monastery of San Paolo fuori le Mura

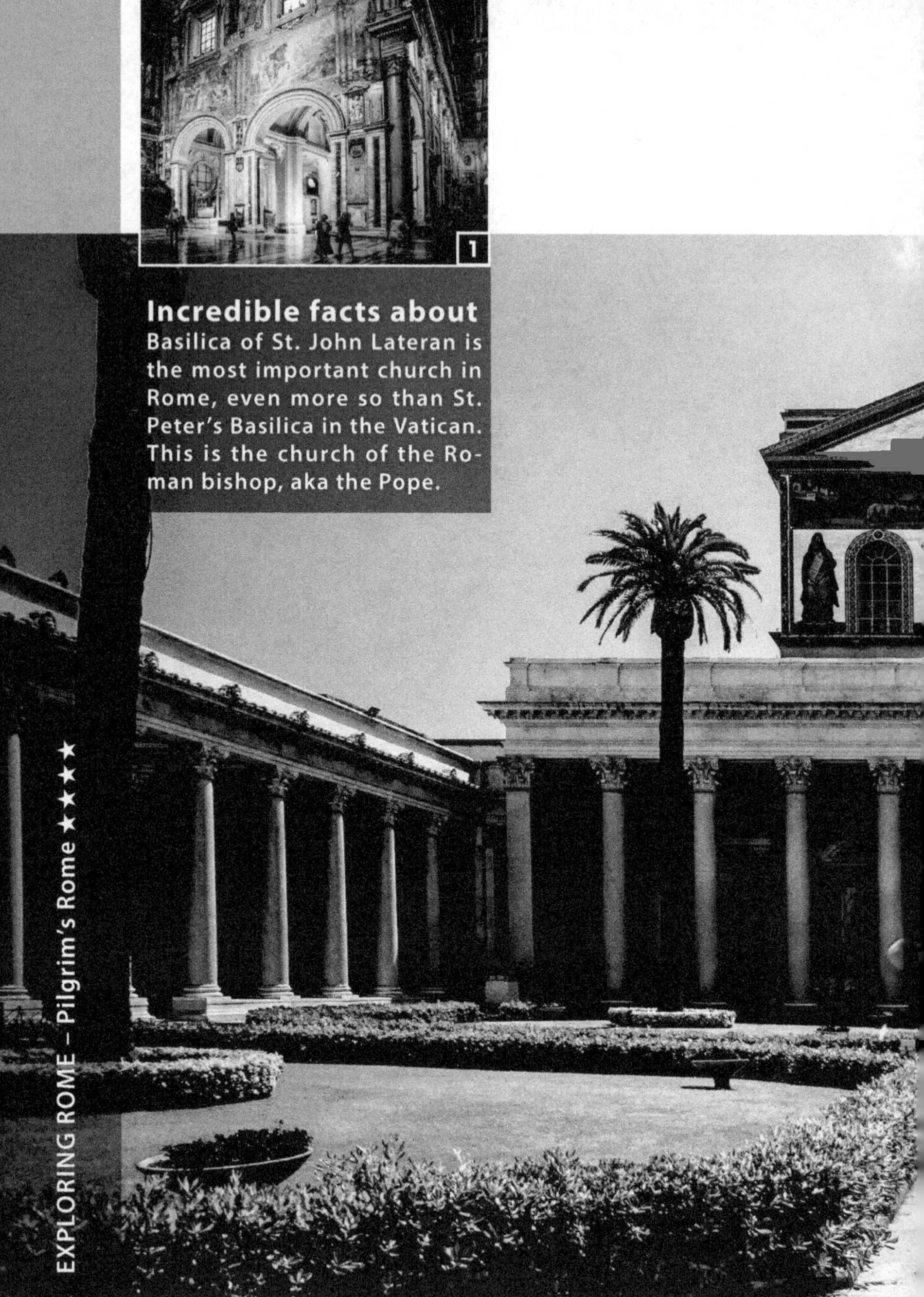

Incredible facts about

Basilica of St. John Lateran is the most important church in Rome, even more so than St. Peter's Basilica in the Vatican. This is the church of the Roman bishop, aka the Pope.

Basilica Papale di San Paolo fuori le Mura

Extra Tip : : :

If you still have trouble picturing the size of a real imperial basilica from the Roman Forum, the Papal Basilica of Saint Paul Outside the Walls can help you with that, it is as close as it gets to a real imperial basilica in terms of proportions and layout.

Seven pilgrim churches of Rome

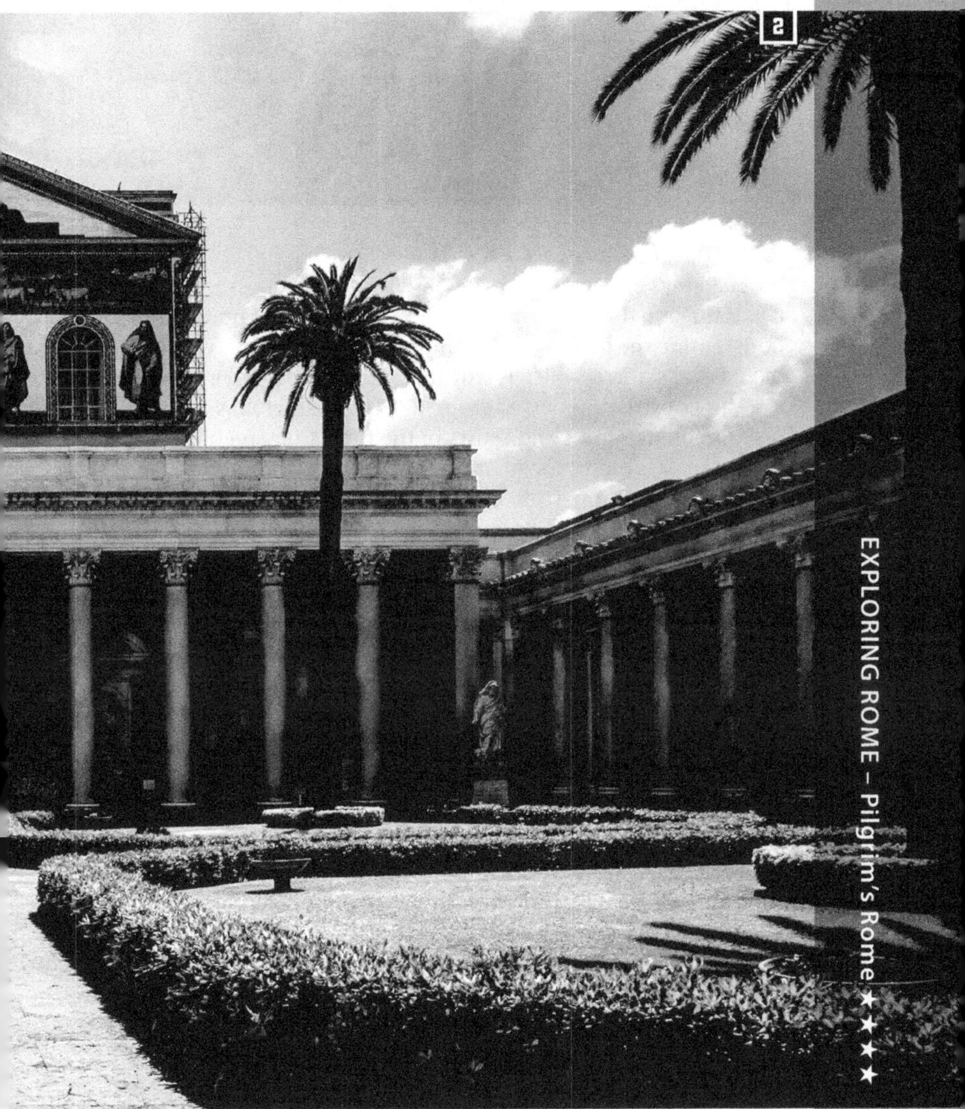

Basilica Papale di San Paolo fuori le Mura
Address: Piazzale San Paolo 1, Roma
Public transportation: Metro B stop Basilica San Paolo | Bus stop Via Ostiense – San Paolo: 23, 769 | Train FC2 Station S. Paolo

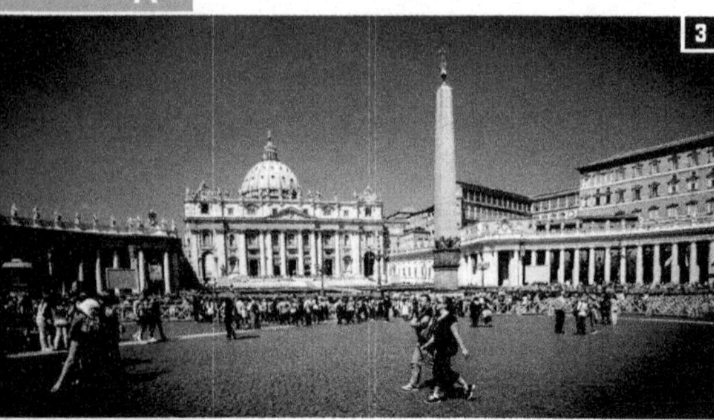

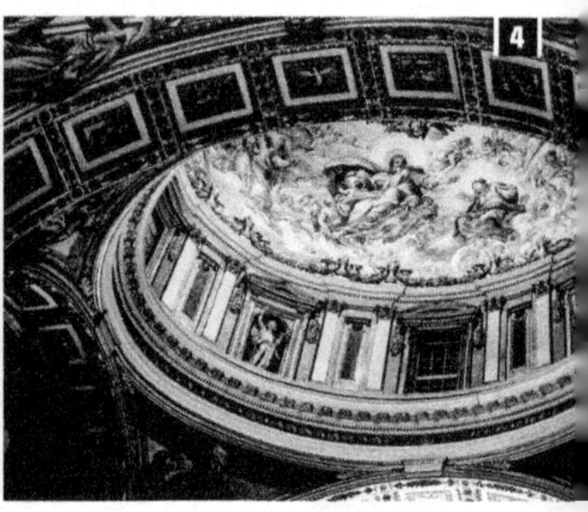

❶ St. Peter's Basilica ★★★★ 3

St. Peter's Basilica is the largest and also the longest church in the world. It was built on the foundations of the old St. Peter's Church from 326, while Constantine the Great was the emperor. Allegedly, this is also the location of St. Peter's grave, which is why this spot was chosen in the first place.

The construction lasted from 1506 to 1626. It was built by the most prominent architects and artists of the time. Chief architects and interior designers were employed, including Donato Bramante, Raphael Santi, Michelangelo Buonarroti, Giacomo Vignola, Carlo Maderno, Francesco Borromini and Lorenzo Bernini. 4

Pope Julius II placed the foundation stone in 1506 below what was to become the base of Veronica's Column. The most valuable relic of the Catholic Church was meant to be stored in it, Veronica's veil.

According to a legend, Veronica gave Jesus her veil, he wiped his face during the Way of Cross and his face was imprinted on the veil. You can read more about this extraordinary building in the chapter about Vatican City State [p.134].

❷ Basilica di San Giovanni in Laterano | Basilica of Saint John Lateran ★★★★ 5

This is the most important church in Rome, even more so than St. Peter's Basilica in the Vatican. This is the church of the Roman bishop, aka the Pope. Since each cardinal is the head of one Roman church, the same goes for the Pope — Pope is the Roman bishop and this is his titular church.

This means that this is also the Roman cathedral, and the throne of the Roman bishop is in the apside of this church. The full title of the church on the façade establishes its dominant position among all Catholic church across the world:

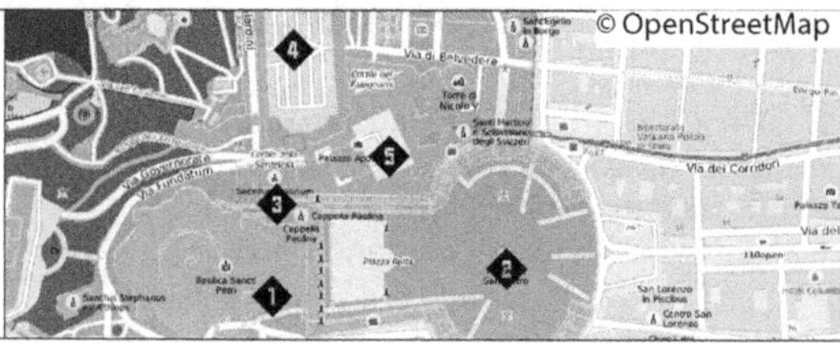

Vatican City State

- ❶ St. Peter's Basilica
- ❷ St. Peter's Square
- ❸ Sistine chapel
- ❹ Vatican Museums
- ❺ Apostolic Palace

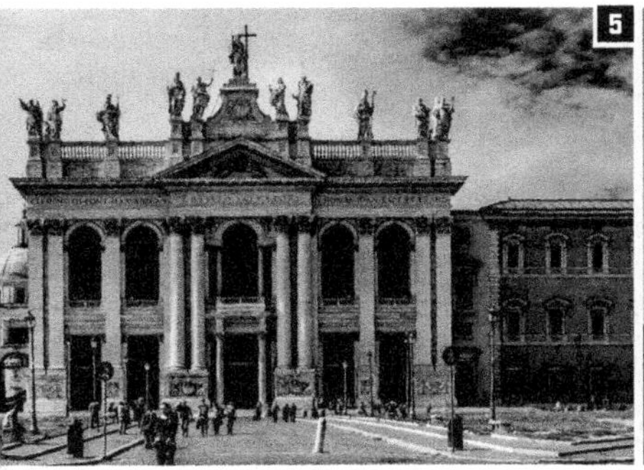

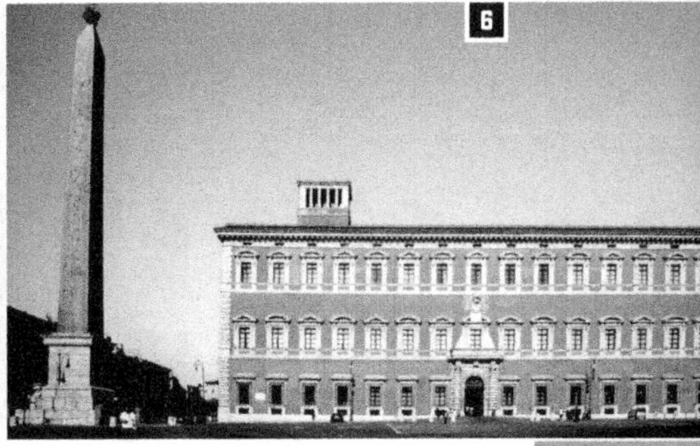

Sacrosancta Lateranensis ecclesia omnium urbis et orbis ecclesiarum mater et caput

Most Holy Lateran Church, of all the churches in the city and the world, the mother and head

The church has five naves. The legend has it that Emperor Constantine had it built in the 4th century and this is also where he was baptized. Over the centuries, the church suffered many blows — it was sacked by the Visigoths in 455, there was an earthquake in 897 and a fire in 1307 and 1361, to name a few. Nevertheless, it always found a way to rise from the ashes, so practically nothing of what we can see today belonged to the original church.

Façade 6 7

The monumental, classicist façade was made by Alexander Galilei in the 18th century.

The bronze doors

The original bronze doors of the Curia Julia or the Senate House were transferred 1660 to the Basilica of St. John Lateran by Pope Alexander VII. 9

Interior of the Basilica

As you can see when you walk into the basilica, the interior does not match the so-called "Golden Basilica", a name given to the original structure. However, architecture and decoration are still very rich. 10 The church was designed by Francesco Borromini at the request of Pope Innocent X. Left of the entrance, there is a sculpture of Emperor Constantine, who was the first builder of this church. 11

Basilica di San Pietro in Vaticano | St. Peter's Basilica in Vatikan City
Address: Piazza San Pietro, Vatican City
Online: www.vaticanstate.va

Public transportation: Metro A stop Ottaviano | Bus stop Largo Di Porta Cavalleggeri – Fornaci: 64 or stop Porta Pinciana: 116 or stop Piazza Della Rovere: 34, 46, 64, 98, 881, 916, 916F, 982 or stop Piazza Pia – Castel Sant'Angelo: 23, 34, 40, 62, 280, 982 | Tram stop Risorgimento – San Pietro: 19 | Train Roma S. Pietro Station: Pisa–Livorno–Grosseto: FL3, FL5

Opening hours:
April to September: Mon – Sun: 7:00 a.m. – 7:00 p.m.
October to March: Mon – Sun: 7:00 a.m. – 6:00 p.m.

Closed: Easter Sunday, the 29th of June (St. Peter and Paul), 25th and 26th of December (Christmas and St. Stephen)

On Wednesdays, if there is the papal audience, the Basilica remains closed until noon.

Every Wednesday at 10:30 a.m. you can see the Pope at St. Peter's Square.

You will need to book the Papal Audience in advance. The tickets are free of charge: www.papalaudience.org

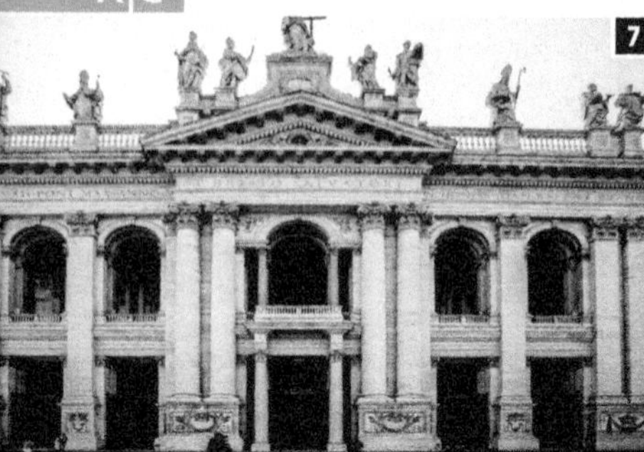

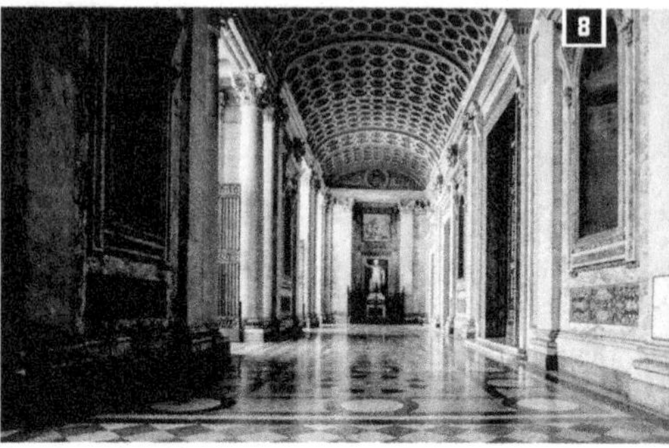

The most impressive sight is opposite the main entrance. It is the apside with the bishop's throne encrusted with a Cosmati mosaic, just like the floor of the main nave. 🔢

Papal tombs

More popes are buried in this church than anywhere outside the Vatican. There are six papal tombs left. The only sarcophagus that survived the legendary Lateran Fires in the 14th century is kept in the Vatican Museums. It is the monumental Sarcophagus of Helena made of red porphyry, originally made for Emperor Constantine's mother, Saint Helena [p.153]. She was kicked out of the sarcophagus to make room for Pope Anastasius IV. The last Pope who was buried outside the Vatican was Leo XIII (1878–1903). His tomb is on the left from the main altar.

① Benedictine monastery

The cloister of the Benedictine monastery is considered one of the most beautiful of Rome. It was built from 1215 to 1232. 🔢

② Lateran Obelisk 🔢

Among the ancient artifacts, the obelisk of Thutmose II is also worth mentioning. It is the largest standing obelisk in the world and it weighs more than 455 tons. In AD 357, Constantius II sent it from Karnak to Rome instead of

Basilica di San Giovanni in Laterano 🔢
Address: Piazza di San Giovanni in Laterano 4, Roma

Online:
www.vatican.va/various/basiliche/
san_giovanni/it/orari/orari.htm

Public transportation:
Metro A and C stop San Giovanni | Bus stop Piazza San Giovanni In Laterano: 16, 51, 85, 87, 186, 650, 666 | Tram stop Porta San Giovanni – Carlo Felice: 8

Opening hours: *see online*

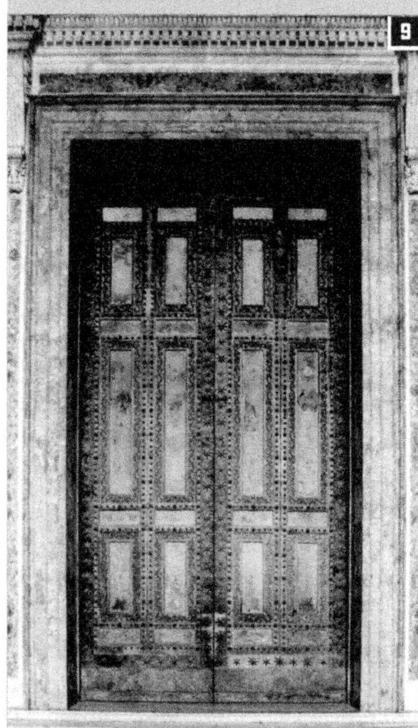

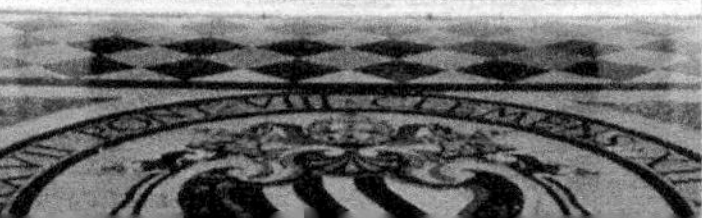

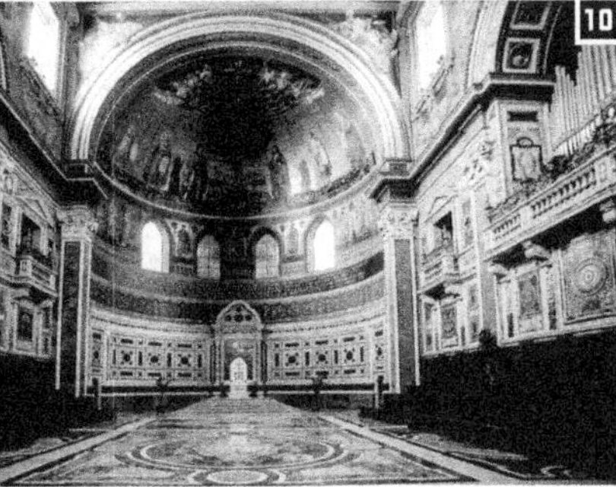

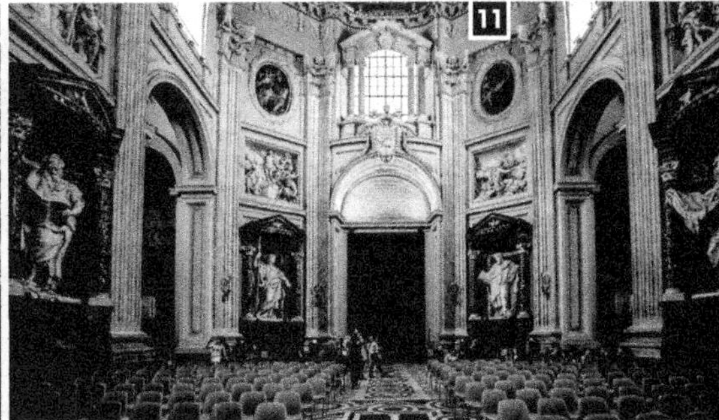

Constantinople, which was Emperor Constantine's wish. First, the obelisk stood at the Circus Maximus. After it broke and fell apart, the obelisk and the fallen statues were buried with honors according to an old Roman tradition. Pope Sixtus V had it excavated and erected in front of the New Lateran Palace, the official residence of the Roman bishop.

Lateran Baptistery

The octagonal plan of the Lateran Baptistery is the first building built as a Christian baptistery (315–440). Francesco Borromini designed frieze of the Baptistery in 1657. The entrance to the Lateran Baptistery has bases, porphyry columns, and the carved capitals (1st century).

Scala Sancta ★

In the 4th century, Scala Sancta or the Holy Stairs were brought to Rome from Jerusalem by St. Helena, mother of Emperor Constantine.

Pilgrim Churches of Rome

Pope John Paul II took the Church of San Sebastiano fuori le mura off the pilgrim's list and included the Santuario della Madonna del Divino Amore. The latter is quite far away and most pilgrims still stick to tradition and follow the old route, which includes San Sebastiano fuori le mura.

Seven Pilgrim Churches of Rome

Four patriarchal basilicas:
1. St. Peter's Basilica
2. Basilica of St. John Lateran
3. Basilica of Saint Paul Outside the Walls
4. Basilica of Santa Maria Maggiore

Three (or four) minor basilicas:
5. San Lorenzo fuori le Mura
6. Santa Croce in Gerusalemme
7. Santuario della Madonna del Divino Amore or San Sebastiano fuori le mura

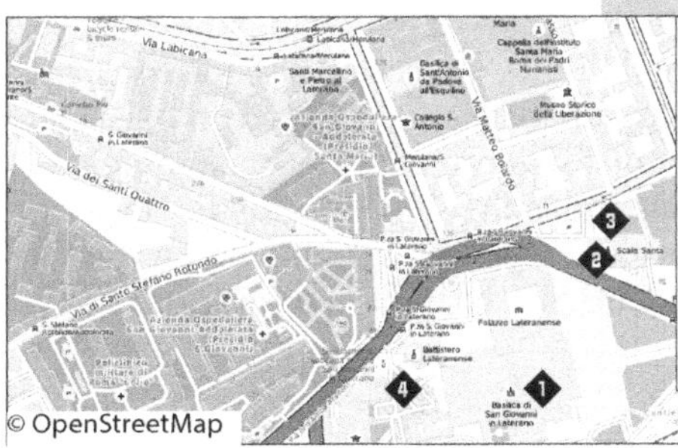

© OpenStreetMap

Lateran
1. Basilica di San Giovanni in Laterano
2. Scala Sancta
3. Sancta Sanctorum Chapel
4. Lateran Baptistery
5. Metro A and C stop San Giovanni

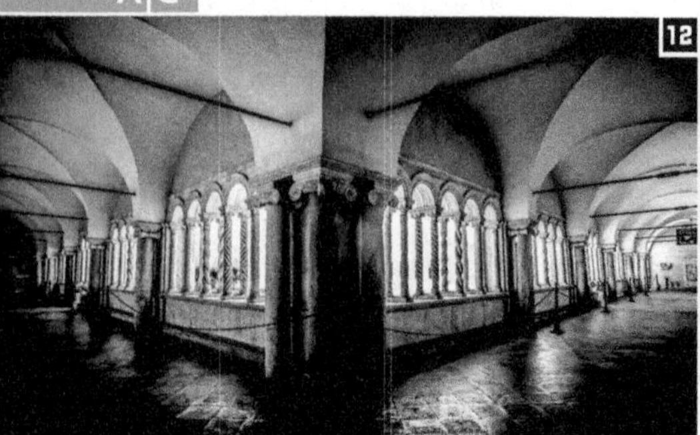
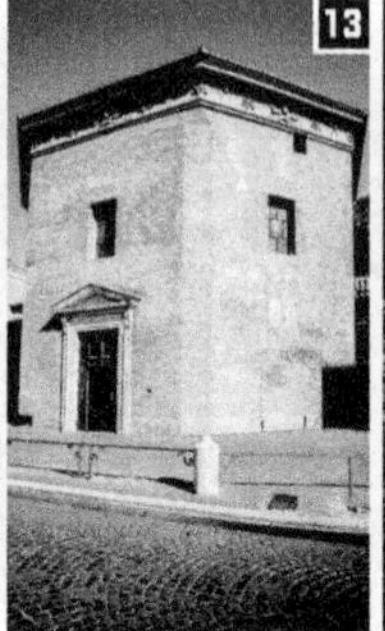
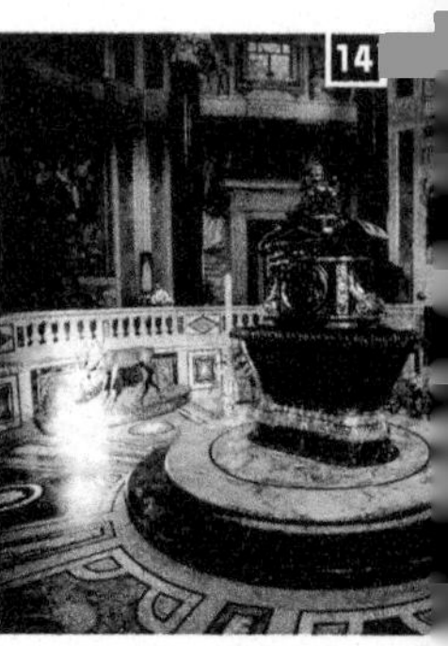

These 28 marble steps led to Pontius Pilate Palace in Jerusalem. Traditionally, Jesus Christ walked on these stairs on his Calvary. Pilgrims who want to pay special respect to the Calvary, walk these 28 marble steps on their knees.

◆ Sancta Sanctorum Chapel ★★

At the end of the stairs, there is a reward for the visitors. It is the Sancta Sanctorum Chapel with the holiest Christian relics brought here from Jerusalem. The chapel stands on soil brought from the Calvary Hill where Jesus was crucified.

There is a mosaic of Christ Pantocrator from the 8th century, along with wonderful frescoes from the 12th and 13th century with Madonna and Child, John the Baptist and John the Evangelist.

Scala Sancta is open to visitors during the same hours as the church. The Sancta Sanctorum Chapel is only open for an hour in the morning and an hour in the afternoon.

Triclinium of Leo III

This building was designed by the architect Domenico Fontana (1585–1590). It was a little further away from the complex but was moved to its present place in the 19th century. The mosaics fell off and were imitated by an engraving of the 17th century. 15 16

◆ Basilica Papale di San Paolo fuori le Mura | The Papal Basilica of Saint Paul Outside the Walls ★★★★ 2

Since this basilica is situated outside Aurelian Walls, the toponym is part of its name. As with all other papal basilicas outside the Vatican, it was granted a special ex-territorial status under the Lateran Agreement, technically allowing it to remain within the jurisdiction of the Holy See.

The construction started under Emperor Constantine on the same place where, according to a legend, St. Paul was buried in AD 67. 17 18 19

Scala Santa and Sancta Sanctorum
Address: Piazza di San Giovanni in Laterano 14, Roma
Online: www.scala-santa.com/en

Public transportation:
Metro A and C stop San Giovanni | Bus stop Piazza San Giovanni In Laterano: 16, 51, 85, 87, 186, 650, 666 | Tram stop Porta San Giovanni – Carlo Felice: 8

Opening hours: *see online*

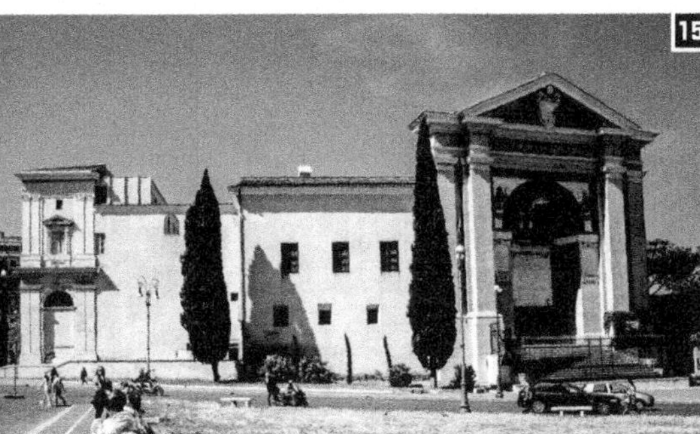

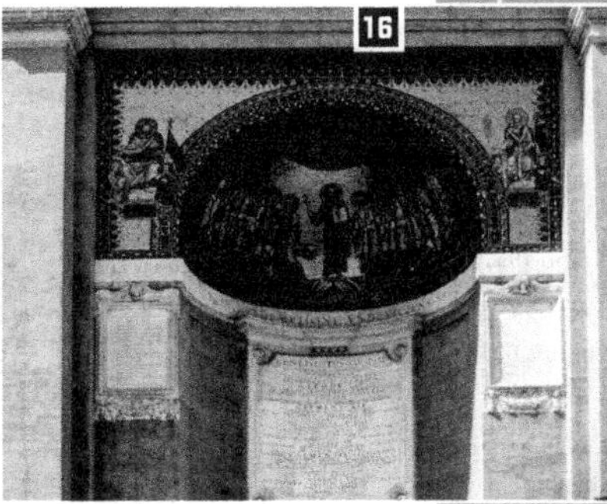

The first basilica was completed in 386. **20** The mosaic on the arch from the 5th century records Emperor Theodosius I as the first builder, then Emperor Honorius who finished it, while restoration and additional decoration was ordered by Empress Galla Placidia during Pope Leo I's pontificate (440–461). The canopy and the apside date back to the 13th century. Everything else was destroyed in a fire in 1823. The basilica was restored in 1845, in accordance with the old layout.

Interior of the Basilica

The basilica with 5 naves is truly spectacular on the inside. Endless rows of columns swim in the light coming from two rows of alabaster windows. The windows were presented as a gift from the Vice-King of Egypt Muhammad Ali.

The windows in the transverse nave were donated by the Russian Emperor Nicholas I. Above the columns, there are 265 papal portraits. The legend goes that Christ would come back to Earth and take over the Holy See when there is no longer room for a portrait of a new pope. Pope John Paul II freed 25 additional places for portraits, just in case.

Basilica Papale di San Paolo fuori le Mura | The Papal Basilica of Saint Paul Outside the Walls
Address: Piazzale San Paolo 1, Roma
Online:
www.basilicasanpaolo.org/en

Public transportation:
Metro B stop Basilica San Paolo | Bus stop Via Ostiense – San Paolo: 23, 769 | Train FC2 Station S. Paolo

Opening hours: *see online*

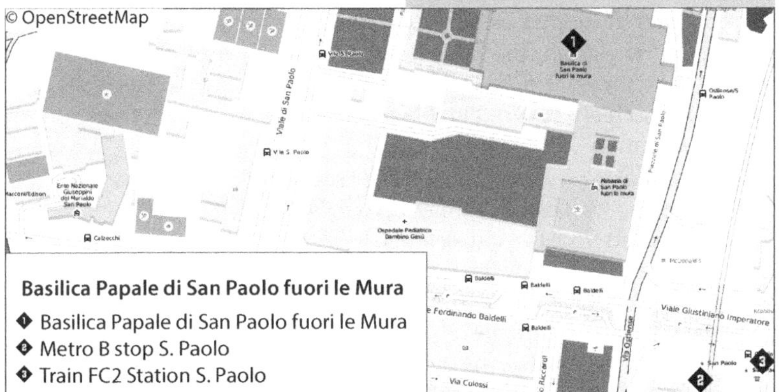

Basilica Papale di San Paolo fuori le Mura

❶ Basilica Papale di San Paolo fuori le Mura
❷ Metro B stop S. Paolo
❸ Train FC2 Station S. Paolo

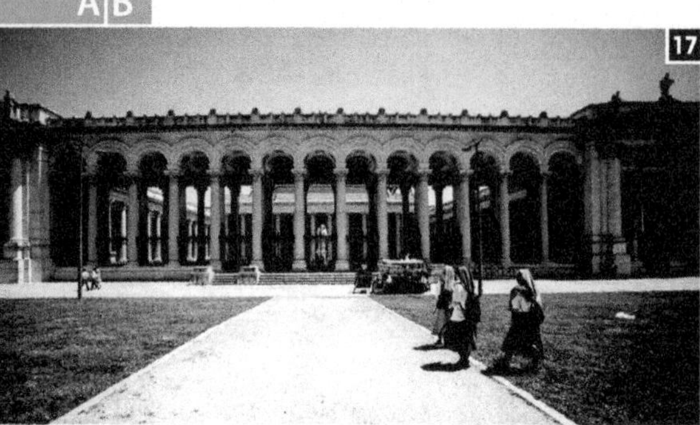

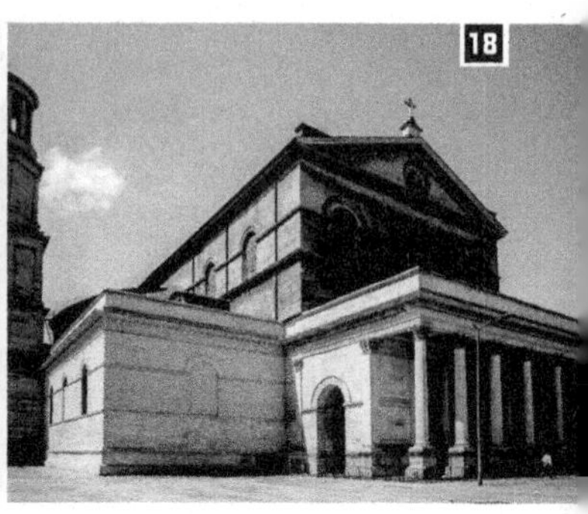

◆ Basilica di Santa Maria Maggiore | Basilica of Santa Maria Maggiore ★ ★ ★ 🔟

Initially, there was a basilica built in the 5th century. Our Lady appeared to John, a wealthy Roman merchant, and his wife, in the night of August 5. She promised they would bear sons if they built a church wherever it snowed in Rome the following day. Next day, they went to Pope Liberius, who had the same dream.

36 antique columns 🔢

Only when you go into the basilica, will you be able to perceive the actual proportions conceived by Pope Sixtus III in 432. The original ancient structure is almost fully preserved. It is a basilica and the aisle is separated by columns. The transversal nave was added in the 13th century, as well as the apside that we see today. In total, the church has 36 columns separating the main nave from the lateral ones. The columns were made of Greek marble and taken from the Temple of Juno on the Aventine Hill. Above them, you can see 27 Roman-style mosaics, also in great condition, depicting the scenes from the life of Moses.

The triumphal arch

The triumphal arch also has mosaics, but they are Byzantine in style, even though they belong to the same period as the ones above the columns. They represent the scenes from the Birth of Jesus Christ. There is an especially attractive representation of Mary's coronation in the apside. Baroque altar canopy was directly inspired by Bernini's altar in St. Peter's Basilica in the Vatican. The stone floor was done by the Cosmati in the 13th century and it is considered to be their best Roman work. The walls of the triumphal arch are covered in 5th-century mosaics with scenes from the Old Testament.

Ceiling 🔢

The ceiling with cassettes features gold ornaments from the 16th century. The gold was donated by the Spanish queen Isabella I, given to her by Christopher Columbus — after he returned from America. To this day, the patrons of this church are Spanish kings.

Basilica di Santa Maria Maggiore
Address: Piazza di Santa Maria Maggiore 42, Roma

Public transportation:
Metro A and B stop Termini | Bus stop Termini: 16, 75, 150F, 360, 590, 649, 717, C3 | Tram stop Termini: 5, 14

Opening hours: *see Google Maps*

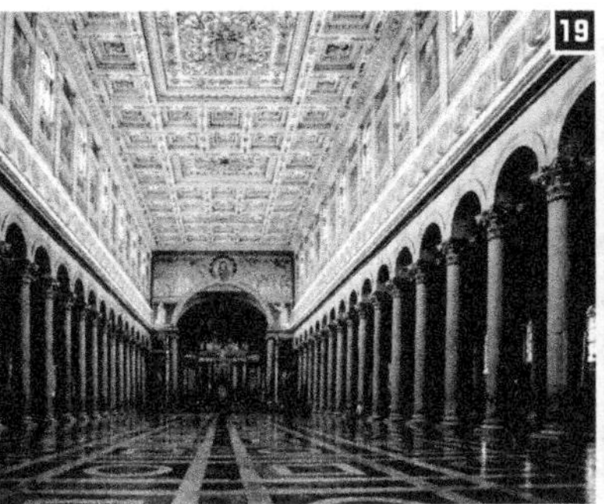

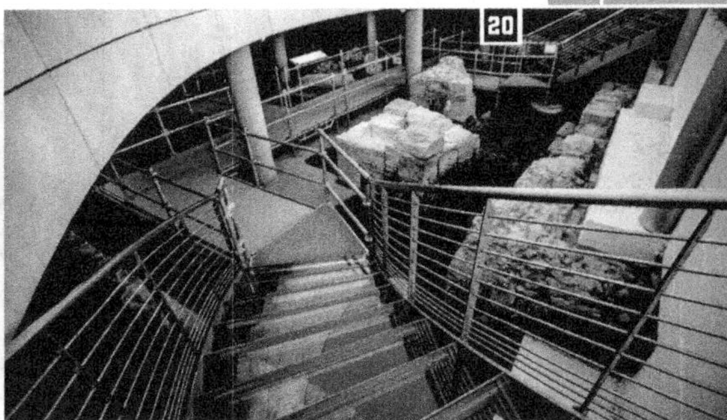

The transversal nave

In the transversal nave, left of the altar, there is the Borghese Chapel or Cappella Paolina.

It was built under the order of Pope Paul V, from the Borghese family.

On the opposite side, in the right section of the transversal nave, there is the Sistine Chapel by Domenico Fontana for Pope Sixtus V. Also, Domenico Fontana made the funeral monument of Pope Nicholas IV.

The Sistine Chapel is reserved for the tombs of Pope Sixtus V and his predecessor Pope Pius V. In front of the chapel, there is the tomb of the greatest baroque architect and sculptor Gian Lorenzo Bernini and his family.

For this church, Bernini authored the sculpture of Saint Cajetan holding the Holy Child opposite the main altar. ▣

Papal tombs

Six out of seven papal tombs are still located in this basilica. Below the altar, in the *Confessio*, there is the most important relic of this church, the remains of Jesus's cradle with the statue of Pope Pius IX in front.

Mary's column ▣

Mary's column on the square in front of the church is 46 ft (14 m) high. Originally, it was placed in the Basilica of Maxentius at the Roman Forum. It is the only remaining column of the original eight identical columns from the Basilica of Maxentius.

Mary's Column, the pedestal and statue rise 138 ft (42 m) in the air. The belfry was built in 1377, as the tallest one in Rome (246 ft or 75 m), to honor the return of the popes from Avignon.

The late antique basilica is not visible from the outside because it is entirely encased by a baroque façade from 1750, work of Ferdinando Fuga. The chorus façade (also baroque) was built in 1670 by Carlo Rainaldi.

Did you know?

The most important Marian relic

Out of the 40 Roman churches dedicated to Mary, this is the biggest one, so it is called Maria Maggiore.

The most important Marian relic is kept here – *Salus Populi Romani* or "Salvation of the Roman People", possibly the oldest representation of Mary in Rome. It is in the Borghese Chapel.

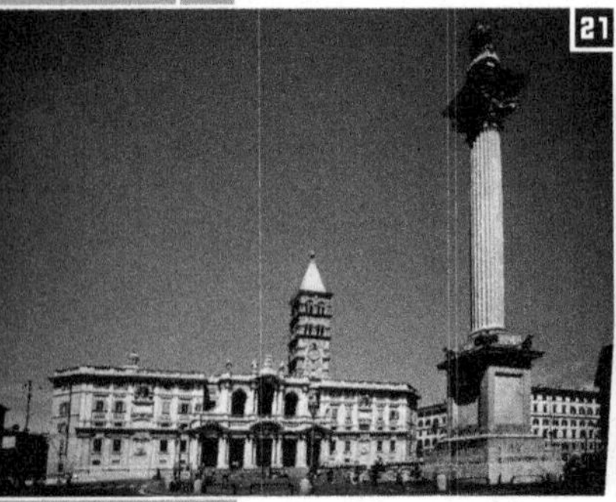

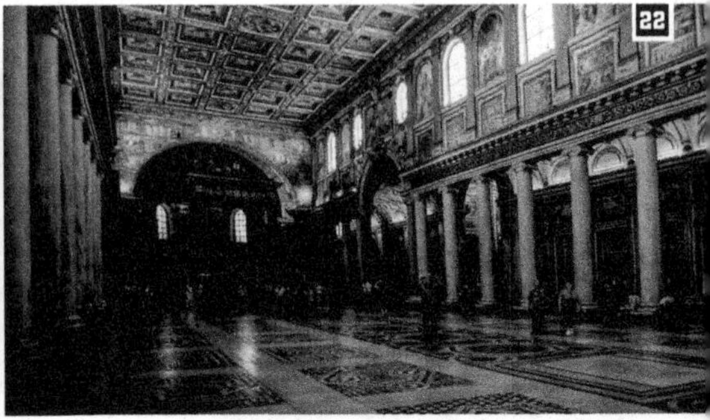

❼ Basilica di Santa Prassede | Basilica of Saint Praxedes ★★★

The church was named after a martyr and daughter of St. Prudens, a senator who was baptized by St. Peter himself. St. Praxedes was St. Pudenziana's sister, who has her own church not far from this one.

Even though the original church was commissioned by Pope Siricius in the late 4th century, the available documents only registered it in 489.

The church was restored in the 16th and 18th century, but still features a lot of the typical elements from the Late Antiquity and the Early Middle Ages.

Besides, it is the most prominent example of Byzantine art in Rome. The belfry is from the 11th century, and it is the oldest belfry in Rome.

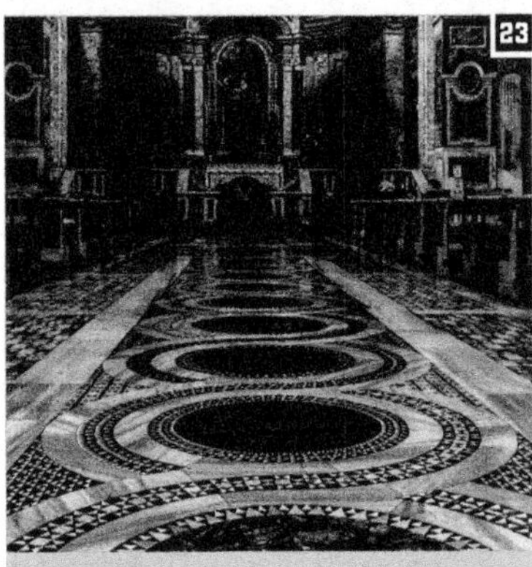

Basilica di Santa Prassede | Basilica of Saint Praxedes
Address: Via di Santa Prassede 9/a, Roma
Online: https://santaprassede.wordpress.com

Public transportation:
Metro A and B stop Termini | Bus stop Termini: 16, 75, 150F, 360, 590, 649, 717, C3 | Tram stop Termini: 5, 14

Opening hours: *see online*

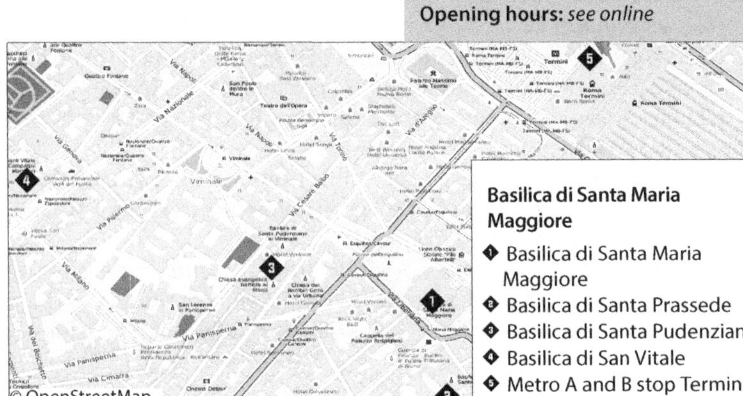

Basilica di Santa Maria Maggiore

❶ Basilica di Santa Maria Maggiore
❷ Basilica di Santa Prassede
❸ Basilica di Santa Pudenziana
❹ Basilica di San Vitale
❺ Metro A and B stop Termini

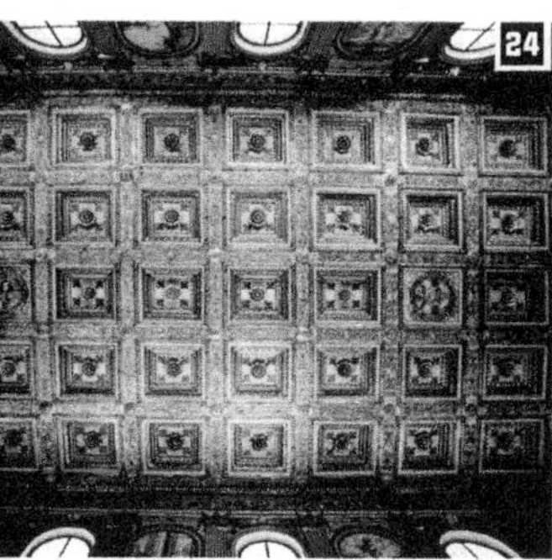
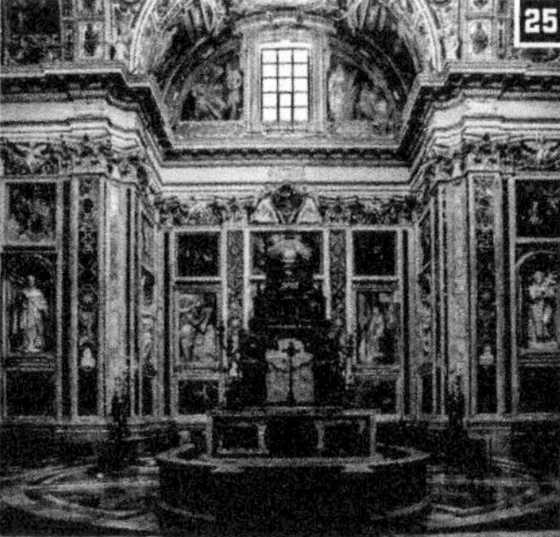
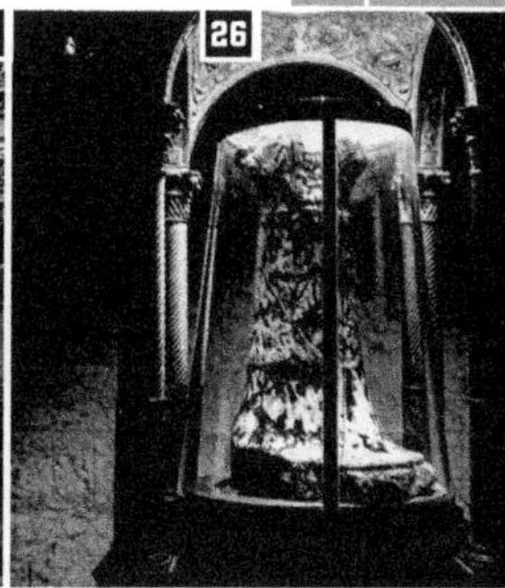

One of the most eye-capturing elements in the church are the mosaics in the arch and apside.

The central mosaic in the apside shows Jesus Christ surrounded by six saints. 27

Pope Paschal I (817–824) is on the right, holding a model of the church.

Instead of a round halo, the Pope has a square one, which means the person was still alive when the scene was designed. St. Praxedes and Paul the Apostle stand next to him.

On the left, we can see Peter the Apostle, St. Pudenziana and another saint, supposedly St. Zenon. Heavenly Jerusalem is represented on the triumphal arch.

The floor of the church has a beautiful, restored Cosmatesque mosaic. 23

The Chapel of Zenon from the 9th century features a relic of the column on which Jesus was tortured before the crucifixion. 26

Pay attention to the vault with the dome and four angels with Christ in the middle. 28

The walls are covered in marble and the floor has a big, round porphyry plates.

The church also holds the posthumous remains of 2,000 martyrs transferred from the catacombs.

Basilica di Santa Pudenziana | Basilica of Santa Pudenziana
Address: Via Urbana 160, Roma
Online: www.stpudenziana.org

Public transportation:
Metro A and B stop Termini | Bus stop Termini: 16, 75, 150F, 360, 590, 649, 717, C3 | Tram stop Termini: 5, 14

Opening hours: *see online*

Did you know?

The oldest churches in Rome
- Santa Pudenziana (4th century) [p.279]
- St. Peter's Basilica (333) [p.136]
- Santa Maria in Trastevere (340) [p.238]
- San Paolo fuori le Mura (386) [p.274]
- Santi Giovanni e Paolo (398) [p.34]
- Santi Nereo e Achilleo (4th century) [p.293]
- Basilica di San Clemente (4th century) [p.33]
- Sant'Agnese fuori le mura (4th century) [p.246]
- Basilica di San Vitale (400) [p.280]
- Basilica di Santa Sabina (422) [p.183]
- Basilica di Santa Maria Maggiore (432) [p.277]
- Santo Stefano Rotondo (455) [p.35]

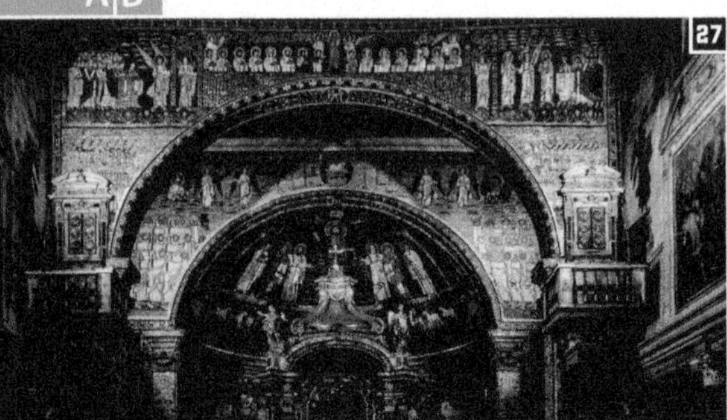
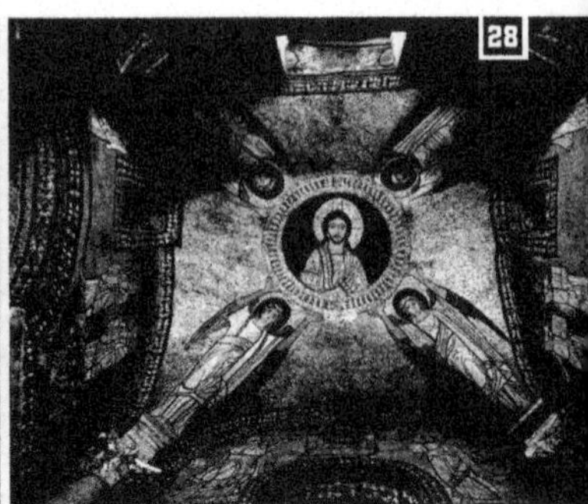

◆ ⑧ Basilica di Santa Pudenziana ★★ 🄌

This basilica is on the Viminal Hill, the smallest of seven Roman hills. There is material evidence that Christians met here in the 2nd century, which makes it the oldest church in Rome. Basilica di Santa Pudenziana also holds a special place in church history as the papal headquarters until 313, when Emperor Constantine the Great offered the Lateran Palace as an alternative. The church honors the martyr St. Pudenziana, St. Praxedes' sister. Like the Basilica of Saint Praxedes, this church is also famous for its mosaic in the apside as one of the most important mosaics of the Late Antiquity. It shows Jesus Christ as a philosophy teacher. He is surrounded by saints, including St. Praxedes on his left and St. Pudenziana on the right, with the symbols of the four evangelists above: the angel (Matthew the Apostle), lion (Mark the Evangelist, bull (Luke the Evangelist) and eagle (John the Evangelist). 🄌

The interior of the dome features a fresco: *Angels and Saints before the Saviour*, by Pomarancio. 🄌 Today, this is the main church of the Roman Filipino community.

◆ ⑨ Basilica di San Vitale ★

Basilica di Santi Vitale e Compagni Martiri in Fovea or Basilica di San Vitale was built in 400 by a wealthy widow Vestina. The floor level of the church is now 20 ft or 6 m below the level of the street.The frescoes in the sanctuary, by Agostino Ciampelli, depict the stoning and torture of St. Vitalis.

◆ ⑩ Porta Maggiore ★★ 🄌

Porta Maggiore is one of 18 major city gates of the imperial Rome. Initially, it was an aqueduct built by Emperor Claudius in AD 52. In the late 3rd century Emperor Aurelian was in a hurry to build the city walls due to the threat of attack by the Germanic tribes, and he built the walls with anything he could find, to buy more time. This is how parts of Aqua Claudia, Pyramid of Cestius, and the tomb of Marcus Vergilius Eurysaces were integrated into the Aurelian Wall.

◆ ⑪ Tomb of Eurysaces the Baker ★★

The tomb of Marcus Vergilius Eurysaces is the largest preserved Roman tomb of a freeman, that is, a former slave. The baker raised this monument for his wife and himself during the Roman Republic (50–20 BC).

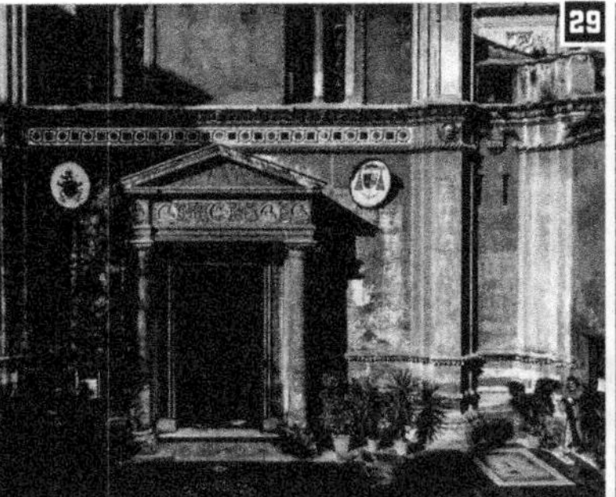

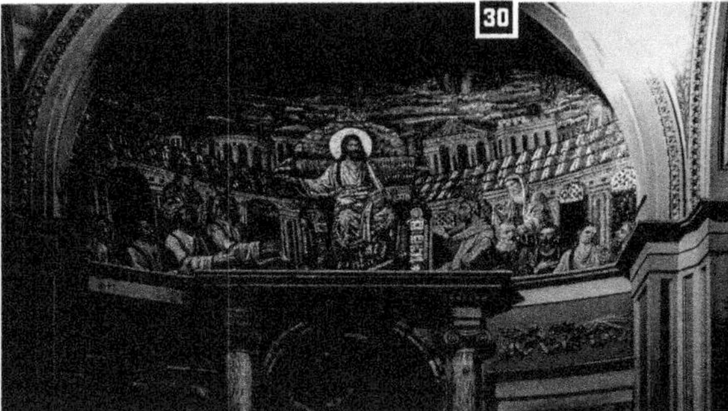

Cylindrical shapes on the mausoleum represent rolling pins. Even the urn was executed as a bread basket. Today, it is kept at the National Roman Museum. The portrait relief was transported to the Capitoline Museums. **33**

⓬ Mausoleum of Helena ★ ★ **34**

When you get off at the Berardi station, go through the entrance of the Santi Marcellino e Pietro al Laterano church towards the cylindrical remains of the Mausoleum of St. Helena, built in AD 326 during Emperor Constantine. The emperor's mother Helena was buried in the mausoleum in AD 328 and later declared saint. At the edges of the dome, you can see amphorae built into the Roman concrete, *opus caementicium*, a special construction method at the time.

By putting in empty amphorae, the weight of the dome was significantly reduced. At the main entrance of the mausoleum, there used to be a monumental sarcophagus made of red porphyry, supposedly made for the emperor himself because it is entirely decorated with battle scenes.

However, he passed on the sarcophagus to his mother, and the saint was thrown out of it in the 12th century by Pope Anastasius IV, so that he could have it for himself. At present, it is on display at the Vatican Museums.

Basilica di San Vitale
Address: Via Nazionale 194B, Roma
Online: https://santivitale.com

Public transportation:
Metro A and B stop Termini | Bus stop Termini: 16, 75, 150F, 360, 590, 649, 717, C3 | Tram stop Termini: 5, 14

Opening hours: *see online*

Porta Maggiore
Address: Piazza di Porta Maggiore, Roma

Public transportation:
Tram stop Piazza di Porta Maggiore: 5, 14, 19

Opening hours:
Public place – always open

Porta Maggiore

- ❶ Porta Maggiore
- ❷ Tomb of Eurysaces the Baker
- ❸ Tram stop Piazza di Porta Maggiore: 5, 14, 19
- ❹ Tram stop Piazza di Porta Maggiore: FC1

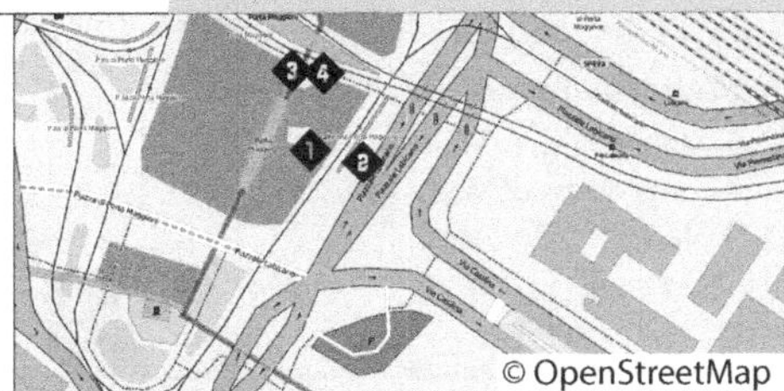

© OpenStreetMap

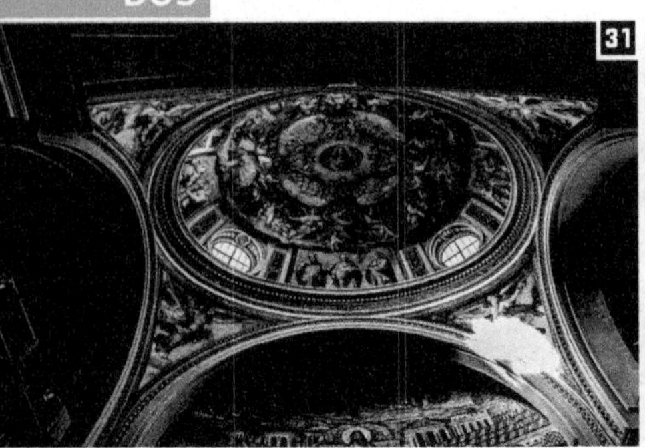

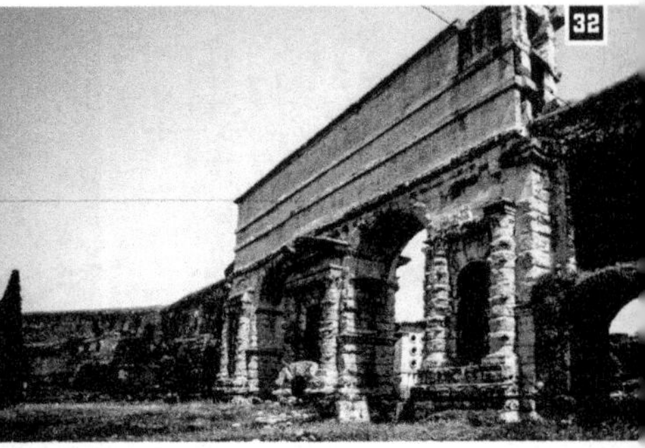

⑬ Catacombs of Marcellinus and Peter ★★

The legend says that these are the catacombs where Christian martyrs St. Marcellinus, St. Peter and St. Tiburtius were buried. Apart from over a thousand skeletons that have been found recently, there are also well-preserved frescoes from the 4th century. Until the early 5th century, more than 20,000 burials were performed here. The catacombs stretch across 3 ha, with 4.5 km of underground galleries on three levels.

They have been open to the public for individual visits only. The ticket includes an expert guide.

⑭ Basilica Papale di San Lorenzo fuori le Mura | Papal Basilica of Saint Lawrence outside the Walls ★★★ 35

The church is devoted to St. Lawrence, one of the first deacons of Rome, who became a martyr in 258. The church was built on a former oratory where St. Lawrence was executed. In fact, the church was created by partitioning the neighboring church of St. Mary, built by Pope Sixtus III (432–440).

When Pope Honorius III attached it to St. Lawrence's church, the former church of St. Mary's was built into the choir of Honorius' St. Lawrence Church.

Mausoleo di Elena | Mausoleum of Helena
Address: Via Casilina 641, Roma
Online:
www.santimarcellinoepietro.it/english

Public transportation: Tram stop Berardi: FC1

Opening hours: *see online*

Catacomba dei SS. Marcellino e Pietro | Catacombs of Marcellinus and Peter
Address: Via Casilina – Via di S. Marcellino, Roma
Online: www.santimarcellinoepietro.it/english

Public transportation: Tram stop Berardi: FC1

Opening hours: *see online*

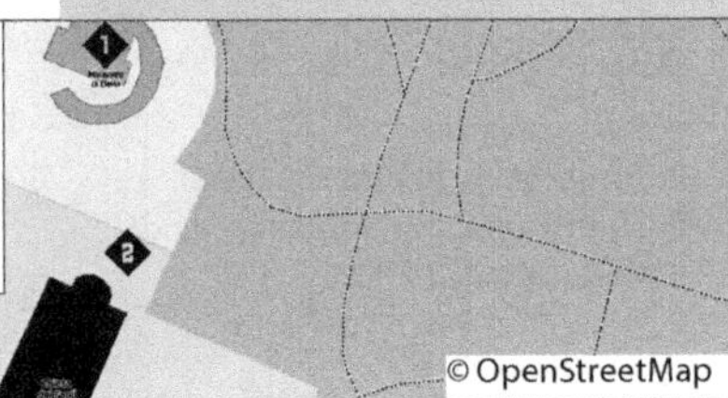

Mausoleum of Helena

◆ Mausoleum of Helena
◆ Catacombs of Marcellinus and Peter
◆ Tram stop Berardi

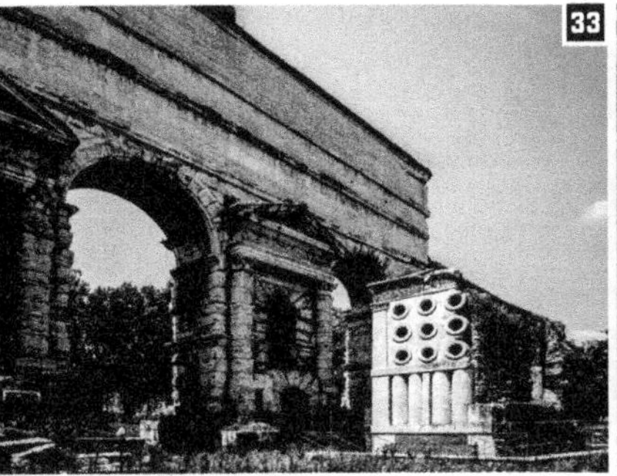

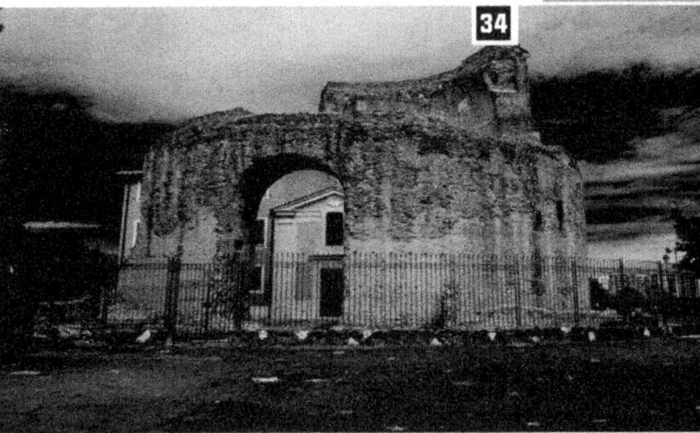

Cosmatesque decorations

Even though the church was badly damaged during the bombings in 1943, it is still covered in medieval mosaics by the Cosmati family from the 12th and 13th century. Look inside the choir, on the pulpit and the Paschal candlestick, all of which are amazing masterpieces by the famous Roman family of artists.

On the papal altar, located behind the main altar, you can even find the artist's name, the Cosmati family and the year 1148, which is when the mosaics were created.

Belfry with a sarcophagus

The belfry was built in the 12th century. What makes it worth the visit is Cardinal Guglielmo Fieschi's tomb, where the cardinal was buried in 1256.

He was buried in a beautiful antique sarcophagus with a representation of a pagan family ceremony.

Basilica Papale di San Lorenzo fuori le Mura | Papal Basilica of Saint Lawrence outside the Walls
Address: Piazzale del Verano, 3, Roma
Online:
https://en.basilicadisanlorenzo.com

Public transportation:
Metro B and B1 stop Policlinico | Bus stop Verano: 88 | Tram stop Verano: 2, 19

Opening hours: *see online*

Basilica Papale di San Lorenzo fuori le Mura

❶ Basilica Papale di San Lorenzo fuori le Mura
❷ Santa Croce in Gerusalemme
❸ National Museum of Musical Instruments
❹ Campo Verano Cemetery

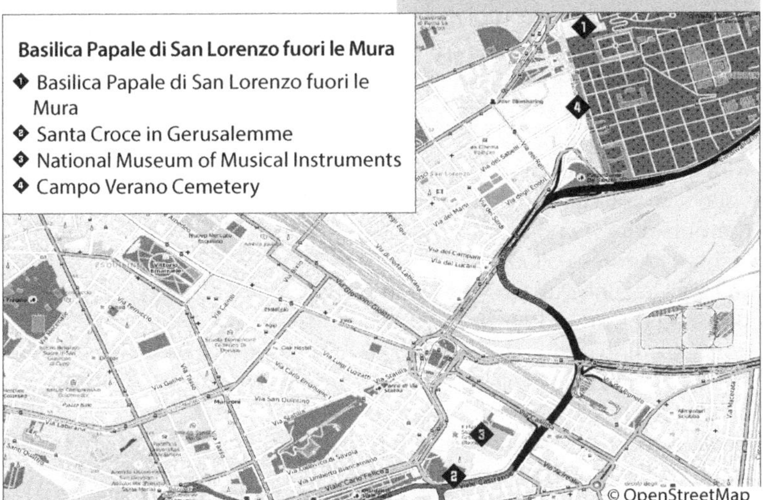

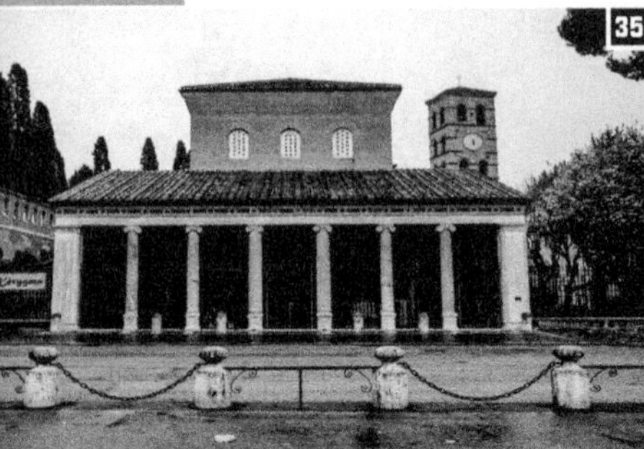

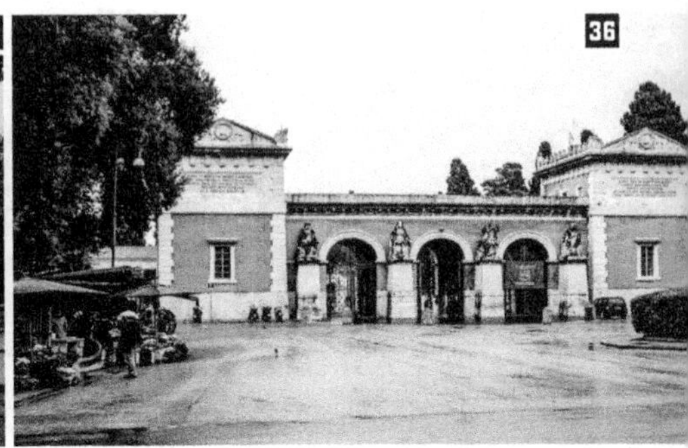

Under the main altar, there is a crypt with relics of St. Lawrence and St. Stephen, and there is also Pope Pius IX's sarcophagus surrounded by relics of all of those who were sanctified by Pius IX. Today, the church is the most relevant funeral church in Rome because it is close to the Campo Verano cemetery, the largest one in Rome. **36**

🖈 Santa Croce in Gerusalemme ★★ **37**

Although the first church rose from the imperial palace of St. Helen, mother of the Roman Emperor Constantine, while she was still alive around AD 330, there are very few elements older than Baroque. However, the floor is still a Cosmati mosaic from the 12th century **38**, and the apside is painted by Antoniazzo Romano's frescoes in 1490. There is also Cardinal Francisco de los Ángeles Quiñones' tombstone, work of Jacopo Sansovino in 1536. **39**

Sessorium

The remains of the Sessorium, an imperial residential palace from the Severan dynasty (193–235), are right of the church, later used by Empress St. Helen herself. You can still see the semicircular walls of *Amphitheatrum Castrense*, the only remaining Roman amphitheater, apart from the Colosseum. The elliptical building is 289 ft or 88 m long and 249 ft or 75.8 m wide. Unfortunately, it is not open for visitors, so you can only admire it from the outside. A famous 16th-century architect Andrea Palladio and French architect Étienne Dupérac studied and sketched the art of Roman construction according to this amphitheater.

The entire vast complex of imperial buildings, which has been repurposed by various Christian orders, also offers accommodation in parts of a 10th-century convent-turned-hotel.

Basilica di Santa Croce in Gerusalemme | The Basilica of the Holy Cross in Jerusalem
Address: Piazza di Santa Croce in Gerusalemme, Roma
Online: www.santacroceroma.it/en

Public transportation:
Metro C Lodi | Tram stop Piazza Santa Croce In Gerusalemme: 8

Opening hours: *see online*

Museo Nazionale degli Strumenti Musicali | National Museum of Musical Instruments
Address: Piazza di Santa Croce in Gerusalemme, 9/a, Roma
Online: http://museostrumentimusicali.beniculturali.it

Public transportation:
Metro C Lodi | Tram stop Piazza Santa Croce In Gerusalemme: 8

Opening hours: *see online*

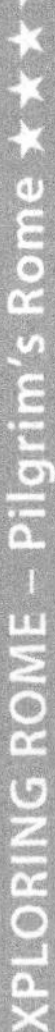

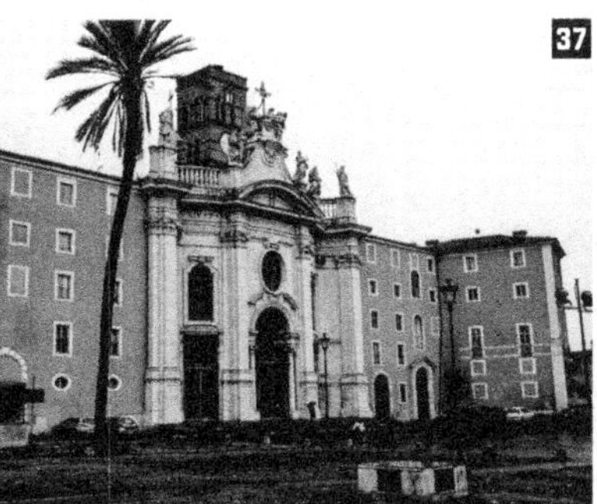

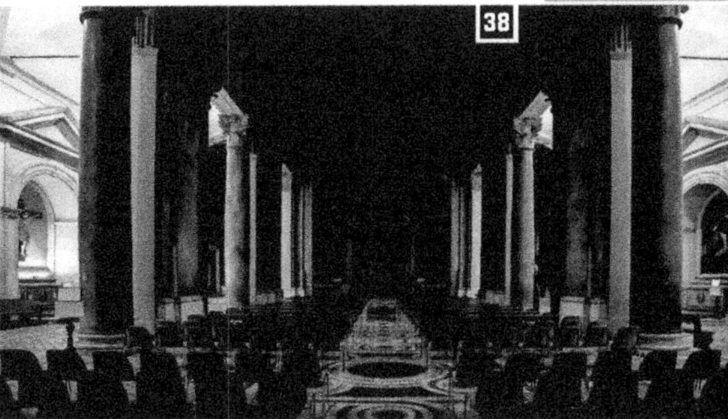

National Museum of Musical Instruments ★★

Left of the Santa Croce in Gerusalemme, there is Museo Nazionale degli Strumenti Musicali.

It holds a particularly interesting collection of musical instruments and it is the best and largest collection of this kind in Europe: instruments from the Far East, ancient Etruscan instruments found during archaeological excavations, late Antique instruments and the famous *Barberini harp*.

⑯ San Sebastiano fuori le mura ★★

The history of the church goes back to the 4th century and Emperor Constantine, while the façade is from the 17th century.

All the way to the Great Jubilee of 2000, this church was one of seven churches that every Roman pilgrim had to visit.

Pope John Paul II replaced San Sebastiano fuori le mura with the Church of Santuario della Madonna del Divino Amore on the pilgrims' list.

Be it tradition, or the fact that the latter is quite far away, most pilgrims stick to the original list and pay regular visits to San Sebastiano fuori le mura.

The bust of the Salvatore —*Salvator Mundi*, was rediscovered in 2001, when the experts have recognized this bust as the last work of Bernini.

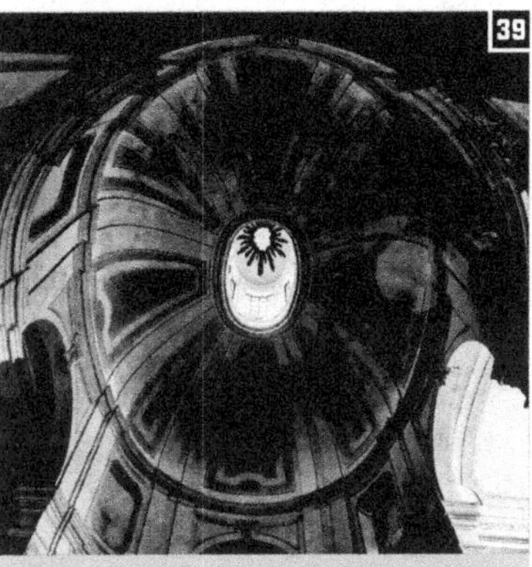

Did you know?

Where to see Domenico Fontana's architecture and fountains in Rome?

▸ Funerary monument of Pope Nicholas IV, Basilica di Santa Maria Maggiore (1574) **[p.277]**

▸ The chapel Cappella Sistina, with the tombs of Pope Sixtus V and Pope Pius V, Basilica di Santa Maria Maggiore (1584–1590) **[p.277]**

▸ The Lateran Palace (1586) **[p.270]**

▸ Triclinium of Leo III (1585–1589) **[p.274]**

▸ Scala Sancta (1586–1588) **[p.273]**

▸ Fontana dell'Acqua Felice (1587) **[p.242]**

▸ San Luigi dei Francesi (1589) **[p.116]**

▸ Quattro Fontane (1588–1593) **[p.230]**

▸ Palazzo del Quirinale (1583) **[p.232]**

▸ Fountain, St. Peter's Square, Vatican (1586) **[p.134]**

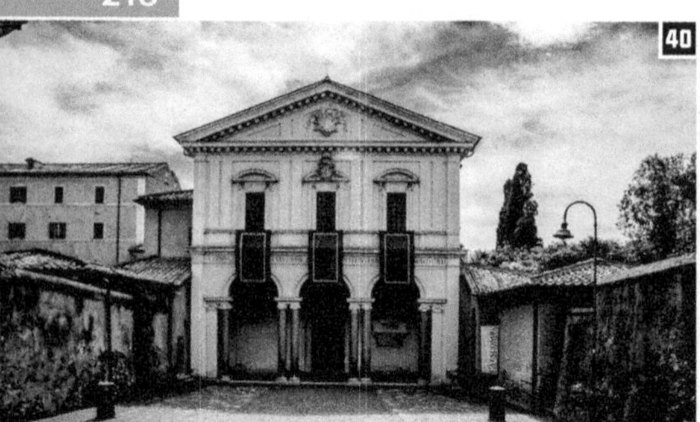

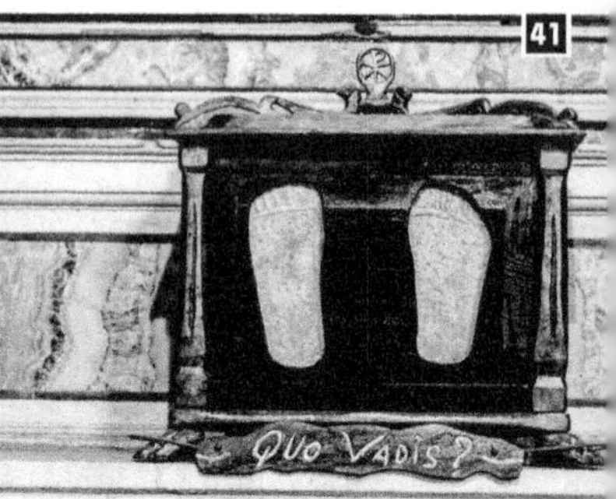

In the Chapel of Relics you can find a stone imprinted with the footprints of Jesus related to the episode of *Quo vadis* or "Where are you marching?" **41** **42**

You can find map with the Saint Sebastian Outside the Walls hier. [p.295]

ⓘ Santuario della Madonna del Divino Amore ★

This church was declared one of seven churches that should be part of any Roman pilgrimage by Pope Paul II in the Holy Year of 2000.

Above the entrance area, there is a medieval fresco with Madonna and Child.

The Holy Mary miraculously appeared exactly at this spot in 1740 and intervened to save a group of pilgrims from certain death when they were attacked by a pack of rabid dogs.

Apart from several other miracles and apparitions over the centuries, the only couple in the history of the Catholic church was beatified in 2001.

They are Luigi Beltrame Quattrocchi (1880–1951) and Maria Corsini-Beltrame Quattrocchi (1884–1965), buried in the crypt.

Pope John Paul II beatified them because "they lived an ordinary life in an extraordinary way."

**San Sebastiano fuori le mura |
Saint Sebastian Outside the Walls**
Address: Via Appia Antica, 136, Roma
Online:
www.sansebastianofuorilemura.org

Public transportation:
Bus stop Basilica San Sebastiano 118

Opening hours: *see online*

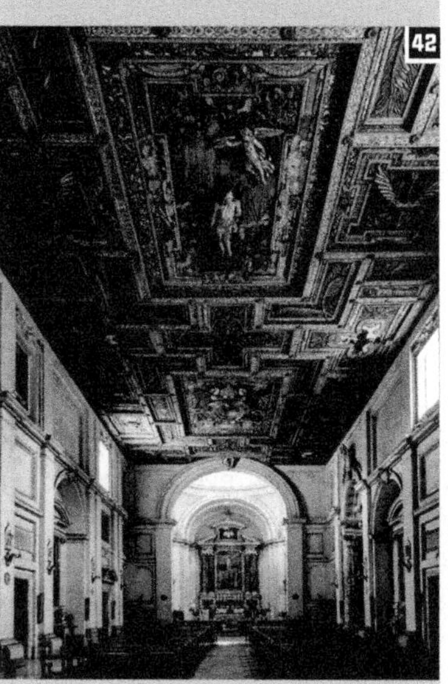

Santuario della Madonna del Divino Amore | The shrine of Our Lady of Divine Love
Address: Via del Santuario 10, Roma
Online: www.santuariodivinoamore.it

Public transportation:
Bus stop Santuario Divino Amore: 074, 218, 702

Opening hours: *see online*

Via Appia Antica

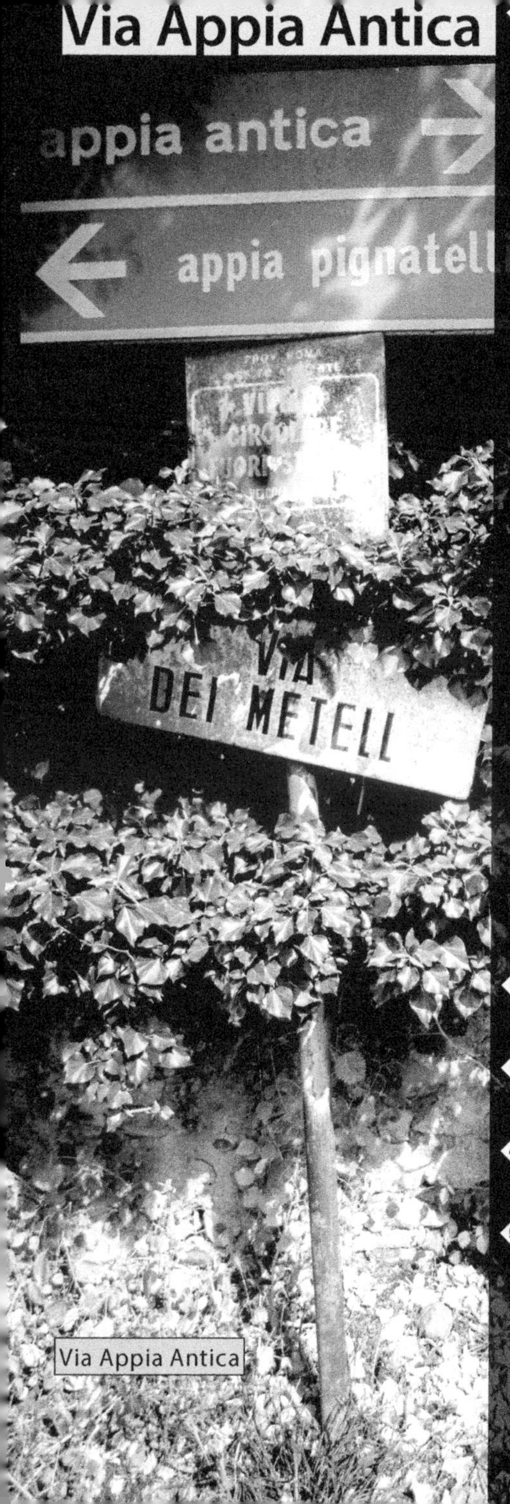

1 **Via Appia Antica**
Monuments dating back to the Classical and Early Christian period. *p. 290*

1 **Porta San Sebastiano**
The best preserved city gates. *p. 291*

2 **Church of Domine Quo Vadis**
On this road St. Peter met Jesus Christ and asked him: *"Domine, quo vadis?"* *p. 292*

3 **Tomb of Priscilla**
It belonged to the wife of a free slave of emperor Domitian. *p. 293*

4 **Catacombe di San Domitilla**
The oldest catacombs. *p. 293*

5 **Catacombe di San Callisto**
The biggest catacombs. *p. 293*

6 **Catacombe di San Sebastiano**
All underground tombs are called catacombs because of these. *p. 294*

7 **San Sebastiano Fuori le Mura**
The last work of Bernini. *p. 295*

8 **Circus of Maxentius**
Over 1,640 ft (500 m) long and 295 ft (90 m) wide. *p. 296*

9 **Mausoleum of Cecilia Metella**
Marcus Licinius Crassus commissioned this mausoleum for his wife. *p. 296*

10 **Villa Capo di Bove**
The ancient Villa with the private thermal baths. *p. 299*

11 **Original Roman pavement**
Via Appia Antica 193. *p. 300*

12 **Villa of the Quintilii**
Villa with nymphaeum, hippodrome and private aqueduct. *p. 300*

2 **Parco della Caffarella**
With still well-preserved tomb built by Herodes Atticus for his wife. *p. 301*

3 **Tombs of Via Latina**
Small archaeological park with well-preserved Roman tombs. *p. 302*

4 **Parco degli Acquedotti**
This unique park has monumental remains of seven aqueducts. *p. 302*

5 **Cinecittà Studios**
The filming location for Ben-Hur and movies of Federico Fellini. *p. 304*

Incredible facts about

In the Church San Sebastiano Fuori le Mura the bust of the Salvatore (Salvator Mundi) was rediscovered in 2001, when the experts have recognized this bust as the last work of the Bernini.

Original Roman pavement on Via Appia Antica

Extra Tip : : :
All underground tombs are called catacombs because of the Catacombs of Saint Sebastian. The place above the catacombs, where the Church of San Sebastiano Fuori le Mura was built, used to be called *ad catacumbas*.

Catacombs and other sights on the Appian Way

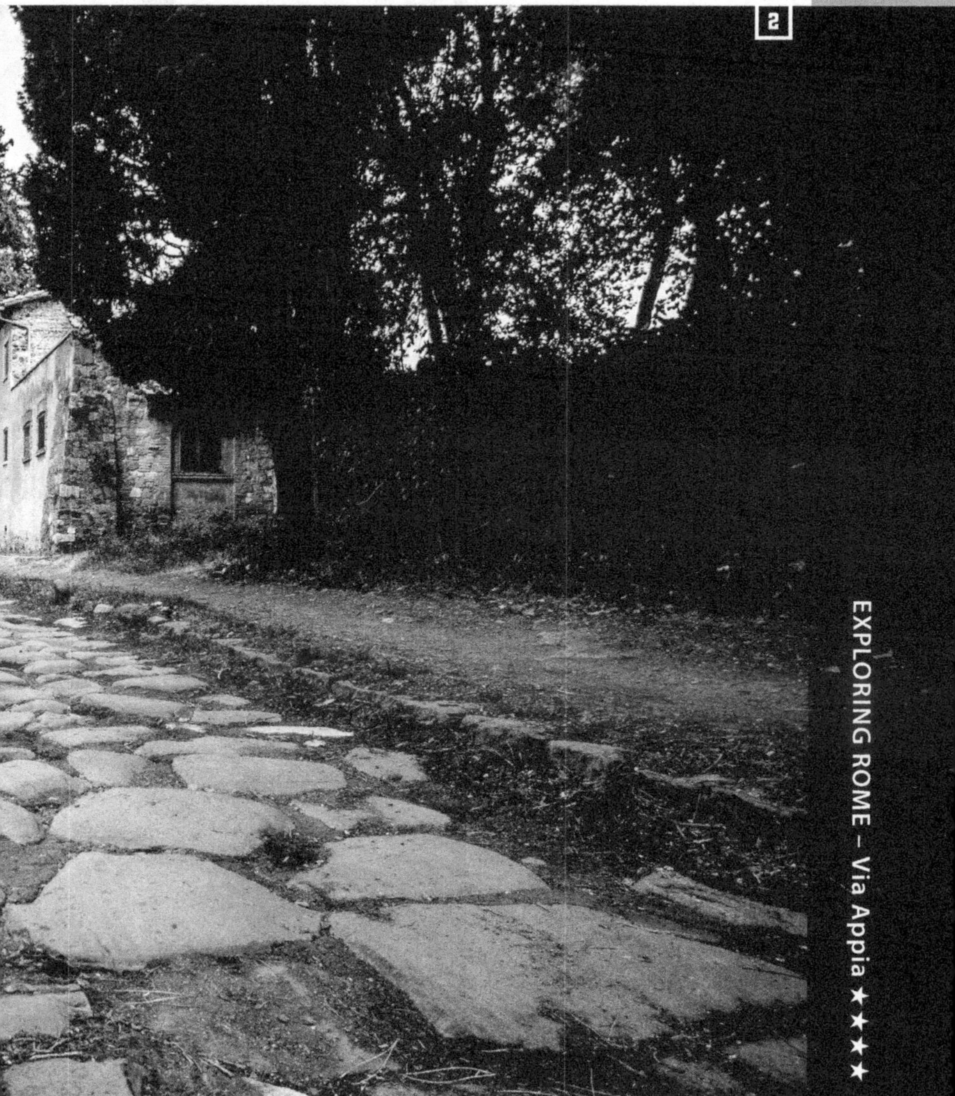

Catacombe di San Sebastiano | Catacombs of Saint Sebastian
Address: Via Appia Antica 136, Roma
Public transportation: Bus stop Basilica San Sebastiano: 118

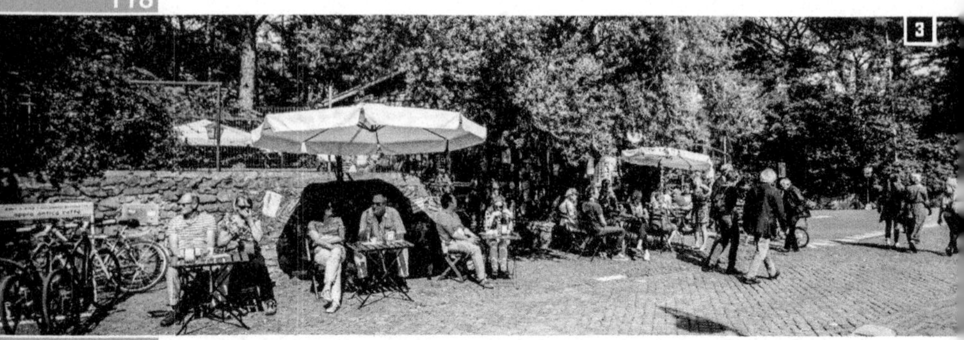

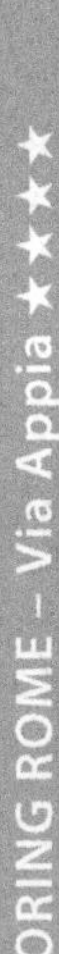

❶ Via Appia Antica ★ ★ ★ ★

Via Appia is now called Via Appia Antica. **3**

The road goes from the San Sebastiano Gate to the Ciampino Airport (7.1 miles or 11.5 kilometers), roughly a two-and-a-half-hour walk. **2** There are many monuments along the way dating back to the Classical and Early Christian period. Step by step, superlatives pile up — Via Appia has the longest flat part of road ever built in Europe, 38.5 mi or 62 km in length. **4**

Also, Via Appia Antica is the longest open-space museum in the world. However, the most important monuments are located on the first 4 miles or 6.5 kilometers.

Via Appia was built to transport armies. It is precisely thanks to the regular movement of troops and supplies that the Romans won in the Second Samnite War (326–304 BC) and extended their rule to the south of the Italian Peninsula. Nevertheless, even after they had established absolute rule over the entire Italian Peninsula, Via Appia was still incredibly significant for the progress of Rome.

This was why it had to reach Brindisi. It took around two weeks to travel from Rome to Brundisium, modern Brindisi, the main port for exchange of goods and slaves from the East.

Did you know?

Spartacus and the Via Appia

The largest slave rebellion happened in 73 BC, lead by Spartacus, a gladiator from Capua. The rebellion was smothered in blood after two years, even though the slaves won several battles. The surviving rebels, circa 6,000 of them, were sentenced to the cruelest of punishments. They were crucified and left to die of thirst along the first 120 miles (200 km) of Via Appia, from Rome to Capua.

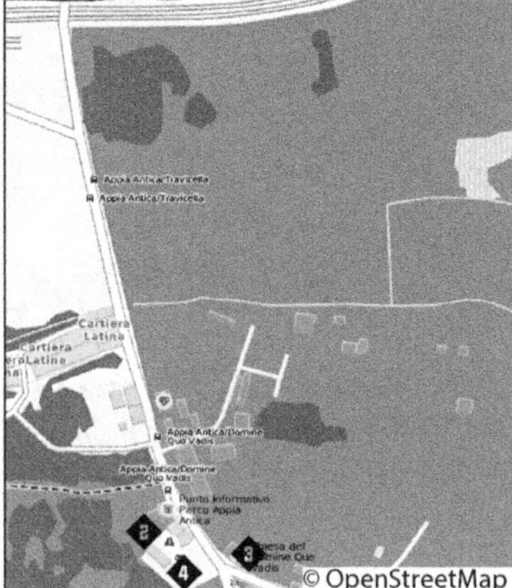

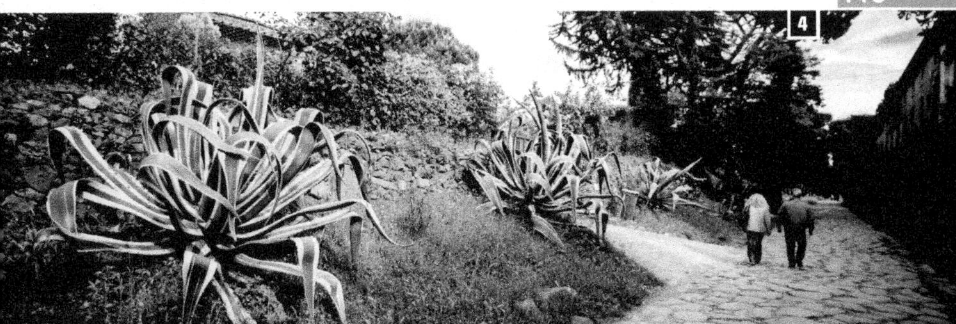

Roman economy depended on slave work and slaves constituted one third of the whole Apennine population.

Porta San Sebastiano ★ ★ 5

Via di Porta San Sebastiano 18

As part of Aurelian fortifications 8, these gates used to be called Porta Appia. They are the largest and best preserved city gates from the Roman period. The Arch of Drusus stands behind the gates, once part of the Aqua Marcia Aqueduct.

Museo delle Mura ★ ★

In the Porta San Sebastiano there is a small, but interesting Museum of the City Walls or Museo delle Mura. It is divided in three collections: ancient, medieval and modern art on the first and second floor, including the towers.

Highlights of the Via Appia Antica

▸ **Porta San Sebastiano & Museo delle Mura**, Via di Porta San Sebastiano 18

▸ **Church of Domine Quo Vadis**, Via Appia Antica 51, 0.5 mi | 0.8 km from Porta San Sebastiano

▸ **Tomb of Priscilla**, Via Appia Antica 76, 0.5 mi | 0.8 km from Porta San Sebastiano

▸ **Catacombe di San Domitilla**, Via delle Sette Chiese 282, 1.37 mi | 2.2 km from Porta San Sebastiano

▸ **Catacombe di San Callisto**, Via Appia Antica 126, 1.43 mi | 2.3 km from Porta San Sebastiano

▸ **San Sebastiano Fuori le Mura & Catacombe di San Sebastiano**, Via Appia Antica 136, 1.49 mi | 2.4 km from Porta San Sebastiano

▸ **Circus of Maxentius**, Via Appia Antica 153, 1.68 mi | 2.7 km from Porta San Sebastiano

▸ **Mausoleum of Cecilia Metella**, Via Appia Antica 161, 1.8 mi | 2.9 km from Porta San Sebastiano

▸ **Roman baths of Villa Capo di Bove**, Via Appia Antica 222, 2.11 mi | 3.4 km from Porta San Sebastiano

▸ **Original Roman pavement on Via Appia Antica**, Via Appia Antica 193, 2.17 mi | 3.5 km from Porta San Sebastiano

▸ **Villa dei Quintili** – with nymphaeum, theater, and baths, Via Appia Antica 290, 3.98 mi | 6.4 km from Porta San Sebastiano

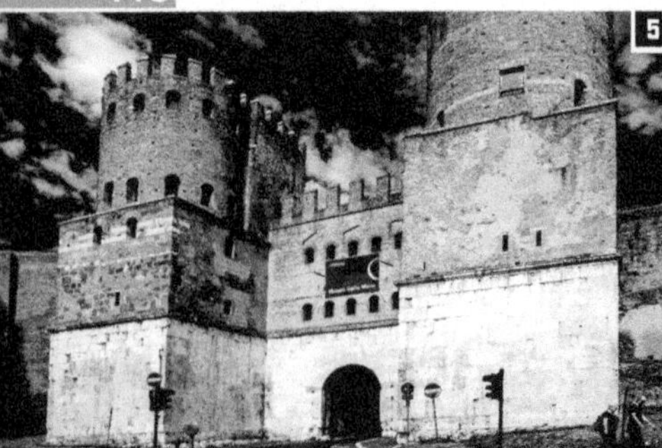

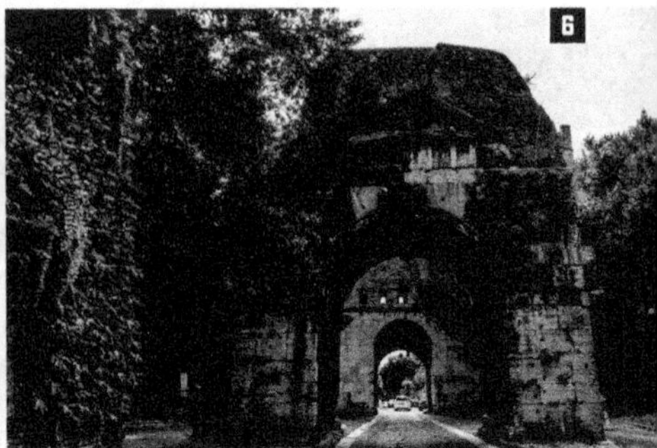

A protected walkway behind a castle battlement or the *Chemin de Ronde* can be visited during the Museum opening hours. Admission is free.

Arch of Drusus ★ ★ 6

Arch of Drusus is nested immediately before Via Appia Antica, next to Porta San Sebastiano. Although the origin of the arch is unknown, it was supposedly part of Aqua Marcia, Caracalla's aqueduct, which means it was never a triumphal arch. It has also been associated with Nero Claudius Drusus Germanicus (38–9 BC), who conquered Germania.

Some say it was Trajan's arc. In any case, the structure seems to have undergone several transformations even in ancient Rome. It is made of travertine, while the inner sides are covered in Numidian marble, with elements of white marble towards the base. Water actually ran through it as part of Aqua Marcia for Caracalla's new baths, and on top of it all, there is a concrete part coated in brick.

② Church of Domine Quo Vadis ★ ★

Via Appia Antica 51, 0.5 mi | 0.8 km from Porta San Sebastiano

Traditionally, Via Appia 7 is the road on which St. Peter met Jesus Christ and asked him: *"Domine, quo vadis?"* or "Lord, where are you going?" Christ responded by saying he was going back to Rome to get crucified again.

These words put St. Peter to shame, so he returned to Rome to be crucified as a martyr.

Allegedly, the place where their meeting took place had a special aura even in ancient Rome — Romans believed Hannibal and his troops managed to go only as far as this point.

In the 9th century, the church of Santa Maria in Palmis was built to mark the spot, but it is better known as Church of Domine Quo Vadis. Cardinal Francesco Barberini renovated it in 1637 in the baroque style, preserved to this day. Christian pilgrims visit regularly. There is a stone plate with the imprints of the feet of Jesus Christ.

On the other hand, archaeologists claim this is a votive plate dedicated to the Roman god of return – *dio Redicolo*. A temple was probably located in the vicinity.

The original plate can be found in the nearby Church of San Sebastiano alle Catacombe, built on top of the most well-known Roman catacombs.

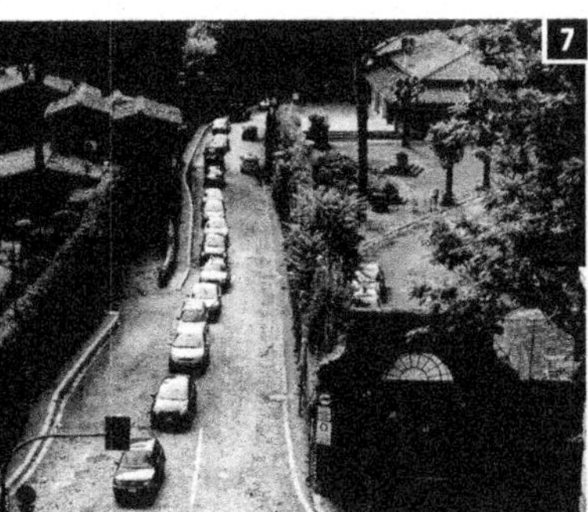

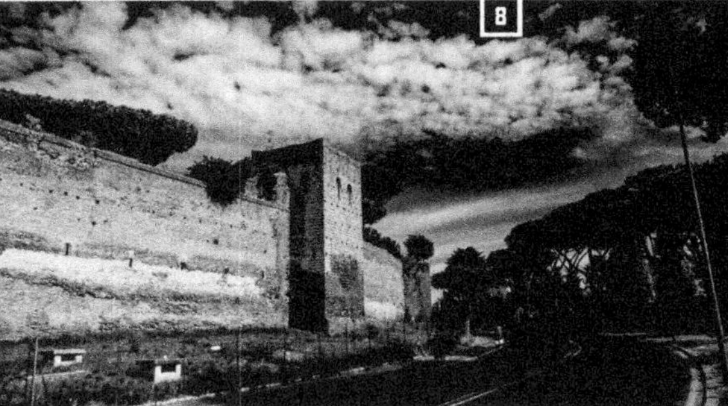

③ Tomb of Priscilla ★ ★

Via Appia Antica 76, 0.5 mi | 0.8 km from Porta San Sebastiano
This tomb is situated opposite the Church of Domine Quo Vadis. It belonged to Priscilla, the wife of a free slave emperor Domitian, Titus Flavius Abascanto. It was used as a fort in the Middle Ages.

④ Catacombe di San Domitilla ★ ★ ★

Via delle Sette Chiese 282, 1.37 mi | 2.2 km from Porta San Sebastiano

These are the oldest catacombs in this area. It is a labyrinth with four underground levels, each of them 16.4 ft or 5 m high. The tombs are from 1st and 2nd century, partly Early Christian. The funeral chambers contain classical and Christian motives. Above them, there is Santi Nereo e Achilleo from the 4th century. Highlights: The most important Early Christian fresco was found here. It is a representation of the *Last Supper* from 2nd century.

⑤ Catacombe di San Callisto ★ ★ ★

Via Appia Antica 126, 1.43 mi | 2.3 km from Porta San Sebastiano

Catacombe di San Callisto are the biggest catacombs found in Rome. They were reserved for Christian burials only. Funeral niches, corridors, chambers and vertical vents for air and light are spread across 37 acres or 15 hectares. All in all, these catacombs are 12.4 mi / 20 km long. Until the 5th century, there was room for more than 370,000 bodies.

Museo delle Mura | Museum of the City Walls
Address: Via di Porta San Sebastiano 18, Roma
Online: www.museodellemuraroma.it/en

Public transportation:
Bus stop Porta San Sebastiano: 118, 218

Opening hours: *see online*
Free entry to the permanent collection

Chiesa di Santa Maria delle Piante | Church of St. Mary in Palmis
Address: Via Appia Antica 51, Roma

Online: www.dominequovadis.com

Public transportation:
Bus stop Appia Antica – Domine Quo Vadis: 118, 218

Opening hours: *see online*

Catacombe di San Domitilla | Catacombe di San Domitillas
Address: Via delle Sette Chiese 282, Roma
Online: www.domitilla.info

Public transportation:
Bus stop Porta San Sebastiano: 118, 218

Opening hours: *see online*
Closed Tuesdays

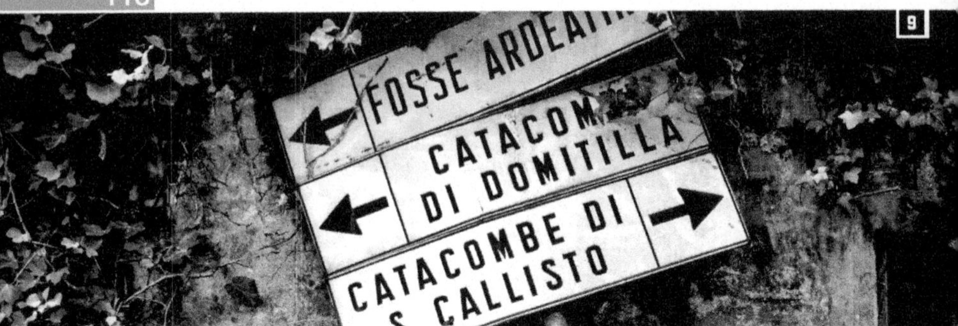

EXPLORING ROME – Via Appia ★★★★

294

Since funeral niches could be used over and over again, it is estimated that more than a million people were buried here. The catacombs were named after Pope Callixtus (217–222), who had them built while Zephyrinus (199–217) was still the Pope. From the 9th to mid-19th century, the catacombs were forgotten. Not only were these the first catacombs under the direct control of the Roman Church, but this is also where 100 martyrs and 16 Roman bishops, i.e. popes found their final resting places. The first inscription stating that the Roman bishop is actually the Pope can be found here. Popes were buried here from the mid-2nd century to late 4th century. By late 9th century, their relics were moved to various shrines. Five broken papal sarcophagi are still here in the Papal Crypt, while another two are kept in the St. Eusebius' Crypt.

Visit to the catacombs is only allowed in the presence of a guide, all included in the price of admission.

◈ Catacombe di San Sebastiano ★★★

Via Appia Antica 136, 1.49 mi | 2.4 km from Porta San Sebastiano

Catacombs di San Sebastiano are 7 mi / 11 km long. The sightseeing, however, takes place in a very small area. All underground tombs are called catacombs because of these.

Catacombe di San Callisto | Catacomb of Callixtus
Address: Via Appia Antica, 126, Roma
Online: www.catacombe.roma.it

Public transportation:
Bus stop Appia Antica – Scuola Agraria: 118

Opening hours: *see online*
Closed Wednesdays

Did you know?

Catacombs around the Via Appia Antica

Via Appia Antica is the most famous and most visited landmark because of the three Roman and Early Christian catacombs spread within a 0.62 mi / 1 km radius.

Each one of these three catacombs is open to visitors 11 months of the year, six days a week. The non-working week or day never coincides, so it is impossible to find yourself on the Via Appia Antica with the catacombs closed. Romans used to bury their dead in catacombs, in sarcophagi placed alongside main roads outside the city, as well as in urns that were kept in niches of the columbarium. Christians were buried in catacombs until the 5th century, when the practice changed to ground burials. There are sixty catacombs in Rome, but only some of them are open to visitors.

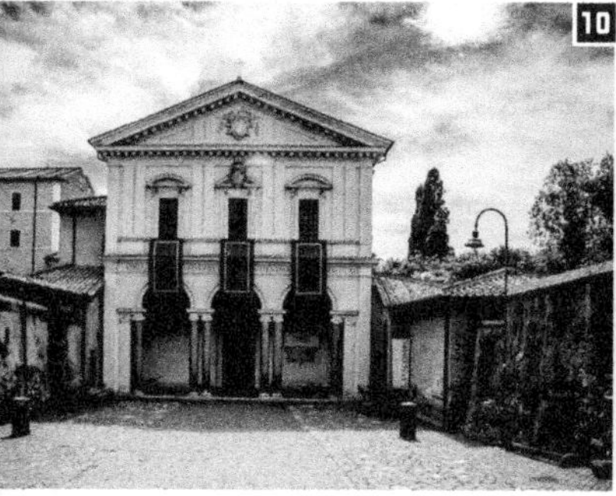

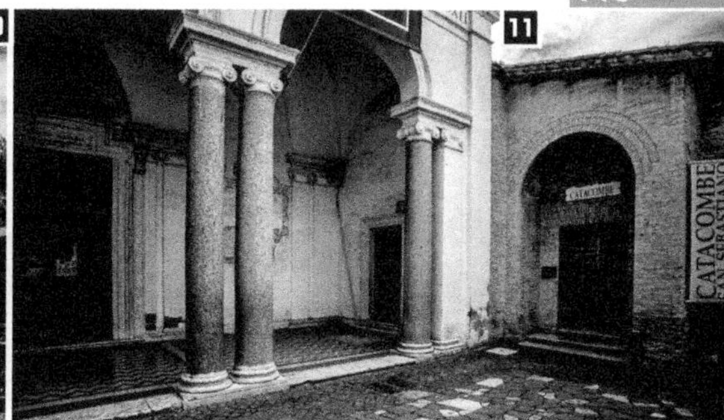

The place above the catacombs, where the Church of San Sebastiano Fuori le Mura was built, used to be called *ad catacumbas,* that is "in the valley". The sag was the result of digging for raw porcelain material. In the Chapel of Relics you can find a stone imprinted with the footprints of Jesus related to the episode of *Quo vadis?* Similar to other catacombs on the Via Appia Antica, there are interesting graffiti and frescoes to be explored. **11**

St. Sebastian's relics are now in the Chapel of Saint Sebastian, in the Basilica San Sebastiano Fuori le Mura. **12**

⑦ Basilica San Sebastiano Fuori le Mura ★ ★ **10**

Via Appia Antica 136, 1.49 mi | 2.4 km from Porta San Sebastiano

The history of the church goes back to the 4th century and Emperor Constantine, while the façade is from the 17th century.

All the way to the Great Jubilee of 2000, this church was one of seven churches that every Roman pilgrim had to visit.

Pope John Paul II replaced San Sebastiano Fuori le Mura with the Church of Santuario della Madonna del Divino Amore on the pilgrims' list.

Be it tradition, or the fact that the latter is quite far away, most pilgrims stick to the original list and pay regular visits to San Sebastiano Fuori le Mura.

Catacombe di San Sebastiano | Catacombs of Saint Sebastian
San Sebastiano Fuori le Mura | Saint Sebastian beyond the Walls
Address: Via Appia Antica 136, Roma
Online: www.catacombe.org

Public transportation:
Bus stop Basilica San Sebastiano: 118

Opening hours: see online

Closed Sundays

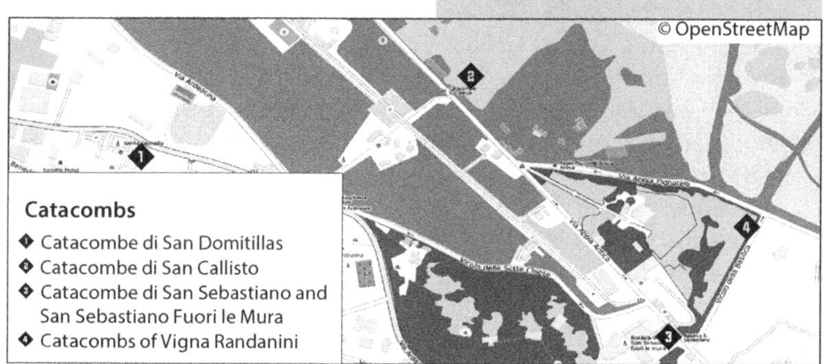

Catacombs

- ◆ Catacombe di San Domitillas
- ◆ Catacombe di San Callisto
- ◆ Catacombe di San Sebastiano and San Sebastiano Fuori le Mura
- ◆ Catacombs of Vigna Randanini

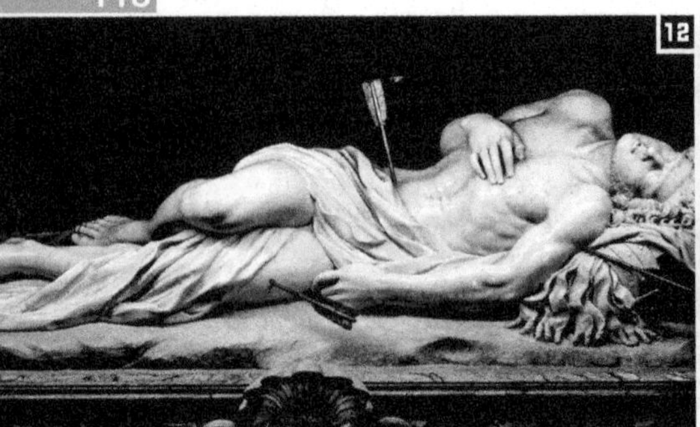

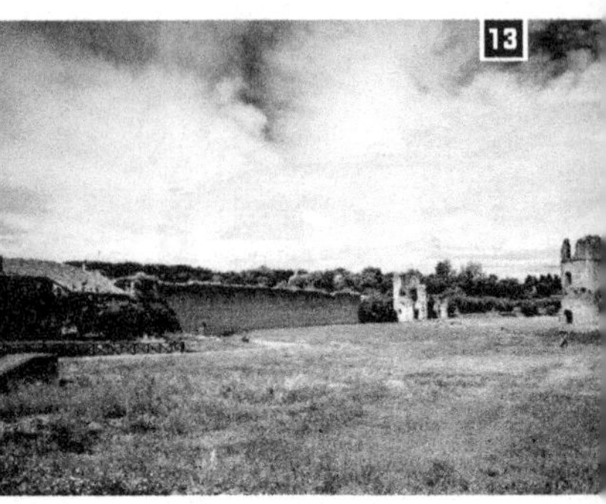

The bust of the Salvatore, or *Salvator Mundi*, was rediscovered in 2001, when the experts have recognized this bust as the last work of the great artist Gian Lorenzo Bernini. **1**

⑧ Villa di Massenzio ★ ★ **13**

Villa di Massenzio, Via Appia Antica 153, 1.68 mi | 2.7 km from Porta San Sebastiano

Maxentius usurped the Roman throne and declared himself emperor in 306, after his father Maximian abdicated with Diocletian on May 5, 305. He was defeated by Constantine in the Battle of the Milvian Bridge in 312, and died. Maxentius ruled for only six years. During that time, he initiated such intensive building projects that even emperors who had been on the throne for decades paled in comparison. Apart from Basilica of Maxentius on the Roman Forum, there is also this circus and a palace close by.

Circus of Maxentius is over 1,640 ft (500 m) long and 295 ft (90 m) wide.

Moreover, this is the best preserved hippodrome to this day and the second largest circus ever built. It was recorded that Circus of Maxentius was only used once for the funeral of Maxentius' son Valerius Romulus, who died in AD 309 and was buried in the nearby palace.

The obelisk that was erected in honor of Valerius Romulus and moved by Bernini to Piazza Navona following the order of Pope Innocent X.

⑨ Mausoleo di Cecilia Metella ★ ★ ★

Via Appia Antica 161, 1.8 mi | 2.9 km from Porta San Sebastiano

Caecilia Metella (100–69 BC) came from a very respectable Republican family of Caecilii Metellii. **14**

Her husband, Marcus Licinius Crassus, was among the wealthiest Romans of his time. He belonged to the First Trumvirate, joined by Caesar and Pompey. It was Marcus Licinius Crassus who commissioned this monumental cylindrical mausoleum for his prematurely deceased wife.

The mausoleum is 36 ft (11 m) high and 95 ft (29 m) in diameter.

Presently, the sarcophagus of Cecilia Metella is situated in the Palazzo Farnese courtyard. The building next to the mausoleum used to belong to the Caetani family. **15**

In the 14th century, the family decided to turn the mausoleum into a fort, to serve as a toll booth.

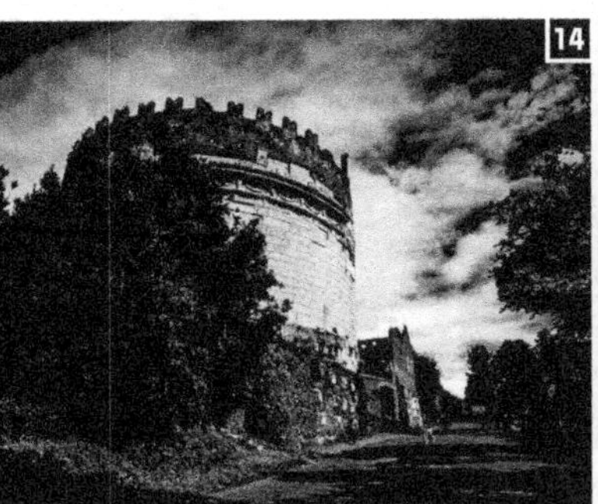

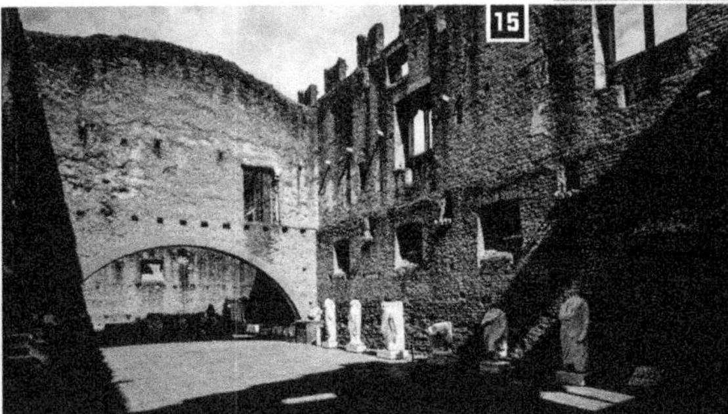

Chiesa di San Nicola a Capo di Bove ★ 🖬

Chiesa di San Nicola a Capo di Bove (1303) is the little Gothic church located opposite Cecilia Metella's tomb.

This was the parish church of the Caetani's fortified village dedicated to San Nicola di Bari.

Capo di Bove Tower ★ 🖬

Immediately after a section of ancient paving you will find the Capo di Bove Tower.

Two plaques affixed to the monument are dedicated to the astronomer Angelo Secchi who measured the straight stretch of the Via Appia Antica (1855).

Heroic relief from the Republican era ★ 🖬

This is the copy of the funeral stele with marble high-relief. It depicts a naked youth, with an imperial mantle and Hellenistic armor at his feet. The original is in the Roman National Museum.

Did you know?

Via Appia Antica as Beverly Hills

Judging by the residents, Via Appia Antica is the Italian version of Beverly Hills — Marcello Mastroianni, Gina Lollobrigida, Anthony Quinn and many others from Italian show business have lived or still live here.

Villa di Massenzio | Villa of Maxentius
Address: Via Appia Antica 153, Roma
Online: www.villadimassenzio.it/en

Public transportation:
Bus stop Basilica San Sebastiano 118

Opening hours: see online
Free entry to the permanent collection

Mausoleo di Cecilia Metella | Tomb of Caecilia Metella
Address: Via Appia Antica 161, Roma
Online:
www.parcoarcheologicoappiaantica.it
Public transportation:
Bus stop Cecilia Metella: 660

Opening hours: *see online*

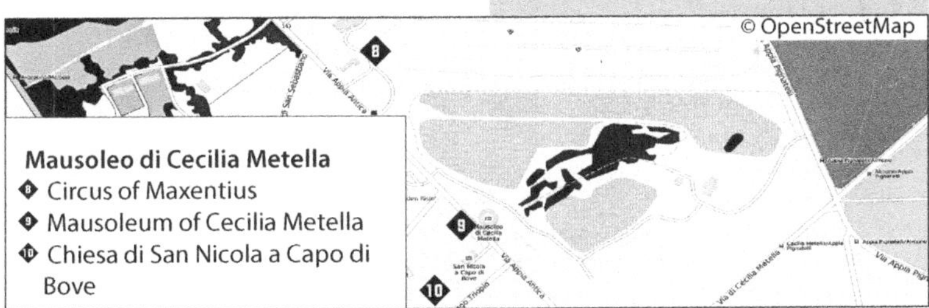

Mausoleo di Cecilia Metella
◆ Circus of Maxentius
◆ Mausoleum of Cecilia Metella
◆ Chiesa di San Nicola a Capo di Bove

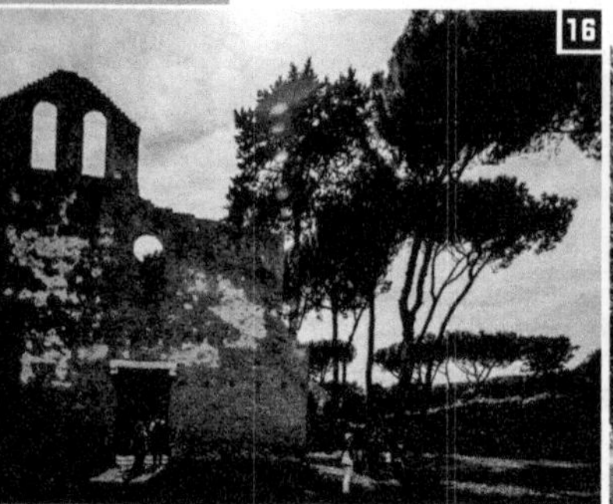
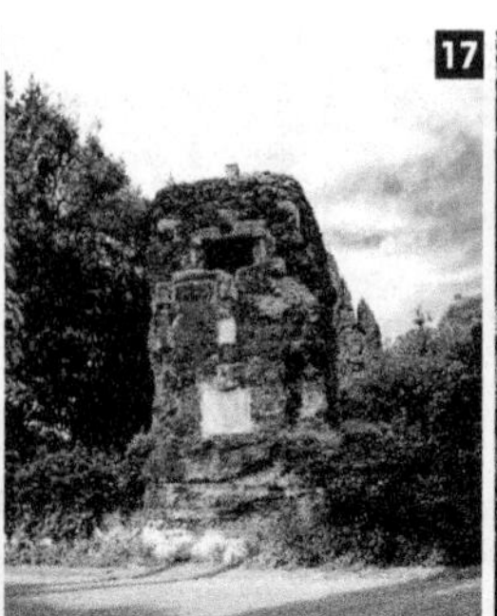
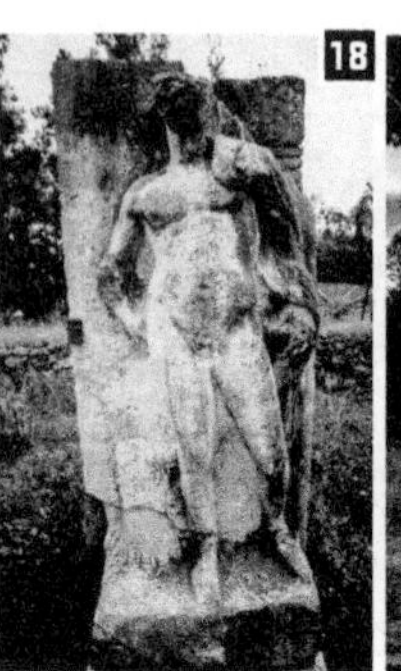
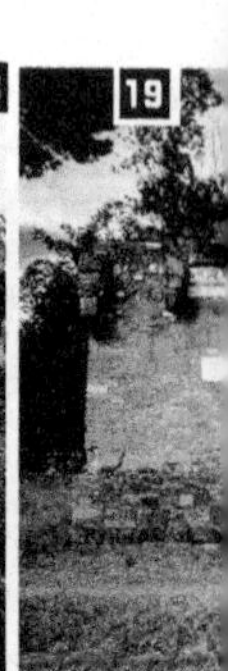

Tomb of freedman Marcus Servilius Quartus ★ 19

Antonio Canova restored this ancient monument in the in the neo-classical style (1808).

Tomb of Seneca ★

The Tomb of Seneca was also constructed by Antonio Canova. The famous Roman Stoic philosopher Lucius Annaeus Seneca owned a villa at the IV Roman mile of the Appia. He was the tutor and later advisor to emperor Nero. Nero ordered him to kill himself.

Circular Mausoleum ★

The entrance to the subterranean burial chamber with four niches for the sarcophagi from the Republican era.

Tomb of the children of Sextus Pompeius Iustus ★

Antonio Canova inserted numerous decorative and architectural fragments which contains an inscription in hexameters in which Sextus Pompeius Iustus remembers the premature death of his children. On one fragment of a sarcophagus you can see the portrait of a married couple inside an open shell.

Doric Monument ★

A funeral monument that featuring a Doric frieze with metopes decorated with a helmet, rosettes and vases, dating from the Republican era.

Tomb of Hilarus Fuscus ★

The tomb of Hilarus Fuscus is a funerary monument. The architecture of the tomb and the analysis of the hairstyle of female portraits allowed dating to the late Republican period.

Tomb of the freedman Tiberius Claudius Secondinus 20

Ti. Claudio
Ti. filio Pal(atina tribu)
Secundino
an(nos) nat(o), IX m(enses) IX,
d(ies) XIIX, equo pub(lico),
f(ilio) dulcissimo,
Flavia Irene
mater

Tiberio Claudio Secondino, son of Tiberio, belonging to the Palatine tribe, who died at nine, nine months, eighteen days, honored with a public horse, sweet son, mother Flavia Irene.

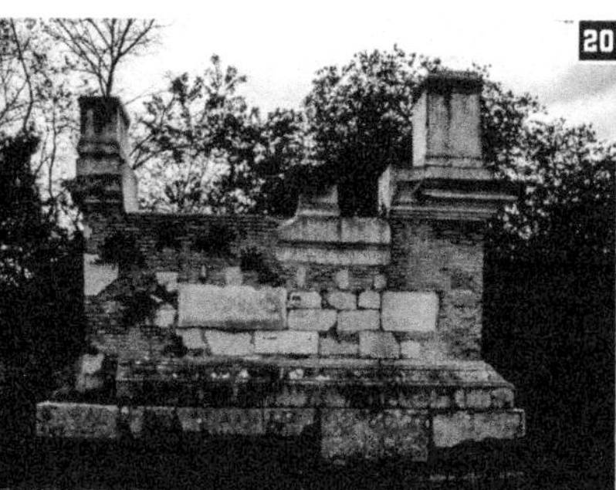
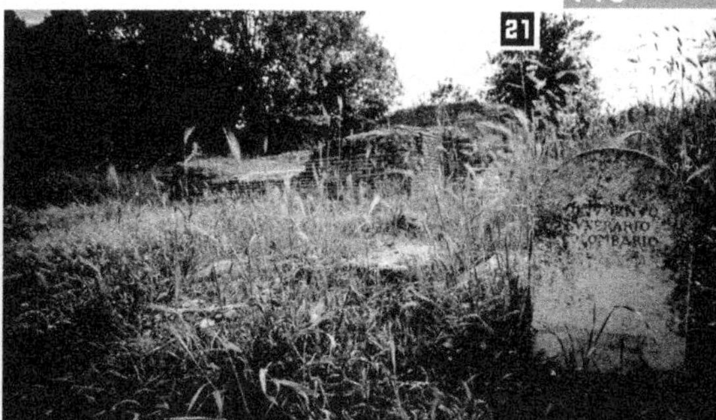

Tiberius Claudius Secundinus was a Freedmen under the Emperor Claudius (41–54).

Columbarium ★

A columbarium is a place for the public storage of cinerary urns. This one is a brickwork construction from the middle of the 2nd century.

Tomb of Quintus Apuleius ★

Here you can see some nice floral fragments and parts of the attic.

Temple-shaped sepulchre ★

This temple and tomb has two stories and an access stairway to the high podium, which led to the upper floor, where funeral ceremonies were held.

The use of two-colour brickwork is a feature of the tomb and typical of the middle of the 2nd century.

The Tomb of Rabiri ★

A tomb with a copy of the original relief, now in the Museum of Palazzo Massimo alle Terme, shows the portraits of three persons: Caius Rabirius Hermodorus, his wife Rabiria Demaris and priestess of Isis, Usia Prima (1st century).

Festoons Tomb ★

The Festoons Tomb belongs to the altar type tombs built in blocks of Peperino stone (1st century BC).

Tomb of the Frontispiece ★ ★

In the center you can see a married couple and on the sides are their two children. The women's hair with a knot tell us that the relief can be dated from the second half of the 1st century BC.

⑩ Villa Capo di Bove or Bagni di Erode Attico ★ ★ ★

Via Appia Antica 222, 2.11 mi | 3.4 km from Porta San Sebastiano

Annia Regilla was from a Roman aristocratic family. Her father arranged for her to be married to a prominent Greek-Roman aristocrat Herodes Atticus.

Her dowry secured the purchase of a large estate, which has stretched between the II and III mile of the Via Appia, deep into the hinterland. Capo di Bove is an archaeological site with the private roman thermal baths (2nd century).

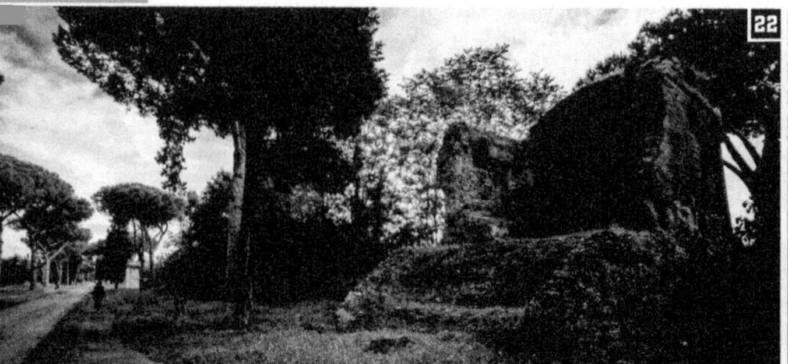

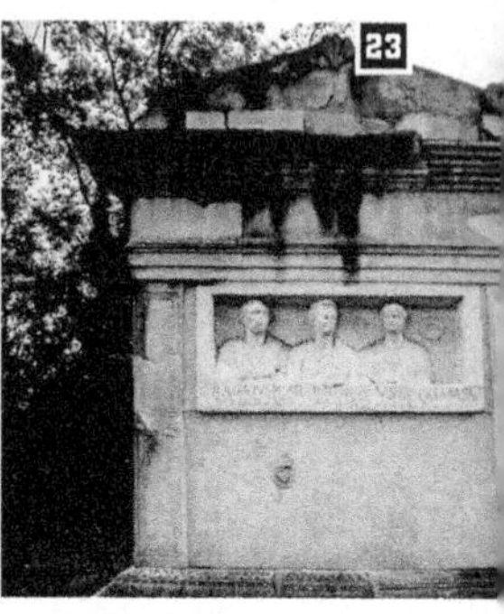

There are several well-preserved mosaics and other typical remains, such as *caldarium*, hot water room, *tepidarium*, tepid water room and *frigidarium*, cold water room. The baths were in function to the 4th century. There is a modern villa next to it with many Roman remains built into the walls. Annia and Herodes lived on this estate for only a couple of years. They spent the rest of their lives in Athens. After Annia was killed in Greece in AD 160, Herodes was charged with murder but soon he was acquitted. Herodes turned his estate into a *Triopium,* a sort of holy area and built here a temple, nymphaeum and tomb for his wife. Later, his estate was incorporated in the suburban residence of Emperor Maxentius built in the 4th century.

⑪ Original Roman pavement ★★

Via Appia Antica 222, 2.11 mi | 3.4 km from Porta San Sebastiano

You can walk on an original Roman pavement from Via Appia Antica 193, that is from 2.2 mi / 3.5 km onwards. The section is about 0.9 ft (1.5 km) long. Only residents' cars are allowed here.

⑫ Villa of the Quintilii ★★

Villa dei Quintili – with nymphaeum, theater, and baths, Via Appia Antica 290, 4 mi | 6.4 km from Porta San Sebastiano

Villa dei Quintili is so spacious that travelers called it Roma Vecchia or

Villa Capo di Bove
Address: Via Appia Antica 222, Roma
Online:
www.parcoarcheologicoappiaantica.it
Public transportation:
Bus stop Cecilia Metella: 660
Opening hours: *see online*

Did you know?

Ideal marriage after the time taste

The Villa Capo di Bove were private property of a wealthy Roman philosopher Herodes Atticus and his wife Annia Regilla, who was from a respectable senatorial Roman family. Annia's grandfather was Faustina the Elder's father, and Faustina was Emperor Antoninus Pius' wife. Annia's husband Herodes Atticus was both of Greek and Roman aristocratic descent. Hadrian named him Prefect of Asia in AD 125. Hadrian's heir, Emperor Antoninus Pius, called Herodes to mentor his stepsons in 140, who were Roman emperors in the making – Marcus Aurelius and Lucius Verus.

Villa dei Quintili | Villa of the Quintilii
Address: Via Appia Nuova 1092, Roma
Online:
www.parcoarcheologicoappiaantica.it
Public transportation:
Bus stop Appia – Bisignano: 118, 664
Opening hours: *see online*

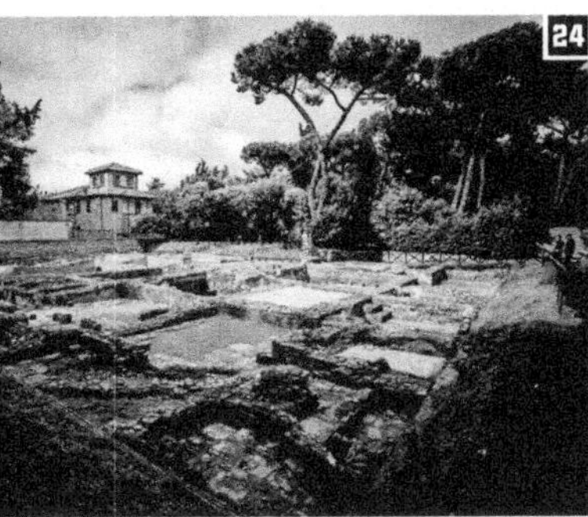

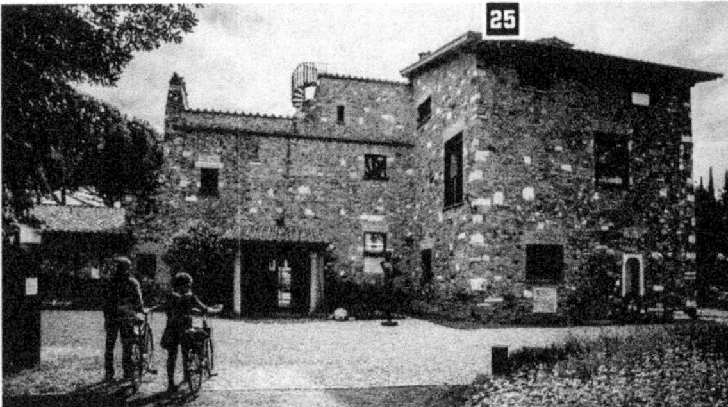

Old Rome even in the 18th century, thinking they came across a Roman settlement. Consuls and brothers Sextus Quintilius Valerius Maximus and Sextus Quintilius Condianus had it built in mid-2nd century.

Emperor Commodus was envious of their large estate and charged them with conspiracy. They were killed in 182, so that Commodus could take the villa.

After that, it became an imperial residence and was extended several times. Until the 4th century, the area gradually grew from Via Appia to the present-day Via Appia Nuova, with nymphaeum, hippodrome, private aqueduct and baths.

❷ Park of the Caffarella s★ ★ ★

Caffarella Park is a large green valley from Via Appia Antica to Via Latina, also part of the Appian Way Regional Park. Even though you can access the park from several angles, such as, from the Roman walls at Porta San Sebastiano, the easiest way to the park is from the Church of Domine Quo Vadis or St. Mary in Palmis.

From there, walk around 50 paces and turn left on Via Appia to Via della Caffarella. Bicycle rental is available at the park on several locations.

Chiesa di Sant'Urbano alla Caffarella ★ ★ ★

This is one of the best preserved temples from the Roman era, mainly because it was turned into a church in the 7th century, which made the harvesting of old stones for construction sites impossible.

The temple is situated outside the Aurelian Walls, so it has been pillaged and destroyed over the years.

It was built by Herodes Atticus who dedicated it to his wife Annia Regilla. The Roman structure is perfectly preserved, with frescoes from the 11th century. Today it is the rectory of St. Sebastian Outside the Walls. It is open for visitors every other Sunday of the month from 11 a.m.

The Nymphaeum of Egeria ★ ★

The fountain was built by Herodes Atticus in mid-2nd century, which can be attributed according to the type of brick used in construction. 26

Tomb of Annia Regilla ★ ★ ★

The tomb was also built by Herodes Atticus for his wife. It has two stories, and the external walls are well preserved. 28

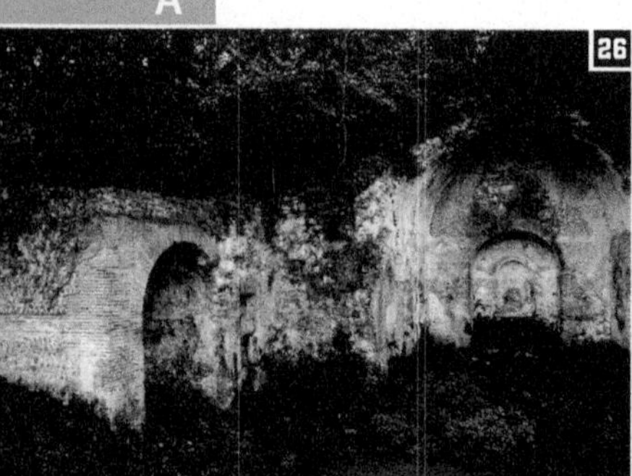

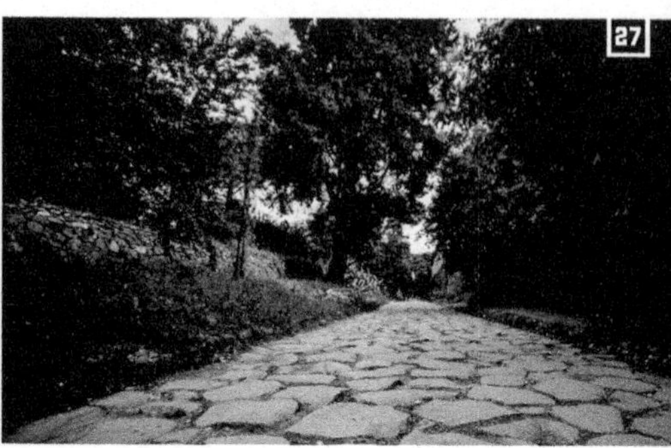

The Sacred Wood ★ ★

This is the only high plateau across from which you can find the Church of Sant'Urbano. Here, you can get an overview of not only the entire area Herodes Atticus inherited after his wife's death, but also the mountains around Rome. Allegedly, it was Herodes Atticus who ordered the Sacred Wood to be planted here.

❸ Tombs of Via Latina ★ ★ ★ 🟦

This well-preserved Roman tombs are now in the small (1,476 ft / 450 m long) archaeological park Parco archeologico delle Tombe di via Latina:

▶ Barberini tomb or *Sepolcro Barberini* in red and yellow bricks, with to floors and an underground burial chamber (2nc century AD),
The Barberini sarcophagus is now in the Vatican Museums, Galleria dei Candelabri, **[p.147]**
▶ Tomb of the Valerii or *Sepolcro dei Valeri* (2nc century AD) is two-story brick tomb,
▶ Tomb of the Pancratii or *Sepolcro dei Pancrazi* contains sarcophagus, good preserved stucco and frescoes.

❹ Parco degli Acquedotti ★ ★ ★ 🟦

This unique park has monumental remains of seven aqueducts and many other buildings, mostly from ancient Roman times. The park and the grandiose arches are still one of the favorite film locations in Italian movies, from Dolce Vita to La Grande Bellezza.

Aqua Claudia and Aqua Anio Novus ★ ★ 🟦

The arcades of the Aqua Claudia and Aqua Anio Novus aqueducts were finished during Emperor Claudius in AD 52. There are 154 remaining connected arches, and the highest one rises to 88.5 ft or 27 m. Aqua Anio Novus was attached to Aqua Claudia, so a single building is the focus of five diverging aqueducts. You can still detect different water systems in some parts. The upper levels have been completely destroyed over time.

Acqua Felice ★ ★

Arcades of the Aqua Felice, built by Pope Sixtus V from 1585 to 1590.

Campo Barbico ★ ★

Campo Barbico as the intersection of Aqua Claudia and Aqua Marcia, was turned into a military camp by the Ostrogoth King Vigiges during the siege of Rome in 539.

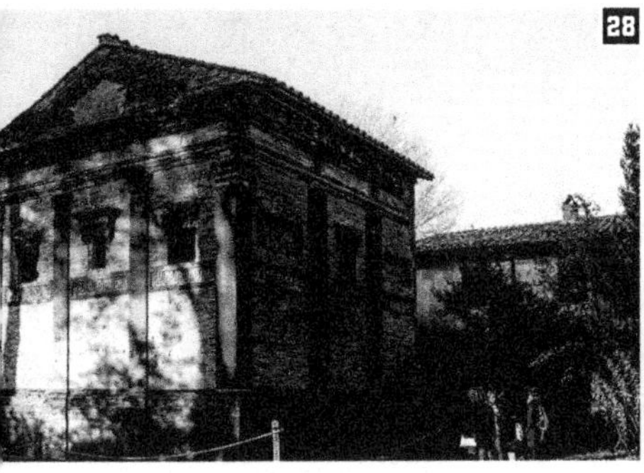

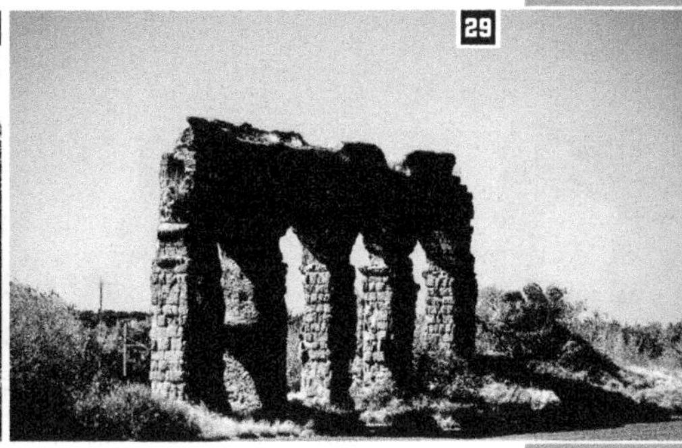

Tor Fiscale ★

Tor Fiscale or the Customs Tower is 98 ft or 30 m high. It was built in the Middle Ages on the intersection of Aqua Claudia and Aqua Marcia.

Villa dei Sette Bassi ★

Villa dei Sette Bassi is on the VI mile of the ancient road Via Latina, presently Via Tuscolana. It was built in the 2nd century, as the second largest villa in the Roman suburbs.

The largest one was the complex of Villa of the Quintilii on Via Appia Antica.

This villa was commissioned by consul and prefect Settimio Basso. Only a small temple, a cistern and a small aqueduct have been preserved.

Villa delle Vignacce ★

Very little can be seen of this villa, because it has not been entirely excavated. It was built sometime between 2nd and 4th century.

The excavated statues were taken to the Vatican Museums.

The walls of the baths and hall of the villa are still here.

Parco archeologico delle Tombe di via Latina | Via Latina archeolocial park
Address: Via dell'Arco di Travertino 151, Roma
Online:
www.parcoarcheologicoappiaantica.it

Public transportation:
Metro A stop Arco di Travertino

Opening hours: *see online*

Parco degli Acquedotti | Aqueduct Park
Address: Via del Quadraro / Via Lemonia / Via delle Capanelle
Online: www.parcodegliacquedotti.it

Public transportation:
Metro A stop Lucio Sestio or Giulio Agricola, Subaugusta or Cinecittà

Archaeological parks

- ❶ Via Appia Antica
- ❷ Park of the Caffarella
- ❸ Parco archeologico delle Tombe di via Latina
- ❹ Parco di Torre Fiscale
- ❺ Parco degli Acquedotti
- ❻ Metro A stop Arco di Travertino
- ❼ Metro A stop Porta Furba Quadraro

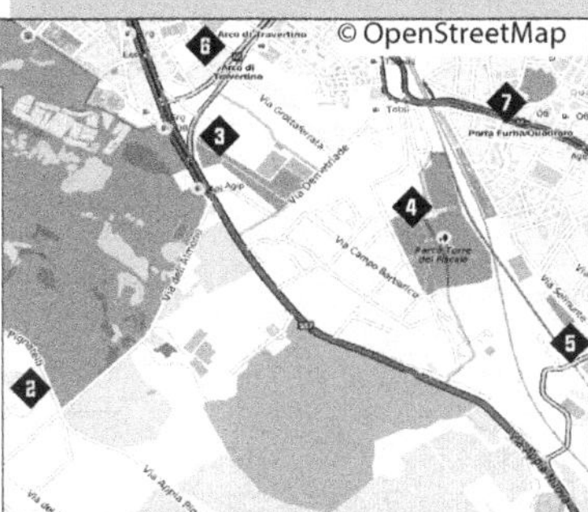

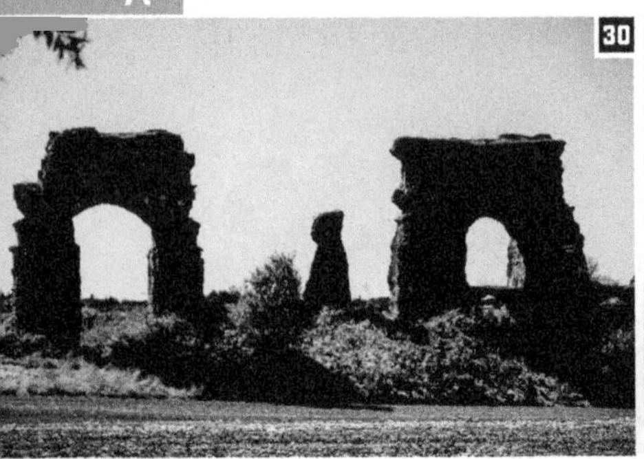

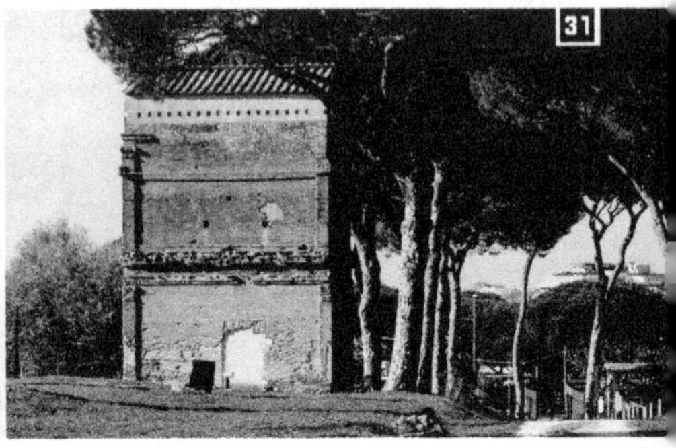

❖ Cinecittà Studios ★ ★ ★ 32

The movie studio was designed during the Fascist regime and inaugurated by the Italian dictator, Benito Mussolini in 1937, himself. As an important instrument in the Fascist propaganda, it released over 300 feature-length films until 1943. After the war, it brought fame to directors such as Roberto Rossellini, Vittorio De Sica and Luchino Visconti. Some of the most important movies by Federico Fellini, e.g., *La dolce vita* (1960) or *Il Casanova di Federico Fellini* (1976) were also shot in these studios.

During the 1950's, Hollywood producers required the services from these studios. It was mostly used for historical dramas, romantic and adventure films, for example, *Quo vadis?* (1959), *Roman Holiday* (1953) and *Ben-Hur* (1959). In the 1960's, Cinecittà released Sergio Leone's westerns. In the 1960's, Cinecittà released Sergio Leone's westerns: *A Fistful of Dollars* (1964), *For a Few Dollars More* (1965) and *The Good, the Bad and the Ugly* (1966).

The Godfather Part III (1990) by Francis Ford Coppola, *Gangs of New York* (2002) by Martin Scorsese, and *The Passion of the Christ* (2004) by Mel Gibson are also some of the films produced in these studios.

More recently, international television producers have taken over most of the studios. For instance, entire sets were built for the TV show *Rome* in 2007, and still used today for film and TV with minor modifications. You can take a tour of the studios with tours in English available every day.

Cinecittà Studios
Address: Via Tuscolana, Roma
Online: www.cinecittastudios.it/en

Public transportation:
Metro A stop Cinecittà

Opening hours: *see online*

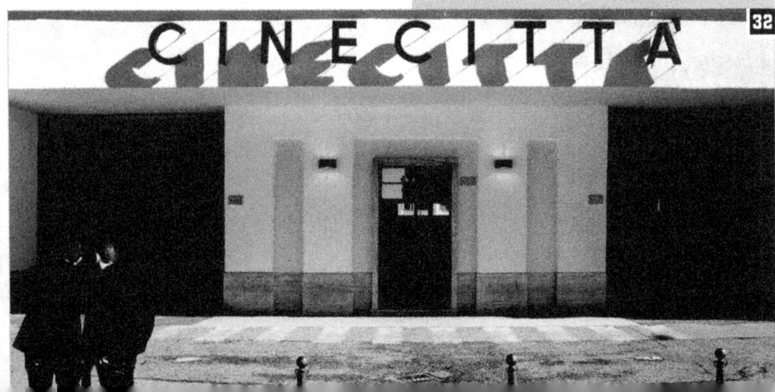

Food & Drink

Restaurant in the Jewish quarter of Rome

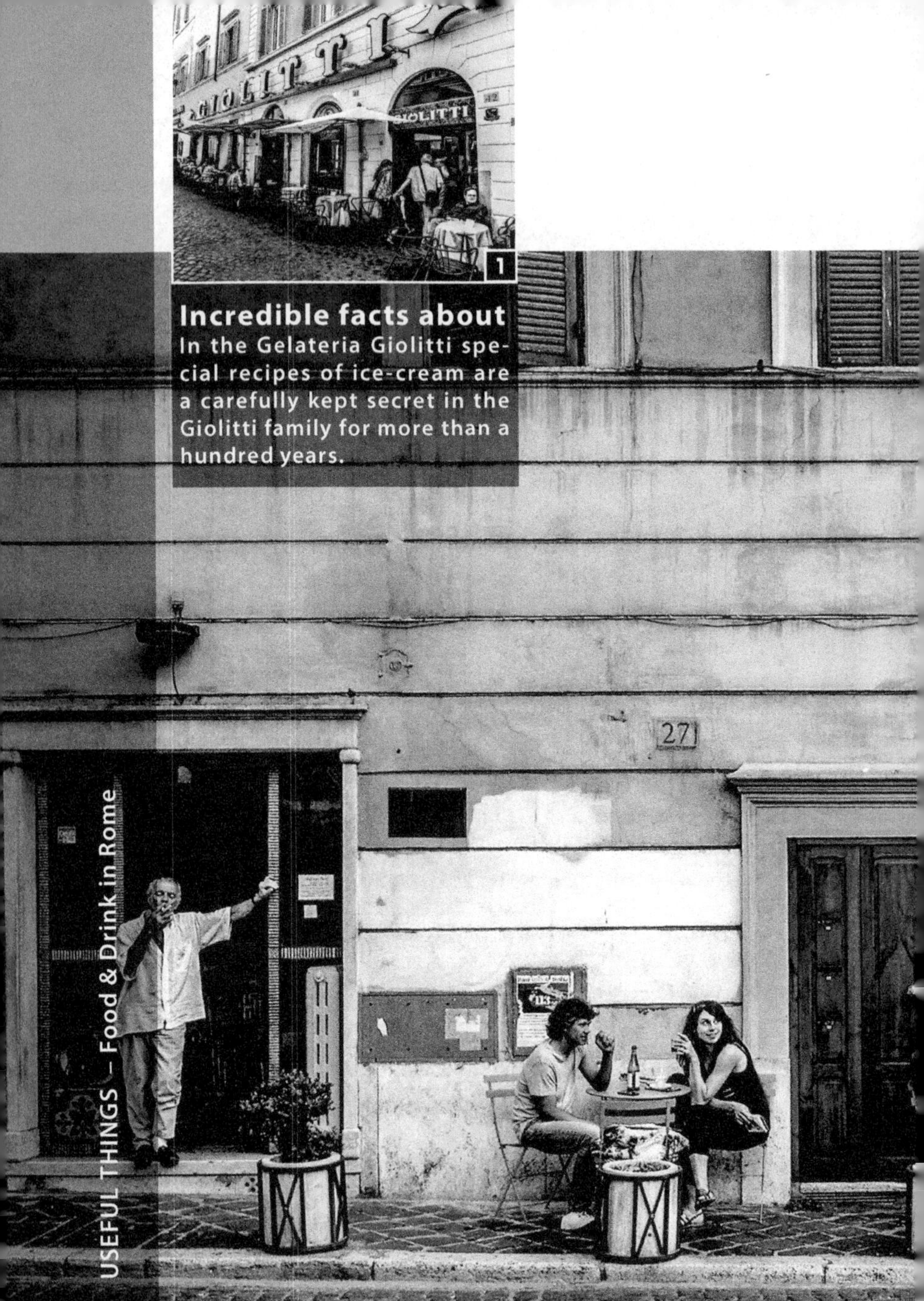

Incredible facts about

In the Gelateria Giolitti special recipes of ice-cream are a carefully kept secret in the Giolitti family for more than a hundred years.

Via dei Coronari

Extra Tip : : :
Whatever you choose, by Giolitti you will be astonished by the rich flavor. It is not easy to find your way among more than a hundred ice cream flavors. When you say your flavors, ice cream server will ask you whether you want topping. It is on the house.

Where and what to eat in Rome?

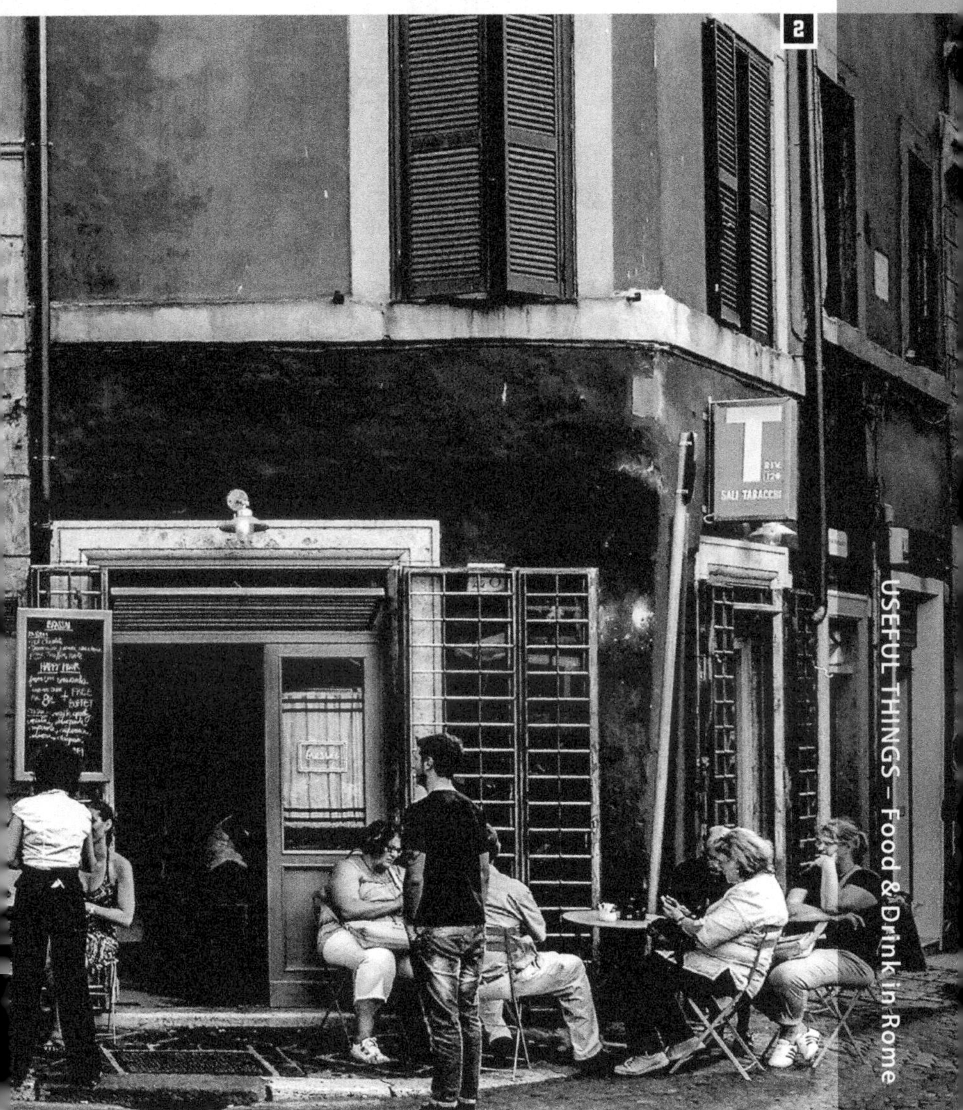

Gelateria Giolitti
Address: Via Uffici del Vicario 40, Roma. **Online:** www.giolitti.it
Public transportation: Bus stop Pie' Di Marmo: 116 or Largo Torre Argentina: 30, 40, 46, 62, 64, 70, 81, 87, 130F, 186, 190F, 492, 628, 916, 916F

Tip ::: THE TOWN OF ARICCIA (LAZIO) HAS BECOME FAMOUS FOR ITS PORCHETTA

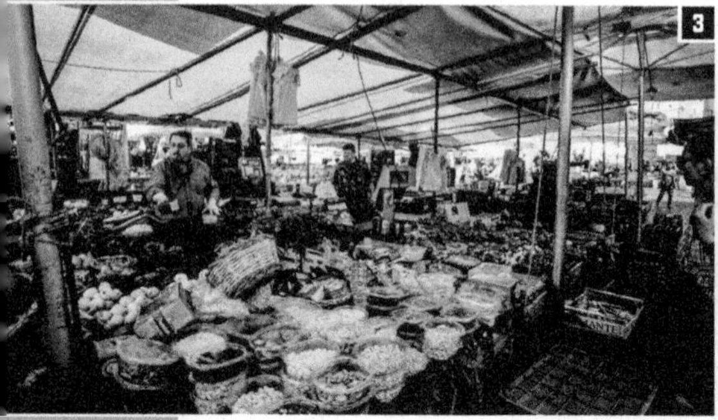
3

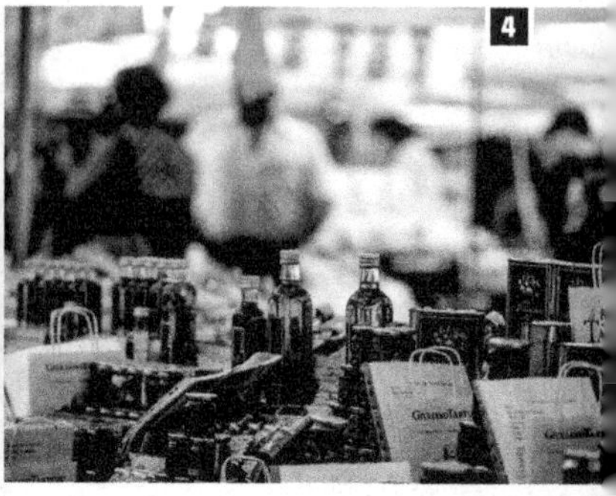
4

❶ Cucina Romana ★★★★ 3

The most important topics of conversation in Rome are not soccer, politics or personal life — it's all about food. Roman cuisine is part of the Italian cuisine, and special in many ways. 5

Out of many different kinds of Italian cuisine, you can only find *quinto quarto* or the fifth quarter category, something considered to be lower quality meat, in Roman recipes. Even with well-known Italian dishes, there are special Roman varieties. Even though pizza is the most popular Italian dish 22, *Pizza Romana* is something completely different from *Pizza Napolitana*. And *Pizza Bianca* is such an authentic Roman dish, it's hard to order it anywhere in Italy outside of Rome. Spaghetti are everywhere, but only the Romans make *Spaghetti alla Carbonara* with *Pecorino Romano*, a local cheese as one of the key ingredients. Pecorino Romano was main meal of Roman legionnaires. *Bucatini all'Amatriciana* is a dish made of round spaghetti-like pasta, with a hole in the middle (*buco* in Italian means hole) and *guanciale*, bacon made of pork cheeks. 9

There are also dishes that traditionally belong to Roman-Jewish cuisine. Jews have lived in Rome since 2nd century BC, even before the arrival of the great Jewish diaspora after the first Jewish-Roman War (66–73). If you did not try *Carciofi alla Giudia* (Jewish style artichokes) or *Fiori alla Zucca* (zucchini flowers), you cannot really say you know Roman cuisine that well. 10

You may opt to eat something on the fly while rushing from one sight to the next. Do as the Romans do, look for a nice porchetta sandwich or vegetarian pizza and you will not regret it. 26

Porchetta is pork glazed with a juicy layer of garlic, rosemary, thyme, oregano, sage and other herbs, rolled and roasted. Sometimes you can see whole piglets roasted like that. Porchetta is part of a *panino* (sandwich), while in Rome and the surrounding area, it is also an ingredient in Pizza Bianca.

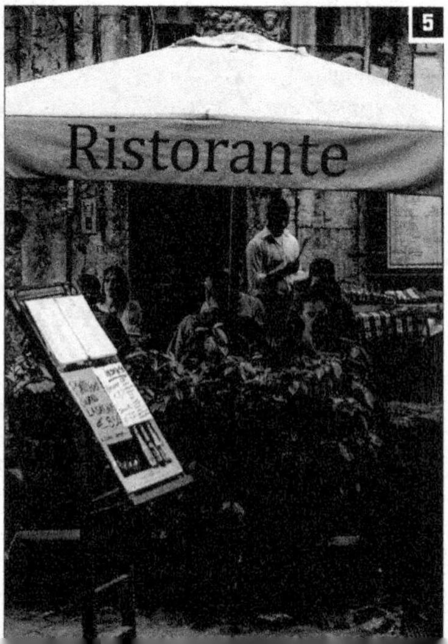

5

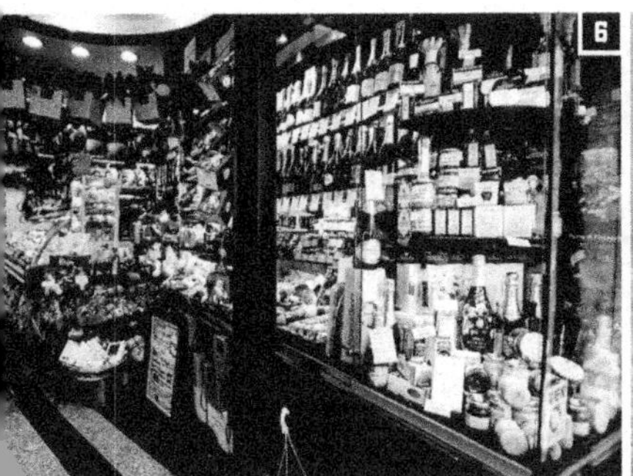

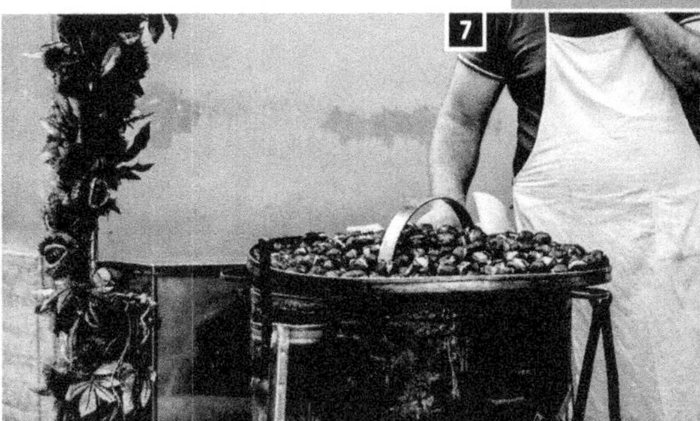

There is a type of Roman fast food called *Supplì alla Romana*. These are fried rice croquettes stuffed with beef liver.

When they are filled with *mozzarella*, they are called *Supplì al Telefono*, because when you bite into a piece of Supplì, the mozzarella stretches out like a telephone chord.

Antipasti

Supplì are usually served cold or heated, and they are called antipasti, or appetizers.

They are joined by the Roman *Bruschetta*, toasted bread with garlic and olive oil.

Bruschetta can have tomatoes, balsamic vinegar, ham or some other great, fresh ingredient close at hand.

Fiori di Zucca is a favorite Roman antipasto. These are fried zucchini flowers stuffed with mozzarella and anchovies.

Carciofi alla Giudia (Jewish style artichokes) are different from *Carciofi alla Romana* (Roman style artichokes) in that they are dipped in frying oil and then served, whereas Roman style artichokes only include the heart of the artichokes boiled in water and lemon juice and then fried with parsley, mint and white wine.

What is *quinto quarto* or the fifth quarter?

Quinto quarto or the fifth quarter are all types of entrails and remaining meat that was not considered to be good enough to be put on the table in front of Roman nobility and clergy. These less appreciated parts of lamb, baby goat or veal, were sold at affordable prices or offered to butcher's as part of their fee in Testaccio Rione, part of the city occupied by butcher's shops. This is why this is still the part of the city with the most authentic Roman cuisine. Famous quinto quarto dishes include *Rigatoni con la Pagliata* – pasta with sauce made of lamb intestine, cooked in spring in trattorias around Testaccio, then *Coratella* – lamb heart, lung and gullet simmered with artichokes or *Testarelle* – roasted lamb head. There is also *Trippa alla Romana*, sheep or cow stomach cooked in tomato sauce with wild mint and served with Pecorino Romano.

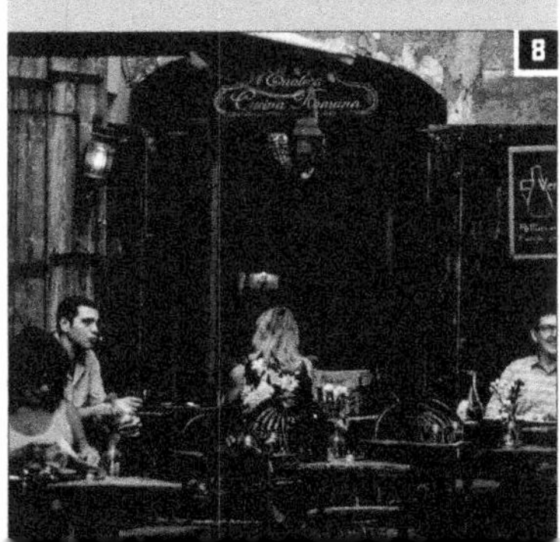

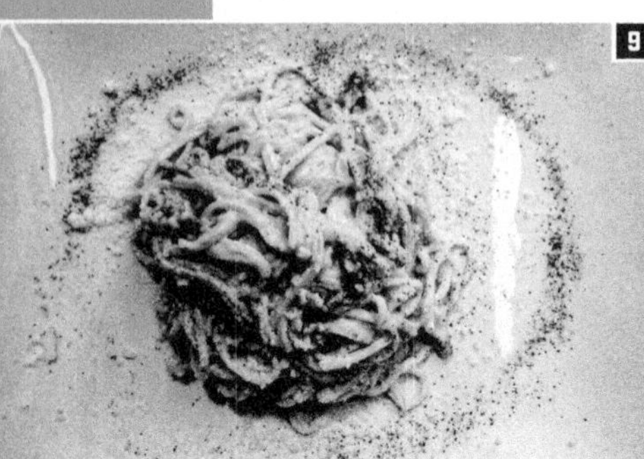

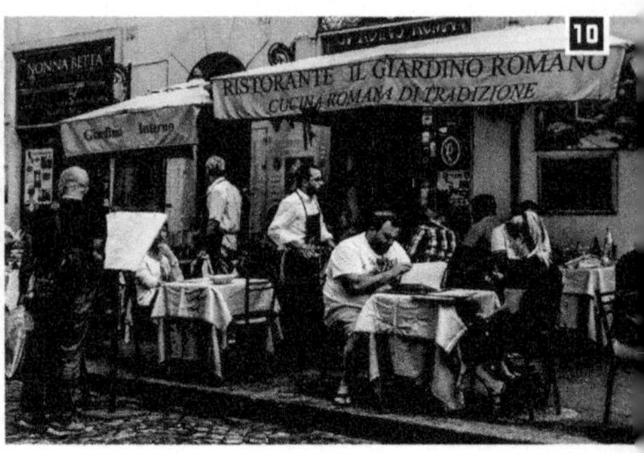

② Primi piatti

Primo piatto is the first course. This is when all the appetizers are served, as well as anything that does not involve the main dish. Usually, these are dishes with tomato sauce. So, dishes like *Coda alla Vaccinara* are sometimes treated as both *primo piatto* and *secondo piatto*, because even though they are meat-based, they contain a lot of tomato sauce.

In terms of typical Roman dishes, primo piatto usually involves pasta, such as, *Spaghetti alla Carbonara* **14**, *Bucatini All'amatriciana*, *Rigatoni con la Pagliata* or *Gnocchi alla Romana*. Gnocchi alla Romana are gnocchi baked with pecorino romano. A famous Roman dish is also *Fettuccine Alfredo* – pasta with *Parmesan* cheese and butter. The dish was invented by Alfredo Di Lelio in his Roman restaurant in the early 20th century.

③ Secondi piatti

The second course usually involves meat and fish. *Saltimbocca alla Romana* is a typical Roman dish with beef, prosciutto and basil rolled and baked in butter and white wine. Saltimbocca means jump in mouth.

Just as delightful are *Scaloppine alla Romana*, thin beef steaks with baby artichokes. *Coda alla vaccinara* (butcher style beef tail), although not considered to be entrails, belong to the quinto quarto category, something considered to be lower quality meat, unsuitable to the fine palates of nobleman and Roman clergy.

Today, it is one of the most venerated dishes of Roman cuisine. In terms of seasonal dishes **7**, the best is *Abbacchio alla Cacciatora* or hunter-style lamb. With the mixture of garlic, rosemary, vinegar, olive oil, sage and anything else the chef might think of, for example Frascati wine, you will remember the Cacciatora lamb for a long, long time.

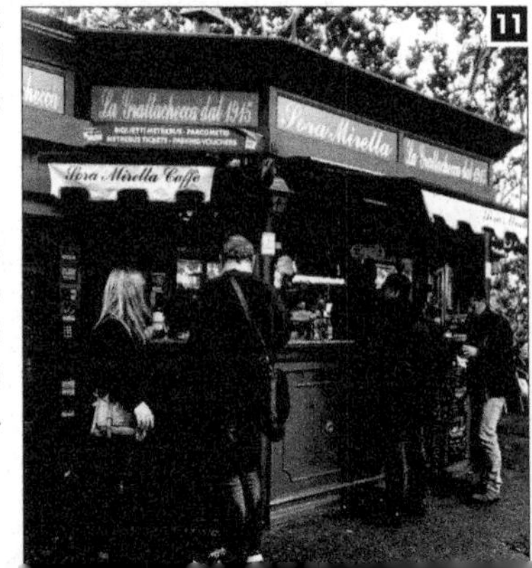

④ Dolce

If you manage to get to the dessert, you have to order *Crostata di Ricotta*. This Roman delicacy is actually a cheesecake with *Ricotta Romana*, a type of cheese made from sheep whey.

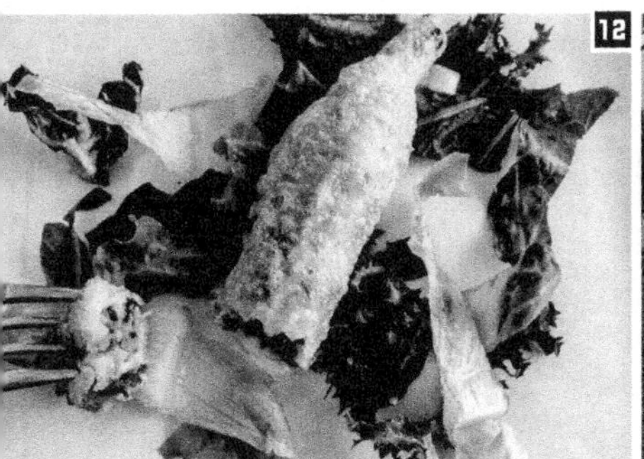

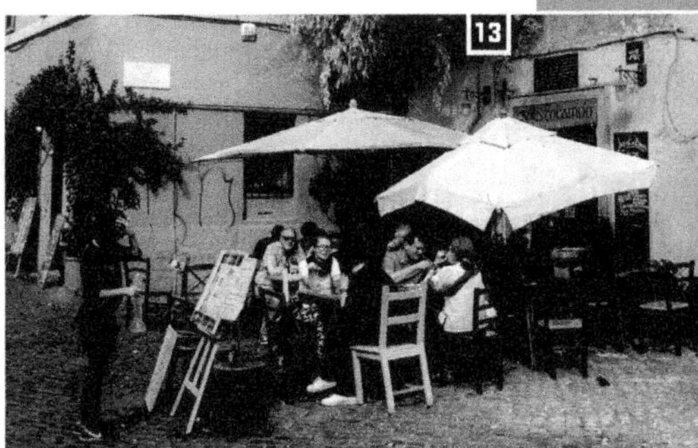

Crostata di ricotta is usually served with lemon or orange and sweet *Marsala* wine.

❷ What to drink?

Wine in Italy is part of the food culture and it is not considered to be an alcoholic beverage in the strictest sense, the same way beer is not really considered alcohol in Germany or Austria.

Vino

Anywhere you eat, there is always *vino* or wine, its doesn't matter if it is an appetizer, main meal or dessert. Antipasti are usually accompanied with a glass of *Prosecco*, primo piatto goes with white wine, while secondo piatto, that is, meat, venison or more robust fish dishes mean it is time for red wine.

Sweet white wines or a liqueur go well with dessert. In any case, you won't go wrong if you order a jug of *vino della casa* (house wine) or *vino da tavola* (table wine), because Italian trattorias and restaurants care about the wine they serve to the customers and you won't get a headache.

Roman wines have been well known for centuries, especially white wines, such as, *Frascati* or *Castelli Romani*, and they go perfectly with Roman dishes.

Did you know?

Grattachecca

If you don't drink alcohol, while in Rome, try their typical summer drink Grattachecca. It's made of grated ice and syrup. You can choose your flavor between amarena (wild cherry), mint, coconut or lemon. On top of this non-alcoholic cocktail, you will get pieces of fresh fruit. Grattachecca is sold at street kiosks. There are only four kiosks with Grattachecca left in Rome.

near to Isola Tiberina

▶ **Grattachecca Sora Mirella** 🔟
Lungotevere Degli Anguillara – corner Ponte Cestio

Public transportation: Tram stop Belli: 8

▶ **Grattachecca Alla Fonte d'Oro**
Lungotevere Raffaello Sanzio – corner Viale di Trastevere

Public transportation: Tram stop Belli: 8

near to Vatican City

▶ Grattachecca della Sora Lella
Via di Porta Cavalleggeri

Public transportation: Bus stop Cavalleggeri/S. Pietro: 34, 46, 98, 190F, 881, 916, 916F, 982

▶ Grattachecca Sora Maria
Via Trionfale – corner Via Bernardino Telesio 37

Public transportation: Metro A stop Cipro: 8

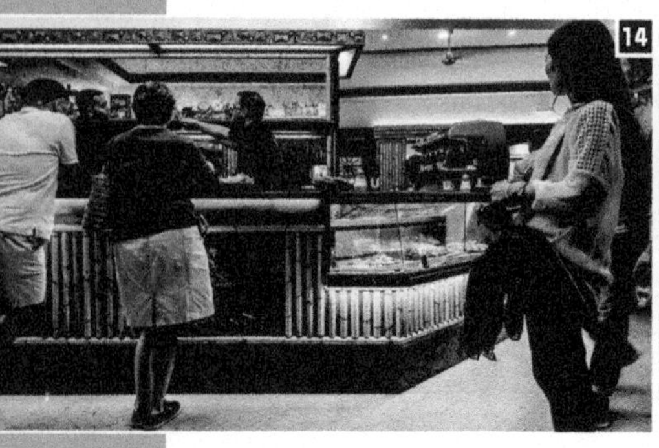
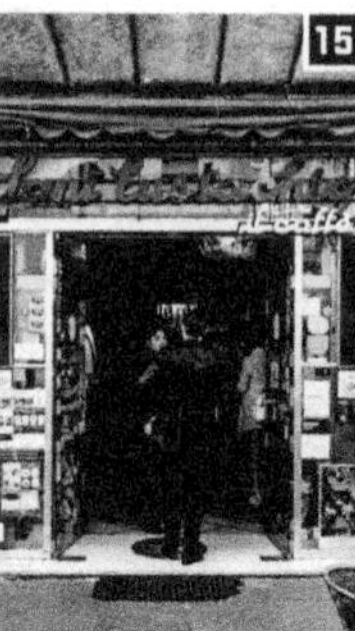
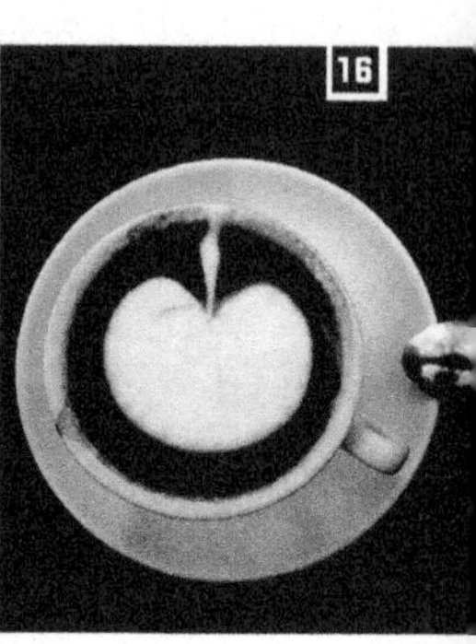

❸ Il caffè

Coffee is an indispensable part of the Roman lifestyle. Coffee is served 24/7. From the early morning to the late evening, espresso is everywhere. Of course, there are a few exceptions.

Un espresso or "un caffè"

In terms of quantity, there is very little coffee in a Roman espresso, but it is extremely powerful. In Rome, espresso is usually drunk at the bar in a hurry. If you want to have an espresso after you've eaten, in Italy it is served after the dessert.

Caffè macchiato

If you want to have milk with a drop of coffee, this is the right combination for you. You will get hot milk in a big cup with a little espresso.

The difference between a *caffè macchiato* and a *caffè latte* is that the milk and coffee in a caffè latte are blended together, while in a caffè macchiato they are put one on top of the other.

Cappuccino

Cappuccino is espresso with foamy, hot milk on top. Remember one thing, there is no whipped cream in an Italian cappuccino. Sometimes there is powdered chocolate on top of the foam.

Caffè latte

Caffè latte is a combination of coffee and hot milk without foam. Pay attention while you order a caffè latte.

If you only say latte, you will get exactly what you ordered, because in Italian that means a glass of milk, no coffee.

La Casa Del Caffè Tazza d'Oro 14
Address: Via degli Orfani 84, Roma
Online: www.tazzadorocoffeeshop.com
Public transport: Bus stop Pie' Di Marmo: 116 or Largo Torre Argentina: 30, 40, 46, 62, 64, 70, 81, 87, 130F, 186, 190F, 492, 628, 916, 916F

Opening hours:
Mon – Sat: 7:00 a.m. – 7:00 p.m

Bar del Cappuccino 16
Address: Via Arenula 50, Roma

Public transportation: Tram stop Arenula – Ministero Grazia E Giustizia 8 | Bus stop Lungotevere de' Cenci – Arenula 23, 63, 280, 810

Opening hours:
Mon – Sun: 6 a.m. – 5 p.m.

Sant'Eustachio Il Caffè 15
Address: Piazza di Sant'Eustacchio 82, Roma
Online: www.caffesanteustachio.com

Public transportation: Bus stop Corso Rinascimento: 30, 70, 81, 87, 116, 130F, 186, 492, 628, C3

Opening hours: *see online*

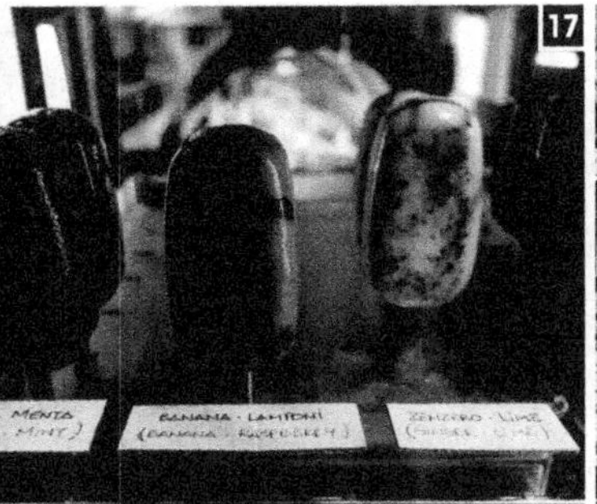

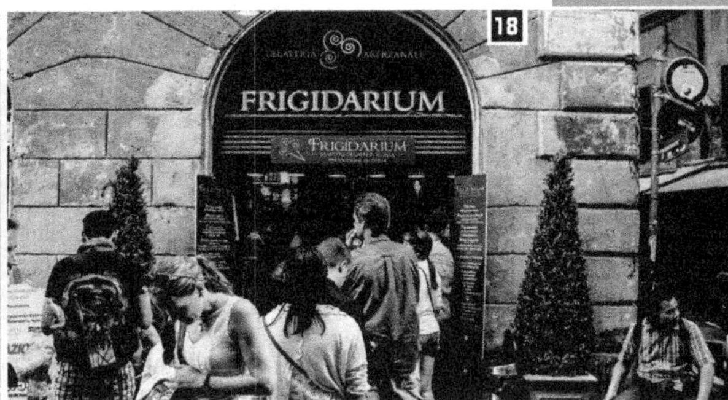

◆ Gelato in the Ice Cream Parlor

There are many places in Rome where you can eat a good gelato. For the Romans, and not just them, Giolitti is unique.

When you try flavors such as *riso* (rice), *mirtilli* (blueberry), *melone* (melon), champagne, *ricotta,* marsala custard, you will know why popes, Italian presidents and Hollywood stars regularly drop in here for ice cream. Besides, prices of the ice cream to go are more than affordable.

The first thing you have to do when you come to Giolitti's will be buying a coupon at the register. You have to decide in advance how many flavors you want.

With that coupon, you wait in line to order your ice cream.

After you decide which flavor you want in your *cornetto* or cup, the vendor will ask you *"con pana?"*, meaning "with whipped cream?" It is on the house.

If you say yes or *si*, you will get an amazingly delicious scoop of whipped cream, which is just as good as the ice cream itself.

◆ Where to eat?

There are three main types of restaurants: *osteria, trattoria* and *ristorante.*

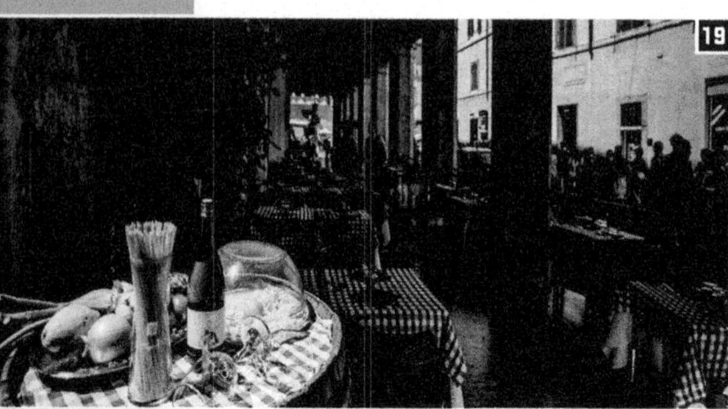

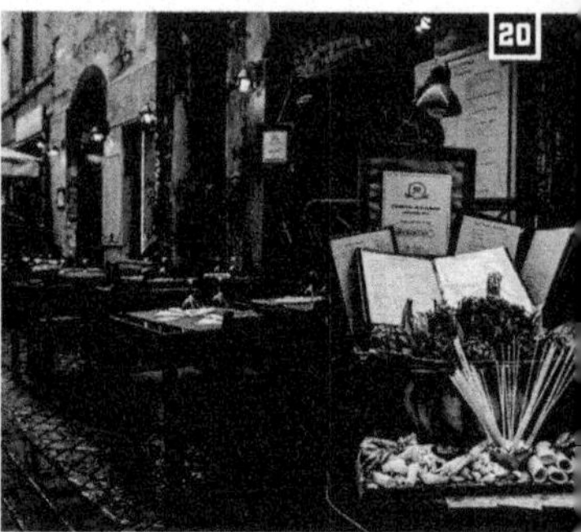

The division used to be straight-forward, but today what is on offer in a trattoria can be classified as a restaurant menu, osteria is similar to a trattoria sometimes, and a ristorante sometimes becomes more of a trattoria due to special demand.

Osteria

Osteria is the most simple type of eatery. It is a tavern with simple meals at affordable prices. 🔳

Trattoria

Trattoria is a simple eatery with medium-priced regional dishes. 🔳

Ristorante 🔳

Ristorante is the most luxurious version, including a full menu with many different dishes with at least four courses. 🔳 🔳 🔳 Ristorante also has a wine list with wines from different regions.

Pasta laboratorio

In the last couple of years, a small snack bar trend has developed, where you can get fresh pasta with a good pasta sauce for 4–7€. If you don't have a lot of experience with authentic Italian cuisine or you find yourself in a hurry, these are the best places to get acquainted with typical Italian pasta dishes. Some of the best, the so-called *pasta labora-torio*, are strategically placed near the Vatican and Castel Sant'Angelo.

❻ Some good places to eat in Rome

near to Campo de' Fiori

► **Taverna Cairoli**
Piazza Cairoli Benedetto 2/A, Roma

Public transportation: Tram stop Arenula/Cairoli: 8

Reservation
Phone +39 06 678 1537
Online: www.tavernacairoli.it

Best choice
► *Fiori di zucca*
► *Pizza Napoletana* (à la Romana with anchovies)
► *Gnocchi* Gorgonzola
► *Spaghetti alla carbonara*
Price: $$

near to Teatro Marcello

► **Nonna Betta**
Via del Portico d'Ottavia 16, Roma

Public transportation: Tram stop Arenula/Cairoli: 8

Reservation
Phone +39 06 6880 6263
Online: www.nonnabetta.it

Best choice
► *Carciofi alla giudia*
► *Aliciotti e Indivia* (anchovies and endive salad)
► *Gnocchi al sugo di castrato* (gnocchi with lamb ragu)
► *Abbacchio al forno con patate* (oven baked lamb with potatoes)
Price: $$–$$$

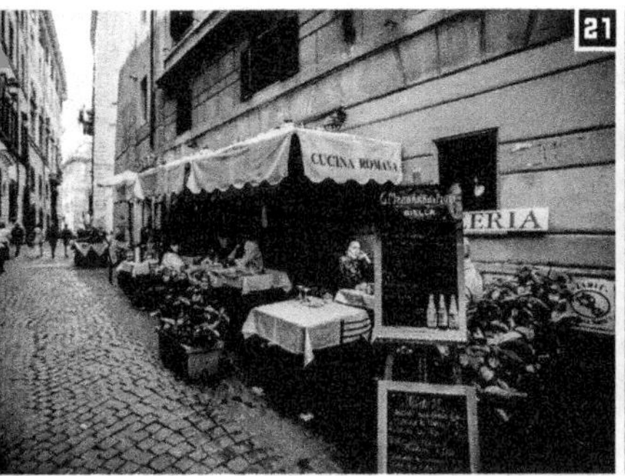

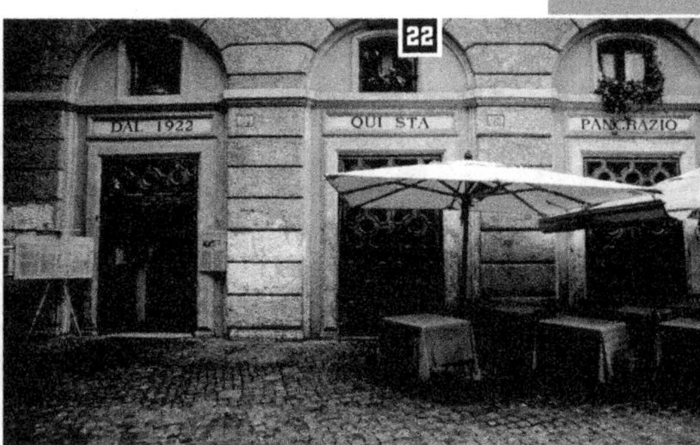

Some good places to eat in Rome

near to Pantheon

► **Armando al Pantheon**
Salita de' Crescenzi 31, Roma

Public transportation: Bus stop Via Torre Argentina: 30, 40, 46, 62, 64, 70, 81, 87, 190F, 492, 628, 916, 916F, C3

Reservation
Phone +39 6 068803034
Online:
www.armandoalpantheon.it/en

Best choice
► *Saltimbocca*
► *Rigatoni con la pagliata*
► *Carbonara*
► *Coda alla vaccinara*
► Good wine from the Lazio region

Price: $$–$$$

near to Fontana di Trevi | Piazza Barberini

► **Hosteria Romana**
Via del Boccaccio 1, Roma

Public transportation: Metro A stop Barberini

Reservation
Phone +39 06 474 5284
Online: www.hostariaromana.it

Best choice
► *Carbonara*
► *Carciofi alla romana*
► *Spaghetti alle vongole*
► *Ossobuco cremolato con funghi e piselli* (cross-cut veal shanksbraised with mushrooms and peas)

Price: $$

Some good places to eat in Rome

Trastevere

► **Antica Trattoria Da Carlone**
Via della Luce 5, Roma

Public transportation: Bus stop Mastai: H | Tram stop Trastevere – Mastai: 8

Reservation
Phone +39 06 580 0039

Best choice
► *Scamorza alla checca* (cow's milk cheese similar to mozzarella and uncooked tomato sauce)
► *Spaghetti alla carbonara, Bucatini all'Amatriciana, Spaghetti cacio e pepe* (spaghetti with pecorino romano cheese and pepper),
► *Pasta alla Gricia* (guanciale with pecorino romano)

Price: $$

near to Pyramid of Cestius

► **Da Bucatino**
Via Luca della Robbia 84, Roma

Public transportation: Metro B and B1 stop Piramide

Reservation
Phone +39065746886
Online: www.dabucatino.it

Best choice
► *Bucatini all'Amatriciana*
► *Rigatoni con la Pagliata*
► Trippa alla romana
► *Abbacchio scottadito e carciofo alla piastra* (lamb grilled with artichoke)

Price: $$–$$$

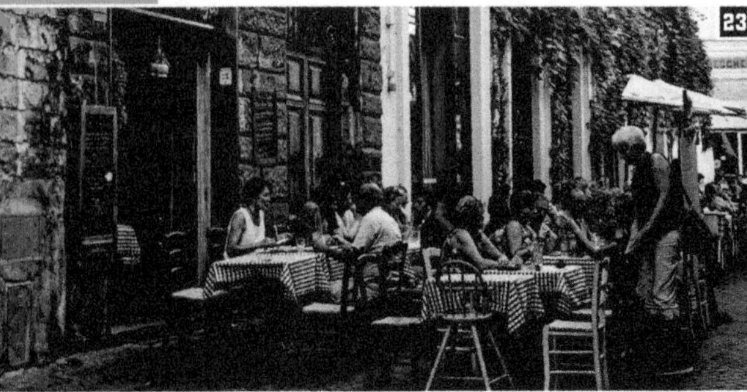
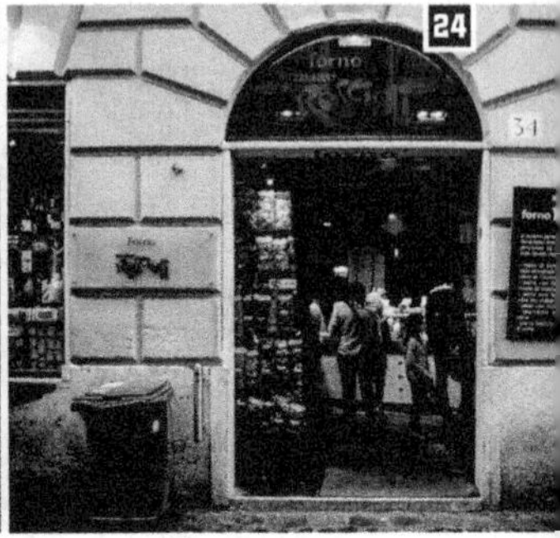

Did you know?

❼ Fast food alla Romana

near to Basilica of San Clemente al Laterano

► Pizzeria Luzzi
Via Celimontana 1, Roma
Online: www.trattorialuzzi.it

Public transportation: Metro B
Colosseo

Best choice
► Pizza or lasagna
Price: $

near to Spanish steps

► Pastificio Guerra
Via della Croce 8, Roma

Public transportation: Metro A
Spagna

Best choice
► Home made fresh pasta
Price: $

near to Campo de' Fiori

► Antico Forno Roscioli 🄳
Via dei Chiavari 34, Roma
Online: www.anticofornoroscioli.it

Public transportation: Tram stop
Arenula/Cairoli: 8

Opening hours
Mon – Sat: 7:00 a.m. – 7:30 p.m.

Best choice
► Pizza or Porchetta to go
Price: $$

near to Campo de' Fiori

►Dar Filettaro a Santa Barbara
Largo dei Librari 88, Roma
Public transportation: Tram stop
Arenula/Cairoli: 8
Opening hours: Daily 5 – 10:40. p.m.

Best choice
► Filetti di baccalà (pan-fried cod fillet)
Price: $

near to Piazza Navona

► Il Pastaio di Roma
Via dei Coronari 102–103, Roma
Online: www.ilpastaiodiroma.it

Public transportation: Bus stop
Paola: 98, 115, 870, 881

Best choice
► Home made fresh pasta
Price: $

near to Piazza Navona

► Pasta Imperiale
Via dei Coronari 160, Roma
Online: www.pastaimperiale.com

Public transportation: Bus stop
Paola: 98, 115, 870, 881

near to Vatican City

► Pastasciutta
Via delle Grazie, Roma
Online: www.pastasciuttaroma.it

Public transportation: Metro A
Ottaviano

Best choice
► Home made fresh pasta
Price: $

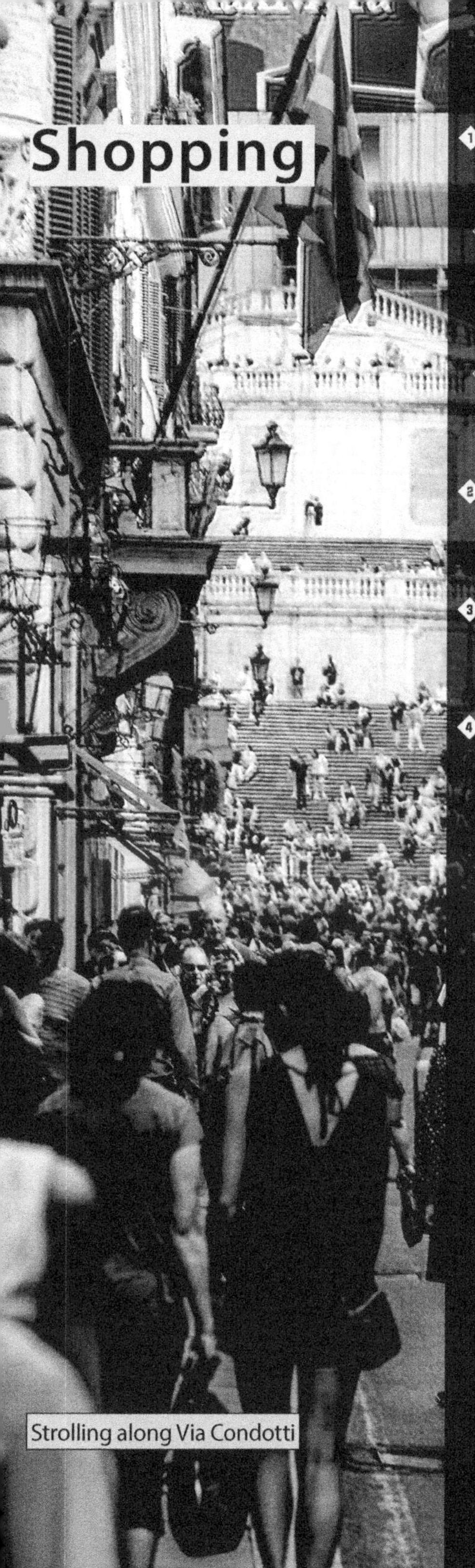

Shopping

1 **Fashion capital**
Rome is one of the global fashion capitals. *p. 320*

1 **High Fashion**
Some of the world's major luxury fashion houses and jewelery chains are headquartered or were founded in Rome. *p. 320*

2 **Mainstream Shopping**
If you want to shop where Romans shop, there are several streets to go. *p. 320*

2 **Antiques**
There are several streets or even districts in Rome that are known for their antiques sellers. *p. 321*

3 **Second Hand Shops**
The vintage shops can be eccentrically priced but you can also find good preserved bargains. *p. 322*

4 **Outdoor Flea Market**
One of the biggest flea markets in Europe is in Rome. *p. 322*

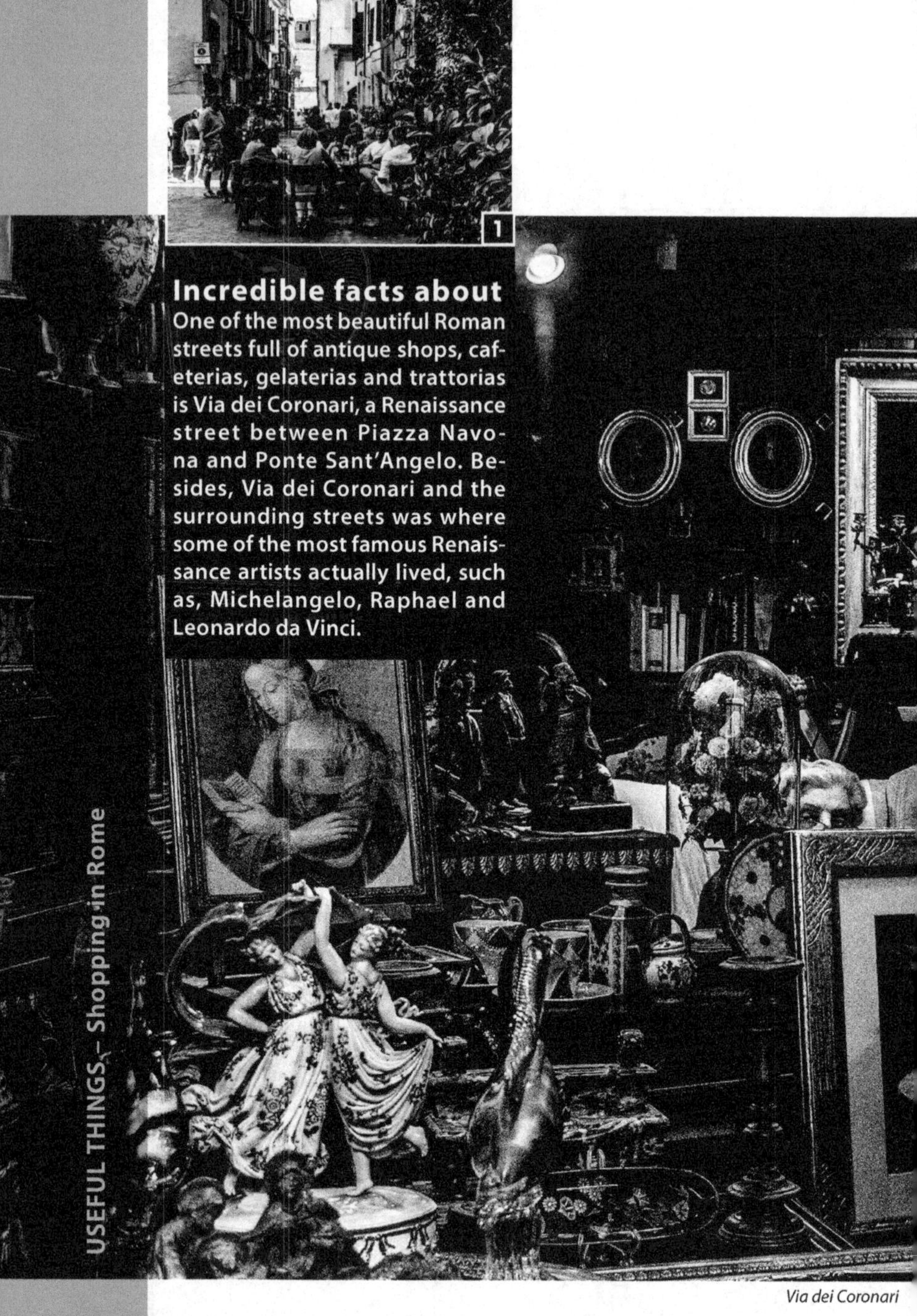

Incredible facts about

One of the most beautiful Roman streets full of antique shops, cafeterias, gelaterias and trattorias is Via dei Coronari, a Renaissance street between Piazza Navona and Ponte Sant'Angelo. Besides, Via dei Coronari and the surrounding streets was where some of the most famous Renaissance artists actually lived, such as, Michelangelo, Raphael and Leonardo da Vinci.

Via dei Coronari

Extra Tip : : :

For food or drinks and souvenirs or gifts for people back home, you should walk around Campo de' Fiori and look at the windows of the delicatessen. Who wouldn't like a nice bottle of Italian wine, olive oil or neatly packaged Italian pasta?

Where to shop in the capital of fashion?

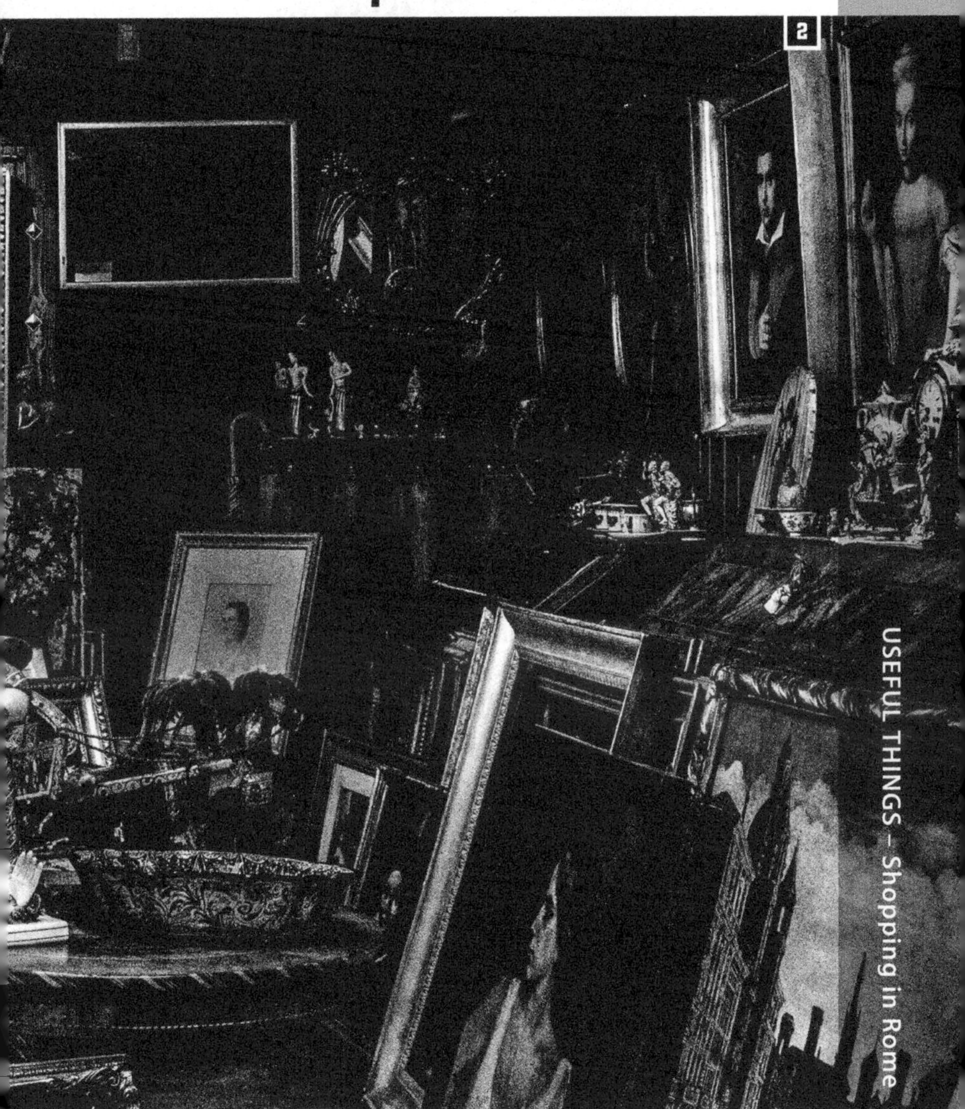

Piazza Campo de' Fiori
Address: Piazza Campo de' Fiori, Roma
Public transportation: Bus stop Corso Vittorio – Sant'Andrea della Valle: 46, 62, 64, 916, 916F or stop Cancelleria: 116 | Tram stop Arenula/Cairoli: 8

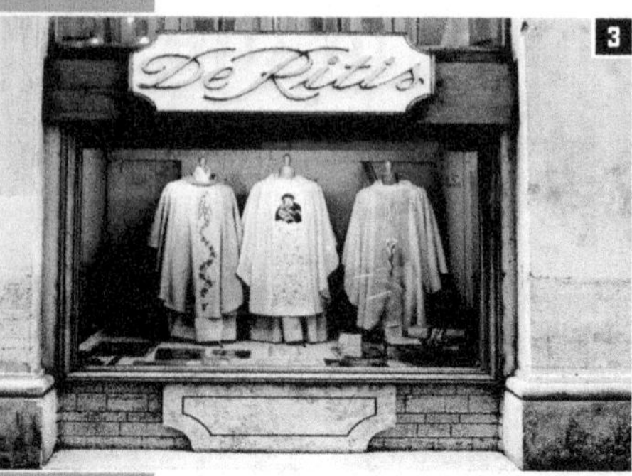

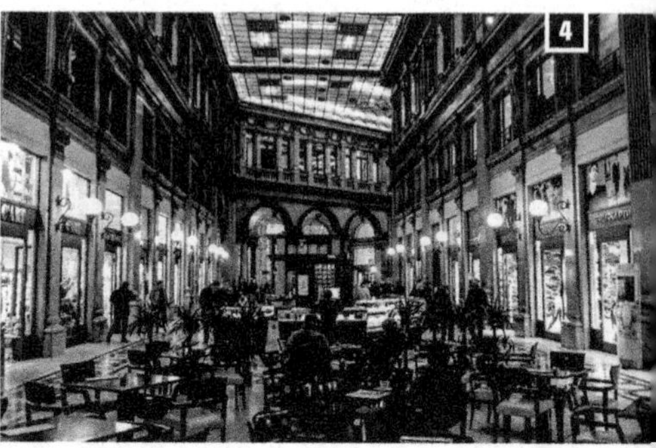

❶ Fashion capital

Rome is the capital of fashion, next to Milan, New York and Paris. Almost every high fashion brand and fashion chain have at least one exclusive store in downtown Rome. Besides, in a city that has been around for over 2,700 years, antique shops, second hand shops and flea markets are places where you can always find rare and exquisite things that are almost impossible to find anywhere else. ❸ Italian fashion brands compete against each other to have the best image. For example, Italian fashion brands put money into the restoration of the Colosseum and Fontana di Trevi.

◈ High Fashion

Some of the most relevant luxury fashion houses and jewelry chains have their headquarters in Rome, and their flagship stores are located in Rome. The highest concentration of famous fashion brands, jewelry, shoes and perfumes is on Piazza di Spagna and the streets around the Spanish Steps, especially Via dei Condotti, Via Borgognona and Via del Babuino.

◈ Mainstream Shopping

On one of the principal street, Via del Corso, you can find the most popular fashion stores and brands. ❹ Via del Corso goes from Piazza Venezia all the way to Piazza del Popolo for 1 mi or 1.6 km. Apart from fashion stores, there are also Italian car shops. In Via Cola di Rienzo, north of the Vatican, there are similar shops, but it's not as crowded as on Via del Corso. Via Cola di Rienzo also has small specialized stores with Italian shoes and bags at surprisingly affordable prices.

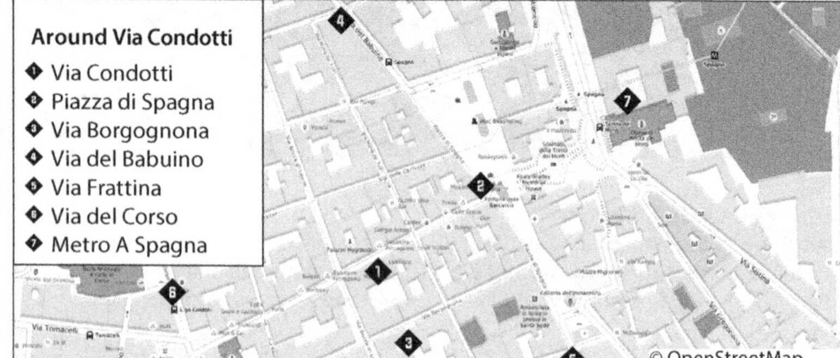

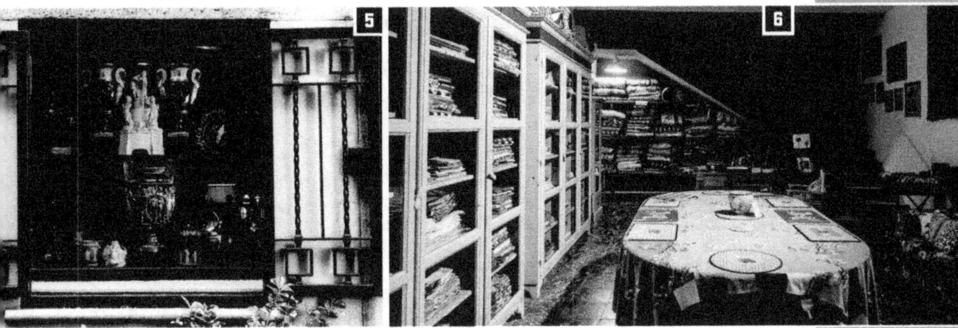

◆ Antiques

Just as there are mostly clothes stores in certain areas of the city, there are others full of antique shops. You will find the antique shop street in the oldest parts of Rome which have usually been looked over for restoration and preservation, so window shopping around these shops also includes taking a coffee break on the cafeteria terrace. One of the most beautiful Roman streets full of antique shops, cafeterias, gelaterias and trattorias is Via dei Coronari, a Renaissance street between Piazza Navona and Ponte Sant'Angelo.

Via dei Coronari dates back to the ancient Rome when it was called Via Recta or straight road, because it's one of the very few streets in Rome that is completely straight all the way (0.31 mi or 500 m). It is not just Via dei Coronari, but the whole quarter Rione Ponte is one of the most picturesque parts of Rome (between Piazza Navona on the east, Corso Vittorio Emanuele II on the south and the Tiber on the north).

Ever since the early Middle Ages, pilgrims walked here on their way to the Vatican, so a lot of churches, relic shops, turned galleries and antique shops, restaurants and old shops, such as, stonemason's, restorers, frame makers, candelabrum and chandelier

Did you know?

Fashion spots of Rome

▸ Via Vittorio Veneto – luxury fashion houses and jewelry chains
Public transportation: Metro A stop Barberini

▸ Via Condotti – luxury fashion houses and jewelry chains
Public transportation: Metro A stop Spagna

▸ Piazza di Spagna – luxury fashion houses and jewelry chains
Public transportation: Metro A stop Spagna

▸ Via Borgognona – luxury fashion houses and jewelry chains
Public transportation: Metro A stop Spagna

▸ Via del Babuino – luxury fashion houses and jewelry chains
Public transportation: Metro A stops Flaminio or Spagna

▸ Via Frattina – high street chains
Public transportation: Metro A stop Spagna

▸ Via del Corso – high street chains
Public transportation: Metro A stops Flaminio or Spagna

▸ Via Cola di Rienzo – designer boutiques
Public transportation: Metro A stop Ottaviano

▸ Galleria Alberto Sordi – designer boutiques
Public transportation: Metro A stop Barberini

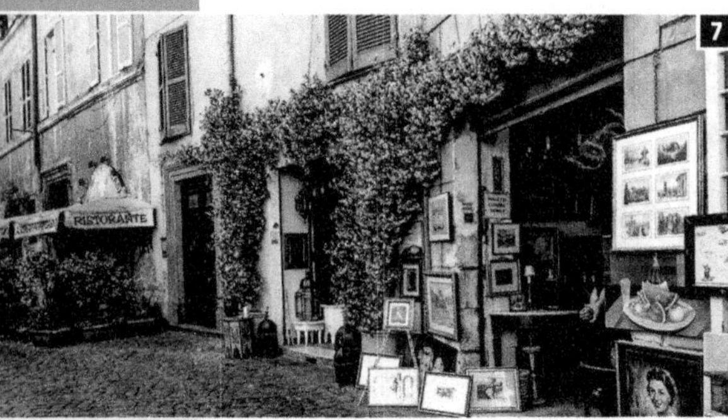

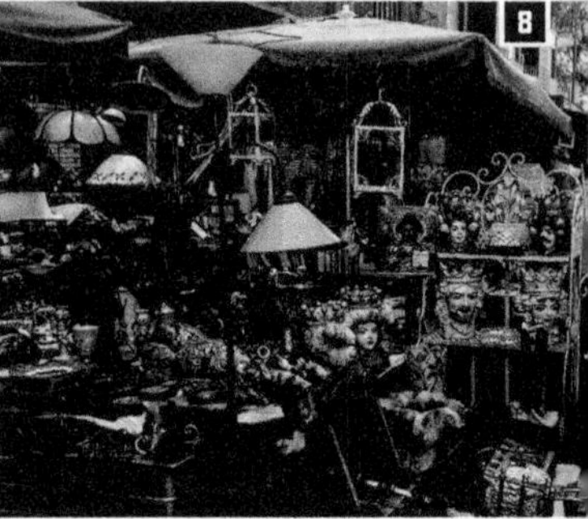

salesmen have been located here for centuries. ▌ Besides, Via dei Coronari and the surrounding streets was where some of the most famous Renaissance artists actually lived, such as, Michelangelo, Raphael and Leonardo da Vinci. Religious and profane pilgrims have left their mark in this street in one way or another. Via dei Coronari owes its name to *corona del rosario*, that is, the rosary, that used be sold here to the pilgrims going to the nearby Vatican. But that's not all.

Via dei Coronari was also Fiammetta Michaelis' address, one of the most famous Roman courtesans and Cesare Borgia's mistress (1465–1512). Cesare Borgia was the son of Pope Alexander VI Borgia. Next to the Via dei Coronari, you can find Piazza Fiammetta, the only square in Rome named after a courtesan. Although Rione Ponte is full of tourists, walking around its streets is particularly refreshing after the crowds on Piazza Navona or the Pantheon. There is another street full of antique stores that is just as interesting called Via Giulia, at the other side of the Corso Vittorio Emanuele II avenue. [p.128]

◆ Second Hand Shops

On the other side of Corso Vittorio Emanuele II, all the way to Via Giulia, there are many second hand shops with clothes and leather goods.The atmosphere in streets and alley between Via dei Banchi Vecchi, Via Giulia and Campo de' Fiori is especially charming. ▌

◆ Outdoor Flea Market

Porta Portese is the largest flea market in Rome. Every Sunday (6:30 a.m. – 2:00 p.m.), a sea of people takes the No. 8 tram to Ippolito Nievo station in Trastevere to shop, sell or just browse anything that can get you to the Porta Portese market – from copies of ancient pieces of decoration to oriental oil lamps, old gramophone records, hats, glasses and things that you will have a hard time figuring out what their original purpose was. ▌

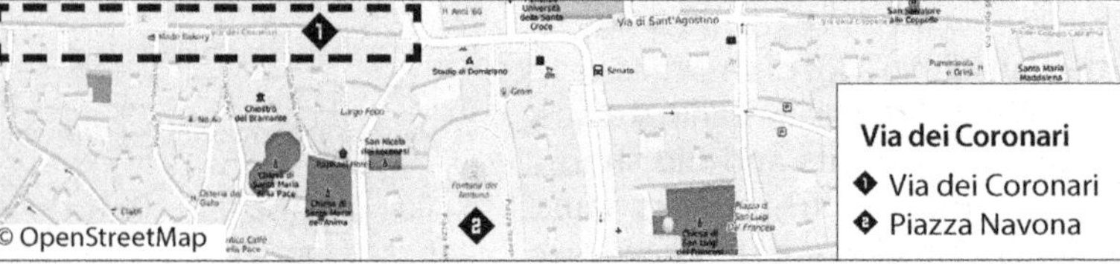

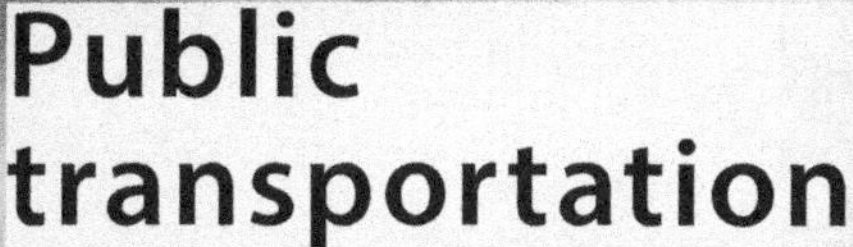

Public transportation

Tram 8: Piazza Venezia – Trastevere

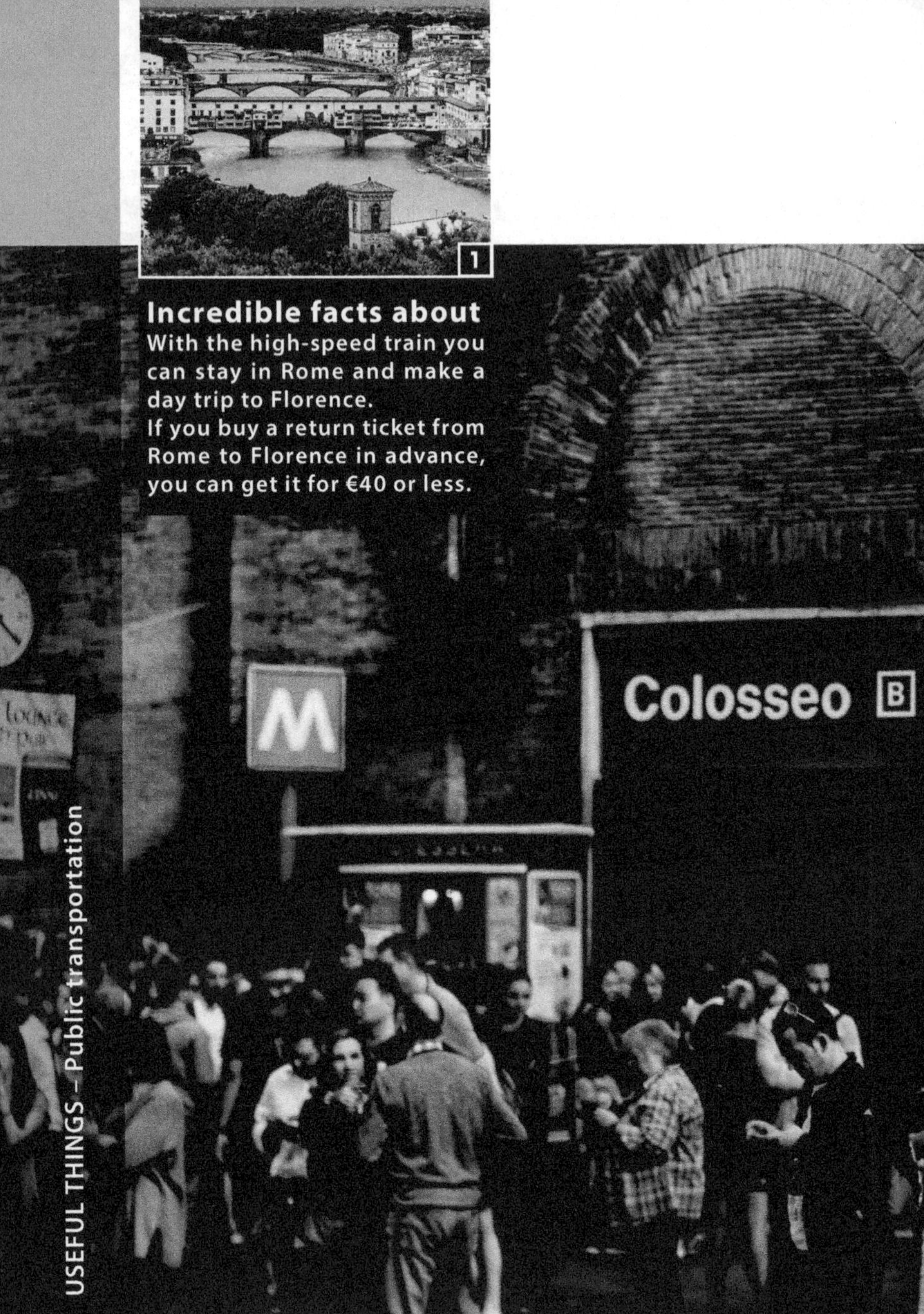

Incredible facts about

With the high-speed train you can stay in Rome and make a day trip to Florence.
If you buy a return ticket from Rome to Florence in advance, you can get it for €40 or less.

Metro B stop Colosseo

Extra Tip : : :
How far you can get outside of Rome depends on the traffic network and on how fast the trains go on specific routes. Major Italian cities are connected via high-speed trains *Frecciarossa* that run 155 mph (250 km/h) to 217 mph (350 km/h).

How to sightseeing using public transportation?

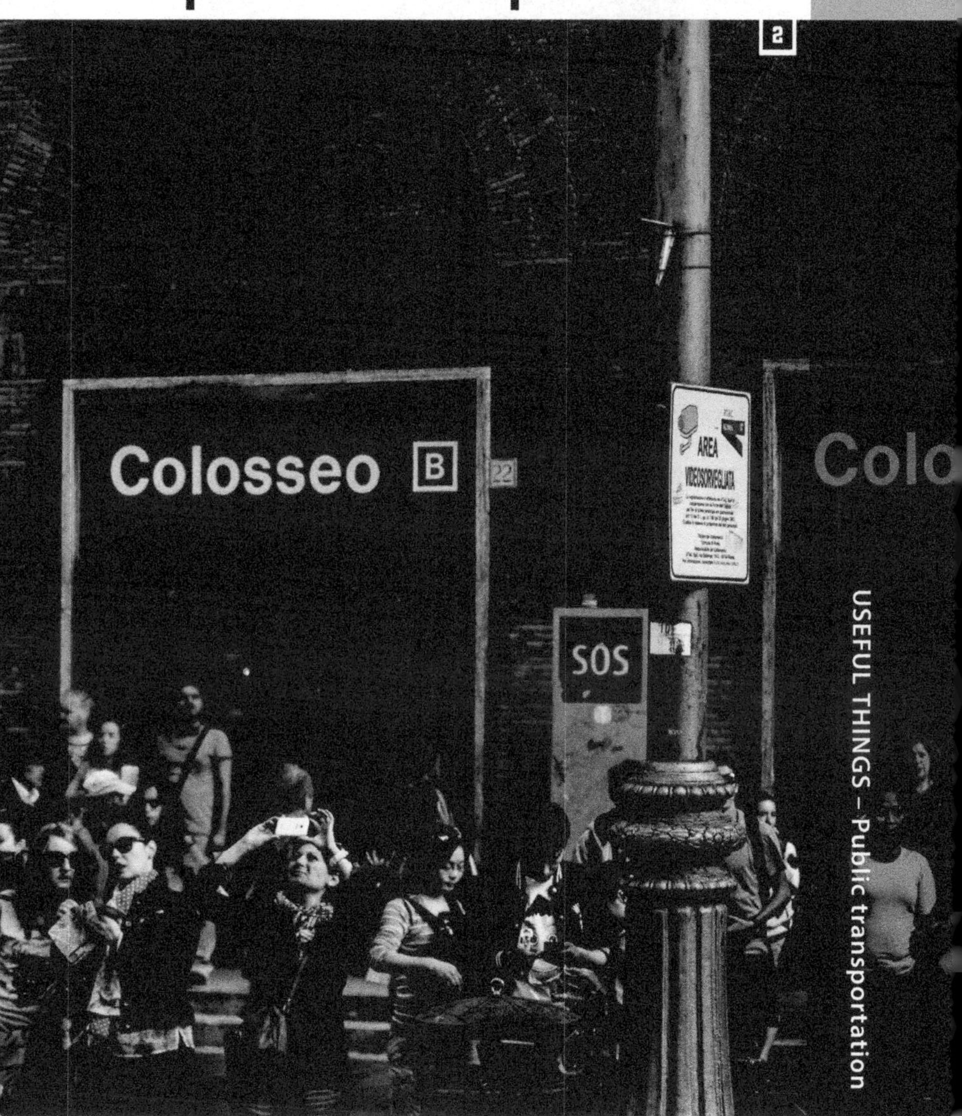

Roma Termini Train Station
Address: Piazzale dei Cinquecento, Roma
Booking tickets online: www.trenitalia.com

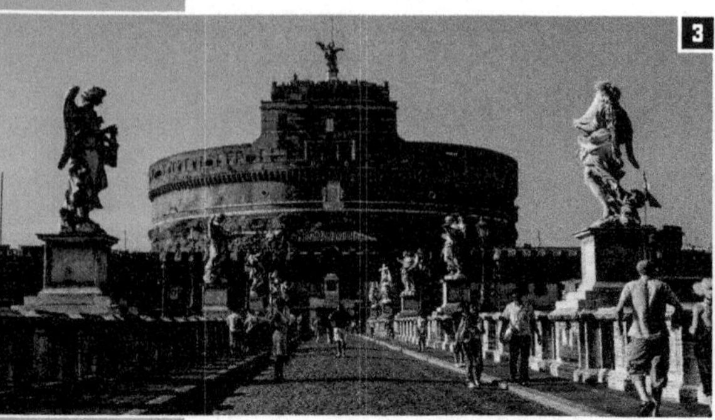

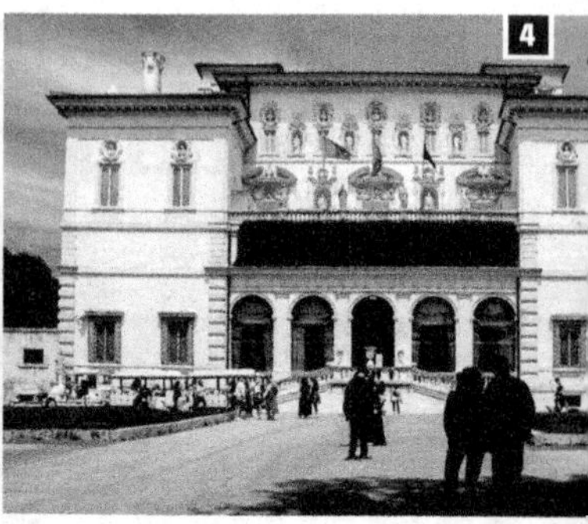

❶ How to get around

By car

You don't want to do that. The traffic is chaotic to say the least, and drivers adhere to a special code of conduct which is not easy to decipher.

Taxi

Taxi is the most expensive way to get around Rome and certainly not the fastest.

Metro

The A and B Line connect at the main train station, Stazione Termini.

Bus

The bus lines are impossible to number. The timetable is rarely respected. Don't wait for a bus that will drive you to your destination, just hop on the first available bus and you will find yourself closer to your destination.

Tram

There are only a few tram lines and they usually operate outside the city center.

Tickets

For all means of public transport, you should use *Biglietto Integrato a Tempo* or a single-ride ticket. It is valid for a 100 minutes.

On foot

This is the most practical and the most beautiful way of getting around Rome.

❷ Day trips outside the city walls

How far you can get outside of Rome depends on the traffic network and on how fast the trains go on specific routes. Major Italian cities are connected via ultra-fast trains that run 155 mph (250 km/h) to 217 mph (350 km/h), so it's easier and faster to get to Florence (1h30min) which is 143 mi (230 km) away, than to Assisi (4h30min) which is only 81 mi (130 km) away from Rome.

You can buy a return ticket from Rome to Florence in advance for 40€ or less. If someone tries to convince you that you can get to Pompeii and back in one day, do not fall for it. A pleasant visit to Pompeii is a one-day trip from Naples, not Rome.

❸ How to travel Italy by train

There is no better way to go from one Italian city to another than riding the train. One-way tickets on the high-speed trains are as low as €9 (Milan – Turin) to €19 (Rome – Florence, Rome – Naples, Rome – Venice).

You can buy the tickets at the ticket office or at one of the many ticket machines at Termini Station. The most affordable option would be to purchase the tickets online via the official Italian railroads website: www.trenitalia.com

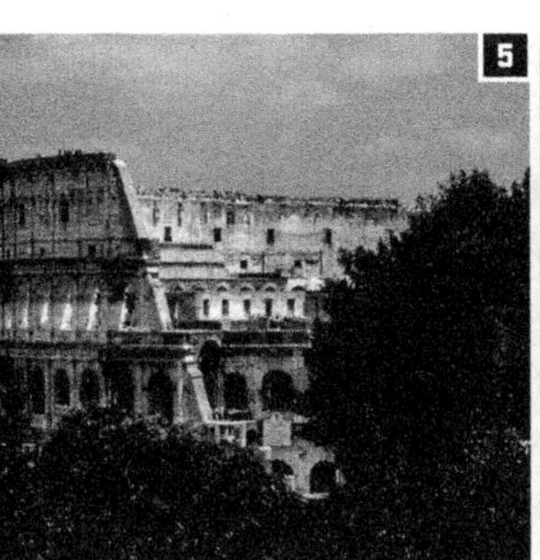 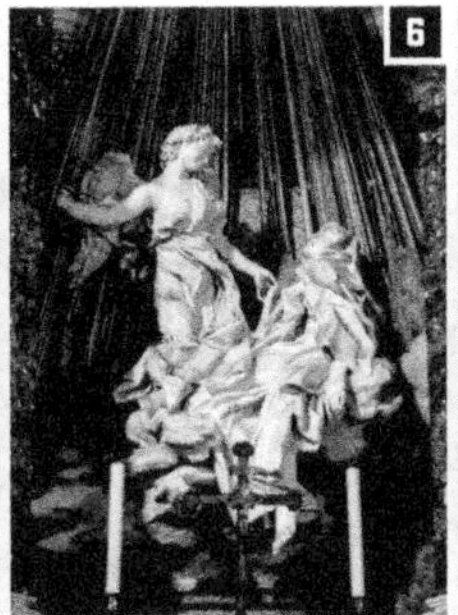 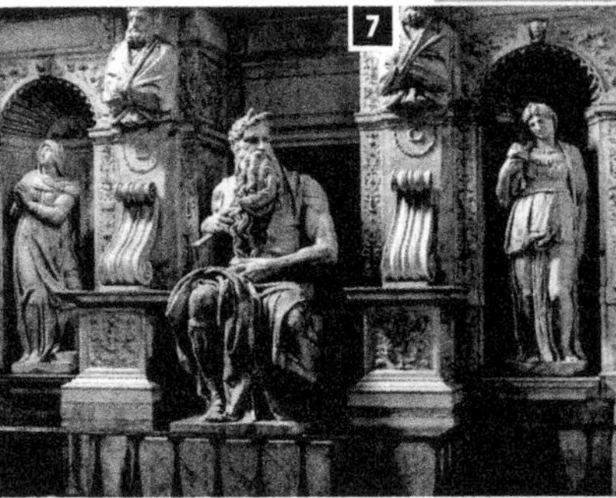

◆ Metro

The subway is the fastest way to visit the most attractions and museums in the least amount of time. The Roman underground has three lines, with A Line (orange line) and B Line (blue line) being the most important ones for visitors. After Bologna stop, B Line is divided into B Line and B1 Line. The C Line (green line) is mostly for locals who live in the suburbs, with only two stations you have to pay attention to: San Giovanni, at the intersection of Lines A and C, and Lodi station.

Ultimately, the C Line will join the B line at Colosseo, with another station between San Giovanni and Colosseo. These two stations will not be finished until 2024. However, this is only an estimate, since digging the tunnels for the underground trains only means more extraordinary archaeological findings, which immediately stops the construction works for at least a few months.

The mission impossible aspect of constructing the Roman metro was most famously depicted by director Federico Fellini in *Fellini's Roma* (1972). You can purchase different types of tickets and travel cards depending on the number of days you will stay in the city: www.atac.roma.it/biglietti-e-abbonamenti/

Did you know?

Day trips outside of city walls

▸ Via Appia Antica — the longest open-space museum in the world [p.290]

▸ Ostia Antica — one of the best preserved Roman towns in general [p.326]

▸ Lido di Ostia Beaches are full of deck chairs and sun loungers [p.326]

▸ Tivoli — The most famous sights are the Renaissance Villa d'Este with an endless water games and the Hadrian's Villa, a large archaeological complex

▸ Orvieto — the site of the city is among the most dramatic in Europe

▸ Florence — almost all you ever wanted to know about the Italian Renaissance 🄳

Rome Termini Train Station 🄱
Address: Piazzale dei Cinquecento, Roma
Online: www.romatermini.com

Public transportation:
Metro A and B stop Termini
Bus stop Termini: 16, 38, 40, 50, 60L, 64, 75, 82, 85, 90, 92, 150F, 105, 170, 223, 310, 360, 590, 649, 714, 717, 910, C2, C3, H
Tram stop Termini: 5, 14

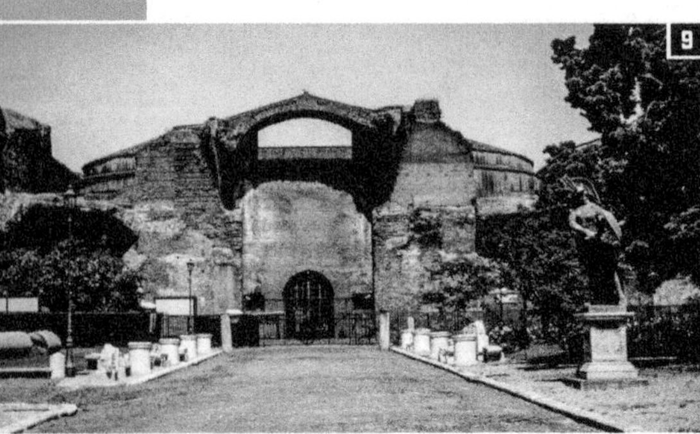

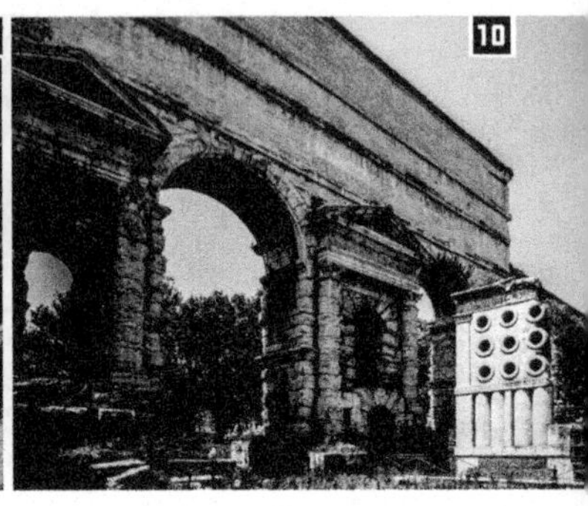

⬟ Rome in Seven Days

Our seven daily walks around Rome are for visitors who want to spend a pleasant, stress-free days in Rome and maximize on the experiences that Rome has to offer. If you opt for our walks, your days in Rome will be minimally impacted by crowds, traffic jams, strikes and other stressful situations that can ruin your whole experience of Rome.

Each day on the list starts and ends with the subway, the most efficient means of transportation in Rome. It is only when you need to leave the city center that you will take a bus (Day 6) or the city rail (Day 7). Day walks always include visits to an important museum or archaeological park, churches, galleries, and historical buildings.

1st day — Imperial Rome
Metro B – Get off at stop Colosseo
1. Colosseum 1–2 h [p.27]
2. Palatine Hill [p.37] & Roman Forum [p.47] 2–3 h
3. Imperial Forums 30 min [p.65]
Afternoon
4. Capitoline Museums 2–3 h [p.75]
Walk From Campidoglio to the Pantheon 30 min
5. Santa Maria Sopra Minerva 30 min [p.106]
6. Pantheon 1 h [p.92]
7. Fontana di Trevi 30 min [p.203]
The nearest metro stop is Metro A Barberini

2nd day — Vatican and Heart of Rome
Metro A – Get off at stop Ottaviano
1. Vatican Museums and Sistine Chapel 3–4 h [p.142]
2. St. Peter's Basilica 1 h [p.136]
3. Castel Sant'Angelo 1 h [p.168]
Afternoon
4. Piazza Navona 1 h [p.110]
5. San Luigi dei Francesi 30 min [p.116]
6. Basilica di Sant'Agostino 30 min [p.116]
7. Spanish Steps 30 min [p.201]
The nearest metro stop is Metro A Spagna

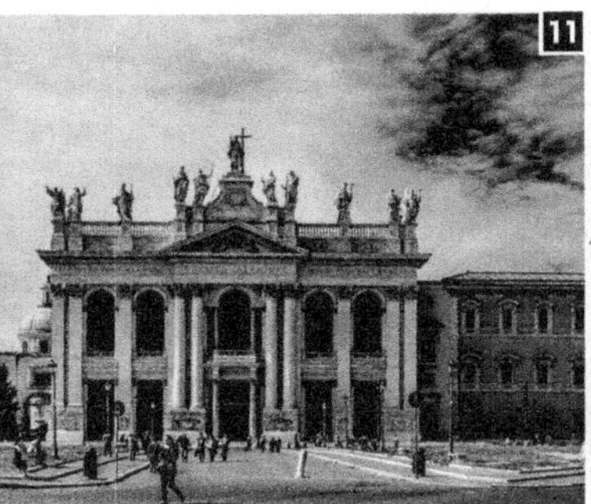

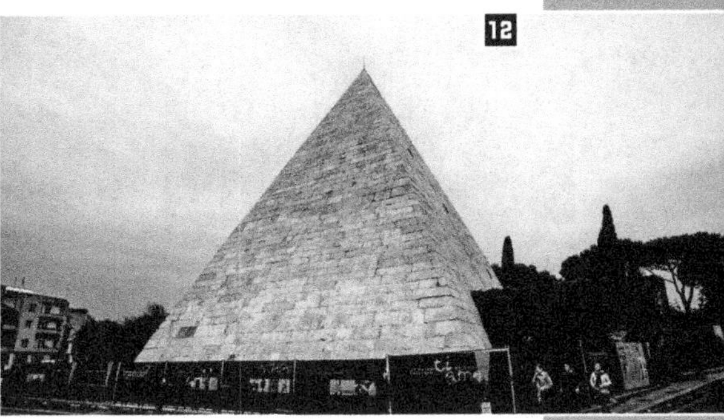

3rd day — Walk around – Art
Metro A – Get off at stop Flaminio
1. Galleria Borghese 2–3 h [p.188]
2. Villa Giulia 1–2 h [p.190]
Afternoon
3. Basilica of Santa Maria del Popolo 1 h [p.195]
4. Piazza del Popolo 30 min [p.194]
5. Ara Pacis 1 h [p.199]
6. Mausoleum of Augustus 1 h [p.200]
7. Palazzo Altemps (Museo Nazionale Romano) 2 h [p.111]
The nearest metro stop is Metro A Barberini

4th day — Walk around – Architecture
Metro A and B – Get off at stop Termini
1. Baths of Diocletian (Museo Nazionale Romano) 1–2 h [p.223]
2. Chiostro di Michelangelo 30 min [p.225]
3. Santa Maria degli Angeli e dei Martiri 30 min h [p.224]
Afternoon
4. Palazzo Massimo alle Terme 2–3 h [p.208]
5. Chiesa di Santa Maria della Vittoria 30 min [p.226]
6. Cripta dei Frati Cappuccini 1 h [p.228]
7. Palazzo Barberini 20 min [p.229]
8. San Carlino alle Quattro Fontane 30 min [p.230]
9. Basilica Sant'Andrea al Quirinale 30 min [p.231]
The nearest metro stop is Metro A Barberini

5th day — Walk around – Archaeology
Metro A and C – Get off at stop San Giovanni
1. Basilica di San Giovanni in Laterano 1 h [p.270]
2. Lateran Baptistery 30 min [p.273]
3. Basilica di San Clemente 2 h [p.33]
Afternoon
4. Domus Aurea 1 h [p.32]
5. Roman Complex Houses at the SS. Giovanni e Paolo 1 h [p.34]
6. Baths of Caracalla 1–2 h [p.46]
7. Circus Maximus 1 h [p.45]
The nearest metro stop is Metro B Circo Massimo

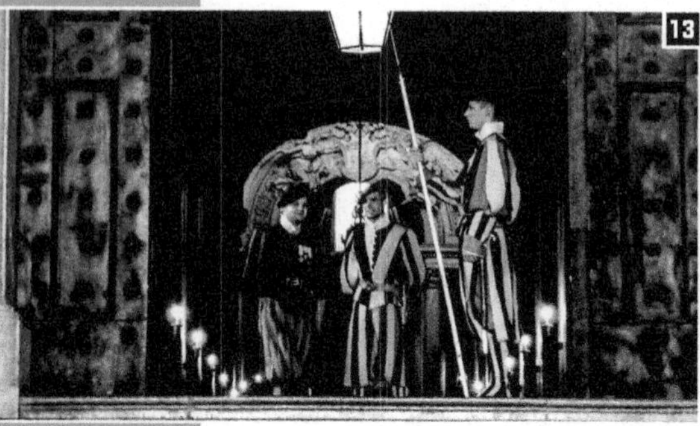

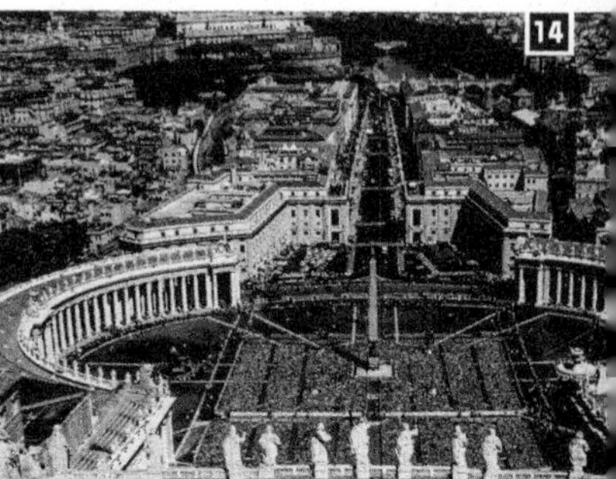

6th day — Catacombs and ancient sights on the Appian Way

Metro B Circo – Get off at stop Massimo to Bus stop Terme Caracalla/ Porta Capena: 118

1. Porta San Sebastiano 30 min [p.291]
2. Church of Domine Quo Vadis 30 min [p.292]
3. Tomb of Priscilla 30 min [p.293]
4. Catacombe di San Domitilla or Catacombe di San Callisto or Catacombe di San Sebastiano 2 h [p.291]
5. San Sebastiano fuori le mura 30 min [p.295]

Afternoon

6. Strolling along the Appian Way 30 min
7. Mausoleum of Cecilia Metella 1 h [p.296]
8. Villa Capo di Bove 30 min [p.299]

Bus 118 stop Catacombe S. Callisto to the Metro B stop Circo Massimo

7th day — On the way to the Sea

Metro B – Get off at stop Piramide

1. Porta San Paolo 20 min [p.254]
2. Piramide di Caio Cestio 20 min [p.254]
3. Protestant Cemetery 1 h [p.255]

Roma Porta San Paolo railway station: Train FC2

4. San Paolo fuori le Mura 1 h [p.257]

Afternoon

5. Ostia Antica 2–3 h [p.262]
6. Lido di Ostia 3 h [p.266]

Train FC2 tp Roma Porta San Paolo railway station. The nearest metro stop is Metro B Piramide

❻ The sights along the Metro Line A

- ► Battistini
- ► Cornelia
- ► Baldo degli Ubaldi
- ► Valle Aurelia
- ► Cipro
- ► **Ottaviano** [13] [14]
    Vatican Museums [p.142]
    St. Peter's Basilica [p.136]

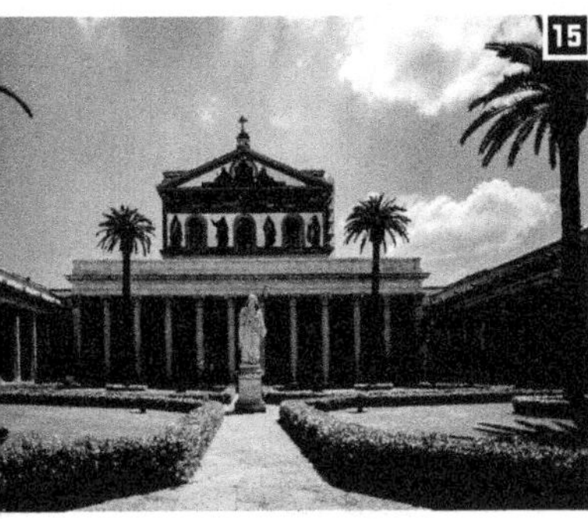
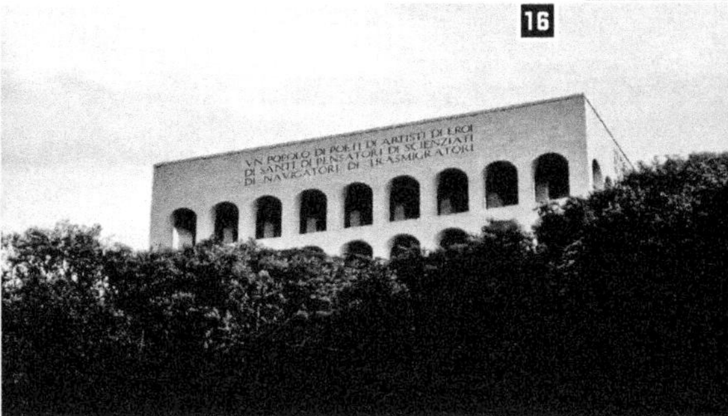

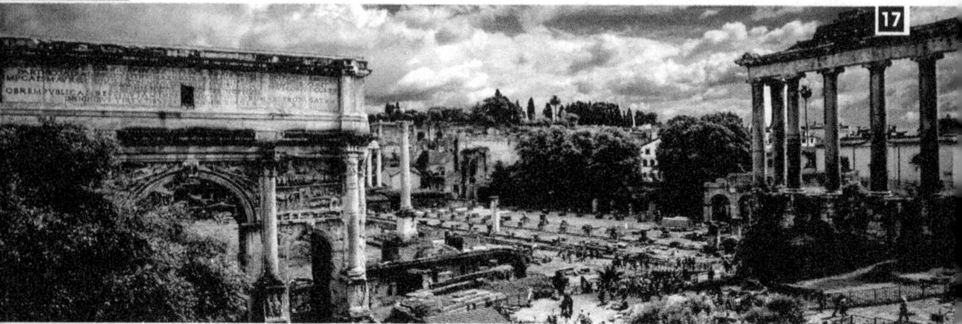

❼ The sights along the Metro Line B

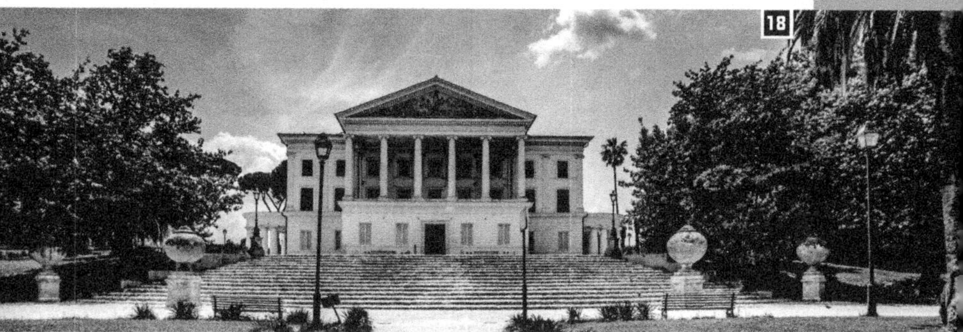
18

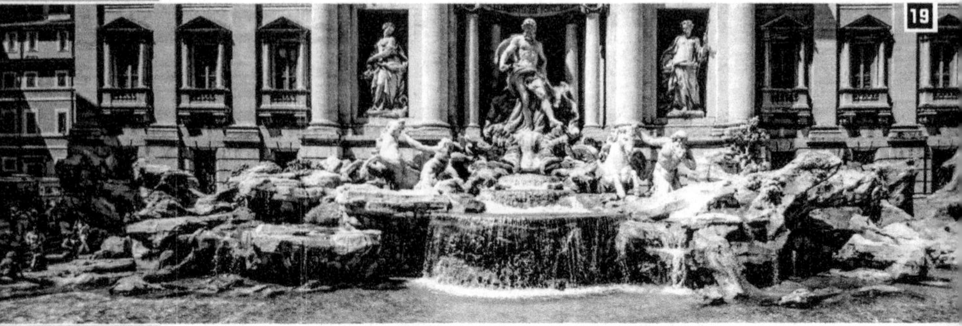

Index of Persons and Places

This index will help you find out the name of the person mentioned in the book and the activity that made the painter, pope or king famous, the year of birth and death of a painter, or the period of reign of popes and kings.

A

B

N

Q

Made in the USA
Las Vegas, NV
21 October 2022

57831618R00201